Environmental Law

The International Library of Essays in Law and Legal Theory
Series Editor: Tom D. Campbell

Schools

Natural Law, Vols I & II *John Finnis*
Justice *Thomas Morawetz*
Law and Economics, Vols I & II *Jules Coleman and Jeffrey Lange*
Critical Legal Studies *James Boyle*
Marxian Legal Theory *Csaba Varga*
Legal Reasoning, Vols I & II *Aulis Aarnio and Neil MacCormick*
Legal Positivism *Mario Jori*
American Legal Theory *Robert Summers*
Law and Language *Fred Schauer*
Sociological Theories of Law *Kahei Rokumoto*
Rights *Carlos Nino*
Law and Psychology *Martin Levine*
Feminist Legal Theory, Vols I & II *Frances Olsen*
Law and Society *Werner Krawietz*
Contemporary Criminological Theory *Francis Cullen and Velmer Burton*

Areas

Criminal Law *Thomas Morawetz*
Tort Law *Ernest Weinrib*
Contract Law, Vols I & II *Larry Alexander*
Anti-Discrimination Law *Christopher McCrudden*
Consumer Law *Iain Ramsay*
International Law *Martti Koskenniemi*
Property Law, Vols I & II *Elizabeth Mensch and Alan Freeman*
Constitutional Law *Mark Tushnet*
Procedure *Denis Galligan*
Evidence and Proof *William Twining and Alex Stein*
Company Law *Sally Wheeler*
Privacy, Vols I & II *Raymond Wacks*
Administrative Law *Denis Galligan*
Child Law *Harry Krause*
Family Law, Vols I & II *Harry Krause*
Welfare Law *Peter Robson*
Medicine and the Law *Bernard Dickens*
Commercial Law *Ross Cranston*
Environmental Law *Michael Blumm*
Conflict of Laws *Richard Fentiman*
Law and Religion *Wojciech Sadurski*
Human Rights Law *Philip Alston*
European Community Law, Vols I & II *Francis Snyder*
Tax Law, Vols I & II *Patricia White*
Media Law *Eric Barendt*

Legal Cultures

Comparative Legal Cultures *Csaba Varga*
Law and Anthropology *Peter Sack*
Hindu Law and Legal Theory *Ved Nanda*
Islamic Law and Legal Theory *Ian Edge*
Chinese Law and Legal Theory *Michael Palmer*
Socialist Law *W. Butler*
Japanese Law and Legal Theory *Koichiro Fujikura*
Law and Development *Anthony Carty*
Jewish Law and Legal Theory *Martin Goldin*
Legal Education *Martin Levine*
Civil Law *Ralf Rogowski*

Future Volumes

Labour Law, African Law and Legal Theory, Postmodernism and Law, Law and History, Law and Ethics and Cumulative index.

Environmental Law

Edited by

Michael C. Blumm

Professor of Law
Northwestern School of Law
Lewis and Clark College, Portland, Oregon

NEW YORK UNIVERSITY PRESS
REFERENCE COLLECTION

First published in the U.S.A. in 1992 by
NEW YORK UNIVERSITY PRESS
Washington Square
New York NY 10003

Library of Congress Cataloging-in-Publication Data
Environmental law / edited by Michael Blumm.
p. cm. — (The International library of essays in law and legal theory. Areas ; 15)
"New York University Press reference collection."
Includes bibliographical references.
ISBN 0-8147-1182-0 (cloth)
1. Environmental law—United States. 2. Environmental law.
I. Blumm, Michael. II. Series.
KF3775.A75E557 1992
344.73'046—dc20
[347.30446] 92-34968
CIP

Contents

PART V BEYOND ENVIRONMENTAL REGULATION

PART VI THE FUTURE OF ENVIRONMENTAL LAW

Acknowledgements

The editor and publishers wish to thank the following for permission to use copyright material.

Columbia Journal of Environmental Law for the essay: Arnold W. Reitze Jr (1989), 'Environmental Policy – It Is Time for a New Beginning', *Columbia Journal of Environmental Law*, **14**, pp. 111–56.

Cornell Law Review for the essay: Daniel R. Coquillette (1979), 'Mosses From An Old Manse: Another Look At Some Historic Property Cases About the Environment', *Cornell Law Review*, **64**, pp. 761–821.

Harvard Environmental Law Review for the essay: Joel A. Mintz (1991), 'Economic Reform of Environmental Protection: A Brief Comment on a Recent Debate', *Harvard Environmental Law Review*, **15**, pp. 149–64. Permission granted by the Environmental Law Review. Copyright © 1991 by the President and Fellows of Harvard College.

Harvard International Law Journal for the essay: Robert W. Hahn and Kenneth R. Richards (1989), 'The Internationalization of Environmental Regulation', *Harvard International Law Journal*, **30**, pp. 421–46. Permission granted by the International Law Journal. Copyright © 1989 by the President and Fellows of Harvard College.

Indiana Law Journal and Fred B. Rothman & Co. for the essay: Charles J. Meyers (1975), 'An Introduction to Environmental Thought: Some Sources and Some Criticisms', *Indiana Law Journal*, **50**, pp. 426–53. Copyright © 1975 by the Trustees of Indiana University. Reprinted by permission.

Law and Contemporary Problems for the essay: Thomas O. McGarity (1983), 'Media-Quality, Technology, and Cost–Benefit Balancing Strategies for Health and Environmental Regulation', *Law and Contemporary Problems*, **46**, pp. 159–233.

Stanford Law Review and Fred B. Rothman & Co. for essays: Bruce A. Ackerman and Richard B. Stewart (1985), 'Reforming Environmental Law', *Stanford Law Review*, **37**, pp. 1333–65. Copyright © 1985 by the Board of Trustees of the Leland Stanford Junior University, and Daniel A. Farber (1989), 'Environmentalism, Economics, and the Public Interest', *Stanford Law Review*, **41**, pp. 1021–43. Copyright © 1989 by the Board of Trustees of the Leland Stanford Junior University.

University of California, Davis Law Review for the essay: Joseph L. Sax (1980), 'Liberating the Public Trust Doctrine From Its Historical Shackles', *University of California, Davis Law Review*, **14**, pp. 185–94. Copyright © 1989 by the Regents of the University of California. Reprinted with permission.

University of California, Los Angeles Law Review and Fred B. Rothman & Co. for the essay: James E. Krier (1971), 'The Pollution Problem and Legal Institutions: A Conceptual Overview', *University of California, Los Angeles Law Review*, **18**, pp. 429–77. Originally published in **18** *UCLA L. Rev* 429. Copyright © 1971, The Regents of the University of California. All Rights Reserved.

Valparaiso University Law Review for the essay: Robert F. Blomquist (1990), '"Clean New World": Toward An Intellectual History of American Environmental Law, 1961–1990', *Valparaiso University Law Review*, **25**, pp. 1–49.

Every effort has been made to trace all the copyright holders, but if any have been inadvertently overlooked the publishers will be pleased to make the necessary arrangement at the first opportunity.

Series Preface

The International Library of Law and Legal Theory is designed to provide important research materials in an accessible form. Each volume contains essays of central theoretical importance in its subject area. The series as a whole makes available an extensive range of valuable material which will be of considerable interest to those involved in the research, teaching and study of law.

The series has been divided into three sections. The Schools section is intended to represent the main distinctive approaches and topics of special concern to groups of scholars. The Areas section takes in the main branches of law with an emphasis on essays which present analytical and theoretical insights of broad application. The section on Legal Cultures makes available the distinctive legal theories of different legal traditions and takes up topics of general comparative and developmental concern.

I have been delighted and impressed by the way in which the editors of the individual volumes have set about the difficult task of selecting, ordering and presenting essays from the immense quantity of academic legal writing published in journals throughout the world. Editors were asked to pick out those essays from law, philosophy and social science journals which they consider to be fundamental for the understanding of law, as seen from the perspective of a particular approach or sphere of legal interest. This is not an easy task and many difficult decisions have had to be made in order to ensure that a representative sample of the best journal essays available takes account of the scope of each topic or school.

I should like to express my thanks to all the volume editors for their willing participation and scholarly judgement. The interest and enthusiasm which the project has generated is well illustrated by the fact that an original projection of 12 volumes drawn up in 1989 has now become a list of some 60 volumes. I must also acknowledge the vision, persistence and constant cheerfulness of John Irwin and the marvellous work done by Mrs Margaret O'Reilly and Mrs Sonia Bridgman.

TOM D. CAMPBELL
Series Editor
The Faculty of Law
The Australian National University

Introduction*

Environmental law is a loose amalgam of common law and (increasingly) statutory provisions designed to protect public health, ecosystems and dependent animal and plant species. The modern regulatory schemes established by the statutes are of recent vintage, but common law remedies for environmental damage have existed for centuries.[1] Widespread public recognition of environmental degradation in the United States culminated in the first Earth Day in 1970, focusing attention on the inadequacies of common law tort and property concepts to prevent environmental damage and ushering in a new era of statutory enactment and administrative implementation. After two decades of statutes largely (although not exclusively) concentrating on environmental impact assessment and 'command and control' regulation, there is now widespread interest in employing economic incentives to encourage environmental improvements (Hahn and Stavins, 1991; Stewart, 1988; Ackerman and Stewart, 1985, 1988).

The essays in this volume, drawn exclusively from legal periodicals, provide an overview of the environmental law field and introduce some of its major themes. The volume is not an attempt to review comprehensively the substance of environmental law. Treatises are available which endeavour to do so (Rodgers, 1986, 1988; Novick, 1987; Skillern, 1981). Rather, this collection is an effort to supply a brief overview of the field and to survey its theoretical underpinnings, characteristic approaches and its future. The emphasis is necessarily on developments in the United States, for that is where modern environmental law was conceived and has been most fully developed, although the themes this volume emphasizes are generic.

The Scope of Environmental Law

One of the chief characteristics of environmental law – which quickly becomes apparent to its students – is its immense scope. Common law concepts of nuisance and trespass, legislation requiring environmental impact assessment, pollution control, natural resource protection and development, species preservation, environmental cleanup, and even land use regulation may all fall under the rubric of environmental law. This section discusses the role which each of these subfields plays, but the essays that follow are aimed at broader concepts such as the scientific and economic basis for environmental regulation (Krier, 1971; Meyers, 1975; McGarity, 1983), alternatives to regulation (Ackerman and Stewart, 1985; Mintz, 1991a), and the prospect of expanding the law's emphasis from environmental residuals to consumption and manufacturing decisions (Reitze, 1989).

---

* By Michael C. Blumm, Professor of Law, Lewis and Clark Law School, Portland, Oregon. Barry Needleman, J.D. 1992, Lewis and Clark Law School, provided valuable research and editorial assistance.

Beginnings of Modern Environmental Law

Environmental conflicts are certainly not new; the first smoke ordinance in England dates from 1273[2] and the first reported case occurred in 1611.[3] But modern nuisance law – the backbone of environmental law – was shaped by the industrial revolution (Rodgers, 1977, 12; Horwitz, 1977). As a result, the nuisance cases of enduring significance are those of the last century (Coquillette, 1979). While nuisance did afford a few environmental plaintiffs some relief, its after-the-fact remedies, its difficult burden of proving damage (especially to health), and its fault and causation requirements made it an inadequate basis upon which to premise a comprehensive scheme of environmental protection, especially due to a pervasive lack of information on the long-term effects of environmental contaminants (Gelpe, 1990).

Not until after World War II was there sufficient interest to pass environmental legislation; that which was enacted was generally limited to the state and local levels and either poorly conceived or badly enforced (Krier and Ursin, 1977). Interest in environmental legislation at the federal level only became widespread after a number of popular studies of environmental degradation were published in the 1960s, most notably Rachel Carson's *Silent Spring* (1962) and a series of polemics by Ralph Nader's study group (Esposito, 1970; Zwick, 1972). Thereafter, the peculiar political dynamics of the day produced a rapid succession of major initiatives concerning environmental assessment and air and water pollution control (Elliot, Ackerman and Millian, 1985).

Contemporaneously, developments in administrative law were granting private citizens the 'standing' to challenge agency actions in court.[4] Moreover, courts began to require agencies to document decision-making in written records explaining how and why particular actions were consistent with authorizing statutes and were reasoned on the basis of available information.[5] These developments gave environmental plaintiffs the opportunity to challenge administrative decisions in court, and many of the early landmark cases involved the environment[6] (Leventhal, 1974; Sive, 1970).

Environmental Impact Assessment

The Magna Carta of American environmental law is the National Environmental Policy Act (NEPA) of 1969[7] (Symposium, 1990; Fogleman, 1990; Mandelker, 1984, 1989). NEPA makes environmental protection the mandate of all federal government agencies. The statute also requires federal agencies to evaluate the environmental effects of their activities in advance, to evaluate alternatives to proposed actions, and to inform and involve the public and other agencies in their decision-making (Blumm, 1988). But Congress included no explicit enforcement mechanism in NEPA. Consequently, it has been left to the courts to enjoin agency actions where they are unaccompanied by sufficient environmental documentation or where that documentation fails to disclose fully the anticipated environmental impacts. Frequently, these court injunctions are premised on adverse comments submitted by agencies with environmental expertise (Blumm and Brown, 1990). However, NEPA supplies no basis for a court to enjoin an agency project on the merits (because it is not the most environmental alternative, or even anti-environmental); all NEPA demands is that the environmental impacts of proposed activities and reasonable alternative courses of action be evaluated, publicly disclosed, and that comments from the public and other agencies be given a 'good faith' written response. This lack of 'substance' in NEPA – this assumption that good environmental information will inevitably produce good environmental decision-making – has led some to call for amendments to strengthen NEPA (Blumm, 1990). No major amendments have occurred during NEPA's two decades, however.

Some other limitations of NEPA warrant mention. First, NEPA only governs federal actions; state, local or private activities are subject to the statute only if they require a federal licence or permit. Many states have, however, enacted 'little-NEPAs' which do demand environmental evaluation of activities not requiring federal approval (Novik, 1987 § 6.03[1](c)). Second, only federal actions with 'significant' environmental effects require detailed analysis in Environmental Impact Statements;[8] federal actions that do not produce significant environmental effects need only briefer analyses, termed Environmental Assessments.[9] Third, a variety of actions have been exempted from NEPA analysis altogether, most commonly because they are subject to expeditious statutory time deadlines[10] or constitute ministerial actions involving no administrative discretion.[11] Finally, it should be noted that the US Supreme Court has consistently interpreted NEPA in a narrow fashion, most recently suggesting that an adequate NEPA analysis need not include a 'worst case analysis' or incorporate a fully developed mitigation plan[12] (Rodgers, 1990; Shilton, 1990; Yost, 1990).

Despite the above limitations, it is not an overstatement to suggest that NEPA has revolutionized environmental law. It has made environmental protection the mandate of all federal officials, led to considerable improvements in inter-agency coordination and given the public an opportunity to participate meaningfully in environmental protection. NEPA has also spawned a number of other statutes requiring environmental assessment on the state, local and international levels. For example, under Canada's statute, a Federal Environmental Assessment Review Office commissions independent panels to review anticipated environmental impacts and underwrites the cost of participation by intervenors, usually environmental organizations (Hunt, 1990). Even more far-reaching is the Michigan Environmental Protection Act which establishes the state's 'paramount concern for the protection of its natural resources' and allows the state or any of its citizens to file suit against anyone likely to impair those resources. The statute generally shifts the burden of proof from plaintiffs to defendants, requiring the latter to justify their actions by showing that there exists 'no feasible and prudent alternative' to their activities (Sax and DiMento, 1974).[13]

Pollution Control

While NEPA and its progeny are aimed at ensuring that governmental activities receive environmental scrutiny, non-governmental activities producing air, water and land pollution are governed by specific statutory schemes such as the Clean Air Act,[14] the Clean Water Act[15] and the Resource Conservation and Recovery Act (RCRA)[16] which controls handling and disposal of hazardous wastes. These are extremely intricate and detailed statutes, and thorough analyses of them must be left to other studies (Rodgers, 1986, 1988; Novick, 1987; Currie, 1981). However, the pollution control statutes do share common approaches that warrant mention here.

First, institutionally, the pollution control statutes all involve federal-state partnerships. The federal role is generally to set standards, provide financial and technical assistance, and enforce against violations. Unlike NEPA, which implicates all federal agencies, the pollution control statutes make standard-setting, financial assistance and enforcement the responsibility of one federal agency, the Environmental Protection Agency (EPA). The state role is generally that of developing plans to achieve federal standards, issuing permits to polluters (where EPA has granted them permit-issuing authority), and enforcing against violators (a role shared by EPA). Except in the case of mobile sources such as automobiles, states may usually set stricter standards for pollution sources within their boundaries than is required federally.

Second, pollution control standards are of two general types: ambient standards (which prescribe maximum total concentration levels from all sources in an environmental medium) and emission standards (which prescribe the amount of emissions a particular pollutant source may discharge). Ambient standards, which usually are set to protect public health, enable particular geographic areas to be divided into 'dirty' or 'clean' classifications, with the former generally requiring stricter source controls than emission standards alone would require in order to bring the area into compliance with ambient standards. Emission standards are set industry-by-industry on a nationwide basis, without regard to local environmental conditions, on the basis of 'best available' technology. Cost is a relevant factor, especially with respect to the technology available to existing sources. New sources must usually meet stricter technological standards. Both ambient and emission standards are reflected in pollution permits that nearly all large pollution sources must obtain from EPA or the states in which they are located.

A third common characteristic of pollution control schemes concerns their enforcement. EPA and the states have concurrent enforcement authority against violators. This authority includes both the ability to file suits seeking injunctions and criminal and civil penalties, as well as the authority to levy administrative fines for small violations without going to court. In addition, the statutes authorize private citizens (such as environmental organizations) to bring suit to enjoin and seek penalties from violators where EPA or the states have chosen not to take enforcement action. Significantly, these 'citizen suits' may be filed not only against polluters, but also against EPA or the states themselves where they have failed to take action made non-discretionary by statute (Miller, 1987; Austin, 1987). Citizen plaintiffs who prevail on the merits may recover attorney and expert witness fees.[17]

Finally, a noticeable shift in pollution control schemes is the growing emphasis placed on economic incentives to promote compliance (Anderson et al., 1977; Hahn and Stavins, 1991). For example, the amount of civil penalties is increasingly being calculated on the basis of removing any economic advantage gained from noncompliance.[18] Even more striking is the movement towards allowing dischargers in compliance with standards to trade emission authorizations among themselves so long as they do not violate ambient standards (Tripp and Dudek, 1989). This 'emissions trading' is an effort to make the pollution control laws more economically efficient (Hahn and Hester, 1989; Stewart, 1988; Ackerman and Stewart, 1985, 1988). Emission taxes have been largely resisted in the US, however, although they have been influential elsewhere, particularly in Germany (Brown and Johnson, 1984; Hahn, 1989).

Brief mention must be made of some of the distinguishing characteristics among the three major pollution control schemes. The Clean Air Act emphasizes federal ambient standards, allowing states considerable flexibility to design individual emission standards so long as the ambient standards are achieved (Currie, 1981; Luneburg, 1978). Under the 1990 amendments to the statute (Symposium, 1991), however, there is an increased federal role in setting emission standards for hazardous air pollutants[19] (Waxman, 1991). The amendments also authorized a prominent role for emissions trading, particularly in their provisions regulating the long-range transport of sulphur emissions (acid rain)[20] (Parker, Poling and Moore, 1991; Fichthorn, 1991). The amendments also tightened emission standards for motor vehicles – the most serious source of urban air pollution – including establishing a new programme to change the composition of petrol in heavily polluted cities[21] (Waxman, Wetstone and Barnett, 1991). However, no attempt was made to provide incentives for reducing reliance on vehicle miles travelled, so improvements in exhaust emissions must remain the exclusive hope for improved urban air quality.

The Clean Water Act has historically relied more heavily on federal emission standards, based on a variety of complex technological availability tests, than the Clean Air Act, (Pedersen, 1988). Ambient standards have been left largely to the states, perhaps because watersheds are more geographically discrete than airsheds, but the EPA has an important (and growing) oversight role (Gaba, 1983). For example, the 1987 amendments required EPA to establish new controls over dischargers on streams that are not achieving water quality standards due to toxic emissions.[22] But the Act still leaves entirely to state discretion the control over 'non-point' pollution (from other than discharge points, such as runoff from farming, forestry and construction activities).[23] Thus, fully one-half of the nation's water pollution is effectively beyond federal control (Fentress, 1989).

Finally, the Clean Water Act has always contained greater reliance on economic subsidies than the other pollution control statutes because a considerable amount of water pollution is due to domestic waste produced by municipal dischargers. In the past, the federal government funded 75 per cent of the cost of municipal treatment facilities, but that subsidy has now been reduced to 55 per cent.[24]

RCRA governs regulation of hazardous waste disposal.[25] RCRA is structurally similar to the Clean Water Act, particularly in its emphasis on federal emission standards. This structural similarity is perhaps fitting, since a chief RCRA concern is prevention of groundwater contamination, something the Clean Water Act, in its concern for surface water, largely overlooked. But RCRA affects more than just the discharge of hazardous wastes; it controls their generation and transportation as well as their disposal in a 'cradle to grave' regulatory scheme (Anderson, Mandelker and Tarlock, 1990, 601–14). Non-hazardous wastes are not subject to this scheme and are left largely to state control.[26] To a degree greater than any other pollution control statute, RCRA spells out detailed standards in the legislation itself.[27] These so-called 'hammer' provisions are among the most complex in all of federal law and are a reflection of Congress' unwillingness to leave hazardous waste standard setting to EPA (Florio, 1986). On the other hand, despite the fact that the statute's goals include increased recycling, there has been little direct federal attention devoted to resource recovery, although the increased costs associated with RCRA compliance have indirectly provided incentives to recycle if, by doing so, RCRA's regulatory net can be avoided.

Environmental Cleanup

The pollution control statutes are focused on prevention or minimization of ongoing and future activities. In contrast, the Comprehensive Environmental Response, Compensation and Liability Act (CERCLA)[28] looks backward, to past disposal of hazardous wastes. For this reason, CERCLA is not a typical regulatory scheme but is in fact a liability scheme. The Act imposes strict and joint and several liability on all generators and transporters of hazardous waste as well as on owners, both past and present, of disposal facilities (responsible parties) for the costs of cleaning up contaminated sites.[29] CERCLA authorizes government cleanups of contaminated sites where the responsible parties fail to (although the latter remain financially liable).[30] The statute also established a fund which pays for government-initiated cleanups. This 'Hazardous Substance Superfund' is authorized at $8.5 billion for 1986–91 and is financed variously by taxes on chemical feedstocks and petroleum, a new environmental corporate tax, general funds, and reimbursements from responsible parties[31] (Barr, 1990).

CERCLA required EPA to evaluate and list sites in need of cleanup; by 1991, the agency had identified nearly 1100 sites,[32] though some estimates of the total number of sites run as high as 30,000 (Findley and Farber, 1991, 535). Costs per site are averaging between $20–30 million for surface and groundwater cleanup. Cleanups, even those undertaken by responsible parties, must undergo extensive public participation, be approved by EPA and meet detailed cleanup standards, including regulatory standards established under most federal and state environmental statutes (Anderson, Mandelker and Tarlock, 1990, 617–18). Because of the severe liability scheme and because all government cleanup costs are reimbursable, responsible parties have strong incentives to negotiate with EPA to provide for cleanup (Weber, 1989; Anderson, 1985).

CERCLA also subjects responsible parties to liability for natural resource damages resulting from hazardous waste releases including damages to land, fish, wildlife, air, water and so forth[33] (Breen, 1984). Liability is limited to the federal government, the states or Indian tribes, depending on the nature of the resource. There is no private recovery under CERCLA for damage to private property, however. The measure of natural resource damages is the cost of restoration of the damaged resources, although at some point (it is not yet clear when), restoration costs must give way to concerns for economic efficiency.[34]

CERCLA contains important provisions that are not concerned with cleanup of, or damages associated with, hazardous waste sites. Title III of the statute, known as the Emergency Planning and Community Right To Know Act,[35] requires local governments to have emergency plans to deal with chemical hazards and also provides the public with information concerning chemical hazards produced in local communities. All owners and operators of chemical facilities must notify local community emergency response organizations whenever a release of hazardous substances occurs.[36] Further, owners and operators must routinely supply state and local authorities with detailed information about the chemicals they use and release into the environment.[37] Like NEPA, the statute assumes that disclosure of this information to the public will induce changes in behaviour, prompting chemical manufacturers to reduce reliance on toxic chemicals and to recycle, rather than dispose of, chemicals wherever possible (Blomquist, 1990b).

Chemical Screening

Rachel Carson's *Silent Spring* sounded the call for chemical regulation in 1962. Three decades later, control of toxic chemicals is a major concern of environmental law. However, there is no single statutory scheme; in fact, both CERCLA and RCRA, as well as the Clean Air and Water Acts, focus extensively on toxic controls[38] (Anderson, Mandelker and Tarlock, 1990, 556–69; Dwyer, 1990; Graham, 1985). Moreover, food additives,[39] pesticides,[40] chemicals in the workplace[41] and manufacture of new chemicals[42] are the subject of separate regulatory schemes (Schoenbaum and Rosenberg, 1991, 332–6; McGarity, 1979).

Chemical regulation is premised on risk assessment, with risk standards varying among the statutes (Gillette and Krier, 1990; Page, 1978). For example, the Delaney clause subjects food additives to a 'zero-risk' standard,[43] but pesticides are not usually considered food additives (Poliner, 1987; Merrill, 1978). EPA registers pesticides under the terms of the Federal Insecticide, Fungicide and Rodenticide Act (FIFRA) to prevent 'unreasonable adverse effects to man or the environment, taking into account the economic, social and environmental costs and benefits of the use of any pesticide'.[44] This explicit call for cost-benefit balancing is unusual in environmental regulation and arguably has led to ineffective public protection (Rodgers, 1988, 102–4). Moreover, workplace standards regulate only 'significant' risks (Rodgers, 1980; Latin, 1982).[45] Regulation of new chemicals under the Toxic Substances Control Act (TSCA) forges a middle-ground risk assessment, rejecting both the Delaney clause's absolutist approach and FIFRA's utilitarian balancing in favour of a pre-market testing scheme designed to prevent unreasonable risk to health or the environment, especially imminent hazards.[46] This standard requires some consideration of costs, but does not require regulation to be premised on showing that adverse health effects outweigh a chemical's benefits (Anderson, Mandelker and Tarlock, 1990, 582–90).

TCSA was recently amended to reduce two prominent public health risks – asbestos hazards in schools and public and commercial buildings and indoor radon emissions.[47] The statute, in tandem with FIFRA, forms the core of federal regulation of the emerging biotechnology field (Shapiro, 1990; McGarity, 1987). TSCA has also been recently promoted as the key to developing an integrated, cross-media approach to chemical regulation in particular and pollution control in general (Guruswamy, 1989).

Special Area Protection

Environmental law extends beyond environmental impact assessment, pollution control and environmental cleanup to include protection of specially designated lands and wildlife. Influenced by nature writers such as Henry David Thoreau and George Perkins Marsh, the US pioneered the concept of setting aside lands for preservation purposes with the establishment of Yellowstone National Park in 1872 (Wilkinson, 1989a). Over the last century and a quarter, numerous national parks have been established to conserve scenery and wildlife and to promote public access to nature preserves.[48] Other land reserves such as national forests, national wildlife refuges, wild and scenic rivers and wilderness areas have been set aside for preservation purposes, although some controlled development is also permissible (Coggins, 1990). Land reserves also exist on the state and local level, but these are small in size compared to the federal lands which constitute one-third of the entire land area of the United States.

The Clean Water Act supplies a limited form of special ecosystem protection by requiring a federal permit prior to the filling of any wetland, regardless of whether or not the area is privately owned[49] (Blumm and Zaleha, 1989). The federal government has also funded state planning efforts under the Coastal Zone Management Act in order to control development along the nation's coastal areas more effectively.[50] Both coastal areas and wetlands have recently been the subject of federal legislation, removing economic subsidies that in the past encouraged development of these fragile ecosystems (Jones, 1991; Tripp and Herz, 1988).

Species Preservation

An increasingly influential area of environmental law is protection of designated species from harvesting and other destructive activities (Bean, 1983). The Marine Mammal Protection Act of 1972 imposed a ban on the taking of marine mammals,[51] while the Migratory Bird Treaty Act regulates the taking of migratory birds.[52]

However the most important species preservation law is the Endangered Species Act (ESA)[53] which generally forbids the hunting, importation or sale of listed species (Rohlf, 1989). The ESA protects both species listed as 'endangered' – defined as those likely to become extinct throughout all or a significant portion of their range – and those listed as 'threatened' – likely to become endangered in the foreseeable future.[54] The ESA has far-reaching consequences due to the fact that it affords protection not only for the listed species, but also for areas designated as critical habitats for species survival. It has thus altered land and water developments, including dam and highway construction, timber harvesting and property development (Coggins and Russell, 1982). However, the ESA does not block all development affecting listed species; projects may proceed with approved habitat conservation plans or with special exemptions granted by an interagency review committee (Thorton, 1991; Kilbourne, 1991). Unlike the Marine Mammal Protection Act, which legislatively extends protection to all marine mammals, the ESA confers protection only on species which are designated through an administrative rulemaking process that includes the opportunity for public review and comment.

Alternative Dispute Resolution

Just as economic alternatives to 'command and control' regulation have won adherents, there has been considerable interest in recent years in employing alternative dispute resolution techniques as a substitute for environmental litigation. Negotiation and settlement agreements are now commonplace in environmental cleanups under CERCLA (Anderson, 1985). Mediated settlements have also been employed in civil enforcement and public land and resource disputes (Grad, 1989). One study of 160 environmental disputes found that 132 of them attempted to reach a negotiated settlement and that 103 (78 per cent) did so successfully (Bingham, 1986).

One particularly controversial form of alternative dispute resolution is negotiated rulemaking. Its defenders claim that it allows interest groups to focus on their real concerns, allows face-to-face negotiations with opposing groups, and reduces the prospects for dilatory litigation (Harter, 1982). The opponents of regulatory negotiation contend that it supplants a public process with an essentially private one and can displace the role of administrative agencies in seeking out and pursuing the public interest (Funk, 1987). Others wonder whether a negotiated rule should receive the same judicial deference to agency expertise as a traditional agency rule when challenged by a party claiming it was not represented in the negotiations (Wald, 1985). Other critics of alternative dispute resolution worry that environmental groups run risks of co-optation and unequal bargaining power when participating in mediation processes (Amy, 1983; Schoenbrod, 1983b); they also allege that negotiation lacks the factfinding capabilities of adversarial litigation (Brunet, 1988). Nevertheless, CERCLA's numerous provisions encouraging settlements[55] seem destined to supply a variety of case studies in the coming years from which to judge the efficacy of environmental alternative dispute resolution.

The Essays in this Volume

Choosing essays for this volume proved to be an excruciating task, given space limitations, the enormity of the subject matter and the quality of the commentary. This selection does not purport to represent the 'best' or 'classic' contributions in the field, although many do fall into that category. It does, however, provide the reader with a broad introduction and survey of the diverse philosophies, themes and debates which have and will continue to animate environmental law. All of the essays are from legal periodicals; shorter papers were preferred over longer ones. Other sources are included in the bibliography which contains numerous additional excellent articles and books for consultation according to readers' interests.

Part I Perspectives on Environmental Law

Charles Meyers provides the initial perspective in this collection by, first, examining in some detail the contributions to environmental thought of Aldo Leopold as representative of nature philosophers (see also Freyfogel, 1990). He skilfully relates Leopold's land ethic to 18th- and 19th-century Deist and Transcendentalist philosophies which sought a more biocentric and less anthropocentric perspective. He also links the preservationist impulse to the American rural ideal, dating back to the Jeffersonian yeoman – the mythical agrarian philosopher tied to no one but the land. Meyers depicts these romantic roots, exemplified by Thoreau, as nostalgia for a simpler life, with fewer people and less complex technologies. He wonders, though, if the environmental writers' rejection of urbanism and technology does not overlook society's dominant cultural values which include the art, literature and music more characteristic of urban than rural life.

Meyers also discusses Barry Commoner's four laws of ecology which he criticizes for being only descriptive; he asserts that the conclusions which Commoner draws from his laws (mostly counselling inaction) are his alone (see also Krier, 1990). Instead of Commoner's ecological laws, Meyers embraces the principles of welfare economies whose solution is to let the market allocate environmental resources, a view that attracts him because it seems to eschew all value judgments except consumer preferences. However, this view has engendered many critics (Blumm, 1992; Sagoff, 1974; Tribe, 1974), who object to equating public decision-making with individuals' ability and willingness to pay and who doubt that monetary values can be assigned to unpriced environmental resources. In a comment on Meyers' essay, Dan Tarlock (1975) reminded his former teacher that environmental decision-making suffers from a pervasive lack of sound information about actual costs and benefits; that past decision-making was premised on an (unwarranted) confidence that the resulting benefits would outweigh the costs; and that the law needs to develop a 'presumption of caution' by expanding the definitions of harm and injury.

Chapter 2 by Robert Blomquist asserts that the complexity which characterizes modern American environmental law is a consequence of three factors: (1) the multiplicity of different contending interests, (2) the evolutionary pace of change of environmental law, and (3) the conflict between absolutist and utilitarian principles that underlie most environmental controversies. He also supplies a valuable narrative bibliography on a wide variety of environmental writings, from the philosophical to the ecological to the futuristic. Along the way, he introduces such influential environmental thinkers as E.F. Schumacher, Barry Commoner,

John Passmore, Samuel Hays, Roderick Nash, and Donald Worster, among others. From his bibliography, the reader can uncover valuable sources about all manner of environmental information, ranging from the influence of the Old Testament on environmental thought to Russian conservation policies to the deep ecology, ecofeminist and animal rights movements.

But Professor Blomquist seeks not just to summarize the existing environmental literature; his aim is to provide an intellectual history of American environmental law by showing how, over the last 30 years, environmental ideas in the fields of ecology, ethics and economics have influenced American law. His survey includes Rachel Carson's vivid account of the unintended consequences of human manipulation of the environment; Garret Hardin and Kenneth Boulding's demonstrations that economic markets fail in allocating environmental resources, producing a tragedy of the commons; Judge Harold Leventhal's introduction of the 'hard look' doctrine, requiring a balancing of environmental and economic considerations in natural resource decision-making; Joseph Sax and Senator Edwin Muskie's collaboration to make citizen suits a hallmark of environmental law; and both the Bruntland Report, which seeks to expand international principles of environmental law, and the Valdez Principles, which attempt to infuse the environmental ethic into corporate decision-making.

The role of economics in environmental decision-making is also the subject of Chapter 3, Daniel Farber's review of Mark Sagoff's (1988) book, *The Economy of the Earth*. The book asserts that economic cost-benefit analysis is an inappropriate basis for setting environmental policy. Sagoff contends that while economic efficiency may be appropriate in the pursuit of personal preferences or individual wants, it is inappropriate in the case of collective values like environmentalism which are dependent on political, moral and cultural convictions (see also Sagoff, 1981). Farber concludes that Sagoff is only partly right: he agrees that mechanistic cost-benefit analysis cannot resolve essentially political questions like environmental standard setting, but he thinks economic efficiency is a valid social goal that should not be wholly ignored in environmental decision-making.

Farber also suggests that Sagoff is wrong to dismiss private preferences and the virtues of ordinary life in the belief that government can easily modify these preferences. Farber cites the inability of the former Soviet government to motivate workers on collective farms and observes that cultural traditions and private preferences have considerable force irrespective of paternalistic government policies. Farber claims Sagoff is both too cynical about private life and too romantic about public life – the opposite end of the political spectrum from the new Public Choice theorists (who include many law and economics proponents), a philosophy that Farber has studied in some detail (Farber and Frickey, 1987).

Farber criticizes Sagoff's approach to risk management as simplistic; he then proceeds to give a lucid overview of the unreliable nature of risk-benefit methodologies. He notes that cognitive psychology studies show that individuals are notoriously poor at processing risks, and then discusses the usual factors that influence people's risk perceptions such as cause of death, age of the individual, clusters of deaths, unfamiliarity of the risk and voluntariness of the exposure (although he questions the relevance of the latter two). He observes with some wonder that an emphasis on voluntariness can lead to perverse results: for example, a tolerance for 350,000 smoking deaths per year, yet intolerance for minute amounts of hazardous wastes.

Farber does concur with Sagoff's characterization of the public outrage over toxic chemicals as a consequence of 'feeling that someone secretly imposed a risk on others; it is this feeling of powerlessness that gives rise to anger'. He therefore endorses a kind of 'environmental due process' approach to toxic controls that emphasizes full disclosure and public participation. Ultimately, he agrees with Sagoff that the difficulty of assigning values to the costs and benefits of health regulation forecloses reliance on mechanistic cost-benefit tests; 'we must rely', he concludes, 'on such political virtues as dialogue, open-mindedness, clarity, participation, and intelligence'. For Farber, the public interest is not simply the sum of individual preferences, but a product of the political process itself: 'in a democracy, the political process creates the public interest in the process of searching for it. The public interest can best emerge from a political process possessing the liberal virtues of broad participation, tolerance and intelligent deliberation.'

Part II Common Law Remedies and the Environment

In Chapter 4, Daniel Coquillette supplies a useful historical perspective to the common law's approach to the environment, 'exhum[ing] three famous cases on Anglo-American property doctrine'. The first, *William Aldred's Case*[56] in the early 17th century, held that the nuisance doctrine forbade any material interference with certain natural rights necessary for the enjoyment of land, such as 'wholesome air and light' (although aesthetic injuries were not recoverable). Thus, ancient nuisance doctrine espoused a protectionist, absolutist approach to the environment that specifically rejected balancing the utility of neighbouring activities.

In the 19th century the urge to balance gradually overwhelmed the old rule, however, and now dominates nuisance law (Bone, 1986). Professor Coquillette disputes the origins of the balancing test, claiming that what was widely considered to be the foundation case, *St. Helens Smelting Co. v. Tipping*,[57] actually affirmed the old absolutist rule. Nevertheless, over the past century the courts have almost uniformly adopted a balance of utilities test in an effort to determine the reasonableness of the conduct alleged to be a nuisance.[58] This balancing accommodated industrial growth by allowing defences such as 'coming to the nuisance', changed conditions and use of best available technology, as well as a determination that the utility of the defendant's conduct outweighed the gravity of harm to the plaintiff (Horwitz, 1977; Bryson and Macbeth, 1972). Having courts conduct such cost-benefit balancing was arguably beyond their institutional capacities and prompted legislatures to shift this responsibility to administrators under modern pollution control legislation. Still, the modern statutes have not pre-empted nuisance doctrine;[59] indeed, it is often the only vehicle available for plaintiffs to receive compensation for their injuries. Plaintiffs must, however, overcome substantial problems in proving causation, especially with regard to the low-level, long-term exposures that typically characterize toxic pollution (Farber, 1987; Rosenberg, 1984; Gelpe and Tarlock, 1974).

Professor Coquillette's third exhumed case, *Illinois Central Railroad v. Illinois*,[60] concerns the public trust doctrine under which certain resources (traditionally lands adjoining or submerged by water) are held as *res communes* in trust for the public. Grants of these resources in derogation of public uses are voidable. Citizens have standing to enforce this trust in court, and Coquillette argues that they enjoyed a shift in the burden of proof which normally assumes regularity of government action.[61] He welcomes recent developments expanding the public trust doctrine[62] (even more have taken place since he wrote, see Meyers, 1989; McCurdy, 1989), but he criticizes the chief intellectual proponent of the doctrine, Professor Sax (1970), for advocating it as a principle of administrative law rather than as a public ownership concept. Coquillette does not make the nature of his concerns clear; it may be that he misunderstood Sax's argument that one of the chief virtues of the public trust doctrine is the flexible remedies it can provide to resolve different resource conflicts (Blumm, 1989).

Joseph Sax, the intellectual father of the modern public trust doctrine (1970), seeks to 'liberate' the doctrine from its 'historical shackles' in Chapter 5. Sax believes that, to the extent that the doctrine is perceived as a rigid prohibition preventing the disposition of tidelands or freezing their uses to traditional ones, it is misunderstood. For Sax, the trust doctrine is neither limited to tidal areas nor an absolute bar to transfer or development, but instead a property law doctrine premised on protecting reasonable public expectations: 'the central idea of the public trust is preventing the destabilizing disappointment of expectations held in common but without formal recognition of title'. The trust doctrine therefore seeks stable relationships and evolutionary changes.

Sax draws an analogy from the English experience with customary rights, where public uses could be protected despite private ownership. He suggests that public versus property disputes will be resolved not by mechanistic title searches nor rigid adherence to customary uses, but by pursuing feasible alternatives that avoid destabilizing expectations which support social, economic and ecological systems. He relies on a California Supreme Court decision that protected public uses (despite 100 years of private title) because these public uses continued during private ownership.[63] His emphasis on feasible alternatives to resolve public/private rights conflicts perceptively anticipated another California Supreme Court decision, the *Mono Lake* case[64] – perhaps the most famous modern trust doctrine case (Dunning, 1985) – by three years.

Sax concludes by suggesting that the public trust doctrine demands explicit and fully considered legislative judgments. Administrative decisions allocating trust resources, he contends, should fail absent legislation that attempts to minimize destabilizing expectations. Other commentators have subsequently explored the trust doctrine's application to legislative and administrative decision-making as well as its public access and democratic decision-making themes. A number have devoted attention to the doctrine's geographic expansion beyond tidal areas to water allocation and wetlands and to wildlife protection (Symposium, 1989). One commentator has located the roots of public trust in the federal 'equal footing' doctrine (Wilkinson, 1989b); another has advocated its application in water pollution cases (Johnson, 1989), while a third has urged property law scholars to understand its relevance to property jurisprudence (Dunning, 1989, see also Hunter, 1988).

The public trust doctrine has also engendered critics, the most persistent of whom is James Huffman (1989; see also Lazarus, 1986). Huffman has forcefully criticized the views of Professor Sax for threatening to replace the democratic decisions of legislative bodies with subjective preferences claiming judicial protection (Huffman, 1986). He considers the public trust a dangerous doctrine, first, because it gives courts too much power to allocate natural resources and, second, because it effectively evades the constitutional requirement of paying 'just compensation' for the taking of private property for public uses[65] (Huffman, 1987). A recent account comparing the perspectives of Sax and Huffman argues that both fail to analyse explicitly the social goods at stake in public trust decision-making, suggesting instead that useful principles may be found in an examination of the natural resources damage provisions of CERCLA and the Clean Water Act[66] (Reiser, 1991).

Part III Environmental Regulation

The most venerable essay in the collection is James Krier's 1971 timeless classic, supplying a conceptual overview of the pollution problem and legal institutions (Chapter 6). Krier provides a concise summary of the market's imperfections in allocating environmental resources due to the lack of 'marketable packages' for collective goods like clean air and water and the 'free rider'[67] problem. These imperfections justify government intervention to correct the market's failure to allocate environmental resources efficiently. Consideration of the type of government intervention leads Krier to examine the famous Coase analysis, which maintains that environmental conflicts are reciprocal in nature and that, where rational individuals can bargain without costs, they will achieve efficient resource allocation without government intervention (Coase, 1960).

Krier appreciates that the Coase Theorem describes a world which – because of a pervasive lack of information concerning the costs and benefits of environmental controls, high transaction costs and the frequent lack of rational bargaining – does not exist (as Coase himself also recognized). Nevertheless, Krier's lucid discussion of the lessons of Coasian analysis allows him to posit important principles for delineating environmental rights and liabilities in a world where collective guesses are the inevitable rule. He suggests delineating environmental rights in ways (1) in which, if wrong, market action can be corrected most cheaply, and (2) which serve goals other than economic efficiency (redistributing wealth, for example), so long as there is no apparent adverse effect on resource allocation. These principles lead him to conclude that, in a typical case where the number of receptors outnumber the number of polluters, bargaining costs are lowest when liability is imposed on the polluters. He thus develops a theory of common law liability based on resource allocation efficiency (as opposed to moral principle), grounded on factors such as transaction costs, access to information and the free rider problem. But Krier also vividly illustrates the inadequacies of reliance on common law rules to resolve environmental problems, including the substantive and procedural burdens of proof that disadvantage environmental plaintiffs, as well as the court's institutional inadequacy in resolving complex pollution problems. He concludes (like Farber in Chapter 3) that the pollution problem 'is an essentially political one, ideally to be decided by the democratic process'.

Krier then proceeds to consider legislative approaches to environmental quality. Examining the Clean Air Act, he illustrates how key decisions, based almost wholly on subjective factors of value choices, can appear to be technical issues assigned to experts and advisory committees. He believes leaving such questions to technocrats is undemocratic and inappropriate considering 'the distinctly subjective nature of environmental quality decisions'.

Krier then surveys the variety of forms that governmental information may take, from regulation to subsidies to pricing techniques. He asserts that the American preference for regulation is imbalanced – 'and barren' – due largely to (an unfortunate) 'catastrophe theory of planning', a (misguided) desire to punish 'wrongdoers', a (short-sighted) desire to incur least near-term costs, and poor public understanding of the nature of the pollution problem (see also Krier and Ursin, 1977). Where regulation is employed, Krier prefers 'performance' to 'specification' standards because the former regulate only results, not methods to achieve them, thus allowing pollution sources to develop least-cost strategies and imposing lower administration costs as well. But his principal argument is for increased reliance on

pricing strategies, particularly establishing a pollution ceiling and then conducting an auction of transferable, limited-term pollution rights. This proposal seems remarkably prescient in light of the increasing attention it has drawn in recent years (Ackerman and Stewart, 1985, 1988).

In Chapter 7, Thomas McGarity examines three distinct approaches to environmental regulation in his case study on the chemical industry: (1) media-quality-based, focused on the quality of the receiving air or water; (2) technology-based, focused on available control technologies; and (3) balancing approaches that require cost–benefit calculations. Like Krier, he discusses in some detail the reasons the market fails to allocate environmental resources efficiently (the inaccuracy of the economists' 'full knowledge' assumption, the persistence of transaction costs and the exclusive emphasis on anthropocentric utility) and the inability of the common law tort system to remedy those deficiencies (due to problems in proving causation, transaction costs and the general passivity of the tort system).

McGarity points out that the Coase Theorem's assumption that bargaining will produce the same amount of resources devoted to pollution or workplace safety control irrespective of industry liability is not even theoretically true; this is because different results will be obtained if unpriced resources are valued under a 'willingness to pay' model rather than under a 'willingness to sell' model. Choosing which model to employ is fundamentally a value choice (more resources will be devoted to environmental controls under the latter than the former which generally undervalues the benefits of environmental protection). And McGarity cautions that economists have no better qualifications to make that choice than the general public (see also Latin, 1988). For all of these reasons, he suggests that government intervention is necessary.

McGarity sees the advantages of government controls as including lower causation requirements, anticipatory controls, broader planning horizons, reduced transaction costs through generic controls and government enforcement, and greater scientific expertise and political accountability. Understanding these advantages does not, however, answer the question of the type of governmental intervention likely to be most effective. Thus McGarity proceeds to examine three governmental decision-making models: cost–benefit balancing, media-based controls that are frequently based on absolutist goals, and technology-based regulation.

McGarity rejects cost–benefit balancing in setting of environmental goals because of insurmountable difficulties in accurately valuing costs and risks, the (frequently hidden) value judgments underlying cost–benefit models, and the economic model's inattention to the wealth shifting implications of governmental intervention among polluters, consumers and victims (see also Latin, 1988; Rodgers, 1980). Not only does McGarity claim that Congress has been justified in largely rejecting cost–benefit balancing, he shows how its frequent resort to absolutist, inefficient environmental goals can be supported on symbolic grounds and resort to nonutilitarian moral judgments, a theme pursued extensively in a recent study by Mark Sagoff (1986). However, he acknowledges that there are extreme difficulties in achieving such aspirational goals (see also Dwyer, 1990; Henderson and Pearson, 1978) which explains why implementation of pollution control policy is a function of media-based or technology-based regulation, and usually a combination of both, that allows for some consideration of costs and feasibility.

Although both approaches characterize modern pollution control, McGarity supplies a valuable critical analysis of the strengths and weaknesses of each. He finds the media-quality

approach superior in terms of its ability to be implemented in an economically efficient manner, its likelihood of surviving court challenges, and its potential to spur technological innovation. However, the approach has never been able to draw clear links between ambient media-quality and particular source emissions, nor can it predict the health effects of low-dose exposures with any reasonable accuracy. Moreover, it is subject to administratively irresistible pressures to convert ambient media levels to technology-based source controls.

Technology-based standards, on the other hand, are attractive to regulatory entities because they allow for considerable administrative discretion in setting targets, are easy to enforce, and do not threaten the industry with economic shutdown. Yet they have proved vulnerable to court challenge, require considerable administrative expertise, arguably give industry too large a role in the standard-setting process, and do not address intercompany inequities or encourage technological innovation as well as does the media-based approach.

McGarity ultimately opts for a mixed system of media-based and technology–based controls. He defends absolutist goals, even if they are unachievable, because he believes that 'reaching El Dorado is not always as important as the attempt'. He argues for retaining two–tiered technology–based controls on old and new sources, with sufficient administrative flexibility to avoid providing incentives to firms to extend the life of existing, more polluting sources. Interestingly, he disagrees with Krier's preference for performance rather than specification standards, contending that the theoretical efficiency benefits of the former are not worth the increased transaction costs (particularly court challenges) involved in demonstrating the level of pollution removal which a given technology is capable of producing.

McGarity would also levy a media-quality-based charge on all units of pollution to supply a continuing incentive to reduce emissions beyond existing technologies. This revenue would provide money to be used for pollution control research and development, and perhaps even to fund a victim compensation programme. He contends that such a charge would not be expensive to administer because it would not attempt to induce a particular level of media quality – its dual purposes would be only to reinforce society's absolutist goals and to encourage development of more sophisticated control technologies. Thus, no complex risk assessment or technology assessment would precede imposition of the charge. McGarity's thought-provoking proposal is not one that economic-minded reformers like Ackerman and Stewart (1985, 1988) are likely to embrace, however.

Part IV Economic Incentives and the Environment

Bruce Ackerman and Richard Stewart are among the leaders of a group of law and economics critics of the current system of environmental regulation. Chapter 8 is a response to an article by Howard Latin (1985) which would have been included in this collection had not space limitations interfered. Latin criticized the preoccupation of reformers like Ackerman and Stewart with theoretical efficiency, while giving inadequate attention to real decision-making costs and implementation constraints. He conceded that the current system of regulatory standards might be economically inefficient but contended that the characteristics of environmental regulation – including pervasive uncertainties about costs, risks and benefits, high decision-making costs, and manipulative strategic behaviour by both public and private interests – would eviscerate any superior theoretical efficiencies of alternative 'economically sensitive' models. Latin charged that Ackerman and Stewart were unwitting

academic water-carriers for the political deregulation army that has dominated national politics since 1980.

Ackerman and Stewart do not respond directly to Latin's charges in this chapter, but instead levy a renewed attack on the existing system. They claim that the current regulatory emphasis wastes billions of dollars by ignoring the individual differences among plants, penalizes new products and industries (adversely affecting international competitiveness), provides no incentives for new technologies, imposes massive information-gathering costs on regulators (and an incentive to litigate), and encourages administrators to regulate only a few pollutants. They also argue that the existing system is deficient because it issues pollution permits without charge and fails to allow for transfers of pollution permits.

Under Ackerman and Stewart's proposal, pollution permits would be capped at existing levels, issued at an auction, be tradeable, be for limited terms only, and eliminate the distinction between old and new sources. They contend that such a system would (1) save billions of dollars, (2) reward innovation in cleanup techniques, (3) eliminate the current penalty on new (they assume, productive) investment, (4) reduce administrative costs, (5) reduce litigation, (6) offer 'a rich source of budgetary revenue', and (7) free administrative resources for enforcement (see also Stewart, 1988).

Ackerman and Stewart envision only four tasks for the bureaucracy: (1) to ascertain the current level of allowable emissions; (2) to conduct a fair auction that would sell pollution rights for limited terms; (3) to maintain an efficient title registry; and (4) to consistently penalize permit violators. They claim that environmental quality could be improved by reducing existing emissions through increased charges over time, although they admit that their proposals do not resolve the problem of toxic 'hot spots'. Nevertheless, they profess not to worry because their proposal caps emissions at existing levels, while producing 'a more democratic, and more enlightened, dialogue on the nature of America's evolving environmental objectives'. However, a 'second generation' of reforms which they propose (to be implemented some years after the marketable permit auction) would allow different regions of the country to reduce permitted emissions on the basis of cost-effectiveness tests and special regional conditions. One might doubt their claim that enabling regulators to cut back three times more in some areas than in others would produce less litigation.

Finally, Ackerman and Stewart contend that, in scrapping the current system of technology-based limitations, their system would encourage administrators to conduct risk-benefit assessments on new pollutants. They claim that because the bureaucracy would share in revenues produced by the marketable permit auctions, there would be economic incentives to control new risks. This large role they envisage for government risk assessment stands in marked contrast to McGarity's proposal, which seeks a reduced governmental role in risk assessment.

Joel Mintz provides a synopsis of both the Latin and Ackerman/Stewart approaches in Chapter 9. He maintains that Ackerman and Stewart's characterization of the existing system as one dominated by a search for best available technology is a 'misleading oversimplification' since many pollution control limits are set on the basis of other standards. And he doubts that Ackerman and Stewart's 'first generation' reforms will produce significant benefits because the government will remain responsible for setting overall pollution limits within which the auction will function. It will thus remain subject to the problems of bureaucratic centralization, procedural delay and litigation. He does not think the reforms will reduce the government's information processing burden, and he claims that improved enforcement is more a function

of professional staff turnover than economic incentives to enhance agency budgets (see also Mintz, 1988).

Mintz also questions the reliance of Ackerman and Stewart's 'second generation' reforms on risk assessment. He suggests that not enough is known about the operation of ecological systems or the health effects of chemicals to justify extensive reliance on models that attempt to balance costs and benefits technocratically. In addition, he doubts that such a system will produce democratic decision-making more sensitive to the public will. But he does not dismiss Ackerman and Stewart's reforms because he agrees that the current system is dilatory and wasteful, nor is he persuaded (as Latin is) that the only choices are crude regulation or no regulation at all. He therefore endorses local marketable permit schemes, capped by existing regulatory standards, on a demonstration project basis to allow empirical testing of the concept.

Part V Beyond Environmental Regulation

Adam Babich (Chapter 10) agrees with the law and economics critics that the current regulatory system is neither efficient nor comprehensive enough to force basic societal behaviour changes necessary to resolve environmental problems. However, he does not advocate a change to marketplace principles; instead, he argues that new threats of civil liability for environmental damage will motivate improved environmental action. And he claims that this new liability-based approach to environmental protection has already been instituted in the statutes of Congress enacted in the 1980s – principally CERCLA[68] – which 'disrupt the normal routines of business and consumers'.

Like Ackerman and Stewart, Babich criticizes the current system's reliance on 'command and control' regulation because it rests on false assumptions about the government's ability to identify environmental problems, set priorities, and develop workable and enforceable regulations. But he also adds telling criticisms of the regulatory system's tolerance of exemptions for special interests, most notably for the federal government's own pollution sources. He characterizes the existing system as one in which Congress sets absolutist, symbolic goals, then tolerates administrative regulations which implicitly and explicitly embrace cost-benefit balancing. This arrangement may constitute good politics, but he claims it erodes public confidence in environmental protection.

Like Ackerman and Stewart (1985, 1988), Babich also decries the regulatory system's ponderous implementation speed. However, he notes that delays are not only the consequence of litigation, but also of interference by the President's Office of Management and Budget and of cumbersome and complex enforcement (for example, the current regulatory definition of hazardous waste is ten pages long). He faults the current system's reliance on government planning and its lack of incentives for self-policing.

For Babich, economic reforms, such as Ackerman and Stewart's marketable permit approach, are not a complete answer to the shortcomings of the regulatory system. He acknowledges that they may reduce some of the costs of environmental protection, but worries about their inability to prevent toxic 'hot spots', their heavy reliance on government risk assessments, and their failure to force the private sector to bear the risk if permitted discharges fail to protect public health.

Babich maintains that a new era of environmental law began with the enactment of CERCLA in 1980, which shifted the primary focus from 'prospective regulation to retrospective liability'.

He claims that CERCLA's imposition of strict (no-fault) joint and several and retroactive liability imposes 'new planning and cleanup obligations on all segments of the economy'. The statute makes all 'responsible parties' (that is, all past and present owners of waste facilities, as well as generators and transporters of hazardous waste) liable for investigation, cleanup and litigation costs and also damages to natural resources. Moreover, it authorizes not only government cleanups but also cleanups by responsible parties and others (who then may recover their expenses from responsible parties).

Babich shows how this liability scheme has created powerful new incentives for responsible parties to police their own conduct as well as that of their peers (see also Dechert and Smith, 1988). Environmental audits are now commonplace prior to property transfers, for example. This self-policing is taking place without waiting for government action and is not tied directly to regulatory standards. Further, Babich argues that uncertainties over potential liability and the prospect of extremely expensive (and likely wasteful) government cleanups actually increase incentives for responsible parties to clean up quickly and to maintain compliance with all regulatory standards (see also Frost, 1988). Thus, the liability system supplies continuous incentives to businesses to avoid pollution problems in ways that the regulatory system does not. However, Babich does suggest that the liability scheme could be improved by expanding the legal remedies available to victims of toxic pollution and by lowering their burden of proof.

Arnold Reitze, author of one of the pioneering textbooks on environmental law (1974), charges that current environmental law lacks focus. In Chapter 11 he contends that too much time, effort and expense are devoted to pollution control when, in reality, the marginal benefits of increased controls seldom justify their marginal costs (see also Krier, 1990). He makes a number of unsettling comparisons, including (1) a national preoccupation with low-level exposures to hazardous waste and a national tolerance for over 300,000 smoking-related deaths per year (see also Chapter 3); (2) preoccupation with automotive exhaust emissions while rejecting mandatory airbags for passengers who perish at a rate of 50,000 per year; and (3) extreme scrutiny devoted to groundwater contamination while allowing massive groundwater exploitation for low-value agricultural crops, many of which require government subsidies. Reitze wants the government to restore some perspective to environmental policy by expanding its pollution control measures into a comprehensive environmental policy that includes population control, materials conservation and energy policy components.

Reitze recounts a sorry history of national population control and materials conservation policies: the former now consists essentially of the Administration's pro-natal, anti-abortion policy; the latter is nonexistent (not surprising in a nation which consumes 11 times the world's per capita rate of energy, six times as much steel, and four times as much grain). Reitze then examines the potential of a number of unimplemented provisions of the Resource Conservation and Recovery Act to improve materials conservation. He also reviews the dismal track record of national energy policy vacillations during the 1970s and 1980s, from President Carter's 'soft' paths to President Reagan's 'hard' ones, noting that despite the ineffectiveness of government conservation efforts, price increases induced six times more energy saving in efficiency improvements than that generated by new sources. He cites the government's weakening of fuel efficiency standards as particularly inane, observing that the average car generates its weight in carbon emissions each year and that, if the 50 miles per gallon level that is technically available were reached, global gasoline consumption could be reduced by a quarter, with corresponding improvement in national security.

Reitze's prescription for the future comprises five parts. He would first reorder the Department of Energy's budget so that it becomes a real energy agency instead of expending two-thirds of its resources on nuclear weapons production. Second, he would tax petrol to increase its price to reflect its real costs, including defence costs necessary to keep imported oil flowing. Third, he recommends a major effort to reduce energy used in agriculture, including soil conservation efforts. Fourth, he posits three criteria for energy technologies to replace petroleum; he would support only those that (1) are sustainable without serious harm to ecosystems, (2) are decentralized and (3) produce net energy. These criteria would rule out increased use of nuclear power or conversion to alcohol fuels and would instead emphasize solar, wind and hydropower. Finally, Reitze would charge the President's Council on Environmental Quality with developing a coherent national population policy. These reforms, he suggests, would rescue environmental law from becoming merely a technician's field and return it to its proper role of 'honestly confront[ing] the physical and biological limits of our world and seek[ing means] to live within these limits'.

Part VI The Future of Environmental Law

Robert Hahn and Kenneth Richards (1989), then staff members of the President's Council of Economic Advisors, attempt to establish a framework that helps explain the increasing prevalence of international environmental agreements. In Chapter 12 they supply a brief history of international regulation of the environment and sketch a general model of how international environmental agreements – increasingly popular due to economic growth and reduced costs of exchanging information – emerge.

In Hahn and Richards' view, the well-known fable of the 'Prisoner's Dilemma', under which the rational outcome is not to cooperate, fails to depict accurately the dynamic forces that influence the emergence of international environmental agreements. These forces include scientific consensus about the causes and seriousness of a problem, public concern, perceptions of fairness among the negotiating parties, economic costs, the number of negotiating participants and the existence of previous agreements. But the dominant force is domestic political concerns. By identifying these factors, Hahn and Richards are able to explain such matters as why developing countries favour standards on a per capita basis, why Europeans favour percentage reductions, while the US promotes state-of-the-art control technologies with credits for prior pollution reductions. They also suggest why agreements tend to have grace periods prior to going into effect so as to postpone economic costs, why they tend to be characterized by weak enforcement and self-monitoring, and how the choice of a negotiating and sponsoring forum (like the UN Environment Programme or the UN Economic Committee for Europe) can affect the development and enforcement of an agreement.

Hahn and Richards use their framework to draw some lessons for US policy and to make predictions about the likelihood of an agreement on global warming. They suggest that the White House should not formulate policies based on world opinion because, according to their theory, many international environmental agreements will emerge, some of which may have negative net economic effects. Instead, they contend that the President should define and articulate clear priorities that are sensitive to domestic economic costs, attempt to shape both domestic and world opinion, and sign only 'effective and meaningful' agreements. Their framework predicts that a global warming agreement is not likely very soon because its

benefits would be spread unevenly and its costs would be high. For these reasons, they conclude that a global warming treaty will require a 'much greater consensus on the scientific aspects of the problem and a much greater level of public concern', factors which led to the Montreal Protocol on stratospheric ozone pollution (see also Mintz, 1991b; Morrisette, 1989).

William Reilly (1989), President Bush's Environmental Protection Agency Administrator, discusses the kinds of changes environmental law has witnessed over the past decade and makes predictions for its future in Chapter 13. He discusses the evolution of the focus of environmental law from the national to the global level, noting that the pressing environmental problems of the 1990s – global warming, stratospheric ozone depletion and tropical rain forest destruction – will require international collaboration on an unprecedented scale.

Discussing the environmental initatives of the 1970s and 1980s as 'one of the great success stories of American life and history', he points to the challenge of shifting the emphasis from a relatively few large sources of pollution to millions of small, highly decentralized and diverse sources. For example, ground-level ozone pollution is the product of automobiles and many small businesses such as print shops, bakeries and dry cleaners. Lawn fertilizers and garden insecticides contribute to estuarine pollution. These sources have never been subjected to regulation, and their cleanup will require a coordinated effort from business, individuals and government. Environmental education will be necessary to change personal behaviour and enable the public to make more informed risk-benefit decisions.

Reilly acknowledges that EPA must often make decisions on the basis of data that is incomplete, contradictory and ambiguous. Nevertheless, he suggests that if regulatory disagreements can be kept to 'a more scientific plane', the public will have more trust in regulatory decisions.

Reilly claims that the future of environmental law will involve more international law and diplomacy (see also Developments, 1991; Kay and Jacobson, 1983; Gaines, 1989). He also predicts, somewhat paradoxically, an increasing emphasis on state and local initiatives, contending that one of the failures of the past has been the inability to organize in the state capitals as effectively as in Washington. He also foresees greater attention to both enforcement and economic incentives in the future and maintains that waste reduction in the 1990s must receive attention equivalent to energy conservation in the 1970s, when energy use was reduced by 40 per cent.

Reilly calls upon the environmental lawyers of the future to help eliminate the inconsistencies and conflicts in current environmental law by thinking in terms of systems, incentives and multimedia approaches. Finally he suggests that, in order to prepare adequately for the environmental challenges of the 21st century, this decade must witness a national and global transformation of the environment from the margins of public policy to the mainstream of domestic policy and foreign affairs.

Notes

1 See for instance, William Aldred's Case, 9 Co. Rep. 57b, 79 Eng. Rep. 816 (1611) (allowing an adjacent landowner to recover in nuisance against an owner of a pigsty).

2 See Chass and Feldman (1954), 'Tears for John Doe', *Southern California Law Review*, **27**, 349, 352, citing W. Steer (1945), *The Law of Smoke Nuisance*, National Smoke Abatement Society, 2d ed.

3 See *supra* note 1.

4 Sierra Club v. Morton, 405 U.S. 727 (1972); Duke Power v. Carolina Environmental Study Group, 438 U.S. 59 (1978). But see Lujan v. National Wildlife Federation, 110 S. Ct. 3177 (1990) (denying standing to an environmental group for failing to allege facts specific enough to show injury resulting from agency action).
5 Citizens To Preserve Overton Park v. Volpe, 401 U.S. 402 (1971); Motor Vehicle Manufacturers Ass'n v. State Farm Mutual Automobile Insurance Co., 463 U.S. 29 (1983).
6 E.g., Scenic Hudson Preservation Conference v. Federal Power Commission, 354 F.2d 608 (2d Cir. 1965), cert. denied, 384 U.S. 941 (1966); Udall v. Federal Power Commission, 387 U.S. 428 (1967).
7 42 U.S.C. §§ 4321–70c.
8 *Id.* § 4332 (2)(C); see 40 C.F.R. §§ 1502 (contents of an Environmental Impact Statement), 1508.27 (definition of 'significance').
9 40 C.F.R. § 1508.9 (contents of an Environmental Assessment).
10 Flint Ridge Development Co. v. Scenic Rivers Ass'n of Oklahoma, 426 U.S. 776 (1976).
11 South Dakota v. Andrus, 619 F.2d 1190 (8th Cir. 1980); Natural Resources Defense Council v. Berkland, 609 F.2d 553 (D.C. Cir. 1979); see also Pacific Legal Foundation v. Andrus, 657 F.2d 829 (6th Cir. 1981).
12 Marsh v. Oregon Natural Resources Council, 490 U.S. 360 (1989); Robertson v. Methow Valley Citizens Council, 490 U.S. 332 (1989).
13 Mich. C.L.A. § 691.1203; see Ray v. Mason County Drain Commissioner, 224 N.W. 883 (Mich. 1975).
14 42 U.S.C. §§ 7401–7671q.
15 33 U.S.C. §§ 1251–1387.
16 42 U.S.C. §§ 6901–6992k.
17 Ruckelshaus v. Sierra Club, 463 U.S. 680 (1983).
18 See, e.g., 42 U.S.C. § 7420 (noncompliance penalties under the Clean Air Act).
19 *Id.* § 7412.
20 *Id.* §§ 7651–7651o.
21 *Id.* §§ 7521–54 (auto emission controls); 7581–90 (new fuels).
22 33 U.S.C. § 1314(1).
23 *Id.* §§ 1288, 1329.
24 *Id.* § 1282.
25 42 U.S.C. §§ 6901–6992k (also known as the Solid Waste Disposal Act).
26 *Id.* §§ 6941–6949a.
27 See, e.g., *id.* § 6924(o)(5)(B) (minimum technological requirements for hazardous waste disposal facilities).
28 42 U.S.C. §§ 9601–75.
29 42 U.S.C. § 9607.
30 *Id.* § 9604.
31 *Id.* § 9611.
32 See 40 C.F.R. § 300, App. B.
33 *Id.* § 9607(f).
34 Ohio v. U.S. Dept. of the Interior, 800 F.2d 432 (D.C. Cir. 1989).
35 42 U.S.C. §§ 11001–50.
36 *Id.* § 11004.
37 *Id.* §§ 12022–23.
38 42 U.S.C. § 7412 (regulation of hazardous air pollutants); 33 U.S.C. § 1317 (regulation of toxic water pollutants). See also Safe Drinking Water Act, 42 U.S.C. § 300(f) (safe drinking water maximum contaminant levels).
39 Federal Food, Drug, and Cosmetics Act, 21 U.S.C. §§ 301 *et seq.*
40 Federal Insecticide, Fungicide and Rodenticide Act, 7 U.S.C. §§ 136–136y.
41 Occupational Safety and Health Act, 29 U.S.C. §§ 651–678.
42 Toxic Substances Control Act, 15 U.S.C. §§ 2601–29.
43 21 U.S.C. § 348(c)(3)(A) ('no additive shall be deemed to be safe if it is found to induce cancer when ingested by man or animal . . . ').

44 7 U.S.C. § 136(bb).
45 Industrial Union Dept., AFL-CIO v. American Petroleum Inst., 448 U.S. 607 (1980).
46 15 U.S.C. § 2604(a)(1)(A).
47 *Id.* §§ 2650–53 (asbestos); 2661–71 (radon).
48 16 U.S.C. § 1.
49 33 U.S.C. § 1344.
50 16 U.S.C. §§ 1451–64.
51 *Id.* §§ 1361–1407.
52 *Id.* §§ 703–12.
53 *Id.* §§ 1531–44.
54 *Id.* §§ 1532(6), (20).
55 See generally 42 U.S.C. § 9622, which authorizes settlement agreements, including provisions for 'covenants not to sue' (§ 9222(f)), non-binding allocation of responsibility (§9622(e)(3)(C)), and de minimus settlements (§ 9222(g)).
56 77 Eng. Rep. 816 (K.B. 1611).
57 11 Eng. Rep. 1483 (H.L. 1865).
58 American Law Inst., Restatement (Second) of Torts § 826; see also *id.* §§ 827–28 (factors in determining unreasonableness). Two exceptions noted by Coquillette are Morgan v. High Penn Oil Co., 77 S.E.2d 682 (N.C. 1953); and Jost v. Dairyland Power Coop., 172 N.W.2d 647 (Wis. 1969).
59 See, for instance, 42 U.S.C. § 7604(e) (Clean Air Act); 33 U.S.C. § 505(e) (Clean Water Act); 42 U.S.C. § 6972(f) (Resource Conservation and Recovery Act). But see Milwaukee v. Illinois, 451 U.S. 304 (1981) (federal common law preempted); International Paper Co. v. Oullette, 479 U.S. 481 (1987) (common law of state of discharge preserved).
60 146 U.S. 387 (1892).
61 Citing Texas Eastern Transmission Corp. v. Wildlife Preserves, Inc., 225 A.2d 130 (N.J. 1966).
62 See Boston Waterfront Development Corp. v. Commonwealth, 393 N.E.2d 356 (Mass. 1979); Paepcke v. The Public Building Commission of Chicago, 263 N.E.2d 11 (Ill. 1970). A more recent famous case is National Audubon Society v. Superior Court, 658 P.2d 709 (Cal. 1983).
63 City of Berkeley v. Superior Court, 26 Cal. 3d 515, 606 P.2d 362, 162 Cal. Rptr. 327, cert. denied, 449 U.S. 840 (1980).
64 National Audubon Soc'y. v. Superior Court, 33 Cal. 3d 419, 658 P.2d 709, 189 Cal. Rptr. 346, cert. denied, 464 U.S. 977 (1983).
65 U.S. Const. amends. V, XIV § 1.
66 42 U.S.C. §§ 9607(a)(4)(C), (f)(1) (CERCLA); 33 U.S.C. §§ 1321(f)(4), (5) (Clean Water Act).
67 The 'free rider' problem involves efforts to extract contributions from members of a group in order to carry out transactions that will confer collective, nonexclusive benefits on the group. Since these benefits are shared by contributors and noncontributors alike, there are economic incentives not to contribute and instead take a 'free ride' on the efforts of the contributors.
68 See *supra* notes 28–37 and accompanying text.

References

Ackerman, B. and Stewart, R. (1988), 'Reforming Environmental Law: The Democratic Case for Market Incentives', *Columbia Journal of Environmental Law*, **13**, 171.

Ackerman, B. and Stewart, R. (1985), 'Reforming Environmental Law', *Stanford Law Review*, **37**, 1333.

Amy, D. (1983), 'The Politics of Environmental Mediation', *Ecology Law Quarterly*, **11**, 1.

Anderson, F. (1989), 'Natural Resource Damages, Superfund, and the Courts', *Boston College Environmental Affairs Law Review*, **16**, 405.

Anderson, F. (1985), 'Negotiation and Informal Agency Action: The Case of Superfund', *Duke Law Journal*, 261.

Anderson, F., Kneese, A., Reed, P., Stevenson, R. and Taylor, S. (1977), *Environmental Improvement through Economic Incentives*, Johns Hopkins.

Anderson, F., Mandelker, D. and Tarlock, A. (1990), *Environmental Protection: Law and Policy*, 2d ed., Little, Brown.

Andreen, W. (1989), 'In Pursuit of NEPA's Promise: The Role of Executive Oversight in the Implementation of National Environmental Policy', *Indiana Law Journal*, **64**, 205.

Andreen, W. (1987), 'Beyond Words of Exhortation: The Congressional Prescription for Vigorous Federal Enforcement of the Clean Water Act', *George Washington Law Review*, **55**, 202.

Austin, J. (1987), 'The Rise of Citizen-Suit Enforcement in Environmental Law: Reconciling Private and Public Attorneys General', *Northwestern University Law Review*, **81**, 220.

Babich, A. (1990), 'Understanding the New Era in Environmental Law', *South Carolina Law Review*, **41**, 733.

Barr, L. (1990), 'CERCLA Made Simple: An Analysis of the Cases Under the Comprehensive Environmental Response, Compensation, and Liability Act of 1980', *Business Lawyer*, **45**, 923.

Bean, M. (1983), *The Evolution of Nation Wildlife Law*, 2d ed., Praeger.

Bingham, G. (1986), *Resolving Environmental Disputes: A Decade of Experience*, Conservation Foundation.

Blomquist, R. (1990), 'The Logic and Limits of Public Information Mandates Under Federal Hazardous Waste Law: A Policy Analysis', *Vermont Law Review*, **14**, 559.

Blumm, M. (1992), 'The Fallacies of Free Market Environmentalism', *Harvard Journal of Law and Public Policy*, **15**, 371.

Blumm, M. (1990), 'The National Environmental Policy Act At Twenty: A Preface', *Environmental Law*, **20**, 447.

Blumm, M. (1989), 'Public Property and the Democratization of Western Water Law: A Modern View of the Public Trust Doctrine', *Environmental Law*, **19**, 573.

Blumm, M. (1988), 'The Origin, Evolution, and Direction of the U.S. National Environmental Policy Act', *Environmental and Planning Journal*, **5**, 179.

Blumm, M. and Brown, S. (1990), 'Pluralism and the Environment: The Role of Comment Agencies in NEPA Litigation', *Harvard Environmental Law Review*, **14**, 277.

Blumm, M. and Zaleha, B. (1989), 'Federal Wetlands Protection Under the Clean Water Act: Regulatory Ambivalence, Intergovernmental Tension, and a Call for Reform', *University of Colorado Law Review*, **60**, 695.

Bone, R. (1986), 'Normative Theory and Legal Doctrine in American Nuisance Law: 1850 to 1920', *Southern California Law Review*, **59**, 1101.

Breen, B. (1984), 'CERCLA's Natural Resource Damage Provisions: What Do We Know So Far?', *Environmental Law Reporter*, **14**, (Environmental Law Institute) 10306.

Brown, G. and Johnson, R. (1984), 'Pollution Control by Effluent Charges: It Works in the Federal Republic of Germany, Why Not in the U.S.?', *Natural Resources Journal*, **24**, 929.

Brunet, E. (1988), 'The Costs of Environmental Alternative Dispute Resolution', *Environmental Law Reporter* (Environmental Law Institute), **18**, 10,515.

Bryson, J. and Macbeth, A. (1972), 'Public Nuisance, The Restatement (Second) of Torts, and Environmental Law', *Ecology Law Quarterly*, **2**, 241.

Carson, R. (1962), *Silent Spring*, Houghton Mifflin.

Coase, R. (1960), 'The Problem of Social Cost', *Journal of Law and Economics*, **3**, 1.

Coggins, G. and Russell, I. (1982), 'Beyond Shooting Snail Darters in Pork Barrels: Endangered Species and Land Use in America', *Georgetown Law Journal*, **70**, 1433.

Coggins, G. (1990), *Public Natural Resources Law*, Clark Boardman.

Coquillette, D. (1979), 'Mosses from an Old Manse: Another Look at Some Historic Property Cases about the Environment', *Cornell Law Review*, **64**, 761.

Costle, D. (1982), 'Environmental Regulation and Regulatory Reform', *Washington Law Review*, **57**, 409.

Cross, F. (1989), 'Natural Resource Damage Valuation', *Vanderbilt Law Review*, **42**, 269.

Currie, D. (1981), *Air Pollution: Federal Law and Analysis*, Callaghan.

Dechert, W. and Smith, J. (1988), 'Environmental Liability and Economic Incentives for Hazardous Waste Management', *Houston Law Review*, **25**, 935.

Developments in the Law (1991), 'International Environmental Law', *Harvard Law Review*, **104**, 1484.
Dunning, H. (1989), 'The Public Trust: A Fundamental Doctrine of American Property Law', *Environmental Law*, **19**, 515.
Dunning, H. (1985), 'The Public Trust Doctrine and Western Water Law: Discord or Harmony?', *Rocky Mountain Mineral Law Institute*, **30**, 17–1.
Dwyer, J. (1990), 'The Pathology of Symbolic Legislation', *Ecology Law Quarterly*, **17**, 233.
Elliot, D., Ackerman, B. and Millian, J. (1985), 'Toward a Theory of Statutory Evolution: The Federalization of Environmental Law', *Journal of Law, Economics and Organization*, **1**, 313.
Esposito, J. (1970), *Vanishing Air: The Ralph Nader Study Group on Air Pollution*, Grossman.
Farber, D. (1987), 'Toxic Causation', *Minnesota Law Review*, **71**, 1219.
Farber, D. and Frickey, P. (1987), 'The Jurisprudence of Public Choice', *Texas Law Review*, **65**, 873.
Fentress, R. (1989), 'Nonpoint Source Pollution, Groundwater, and the 1987 Water Quality Act: Section 208 Revisited?', *Environmental Law*, **19**, 807.
Fichthorn, N. (1991), 'Command and Control vs. The Market: The Potential Effects of Other Clean Air Act Requirements on Acid Rain Compliance', *Environmental Law*, **21**, 2069.
Findley, R. and Farber, D. (1991), *Cases and Materials on Environmental Law*, 3d ed., West.
Florio, J. (1986), 'Congress As a Reluctant Regulator: Hazardous Waste Policy in the 1980s', *Yale Journal on Regulation*, **3**, 351.
Fogleman, V. (1990), *Guide to the National Environmental Policy Act: Interpretations, Applications and Compliance*, Quorum Books.
Freyfogle, E. (1990), 'The Land Ethic and Pilgrim Leopold', *University of Colorado Law Review*, **61**, 217.
Frost, E. (1988), 'Strict Liability as an Incentive for Cleanup of Contaminated Property', *Houston Law Review*, **25**, 951.
Funk, W. (1987), 'When Smoke Gets in Your Eyes: Regulatory Negotiation and the Public Interest – EPA's Woodstove Standards', *Environmental Law*, **18**, 55.
Gaba, J. (1983), 'Federal Supervision of State Water Quality Standards Under the Clean Water Act', *Vanderbilt Law Review*, **36**, 1167.
Gaines, S. (1989), 'International Principles for Transnational Environmental Liability: Can Developments in Municipal Law Break the Impasse?', *Harvard International Law Journal*, **30**, 311.
Gelpe, M. (1990), 'Organizing Themes of Environmental Law', *William Mitchell Law Review*, **16**, 897.
Gelpe, M. and Tarlock, A. (1974), 'The Uses of Scientific Information in Environmental Decisionmaking', *Southern California Law Review*, **48**, 371.
Gillette, C. and Krier, J. (1990), 'Risk, Courts and Agencies', *University of Pennsylvania Law Review*, **138**, 1027.
Grad, F. (1989), 'Alternative Dispute Resolution in Environmental Law', *Columbia Journal of Environmental Law*, **14**, 157.
Graham, J. (1985), 'The Failure of Agency-Forcing: The Regulation of Airborne Carcinogens Under Section 112 of the Clean Air Act', *Duke Law Journal*, 100.
Guruswamy, L. (1989), 'Integrating Thoughtways: Re-Opening of the Environmental Mind?', *Wisconsin Law Review*, 463.
Hahn, R. (1989), 'Economic Prescriptions for Environmental Problems: How the Patient Followed Doctor's Orders', *Journal of Economic Perspectives*, **3**, 95.
Hahn, R. and Hester, G. (1989), 'Marketable Permits: Lessons For Theory and Practice', *Ecology Law Quarterly*, **16**, 361.
Hahn, R. and Richards, K. (1989), 'The Internationalization of Environmental Regulation', *Harvard International Law Journal*, **30**, 421.
Hahn, R. and Stavins, R. (1991), 'Incentive-Based Environmental Regulation: A New Era From An Old Idea?', *Ecology Law Quarterly*, **18**, 1.
Harter, P. (1982), 'Negotiating Regulations: A Cure for Malaise', *Georgetown Law Journal*, **71**, 1.
Henderson, J. and Pearson, R. (1978), 'Implementing Federal Environmental Policies: The Limits of Aspirational Commands', *Columbia Law Review*, **78**, 1429.
Horwitz, M. (1977), *The Transformation of American Law, 1780–1860*, Harvard.

Huffman, J. (1989), 'A Fish Out of Water: The Public Trust in the Constitutional Democracy', *Environmental Law*, **19**, 527.
Huffman, J. (1987), 'Avoiding the Takings Clause Through the Myth of Public Rights: The Public Trust and Reserved Rights Doctrines at Work', *Journal of Land Use and Environmental Law*, **3**, 171.
Huffman, J. (1986), 'Trusting the Public Interest to Judges: A Comment on the Public Trust Writings of Professors Sax, Wilkinson, Dunning, and Johnston', *Denver University Law Review*, **63**, 565.
Hunt, C. (1990), 'A Note on Environmental Impact Assessment in Canada', *Environmental Law*, **20**, 789.
Hunter, D. (1988), 'An Ecological Perspective on Property: A Call for Judicial Protection of the Public's Interest in Environmentally Critical Resources', *Harvard Environmental Law Review*, **12**, 311.
Johnson, R. (1989), 'Water Pollution and the Public Trust Doctrine', *Environmental Law*, **19**, 485.
Jones, E. (1991), 'The Coastal Barrier Resources Act: A Common Cents Approach to Coastal Protection', *Environmental Law*, **21**, 1015.
Kay, D. and Jacobson, H. (eds) (1983), *Environmental Protection: The International Dimension*, Allanheld, Osmun & Co.
Kilbourne, J. (1991), 'The Endangered Species Act Under the Microscope: A Closeup Look From a Litigator's Perspective', *Environmental Law*, **21**, 499.
Krier, J. (1990), 'The Political Economy of Barry Commoner', *Environmental Law*, **20**, 11.
Krier, J. (1971), 'The Pollution Problem and Legal Institutions: A Conceptual Overview', *U.C.L.A. Law Review*, **18**, 429.
Krier, J. and Ursin, E. (1977), *A Case Essay on the California and Federal Experience with Motor Vehicle Air Pollution, 1940–1975*, University of California.
Large, D. and Michie, P. (1981), 'Proving That the Strength of the British Navy Depends on the Number of Old Maids in England: A Comparison of Scientific Proof with Legal Proof', *Environmental Law*, **11**, 557.
Latin, H. (1988), 'Good Science, Bad Regulation and Toxic Risk Assessment', *Yale Journal on Regulation*, **5**, 89.
Latin, H. (1985), 'Ideal Versus Real Regulatory Efficiency: Implementation of Uniform Standards and "Fine-Tuning" Regulatory Reforms', *Stanford Law Review*, **37**, 1267.
Latin, H. (1982), 'The "Significance" of Toxic Health Risks: An Essay on Legal Decisionmaking under Uncertainty', *Law Quarterly*, **10**, 339.
Lazarus, R. (1986), 'Changing Conceptions of Property and Sovereignty in Natural Resources: Questioning the Public Trust Doctrine', *Iowa Law Review*, **71**, 631.
Leventhal, H. (1974), 'Environmental Decisionmaking and the Role of the Courts', *University of Pennsylvania Law Review*, **122**, 509.
Luneburg, W. (1978), 'The National Quest For Clean Air, 1970–1978: Intergovernmental Problems and Some Proposed Solutions', *Northwestern University Law Review*, **73**, 397.
Mandelker, D. (1984, 1989), *NEPA Law and Litigation*, Callaghan.
McCurdy, M. (1989), 'Public Trust Protection for Wetlands', *Environmental Law*, **19**, 683.
McGarity, T. (1987), 'Federal Regulation of Agricultural Biotechnologies', *University of Michigan Journal of Law Reform*, **20**, 1089.
McGarity, T. (1983), 'Media-Quality, Technology and Cost-Benefit Balancing Strategies for Health and Environmental Regulation', *Law and Contemporary Problems*, **46** (Summer), 159.
McGarity, T. (1979), 'Substantive and Procedural Discretion in Administrative Resolution of Science Policy Questions: Regulating Carcinogens in EPA and OSHA', *Georgetown Law Journal*, **67**, 729.
Merrill, R. (1978), 'Regulating Carcinogens in Food: A Legislator's Guide to the Food Safety Provisions of the Federal Food, Drug, and Cosmetic Act', *Michigan Law Review*, **77**, 171.
Meyers, G. (1989), 'Variation on a Theme: Expanding the Public Trust Doctrine to Include the Protection of Wildlife', *Environmental Law*, **19**, 723.
Miller, J. (1987), *Citizen Suits: Private Enforcement of Federal Pollution Control Laws*, Wiley Law Publications.
Mintz, J. (1991a), 'Economic Reform of Environmental Protection: A Brief Comment on a Recent Debate', *Harvard Environmental Law Review*, **15**, 149.

Mintz, J. (1991b), 'Progress Toward a Healthy Sky: An Assessment of the London Amendments to the Montreal Protocol on Substances That Deplete the Ozone Layer', *Yale Journal of International Law*, **16**, 571.
Mintz, J. (1988), 'Agencies, Congress, and Regulatory Enforcement: A Review of EPA's Hazardous Waste Enforcement Effort, 1970–87', *Environmental Law*, **18**, 683.
Morrisette, P. (1989), 'The Evolution of Policy Responses to Stratospheric Ozone Depletion', *Natural Resources Journal*, **19**, 793.
Novick, S. (ed.) (1987), *Law of Environmental Protection*, Environmental Law Institute.
Page, T. (1978), 'A Generic View of Toxic Chemicals and Similar Risks', *Ecology Law Quarterly*, **7**, 207.
Parisi, F. and Ricci, P. (1991), 'Environmental Policy in the 1990s', *Ecology Law Quarterly*, **18**, 459.
Parker, L., Poling, R. and Moore, J. (1991), 'Clean Air Act Allowance Trading', *Environmental Law*, **21**, 2021.
Pedersen, W. (1988), 'Turning the Tide on Water Quality', *Ecology Law Quarterly*, **15**, 69.
Poliner, E. (1987), 'The Regulation of Carcinogenic Pesticide Residues in Food: The Need to Reevaluate the Delaney Clause', *Virginia Journal of Natural Resources Law*, **7**, 111.
Reilly, W. (1989), 'The Future of Environmental Law', *Yale Journal on Regulation*, **6**, 351.
Reiser, A. (1991), 'Ecological Preservation as a Public Property Right: An Emerging Doctrine in Search of a Theory', *Harvard Environmental Law Review*, **15**, 393.
Reitze, A. (1989), 'Environmental Policy – It Is Time for a New Beginning', *Columbia Journal of Environmental Law*, **14**, 111.
Reitze, A. (1974), *Environmental Planning: Law of Land and Resources*, North American Institute.
Rodgers, W. (1990), 'NEPA at Twenty: Mimicry and Recruitment in Environmental Law', *Environmental Law*, **20**, 485.
Rodgers, W. (1986, 1988), *Environmental Law: Air, Water, Pesticides and Toxic Substances*, 3 vols, West.
Rodgers, W. (1981), 'Judicial Review of Risk Assessments: The Role of Decision Theory in Unscrambling the Benzene Decision', *Environmental Law*, **11**, 301.
Rodgers, W. (1980), 'Benefits, Costs and Risks: Oversight of Health and Environmental Decisionmaking', *Harvard Environmental Law Review*, **4**, 191.
Rodgers, W. (1977), *Environmental Law*, West.
Rohlf, D. (1989), *The Endangered Species Act: A Guide to its Protections and Implementation*, Stanford.
Rosenberg, D. (1984), 'The Causal Connection in Mass Exposure Cases: A "Public Law" Vision of the Tort System', *Harvard Law Review*, **97**, 849.
Sagoff, M. (1988), *The Economy of the Earth: Philosophy, Law and the Environment*, Cambridge.
Sagoff, M. (1986), 'The Principles of Federal Pollution Control Law', *Minnesota Law Review*, **71**, 19.
Sagoff, M. (1981), 'Economic Theory and Environmental Law', *Michigan Law Review*, **79**, 1393.
Sagoff, M. (1974), 'On Preserving the Natural Environment', *Yale Law Journal*, **84**, 205.
Sax, J. (1970), 'The Public Trust Doctrine in Natural Law: Effective Judicial Intervention', *Michigan Law Review*, **68**, 471.
Sax, J. and DiMento, J. (1974), 'Environmental Citizen Suits: Three Years' Experience Under the Michigan Environmental Protection Act', *Ecology Law Quarterly*, **4**, 1.
Schoenbaum, T. and Rosenberg, R. (1991), *Environmental Policy Law*, 2d ed., Foundation.
Schoenbrod, D. (1983a), 'Goals Statutes or Rules Statutes: The Case of the Clean Air Act', *U.C.L.A. Law Review*, **30**, 740.
Schoenbrod, D. (1983b), 'Limits and Dangers of Environmental Mediation: A Review Essay', *New York University Law Review*, **58**, 1453.
Shapiro, S. (1990), 'Biotechnology and the Design of Regulation', *Ecology Law Quarterly*, **17**, 1.
Shilton, D. (1990), 'Is the Supreme Court Hostile to NEPA? Some Possible Explanations For a 12–0 Record', *Environmental Law*, **20**, 551.
Sive, D. (1970), 'Some Thoughts of an Environmental Lawyer in the Wilderness of Administrative Law', *Columbia Law Review*, **70**, 612.
Skillern, F. (1981), *Environmental Protection: The Legal Framework*, McGraw-Hill.
Stewart, R. (1988), 'Controlling Environmental Risks Through Economic Incentives', *Columbia Journal of Environmental Law*, **13**, 153.

'Symposium on the Clean Air Act Amendments of 1990' (1991), *Environmental Law*, **21**, 1549–2322.
'Symposium on the National Environmental Policy Act At Twenty' (1990), *Environmental Law*, **20**, 447–810.
'Symposium on the Public Trust and the Waters of the American West: Yesterday, Today, and Tomorrow' (1989), *Environmental Law*, **19**, 425–735.
Tarlock, A.D. (1975), 'A Comment on Meyers' Introduction to Environmental Thought', *Indiana Law Journal*, **50**, 454.
Thorton, R. (1991), 'Searching For Consensus and Predictability: Habitat Conservation Planning Under the Endangered Species Act of 1973', *Environmental Law*, **21**, 605.
Tribe, L. (1975), 'From Environmental Foundations to Constitutional Structures: Learning From Nature's Future', *Yale Law Journal*, **84**, 545.
Tribe, L. (1974), 'Ways Not To Think About Plastic Trees: New Foundations For Environmental Law', *Yale Law Journal*, **83**, 1315.
Tripp, J. and Dudek, D. (1989), 'Institutional Guidelines For Designing Successful Transferable Rights Programs', *Yale Journal on Regulation*, **6**, 369.
Tripp, J. and Herz, M. (1988), 'Wetland Preservation and Restoration: Changing Federal Priorities', *Virginia Journal of Natural Resources Law*, **7**, 221.
Wald, P. (1985), 'Negotiation of Environmental Disputes: A New Role for the Courts?', *Columbia Journal of Environmental Law*, **10**, 1.
Waxman, H. (1991), 'An Overview of the Clean Air Act Amendments of 1990', *Environmental Law*, **21**, 1721.
Waxman, H., Wetstone, G. and Barnett, P. (1991), 'Cars, Fuels and Clean Air: A Review of Title II of the Clean Air Act Amendments of 1990', *Environmental Law*, **21**, 1947.
Weber, A. (1989), 'Misery Loves Company: Spreading the Costs of CERCLA Cleanup', *Vanderbilt Law Review*, **42**, 1469.
Wilkinson, C. (1989a), *The American West: A Narrative Bibliography and a Study in Regionalism*, University of Colorado.
Wilkinson, C. (1989b), 'The Headwaters of the Public Trust: Some Thoughts on the Source and Scope of the Traditional Doctrine', *Environmental Law*, **19**, 425.
Yost, N. (1990) 'NEPA's Promise – Partially Fulfilled', *Environmental Law*, **20**, 533.
Zwick, D. (1972), *Water Wasteland: Ralph Nader's Study Group Report on Water Pollution*, Bantam Books.

Part I
Perspectives on Environmental Law

[1]

An Introduction to Environmental Thought: Some Sources and Some Criticisms

CHARLES J. MEYERS*

Natty Bumppo, the leather-clad, direct-speaking frontiersman in James Fenimore Cooper's *Leather-Stocking Tales*, once asked, "[W]hat has a man who lives in the wilderness to do with the ways of the law?"[1] As a legal scholar concerned with resource management and environmental protection, and not as a philosopher or historian, I am inclined to rephrase Natty's question: "How does the law derive from the ways of man and the wilderness?" This article will attempt to sketch out some answers to that question. The task is a formidable one. A historian of ideas could spend a lifetime on this subject and barely identify, much less analyze, the vast number of strands that make up the fabric of environmentalism. Nonetheless, I believe that legal scholars, practicing lawyers, judges, and law students should be concerned with the intellectual and cultural history of major ideological movements affecting the development of law. This is so because, at root, law reflects cultural attitudes and value choices of the society. To be sure, the law may alter by a few degrees the course of a cultural or ideological movement. Nevertheless, within broad limits, the direction of social action is ultimately set by ideas whose roots typically lie outside the legal system and the legal profession.

This article is limited to just three major contributions to environmental thought. These three do not begin to exhaust the catalog, but they are probably the dominant ideas influencing environmental thought today, and they are likely to continue to be the chief elements in environmental thinking in the future. These three intellectual forces are: (1) nature and wilderness philosophy, (2) ecology, and (3) economics. Each will be examined in turn, in an attempt to discover their fundamental

---

* Charles A. Beardsley Professor of Law, Stanford University; Co-author, *Oil and Gas Law* (1959, 1964), *Cases on Oil and Gas Law* 3d ed. 1974), *Water Resource Management* (1971). B.A. 1949, Rice University; LL.B. 1949, University of Texas; LL.M. 1953, J.S.D. 1964, Columbia University.

This article is a revision of the Addison C. Harris Lectures given at the Indiana University School of Law on November 11–12, 1974. I wish to thank James Baer, J.D.–M.B.A. [1976], Stanford University, for his research assistance in the preparation of the lectures, and Professors Gerald Gunther, Kenneth E. Scott, and A. Dan Tarlock for valuable suggestions on the revision.

[1] J. COOPER, THE PIONEERS 318 (1959).

premises and the effects they have had on the environmental movement. As shall be seen, this tripartite division is not nearly so neat as the classifications might suggest. The strands of thought are interwoven; and, as in a balanced natural ecology, to remove one element without disturbing the others is altogether impossible.

I

Let us begin with nature and wilderness values. In 1973, *Not Man Apart*, a magazine published by Friends of the Earth, conducted a poll of prominent environmentalists to name the books to enter an Environmental Hall of Fame. *Silent Spring* by Rachel Carson and *A Sand County Almanac* by Aldo Leopold easily led the field. Leopold's classic provides an ideal starting point for a discussion of wilderness values.

Leopold, both scholar and outdoorsman, was a man who learned the value of wilderness through direct experience. Trained as a forester at Yale University, Leopold spent 15 years in the United States Forest Service and the rest of his career at the University of Wisconsin. That blend of experience is reflected in *A Sand County Almanac*, first published in 1948 and still a strong influence on enviromental thinking. A collection of essays, the book is at once graceful and exhorting, poetic and gently resigned. Shortly after its publication, Leopold died tragically, fighting a brush fire on a neighbor's land, just a short distance from his beloved farmhouse on the Wisconsin River. In the foreword Leopold writes:

> Conservation is getting nowhere because it is incompatible with our Abrahamic concept of land. We abuse land because we regard it as a commodity belonging to us. When we see land as a community to which we belong, we may begin to use it with love and respect. . . . That land is a community is the basic concept of ecology, but that land is to be loved and respected is an extension of ethics. That land yields a cultural harvest is a fact long known, but latterly often forgotten.[2]

Leopold celebrates nature and all the little things in it—including man. Leopold is no misanthrope: he assures us that man has his place in nature if only he would keep it. Man keeps his place through ethics, which Leopold terms "a limitation on freedom of action in the struggle for existence."[3] But what values in nature and the wilderness are strong enough to temper man's struggle for existence? Leopold suggests three.

[2] A. Leopold, A Sand County Almanac viii–ix (1974).
[3] *Id.* at 202.

There is, first, the value of an experience that recalls to memory our distinctive national origins and history. Leopold calls this the "split-rail value"[4] and points to the Boy Scout who is reminded of Daniel Boone when he ventures into the forest; the Scout is reenacting a small bit of American history. Secondly, the wilderness experience reaffirms man's membership in the ecological chain. Leopold repeatedly emphasizes this theme of the interrelationship of all natural things, insisting that man's efforts must move toward the soil and not away from it.[5] Leopold's third value is the collection of restraints on behavior called "sportsmanship."[6] Wilderness sportsmanship is largely an internal force, for the hunter or angler is solitary—he appeals to no gallery and is applauded by no grandstand. He is dependent, therefore, on his own conscience and his own moral judgment to uphold the ethic. And that ethic teaches self-reliance, hardihood, and thrift.

Of these three values, the first—the "split-rail value"—is the most uniquely American, for American culture has developed, at every stage, with an acute awareness of wilderness—although more often in the direction of clearing the land, rather than saving it.[7] Nevertheless, consciousness of wilderness has been essential to the American character, and a constant source of national pride. Columbus wrote of "fields

---

[4] *Id.* at 177–78.

[5] *Id.* at 178.

[6] *Id.*

[7] Nature as a formidable adversary is a counter, though secondary, theme in the American consciousness.

The *Chronicles* of Nathaniel Morton, keeper of the records of Plymouth Colony, record the Pilgrims' reaction upon encountering North America:

> Besides, what could they see but a hideous and desolate wilderness, full of wilde beasts and wilde men? and what multitudes of them there were, they then knew not: for which waysoever they turned their eyes (save upward to Heaven) they could have but little solace or content in respect of any outward object; for summer being ended, all things stand in appearance with a weather-beaten face, and the whole country, full of woods and thickets, represented a wild and savage hew.

Quoted in Wall St. J., Nov. 27, 1974, at 16, col. 1. And Willa Cather echoes the attitude:

> But the great fact was the land itself, which seemed to overwhelm the little beginnings of human society that struggled in its somber wastes. It was from facing this vast hardness that the boy's mouth had become so bitter; because he felt that men were too weak to make any mark here, that the land wanted to be let alone, to preserve its own fierce strength, its peculiar, savage kind of beauty, its uninterrupted mournfulness.

W. CATHER, O PIONEERS! 15 (1941).

A powerful, contemporary novel portrays the struggle of man against nature and its denizens (including other men as barbaric as nature itself). J. DICKEY, DELIVERANCE (1970).

For a fuller development by a philosopher of the cultural and intellectual history developed in Part I of this article, see Sagoff, *On Preserving the Natural Environment*, 84 YALE L.J. 205 (1974).

very green and full of an infinity of fruits as red as scarlet, and everywhere there was the perfume of flowers and the singing of birds very sweet."[8] Similarly, early American writers—William Cullen Bryant, Washington Irving, and James Fenimore Cooper—boasted of America's wild beauty. In *The Sketch Book*, Washington Irving wrote:

> I visited various parts of my own country; and had I been merely a lover of fine scenery, I should have felt little desire to seek elsewhere its gratification, for on no country have the charms of nature been more prodigally lavished.[9]

That reverence for the American wilderness lit the inner eye with which early Americans saw nature. Certainly Daniel Boone's relation to wilderness exemplifies that love and respect for the community of nature advocated by Leopold. A further dimension is thus added to the "split-rail value," for the hiker who likens his wilderness adventure to the pioneering of Daniel Boone does so not only with Leopold's notion of patriotism, but also with a profound sense of responsibility—a responsibility to live up to Boone's values. What does our hiker imagine Boone's values to be? Precisely the final two values which Leopold himself emphasizes: membership in the ecological chain, and wilderness sportsmanship.

The second of Leopold's values—man's recognition of his place in the ecological chain—is representative of the thinking of many environmentalists and natural philosophers. His analysis is in two parts: the rejection of private property and capitalist institutions, and their replacement with a land ethic based on adherence to belief in the laws of nature. Leopold's condemnation of ownership institutions goes beyond the traditional debate between economists and environmentalists over the sources of human behavior. The economist holds that private ownership protects the land because man is self-interested and will protect what he owns outright, but will not care for what is collectively owned—"The Tragedy of Commons" as it is called by Garret Hardin.[10] Many environmentalists take a sharply different view of human behavior, contending that private ownership fosters greater abuses than does public ownership. Leopold, however, goes further: he suggests that *any* notion of land ownership is abusive. Remember his statement: "We abuse land because we regard it as a commodity belonging to us."[11]

---

[8] *Quoted in* R. Lord, Behold Our Land 77 (1938).
[9] W. Irving, The Sketch Book 2 (1963).
[10] Hardin, *The Tragedy of the Commons*, 162 Science 1243 (1968).
[11] A. Leopold, *supra* note 2, at viii.

This concept is more fully developed in his essay, *The Land Ethic.*[12] It recalls that Ulysses, returning from the Trojan Wars, hanged on one rope a dozen slave girls suspected of misbehavior. The hanging was considered proper, Leopold tells us, because the girls were property. With this illustration, Leopold makes his key point: land, like the slave girls, when viewed as property, entails privileges without obligations. Leopold calls for neither private nor collective ownership. Instead, he proposes a land ethic based on recognition of nature as a community to which man belongs. Man's role changes from conqueror of the land-community to citizen. What we might characterize as "Leopold's Basic Law" states: "A thing is right when it tends to preserve the integrity, stability, and beauty of the biotic community. It is wrong when it tends otherwise."[13]

Leopold's ethic is based on the interdependence of man and nature. A related concept, the harmony of man and nature, can be traced to the 18th century religious philosophy called Deism. Deism was a product of the Enlightenment, which was itself primarily a product of Sir Issac Newton's scientific discoveries. As Alexander Pope wrote:

> Nature and Nature's law lay hid in night,
> God said: "Let Newton be," and all was light.[14]

Prior to Newton and the Enlightenment philosophers, religious thinkers considered man the central character in an intricately ordered universe. God alertly governed three interconnected domains—the universe, the world of created objects, and human society—with man as the focal point of each. The earth was at the center of the celestial domain; man stood at the center of the ranks of created beings; and nobles ruled society by divine right. In this anthropocentric world view, man did not consider himself a citizen of the community of nature. Western Man saw himself as something separate, distinct, and somehow above the workings of nature. All this changed with Newton's theories of the universe. Newton's universe resembled an infinite cosmic ocean, throughout which the laws of physics and nature reigned uniformly over the tiniest things on earth as well as over the farthest stars.

This mechanical model of the universe disrupted the older hierarchical world view. Nature came to be seen as a system of harmoniously interrelated parts subject to immutable laws of science. And man came to be regarded as an integral element of the natural world; he was neither

---

[12] *Id.* at 201–02.
[13] *Id.* at 224–25.
[14] *Quoted in* DEISM AND NATURAL RELIGION vi (E. Waring ed. 1967).

separated from nature by Original Sin, nor elevated above the workings of natural law. "Why should God interpose to alter the determinations of human will, more than the operations of nature?" a contributor of *The American Magazine* asked in 1769,[15] as did many contemporary American leaders. George Washington, Benjamin Franklin, Thomas Jefferson, Elihu Palmer, and Revolutionary War heroes Charles Lee and Ethan Allen were all among the advocates of the pure and simple Religion of Nature espoused by the Deists. Jonathan Dickinson, President of the College of New Jersey, praised "the glorious art and contrivance of [this] admirable frame of nature."[16] Similarly, the eminent Boston preacher, Jonathan Mayhew, lectured about the regularity and harmony of the natural order. But it was Thomas Paine who best expressed the Deist ethic:

> When we survey the works of Creation, the revolutions of the planetary system, and the whole economy of what is called Nature, which is not other than the laws the Creator has prescribed to matter, we see unerring order and universal harmony reigning throughout the whole. No one contradicts another. . . . Everything keeps its appointed time. . . . Here then is the standard to which everything must be brought that pretends to be the work or word of God.[17]

In Deism, we find a philosophical origin of environmental awareness, an early expression of a land ethic comparable to Leopold's. For Deists, nature was not merely an economic resource, but the work and representation of God in which one could contemplate His power, His wisdom, and His munificence. In that God and nature came to be seen as inseparable, man's ideal relation to nature became one of adoration, and tenderness. As the British Deist, Charles Blount, insists: "Our Religion must necessarily be this, to do good to [His] Creatures; for therein we concur with the will of God."[18] This sounds much like Leopold's Basic Law[19]—right consists of obedience to and respect for nature.

Deism was too impersonal to satisfy the spiritual requirements of most Americans. They were engaged in a difficult struggle for survival and needed assurance that salvation would come. Yet, the impact of Deism on environmental thought has been significant. By identifying the

---

[15] *Quoted in* H. MORAIS, DEISM IN EIGHTEENTH CENTURY AMERICA 89 (1934).
[16] *Id.* at 54.
[17] T. PAINE, *The Prospect Papers,* in 4 WRITINGS OF THOMAS PAINE 339 (M. Conway ed. 1896).
[18] Blount, *The Oracles of Reason, quoted in* H. MORAIS, *supra* note 15, at 31–32.
[19] A. LEOPOLD, supra note 2, at 224–25.

universe as a body of parts harmoniously interrelated, and subject to uniform and purposeful laws, several of the more stifling beliefs of Christianity were eroded: (1) Man was not debased and separated from nature, as in Calvinism, but a participant in the workings of nature; (2) God did not predetermine all activity, so the study of nature was no longer discouraged as a form of heresy; (3) Nature was a representation of God—a community to which man owed reverence and obedience.

Wilderness experience reaffirms man's membership in the community of nature and of God: that has been a central theme of almost all American environmentalists since the Deists. The Transcendentalists, for example, fully recognized the mystical relation between man and nature. Ralph Waldo Emerson, the most influential of the Transcendentalists, praised the mystical qualities of nature in his first essay, *Nature*, published in 1836: "In the woods, we return to reason and faith. . . . I become a transparent eye-ball; I am nothing; I see all; the currents of the Universal Being circulate through me; I am part and parcel of God."[20] "The whole of nature addresses itself to the whole man," Emerson tells us, and "It is more than a medicine. It is health."[21]

No American celebrates the sweetness of nature more lyrically than Henry David Thoreau:

> The true harvest of my daily life is somewhat as intangible and indescribable as the tints of morning or evening. It is a little star-dust caught, a segment of the rainbow which I have clutched.[22]

He communes with nature, "I go and come with a strange liberty in Nature, a part of herself,"[23] and he urges us "To anticipate not the sunrise and the dawn merely, but, if possible, Nature herself!"[24] Yet, in all of Thoreau's writing there is an undercurrent of discontent, almost at times to the point of despair. He protests the materialist obsession of society:

> Most men, even in this comparatively free country, through mere ignorance and mistake, are so occupied with the factitious cares and superfluously coarse labors of life that its finer fruits cannot be plucked by them.[25]

The Transcendentalists' rejection of American social values was

---

[20] R. EMERSON, *Nature*, in SELECTED WRITINGS OF EMERSON 6 (B. Atkinson ed. 1950).

[21] 3 EMERSON JOURNALS 453 (E. Emerson & W. Forbes eds. 1910).

[22] H. THOREAU, WALDEN 148–49 (1960).

[23] *Id.* at 89.

[24] *Id.* at 11.

[25] *Id.* at 3.

too radical for the expansion-minded temper of their times; just as the Deists' creed, the pantheism of the Transcendentalists failed to win broad support. Nevertheless, the Transcendental philosophy of nature persisted as a force in environmental thought. The imaginative and influential conservationist, John Muir, describes the wilderness as "godful" in a manner reminiscent of the Transcendentalists. In his book, *My First Summer in the Sierra,* Muir writes: "The whole landscape showed design, like man's noblest sculptures. How wonderful the . . . beauty. . . . More and more, in a place like this, we feel ourselves part of wild Nature, akin to everything."[26] Muir's sentiment—like Emerson's, Thoreau's, and the Deists'—returns us, at last, to Aldo Leopold's second wilderness value: the appreciation of what he calls "the fundamental organization of the biota."[27]

Undoubtedly, it was Leopold's experience as an outdoorsman that fostered the development of his third set of values—a collection of voluntary limitations on behavior that he calls "sportsmanship."[28] Sportsmanship is voluntary, good behavior deriving from the recognition of one's involvement in the ecological chain. The sportsman's actions are voluntary because he performs without an audience. "Whatever his acts," Leopold stresses, "they are dictated by his own conscience, rather than by a mob of onlookers."[29] Ethical self-dependence teaches self-reliance, hardihood, thrift. It is difficult to exaggerate the importance of these qualities (particularly self-reliance) in the fabric of environmental thought.

These virtues spring from the depths of the American consciousness, for they are closely related to the Jeffersonian ideal of the independent yeoman farmer. Much as Leopold's sportsman must rely on his own sense of values throughout his wilderness sojourn, so must the land-holding yeoman depend on his own conscience concerning the use of his land and its resources. Both the farmer and the sportsman ultimately lack access to outside sources for moral guidance. They stand alone—powerful, and personally responsible for maintaining or violating the stability, integrity, and beauty of the natural community.

The Agrarian philosopher finds even greater significance in this ethical self-reliance than does Leopold. For Jefferson and other advocates of agrarianism, *all* virtues stem from self-sufficiency and self-reliance. Jefferson emphasizes this:

---

[26] J. MUIR, MY FIRST SUMMER IN THE SIERRA 18, 326 (1911).
[27] A. LEOPOLD, *supra* note 2, at 178.
[28] *Id.*
[29] *Id.*

> Corruption of morals in the mass of cultivators is a phenomenon of which no age nor nation has furnished an example. . . . [G]enerally speaking, the proportion which the aggregate of the other classes of citizens bears in any state to that of its husbandmen, is the proportion of its unsound to its healthy parts . . . .[30]

Two principles underlie the agrarian belief that self-reliance is necessary for the development of all virtues: (1) self-reliance places one in partnership with God; and (2) self-reliance is a fundamental component of democracy.

The first of these principles—that self-reliance places one in partnership with God—is a concept that develops syllogistically. Farming is an organic event, whereby one learns at first hand the truth that nature can be commanded only by delicate obedience. Through this discovery, one becomes involved in the biotic community as a guardian and protector. This protective and benevolent relation with nature is compatible with the work of God and places one in His partnership. Jefferson states the conclusion conscisely:

> Those who labour in the earth are the chosen people of God, if ever he had a chosen people, whose breasts he has made his peculiar deposit for substantial and genuine virtue.[31]

Thus, in full cooperation with God, and in gentle harmony with the natural community, one is able to attain the nobility of character for which one is intended.

The second tenet of agrarianism is that self-reliance is essential for democracy. Jefferson envisioned an American society based upon a system of land ownership which minimized the likelihood of a peasant-based economy. His yeoman class of cultivators would be above corruption by virture of the self-sufficiency of its members. And, the free exercise of their diverse talents would improve the quality of the citizenry and ultimately the state. During the formative years of the Republic, rural life came to be associated with rarefied notions of pure government, ideal politics, and democracy. This is illustrated by Jefferson's contemptuous description of "the mobs of great cities" as adding to the support of pure government as do sores "to the strength of the human body."[32]

Early American visions of an agrarian democracy were admixtures of political reality and philosophical idealism. Throughout Jefferson's political life, 90 percent of all Americans were farmers; and it was

---

[30] T. JEFFERSON, NOTES ON THE STATE OF VIRGINIA 165 (W. Peden ed. 1955).
[31] *Id.* at 164–65.
[32] *Id.* at 165.

generally believed that there was no limit to the land available for small farms. Beyond these factual foundations, however, were the egalitarian impulses implicit in early environmental thinking. "In this admirably planned universe," an Enlightenment philosopher would explain, "every man has natural liberty." Similarly, the Declaration of Independence appeals to the "Laws of Nature and of Nature's God" for liberty and justice. In short, rudimentary beliefs in liberty and equality are closely tied to environmental thought and its respect for nature. All men are equally endowed with the capacity to work the land and appreciate nature; all virtues stem from these activities; respect for man and for nature are correlative.

Jefferson's concept of agrarian democracy cannot survive serious analysis. Nevertheless, the importance of farming during the early years of the Republic led to an irrational but persistent blending of the virtues of democracy with those of agrarianism. Those themes are so deeply rooted in the American experience that they are applied to many nonfarm contexts. The creation of parks, wildlife reserves, and open spaces in urban centers is justified by lawmakers and politicans in terms of agrarian ideology—a continuing belief that the best in American private and social character is to be found in the preservation of rural life and the wilderness experience.

In each of the three nature values just discussed one finds a seed-bed of another major line of environmental thought—a nostalgia for a simpler life, with fewer people, more wilderness, and less complexity. This longing for simplicity is expressed by many environmentalists as distrust of, if not outright aversion to, two main components of modern civilization: technology and urbanism. As John Muir insisted: "Compared with the intense purity, cordiality, and beauty of nature, the most delicate refinements and cultures of civilization are gross barbarisms."[33] For Leopold, the barbarism of civilization consists in thoughtless application of machinery in a wilderness context. He contrasts the pioneer methods of "go light" and "one-bullet-one-buck" with gadgeteering of modern sportsmen. "Gadgets fill . . . the auto-trunk, and also the trailer," Leopold laments.[34] Mechanization debases the wilderness adventure. It deprives us of the primitive, atavistic experience that is necessary to remind us of our national heritage; it separates us from the community of nature; and it erodes our self-reliance. In short, Leopold feels that immoderate use

[33] J. Muir, *supra* note 26, at 106–07.
[34] A. Leopold, *supra* note 2, at 180.

of machinery destroys the cultural values of nature.

These modern misgivings about technological progress echo views commonly held by 19th century naturalists. Thoreau repeatedly criticized the materialism and insensitivity which he saw dominating society. He decried "modern improvements":

> [T]here is an illusion about them; there is not always a positive advance. The devil goes on exacting compound interest to the last for his early share and numerous succeeding investments in them. Our inventions are wont to be pretty toys, which distract our attention from serious things. They are but improved means to an unimproved end . . . .[35]

During roughly the same period that Thoreau was writing *Walden*, Samuel Butler described the problem of mechanization with an eye to the future: "We are daily giving them [the machines] greater power," Butler comments; "in the course of ages, we shall find ourselves the inferior race."[36] The 19th century naturalist was apprehensive about technology: characteristically he foresaw a mechanical world antagonistic to natural and humane values. But his concern was vague and ill-defined, perhaps because technology was just emerging as a force in the affairs of men. By the 20th century, technology had fully arrived, and so we turn to contemporary thinkers to discover the nature of the problem.

Some eminent writers, Lewis Mumford, Hans J. Morgenthau and Rene Dubós among them, identify the problem of technology as the failure of man to integrate his scientific pursuits with higher social values. When we experiment with the creation of life and tinker with the evolutionary process, we stray too far from valued ends. Our egoist drive to dominate causes us to fashion more tools and build more machinery in order to dominate the world and decide its future.

Implicit in the idea that technology is misdirected and fails to pursue the public interest is a strong sense of the capacity of human beings to exert control. As Mumford writes:

> Technics and civilization as a whole are the result of human choices. . . . No matter how completely technic relies on the objective procedures of the sciences, it does not form an independent system. . . . The machine itself makes no demands and holds out no promises: it is the human spirit which makes demands and keeps promises.[37]

---

[35] H. THOREAU, *supra* note 22, at 36.

[36] *Quoted in* W. KUHNS, POST-INDUSTRIAL PROPHETS 16 (1971).

[37] *Quoted in* MODERN TECHNOLOGY AND CIVILIZATION 12 (C. Walker ed. 1962).

Our technological predicament, according to this school of thought, must be resolved by purposive reorientation of our institutions, and by serious reevaluation of the nature of our scientific investigations. While these thinkers are far from optimistic, they maintain that it is within our power to correct the course and put technology on the proper heading.

In sharp contrast to this view stands the grim critique of the French philosopher, Jacques Ellul. Ellul claims that machines are only symptomatic of the problem. Technology's true impact, he holds, is found in its total domination of life. He makes this clear in his definition of "technique":

> The term *technique*, as I use it, does not mean machines, technology, or this or that procedure for attaining an end. In our technological society, *technique* is the *totality of methods rationally arrived at and having absolute efficiency* . . . in *every* field of human activity.[38]

This description of technique differs significantly from Mumford's. Ellul does not see technology as a problem of machines, scientists, and poorly chosen objectives. He refuses to accept the notion that men are to blame for the abuses of technology. Such a belief rests on the supposition that men are able to orient technology for moral, and consequently, nontechnical reasons. For Ellul, this concept ignores technical reality. In his words:

> [A] principal characteristic of technique . . . it its refusal to tolerate moral judgments. It is absolutely independent of them and eliminates them from its domain. Technique never observes the distinction between moral and immoral use. It tends, on the contrary, to create a completely technical morality.[39]

The technical morality Ellul speaks of is unwavering adherence to the goal of absolute efficiency. Technology becomes more than neutral matter; it is a self-contained force that functions outside the bonds of human constraint, ever pursuing efficiency.

As Ellul sees it, technique has three chilling faces. It does not allow freedom of choice, for it insists on selection of the more efficient means. Moreover, it is self-augmenting. "[A]lmost without deliberate will, by a simple combination of new data, incessant discoveries take place everywhere," Ellul explains. "The qualities which technique requires for its advance are precisely those characteristics of a technical

---

[38] J. ELLUL, THE TECHNOLOGICAL SOCIETY xxv (J. Wilkinson transl. 1964) (emphasis in original).

[39] *Id.* at 97.

order which do not represent the individual intelligence."[40]

The autonomous and self-augmenting facets of technique form a monistic whole which embraces all of the separate components. Technique and the use to which it is put are indistinguishable. Both polio vaccinations and bacteriological warfare are of the same nature: each adds dimension, without direction, to the technical mass—and both are born only of efficiency, evolving toward still greater efficiency, altogether lacking regard for illness as opposed to health or life as opposed to death. Whatever the objectives may be, they are pursued with equal fervor and equal skill. Such is the world inhabited by Ellul's technical phantasm.

We have seen thus far how nature values derive from Deism, Agrarianism and Transcendentalism, and how those sources can lead to the rejection of materialism, urbanism and technology. Undoubtedly, the nature and wilderness philosophers' values (and anti-values) embody the beliefs of some Americans and probably some part of the beliefs of many Americans.

There are, however, conflicting values which seem to me to be closer to the mainstream of Western thought and culture: the values of art, literature and music—the values of the created as opposed to the natural. These values, too, are embraced by many Americans and in some part, I venture to say, by most Americans.

It can be plausibly maintained that our dominant cultural values derive from the city. The rise of Florence in the 15th century led to a cultural explosion providing a richness and variety to life theretofore unknown in Western Europe. By the end of the 16th century, the Renaissance had established artistic and cultural values which have ever since tended to represent the highest aspirations of mankind—and these are essentially urban values, for they depend on the city for nurture. Perhaps the greatest creative achievements in Western civilization are found in the works of Michelangelo, Shakespeare, Rembrandt and Mozart, all men of the city. Without trade and commerce, which rest on a base of technology and urban organization, an artistic culture cannot exist, for there are no social resources to support it.

Should we conclude, then, that Leopold and the nature philosophers do no more than express a personal preference for wilderness values over urban values? Do they establish for the rest of us the supremacy of wilderness values? Does the wilderness remind us of our origins and our history any more than Shakespeare? Are the ethical restraints

[40] *Id.* at 91–93.

of wilderness sportsmanship any more compelling than the moral imperatives of urban life? Leopold and other naturalists have a single vision of man's nature and needs. And in many respects it is an intensely American view, American in feeling a separation from Europe, in celebrating our frontier, in surveying a country of spacious skies, of amber waves of grain, and purple mountains' majesties. But do they not ignore another vision, also widely shared? That other vision appeared in a newspaper in the fall of 1974. The article recounts the arrival of transfer students at Stanford University, a campus of 9000 acres, with spacious skies, some amber fields, and purple hills, if not mountains, of some pretense to majesty. When asked to compare Stanford with City University of New York, one student said, perhaps inelegantly but with obvious deep feeling: "You could stagnate in a college community like this . . . not enough diversity. Where the city is, that's where things are happening."[41]

How do the environmentalists respond to this? A modern answer may be found in the science of ecology and the rules of behavior some commentators have founded upon it. And a contradiction of that answer may be found in the work of neoclassical economists. Those two schools of thought are considered next.

II

In treating Leopold's *A Sand County Almanac* as the epitome of environmental thinking, we have focused so far on his poetic and instinctive treatment of the values of wilderness experience. But Leopold was a scientist, and his book is permeated with insights from the science of ecology. "Land, then, is not merely soil; it is a fountain of energy flowing through a circuit of soils, plants, and animals," and "When a change occurs in one part of the circuit, many other parts must adjust themselves to it."[42]

Leopold was by no means the first to recognize the interworkings of the natural world. In fact, the word "ecology" was coined nearly a century earlier by the German zoologist, Ernst Haeckel, to describe the life science dealing with the relationships between organisms and the environment.[43] Ironically, the word "ecology" was formed from the word "economy," which preceded it by some 350 years; both words derive from the Greek *oikos*, which means home or dwelling place. Even before Haeckel and the advent of the science of ecology, natural-

[41] San Francisco Sunday Examiner & Chronicle, Sept. 8, 1974, § 5, at 5, cols. 1 & 2.
[42] A. Leopold, *supra* note 2, at 216.
[43] *See* Principles of Animal Ecology (1949).

ists appreciated the seamless unity of Nature and extrolled its innate wisdom. Ralph Waldo Emerson, for example, portrayed nature as more than just material, but also as process and result. "All the parts incessantly work into each other's hands," Emerson wrote in one of his early essays. He continued:

> The wind sows the seed; the sun evaporates the sea; the wind blows the vapor to the field; . . . the rain feeds the plant; the plant feeds the animal: and thus the endless circulations of the divine charity nourish man.[44]

A more scientific contributor to ecological thought was the American diplomat and scholar George Perkins Marsh. Marsh's book, *Man and Nature; Or, Physical Geography as Modified by Human Action,* first published in 1864, has been praised as the first significant study of the impact of man on his environment.[45] His thesis is that manmade changes in the environment have effects on the fundamental harmony and balance of nature more extensive and disruptive than may be intended or foreseen. He remarks:

> [T]he organic and inorganic worlds are . . . bound together by such mutual relations and adaptations as secure, if not the absolute permanence and equilibrium of both, a long continuance of the established conditions at any given time. . . . But man is everywhere a disturbing agent.[46]

Despite the observations and admonitions of this early American naturalist, the science of ecology was not popularized until 1962, when Rachel Carson's book, *Silent Spring,* was first serialized in *The New Yorker* magazine. *Silent Spring* reiterates much of Marsh's theme—that the balanced interaction between living things and their surroundings has been upset by man's reckless domination of nature. Carson's book was immensely influential, for she provided a vivid and passionate evaluation of the damaging effects of chemical agents—primarily DDT—on the quality of all forms of life. "We stand now where two roads diverge," Carson warned.[47] In order to choose the road to salvation, it is essential, she averred, to understand the rules of ecology.

For me, Barry Commoner's collection of essays entitled *The Closing Circle: Nature, Man and Technology* provides the most accessible discourse on the principles of ecology and their relevance to social policy. It is difficult to introduce *The Closing Circle* in a word or two,

---

[44] R. Emerson, *supra* note 20, at 5.
[45] Lacey, *Man, Nature and the Ecological Perspective,* 8 Am. Studies 15 (1970).
[46] G. Marsh, Man and Nature 36 (1865).
[47] R. Carson, Silent Spring 277 (1962).

just as it is difficult to characterize Professor Commoner briefly. He is foremost a scientist—a biological scholar of renown—but he is also a sensitive social philosopher and a colorful and expressive author. All of these facets of the man are reflected in his essays: they are at once vivid, straightforward and moralistic. Commoner constructs hypotheses regarding air pollution, contamination of waters, and threats of atomic radiation—all based on measurable data. He argues in terms of right and wrong with an urgent sense of moral duty. And he adeptly uses metaphors which evoke in us his desired responses. "The environmental crisis is a sign that the finely sculptured fit between life and its surroundings has begun to corrode." And he asks: "Where did the fabric of the ecosphere begin to unravel?"[48] But Commoner's central metaphor is "the circle of life."[49] These figures of speech are, of course, more than simple literary devices: they *do* convey the essence of the science of ecology; they *do* remind us of the cyclical flow of energy and life, and of the impact of human activity on this cycle.

However, it is neither Commoner's scientific accomplishment nor his literary style which interests me most. Instead, I will focus on Commoner the social philosopher, the biologist who extracts from scientific principles a code for human conduct. He calls his informal prescriptions the Laws of Ecology;[50] there are four of these:

(1) Everything is connected to everything else;
(2) Everything must go somewhere;
(3) Nature knows best; and
(4) There is no such thing as a free lunch.

Although these prescriptions may be based on scientific principles, they are normative, and therefore debatable, propositions.

The first law states that "everything is connected to everything else." This may seem to be a simple iteration of the observations of Marsh, Leopold, Carson and other ecologists, all of whom believed in an elaborate web of interconnection among all organisms. Commoner, however, analyzes the functioning of this network of interrelationships in greater detail and with the benefit of modern scholarship. He contends that balance within the ecosphere is achieved by dynamic, self-compensatory properties of the system, and he develops several examples of this self-regulatory process. Consider the freshwater ecological cycle: fish—organic waste—bacterial decay—inorganic nutrients—algae—fish.

[48] B. Commoner, The Closing Circle 11 (1971).
[49] *Id.* at 12, 299.
[50] *Id.* at 33–48.

If, due to unusually warm weather, there is a rapid growth of algae, the supply of nutrients becomes depleted so that algae and nutrients are temporarily out of balance. But through self-correction the system re-establishes equilibrium. The surplus algae increase the available food supply for fish; the fish eat the algae, thereby reducing the algal population and in turn increasing their own waste production, which, as the waste decays, leads once again to a higher level of nutrients. Thus, the freshwater ecosystem returns to proper balance.

In such a precariously balanced system there is always danger that the entire chain may collapse if the self-compensating properties of the system come under too much stress. When large amounts of human wastes are introduced into the freshwater system, the bacterial activity and oxygen consumption may increase so disproportionately to the production of oxygen by algae that the oxygen level goes to zero, and the system collapses. In short, the self-correction that normally restores balance cannot occur. Implicit in this law of limited self-regulation and total interconnection within an ecosystem is a rule of conduct. The lesson to be learned is: "Do not interfere with the system."

In my view, however, a prescription for behavior does not necessarily follow from a description of scientific fact. Even without human intrusion, life systems may strike ecological balances at quite different levels, and sometimes the operation of natural processes may change their basic structures. Both the coming of the Ice Age and its retreat, for example, had enormous impacts on the ecology of North America. Yet, we make no judgments about the quality of the ecosystems before and after the Ice Age; we merely observe that they were different. Thus, the realization that everything is connected with everything else and that intrusion into the life cycle may produce new ecological balance points does not tell society whether, when, or how to act.

It is conceivable, for example, that depositing human wastes in Lake Erie may be desirable, even though this will certainly change the ecology of the lake. Simply knowing that human intrusion causes a change in the system does not tell us whether that change is good or bad. Ecology enables us to describe likely consequences of specific acts, and it may even allow us to recognize that certain conduct produces unknown and potentially dangerous effects. But the decision whether or not to engage in specific activities cannot be answered merely by reference to the first law of ecology—that everything is connected to everything else. That is true of everything good as well as everything bad. It may seem intuitively right to extrapolate an ethic against all human intrusion on the basis of ecological observations; but it is, nonetheless, an assignment of conservative values that we do not find anywhere else in nature.

The second law of ecology—"everything must go somewhere"—is an informal restatement of a basic premise of classical physics: matter is indestructible. Commoner's use of this principle, however, is highly didactic. He dispels the prevalent notion that discarded items simply "go away" by tracing the ecological path of a common "throw-away," a dry-cell battery containing mercury.[51] The battery is burned as rubbish. The fire vaporizes the mercury which, carried by the wind, eventually comes to earth in precipitation. It then flows into a mountain lake, where it condenses and sinks to the bottom. By chemical reaction it is converted to a soluble mercury compound which enters fish, and after the fish encounter hook and frying pan, the mercury eventually enters man.

Underlying the law that everything must go somewhere is Commoner's directive that we avoid "artificial" materials—those not created by nature—because of the dangers of introducing foreign substances into the life cycle. He asserts:

> One of the chief reasons for the present environmental crisis is that great amounts of materials have been extracted from the earth, converted into new forms, and discharged into the environment. . . . The result, too often, is the accumulation of harmful amounts of material in places where, in nature, they do not belong.[52]

This guide is not a certain one; it lacks discrimination. Natural processes may cause mercury poisoning as surely as do artificial conversions. Similarly, disposal of nondegradable plastic wastes poses problems different in kind from those of atomic waste disposal. Commoner's second law does not provide for such distinctions. Knowledge that "everything goes somewhere" is not sufficient to resolve questions regarding the wisdom of producing a particular artificial material.

The third law of ecology—that nature knows best—largely coincides with arguments presented by opponents of technology. Commoner infers from that law "that any major man-made change . . . is likely to be *detrimental* to the system."[53] Proof of this proposition is characteristically broad and proceeds by vivid analogy. Commoner asks us to open our watches, close our eyes, and poke a pencil into the works. This action is likely to cause damage, because the watchmaker has a well-conceived design—just as nature does. Thus, interference with natural design is probably harmful. Commoner's counsel is one of

[51] *Id.* at 40.
[52] *Id.* at 40–41.
[53] *Id.* at 41 (emphasis in original).

caution and prudence; he is no Luddite. But his suggestion that we regard manmade environments and manmade chemical compounds as deleterious to the natural life cycle can be easily exaggerated by others. At its extreme, the Third Law of Ecology encourages public policies forbidding technological innovation.

The question that arises in the skeptical legal mind is whether we can formulate sound policy on the presumption that natural things are better than artificial ones. As John Maddox asks, was "the discovery of bacteria and then of means of preventing infectious disease"[54] detrimental to the system? Some might answer that, viewed in full perspective, man's disease-fighting efforts do indeed seriously upset the design of nature. Others insist that man's mastery of nature—his artificial structures, machines, and synthetics—are as natural as was his use of stones and branches for tools. Clearly, the issue of natural process versus artificial intrusion needs a more precise evaluation than is provided by the aphorism, "nature knows best."

The fourth and final law of ecology states that "there is no such thing as a free lunch." This, needless to say, is not a postulate of physical science. Rather, it is Commoner's application to environmental management of a familiar economic maxim, that benefits entail costs. Commoner explains:

> Because the global ecosystem is a connected whole, in which nothing can be gained or lost and which is not subject to over-all improvement, anything extracted from it by human effort must be replaced. Payment of this price cannot be avoided; it can only be delayed.[55]

It is good to recognize this fact. However, the conclusion that man should be slow to disturb natural processes outstrips the premise. The proposition that every lunch has its price is not truly an answer; it is merely a question. And the ultimate question is, how high the price and how good the lunch. Ecology may be able to tell us the price, but it is no Michelin guide to the quality of the forthcoming meal.

Ecological philosophy, as represented by Commoner, contains two contradictory premises: the first is the value-free proposition that interrelations of nature's organisms may be observed and hypotheses then constructed to allow prediction of the consequences of certain acts. The second proposition is that because there are consequences which have costs, certain acts should be avoided. At some level of cost, we may all agree. But at lower cost levels there is bound to be disagreement. Even

[54] J. Maddox, The Doomsday Syndrome 170 (1972).
[55] B. Commoner, *supra* note 48, at 46.

if the costs are indisputable, the benefits will be valued differently by different individuals. The value judgment made by Commoner seems to emphasize the costs and minimize the benefits. All four laws of ecology counsel inaction: do not change nature; avoid technological change; nature's way of doing things is best. Yet, when we ask the ecologist, "why?" we seem to be no farther along than we were before the science of ecology arrived. His science does not answer; his value system merely tells us his preferences, how *he* would weigh benefits and costs. The ecologist-philosopher's premises, once distilled, rest on ethical and aesthetic beliefs, not scientific facts. In my view, the Four Laws of Ecology are philosophical heirs of the wilderness philosophers. In short, the science of ecology may teach us a great deal about the workings of nature, but the philosophy of ecology takes us little farther than Leopold's intuitive Basic Law: "A thing is right when it tends to preserve the integrity, stability, and beauty of the biotic community. It is wrong when it tends otherwise."[56]

III

A third major intellectual influence on environmentalism is that dismal science, economics. If environmentalists were to characterize themselves as revolutionaries, they would almost certainly depict economists as counterrevolutionary adversaries. Leopold, for one, complains that "some economists see the whole of society as a plaything for [their] processes";[57] while Commoner argues that "[i]f we are to survive, ecological considerations must guide economic and political ones"[58] and not vice versa. The environmentalists' disdain for economics is understandable, especially with respect to traditional or neoclassical economic philosophy. Yet not all economic theories are antithetical to the value system of environmentalists. This may be demonstrated by examining the Neo-Marxist school of economic thought, before we turn to the neoclassical, capitalist precepts which are prevalent in our own society.

Neo-Marxism is, of course, an outgrowth of the thought of Karl Marx. The principal contemporary refinement of Marxist doctrine is set forth by Paul A. Baran and Paul M. Sweezy in their book *Monopoly Capital* and is the perception that monopoly is the dominant economic force in capitalist society. Monopoly capitalism derives its power from the tendency of economic surplus to rise to the higher echelons of

[56] A. LEOPOLD, *supra* note 2, at 224–25.
[57] *Id.* at 186.
[58] B. COMMONER, *supra* note 48, at 292.

society.[59] In this analysis, the difference between what a society produces and the cost of production comprises the surplus which comes under the control of corporate managers and owners. Baran and Sweezy state:

> The size of the surplus is an index of productivity and wealth, of how much freedom a society has to accomplish whatever goals it may set for itself. The composition of the surplus shows how it uses that freedom.[60]

Maintaining still the Hegelian-Marxist dialectic of thesis, antithesis and synthesis, Baran and Sweezy see monopoly capitalism as the thesis which, by its irrationality, creates its own antithesis, leading to a new synthesis. The thesis of capitalism—maximization of profits—dictates the modes of surplus utilization—for example, advertising and militarism—which promote the interests of the capitalist class. Such use of surplus, however, inevitably generates contradiction or antithesis. The contradiction lies in the wide disparity between capitalists' use of surplus and true human desires. Rather than stressing class struggle, Neo-Marxists perceive a fundamental conflict between the objectives of monopoly capitalism, with its misapplication of economic surplus, and the very basis of life. Capitalist ideology, Neo-Marxists assert, clings to anachronistic and moribund concepts, and, by manipulating surplus, it perpetrates half-truths that frustrate mankind by creating expectations which cannot be satisfied and represses impulses which are neutral and healthy.

Richard England and Barry Bluestone present a Neo-Marxian analysis of the pollution problem. At the root of the crisis, they state,

> is the high premium we have put on material growth. So long as either population *or* the material standard of living is growing the total volume of pollution will eventually reach intolerable levels.[61]

The only way to avert that ecological Armageddon is to assure the continual and rapid decline in the amount of pollution per unit of production, and this is not likely to occur unless all production and consumption activities recycle all wastes. Alternatively, "if ecological disasters are to be prevented and not simply postponed, material growth must eventually be restricted."[62] But the capitalist system requires rapid and continuous growth to avoid mass unemployment and depression. Thus, the private market economy operates on a treadmill: in order to

[59] P. Baran & P. Sweezy, Monopoly Capital 52–78 (1966).

[60] *Id.* at 9.

[61] England & Bluestone, *Ecology and Social Conflict*, in Toward a Steady-State Economy 198 (H. Daly ed. 1973) (emphasis in original).

[62] *Id.*

forestall mass unemployment, growth patterns must be accelerated and ever higher levels of consumption must be stimulated, adding endlessly to pollution and eventually causing environmental collapse.

The Neo-Marxist prescription for escape from ecological disaster is socialization of the economy. The premises of the argument are broader than environmentalism, however; they rest on the character of production in advanced societies and on the nature of man. All production, it is contended, is social and not private. Consumption or production by any one person affects the welfare of others. Therefore, economic policymaking should not rest with a few select individuals; to assure responsible and equitable decisionmaking, everyone should participate in determining what is produced, how it is produced, and how it is distributed. Environmentally conscious groups in a socialist, participatory system, Bluestone and England contend, will direct consumptive energies toward public transport, communal shelter, and community-owned property.

While the Neo-Marxist vision of environmental betterment through social control and restraint of production appeals to the idealism of many, much of the reasoning seems naive and muddled. Relying on Marx's notion that the "essence of human nature"[63] is realizable only through the active relating of oneself to others and to nature, the Neo-Marxists suggest that the new socialist society will assure a spiritually overhauled citizenry. Instinctive drives and natural, transcendent values will not be repressed or manipulated as in capitalist society. As true human qualities emerge, values will become objective rather than subjective because there will be no basis for disagreement as to an object's worth. According to the Neo-Marxists, wilderness and nature values will emerge as objective and inviolable truths in a socialist state. Thus, at the extreme limits of their idealism, some Neo-Marxist economists ultimately endorse the naturalists' preference for wilderness values.

Optimistic as the Neo-Marxist ideal appears to be, England and Bluestone concede that no existing socialist model has been wholly successful in dealing with the environmental crisis. Industrial pollution has not been controlled; wilderness values have not triumphed. The Soviet Union is roundly condemned for its authoritarian economic policies which establish production quotas "without regard for controlling waste and pollution"[64] and which encourage personal consumerism. Although the Maoist model receives better marks because of its emphasis on

---

[63] *Quoted in* Fromm, *Marx's Contribution to the Knowledge of Man*, in MARX AND CONTEMPORARY SCIENTIFIC THOUGHT 458 (1969).

[64] England & Bluestone, *supra* note 61, at 207.

communalism and because of its willingness to temper the rate of material growth, it does not, they concede, offer an acceptable program for America.[65] Thus, for an analysis that fits our institutions and conforms to prevailing ideology, we turn to neoclassical economic theory.

The neoclassical economist sees man as a rational being who seeks to maximize his own welfare. As a consumer he purchases goods and services of various types up to the point where, for him, the value of one more item *just equals* the value of some other alternative. Similarly, the producer of goods and services manufactures up to the point where the incremental cost of producing one more item *just equals* the price he can obtain for it in the marketplace. Thus, the neoclassical economist sees an allocation of resources that maximizes the public good by providing just the right amount and mix of goods and services that consumers desire. The price system provides signals to producers indicating that more or less of certain items are desired; it also rations scarce goods and services among consumers. The operation of the price system to produce this equilibrium is dependent on three conditions: (1) perfect competition, manifested by the inability of any producer or consumer to affect price by his conduct; (2) good information about supply, demand, and price; and (3) the absence of external diseconomies. It is this latter concept with which we are primarily concerned.

External diseconomies may be defined as the use of resources without cost to the user, but at a cost to others. Since the user does not pay a price for the use of the resource, the price system fails in its function of telling users how much to consume, and it further fails to ration the resource adequately. This market failure results in pollution, an external diseconomy that distorts resource allocation. The air is polluted, the traditional economists tell us, because the manufacturer can discharge wastes into the sky without paying a price for the use of clean air. Nobody owns the air and hence nobody can sell it for waste disposal.

In theory, a group of citizens wishing to breathe clean air may approach the manufacturer and pay him to reduce his emissions. But in practice, the group cannot accomplish this because the costs of getting together are prohibitive.[66] For example, suppose that a manufacturer is willing to install pollution control equipment in return for a $100,000 payment. And, suppose that each of 100,000 affected citizens is willing to pay $1.10 to have cleaner air. If the formation of the citizen group

[65] *Id.* at 209.

[66] *See* Coase, *The Problem of Social Costs*, 3 J. LAW & ECON. 1 (1960).

were costless, the group and the manufacturer would strike a bargain for the installation of the pollution equipment at some figure between $100,000 and $110,000. But, if it costs $20,000 for mailings, collection of contributions, and other organizational expenses, no bargain can be reached, since the clean air group has only $90,000 to offer the manufacturer. Even if transaction costs are reduced, the motivational problem of free riders exists: can a clean air group be organized in the first place, in view of the individual's incentive to say, "Let George do it"?

This analysis—familiar enough to those who have considered the economics of pollution—provides the basis for the neoclassical economists' solution to the problem of pollution. That solution is to create a simulated market condition by establishing prices for the resources used for the disposal of wastes. The most common suggestion is to establish effluent taxes to be measured at the equilibrium point, that is, the point at which the cost of removal of one more unit of pollution just equals the amount of damages saved by the removal. It is at this point that the resource is most efficiently used by society—partly clean and partly dirty.

The implications of the neoclassical view of environmental protection now become clear. Society must strive to count the costs of pollution and the costs of cleaning up. Yet there are no absolutes: totally clean air, or 100 percent pure water, is not the goal of social action. Instead, we must try to quantify the benefits of clean air and water, and we should not spend money on pollution abatement in amounts greater than the benefits. We should not, in short, have a national goal like that of the 1972 Water Pollution Act:[67] zero discharge of pollutants. Indeed, we should not have standards at all, for standards, except by accident, are going to be too high or too low in relation to the damage imposed by pollution.

Other proposals for social action stem directly from the economists' model and are even more imaginative. One that has yet to be tried but that derives directly from economic theory, was first proposed by Professor Dales and has since attracted other academic support.[68] Instead of shadow prices by way of effluent charges, Dales proposed that we create property interests in pollution rights (or, to economists, the allocational equivalent: property interests in pollution no-rights) and then let bargaining determine the optimum level of pollution.

[67] 33 U.S.C. §§ 1251–1376 (1970). *See* text at note 71 *infra*.
[68] J. Dales, Pollution, Property and Prices (1968).

While most of the neoclassical economic thinking on environmental issues has been directed toward pollution problems, some economists have considered the significance of wilderness and nature values in formulating sound social policy. Here, too, the gulf between the economist and the natural philosopher is wide. As we have seen, the naturalists' value scheme expresses a preference for natural processes over the artificial, for wilderness over urbanization. The naturalists' reasoning proceeds as follows: an individual is mentally healthier, whether he knows it or not, if he can escape to nature; given such healthy individuals, society will be better off; and even if this is not the case, nature is irreplaceable and the minority who embrace wilderness values are entitled to protection against irreparable loss. The latter argument is usually bolstered by invoking the claims of future generations of nature-lovers—who may or may not be in the minority.

Some economists would scoff at these claims. They proceed from a different set of assumptions—that each individual knows what is best for himself (or at least knows better than anyone else), and that through bargaining and the free exercise of consumer sovereignty, social welfare will be maximized. "Social welfare" in this usage is not an independent value with normative content. It is comprised of the sum of individual preferences, whether they be "good" or "bad" from the standpoint of these economists' personal set of preferences.

Thus, wherever property interests in natural values can be created, these economists would allow the market to allocate the resources. Take the Grand Canyon National Park as an illustration. Assume that exclusive rights of use may be enforced at negligible cost, since access to the park is easily controlled. In such a situation, a traditional economist such as Milton Friedman would propose that the park be sold to the highest bidder.[69] If a power company or Walt Disney Enterprises offers more for the property than the Sierra Club or the Friends of the Earth, it is because the greater social benefit, as perceived by consumers, lies in commercial development of the canyon.

It is not that this economist personally believes that society is better off with a pleasure palace or a power dam at the Grand Canyon; he sees himself as value-free on the question of how the resource is to be used. His value attaches to the process of allocation; he desires a procedure that will allocate the resource in a manner that will produce the greatest net consumer satisfaction. He accepts the results of dollar voting.

Other economists working within the neoclassical tradition strain

---

[69] *See* M. FRIEDMAN, CAPITALISM AND FREEDOM 31 (1962).

to avoid conclusions from a theory that calls for the sale of a Grand Canyon.[70] They postulate an option demand—a consumer preference that the Grand Canyon remain unspoiled—for which the consumer will pay even though he never intends to visit the park. Having hypothesized this option demand, these economists can summon the standard analysis of market failure to support government intervention. One can never measure the aggregate value of the option demand because of the free rider problem. Why should I contribute to the preservation of the Grand Canyon if I think others will carry the day and me along with it?

Just how these theorists justify "No Sale" when their theory hypothesizes an inability to determine consumer preference is somewhat obscure. To the lawyer, they appear to be playing the legal game of burden of proof: make no change in the status quo until proponents of change establish their case. But note that the fighting is internecine; both groups of economists work within the constraints of consumer preference. Their disagreement arises over measurement of aggregate demand, not over how to act once demand is established.

The differences between the environmental philosopher and the neoclassical economist are even wider and deeper than I have described so far. They differ not only over the nature of man but over the proper role of government in ordering society. Aldo Leopold represents a long tradition in environmental thought in believing that man is a part of nature, that his physical and mental wellbeing depend on rapport with nature. When man seeks to escape the chain of nature, when technology insulates him from primeval pursuits such as fishing, hunting, and farming, he loses a vitality that makes for a healthy man and a good society. The neoclassical economists regard man as both selfish and rational: man seeks to maximize pleasure and minimize pain and has the ability, through the exercise of reason, to make that calculus and to act on its product. And the economists allow for a vast number of different products in the sum of those individual calculations, for one man's pain is another's pleasure.

The difference then between the environmental philosopher and the economist is that the environmentalist discerns in all mankind certain universal traits or common characteristics that lead man to construct a hierarchy of values and that require society to adopt a set of policies to implement those values. While the economist also perceives a basic characteristic in all mankind, self-interest, his perception leads him to

[70] Krutilla, *Conservation Reconsidered*, 57 Am. Econ. Rev. 777, 778–80 (1967).

adopt not a value hierarchy against which to test public policy, but to devise a process for accommodating a great variety of competing human desires. The environmentalist would base public policy on a set of values he holds to be transcendent and absolute, inherent in the nature of man and therefore ineluctable. The economist rejects absolutes: what is good is what the individual prefers; a good society is one that maximizes freedom of choice. The economists' values speak to the question of *how* society should be organized in order to satisfy individual desires, whatever they may be.

This difference in attitude toward the nature of man and what is good for him produces a fundamental conflict between the two schools of thought over the proper role of government in resource allocation and environmental protection. While Leopold himself may recognize that his cherished wilderness values may not be shared by the majority, and while his writings may constitute an appeal to individuals to know themselves and change their ways, the environmental movement itself would go further to employ government's power to protect society from itself. The justification for government decree inheres in the environmentalists' fundamental beliefs: if it is true that mankind withers, that society decays when we fail "to preserve the integrity, stability and beauty of the biotic community," when we violate the Four Laws of Ecology, then it easily follows that all possible actions must be taken to avoid ecocide.

I must confess my unease with environmental postulates carried to these conclusions. The result, too often, is the imposition by government of flat rules reflecting absolutist values. The Federal Water Pollution Control Act Amendments of 1972[71] are an example. The stated national goal, to be achieved by 1985, is the elimination of the discharge of *all* pollutants into the nation's waters. After 100 years of population growth and industrialization, our waters are to be restored to their natural purity in 13 years. The goal is not likely to be achieved, for the cost would run to hundreds of billions of dollars—some part of which many would prefer to remain in the private sector to be spent by individual decision, and the other part of which, the dollars left in the public sector, might bring greater satisfactions if spent on housing, education and jobs.

The economists' model—and of course they neither invented it nor does it belong to them exclusively—seems to me more in keeping

[71] 12 U.S.C. § 24; 15 U.S.C. §§ 633, 636; 31 U.S.C. § 711; 33 U.S.C. §§ 1251–65, 1281–92, 1311–28, 1341–45, 1361–76 (Supp. III, 1973).

with democratic theory in a pluralistic society. I would argue that the proper role of the government in resource allocation and environmental protection is to define property rights, so that market exchanges can occur; to enforce those bargains and protect property rights so defined; and to intervene in the economy when market failure produces external diseconomies such as water and air pollution. But the intervention should not be based on absolutist values of 100 percent pure water and pure air, for some individuals (probably more than a few) would prefer the alternative goods and services that could be produced by the resources that environmentalists would devote to their absolutist goals.[72]

That the controversy over environmental protection should exhibit a conflict between absolutism and pluralism should surprise no one: that conflict has characterized many an earlier controversy. As a society, we seem to swing back and forth between the two poles, and as individuals many of us do the same inside ourselves. But I would hope as we face the environmental issues of the future that we would recall the admonitions of Learned Hand: "[W]e never shall get along in matters of large public interest, if we proceed by generalizations, indeed, if you insist, by principles, put forward as applicable in all circumstances."[73] Liberty, the great judge says elsewhere,

> is secure only . . . in that sense of fair play, of give and take, of the uncertainty of human hypothesis, of how changeable and passing are our surest convictions, which has so hard a chance to survive in any times, perhaps especially in our own.[74]

What is required is Hand's Spirit of Liberty, "the spirit that is not too sure that it is right."[75]

---

[72] For a philosopher's attempt to justify an obligation to protect natural environments, see Sagoff, *supra* note 7, at 264–67. Professor Tribe has examined the argument critically in Tribe, *From Environmental Foundations to Constitutional Structures: Learning from Nature's Future*, 84 YALE L.J. 545 (1975). Building on his earlier thought-provoking article, Tribe, *Ways Not to Think About Plastic Trees: New Foundations for Environmental Law*, 83 YALE L.J. 1315 (1974), he seeks to develop a value system that goes beyond the satisfaction of wants in utilitarianism and recognizes rights in natural objects, with Kant rather than Bentham as the starting point for new thinking. Moreover, Professor Tribe is vitally concerned with process in building the new value system: "[I]ts central characteristic must be communal choice in terms of principles 'capable of evolution as we change in the process of pursuing them.'" 84 YALE L.J. at 552 (footnote omitted).

[73] L. HAND, THE SPIRIT OF LIBERTY 227 (1953).

[74] *Id.* at 76.

[75] *Id.* at 190.

[2]

Valparaiso University Law Review

Volume 25 | Fall 1990 | Number 1

ARTICLE

"CLEAN NEW WORLD": TOWARD AN INTELLECTUAL HISTORY OF AMERICAN ENVIRONMENTAL LAW, 1961-1990

PROFESSOR ROBERT F. BLOMQUIST*

I. INTRODUCTION

I am greatly honored by your attendance at my Inaugural Lecture. Mindful of John Dryden's warning about those "who think too little and who talk too much"[1] and cognizant of Ben Johnson's observation that "talking and eloquence are not the same.... A fool may talk, but a wise man speaks,"[2] I shall try to speak much but talk little.

Indeed, my lecture today will reveal that my thoughts on the intellectual history of modern American environmental law are incomplete and still evolving. As the title of my lecture implies, I present you with a work-in-progress -- with an impressionistic painting only partially shaded; with a bas

---

* Professor of Law, Valparaiso University School of Law. B.S., University of Pennsylvania (Wharton School) 1973; J.D., Cornell University 1977. Portions of this paper were originally delivered at my Inaugural Lecture at the Valparaiso University School of Law on March 28, 1990. I gratefully acknowledge the helpful comments and criticisms that George Priest, Richard Brooks, Jack Hiller, Richard Stith, Phil Gilbertson, Ed Gaffney, Charles Ehren, Jr., Paul Brietzke, Dave Myers, Roger W. Findley, and L. Diane Schenke provided of earlier drafts or summaries of this article.

1. J. DRYDEN, ABSALOM AND ACHITOPHEL (1680), *quoted in* J. BARTLETT, FAMILIAR QUOTATIONS 304 (15th ed. 1980).

2. B. JOHNSON, TIMBER; OR DISCOVERIES MADE UPON MEN AND MATTER (1640), *quoted in* J. BARTLETT, FAMILIAR QUOTATIONS 257 (15th ed. 1980).

relief still rough around the edges. Today's lecture represents the cornerstone for a long-term project that will, I hope, lead to further articles and, possibly, a book on the subject a few years from now.

Two main questions that I would like to consider with you can be stated as follows: First, will our knowledge of the dynamics of political give and take between opposing interest groups -- both organized and disorganized, either now or in the future -- suffice to explain all aspects of contemporary American environmental law? On the supposition that the answer to the initial question is in the negative, the second question is: What role have diverse and eclectic intellectual ideas from scholars, writers, and government officials had in the evolution of American environmental law during the past three decades? You will observe at once, I am sure, that the answer to the second question -- in light of a presumed negative answer to the first question -- depends on two crucial details: (1) the quality and quantity of the record of intellectual writings about environmental issues during the sixties, seventies, and eighties; and (2) whether, and to what extent, lawyers and legal decisionmakers in legislatures, courts, and administrative agencies have relied directly or indirectly upon this diverse body of writing.

To probe and ponder the answers to these two overarching questions and related points, I propose to proceed as follows. Initially, I will consider the nature of the staggering complexity in the structure, process and content of modern American environmental law.[3] Second, I shall briefly explain and survey existing historical literature about "things environmental": from ecological histories to histories of environmental ethics to environmental political histories to futuristic writings about the environment based on historical trends.[4] Third, the lecture will explain the difference of my proposed focus on the *intellectual* history[5] of modern American environmental law in comparison to

3. *See infra* notes 12-41 and accompanying text.

4. *See infra* notes 42-80 and accompanying text.

5. Intellectual history is predominantly the history of ideas and the intellectuals who profered those ideas. For general world intellectual histories, see generally F. BAUMER, MAIN CURRENTS OF WESTERN THOUGHT: READINGS IN WESTERN EUROPEAN INTELLECTUAL HISTORY FROM THE MIDDLE AGES TO THE PRESENT (rev. 2d ed. 1964); F. BAUMER, MODERN EUROPEAN THOUGHT: CONTINUITY AND CHANGE IN IDEAS, 1600-1950 (1977); J. BRONOSKI & B. MAZLISH, THE WESTERN INTELLECTUAL TRADITION: FROM LEONARDO TO HEGEL (1960); A. BULLOCK, THE HUMANIST TRADITION IN THE WEST (1985); F.E. & F.P. MANUEL, UTOPIAN THOUGHT IN THE WESTERN WORLD (1979); MODERN EUROPEAN INTELLECTUAL HISTORY: REAPPRAISALS AND NEW PERSPECTIVES (D. La Capra & S. Kaplan eds. 1982); R. NISBET, HISTORY OF THE IDEA OF PROGRESS (1980); B. SCHWARTZ, THE WORLD OF THOUGHT IN ANCIENT CHINA (1985); R. STROMBERG, AFTER EVERYTHING: WESTERN INTELLECTUAL HISTORY SINCE 1945 (1975); R. STROMBERG, EUROPEAN INTELLECTUAL HISTORY SINCE 1789 (4th ed. 1986).

For American intellectual histories, see generally THE AMERICAN INTELLECTUAL TRADITION (C. Capper & D. Hollinger eds. 1989); T. BENDER, NEW YORK INTELLECTUAL: A HISTORY OF

existing environmental histories and legal analyses, while placing the proposed study of the intellectual history of American environmental law within the larger tradition of the sociological school of jurisprudence.[6] Finally, I will sketch a

---

INTELLECTUAL LIFE IN NEW YORK CITY FROM 1750 TO THE BEGINNINGS OF OUR TIME (1988); S. BERCOVITCH, THE AMERICAN JEREMIAD (1978); N. BIRNBAUM, THE RADICAL RENEWAL: THE POLITICS OF IDEAS IN MODERN AMERICA (1988); A. BLOOM, PRODIGAL SONS: THE NEW YORK INTELLECTUALS AND THEIR WORLD (1986); D. BOORSTIN, THE LOST WORLD OF THOMAS JEFFERSON (1948); P. BOYER, BY THE BOMB'S EARLY LIGHT: AMERICAN THOUGHT AND CULTURE AT THE DAWN OF THE ATOMIC AGE (1985); H. COMMAGER, THE AMERICAN MIND: AN INTERPRETATION OF AMERICAN THOUGHT AND CHARACTER SINCE THE 1880s (1950); J. DIGGINS, THE LOST SOUL OF AMERICAN POLITICS: VIRTUE, SELF-INTEREST, AND THE FOUNDATIONS OF LIBERALISM (1984); R. HOFSTADTER, ANTI-INTELLECTUALISM IN AMERICAN LIFE (1963); D. HOLLINGER, IN THE AMERICAN PROVINCE: STUDIES IN THE HISTORY AND HISTORIOGRAPHY OF IDEAS (1985); R. JACOBY, THE LAST INTELLECTUALS: AMERICAN CULTURE IN THE AGE OF ACADEME (1987); P. JOHNSON, INTELLECTUALS (1988); H. KALVEN, JR., A WORTHY TRADITION: FREEDOM OF SPEECH IN AMERICA (1988); C. LASCH, THE CULTURE OF NARCISSISM (1979); C. LASCH, THE NEW RADICALISM IN AMERICA, 1889-1963: THE INTELLECTUAL AS A SOCIAL TYPE (1965); H. MAY, THE END OF AMERICAN INNOCENCE: A STUDY OF THE FIRST YEARS OF OUR OWN TIME, 1912-1917 (1960); L. PERRY, INTELLECTUAL LIFE IN AMERICA: A HISTORY (1984); M. PETERSON, THE JEFFERSON IMAGE IN THE AMERICAN MIND (1960).

6. *See infra* notes 81-83 and accompanying text. Sociological jurisprudence is "[t]he general name for those approaches to the study of law, in general, which have more regard to the working of law in society than to its form or content." D. WALKER, THE OXFORD COMPANION TO LAW 1153 (1980). Indeed, "[s]ociological jurists look on legal institutions, doctrines, and precepts functionally; the form of legal precepts is the means only. They have very divergent philosophical views." *Id.* An appreciation of the history of the sociological school of jurisprudence is helpful as a predicate for exploring more specific intellectual histories of law.

> Montesquieu may be looked on as the forerunner of the school; he tried to trace the effect of social environment on the law. The initial steps were taken by Jhering whose *Der Zweck im Recht (Purpose in Law, translated as Law as a Means to an End)* develops aspects of analytical positivism and combines them with some utilitarian ideas; the purpose was the protection of interest. In Germany the move for a sociological jurisprudence was led by Ehrlich and Kantorowicz and this led in Germany to the "Jurisprudence of Interests" school of which the leader was Heck.
>
> In the U.S., the forerunner was Mr. Justice Holmes, succeeded by Mr. Justice Cardozo and, among academics, Roscoe Pound, followed in Australia by Stone and Paton. Pound stated the [program] of the sociological school as comprising: study of the actual social effects of legal institutions, precepts and doctrines; study in preparation for lawmaking; study of the means of making legal precepts effective in action; study of judicial method; sociological legal history; recognition of the importance of individualized application of legal precepts; a ministry of justice; and to make effort more effective in achieving the purpose of the legal order. Much attention is devoted to the interests which law seeks to protect, individual interests, social interests and public interests. This study does not, however, help to decide the crucial issues, how particular interests are to be weighed and compared one with another.
>
> A divergent branch of sociological jurisprudence is realism, the approach of jurists principally in the U.S. who regard what the courts will, in fact, do in particular cases as being the law. Notable figures adopting this standpoint have been Gray, Mr. Justice Holmes, Frank, and Llewellyn.

Id. An intellectual history of American environmental law, therefore, is consistent with broad tenets

historical inventory and prospectus of several categories of intellectual ideas drawn from fields as diverse as biology, economics, and ethics, which have impacted the development of American environmental law over the last thirty years, and in some cases, are still affecting the development today.[7]

In proposing this intellectual synthesis, I draw for inspiration and guidance on two key propositions about the nature of ideas, in general, and the history of ideas, in particular. As the philosopher Immanuel Kant reasoned, ideas are the conceptions by which we think about things. Ideas are the terms in which we state fundamental problems as well as the notions we employ in defining issues and discussing them. As the chief substance of our thought, they are *what* we think as well as what we think *about*.[8] Moreover, as stated by Professors Jacob Bronoski and Bruce Mazlish in their masterful work *The Western Intellectual Tradition*:[9]

> The history of ... ideas ... is necessarily a history of movement. The movement is created by that which gives life to ideas: by the interplay of all the interests of the mind, by the pressure of events, and by the expression of personalities.[10]

Bronoski and Mazlish went on to observe that intellectual history should be approached as "[a] complex of people and groups with conflicting ideas which yet have a common direction...."[11]

II. Environmental Law: The Beauty of Complexity

In seeking to better understand and describe the major intellectual contributions to the evolving sweep of American environmental law from 1961 to the present, it is instructive to begin discussion with a general qualitative description of the prevalent structure, processes and content of the environmental legal regime.[12] T.S. Eliot noted that: "As we grow older, the world becomes

---

of sociological jurisprudence if the history seeks to identify diverse economic, ethical, and ecological ideas as a means to the social ends of environmental protection and enhancement.

7. *See infra* notes 84-228 and accompanying text.

8. *See generally Idea* in 2 GREAT IDEAS OF THE WESTERN WORLD 761 (M. Adler ed. 1985).

9. J. BRONOSKI & B. MAZLISH, *supra* note 5.

10. *Id.* at xiii.

11. *Id.*

12. There are several excellent casebooks and treatises that describe the structure, processes, and content of American environmental law. *See generally* ENVIRONMENTAL POLICY LAW: CASES, READINGS AND TEXT (T. Schoenbaum ed. 1985); ENVIRONMENTAL PROTECTION: LAW AND POLICY (F. Anderson, D. Mandelker & A.D. Tarlock eds., 2d ed. 1990); R. FINDLEY & D. FARBER, ENVIRONMENTAL LAW: CASES AND MATERIALS (2d ed. 1985); F. GRAD, ENVIRONMENTAL LAW (3d ed. 1985); THE LAW OF ENVIRONMENTAL PROTECTION: CASES-LEGISLATION-POLICIES (J.

stranger, its pattern more complicated."[13] Such is the lot of modern environmental law: As it has grown older it has become stranger, its patterns more complicated. Indeed, the overarching *idea of complexity* is essential to understanding the meaning and operation of modern environmental law and policy.

As I previously concluded in a book review[14] of Professor William Rodgers' two-volume treatise on environmental law, *Environmental Law: Air and Water*,[15] the idea of complexity in modern American environmental law can be subdivided into three parts: (1) the multiplicity of *different interest groups*; (2) the notion of *evolutionary change* in environmental law; and (3) the bipolar principles of *absolutism* and *utilitarianism* that are at work in current environmental statutes, case decisions, and administrative regulations.[16]

With regard to the first aspect of complexity -- the multiplicity of *different interest groups* in modern environmental law -- Professor Rodgers has elegantly observed that:

> In this field, each statement of facts is a multidisciplinary saga, with loose ends trailing off to the limits of the knowledge of a variety of scientific disciplines. Environmental law arises in a world of many parties, where issues are linked together in mysterious ways, and each 'definitive' resolution is but the prelude to future bargaining, compromise, and defection. The field presents an ongoing kaleidoscope of tussling organizations, interests, jurisdictions, and states where strategies, goals and outcomes are subject to constant redefinition.[17]

In a word, American environmental law is infused and suffused with "politics." Stated differently, environmental law involves competing ideologies of the public good. As noted by political scientist Professor Samuel Hays of the University of Pittsburgh, most environmental debate in recent years has been

---

Bonine & T. McGarity eds. 1984). *See also* T. HOBAN & R. BROOKS, GREEN JUSTICE: THE ENVIRONMENT AND THE COURTS (1987); LAW OF ENVIRONMENTAL PROTECTION (S. Novick, D. Stever & M. Mellon eds. 1988); W. RODGERS, JR., ENVIRONMENTAL LAW (1977); W. RODGERS, JR., ENVIRONMENTAL LAW: AIR AND WATER (1986); W. RODGERS, JR., ENVIRONMENTAL LAW: PESTICIDES AND TOXIC SUBSTANCES (1988); F. SKILLERN, ENVIRONMENTAL PROTECTION: THE LEGAL FRAMEWORK (1981).

13. T.S. ELIOT, EAST COKER, PART V (1940), *quoted in* J. BARTLETT, FAMILIAR QUOTATIONS 807 (15th ed. 1980).

14. Blomquist, *The Beauty of Complexity* (Book Review), 39 HASTINGS L.J. 555 (1988).

15. W. RODGERS, JR., ENVIRONMENTAL LAW: AIR & WATER *supra* note 12.

16. Blomquist, *supra* note 14, at 566-70.

17. 1 W. RODGERS, JR., *supra* note 15, at v.

engendered "through personal circumstances and immediate needs, shared with others through common experiences."[18] Indeed, Hays goes on to contend that "environmental affairs [in America] have provoked much action but little focused reflection."[19] On the other hand, Professor Thomas Schoenbaum of the University of Georgia Law School makes a more refined point about the interdisciplinary nature of environmental law and politics by observing that while American environmental law "cannot be separated from politics.... [n]evertheless, the political debate is usually carried on not directly, but in the context of the legal issues involved."[20]

In my judgment, Professor Schoenbaum's view is more accurate and informed than Professor Hays' critical legal studies perspective that environmental law is essentially equivalent to environmental politics or environmental ideology.[21] Indeed, Professor Schoenbaum's *contextual view* of the indirect effect of political ideologies and interest groups on the development of environmental law implicitly acknowledges the role of larger, more dispassionate, intellectual concepts in the formulation and evolution of American environmental law.

With regard to the second part of the tripartite nature of complexity in modern American environmental law -- the notion of recurring *evolutionary* change -- it has been argued that each new environmental regulatory effect "produces its own dissatisfactions, gives rise to new 'gaps' to be filled, and creates its own demands for more regulation."[22] Continued evolutionary change tends to characterize modern American environmental law "because the facts, players, policies, rules, and strategies invariably drift and move when plotted over time."[23] Evolutionary change, then, as an aspect of the overarching complexity of environmental law, can best be understood as an inherent intellectual taproot that, while hidden and beneath the surface, nourishes and affects the continued growth of environmental laws and policies.

With regard to the third part of the tripartite nature of complexity in modern American environmental law, Professor Rodgers, again, sheds penetrating light on the subject of different, apparently diametrically opposed,

18. S. HAYS, BEAUTY, HEALTH AND PERMANENCE: ENVIRONMENTAL POLITICS IN THE UNITED STATES, 1955-1985 65 (1987).

19. *Id.* at 10.

20. T. SCHOENBAUM, *supra* note 12, at xxii.

21. *See generally* THE HARVARD SOCIETY FOR LAW AND PUBLIC POLICY AND THE FEDERALIST SOCIETY FOR LAW & PUBLIC POLICY STUDIES, A DISCUSSION ON CRITICAL LEGAL STUDIES AT THE HARVARD LAW SCHOOL (1986); THE POLITICS OF LAW: A PROGRESSIVE CRITIQUE (D. Kairys ed. 1982).

22. 1 W. RODGERS, JR., *supra* note 15, at 17.

23. *Id.* at v.

legal standards at work in current environmental statutes, case decisions, and administrative regulations. In his writings, Rodgers has pointed out the existence of "dramatic collisions between absolute rights and utilitarianism" found, for instance, in the common law principles of nuisance, and in the statutory enactments of the Clean Air and Clean Water Acts.[24] According to Rodgers, "[t]hrough the lens of *absolute rights*, on the one hand, health standards or environmental quality regulations are paramount, while pleas for economic efficiency are viewed as irrelevant and greeted with a 'dollars-be-damned-attitude.'"[25] Examples of *absolutist rules* under the Clean Air Act, for example, include: statutory principles of no significant deterioration of air quality; visibility provisions; and best technology rules for pollution control equipment.[26] Likewise, the Clean Water Act -- by way of further illustration -- reflects absolutism in several statutory provisions. Potent examples include: oil spill provisions that "forbid all discharges causing so much as a sheen on the surface of the water;"[27] "the [goal] ... [of] fishable/swimmable waters everywhere by July 1, 1983 and no discharges anywhere by January 1, 1985"[28] promulgated by Congress in 1972;[29] several "best technology" formulations that press technology "beyond the limits of benefit-cost dictates;"[30] and, the mandate to clean up hazardous pollutants in the nation's waters without regard to costs.[31]

At the other end of the jurisprudential spectrum, several provisions of modern environmental statutes take a *utilitarian* -- or balancing -- approach to problems of pollution and resource depletion. For example, under the federal Clean Air Act, the penalty provisions for violation of air standards can be viewed "as a model of economic efficiency."[32] Similarly, the Clean Air Act's

> offset emission regulations and the bubble proposals offer a splendid [utilitarian] opportunity for the market analyses popular now in the law schools. Congress even found it necessary to make clear that ... oil companie[s] could recover in price increases the costs of installing a vapor recovery system, a proposition some might consider self-evident.[33]

---

24. *Id.* at 19.
25. *Id.*
26. *Id.*
27. 1 W. Rodgers, Jr., Environmental Law: Air and Water (1986).
28. *Id.*
29. Federal Water Pollution Control Act of 1972, Pub. L. No. 92-500, § 2, 86 Stat. 896.
30. 1 W. Rodgers, Jr., *supra* note 27, at 21.
31. *Id.*
32. *Id.* at 8.
33. *Id.*

The Clean Water Act, by way of comparison, also contains "a host of cost-effectiveness formulations"[34] that suggest an endorsement of economic efficiency. "Examples of utilitarianism include the municipal sewer construction grants program, the dredge and fill rules, and provisions that pertain to review of water quality standards."[35]

The dichotomy between absolutism and utilitarianism demonstrates the divergent themes and apparently "contradictory impulses" found in modern American environmental law.[36] These contradictory impulses can be explained by pure political theory -- what Professor Hays refers to as the product of "reaction by long-established commodity producers to ... new consumer politics," which by way of persistent challenge and opposition to absolutist tendencies by grass roots and national environmental groups "succeeded in turning back, muting [and] restraining many an environmental effect" through "maximum feasible opposition and minimum feasible retreat."[37] Yet, like my earlier disagreement with Professor Hays, I think that this uni-dimensional political explanation is misinformed or uninformed about the potential influence of broader, intellectually-inspired ideas in the makeup and development of modern American environmental law.[38] As I have argued elsewhere, a

---

34. *Id.*

35. Blomquist, *supra* note 14, at 569.

36. 1 W. RODGERS, JR., *supra* note 27, at 19.

37. S. HAYS, *supra* note 18, at 288.

38. I am grateful to Professor Richard O. Brooks, Director of the Environmental Law Center and Professor of Law at the Vermont Law School, for providing me with the insight that intellectual ideas have not fulfilled their full potential in influencing the content of environmental law. In this regard, Brooks has observed in a draft unpublished manuscript:

> Although the environmental movement introduced new forms of ecological thought and practice which might have implied a revolution in conventional legal thought and practice -- that revolution, in many important ways is unrealized. For example, the moral and intellectual insights of the new discipline of ecology are barely visible in the corpus of environmental law. (The one exception may be the National Environmental Policy Act). The failure of that potential revolution is not the fault of the American people nor of the legions of committed environmentalists. The fault lies at the feet of us bureaucrats, lawyers, and scholars who have tarnished that dream with unimaginative legal responses.

R. BROOKS, A NEW AGENDA FOR MODERN ENVIRONMENTAL LAW (Vermont Law School's Environmental Law Center, draft July, 1989) (unpublished manuscript) 1 (footnotes omitted).

Professor Brooks asserts that the conventional legal regime fails to fully utilize innovative and exciting intellectual ideas. He notes:

> When Earth Day [1970] was celebrated, environmental problems were viewed in global perspective, as threats to the viability of our earth's ecosystem. We all felt the pull of grand and exciting environmental ideals, requiring the earth saving action of everyone. Over the past two decades, the charisma of the environmental response has been routinized into bureaucracy and law; a conventional legal organization, manned by tired and overworked officials, has been established to cope, day-in, day-out, with environmental problems.

plausible intellectual mode of unity between absolute rights and principles of utilitarianism can be discerned by analogy to various equitable maxims of chancery practice where apparently antipodal concepts are blended together in the legal process.[39] Jurists have intellectually expressed the need "for law to balance competing interests using general notions of justice, fair play, and practicality" in such equitable maxims as: "Equity suffers no right to be without a remedy;" "Equity regards substance rather than form;" "Equity follows the law;" "Equity will not order the doing of an impossible act;" and, "Equity prevents mischief."[40] Therefore, understood as a potentially synthesizing *intellectual pursuit* conducted within the *context* of political interaction, environmental law can be usefully viewed as "an elaborate balancing process between the rights of individuals and the needs of the social community."[41]

> The current legal approach to environmental problems illustrates a social engineering approach to these problems. The conventional pattern of environmental law conceives its problem to be the effective achievement of prosaic objectives, often stated in dull engineering prose. These objectives specify levels of ambient clean air and water, planned protection of selected ecologically-sensitive land areas such as wetlands, and proper marketing, use, or disposal of toxic substances. In short, we have taken a business-as-usual cautious legal approach.
>
> No constitutional changes, no new forms of laws, no major new institutions were deemed to be required to transform our way of life. Instead, traditional positive law in the form of a complex array of statutes are adopted by centralized government -- the federal legislature. Federal administrative bureaucracies, manned by lawyers and environmental specialists, employ plans and exhaustive and exhausting regulations as the first step in the cleanup or pollution prevention process. (When excited environmental law students meet these statutes, plans and regulations for the first time, their collective heart sinks under the boring technicality of the enterprise.) These federal bureaucracies are assisted by the states and their state bureaucracies in what some have called 'administrative federalism, in which states are simply viewed as enforcement arms of the federal government.'
>
> * * *
>
> Under the bureaucratic regime of traditional environmental protection, the abstract disciplines of law, economics, environmental sciences and policy sciences, i.e. risk assessment, ecosystem modelling and benefit/cost analysis become the opera glasses through which the Green Globe is viewed. The starting point of the legal process is the environmental symptom -- usually some form of pollution; the ending point is the removal or control of this symptom.
>
> This conventional legal model dominates the attention of legal scholarship, guides the content of formal education programs of environmental lawyers, planners and administrators, and creates the large bureaucracies which in turn hire environmental law graduates. * * * But I grow more upset when I realize that the conventional legal model the students have learned guides the way in which they and most environmental lawyers, administrators and planners see and think about the environment and the law, and the way in which scholars explore the needs for reform of that law.

Id. at 2-4 (footnotes omitted). *See also infra* note 83 and accompanying text.

39. Blomquist, *supra* note 14, at 569-70.

40. *Id.* (quoting 27 AM. JUR. 2D, *Equity* § 119 (1968)).

41. *Id.* at 570.

III. A Survey of Important Writings on Environmental History

For the reader interested in broadly pursuing historical studies of "things environmental," there is a wide assortment of books and articles -- largely written in the years following World War II -- to choose from.[42] These diverse environmental histories can be roughly sorted into four categories: (1) socio-economic-political histories of environmentalism; (2) philosophical and theological histories of environmental issues; (3) histories of ecology; and (4) "future histories" (involving projections and forecasts and speculations based on environmental trends). Without attempting to exhaustively catalog every environmental historical study, a few of the most interesting and important historical works in each of the four categories should be briefly reviewed to give a flavor for the existing historical literature on the subject.

First, with regard to *socio-economic-political histories*, E.F. Schumacher's 1973 book *Small is Beautiful: Economics as if People Mattered*[43] is a classic historical study. "Schumacher's book [r]eache[s] backward, ... embrac[ing] communal, handicraft, tribal, guild, and village lifestyle[s] as old as the neolithic cultures. In that sense, it is not an ideology at all, but a wisdom gathered from historical experience."[44] Another historical classic in this genre is Barry Commoner's 1971 book *The Closing Circle: Nature, Man & Technology.*[45] Commoner concludes his book by stating:

> Human beings have broken out of the circle of life, driven not by biological need, but by the social organization which they have devised to 'conquer' nature: means of gaining wealth that are governed by requirements conflicting with that which govern nature.
>
> * * *
>
> [T]he world is being carried to the brink of ecological disaster not by a singular fault, which some clever scheme can correct, but by the

---

42. *See generally* T. HOBAN AND R. BROOKS, GREEN JUSTICE: THE ENVIRONMENT AND THE COURTS 231-46 (1987) (bibliography of general philosophical works; biological and ecological works; literary ecological classics; planning works; planning, law, and the environment; basic causes of environmental problems; economics; political science, public administration, history and the environment; statewide experiences; ethics and psychology; the history of ideas; jurisprudential works; environmental works dealing with specific problems or environments; other ideas of law having relevance to environmental law). *See also* R. NASH, THE RIGHTS OF NATURE: A HISTORY OF ENVIRONMENTAL ETHICS 273-78 (1989) (selected annotated bibliography of literature on the history of environmental ethics, broadly conceived).

43. E. SCHUMACHER, SMALL IS BEAUTIFUL: ECONOMICS AS IF PEOPLE MATTERED (1973).

44. T. Roszak, *Introduction*, to *id.* at 4.

45. B. COMMONER, THE CLOSING CIRCLE: NATURE, MAN & TECHNOLOGY (1971).

> phalanx of powerful economic, political, and social forces that constitute the march of history. Anyone who proposes to cure the environmental crisis undertakes thereby to change the course of history.[46]

Samuel P. Hays has made an important contribution to the political history of environmental matters in America by his 1987 study *Beauty, Health and Permanence: Environmental Politics in the United States, 1955-1985*.[47] According to Professor Hays, his book traces the post-World War II

> .... transition from an older stress on efficient development and use of material resources such as water, forests, and soils known as the conservation movement, which took place in the first four decades of the twentieth century. Conservation gave way to environment after World War II amid a rising interest in the quality of life beyond efficiency in production.[48]

Another significant socio-economic-political history of environmentalism written in the last three decades includes James Whorton's 1974 book, *Before Silent Spring: Pesticides & Public Health in Pre-DDT America*,[49] which examines the period of time toward the turn of the twentieth century where "economic necessities, technological limitations, and pressures on regulatory agencies" brought America to its "dilemma of seemingly having to poison our food in order to protect it."[50] In another significant book, Douglas Weiner has written about the socio-political origins of Soviet conservation policies in his 1988 book *Models of Nature: Ecology, Conservation and Cultural Revolution in Soviet Russia*.[51]

---

46. *Id.* at 298-99. For an updated version of Barry Commoner's thinking, see B. COMMONER, MAKING PEACE WITH THE PLANET (1990) (planned to coincide with Earth Day 1990).

47. S. HAYS, *supra* note 18.

48. *Id.* at 3. Professor Hays also points out that:

> Evolving environmental values were closely associated with rising standards of living and levels of education. These changed markedly after the war. Personal real income grew and the percentage of Americans with college education increased. The social context within which environmental values flourished was twofold: younger people and the more educated. With each level of age from younger to older, environmental interest fell; and with each level of education from elementary school to college degree, it rose.

Id.

49. J. WHORTON, BEFORE SILENT SPRING: PESTICIDES AND PUBLIC HEALTH IN PRE-DDT AMERICA (1974).

50. *Id.* (book jacket synopsis).

51. D. WEINER, MODELS OF NATURE: ECOLOGY, CONSERVATION AND CULTURAL REVOLUTION IN SOVIET RUSSIA (1988).

The author describes the socio-political origins of Soviet conservation policies. After

The second major category of environmental historical works pertains to *philosophical and theological histories* of things environmental. In this category, two books are of particular importance: John Black's 1970 book, *The Dominion of Man: The Search for Ecological Responsibility*[52] and William Leiss' book, *The Domination of Nature*[53] published in 1972. These books review the ideas -- some going back to the Old Testament's charge for humans to have dominion over nature[54] -- that have contributed to present environmental problems. A 1980 book by Australian philosopher John Passmore, *Man's Responsibility for Nature: Ecological Problems and Western Traditions*,[55] provides insights to both environmental philosophy and intellectual history. Passmore concomitantly identifies grounds for environmental responsibility in Western traditions and values, while demonstrating the heritage of resistance to this idea encountered in Western thought. Eugene C. Hargrove extends Passmore's study of the ebb and flow of environmental ethics in Western philosophical thought in his 1988 book *Foundations of Environmental Ethics*.[56]

> describing the emergence of a 'conservation sensibility' among a small section of Russia's educated elite before the October 1917 Revolution, the author analyzes the way in which changes in the political regime and national mood affected Russian attitudes toward nature. He points out, for example, that while the period of Lenin's rule and of the new Economic Policies of the mid-1920's spurred the adoption of pioneering approaches to the environment featuring the creation of a network of virgin nature reserves dedicated to ecological study, the succeeding turbulence of Stalin's Five Year Plans in the 1930's proved inhospitable to ecologically informed conservation. Indeed, the book points out in stark political terms that because Soviet conservationists, using ecological arguments, sought to halt or modify such central, heroic development projects as collectivization, the introduction of exotic fauna and flora, and the construction of huge hydroelectric installations, they became vulnerable to the charge of purveying counterrevolutionary scientific theories.

Id. (book jacket synopsis).

For further interesting socio-economic-political histories of environmentalism, see also M. BROWN, LAYING WASTE: THE POISONING OF AMERICA BY TOXIC CHEMICALS (1979); CONGRESSIONAL QUARTERLY INC., THE BATTLE FOR NATURAL RESOURCES (1983); J. LASH, K. GILLMAN & P. SHERIDAN, A SEASON OF SPOILS: THE STORY OF THE REAGAN ADMINISTRATION'S ATTACK ON THE ENVIRONMENT (1984).

52. J. BLACK, THE DOMINION OF MAN: THE SEARCH FOR ECOLOGICAL RESPONSIBILITY (1970).

53. W. LEISS, THE DOMINATION OF NATURE (1972).

54. *See Genesis* 1:28.

55. J. PASSMORE, MAN'S RESPONSIBILITY FOR NATURE: ECOLOGICAL PROBLEMS AND WESTERN TRADITIONS (1980).

56. E. HARGROVE, FOUNDATIONS OF ENVIRONMENTAL ETHICS (1988). *But cf.* D. SHI, THE SIMPLE LIFE: PLAIN LIVING AND HIGH THINKING IN AMERICAN CULTURE (1975) (shows how from Jefferson to Thoreau to Louis Mumford to Scott Nering and the hippies of the 1960s, advocates of the "simple life" in relation to the environment have formed a rich and diverse American cultural tradition).

Two books by intellectual historian Roderick Nash are particularly important in probing the roots and recent past of American ethical views about the environment. In his 1967 book, *Wilderness and the American Mind*,[57] Nash contends: "Wilderness was the basic ingredient of American civilization. From the raw materials of the physical wilderness Americans built a civilization; with the idea or symbol of wilderness they sought to give that civilization identity and meaning."[58] In his recent book, *The Rights of Nature* (1989),[59] Nash elegantly focuses on more contemporary times including historical discussions of the deep ecology movement,[60] animal rights,[61] and ecofeminism.[62]

---

57. R. NASH, WILDERNESS AND THE AMERICAN MIND (1967).

58. *Id.* at vii.

59. R. NASH, *supra* note 42.

60. *Id.* at 146-47.

> Deep ecology, as George Sessions has pointed out, owes much to Norwegians. As early as 1941 Peter Zapffe outlined a non-anthropocentric theory of human-environment relations that he called 'biosophy.' And in 1974 another Norwegian, Sigmund Kvaloy, coined 'ecophilosophy' in an article in *North American Review*. But it remained for Arne Naess, the eminent Norwegian philosopher, Nazi resister, and mountaineer to exert the most impact on the new American environmentalism when he proposed 'deep ecology.' Naess also believed that ecologists and philosophers should pool their wisdom in a new discipline called 'ecosophy.' He first announced his concepts in a lecture in 1972 and published the paper in English the following year. The year 1973, then, saw the genesis of both the modern animal-rights approach to ethical extension (Peter Singer's essay was also published in that year) and deep ecology. Although professional philosophers inspired both perspectives, the two viewpoints proved ... to be uneasy allies in the new environmentalism.
>
> For Arne Naess and the American exponents of deep ecology whom he inspired, notably George Sessions and Bill Devall, the rise of ecology entailed philosophical and religious principles that completely undermined traditional ways of understanding the human-environment relationship, or what deep ecologists frequently called the 'dominant paradigm' of Western thought regarding nature. The most radical component of the new paradigm was what Naess called 'ecological egalitarianism.' Other deep ecologists commonly used 'biocentrism' or 'anti-anthropocentrism' to refer to the same philosophy, and Naess spoke of 'a core democracy in the biosphere.' The central idea was the right of every form of life to function normally in the ecosystem or, in Naess' words, 'the equal right to live and blossom.'

Id. (footnotes omitted). *See also* B. DEVALL & G. SESSIONS, DEEP ECOLOGY: LIVING AS IF NATURE MATTERED (1985); DEEP ECOLOGY (M. Tobias ed. 1985).

61. R. NASH, *supra* note 42 at 5-6.

> But 'speciesism' or 'human chauvinism' persisted [after extension of rights to blacks and women] and animal rights was the next logical stage in moral extension. By the 1970s there was growing support in Anglo-American thought for what Peter Singer was the first to call 'animal liberation.'

Id. (footnotes omitted). *See also id.* at 22-23, 24-28, 151-52, 159-60.

62. *Id.* at 145.

> Almost every feminist writer noted the parallels between the 'rape' of the 'virgin' land and abuse of women. Consequently the woman's movement of the 1960s and 1970s – coupled with growing public understanding of ecology, Indian religions, and Asian ying-yang theology – focused attention on nature as an exploited female presence.

There are a few good historical treatments of environmental theological issues. A good collection is the 1986 work, edited by Eugene Hargrove, *Religion and Environmental Crisis*.[63] In this book, various authors take a new look at the contributions that Western as well as Eastern religions have made to modern environmentalism. In a similar vein, the editors of the 1989 book, *Environmental Philosophy: The Nature of Nature in Asian Traditions of Thought*[64] take an approach that is organized around various Asian worldviews of the sacredness of nature.

In the third major category of historical environmental works -- *histories of ecology* -- there are only a handful of good books. Two books are particularly significant. In his 1977 work, *Nature's Economy: The Roots of Ecology*,[65] Donald Worster makes an important contribution to the literature by pointing out that:

> The term 'ecology' did not appear until 1866, and it took almost another hundred years for it to enter the vernacular. But the *idea* of ecology is much older than the name. Its modern history begins in the eighteenth century, when it emerged as a more comprehensive way of looking at the Earth's fabric of life: a point of view that sought to describe all of the living organisms of the Earth as an interacting whole, often referred to as the 'economy of nature.' This phrase gave

---

> If nature and women were perceived as partners in subjugation, campaigns for their ethical consideration could be mutually supportive. Indeed, many bridged the two causes under labels such as 'ecofeminism,' 'ecosophy,' and 'gyn/ecology.' According to Ynestra King, 'Ecology, feminism, and liberation for all of nature, including ourselves, are joined.' But how did this connection work? Many contended that because of their role in the creation of life, women have traditionally been 'closer' to nature than men. The feminine mind knows best how to think about the human-nature relationship. 'Ecology,' King writes, 'requires a feminist perspective,' and Jim Cheney believes that 'holistic deep ecology is somehow feminist.' Susan Griffin makes the point more poetically: 'Woman speaks with nature ... she hears voices from under the earth ... wind blows in her ears and trees whisper to her.' The whispered message, according to Griffin and most feminist writers on environmentalism, is that interrelatedness, not hierarchy, is the way of nature and should become the central support for a new moral philosophy.

Id. (footnotes omitted).

63. RELIGION AND ENVIRONMENTAL CRISIS (E. Hargrove ed., 1986).

64. ENVIRONMENTAL PHILOSOPHY: THE NATURE OF NATURE IN ASIAN TRADITIONS OF THOUGHT (J. Callicott & R. Ames ed. 1989). *See also* EARTH MIGHT BE FAIR: REFLECTIONS ON ETHICS, RELIGION AND ECOLOGY (I. Barbour ed. 1972); ECOLOGY AND RELIGION IN HISTORY (D. Spring & E. Spring ed. 1974); J. Hughes, American Indian Ecology (1983); P. SANTMIRE, THE TRAVAIL OF NATURE: THE AMBIGUOUS ECOLOGICAL PROMISE OF CHRISTIAN THEOLOGY (1985); C. STEWART, JR., NATURE IN GRACE: A STUDY IN THE THEOLOGY OF NATURE (1983); WESTERN MAN AND ENVIRONMENTAL ETHICS (I. Barbour ed. 1973).

65. D. WORSTER, NATURE'S ECONOMY: THE ROOTS OF ECOLOGY (1977).

> birth to a rich set of ideas out of which emerged the [biological] science of [ecology]....[66]

In the course of his historical study of ecology, Worster discusses such thinkers as Linnaeus -- the great Swedish "man of flowers," the evolutionary theories of Charles Darwin and Alfred North Whitehead's view of the "organic unity" of all nature.[67]

Similarly, Anna Bramwell in her 1989 book *Ecology in the 20th Century: A History*[68] traces the scientific and political history of ecology. An implicit insight of her work is that a combined scientific and political study of ecology is essential. She observes that:

> The word ecology is widely used today in the normative sense, not in the biological sense. The science of ecology is one that considers energy flows within a closed system. The normative sense of the word has come to mean the belief that severe or drastic change within that system, or indeed any change which can damage any specie within it, or that disturbs the system, is seen as wrong. Thus, ecological ideas have come to be associated with the conservation of specific patterns of energy flows. These patterns can be relatively small in scale, such as a one-acre wetland site; or it can be the weather pattern resulting from the Amazon rain forests, or larger patterns that affect the continuity of human existence.[69]

The fourth category of environmental histories entails what I have labeled *"futuristic" environmental histories*. An enormous number of books and articles providing environmental projections, forecasts and speculations based on historical records or trends have appeared in recent years. Some of the more significant include the following. In 1980, the United States Council on Environmental Quality and the United States Department of State issued their

---

66. *Id.* at x.

67. R. NASH, *supra* note 42 at 59-60.

> Utilizing new findings that constantly interacting electromagnetic particles were the essence of matter, Whitehead contended that the identity and purpose of every object in the universe arose from its relationship to everything else. All things were in flux at all times. This continuing interaction at the molecular level of all matter -- animate and inanimate -- defined reality. It followed for Whitehead that every organism, indeed every atom, had intrinsic value if only for the contribution it made to the ongoing reality of the universe on what he called 'process.'

Id.

68. A. BRAMWELL, ECOLOGY IN THE TWENTIETH CENTURY: A HISTORY (1989).

69. *Id.* at 4. *See also* S. FLADER, THINKING LIKE A MOUNTAIN: ALDO LEOPOLD AND THE EVOLUTION OF AN ECOLOGICAL ATTITUDE TOWARD DEER, WOLVES AND FORESTS (1974).

ponderous report, *The Global 2000 Report to the President: Entering the Twenty-First Century*.[70] The report summarized its key holdings by noting that:

> If present trends continue, the world in 2000 will be more crowded, more polluted, less stable ecologically, and more vulnerable to disruption than the world we live in now. Serious stresses involving population, resources, and environment are clearly visible ahead. Despite greater material output, the world's people will be poorer in many ways than they are today.[71]

One of the more important contributors to "futuristic" environmental histories is the Washington, D.C.-based Worldwatch Institute, which has issued annual "state of the world" reports from 1984 through 1990.[72] These reports focus on major ecological, environmental, and demographic trends and the Institute uses these trends to propose major policy initiatives needed to stabilize the climate, improve air quality and reduce poverty. They focus on developing a "sustainable" society.[73] Moreover, a number of citizen environmental conferences have led to the generation of "futuristic" environmental histories. Prime examples include the 1989 book *Earth Conference One: Sharing a Vision*

---

70. UNITED STATES COUNCIL ON ENVIRONMENTAL QUALITY AND UNITED STATES DEPARTMENT OF STATE, THE GLOBAL 2000 REPORT TO THE PRESIDENT: ENTERING THE TWENTY-FIRST CENTURY (1980).

71. *Id.* at 1.

72. *See* STATE OF THE WORLD (L. Brown ed. 1984); STATE OF THE WORLD (L. Brown ed. 1985); STATE OF THE WORLD (L. Brown ed. 1986); STATE OF THE WORLD (L. Brown ed. 1987); STATE OF THE WORLD (L. Brown ed. 1988); STATE OF THE WORLD (L. Brown ed. 1989); STATE OF THE WORLD (L. Brown ed. 1990).

73. Lester Brown discusses the idea of sustainability in the 1984 STATE OF THE WORLD report, *supra* note 72, as follows:

> Over the past generation the world has yielded to an excessive dependence on oil, moved from farming soils to mining them, and begun to consume the economy's biological support systems. In short, the world economy has moved onto a development path that is unsustainable. Although at least some political leaders and their economic advisers are vaguely aware of this, the effort to return to a sustainable development path is not well defined. Most national governments, lacking a clearly defined development strategy, are attempting to "muddle through." As a result, successes are infrequent, often outnumbered by failures.
>
> The essential components of a sustainable development strategy are straightforward. They include stabilizing population, reducing dependence on oil, developing renewable energy resources, conserving soil, protecting the earth's biological support systems, and recycling materials. The good news is that in each case at least a few countries are making some impressive progress, providing a model for others. The bad news is that in only one area, reducing dependence on oil, is the worldwide performance close to adequate.

Id. at 2-3.

for Our Planet,[74] the 1988 book edited by P. Borrelli entitled *Crossroads: Environmental Priorities for the Future*[75] and the 1985 book *An Environmental Agenda for the Future*.[76]

---

74. A. VITTACHI, EARTH CONFERENCE ONE: SHARING A VISION FOR OUR PLANET (1989). One of the declarations to come out of the conference observed:

> We recognize that it is not only human survival but the survival of the whole planet, with its interdependent forms of life, which is threatened. The Earth, as recent environmental evidence confirms, is delicately balanced and vulnerable. Each one of us must accept the responsibility to care for and protect the Earth, which is our home.
>
> We have derived from our meeting a vivid awareness of the essential oneness of humanity and also the realization that each human person has both a spiritual and a political dimension. We acknowledge the inadequacy of attitudes and institutions within all our traditions to deal with our present global crisis.
>
> *We therefore now affirm our shared vision of survival, and we commit ourselves to work for a fundamentally changed and better world. We urge the leaders of the world to adopt new attitudes and to implement new policies based on sustainability and justice.*

Id. at 139-40 (emphasis in original).

75. CROSSROADS: ENVIRONMENTAL PRIORITIES FOR THE FUTURE (P. Borrelli ed. 1988). One of the chapters, Berle, *Managing the Future, If We Want To* in CROSSROADS, *supra*, melds past environmental trends with future projections in an elegant and powerful way. For example, lawyer Berle writes:

> The challenge then is to influence the nature of change so that a healthy Earth survives and we can have a significant impact on ... outcome. We can do it by defining our national security in terms of fostering a sound global environment rather than simply achieving an arms advantage. We can do it through economic activity and aid that assists worldwide efforts to limit population growth. We can do it by ensuring that the varying demands on our resources are considered before those resources are taken over by special interests.
>
> We need to do a better job of measuring the benefits of environmental protection. Every plant manager can describe to the penny how much control technology will cost, but the benefit of a pollution-free environment is much less quantifiable. Long-term impact on ecosystems cannot always be calculated. Putting a dollar value on the unknown risk of sustaining an undefined damage is impossible. But the lack of mechanisms to quantify does not mean that environmental protection is without value. When the damage becomes quantifiable, it may be too late to reverse or mitigate it. Since long-term costs and benefits frequently are impossible to calculate or compensate, one cannot make environmental policy decisions solely on the basis of currently anticipated cost figures. Everyone who argues that the cost of some environmental strategy is too high must be asked whether benefits of that strategy have been analyzed, whether all costs and all benefits have been considered, and what costs and benefits are also involved that cannot be measured.

Id. at 209-10.

76. AN ENVIRONMENTAL AGENDA FOR THE FUTURE (J. Adams, et al., ed. 1985). The editors provide a brief synopsis of American environmentalism from citizen actions spurring congressional protection of Yellowstone as the world's first national park in 1872; the "conservation movement" of the late nineteenth and early twentieth centuries; the environmental problems of the 1950s where "[t]he pressures of a burgeoning population led to a passion for acquisition and development of land and resources that overtook the nation;" the flurry of legislative activity in the 1970s after "Earth Day 1970." *Id.* at 2-4. In speaking of the future, the editors assert:

A recent special issue of the prestigious publication *Scientific American*, published in September 1989, focused on the theme *Managing Planet Earth.*[77] In a series of scientific and policy-based articles examining environmental and global trends, a number of prominent technical and policy thinkers examined prospects for managing environmental problems.[78] In a similar vein, Bill

---

> Marked progress has been made in the ... years since passage of NEPA, but many of the problems it was meant to solve still remain. Congress has passed a multitude of laws, and the courts have in many instances upheld the lawsuits brought by citizens to force compliance with some recalcitrant elements in industry and government agencies. But compliance and enforcement are still spotty and not adequately achieving the purposes of the laws. And because the laws and regulations often have not dealt with root causes, they have been inadequate to cope with added problems that have arisen, partly from new technologies.
>
> Many of today's problems are global in scope and make local, regional, or even national solutions difficult. These problems include human population growth that is exceeding the capacity of some countries to feed and sustain their burgeoning numbers; toxic chemicals, developed with the intent of benefiting humankind, that turn out to be serious threats to health with side effects that kill and maim; the greatly increased burning of fossil fuels, producing atmospheric effects that could melt icecaps and flood coastal cities. Looming over all is the spectre of nuclear war with its massive immediate death and destruction, which could be followed by the cold and dark of nuclear winter spreading climatic change throughout the world, destroying the life support system, eliminating many species of plants and animals, and even threatening the survival of the human species.
>
> These and other global problems call for pragmatic approaches and an agenda that can help the nation look toward ways of meeting the environmental challenges of the next 15 years and on into the next century. Building upon the strategies that have brought results in the past two decades, citizens, working with government, must continue to find new ways to achieve solutions.

Id. at 4.

77. 261 *Sci. Am.* 46-175 (1989).

78. Clark, *Managing Planet Earth* in *id.* at 46 ("In the millennia since our species emerged, it has colonized the planet exuberantly. Can we summon the intelligence to understand the biological and physical systems of which we are a part, so that we can pursue economic growth and development in ecologically sustainable ways?"); Crosson & Rosenberg, *Strategies for Agriculture* in *id.* at 128 ("Agricultural science and technology may indeed find ways to feed 10 billion people 100 years from now, but social and economic changes will have to be made to persuade individual farmers to adopt methods that will boost food production without further degrading the environment"); Frosch & Gallopoulos, *Strategies for Manufacturing*, in *id.* at 144 ("Can the industrial way of life be maintained without exhausting resources, generating unmanageable amounts of waste and poisoning the environment? Creative engineering can provide an 'industrial ecosystem,' characterized by dematerialization and closed-system manufacturing"); Gibbons, Blair & Gwin, *Strategies for Energy Use* in *id.* at 136 ("Nuclear power, solar cells, wind and tide will all have roles in supplying energy for growth and development without aggravating the greenhouse effect. Yet exotic new energy sources alone cannot meet the challenge. Significant improvement in the efficiency of energy use is the real hope"); Graedel & Crutzen, *The Changing Atmosphere*, in *id.* at 58 ("The chemistry of the atmosphere is changing, in large measure because of gases emitted by such human activities as farming, manufacturing and the combustion of fossil fuels. The deleterious effects are increasingly evident; they may well become worse in the years ahead"); Keyfitz, *The Growing Human Population* in *id.* at 118 ("Populations will stabilize as development

McKibben in his 1989 book *The End of Nature*[79] examines scientific trends and writes eloquently about the meaning of environmental change: about the sadness of a world where there is no escaping human beings. McKibben points out that although for decades civilization has polluted the earth, in the past those attacks were relatively local. In the present age -- with the global changes caused by planetary warming and depletion of the protective ozone shield -- humankind has altered the most elemental processes of life everywhere. McKibben points out that in a basic inversion of history the basic forces of nature (once beyond human reach) are now and will be forever the subject of human dominion.[80]

IV. Toward an Intellectual History of American Environmental Law

Why, you may ask, do I propose to add yet another environmental history to the mass of existing histories on "things environmental"? I offer three reasons in response to this preliminary question of purpose. First, there is no comprehensive study of the intellectual history of modern American

brings economic and social advances. Yet even as rates of increase decline, absolute numbers soar. How can poor nations progress when population growth not only hastens degradation of the environment but also threatens development itself?"); MacNeill, *Strategies for Sustainable Economic Development* in *id.* at 154 ("Economic growth in developing countries must accelerate to meet the needs of larger populations. Growth can be attained by means that do not damage the environment, and governments -- north and south -- will have to muster the determination to follow these alternative paths to development"); Maurits la Rivière, *Threats to the World's Water* in *id.* at 80 ("Water, most precious of all resources, is in short supply in many regions; almost everywhere increasing amounts of organic waste and industrial pollutants threaten its quality. Only international cooperation in the integrated management of water resources can ameliorate the situation"); Ruckelshaus, *Toward a Sustainable World* in *id.* at 166 ("Moving people and nations toward sustainability requires changes in values and social institutions on a scale comparable to two other transforming events in the history of humankind: the agricultural revolution and the Industrial Revolution. Some initial strategies are proposed"); Schneider, *The Changing Climate* in *id.* at 70 ("The earth owes its hospitable climate to the greenhouse effect, but now the effect threatens to intensify, rapidly warming the planet. Rising concentrations of carbon dioxide and other gases are the cause. The danger of warming is serious enough to warrant prompt action"); Wilson, *Threats to Biodiversity* in *id.* at 108 ("The elimination of habitats -- and in particular the felling of species-rich tropical rain forests -- is driving plant and animal species to extinction in unprecedented numbers. The accelerating loss of diversity is nothing less than a moral, scientific and economic tragedy"). (Summaries quoted from *id.* at 4-5.) *Cf.*, 263 *Sci. Am.* 54-163 (1990) (special symposium edition on *Energy for Planet Earth*); 174 *Nat'l Geog.* 765-945 (1988) (special symposium edition on global environmental problems).

79. B. McKibben, The End of Nature (1989).

80. *Cf.* J. McPhee, The Control of Nature (1989). *See also*, L. Timberlake, Only One Earth: Living for the Future (1987).

environmental law.[81] Second, such a history would give us a glimpse of the extent and influence of *ideas* -- as well as politics and ideology -- in the evolution of modern American environmental law. Finally, other intellectual histories of topics in American law have proven fruitful and have fit well within the tradition of the sociological school of jurisprudence (a counterweight to the law and economics and political analyses of law).[82]

Indeed, it is my thesis that ideas from a diverse spectrum of disciplines -- including economics, ecology and ethics -- have subtly influenced and continue

81. A few scholars have provided useful excerpts and summaries of the intellectual roots of modern American environmental law. *See generally, What is Environmentalism, and What are its Intellectual Origins, Foundations, and Legal Ramifications?* in F. Anderson, D. Mandelker, & A. Tarlock, *supra* note 12, at 1-82 (discussing *inter alia* F. ANDERSON, A. KNEESE, P. REED, R. STEVENSON & S. TAYLOR, ENVIRONMENTAL IMPROVEMENT THROUGH ECONOMIC INCENTIVES (1977); M. COHEN, THE PATHLESS WAY: JOHN MUIR AND AMERICAN WILDERNESS (1984); L. DYE, BLOWOUT AT PLATFORM A: A CRISIS THAT AWAKENED A NATION (1971); S. FOX, JOHN MUIR AND HIS LEGACY: THE AMERICAN CONSERVATION MOVEMENT (1980); S. HAYS, CONSERVATION AND THE GOSPEL OF EFFICIENCY: THE PROGRESSIVE CONSERVATION MOVEMENT 1890-1920 (1959); A. LEOPOLD, A SAND COUNTY ALMANAC AND SKETCHES HERE AND THERE (1949); J. LOVELOCK, THE AGES OF GAIA: A BIOGRAPHY OF OUR LIVING EARTH (1988); L. MARX, THE MACHINE AND THE GARDEN: TECHNOLOGY AND THE PASTORAL IDEAL IN AMERICA (1964); D.H. MEADOWS, D.L. MEADOWS, J. RANDERS & W. BEHRENS, THE LIMITS TO GROWTH (1972); C. MEINE, ALDO LEOPOLD: HIS LIFE AND WORK (1988); E. ODUM, FUNDAMENTALS OF ECOLOGY (2d ed. 1959); W. OPHULS, ECOLOGY AND THE POLITICS OF SCARCITY (1977); J. PASSMORE, MAN'S RESPONSIBILITY FOR NATURE (1974); J. PETULLA, AMERICAN ENVIRONMENTAL HISTORY: THE EXPLOITATION AND FOUNDATIONS OF AMERICAN ENVIRONMENTAL ATTITUDES (2d ed. 1987); E. PURCELL, THE CRISIS OF DEMOCRATIC THEORY: SCIENTIFIC NATURALISM AND THE PROBLEM OF VALUE (1973); STONE, EARTH AND OTHER ETHICS (1987); I.K. THOMAS, MAN AND THE NATURAL WORLD: A HISTORY OF MODERN SENSIBILITY (1983); F. TURNER, REDISCOVERING AMERICA: JOHN MUIR IN HIS TIME AND OURS (1985); B. WARD & R. DUBOS, ONLY ONE EARTH (1972); P. WENZ, ENVIRONMENTAL JUSTICE (1988); COMPANION TO A SAND COUNTY ALMANAC (B. Callicott ed. 1988); Ackerman & Stewart, *Reforming Environmental Law,* 37 STAN. L. REV. 1333, 1346 (1985); Hargrove, *The Historical Foundations of American Environmental Attitudes,* 1 ENVT'L ETHICS 209 (1979); Jenkins, *Nature's Rights and Man's Duties* in LAW AND THE ECOLOGICAL CHALLENGE 91 (E. Dais ed. 1978); Stroup, *Environmental Policy* in THE REAGAN RECORD AND THE TASK AHEAD, REGULATION 47 (No. 3 1988)).

See also Environmental Policy Perspectives, in T. Schoenbaum, *supra* note 12, at 1-74. Professors Bruce Ackerman and W. Hisser in their book CLEAN COAL/DIRTY AIR (1982) provide an insightful political and intellectual history of the Clean Air Act from its 1970 origin to its 1977 amendments. In a similar respect, Professor Peter Schuck's book, AGENT ORANGE: MASS TOXIC DISASTERS IN THE COURTS (1987) affords a remarkable mixture of factual analysis, case reportage, intellectual analysis and political review of Vietnam veterans' mass toxic tort suits for personal injuries and latent diseases allegedly suffered during the war. Professor William Rodgers, Jr., while he has not provided a complete and comprehensive intellectual history of American environmental law, does frequently refer to the influence and interrelationship of intellectual thought on environmental law and policy. *See generally* Blomquist, *supra* note 14, at 565.

82. *See* G.E. WHITE, TORT LAW IN AMERICA: AN INTELLECTUAL HISTORY (1980); Priest, *The Invention of Enterprise Liability: A Critical History of the Intellectual Foundations of Modern Tort Law,* 14 J. LEGAL STUD. 461 (1986).

to have potential influence on the development and evolution of modern American environmental law, albeit within a highly-charged political milieu. If we were able to document and understand the way that these ideas have been received by the courts, legislatures, and other legal decisionmakers; and, how governmental rules and decisions, in turn, have influenced further development of ideas, we would gain a richer, more complete understanding of the dynamics of contemporary American environmental law. I propose, then, to study ideas of intellectual elites -- such as scholars, judges, legislators and administrative staff persons -- as "social facts" in the continuing evolution of American environmental law.[83]

I end my lecture with an inventory and prospectus of several key intellectual congeries of ideas and persons that emerged during the period 1961-90 and that have had significant influences on modern American environmental law. This classification, of course, is tentative and open to further expansion, elaboration, and research. It, nevertheless, forms a blueprint of sorts for my work-in-progress over the next several years.[84]

---

83. *See supra* notes 5-6 and accompanying text. I hope that in some small measure this work can remedy the scholarly deficiencies identified by Professor Richard Brooks. He writes:

> Rather than beginning with a fixed series of prosaic environmental objectives, environmental law should be guided by modern ecological perspectives which can offer a modern reinterpretation of a series of traditional ethical [and other] ideals embodied in our tradition. These ideals -- holding the environment in trust for future generations, respecting non-human nature, making secure the citizens' health and lives, especially vulnerable citizens, protecting nature's beauty, community sharing of renewable resources, encouragement of ecologically sensitive lifestyles -- should be the starting point for reformulating environmental policy and law. The importance of these ideals is that they carry a rich tradition, and consequently are ensconced, more or less, in American culture. For example, the rights of non-human nature is an extension of the ever-expanding circle of recognized rights. Some of these ideals already have certain institutions corresponding to them; e.g., the trust ideal has private land trust institutions and the court interpretations of the public trust doctrine. These ideals are built into the ongoing enterprise of our society.
>
> Fortunately, these ideals have been subjected to extensive analysis in the field of philosophical ethics which has fleshed out their dimensions and implications. Unfortunately, this ethical analysis has often been hermetically separated from a historical and legal study of the question of [the] history of the operation of these ideals and the ways in which these ideals are institutionalized in everyday institutions and practices.

Brooks, *supra* note 38, at 13-14 (emphasis omitted).

84. Follow-up articles should, among other things, amplify and expand the discussion and bibliography of intellectual ideas addressed in this brief account; explore reasons why some ideas influenced lawmaking while others had less impact; and, compare and contrast the dynamics of the intellectual history of modern American law with the intellectual histories of other branches of American law, such as tort law. The logical synthesis of my work would eventually culminate in a book.

1. Rachel Carson and the Idea of "Silent Spring"

Like Aldo Leopold, her intellectual forebear, Rachel Carson neither earned nor cared to earn a Ph.D. "Her forte was not original research but old-fashioned natural history, colored in every respect with something many modern ecologists have forgotten: love of nature."[85] Born in 1907, she joined the U.S. Bureau of Fisheries -- later to become the U.S. Fish and Wildlife Service -- in 1935 as a writer and editor, after earning a Master's degree in biology. As explained by Roderick Nash:

> Her first book, *Under The Sea Wind* (1941), attracted comparatively little attention, but her next, *The Sea Around Us* (1951), was a publishing sensation. It appeared on non-fiction best-seller lists for nearly two years, won a National Book Award, enjoyed translations into thirty-two foreign languages and, incidentally, provided Carson with sufficient royalty income to retire from government bureaucracy. With her new leisure she completed *The Edge of the Sea* in 1955. The marine ecology books profess no overt environmental ethic, but they testify on almost every page to the author's awe in the face of the vast community of life centered on the oceans. Carson emphasized not just well-known forms of sea life but species that humans never use and seldom see. Respect for these creatures ... suffused Carson's thought and behavior. Paul Brooks, her editor ... recalled how after examining living specimens with her microscope, Carson would conclude the day by placing them in a basket and returning them, alive, to the sea.[86]

Rachel Carson published her classic polemic, *Silent Spring*, in 1962[87] -- one year after John F. Kennedy took the oath of office as the youngest elected president in United States history. In this book, Carson attacked, on scientific and ethical levels, the widespread use of DDT and other chemical pesticides and insecticides by American agriculture. "Carson preferred to think about DDT and the like not as pesticides but as biocides -- killers of life."[88] She was well aware that the chemical poisons "seldom stopped working at a convenient or expected point in the food chain. Creatures that ate the poisoned insects sickened and died. Other forms of life became intended victims of indiscriminate sprayings. Ultimately, the insecticides infected the entire

---

85. R. NASH, *supra* note 42, at 78.

86. *Id.* at 78-79. *See also* P. BROOKS, THE HOUSE OF LIFE: RACHEL CARSON AT WORK (1972); C. GARTNER, RACHEL CARSON (1983); P. STERLING, SEA AND EARTH: THE LIFE OF RACHEL CARSON (1970).

87. R. CARSON, SILENT SPRING (1962).

88. R. NASH, *supra* note 42, at 79.

ecosystem. A 'silent spring' where no birds sang was a distinct possibility. And so, Carson reasoned, was a sick human society, poisoned as an ironic side-effect of the drive to conquer and dominate nature."[89]

In the final paragraph of *Silent Spring*, Carson attacked the notion of "the control of nature" -- curiously the title of a book recently published by John McPhee.[90] The "'control of nature,'" wrote Carson, "is a phrase conceived in arrogance, borne of the Neanderthal age of biology and philosophy, when it was supposed that Nature exists for the convenience of man."[91] As a substitute idea, Carson proposed "reasonable accommodation" between the natural world and people.[92]

The ideas articulated by Rachel Carson in *Silent Spring* and fervently debated throughout the country thereafter were the direct antecedents of legal principles adopted by Congress seven years later in the National Environmental Policy Act of 1969 (NEPA).[93] Drawing directly upon Carson's insights, Congress acknowledged in NEPA's preamble that it recognized "the profound impact of man's activity on the interrelations of all components of the natural environment."[94] Likewise, in framing more specific planning principles under the statute, Congress reiterated Carson's wisdom by proposing national goals to:

- "fulfill the responsibilities of each generation as trustee of the environment for succeeding generations,"[95]
- "assure for all Americans safe, healthful, productive, and aesthetically and culturally pleasing surroundings,"[96] and
- "attain the widest range of beneficial uses of the environment without degradation, risk to health or safety, or other undesirable and unintended consequences."[97]

In addition to its obvious impact on the enactment of NEPA, it was pointed out by the United States Court of Appeals for the District of Columbia[98] that "[o]ne of the most influential publications in the eventual enactment of the [1972 amendments to the Federal Insecticide, Fungicide and Rodenticide Act] was [Rachel Carson's] *Silent Spring* which devoted considerable attention to the

---

89. *Id.*
90. J. MCPHEE, *supra* note 80.
91. R. CARSON, *supra* note 87, at 297.
92. *See supra* note 87.
93. National Environmental Policy Act of 1969, 42 U.S.C. §§ 4321 to 4370(b) (1988).
94. 42 U.S.C. § 4331(a) (1986).
95. 42 U.S.C. § 4331(b)(1) (1986).
96. 42 U.S.C. § 4331(b)(2) (1986).
97. 42 U.S.C. § 4331(b)(3) (1986).
98. Environmental Defense Fund v. EPA, 598 F.2d 62 (D.C. Cir. 1978).

carcinogenic nature of some heavy metals and some chlorinated hydrocarbon pesticides."[99] After the publication of Carson's book, the phrase "silent spring" became a shorthand way of expressing the unintended consequences of human manipulation of the natural environment. Several judicial opinions make this type of shorthand reference, including the United States Court of Appeals for the Second Circuit,[100] the United States Court of Appeals for the Fifth Circuit,[101] the Rhode Island Supreme Court,[102] and the United States District Court for the Southern District of Georgia.[103] Other courts cited *Silent Spring* for various scientific facts and views.[104]

2. *Garret Hardin and Kenneth Boulding: "The Tragedy of the Commons" on "Spaceship Earth"*

A second congery of intellectual ideas drawn from the field of economics has had a significant impact on the development of American environmental law in the last thirty years. Two academics, Garret Hardin and Kenneth Boulding, added intellectual ferment to environmental issues by publication of a technical article and a non-fiction book chapter, respectively. The conceptual phrases that they coined had a profound effect on environmental legal analysis.

Hardin's article, published in a 1968 issue of the journal *Science*, was entitled "The Tragedy of the Commons."[105] In elegant prose, Hardin noted that:

> The tragedy of the commons develops in this way. Picture a pasture open to all. It is to be expected that each herdsman will try to keep as many cattle as possible on the commons. Such an arrangement may work reasonably satisfactory for centuries because tribal wars, poaching, and disease keep the numbers of both man and beast well below the carrying capacity of the land. Finally, however, comes the day of reckoning, that is, the day when the long-desired goal of social stability becomes a reality. At this point the inherent logic of the commons remorselessly generates tragedy.

---

99. *Id.* at 72, n. 32 (citing Federal Insecticide, Fungicide and Rodenticide Act, 7 U.S.C. §§ 136 to 136y).

100. Morningside Renewal Council, Inc. v. United States Atomic Energy Comm'n, 482 F.2d 234 (2d Cir. 1973).

101. Zabel v. Tabb, 430 F.2d 199 (5th Cir. 1970).

102. Wood v. Picillo, 443 A.2d 1244 (R.I. 1982).

103. United States v. Lewis, 355 F. Supp. 1132 (S.D. Ga. 1973).

104. Hercules, Inc. v. EPA, 598 F.2d 91, 98 n.4 (D.C. Cir. 1978); Edwards v. Nat'l Audubon Soc'y, Inc , 556 F.2d 113 (2d Cir. 1977); United States v. Goodman, 486 F.2d 847, 850 n.12 (7th Cir. 1973); Zepeda v. Zepeda, 41 Ill. App. 2d 240, 190 N.E.2d 849 (1963).

105. Hardin, *The Tragedy of the Commons*, 162 SCI. 1243 (1968).

* * *

> Each man is locked into a system that compels him to increase his herd without limit in a world that is limited. Ruin is the destination toward which all men rush, each pursuing his own best interest in a society that believes in the freedom of the commons. Freedom in a commons brings ruin to all.[106]

Hardin's article made a big impact on economists. To an economist, Hardin had provided a parable for a problem that they referred to as "market failure" or the "externality problem."[107] Externalities "occur whenever the activity of one person affects the welfare of other persons who have no direct means of control over those activities."[108] In partial response to Hardin's article, the Congress, and ultimately the EPA, took the problem of externalities more seriously. To alleviate "the tragedy of the commons," environmental regulators started to improve pollution penalties which, at a minimum, would recoup the "economic benefit" externality derived by a polluter in failing to conform to a pollution standard when other companies had internalized the cost of pollution by spending the necessary funds to abate discharges into the air and water. Indeed, Section 120 of the Clean Air Act[109] and Section 309 of the Clean Water Act[110] are the intellectual offspring of Hardin's idea for

---

106. *Id.* at 1244-45.

107. *See* T. Schoenbaum, *supra* note 12, at 25.

108. *Id.*

109. 42 U.S.C. § 7420 (1988). Subsection (d)(2) provides in pertinent part that:

> The amount of the penalty which shall be assessed and collected with respect to any source under this section shall be equal to –
>
> (A) The amount determined in accordance with regulations promulgated by the Administrator ... which is no less than the *economic value which a delay in compliance* beyond July 1, 1979, may have for the owner of such source, including the quarterly equivalent of the capital costs of compliance and debt service over a normal amortization period, not to exceed ten years, operation and maintenance costs foregone as a result of noncompliance, and any additional economic value which such a delay may have for the owner or operator of such source, minus
>
> (B) The amount of any expenditure made by the owner or operator of that source during any such quarter for the purpose of bringing that source into, and maintaining compliance with, such requirement, to the extent that such expenditures have not been taken into account in the calculation of the penalty under subparagraph (A).

Id. (emphasis provided).

110. 33 U.S.C. § 1319 (1988). Subsection (d) provides in pertinent part:

> Any person who violates [the permit and effluent provisions of the Clean Water Act] shall be subject to a civil penalty not to exceed $25,000 per day for each violation. In determining the amount of a civil penalty the court shall consider the seriousness of the violation or violations, *the economic benefit (if any) resulting from* the violation, any history of such violations, any good-faith efforts to comply with the applicable requirements, the economic impact of the penalty on the violator, and such other matters as justice may require.

Id. (emphasis provided).

preventing "the tragedy of the commons" through coercive governmental measures to recoup economic benefit derived from legal violation of the commons. Hardin's idea has been cited with regularity by scholars[111] and the courts.[112] For example, in an action by an Oregon orchard owner to recover for damages caused by an aluminum plant's emissions, the court in *Orchard View Farms, Inc. v. Martin Marietta Aluminum*[113] observed:

> Our system of law attempts to insure that businesses are, on balance, socially beneficial by requiring that each enterprise bear its total production costs, as accurately as the costs can be ascertained. A fundamental means to this end is the institution of tort liability, which requires that persons harmed by business or other activity be compensated by the perpetrator of the damage. In the context of pollution, however, the tort system does not always operate smoothly to impose liability for compensatory damages. Among the difficulties encountered are: (1) that the harm be gradual or otherwise difficult to perceive; (2) that the cause of the harm may be difficult to trace to the pollution and from pollution to its source; and (3) that the harm may be inflicted in small amounts upon a large number of people, none of whom individually suffer sufficient damage to warrant the time and expense of legal action and whose organization into a plaintiff class is hindered by what has come to be known as the *tragedy of the commons*.[114]

Likewise, the federal appellate court in *Natural Resources Defense Council v. Costle*[115] noted that "the primary purpose of the effluent limitations and guidelines [under the Clean Water Act] was to provide uniformity among the federal and state jurisdictions enforcing the ... program and prevent the 'Tragedy of the Commons' that might result if jurisdictions can compete for industry and development by providing more liberal limitations than their neighboring states."[116]

Inspired by the space-eye view of the planet from an Apollo Moon

---

111. *See generally,* F. Anderson, D. Mandelker & A. Tarlock, supra note 12, at 20-25; FINDLEY & FARBER, *supra* note 12, at 32-35; Pierce, *State Regulation of Natural Gas in a Federally Deregulated Market: The Tragedy of the Commons Revisited*, 73 CORNELL L. REV. 15 (1987); T. Schoenbaum, *supra* note 12, at 92-24.

112. *See infra* notes 113-16 and accompanying text. *See also* Northwest Central Pipeline Corp. v. State Corp. Comm'n of Kansas, 109 S. Ct. 1262 (1989) (citing Pierce, *supra* note 111 at 1269).

113. 500 F. Supp. 984 (D. Or. 1980).

114. *Id.* at 989 (emphasis added).

115. 568 F.2d 1369 (D.C. Cir. 1977).

116. *Id.* at 1378.

shot,[117] Kenneth Boulding formulated the idea of "Spaceship Earth" in a book chapter called "The Economics of the Coming Spaceship Earth" published in the volume *Environmental Quality in a Growing Economy.*[118] According to Boulding, society might place too much emphasis on maximizing wealth and consumption. Boulding wrote:

> The closed Earth of the future requires economic principles which are somewhat different from those of the open Earth of the past. For the sake of picturesqueness ... call the open economy the 'cowboy economy;' the cowboy being symbolic of the illimitable plains and also associated with reckless, exploitive, romantic, and violent behavior, which is characteristic of open societies. The closed economy of the future might similarly be called the 'spaceman' economy, in which the Earth has become a single spaceship, without unlimited reservoirs of anything, either for extraction or for pollution, and in which, therefore, man must find his place in a cyclical ecological system.... The differences between the two types of economy become most apparent in the attitude towards consumption. In the cowboy economy, consumption is regarded as a good thing and production likewise; and the success of the economy is measured by the amount of the throughput from the 'factors of production,' a part of which, at any rate, is extracted from the reservoirs of raw materials and non-economic objects, and another part of which is output into the reservoirs of pollution. By contrast, in the spaceman economy, throughput is by no means a [desirable thing] and is indeed to be regarded as something to be minimized rather than maximized.[119]

Despite the rather esoteric nature of Boulding's thinking, environmental legal scholars have incorporated his view into the case against the "efficiency criterion."[120] Moreover, at least one court in the case of *Manufacturing Chemists Association v. Costle*[121] has cited Kenneth Boulding's idea with approval in a case involving the efficacy of hazardous waste regulations.[122]

---

117. T. FERRIS, SPACESHOTS: THE BEAUTY OF NATURE BEYOND EARTH 111, 141 (1984).

118. Boulding, *The Economics of the Coming Spaceship Earth* in ENVIRONMENTAL QUALITY IN A GROWING ECONOMY (H. Jarrett ed. 1971).

119. *Id.* (quoted in T. Schoenbaum, *supra* note 12, at 42).

120. *See, e.g.*, T. Schoenbaum, *supra* note 12, at 42-45.

121. 451 F. Supp. 902 (W.D. La. 1978), 455 F. Supp. 968 (W.D. La. 1978).

122. 455 F. Supp. at 981. *In dicta* prior to quoting from the Boulding chapter, the court noted:

> We do not view this decision as a victory for those who would pollute our waters with impunity...nor as a defeat for those who are fighting the worthy battle to protect our environment. No one could possibly be happy with a system which produces goods at the ultimate expense of the health and well-being of the inhabitants of our planet.
>
> 'The essential measure of the success of the economy is not production and

3. Professor Christopher Stone & Justice William Douglas: "Should Trees Have Standing"

A third intellectual idea drawn from the field of ethics has had a significant impact on the development of American environmental law in recent years. This basic intellectual idea posits the notion that instead of requiring human beings to assert "standing" to come before courts of law on behalf of natural objects such as trees, rocks, or river valleys, it makes sense that these natural objects should have standing in their own right.

Professor Christopher Stone of the University of Southern California Law School originated this idea in a 1972 law review article entitled "Should Trees Have Standing? -- Toward Legal Rights for Natural Objects."[123] This intellectual idea was given real-world currency by Justice William Douglas' dissenting opinion in the 1972 case of *Sierra Club v. Morton*.[124] Drawing upon Stone's insights, Justice Douglas observed that:

> The critical question of "standing" would be simplified and also put neatly in focus if we fashioned a federal rule that allowed environmental issues to be litigated before federal agencies or federal courts in the name of the inanimate object about to be despoiled, defaced, or invaded by roads and bulldozers and where injury is the subject of public outrage. Contemporary public concern for protecting nature's ecological equilibrium should lead to the conferral of standing upon environmental objects to sue for their own preservation. *See* Stone, 'Should Trees Have Standing? -- Toward Legal Rights for Natural Objects,' 45 S. CAL. L. REV. 450 (1972).
>
> * * *
>
> Inanimate objects are sometimes parties in litigation. A ship has a legal personality, a fiction found useful for maritime purposes. The corporation sole -- a creature of ecclesiastical law -- is an acceptable adversary and large fortunes ride on its cases. The ordinary corporation is a 'person' for purposes of the adjudicatory processes, whether it represents proprietary, spiritual, aesthetic, or charitable causes.

---

consumption at all, but the nature, extent, quality and complexity of the total capital stock, including in this the state of the human bodies and minds involved in the system.' *Id.* (quoting Boulding, *supra* note 118).

123. Stone, *Should Trees Have Standing? -- Toward Legal Rights for Natural Objects*, 45 S. CAL. L. REV. 450 (1972).

124. 405 U.S. 727 (1972) (Douglas, J. dissenting).

> So it should be as respects valleys, alpine meadows, rivers, lakes, estuaries, beaches, ridges, groves of trees, swampland, or even air that feels the destructive pressures of modern technology and modern life. The river, for example, is the living symbol of all the life it sustains or nourishes -- fish, aquatic insects, water ouzels, otter, fisher, deer, elk, bear, and all other animals, including man, who are dependent on it or who enjoy it for its sight, its sound, or its life. The river as plaintiff speaks for the ecological unit of life that is part of it. Those people who have a meaningful relation to that body of water -- whether it be a fisherman, a canoeist, a zoologist, or a logger -- must be able to speak for the values which the river represents and which are threatened with destruction.[125]

Other categories of intellectual ideas having significant impact on American environmental law are as follows:

4. *Judge Harold Leventhal as Environmental Theorist: "Hardlook" Judicial Review of Agency Decisionmaking*

Prior to his appointment to the United States Court of Appeals for the District of Columbia Circuit in 1965 at the age of fifty, Harold Leventhal already had a distinguished legal career.[126] Just four years after his appointment to the bench, Judge Leventhal originated an intellectual idea that "through forcefulness of concept and simplicity of expression [was] ... as important in the evolution of the law as the specifics of the holdings that spawned it."[127] In a pair of 1969 opinions -- *Pikes Peak Broadcasting Co. v. F.C.C.*[128] and *Women Strike For Peace v. Hickel*[129] -- Judge Leventhal first

---

125. *Id.* at 741-43.

126. Born in 1915, Leventhal obtained both his undergraduate and law degrees at Columbia University. After his graduation from law school and admission to the New York Bar in 1936, Leventhal clerked for U.S. Supreme Court Justice Harlan F. Stone (1936-37) and then for U.S. Supreme Court Justice Stanley Reed (1938). From 1938-39 he worked on the staff of the Office of Solicitor General; from 1939-40 he was chief of litigation of the Bituminous Coal Division of the U.S. Department of Interior; from 1940-43 he was assistant general counsel to the federal Office of Price Administration (OPA). At the end of World War II Leventhal embarked on the fascinating experience of working on the staff of Justice Robert Jackson in his role of one of the judges of the Nuremberg Trials (1945-46). Thereafter, Leventhal practiced law with the New York law firm of Ginsburg and Leventhal, until his appointment to the federal bench by President Lyndon B. Johnson in 1965. Some of his "activities" while practicing law in New York included the following: general counsel to the Democratic National Committee (1952-65); visiting lecturer at Yale Law School (1957-62). BIOGRAPHICAL DICTIONARY OF THE FEDERAL JUDICIARY 164-65 (H. Chase, S. Krislov, K. Boyum, J. Clark eds. 1976).

127. J. Bonine & T. McGarity, *supra* note 12, at 132.

128. 422 F.2d 671, 682 (D.C. Cir. 1969) (upholding agency).

129. 420 F.2d 597, 603 (D.C. Cir. 1969) (reversing agency).

stated that an agency must take a "hard look" at contentions by the litigants, or the underlying facts bearing on a particular agency decision, in review of administrative decisions. "He then labored to give the term currency in succeeding opinions that he issued, each citing his preceding ones and each putting the phrase in quotes, drawing attention to it."[130] In time, other judges on the D.C. circuit and elsewhere began using the phrase "hard look" in F.C.C. cases.[131] In 1971 Judge Leventhal expanded use of the phrase to cases involving the Federal Power Commission and the Securities and Exchange Commission (still using quotes and citing his earlier opinions).[132]

In 1972 Judge Leventhal "became the first judge in the nation to call for a 'hard look' in environmental cases."[133] He justified the need for "hard look" review in *Natural Resources Defense Council (NRDC), Inc. v. Morton*[134] and *EDF, Inc. v. EPA.*[135] These opinions had an immediate and substantial impact on judicial reasoning in cases involving interpretation of the National Environmental Policy Act.[136] In a few years, the United States Supreme Court "joined the throng" of courts that acknowledged and applied the idea of "hard look" judicial review in environmental cases by its discussion in the 1975 decision, *Aberdeen & Rockfish Railroad Co. v. Students Challenging Regulatory Agency Procedures*,[137] and the 1976 decision in *Kleppe v. Sierra Club.*[138] Later on, in the 1983 decision in *Baltimore Gas & Electric Co. v. Natural Resources Defense Council, Inc.*,[139] the Supreme Court referred to its *Kleppe* decision for the propriety of utilizing the "hard look" doctrine in NEPA cases.[140]

---

130. J. Bonine & T. McGarity, *supra* note 12, at 133 (citing WAIT Radio v. FCC, 418 F.2d 1153, 1156 n.8, 1157, 1160 (D.C. Cir. 1969) (reversing agency) and Greater Boston Television Corp. v. FCC, 444 F.2d 841, 851 (D.C. Cir. 1970) (upholding agency)).

131. *Id.*

132. *Id.* (citing Alabama Power Co. v. FPC, 454 F.2d 716, 721 (D.C. Cir. 1971); City of Lafayette v. SEC, 450 F.2d 941, 954 (D.C. Cir. 1971)).

133. *Id.*

134. 458 F.2d 827, 838 (D.C. Cir. 1972).

135. 465 F.2d 528, 541 (D.C. Cir. 1972).

136. 42 U.S.C. § 4321 (1988).

137. 422 U.S. 289, 327 n. 28 (1975).

138. 427 U.S. 390, 410 n. 21 (1976).

139. 462 U.S. 87 (1983).

140. *But see* the Supreme Court's emphasis on the limited role of the judiciary in reviewing environmental impact statements under NEPA in *Vermont Yankee Nuclear Power Corp. v. NRDC, Inc.*, 435 U.S. 519, 558 (1978) (courts should simply "insure a fully informed and well-considered decision [by the agency]," setting aside agency decisions only for "substantial procedural or substantive reasons ..., not simply because the court is unhappy with the result reached"); Strycker's Bay Neighborhood Council v. Karlen, 444 U.S. 223, 227 (1980) (*per curiam*); Baltimore Gas & Elec. Co. v. NRDC, Inc., 462 U.S. 87 (1983).

Judge Leventhal added intellectual force to his "hard look" conception by a 1974 article in the *University of Pennsylvania Law Review* entitled *Environmental Decisionmaking and the Role of the Courts*.[141] Judge Leventhal argued that substantive review of environmental agency decisions by the judiciary was worthwhile because of "the check it could place on agency decisionmaking."[142] In this regard, he wrote:

> The common theme one can draw from these observations on the role of the courts in environmental matters is the court's central role of ensuring the principled integration and balanced assessment of both environmental and nonenvironmental considerations in federal agency decisionmaking. The rule of administrative law, as applied to the congressional mandates for a clean environment, ensures that mission-oriented agencies ... will take due cognizance of environmental matters. It ensures at the same time that environmental protection agencies will take into account the congressional mandate that environmental concern be reconciled with other social and economic objectives of our society.[143]

In addition to the ferment among fellow judges,[144] Judge Leventhal's "hard look" conception engendered important intellectual debate in the law reviews among scholars and jurists -- not only in the area of judicial review of administrative decisions,[145] but also with regard to judicial assessment of scientific evidence in general.[146]

5. *Professor Joseph Sax, Senator Edmund Muskie and the Development of Environmental Citizen Suits*

In the early 1970s "[a]s interest in environmental protection grew,

---

141. Leventhal, *Environmental Decision Making and the Role of the Courts*, 122 U. PA. L. REV. 509 (1974).

142. F. Anderson, D. Mandelker & A.D. Tarlock, *supra* note 12, at 126.

143. Leventhal, *supra* note 141, at 604.

144. *See supra* notes 130-143 and accompanying text.

145. *See* Bazelon, *Coping With Technology Through the Legal Process*, 62 CORNELL L. REV. 817 (1977); Byse, *Vermont Yankee and the Evolution of Administrative Procedure: A Somewhat Different View*, 91 HARV. L. REV. 1823 (1978); Oakes, *The Judicial Role in Environmental Law*, 52 N.Y.U. L. REV. 498 (1977); Rodgers, *A Hard Look at Vermont Yankee: Environmental Law Under Close Scrutiny*, 67 GEO. L. J. 699 (1979); Siegel, *The Aftermath of* Baltimore Gas & Electric Co. v. NRDC: *A Broader Notion of Judicial Deference to Agency Expertise*, 11 HARV. ENVTL. L. REV. 331 (1987); Stewart, *Vermont Yankee and the Evolution of Administrative Procedure*, 91 HARV. L. REV. 1805 (1978).

146. *See* Brennan, *Helping Courts With Toxic Torts: Some Proposals Regarding Alternative Methods for Presenting and Assessing Scientific Evidence in Common Law Courts*, 51 U. PITT. L. REV. 1 (1989).

awareness of the lack of credible enforcement mechanisms and credible state and federal enforcement programs also increased."[147] This, in turn, spurned dissatisfaction with the prevailing environmental regulatory scheme and "led directly to the significant enhancement of federal enforcement tools in the environmental legislation of the 1970s and to the creation of citizen suits."[148]

Two individuals -- one a legal academic and the other a United States senator -- had a profound intellectual influence on the genesis of the idea of citizen environmental suits and the crafting of specific laws to implement that idea. The academic, Professor Joseph L. Sax, was a Professor of Law at the University of Michigan Law School at the time of this activity in the early seventies.[149] The senator, Edmund Muskie, was, in the early 1970s, United States Senator for Maine and Chair of the Senate Public Works' Subcommittee in charge of pollution and environmental control.[150]

Professor Sax authored and championed Michigan's environmental citizen suit provisions, passed into law in 1970.[151] As explained in his academic writings about the Michigan citizen suit provision,[152] Michigan's law gave citizens the right to enforce state environmental policies not being enforced by

---

147. J. MILLER, CITIZEN SUITS: PRIVATE ENFORCEMENT OF FEDERAL POLLUTION CONTROL LAWS 3 (1987).

148. *Id.* at 3-4 (footnotes omitted).

149. Sax is now the House/Hurd Professor of Environmental Law at the University of California School of Law at Berkeley. After graduating from the University of Chicago School of Law in 1959 (and serving as editor-in-chief of the University of Chicago Law Review), Sax served as Assistant and later Associate Professor of Law at the University of Colorado School of Law (1962-65); and Professor of Law at the University of Michigan School of Law (1966-87) with visiting professorships at Berkeley (1965-66 and 1986) and the University of Paris (1982). ASSOCIATION OF AMERICAN LAW SCHOOLS, DIRECTORY OF LAW TEACHERS 702 (1988-89).

150. Senator Muskie was born in Rumford, Maine in 1914. After graduating from Cornell Law School in 1939, he commenced the practice of law in Waterville, Maine, in 1940. During the second World War he enlisted in the United States Navy and served in both the Atlantic and Asiatic-Pacific Theaters from 1942-45. After holding a series of local offices, he was elected to the Maine House of Representatives in 1946, 1948, and 1950 and was Democratic Floor Leader from 1949-51. From 1955-59, Muskie served as Governor of Maine. In 1958 he was elected as United States Senator from Maine and reelected in 1964, 1970 and 1976. In May 1980 he became U.S. Secretary of State under President Jimmy Carter. In 1987 he served on the President's Special Review Board ("Tower Commission"). He presently practices law and resides in Washington, D.C. *See*, JOINT COMMITTEE ON PRINTING, CONGRESS OF THE UNITED STATES, BIOGRAPHICAL DIRECTORY OF THE UNITED STATES CONGRESS 1774-1989 1555 (1989). *See also*, ASBELL, THE SENATE NOBODY KNOWS (1978); COHEN, ROLL CALL: ONE YEAR IN THE UNITED STATES SENATE (1981); MUSKIE, JOURNEYS (1972).

151. MICH. COMP. LAWS ANN. §§ 691.1201-691.1207 (West 1987).

152. *See* Sax and Conner, *Michigan's Environmental Protection Act of 1970: A Progress Report*, 70 MICH. L. REV. 1004 (1972); Sax and DiMento, *Environmental Citizen Suits: Three Years Experience Under the Michigan Environmental Protection Act*, 4 ECOLOGY L.Q. 1 (1974).

the executive branch of state government.[153] As a result of Michigan's example, a number of states enacted state environmental citizen suit provisions in ensuing years.[154]

Senator Muskie led congressional efforts at formulating the first federal citizen environmental enforcement provisions. These were contained in the Clean Air Act of 1970.[155] During Senate debates on this legislation on September 21, 1970, Senator Muskie noted that "state and local governments have not responded adequately [to the challenge of enforcement].... It is clear that enforcement must be toughened if we are to meet the national deadline. More tools are needed, and the federal presence and backup authority must be increased."[156]

With the intellectual spur of Professor Sax and Senator Muskie, the idea of citizen suits as a supplemental means of enforcing environmental laws was developed at the state and federal levels during the early 1970s. After passage of the Clean Air Act, statutory citizen suit provisions were included in virtually all new federal environmental statutes or major amendments to existing regulatory statutes.[157]

Citizen suits in environmental litigation have instigated considerable litigation in recent years with vigorous debate taking place among jurists and scholars about the meaning and significance of these provisions.[158]

---

153. *See also* Haynes, *Michigan's Environmental Protection Act in its Sixth Year: Substantive Environmental Law from Citizen Suits* 53 J. URB. L. 589 (1976).

154. *See, e.g.*, CAL. GOV'T CODE §§ 12600 to 12612 (West 1980); CONN. GEN. STAT. ANN. §§ 22a-14 to 22a-20 (West 1985 and Supp. 1990); FLA. STAT. ANN. § 403.412 (West 1986 and Supp. 1990); IND. CODE ANN. §§ 13-6-1-1 to 13-6-1-6 (West 1990); MD. NAT. RES. CODE ANN. §§ 1-501 to 1-508 (1989); MASS. GEN. LAWS ANN. ch. 214, § 7A (West 1989); MINN. STAT. ANN. §§ 116B.01 to 116B.13 (West 1987); NEV. REV. STAT. ANN. §§ 41.540 to 41.570 (Michie 1986); N.J. STAT. ANN. §§ 2A:35A-1 to 2A:35A-14 (West 1987); S.D. CODIFIED LAWS ANN. §§ 34A-1 to 34A-15 (1986 and Supp. 1990).

155. Clean Air Act § 304, 42 U.S.C. § 7604 (1988).

156. J. Miller, *supra* note 147, at 4, n. 2 (quoting ENVIRONMENTAL POLICY DIVISION, CONGRESSIONAL RESEARCH SERVICE, A LEGISLATIVE HISTORY OF THE CLEAN AIR ACT AMENDMENTS OF 1970 at 226).

157. *See* Federal Water Pollution Control Act § 505, 33 U.S.C. § 1365 (1988); Noise Control Act § 12, 42 U.S.C. § 4911 (1988); Resource Conservation and Recovery Act § 7002, 42 U.S.C. § 6972 (1988); Safe Drinking Water Act § 1449, 42 U.S.C. § 300j-8 (1988); Toxic Substances Control Act § 20, 15 U.S.C. § 2619 (1988). The one exception is the Federal Insecticide, Fungicide, and Rodenticide Act (FIFRA), 7 U.S.C. §§ 135-136y (1988), which does not contain a citizen suit provision.

158. *See generally* Blomquist, *Rethinking the Citizen as Prosecutor Model of Environmental Enforcement Under the Clean Water Act: Some Overlooked Problems of Outcome-Independent Values*, 22 GA. L. REV. 337 (1988) (collecting sources).

6. *Bureaucrats as Intellectuals: Reports of the Council on Environmental Quality (CEQ) and the Office of Technology Assessment (OTA)*

Professor William H. Rodgers, Jr. has observed that American law mandates the "establishment of ... national commissions, and a host of lesser study provisions."[159] He goes on to note, however, that this penchant for study and analysis is "consistent with a theory of legislation as dynamic, ever-changing, and as tending towards the provisional solution."[160] "It is," he asserts, "as if the 'more study' outcome is the natural equilibrium point between opponents and proponents of regulation in pollution conflicts of high uncertainty."[161]

Two federal government agencies -- one in the Executive Office of the President, the other a congressional appendage for policy advice -- have had a significant impact during the last two decades in providing raw information about environmental degradation and in also generating ideas for resolving these problems. The former agency, the Council on Environmental Quality (CEQ), was established by the National Environmental Policy Act of 1969[162] to formulate and recommend national policies to promote the improvement of the quality of the environment. Additional responsibilities were provided by the Environmental Quality Improvement Act of 1970.[163] The Council consists of three members appointed by the President with the advice and consent of the Senate. CEQ's research and analytical responsibilities entail the following work:

> The Council develops and recommends to the President national policies that further environmental quality; performs a continuing analysis of changes or trends in the national environment; reviews and appraises programs of the Federal Government to determine their contribution to sound environmental policy; conducts studies, research, and analyses relating to ecological systems and environmental quality; assists the President in the preparation of the annual environmental quality report to the Congress; and oversees implementation of the National Environmental Policy Act.[164]

---

159. 2 W. RODGERS, JR., *supra* note 12, at 8.

160. *Id.*

161. *Compare* Blomquist, *Beyond the EPA and OTA Reports: Toward a Comprehensive Theory and Approach to Hazardous Waste Reduction in America*, 18 ENVTL. L. 817, 822-30 (1988) (discussing the dynamics of "policymaking by study reports" under the Hazardous and Solid Waste Amendments of 1984, Pub. L. No. 98-616, 98 Stat. 3221 (1984)).

162. 42 U.S.C. §§ 4321, 4331-4335, 4341-4347 (1988).

163. 42 U.S.C. §§ 4371-4375 (1988).

164. OFFICE OF THE FEDERAL REGISTER, NATIONAL ARCHIVES AND RECORDS ADMINISTRATION, THE UNITED STATES GOVERNMENT MANUAL 1989/90 96 (1989).

While CEQ has provided a plethora of good environmental analysis in the twenty years of its existence,[165] three categories of studies contain pathbreaking conceptual analyses of environmental problems and are worthy of special note as truly intellectual sources. The first category consists of two outstanding environmental quality reports: *The Tenth Annual Report*,[166] published in 1979; and *The Twentieth Annual Report*, released in 1990.[167] In a prologue and twelve substantive chapters[168] joined with several special appendices, the *1979 Report* went beyond past annual reports to provide a synoptic view of the record of environmental progress during the decade of the 1970s. Quite properly, CEQ compared the flurry of new environmental legislation during the decade to other legal watersheds in American history. As noted in the *1979 Report*:

> In 1970, Congress began to enact a body of legislation which by the end of the decade would have a major impact on people's lives and the nation's way of doing business, possibly comparable with such earlier political changes as the New Deal in the 1930s, or the civil rights reforms of the 1950s and 1960s.[169]

Indeed, the *1979 Report* provided one of the first clear intellectual links between the "environmentalism" of the seventies and America's nineteenth century conservation movement and municipal concern for air and water pollution in the first few decades of the twentieth century. The CEQ characterized the similarity as constituting pursuit of "a new direction."[170] In particular, with a parting reference to Rachel Carson, CEQ concluded:

> That is not to say that no choking exhaust will ever again leave a tailpipe, that no worker will ever again breathe in a cancer-causing chemical, that no endangered plant or animal will ever be in jeopardy, that no pristine or unique wilderness area will ever be despoiled or that global resources, even the planet's atmosphere, will be proof against degradation from the actions of billions of humans. There is an immense amount to be done on these and many other environmental issues. And as the needs and goals of the nation change over the

165. From 1970 to 1990, CEQ issued twenty annual reports on environmental quality and occasional technical reports.

166. U.S. COUNCIL ON ENVIRONMENTAL QUALITY, TENTH ANNUAL REPORT (1979).

167. U.S. COUNCIL ON ENVIRONMENTAL QUALITY, TWENTIETH ANNUAL REPORT (1990).

168. The prologue is entitled *An Environmental Decade*. The twelve substantive chapters address the following: air quality, water quality, toxic substances and environmental health, municipal solid waste, energy, natural resources, coastal ecology and shellfish, human settlement and land use, noise, NEPA, the global environment, and economics.

169. 1979 CEQ REPORT, *supra* note 166, at 1.

170. *Id.* at 1-15 (prologue).

coming decades, no doubt new environmental problems and issues will arise and have to be faced.

What has changed in an important way is the nation's method of going about its business. Embedded not just in the law, but in the nation's consciousness, is now the belief that no new project should be undertaken without first seriously considering its effect on the ecosystem of which we are all a part.***

***

Rachel Carson in 1962 prefaced *Silent Spring* with the following statement by Albert Schweitzer: 'Man has lost the capacity to foresee and to forestall. He will end by destroying the earth.' In the early 1960s, for people thinking and writing about environmental problems, there was considerable agreement with this pessimistic view. But since then, much has in fact changed. The commitment to environmental progress has been made, and seems to be here to stay. While there is still much to learn, understand, and work out before the nation achieves and maintains a healthful, livable environment that can sustain people for centuries, we have embarked upon that journey.[171]

Although the quality of CEQ annual reports languished during the administration of Ronald Reagan,[172] CEQ redeemed its past reputation with publication of the *1990 Report*.[173] In an elegant report, suffused with an accumulation of data and experience over twenty years, CEQ emphasizes the "historical perspective" in all eight substantive chapters in the report.[174] In commenting on two particularly important historical trends in environmental law and policy from 1970 to 1990, CEQ observes:

Unlike 1970 environmental pollution today is considered not only harmful and irresponsible, but -- in many instances -- *criminal* as well. Environmental laws are enforced now at every level of government, by a number of federal, state, and local agencies, and with a much-expanded array of tools. Although violation of environmental laws continue to present problems, law enforcement officials today are much better equipped to address them.

171. *Id.*

172. J. Lash, K. Gillman, and D. Sheridan, *supra* note 51.

173. *See supra* notes 166 to 167 and accompanying text.

174. The eight substantive chapters are as follows: Twenty Years of Change, The National Environmental Policy Act, Environmental Data and Trends, Environmental Science and Technology, Environmental Enforcement, Pollution Prevention, International Issues, and The Great Lakes.

> One of the most fundamental changes that has occurred over the past 20 years is the response of American businesses to their environmental responsibilities. Many corporations today are interested not simply in their legal responsibilities to control pollution before it escapes to the environment, but in the broad corporate benefits that attend efforts to reduce pollution at its source. Widespread efforts to redesign manufacturing processes, substitute less harmful production materials, and recycle wastes are beginning to play a major role in protecting the environment.[175]

Closely related to CEQ's annual reports is the second category of significant intellectual projects it has undertaken in the last twenty years: preparation of an original national environmental database in its 1981 publication, *Environmental Trends*,[176] and updating of that database in 1989.[177] In its initial trend report, the CEQ broached the idea that there was no "single index of environmental quality, and environmental GNP."[178] Indeed, the CEQ "found that no single measure and no single index could tell ... in a meaningful and valid way what the state of the environment was and whether or not it was improving."[179] Alternatively, CEQ sought to "sort out the useful [environmental information] from the less useful and bring together the most important and informative data on environmental conditions and trends that could be found."[180] Based on criteria of relevancy, selectivity, availability, statistical quality, and scope of coverage the authors of the *1981 Environmental Trends* presented hundreds of graphs and tables on environmental indicators in thirteen areas: people and the land; critical areas; human settlements; transportation; material use and solid waste; toxic substances; croplands, forests and rangeland; wildlife; energy; water resources; water quality; air quality; and the biosphere.[181]

Building on the original data compilation, CEQ refined and improved the database in its *1989 Environmental Trends*.[182] The *1989 Environmental Trends* report sets forth environmental information in 367 graphics and condenses the material into nine chapters: minerals and energy; water; imate and air quality; land resources; wetlands and wildlife; protected areas; population; transportation; and environmental risks and hazards. The changes in data format

---

175. 1990 CEQ REPORT, *supra* note 167, at 12-13.
176. U.S. COUNCIL ON ENVIRONMENTAL QUALITY, ENVIRONMENTAL TRENDS (1981).
177. U.S. COUNCIL ON ENVIRONMENTAL QUALITY, ENVIRONMENTAL TRENDS (1989).
178. 1981 ENVIRONMENTAL TRENDS, *supra* note 176, at iv.
179. *Id.*
180. *Id.*
181. *Id.* at iii (table of contents).
182. 1989 ENVIRONMENTAL TRENDS, *supra* note 177.

and compilation were undertaken by CEQ so that the following key conceptual questions could be addressed by policymakers and citizens:

> Are environmental conditions getting better or worse? What aspects of the environment are most improved, most degraded? Where do environmental conditions pose a health hazard? Are the data monitored sufficiently to give confidence in making accurate assessments? Have environmental legislation and programs resulted in any measurable improvements? In what areas is change most noticeable?[183]

Finally, CEQ's collaboration with the U.S. Department of State in producing the *Global 2000 Report to the President* -- briefly discussed above[184] -- was an outstanding intellectual contribution to the development of American environmental law in the last thirty years. Its primary importance lies in conceptually *internationalizing* environmental problems in a comprehensive and analytical way. After the *Global 2000 Report*, experts might disagree as to the specific transnational impacts of environmental problems but they would find it hard to argue against the idea of international environmental problems and the need for international environmental law in resolving these problems.

The Congressional Office of Technology Assessment (OTA) was created by the Technology Assessment Act of 1972[185] to serve Congress by providing objective analyses of major public policy issues relating to scientific and technological change. The OTA began operations in January 1974.

Although the OTA has a somewhat cumbersome organizational structure,[186] the comprehensive reports prepared by its staff over the years

---

183. *Id.* at vii.

184. *See supra* notes 70 to 71 and accompanying text.

185. 2 U.S.C. § 472 (1986).

186. OTA's Enabling Act, 2 U.S.C. §§ 472, 475, 476 (1988) specifies that it shall consist of a Technology Assessment Board, a Director, a Technology Advisory Council, and such other employees and consultants as may be necessary in the conduct of OTA's work.

> The bipartisan 13-member Board includes six Senators appointed by the President pro tempore, six members of the House of Representatives appointed by the Speaker, and the Director of OTA, who is a non-voting member. The Board selects a Chairman and a Vice Chairman from among its members at the beginning of each Congress. The Chairmanship and Vice Chairmanship alternate between the Senate and the House of Representatives with each Congress. The Director is appointed by the Board and serves a 6-year term. Their Director has full authority and responsibility for organizing and managing OTA's resources according to policies set by the Board.
>
> The Technology Assessment Advisory Council comprises 10 public members eminent in science and technology. The Council is appointed by the Board and advises the Board and OTA on assessments and other matters. The Comptroller General of the

have synthesized important environmental and technical research while providing new ideas and new paradigms for addressing environmental issues. OTA has tended to focus its assessments on the area of hazardous, toxic, or radioactive wastes, publishing several reports in this area in the last decade.[187] Two of these reports, *Serious Reduction of Hazardous Waste*, published in 1986[188] and *Coming Clean: Superfund Problems Can Be Solved*,[189] published in 1989 have had a profound impact on changing national environmental policy. The former report articulated and refined a vision of "waste reduction" over "waste treatment" while "urging primacy of waste reduction over waste treatment, and focusing on careful definition of terms."[190]

The latter report, *Coming Clean*,[191] led the EPA to "tighten oversight of Superfund cleanups by requiring federal or state officials to conduct health risk studies because private companies may be underestimating the threats to

---

United States and the Director of the Congressional Research Service of the Library of Congress are also members.

The office's assessments explore complex issues involving science and technology, helping Congress resolve uncertainties and conflicting claims, identifying alternative policy options, and providing foresight or early alert to new developments that could have important implications for future Federal policy. Requests for assessments may be made by the chairman of any congressional committee acting for himself or on behalf of a ranking minority member, or a majority of committee members; by the OTA Board; or by the OTA Director, in consultation with the Board.

The office's work centers on comprehensive assessments that may take 1 to 2 years to complete. It also draws upon its past and current work to provide a variety of responses to meet immediate congressional needs, such as briefings, testimony and special reports.

U.S. GOVERNMENT MANUAL, *supra* note 164, at 61.

187. *See, e.g.*, U.S. OFFICE OF TECHNOLOGY ASSESSMENT, COMING CLEAN: SUPERFUND PROBLEMS CAN BE SOLVED (1989); U.S. OFFICE OF TECHNOLOGY ASSESSMENT, FROM POLLUTION TO PREVENTION: A PROGRESS REPORT ON WASTE REDUCTION (1987); U.S. OFFICE OF TECHNOLOGY ASSESSMENT, MANAGING THE NATION'S COMMERCIAL HIGH-LEVEL RADIOACTIVE WASTE (1985); U.S. OFFICE OF TECHNOLOGY ASSESSMENT, NEUROTOXICITY: IDENTIFYING AND CONTROLLING POISONS OF THE NERVOUS SYSTEM (1990); U.S. OFFICE OF TECHNOLOGY ASSESSMENT, OCEAN INCINERATION: ITS ROLE IN MANAGING HAZARDOUS WASTE (1986); U.S. OFFICE OF TECHNOLOGY ASSESSMENT, PARTNERSHIPS UNDER PRESSURE: MANAGING COMMERCIAL LOW-LEVEL RADIOACTIVE WASTE (1989); U.S. OFFICE OF TECHNOLOGY ASSESSMENT, SERIOUS REDUCTION OF HAZARDOUS WASTE: FOR POLLUTION PREVENTION AND INDUSTRIAL EFFICIENCY (1986); U.S. OFFICE OF TECHNOLOGY ASSESSMENT, SUPERFUND STRATEGY (1985); U.S. OFFICE OF TECHNOLOGY ASSESSMENT, TECHNOLOGIES AND MANAGEMENT STRATEGIES FOR HAZARDOUS WASTE CONTROL (1983); U.S. OFFICE OF TECHNOLOGY ASSESSMENT, TRANSPORTATION OF HAZARDOUS MATERIALS (1986); U.S. OFFICE OF TECHNOLOGY ASSESSMENT, WASTES IN MARINE ENVIRONMENTS (1987).

188. *See* SERIOUS REDUCTION, *supra* note 187. This report was followed by the rebuttal report, FROM POLLUTION TO PREVENTION, *supra* note 187, published in 1987.

189. *See* COMING CLEAN, *supra* note 187.

190. Blomquist, *supra* note 161, at 867.

191. COMING CLEAN, *supra* note 187.

residents near the sites."[192] Indeed, OTA's 1989 report argued that "the government should do all the studies and design plans for Superfund cleanups and limit responsible parties to doing only the actual cleanup work."[193]

7. *Prime Minister Gro Brundtland and the Report of the World Commission on Environment and Development*

Prior to becoming Prime Minister of Norway in 1981, Mrs. Gro Harlem Brundtland had served as Norway's Minister of Environment from 1974-79 and a member of the Norway Parliament from 1977.[194] Relating her personal reaction to the Secretary-General of the United Nations' request in December 1983 for her to "establish and chair a special, independent commission to address"[195] world environmental problems, Brundtland acknowledged that she "was acutely aware that this was no small task and obligation."[196] But she went on to muse:

> What the general assembly asked for ... seemed to be unrealistic and much too ambitious. At the same time, it was a clear demonstration of the widespread feeling of frustration and inadequacy in the international community about our own ability to address the vital global issues and deal effectively with them.
>
> ***
>
> All this was on my mind when the Secretary-General presented me with an argument to which there was no convincing rebuttal: No other political leader had become Prime Minister with a background of several years of political struggle, nationally and internationally, as an environment minister. This gave some hope that the environment was not destined to remain a side issue in central, political decisionmaking.[197]

It is interesting that Prime Minister Brundtland compared her task to the "formula[tion] [of] a third and compelling [international] call for political action:

192. 21 *Env't Rep.* (BNA) 414-15 (June 29, 1990).

193. *Id.*

194. WORLD COMMISSION ON ENVIRONMENT AND DEVELOPMENT, OUR COMMON FUTURE 353 (1987) [hereinafter OUR COMMON FUTURE].

195. *Id.* at ix.

196. *Id.*

197. *Id.* at ix-x.

After Brandt's *Programme for Survival* and *Common Crisis*, and after Palme's *Common Security*."[198]

After beginning her work in 1983, Brundtland named the other Commissioners.[199] At its inaugural meeting in October 1984, the Commission selected eight key issues for analysis during the course of its work:

- Perspectives on Population, Environment and Sustainable Development;
- Energy: Environment and Development;
- Industry: Environment and Development;
- Food Security, Agriculture, Forestry, Environment, and Development;
- Human Settlements: Environment and Development;
- International Economic Relations, Environment and Development;
- Decision Support Systems for Environmental Management; and
- International Cooperation.[200]

Resolving to "receiv[e] the broadest range of views and advice on the key issues it was addressing,"[201] the Commission "decided that it would hold deliberative meetings in all regions of the world and that it would take the occasion of those meetings to get a first-hand view of environment and development issues in those regions."[202] These views were incorporated into the final text of *Our Common Future* with the assistance of staff, experts, and advisory panels.

Drawing on past intellectual concepts of "Spaceship Earth,"[203] and sustainable development,[204] the report articulated a new international environmental construct: "From one earth to one world."[205] This construct is composed of "six priority areas": (1) "getting at sources" to "make the key national, economic, and sectorial agencies directly responsible and accountable for ensuring that their policies ... support development that is economically and

---

198. *Id.* at x.

199. The Commission consisted of 23 members. This included the United States' representative, William Ruckelshaus, former Administrator of the EPA. *See* OUR COMMON FUTURE, *supra* note 195, at 353-56 (listing members).

200. *Id.* at 358.

201. *Id.* at 359.

202. *Id.*

203. *See supra* notes 117 to 122 and accompanying text.

204. *See supra* note 73 and accompanying text.

205. OUR COMMON FUTURE, *supra* note 195, at 1-23.

ecologically sustainable;"[206] (2) "dealing with the effects" by having governments "reinforce the roles and capacities of environmental protection and resource management agencies;"[207] (3) "assessing global risks" by improving "[t]he capacity to identify, assess, and report on risks of irreversible damage to natural systems and threats to the survival, security, and well-being of the world community;"[208] (4) "making informed choices" by encouraging "widespread support and involvement of an informed public and of non-governmental organizations, the scientific community, and industry;"[209] (5) "providing the legal means" to fill "major gaps in existing national and international law related to the environment, to find ways to recognize and protect the rights of present and future generations to an environment adequate for their health and well-being, [and] to prepare under UN auspices a universal Declaration on environmental protection and sustainable development;"[210] and (6) "investing in our future" by World Bank lending practices that focus on "renewable energy development, pollution control, and achieving less resource-intensive forms of agriculture."[211]

The six priority areas are addressed in twenty-two "proposed legal principles" for environmental protection and sustainable development" adopted by the Commission.[212]

---

206. *Id.* at 20.
207. *Id.*
208. *Id.*
209. OUR COMMON FUTURE, *supra* note 195, at 21.
210. *Id.*
211. *Id.*
212. *Id.* at 348-51.

I. GENERAL PRINCIPLES, RIGHTS, AND RESPONSIBILITIES

Fundamental Human Right

1. All human beings have the fundamental right to an environment adequate for their health and well-being.

Inter-Generational Equity

2. States shall conserve and use the environment and natural resources for the benefit of present and future generations.

Conservation and Sustainable Use

3. States shall maintain ecosystems and ecological processes essential for the functioning of the biosphere, shall preserve biological diversity, and shall observe the principle of optimum sustainable yield in the use of living natural resources and ecosystems.

Environmental Standards and Monitoring

4. States shall establish adequate environmental protection standards and monitor changes in and publish relevant data on environmental quality and resource use.

Prior Environmental Assessments

5. States shall make or require prior environmental assessments of proposed activities which may significantly affect the environment or use of a natural resource.

Prior Notification, Access, and Due Process

6. States shall inform in a timely manner all persons likely to be significantly affected by a planned activity and to grant them equal access and due process in administrative and judicial proceedings.

Sustainable Development and Assistance

7. States shall ensure that conservation is treated as an integral part of the planning and implementation of development activities and provide assistance to other States, especially to developing countries, in support of environmental protection and sustainable development.

General Obligation to Co-operate

8. States shall co-operate in good faith with other States in implementing the preceding rights and obligations.

II. PRINCIPLES, RIGHTS, AND OBLIGATIONS CONCERNING TRANSBOUNDARY NATURAL RESOURCES AND ENVIRONMENTAL INTERFERENCES

Reasonable and Equitable Use

9. States shall use transboundary natural resources in a reasonable and equitable manner.

Prevention and Abatement

10. States shall prevent or abate any transboundary environmental interference which could cause or causes significant harm (but subject to certain exceptions provided for in Art. 11 and Art. 12 below).

Strict Liability

11. States shall take all reasonable precautionary measures to limit the risk when carrying out or permitting certain dangerous but beneficial activities and shall ensure that compensation is provided should substantial transboundary harm occur even when the activities were not known to be harmful at the time they were undertaken.

Prior Agreements When Prevention Costs Greatly Exceed Harm

12. States shall enter into negotiations with the affected State on the equitable conditions under which the activity could be carried out when planning to carry out or permit activities causing transboundary harm which is substantial but far less than the cost of prevention. (If no agreement can be reached, see Art. 22.)

Non-Discrimination

13. States shall apply as a minimum at least the same standards for environmental conduct and impacts regarding transboundary natural resource and environmental interferences as are applied domestically (i.e., do not do to others what you would not do to your own citizens).

General Obligation to Co-operate on Transboundary Environmental Problems

14. States shall co-operate in good faith with other States to achieve optimal use of transboundary natural resources and effective prevention or abatement of transboundary environmental interferences.

Exchange of Information

15. States of origin shall provide timely and relevant information to the other concerned States regarding transboundary natural resources or environmental interferences.

Prior Assessment and Notification

16. States shall provide prior and timely notification and relevant information to the other concerned States and shall make or require an environmental assessment of planned activities which may have significant transboundary effects.

While it is probably premature to assess the intellectual impact of *Our Common Future*, it is reasonable to assume that the report will have a substantial impact on federal legislation considered by the United States Congress on international legal issues such as ozone depletion, global warming, and transboundary export of hazardous waste.

8. Environmental Groups and Development of the Valdez Principles

On March 24, 1989, the Exxon Valdez spilled 10.92 million gallons of crude oil into Prince William Sound, after running aground.[213] While cleanup operations were underway during the summer and autumn of 1989, a group of environmentalists, money managers, and other social activists drafted a set of ten corporate management guidelines, which they called the "Valdez Principles." "The drafters, the Coalition for Environmentally Responsible Economies (CERES), called on companies to adopt these principles, suggesting that their implementation would help consumers, shareholders, and the general public to

---

Prior Consultations

17. States of origin shall consult at an early stage and in good faith with other concerned States regarding existing or potential transboundary interferences with their use of a natural resource or the environment.

Co-operative Arrangements for Environmental Assessment and Protection

18. States shall co-operate with the concerned States in monitoring, scientific research and standard setting regarding transboundary natural resources and environmental interferences.

Emergency Situations

19. States shall develop contingency plans regarding emergency situations likely to cause transboundary environmental interferences and shall promptly warn, provide relevant information to and co-operate with concerned States when emergencies occur.

Equal Access and Treatment

20. States shall grant equal access, due process and equal treatment in administrative and judicial proceedings to all persons who are or may be affected by transboundary interferences with their use of a natural resource or the environment.

III. STATE RESPONSIBILITY

21. States shall cease activities which breach an international obligation regarding the environment and provide compensation for the harm caused.

IV. PEACEFUL SETTLEMENT OF DISPUTES

22. States shall settle environmental disputes by peaceful means. If mutual agreement on a solution or on other dispute settlement arrangements is not reached within 18 months, the dispute shall be submitted to conciliation and, if unresolved, thereafter to arbitration or judicial settlement at the request of any of the concerned States.

Id. at 348-51.

213. Note, *The Valdez Principles: A Corporate Self-Governance Code on Environmental Conduct*, 2 GEO. INT'L ENVTL L. REV. 237 (1989).

determine which companies are environmentally responsible and which placed the environment at risk."[214]

The Social Investment Forum, a national trade group of money managers, brokers, bankers, analysts and other social investors combined forces with leading national environmental groups, including the Sierra Club and the National Audubon Society to form CERES. "Based on the Sullivan Principles, which are intended to guide business decisions in South Africa in an attempt to end apartheid, the Valdez Principles are intended to focus the pressure of socially-conscious investors in order to improve the environmental conduct of publicly owned corporations."[215]

While CERES first issued the Valdez Principles in September 1989, the group has been at work during the ensuing months "on guidance to articulate the underlying concepts and expectations behind the Principles."[216] The present version of the ten Valdez Principles state the following:

1. Protection of the Biosphere
   We will minimize and strive to eliminate the release of any pollutant that may cause environmental damage to the air, water, or earth or its inhabitants. We will safeguard habitats in rivers, lakes, wetlands, coastal zones and oceans and will minimize contributing to the greenhouse affect, depletion of the ozone layer, acid rain, or smog.
2. Sustainable Use of Natural Resources
   We will make sustainable use of renewable natural resources, such as water, soils and forests. We will conserve nonrenewable natural resources through efficient use and careful planning. We will protect wildlife habitat, open spaces and wilderness, while preserving biodiversity.
3. Reduction and Disposal of Waste
   We will minimize the creation of waste, especially hazardous waste, and wherever possible recycle materials. We will dispose of all wastes through safe and responsible methods.
4. Wise Use of Energy
   We will make every effort to use environmentally safe and sustainable energy sources to meet our needs. We will invest in improved energy efficiency and conservation in our

---

214. Point-Counterpoint, *Can the Valdez Principles Green Corporate America?*, ENVTL FORUM 30 (March/April 1990) [hereinafter *Envtl Forum*]. CERES is the name of the Roman goddess for Mother Earth.

215. *Id.*

216. *Id.*

operations. We will maximize the energy efficiency of products we produce or sell.

5. Risk Reduction
We will minimize the environmental, health and safety risks to our employees and the communities in which we operate by employing safe technologies and operating procedures and by being constantly prepared for emergencies.
6. Marketing of Safe Products and Services
We will sell products or services that minimize adverse environmental impacts and that are safe as consumers commonly use them. We will inform consumers of the environmental impacts of our products or services.
7. Damage Compensation
We will take responsibility for any harm we cause to the environment by making every effort to fully restore the environment and to compensate those persons who are adversely affected.
8. Disclosure
We will disclose to our employees and to the public incidents relating to our operations that cause environmental harm or pose health or safety hazards. We will disclose potential environmental, health or safety hazards posed by our operations, and we will not take any action against employees who report any condition that creates a danger to the environment or poses health and safety hazards.
9. Environmental Directors and Managers
At least one member of the Board of Directors will be a person qualified to represent environmental interest. We will commit management resources to implement these Principles, including the funding of an office of vice-president for environmental affairs or an equivalent executive position, reporting directly to the CEO, to monitor and report upon our implementation efforts.
10. Assessment and Annual Audit
We will conduct and make public an annual self-evaluation of our progress in implementing these Principles and in complying with all applicable laws and regulations throughout our worldwide operations. We will work toward the timely creation of independent environmental audit procedures which we will complete annually and make available to the public.[217]

217. *Id.* at 35.

The Valdez Principles have, already, engendered much public debate and discourse. On the one hand, some commentators argue that the Principles "may prove to be a sophisticated public relations mechanism by which companies can indicate to both investors and shareholders that they are environmentally responsible."[218] Non-complying businesses, according to this line of argument, would risk public scorn and disinvestment.[219] Indeed, the notion of environmentally responsible corporations -- the root idea of the Valdez Principles -- has already been endorsed by a number of corporate executives including the chief executive officers of DuPont and Monsanto.[220] Moreover,

> [o]ther companies are moving in new directions as well. Proctor and Gamble now boasts of using some recycled paper in 70 percent of its product packaging, and its Tide, Cheer, and Downy bottles are now being manufactured from recycled plastics. Kodak has recently announced it would begin recycling its Fling, Stretch, and Weekend disposable cameras, which have been cited as among the worst examples of overpackaged and non-recyclable consumer products. 3M Company has decided to beat the 1998 federal deadline to replace or improve underground storage tanks for liquids and gases, aiming to have all tanks worldwide in compliance five years early by 1993, at a cost of $80 million.[221]

On the other hand, some observers criticize the fact that "CERES completed the Principles without any discussion with industry representatives and has indicated that it will not consider changing them."[222] Likewise, some contend that the Principles are too blunt of a concept: that "they fail to articulate terms that would distinguish truly progressive companies from those that are still recalcitrant in protecting human health and the environment."[223]

The intellectual momentum of the Valdez Principles, however, has increased in recent months. Some thoughtful American legal observers have been inspired to recommend extension or amplification of the Principles by providing such interesting legal changes as the following: "a new defense to civil or criminal antitrust actions for corporations which attempt to develop a voluntary agreement for adherence to the Valdez Principles within a specific

---

218. *The Valdez Principles*, *supra* note 214, at 240-41. *See also* Feder, *Who Will Subscribe to the Valdez Principles?*, N.Y. Times, September 10, 1989, § 3, at 6, col. 1.

219. *The Valdez Principles*, *supra* note 214, at 241.

220. Doyle, *Protecting Planet and Portfolio*, in ENVTL FORUM, *supra* note 215, at 32.

221. *Id.*

222. Friedman, *Don't Sign the Valdez Principles*, in ENVTL FORUM, *supra* note 215, at 32.

223. *Id.*

industry;"[224] requiring that "all [government] contractors receiving federal funds adhere to the Valdez Principles;"[225] "[r]equiring the determination of adherence or non-adherence to the Valdez Principles to be included in a[n] [Environmental Impact Statement]"[226] or, "incorporating adherence to the Valdez Principles in the Federal Acquisition Regulation (FAR)" dealing with federal acquisitions of products and services.[227]

V. Conclusion

An intellectual-historical approach to American environmental law holds considerable promise for three reasons. First, it seeks to identify the rich assortment of ideas, conceptions, and paradigms of intellectual elites including scholars, judges, statespersons, expert government officials, and national environmental leaders. Second, it seeks to assess the real world impact of intellectual ideas on lawmaking -- whether by case law, statute, contractual pledge, agency policy, proposed bill, or scholarly proposal, the idea or ideas have been translated into some legal principle. Third, where appropriate, the flux, or change, of original ideas in response to lawmaking (like a tennis ball bouncing over a net) can be usefully studied and evaluated.

Unfortunately, the prevailing American environmental legal regime, as pointed out by Professor Richard Brooks of Vermont Law School, usually fails to pursue the "big picture"; to think in terms of overarching ideas and conceptions and how the law can use and assimilate these ideas and concepts. But, to assume that all environmental lawmaking in America is the by-product of shallow, uninformed, raw political interaction and compromise is to overstate the case. The intellect as well as the pocketbook plays a part in the continuing evolution of environmental law in this country.

In closing, let me note that while I believe that an intellectual historical approach to American environmental law holds great promise, in the final analysis it, too, is insufficient for complete understanding. Perhaps the poetry of the farmer, Wendell Barry, best expresses this truth:

> And the world cannot be discovered by a journey of miles, no matter how long, but only by a spiritual journey, a journey of one inch, very

224. *The Valdez Principles*, *supra* note 214, at 245.
225. *Id.*
226. *Id.*
227. *Id.* at 245-46 (footnote omitted).

> arduous and humbling and joyful, by which we arrive at the ground at our feet, and learn to be at home.[228]

Only when we learn to truly be "at home" on this planet -- in sustainable balance with other life forms and natural forces -- will we truly fulfill the ultimate purpose of environmental law: to live together in productive harmony.

---

228. Barry, *The Unforeseen Wilderness*, in THE EARTH SPEAKS (S. Van Matre and B. Weiler eds. 1983).

[3]

REVIEW ESSAY

Environmentalism, Economics, and the Public Interest

Daniel A. Farber*

THE ECONOMY OF THE EARTH: PHILOSOPHY, LAW, AND THE ENVIRONMENT. By Mark Sagoff. Cambridge: Cambridge University Press. 1988. ix + 271 pp. $29.95.

Mark Sagoff is probably best known to environmental scholars for his role in the "plastic trees" debate.[1] In response to a suggestion that plastic trees would be cheaper and more durable than real ones, he undertook to explain what was wrong with such a utilitarian calculation. Since then, Sagoff has continued to explore the philosophical basis of environmental law. In *The Economy of the Earth*, he brings together fifteen years of scholarship on the subject of environmentalism. While he has by no means repudiated his early work, this book makes it clear that his thought on the subject has deepened and matured.

Much of the book, like Sagoff's first "plastic trees" article, is dedicated to attacking cost-benefit analysis and the associated standard of economic efficiency.[2] Some scholars, with important support from the Reagan Administration, have contended that economic efficiency is the only proper basis for assessing environmental regulation.[3] Sagoff's ba-

* Henry J. Fletcher Professor of Law, University of Minnesota. I would like to thank Bob Ellickson, Phil Frickey, Dan Gifford, John Merryman, Suzanna Sherry, Gerald Torres, Tom Ulen, and the participants in the Minnesota Political Economy Workshop for their helpful comments.

1. For the major contributions to the debate, see Mark Sagoff, *On Preserving the Natural Environment*, 84 YALE L.J. 205 (1974); Laurence Tribe, *From Environmental Foundations to Constitutional Structures: Learning from Nature's Future*, 84 YALE L.J. 545 (1975); Laurence Tribe, *Ways Not to Think About Plastic Trees: New Foundations for Environmental Law*, 83 YALE L.J. 1315 (1974). Sagoff and Tribe agreed in rejecting utilitarianism, but disagreed sharply in their rationales.

2. Briefly, a government action is economically efficient if its benefits exceed its costs in monetary terms, so that the beneficiaries could afford to compensate the losers and still remain ahead of the game.

3. The Reagan Administration's efforts to mandate cost-benefit analysis are discussed in Cass Sunstein, *Constitutionalism After the New Deal*, 101 HARV. L. REV. 421, 442-63 (1987). For references to the scholarly support for this approach, see pp. 225-26 nn.2-13, 228-30 nn.6-27. Because so much of the book is dedicated to attacking this use of economics, it is important to note that Sagoff is by no means hostile toward the discipline of economics. He believes that economists can provide policymakers with vital information, and in fact he supports some

sic argument is that cost-benefit analysis applies only to personal preferences, whereas environmentalism involves moral values.[4] Such moral issues, he believes, more properly belong to the political process and cannot be resolved through economic analysis.[5] Cost-benefit analysis can only compare the competing weight of arbitrary private wishes, not the moral principles involved in modern social regulation.

I will contend that Sagoff is right in arguing that environmental values are entitled to consideration independent of economic efficiency, but wrong in repudiating economic efficiency as another valid social goal. More generally, he errs in elevating "public values" like environmentalism over the private values of everyday life. He also focuses too exclusively on environmental protection of nature and fails to acknowledge the distinctive problems presented by health regulations. Finally, although Sagoff overly romanticizes politics while unduly deriding private life, he is correct that the political process is the appropriate forum for environmental decisionmaking. Thus, while I reject much of his argument, I agree with his fundamental thesis about the inherently political nature of environmental issues.[6]

Part I of this review essay will consider the relationship between environmental values and economic efficiency, concluding that both are legitimate social goals. Part II will then explore the special problems raised by environmental regulations designed to protect human health. Deciding how to balance safety and cost often involves knotty policy issues. Finally, Part III will return to the more general problem of how to define the public interest. As Sagoff correctly suggests, the public interest cannot be reduced to some objective standard like economic efficiency. What, then, does it mean to say that environmental protection is in the public interest?

---

economists' proposals for using "market-like" mechanisms to control pollution. *See* pp. 205-10, 217. His quarrel with economic theory concerns the goals of environmental law, not the role of economists in devising the means.

4. *See* pp. 8-9, 113-14.

5. *See* pp. 17-18, 26-29.

6. I also agree that environmental problems call for the exercise of practical reason rather than brilliant theorizing:

> [T]o solve policy problems we need to develop the ordinary virtues of inquiry and deliberation . . . even at the expense of developing stimulating theoretical insights in journals of policy and economics. This does not mean that we need to replace the absolutes of welfare economics with other absolutes such as those associated with a "no risk" society. Rather, it means that we have to get along without certainty; we have to solve practical, not theoretical, problems; and we must adjust the ends we pursue to the means available to accomplish them. Otherwise, method becomes an obstacle to morality, dogma the foe of deliberation, and the ideal society we aspire to in theory will become a formidable enemy of the good society we can achieve in fact.

P. 14.

I. Economic Efficiency and Environmental Values

A. *Is Economic Efficiency the Only Value?*

Suppose we were doing a cost-benefit analysis to determine whether to save the whales. On the benefit side we would count the sale of whale products; on the cost side, we would include the expense of whaling. We would also want to evaluate the possibility of preserving a stock of whales so as to extend consumption into the future.[7] Moreover, because whales are part of the ocean's ecological balance, whaling creates externalities that must be considered in a cost-benefit analysis. There are also recreational activities to be taken into account—for example, the amount of money people would be willing to pay for new National Geographic movies about whales. Beyond this, some economists would attempt to take into account the strong feelings many people have about saving the whales. Those people would be unhappy if the whales were exterminated and would be willing to pay something to prevent that outcome. In an attempt to make the cost-benefit analysis complete, the analyst might assign "shadow prices" to environmentalism based on their willingness to pay. Sagoff contends that environmental values cannot properly be considered by including them in the cost-benefit calculation.[8]

Unlike the environmentalist, who unabashedly seeks to advance particular values, the cost-benefit analyst may appear to stand above the fray, seeking only to maximize the satisfaction of consumer preferences.[9] Counting moralisms as externalities may seem to provide a neutral decisionmaking process for combining individual preferences about public policy.[10] But economists know better than to think such a process exists.

Arrow's Theorem shows that no possible methodology can reliably convert individual preferences into a rational social decision. Majority rule, for example, can produce bizarre results with three or more items on the agenda because shifting coalitions can lead to paradoxical "cycles." Although the theorem is often invoked in connection with voting mechanisms, it actually applies to any attempt to transform individual preference orderings into a rational social choice. Every method of social choice inevitably has its flaws. Economic efficiency, in a sense, is even worse than majority voting because it can produce cycles when

7. Whether preservation makes sense on these terms would depend on how the reproduction rate of whales compares with market interest rates: If whales reproduce at a rate of 3% annually, while money reproduces at 5%, we are better off converting the whales to cash and investing the proceeds.

8. *See* pp. 35-39.

9. *See* Charles Meyers, *An Introduction to Environmental Thought: Some Sources and Some Criticisms*, 50 Ind. L.J. 426, 451-52 (1975).

10. *See* p. 40. For a discussion of moralisms from a leading member of the law and economics movement, see Guido Calabresi, Ideals, Beliefs, Attitudes, and the Law: Private Law Perspectives on a Public Law Problem ch. 4 (1985).

there are only two items on the agenda. That is, it is perfectly possible to have situations in which "*A* is more efficient than *B*" and "*B* is more efficient than *A*" are both true.[11]

Sagoff exploits this weakness in the efficiency standard by showing how it can sometimes produce indeterminate results in environmental disputes.[12] Consider the decision to destroy a stand of redwoods. If lumber companies begin with the legal right to harvest the trees—because they owned them, for example—environmentalists might not be willing (or able) to pay the companies enough to get them to stop. A cost-benefit analyst would say that company profits were greater than the external costs imposed on the environmentalists, so logging would be economically efficient.

The loggers' argument assumes, however, that they own the entitlement to control logging. If the environmentalists had the legal right to prevent logging, they might demand a much higher price to sell that right to the lumber companies. One reason for the disparity is that changes in wealth shift the demand curve. Before, the environmentalists may simply have been too poor to pay what it was really worth to them to stop the logging. Owning the trees, they are in a position to demand from the loggers what they themselves could not afford to pay. Thus, if the environmentalists own the entitlement, the cost-benefit analysis may well show that logging is inefficient. We can't decide whether the logging is economically efficient until we know who has the entitlement. Cost-benefit analysis is indeterminate in this situation. We must look elsewhere to decide whether we should allow the trees to be cut.

None of this is news to economists.[13] Even the most fervent believers in economic efficiency concede that "there is more to justice than economics."[14]

B. *Environmentalism As a Preference?*

This argument shows that economic efficiency alone cannot decide environmental disputes. Sagoff, however, wants to show more than this. He wants to show that cost-benefit analysis cannot even consider environmental values. He argues that economists are guilty of what philosophers call a category mistake—that is, that they are attempting to apply an attribute to the wrong category of entities, like trying to

11. This point is developed at greater length in Daniel Farber, *From Plastic Trees to Arrow's Theorem*, 1986 U. ILL. L. REV. 337, 352-54. For a related argument against "wealth maximization" as a principle for social choice, see Donald Keenan, *Value Maximization and Welfare Theory*, 10 J. LEGAL STUD. 409 (1981).

12. *See* pp. 83-84, 184-85, 254 n.24. His argument follows Duncan Kennedy, *Cost-Benefit Analysis of Entitlement Problems*, 33 STAN. L. REV. 387 (1981).

13. For example, the reversibility problem is discussed in Robert Cooter, *Liberty, Efficiency, and Law*, 50 L. & CONTEMP. PROBS. 141, 152-58 (1987).

14. RICHARD A. POSNER, ECONOMIC ANALYSIS OF LAW 25-26 (3d ed. 1986).

attach colors to numbers.[15] In this instance, the attribute is "willingness to pay," which Sagoff claims applies only to personal tastes. As he says, no one would think that the validity of a mathematical proposition depends on whether its backers were willing to pay more in support of their belief than were the skeptics. "No matter how much people are willing to pay, three will never be the square root of six."[16] Just so, he says, for moralisms.[17]

Here, it seems to me, Sagoff is only partially correct. "We should save the whales" is indeed a different kind of statement from "I like Szechuan food."[18] So far, Sagoff is on track. But "we should save the whales" is also quite unlike "2 + 2 = 4" or "the earth is round." In comparing moralisms to mathematical or empirical statements, Sagoff himself may be guilty of mixing categories.

Notably, despite Sagoff's claim that environmentalism is not just a preference but a moral principle "to be judged on the basis of reasons rather than wants,"[19] he makes no real attempt to justify environmentalism rationally. This is a problem, not because environmentalism and other values necessarily need some logical foundation, but because Sagoff wants to call values "principled" and preferences "arbitrary." When he seeks to support environmentalism, he invokes the role of nature in literature and public opinion polls supporting environmentalism.[20] These would not count as rational arguments for a scientific theory or a mathematical theorem, or even, I would think, as valid arguments for a moral philosophy. His treatment raises the question of how seriously he takes his own argument that moralisms differ fundamentally from personal preferences.

Indeed, the distinction between the arbitrary and the principled may itself be rather overdrawn. Some preferences do not fit either category. Friendship is a good example. I cannot reasonably claim that every truly rational creature must like my friends. It would also be odd for me to say that my friendships are based on neutral principles. Yet friendship is not "arbitrary." It is not even purely a matter of choice. Instead, it is to some extent an unmediated response: I can't help but like my friends. The particular things I like about them, the traits that I value, are not themselves arbitrary; rather, they are closely linked with other aspects of my personality and life history. Moreover, to speak of friendship as "arbitrary" would overlook the extent to which the friends make the person; their perceptions of me and my experiences with them are part of what makes me what I am. Much the same is true

15. This term was introduced in GILBERT RYLE, THE CONCEPT OF MIND 11 (1949).

16. Pp. 44-45.

17. *See* pp. 8-9, 55-57, 69, 95.

18. The fact that I like Szechuan food does make me think that other people ought to like it as well, but I would not argue that they are obligated to eat it, whereas the environmentalist would claim that others are obligated to help save the whales.

19. P. 44.

20. *See* ch. 6; *see also* pp. 51, 254 n.23.

of other things that are important to people, including consumer goods like books or music, and nature itself.[21] Basic personal values differ from mere "tastes" not because they are necessarily more rational or principled, but because these "habits of the heart"[22] are so deeply a part of our lives.

In any event, Sagoff's "category mistake" argument does not address the important issue.[23] The real question is not whether environmental values should be ignored in doing cost-benefit analysis. After all, there is no reason for environmentalists to chastise economists for paying too much attention to the environment.[24] Rather, environmentalists claim that environmental values are entitled to independent consideration regardless of whether they can be incorporated into a cost-benefit analysis as well.

Even if efficiency cannot be the exclusive value promoted by government,[25] it might be argued that environmentalism and other moralisms are impermissible values. The strongest argument to this effect has been made by Ronald Dworkin. He contends that liberalism requires the government to remain neutral on the question of "the good," taking no position on what forms of human life are better than others. Ideally, the government would give each individual an equal share of resources, leaving it to the market to determine the allocation of goods and services.[26] If resources are fairly distributed, Dworkin says, the government should not interfere to promote the views of those who value wilderness against those who value increased coal production.[27] As Sagoff and others have argued, however, Dworkin's view

21. For an insightful analysis of the reasons for valuing artistic creations (many of which also have some relevance to environmentalism), see John Merryman, *The Public Interest in Cultural Property*, 77 CALIF. L. REV. — (1989) (forthcoming). Even food preferences, often considered the epitome of arbitrariness, are not wholly arbitrary. They can also reflect, for example, provincialism versus cosmopolitanism.

22. I draw the phrase from HABITS OF THE HEART: INDIVIDUALISM AND COMMITMENT IN AMERICAN LIFE (R. Bellah, R. Madsen, W. Sullivan, A. Swidler, & S. Tipton eds. 1985).

23. Sagoff's argument also proves too much. If the truth of the proposition, "The whales should be saved," is unrelated to its believers' willingness to pay, it is presumably also unrelated to whether they are a majority of the population. Hence, deciding whether to implement that viewpoint on the basis of a majority vote is just as much a "category mistake" as making the same decision based on willingness to pay.

24. It is by no means clear that the government's response to a widespread social belief should turn solely on its truth. If many individuals wrongly believe that some harmless chemical causes cancer, it may be cheaper to eliminate the chemical than to educate the population. If the government can cheaply reassure extremely worried individuals, this seems desirable even if the cause of their anxiety is irrational. So, including moralisms in a cost-benefit analysis is not necessarily illegitimate.

25. The orthodox economic position, of course, is that efficiency is not an exclusive value at all. Rather, according to conventional welfare economics, the distribution of income must also be considered. *See, e.g.*, A. MITCHELL POLINSKY, AN INTRODUCTION TO LAW AND ECONOMICS chs. 2-3 (1983). The question is not whether efficiency should be augmented with other values, but whether environmentalism is one of those supplementary values.

26. *See* RONALD DWORKIN, A MATTER OF PRINCIPLE ch. 8 (1985).

27. *Id.* at 202.

is a caricature of liberalism.[28] While liberals do value tolerance and individual freedom, they need not make a fetish of moral neutrality.

When it adopts moralisms, the government is obviously favoring the views of some citizens over the views of others. Anti-environmentalists cannot be happy that their tax dollars are "wasted" on preservation. But citizens often disagree with government decisions and believe that tax money could be better spent elsewhere. The anti-environmentalist taxpayer seems to have a grievance no different in principle from that of the taxpayer who thinks the defense or social welfare budget is too large. Inevitably in deciding political disputes, the government will favor some views over others; but this does not mean that some groups are receiving unjustified favoritism. In short, the liberal vision of equality need not mean that government is powerless to favor those who want to save the whales over those who would rather kill them.

One way to reveal the flaw in Dworkin's argument is to consider a variant of the reasoning employed by John Rawls, Dworkin's fellow liberal philosopher. Rawls would assess social institutions by asking whether they would be adopted behind "the veil of ignorance," that is, by individuals who are ignorant of their own attributes, moral views, or position in society.[29] As a variation, imagine a group of individuals making plans for society. The individuals are presently all environmentalists, but they are not confident that any of them will retain this belief in the future. This deprives them of any assurance of personal benefit from implementing their present beliefs, since later they may not appreciate living in a world with lots of wilderness. Yet, if they now value wilderness, it would be rational for them to provide safeguards against their possibly anti-environmentalist future selves.

This desire to safeguard against future changes in preferences does not depend on these preferences having any "objective" basis. If, for some reason, a person had reason to think she might later turn against a friend who needed her help, she might well want to take steps now to safeguard her friend's interests, without believing that her friendship had some "objective" basis. On the other hand, if I now like Szechuan food but suspect that I won't in the future, it would be foolish of me to stock up now. In this sense, mere tastes differ from personal values, even if neither one claims to be "objectively" valid.

In one sense, my variation on Rawls is simply a strained hypothetical, but in another sense it is not so different from the ordinary state of the world. We know our preferences today (more or less). But we know much less about what our own preferences will be in the future, and even less about what the preferences of our children and grandchil-

28. *See* ch. 7; *see also* Steven Shiffrin, *Liberalism, Radicalism and Legal Scholarship*, 30 UCLA L. Rev. 1103, 1147-74 (1983); Robin West, *Liberalism Rediscovered: A Pragmatic Definition of the Liberal Vision*, 46 U. Pitt. L. Rev. 673 (1985).

29. *See* John Rawls, A Theory of Justice 11-22 (1971).

dren will be. In thinking about the future of our society, goals like allocational efficiency and distributional equality are all very well. But we can properly hope for more than that, for even more than a society that "takes rights seriously."[30] We can also hope for a future society which has preserved natural beauty, has a vibrant culture, and in other ways fits our own views of the good life.[31] Sagoff is right that these goals need not be subordinated to economic efficiency. He is wrong, however, in thinking that the reason is based on some inherent philosophical distinction between these goals and those that animate private life.

C. *Does Economic Efficiency Have Value?*

Sagoff goes beyond arguing that environmentalism is a legitimate social goal. He also argues that efficiency is itself not a permissible goal and has no intrinsic value at all.[32] The least controversial form of the efficiency standard derives from Pareto. A change is a "Pareto improvement" if someone prefers it and no one else opposes it.[33] Sagoff makes the somewhat startling argument that even Pareto improvements are not inherently worthwhile.

In his view, the fact that something is a Pareto improvement is no reason for the government to support it.[34] According to Sagoff, "[e]fficiency has no merit or worth to begin with and therefore cannot be balanced against substantive values like equality or justice"; hence, a " 'trade-off' between efficiency and equality is conceptually not in the cards."[35] He makes it plain that this applies even to Pareto improvements:

> Even if there are no losers—if at least one person prefers and no one opposes the policy—it is preferable just from that individual's point of view. The idea that it is preferable from *society's* point of view either means nothing or begs the entire question. Why should a policy that benefits *some* be considered, in addition, to benefit *society* or to com-

30. *Cf.* RONALD DWORKIN, TAKING RIGHTS SERIOUSLY (1977).

31. As Sagoff argues persuasively, this is not so much a matter of maximizing the preferences of future generations, as of our responsibility to make a world which will be fit for them to live in. As he points out, it is hard to see how our descendants can have a present right to have their preferences considered; not only do they not yet exist, but our own decisions today will determine who they will be and perhaps what preferences they will have. *See* pp. 63-64.

32. *See* ch. 5.

33. "Pareto optimality" is a more problematic standard. A state is Pareto optimal if no Pareto improvement is possible (that is, at least one individual would oppose a move to any other possible state). Use of this standard is controversial because many Pareto optimal states may exist, some of which may be highly undesirable in other respects. For example, allocating all wealth to one individual may be Pareto optimal, since that individual may object to any reallocation. Thus, the term Pareto optimality may carry a false implication that a state is desirable in some absolute sense. The term "Pareto improvement" does not carry any misleading implication of absolute desirability. It merely expresses a judgment about the relative desirability of two specific states. *See* JAMES HENDERSON & RICHARD QUANDT, MICROECONOMIC THEORY: A MATHEMATICAL APPROACH 255, 279-80 (2d ed. 1971).

34. *See* pp. 99-104, 223-24.

35. P. 107.

mand the consent of *society* as a whole?[36]

Inasmuch as society is composed of individuals, this is a bit baffling. I imagine going out for a pizza with Sagoff and some friends, Muir and Audubon. Audubon really likes mushrooms and the rest of us are indifferent. We prepare to order a large pizza with mushrooms. Sagoff then objects that Audubon's preference for mushrooms gives the *group* no reason to order them. To use one of Sagoff's favorite adjectives, this seems a bit crazy.[37]

If our mushroom-loving friend Audubon is actually extremely allergic to mushrooms, we might not want them on the pizza even though he himself can't resist the temptation to order them. Thus, Sagoff would be on solid ground if he were arguing merely that the existence of an individual preference does not necessarily justify government action. But Sagoff's claim is much stronger; it is that the existence of a preference provides no reason at all for the government to act, even if there are no evident countervailing factors.

The argument against this claim is powerful. Individuals clearly do not always know what is good for them, but then neither does the government. The question is whether individuals are more likely than strangers to know their own welfare. If so, implementing individual preferences will, as a rule, improve individual welfare. Sagoff provides no reason for rejecting the premise that improving individual welfare is a valid social goal. This premise strongly implies that individual preferences presumptively do give the government a reason to take action.[38]

Sagoff's rejection of the Pareto test further reflects his dichotomy between mere preferences and principled moral values. He regards many, perhaps most, preferences as unworthy of satisfaction. He argues that there is a "negative correlation between material improvement and perceived happiness,"[39] once "basic needs" are met. Material progress actually produces dissatisfaction because "[h]appiness and well-being are more likely to spring from overcoming or outgrowing many of our desires than from satisfying them."[40] The pursuit of private satisfactions, he says, is attractive only to hedonists.[41]

36. P. 108 (emphasis in original).

37. Perhaps Sagoff would respond that this situation is different because it is nonpolitical, while he is concerned with government decisionmaking. But one can readily imagine government officials in a similar situation. For example, suppose that a government committee is trying to decide what color to paint their meeting room. The committee has already narrowed the choice down to two colors. Everyone on the committee is indifferent between the two, except for one person who has a strong preference for one of the colors. Should the committee now flip a coin, ignoring that person's preference?

38. In cases of conflicting preferences, the argument for economic efficiency is more problematic because of distributional effects, which must be considered. In many applications of economics to legal problems, however, distributional effects are not substantial. *See* WILLIAM LANDES & RICHARD POSNER, THE ECONOMIC STRUCTURES OF TORT LAW 17-19 (1987).

39. P. 104; *see also* pp. 131-32.

40. P. 104.

41. P. 116.

In contrast, he discusses environmental values in tones of veneration. He speaks of the "reverence" we owe to what is wonderful in nature,[42] and says that values we consider "sacred" cannot be priced in the market.[43] As the following passage illustrates, Sagoff puts environmental values on a higher spiritual plane than mere consumer consumption:

> The wilderness that had served [Americans] had also seduced them, and in destroying it, they destroyed something of their hopes, something of their history, and something of their future as well as of their past. They saw that their prosperity was also an apostasy, their nationalism was also a secularism, and their happiness was also an emptiness. And while they reasoned in terms of wealth, power, comfort, and amenity, they had nothing to serve but themselves.
>
> If, after this time, Americans have remained materialistic, if they have emphasized personal acquisition and wealth, they have done so *faute de mieux*. It is a part of their national character to want a devotion to noble purposes, a respect for great symbols, a commitment to important ideals. Of course, they had only one place to look. If they found collective symbols of freedom, intelligence, virtue, courage, and strength, they did so because a puritan people ascribed these qualities to nature itself.[44]

Despite his rejection of materialism, Sagoff recognizes that economic considerations must be considered in environmental protection. He concedes that expecting people to abandon material comfort completely would be unrealistic. Firms should not be forced to forego all profit in order to protect the environment. However, Sagoff believes that exceeding the reasonable level of environmental protection should be considered "supererogatory," like an act of exceptional heroism.[45] Although the government should not close factories to eliminate the last traces of pollution, Sagoff implies that it would be praiseworthy for a firm to close voluntarily for that reason. Sagoff appears to attach little moral weight to the material losses incurred by shareholders, consumers, and most dramatically, unemployed workers.

One of the standard criticisms of environmentalism is that it is an essentially upper-middle-class movement, dedicated to preserving exotic recreational activities like backpacking and mountain climbing.[46] Although this criticism is in my view unfair (and underrates the breadth of public support for environmentalism), unsettling hints of this attitude appear in Sagoff's writings. When he gives illustrations of con-

42. P. 64; *see also* pp. 141-42.

43. P. 69.

44. Pp. 131-32.

45. *See* pp. 219-20. For example, the EPA "may argue instead that a reduction below reasonably safe levels counts as supererogatory given the technical, economic, and scientific factors bearing on a particular case." P. 220; *see also* pp. 197-98, 209-10.

46. For a general discussion of elitism and environmental law, see Gerald Torres, Book Review, 42 U. PITT. L. REV. 823, 828-33 (1981) (reviewing JOSEPH SAX, MOUNTAINS WITHOUT HANDRAILS: REFLECTIONS ON THE NATIONAL PARKS (1980)).

sumerism, he seems to select examples of plebeian tastes, such as recreational vehicles, romance novels, and velvet paintings.[47]

More troubling is Sagoff's basic premise that personal consumption involves only trivialities. After "basic needs"[48] are met, any further consumption serves no purpose, for "[o]rdinary consumer preferences . . . are usually regarded not as intrinsically good but as arbitrary from a moral point of view."[49] Although this kind of asceticism is probably not unique to Sagoff among environmentalists, it is ultimately untenable, and not just because the flesh is weak. Environmentalism surely does not promote a society that preserves redwoods but bans flowers because only vegetable gardens are needed to meet "basic needs."[50]

Sagoff recognizes that society should "strive to make the conditions under which people live and work cleaner, safer, more natural, and more beautiful," but he endorses these goals while speaking of them as subjects for government regulation.[51] Sagoff does not address the possibility that private life can also seek these goals. This blindness to the moral value of private life underlies his rejection of economic efficiency as a social policy.

II. Environmentalism, Paternalism, and Risk Management

Preserving nature is an important goal of environmental law. In recent years, however, saving human lives has become an equally important goal. Much of the recent growth in environmental law has been in the area of toxics regulation. Sagoff seems to assume that the issues at stake in toxics regulation are philosophically fungible with those of wilderness preservation. I question this assumption.

A. *The Problem of Paternalism*

Sagoff's premise is that "important shared values, for example, health, well-being, safety, cleanliness, and respect and reverence for nature . . . justify governmental intervention in markets, whether or not these markets are efficient."[52] Human health and safety concerns raise quite different problems, however, from programs like protecting endangered species. In deciding how much to spend on saving the

47. *See* pp. 63, 67.

48. *See* p. 100. It is quite unclear to me what Sagoff means by a basic need, beyond the minimum number of calories needed for survival.

49. P. 102.

50. Taken seriously, this kind of asceticism would promote a society in which people did not waste money on architecture but instead lived in pre-fab barracks in which tasteless soy mush was the only available food, and in which the only athletic activities were calisthenics. This picture is not entirely fanciful. It bears resemblance to some of the excesses of the Chinese Cultural Revolution. For example, pets were not necessary to meet "basic needs," and were exterminated as parasites by the Red Guard. *See* William Ewald, *Unger's Philosophy: A Critical Legal Study*, 97 Yale L.J. 665, 742 n.327 (1988).

51. P. 101.

52. P. 7.

whales, we need not worry about what the whales think is the appropriate tradeoff. But the beneficiaries of safety regulations will often have their own views about the appropriate level of protection.

For example, suppose an industry employs 10,000 workers. Current levels of exposure to a toxin will eventually kill five of these individuals. Eliminating the toxin will cost $500 million, or $100 million per life saved.[53] If the employees do not value their own lives that highly, a cost-benefit analysis will be unfavorable. Suppose that the workers actually value their lives at $50 million apiece (which is much higher than the amounts revealed by econometric studies).[54] The employer is then spending $500 million to deliver a benefit that the employees assess as being worth $250 million.[55] Both employer and employees would prefer that the government simply tax the company $300 million and send a check for $30,000 to each worker. From their perspective, the government action is no different from imposing a $500 million tax on the company, burning half of the money, and giving the rest to the workers. Depending on how the safety regulations affect employment, the workers may even find themselves worse off than they were to begin with.[56]

In any event, it is not at all clear how the change can make the employees any better off in their own estimation. Their relative bargaining position limits the total wage which they can extract from the employer. The fact that the employer has just paid out $500 million for safety equipment is hardly likely to make the employer willing to pay higher compensation as well. The government cannot increase their total compensation by ordering that part of it be paid in the form of safety improvements, any more than it could do so by ordering that workers be paid in apples instead of dollars. If workers are unwilling to buy apples (or safety) at the market rate, it is hard to see how their lives can be improved by requiring employers to pay part of their salary in

53. These figures may seem exaggerated, but they are actually of the same order of magnitude as those in a recent Supreme Court case. *See* Industrial Union Dep't v. American Petroleum Inst., 448 U.S. 607, 628-30, 654 (1980) (plurality opinion).

A fuller but more complex presentation of the same hypothetical would treat both the benefits to the workers and the costs to the industry as future cash flows reduced to present value. Also, a similar "stock versus flow" clarification could be made about the risk level, since employees enter and leave the industry constantly. The risk level given in the text should really be understood as the risk per employee work-year, multiplied by the number of employees and the average number of work-years.

54. *See* text accompanying note 72 *infra*. *See also* Richard Pierce, *Encouraging Safety: The Limits of Tort Law and Government Regulation*, 33 VAND. L. REV. 1281, 1311-14 (1980).

55. Taking into account risk aversion would complicate, but not fundamentally change, the analysis.

56. For example, suppose that safety costs are proportional to output and that product demand is not perfectly inelastic. The effect of the safety regulation is then to shift the industry supply curve to the left, where a higher price is required to induce the industry to produce the same quantity. The result is that output falls, bringing about unemployment. The product price also rises, however; hence, part of the safety cost is passed on to consumers.

this form.[57] Thus, the regulation is apparently only worthwhile if we take the paternalistic attitude that the workers misunderstand the facts or undervalue their safety.[58]

Sagoff attempts to sidestep the paternalism issue by arguing that risk preferences are actually irrelevant to the regulatory problem. Even if a risk is sufficiently small that people might be quite willing to assume it voluntarily, he maintains that they have a right to be free from involuntary imposition of the risk.[59] As an example, Sagoff recounts the story of a meeting about a nuclear waste site.[60] Residents were quite unimpressed—rightfully so, he thinks—by the assertion of a state official that "risks they casually accept, for example, by drinking alcohol or by crossing the street, were greater than the risks associated with the buried radioactive residues."[61] The residents were also unimpressed by the official's argument that the waste facility brought enough income and employment into the town to compensate for the hazards. As Sagoff sees it, the real issue was the distribution of power in society, not the relationship between costs and benefits.[62]

Apparently, if they had been consulted in advance, the residents would have agreed to the facility, or at least they would have been irrational if they did not, since the risk was insubstantial and the benefits were significant. But Sagoff argues that hypothetical consent is not enough; the fact that someone would have consented to a transaction means nothing unless they actually did consent.[63]

Sagoff is right, I think, in his analysis of the psychology of the situation. Natural radon emissions are probably a far more serious health hazard than many heavily regulated activities.[64] But only nature is to blame, so this threat arouses relatively little public fervor.[65] Much of

57. It's hard to see, but maybe not impossible. There is an economic model in which destroying a bushel of wheat causes a society-wide Pareto improvement by expediting the creation of futures markets. *See* David Kreps, *In Honor of Sandy Grossman, Winner of the John Bates Clark Medal*, J. ECON. PERSP., Spring 1988, at 111, 121-23. Conceivably, requiring payment in safety improvements may improve social welfare.

58. One way of strengthening the cost-benefit analysis is to appeal to the preferences of members of the public. If 100 million Americans would each be willing to pay five dollars to save the lives of five factory workers, then the cost-benefit analysis would support regulation. But Sagoff correctly rejects this approach as failing to prove anything. There may be another 100 million Americans willing to pay five dollars apiece to save the company and its workers from unwarranted paternalistic intervention. In any case, saying that onlookers would be willing to pay more than the workers themselves to guard the workers' safety does little to advance the analysis. We would still want to know why the onlookers think they are better able to assess the value of worker safety than the workers themselves.

59. *See* pp. 185, 197-98.

60. *See* pp. 24, 46-47.

61. P. 24.

62. P. 24; *see also* pp. 46-48.

63. *See* pp. 108-10, 242 n.31. Although there is a somewhat stronger argument for actual consent in the case of our chemical workers, it is somewhat fanciful to assume that every worker made a conscious tradeoff between this particular risk and increased compensation.

64. *See* Research Note, *Indoor Radon: The Deadliest Pollutant*, 240 SCIENCE 606 (1988).

65. In a national poll, people ranked radon 27th out of 28 hazards, just above microwave

the outrage over toxic chemicals is probably due to the feeling that someone secretly imposed a risk on others; it is this feeling of powerlessness that gives rise to anger. Moreover, Sagoff also seems to be correct in arguing that hypothetical consent is not necessarily sufficient. If a panhandler picks my pocket, it is no defense that I would have given him the money anyway. We have an interest in the fairness of the process that determines what risks we are exposed to, even when we might, in the end, find the risk acceptable.[66]

The independent significance of the decision-making process has some interesting implications for toxics regulation. It suggests that we should pay a great deal of attention to process, to full disclosure, and to public participation in setting levels of acceptable risk.[67] We might, for example, want to encourage collective bargaining on safety issues. But this approach does not resolve the ultimate question of how much safety is enough. Suppose that after full disclosure, workers continue to accept unsafe working conditions. Is society justified in intervening?

Sagoff has little hesitation in embracing paternalistic regulation:

> The transactions that led to child labor, the sixteen-hour workday, and hideous workplace conditions were largely voluntary and informed; no centralized bureaucracy in Washington told workers how old they had to be or what minimum they had to be paid; labor markets were efficient. The resulting levels of death, misery, and disease, even if "optimal" or "efficient" from an economic point of view, cannot be tolerated in any civilized nation.[68]

The reason Sagoff does not find paternalism troubling is that he is convinced that safety regulations change workers' preferences:

> Suppose we were to determine for cost-benefit purposes a value-per-life-saved from *unregulated* but otherwise efficient markets—markets as they were, for example, at the turn of the century. Suppose, in other words, that we were to set an economic value on safety on the basis of the amount traded for it in markets not severely constrained by humanitarian regulation. It might be a very low value indeed. A hundred years of compassionate legislation has produced conditions in which economists can now argue that voluntary markets set an appropriate value on worker safety. This is a result not of more efficient markets but of persistent ethical regulation.[69]

This argument attempts to avoid the paternalism problem by rely-

ovens. *See* Michael Hinds, *Radon: Making the Public Pay Attention*, N.Y. Times, Sept. 24, 1988, at 56, cols. 3, 5.

66. On the other hand, we have much less interest in a process in which the result is a foregone conclusion. This may have been true in the example Sagoff cites, in which the residents would only have rejected the waste facility if they had irrationally overestimated the risks.

67. Of course, we might decide that some risks are too trivial to warrant the costs of such "environmental due process." At some point, presumably, a risk becomes so insubstantial in relation to the benefits that the claim of involuntariness becomes moot.

68. P. 15.

69. Pp. 115-16 (emphasis in original).

ing on preference shifts. Because of the regulations, workers will be accustomed to greater safety and their willingness to tolerate risk will decrease. Hence, after the regulations are in effect long enough, they will fit the workers' own preferences. This argument is unsatisfactory for two reasons. First, it may not be factually accurate. How do we know that workers will be more willing to sacrifice wages for safety after the regulation is in effect? Sagoff's factual premise is not implausible, but plausibility is not proof. Second, as a general matter, reliance on future preference shifts is a dangerous way of avoiding the paternalism problem because it has the capacity to justify almost anything.[70]

Although Sagoff's argument is inadequate, a better response to the paternalism argument is available. We have good reason to question whether the risk preferences revealed by industry wage patterns accurately reflect employees' considered appraisals of their interests. Studies by cognitive psychologists and others show that individuals are quite bad at estimating risk levels. Even where a risk is known, people do not process the information very well. They systematically deviate from rationality in considering combinations of risks; they ignore background information in assessing new data; and they are easily swayed by trivial changes in the presentation of information.[71] Finally, when using labor information as a basis for assessing risk preferences, as is commonly done, we need to be especially cautious. The operation of labor markets is quite poorly understood by economists, which makes interpretation of the data difficult.

The upshot is that the methods used to determine risk preferences are quite unreliable. Not surprisingly, the results are extremely variable, with estimates of the value of life ranging from $15,000 to $10 million.[72] So, we need not be terribly concerned with the claim that a regulation requiring that several million dollars be spent per life saved is oppressively paternalistic. This still leaves, however, the question of how we should set the appropriate level of risk.

70. *See* David Shapiro, *Courts, Legislatures, and Paternalism,* 74 VA. L. REV. 519, 549-50 (1988) (rejecting Sagoff's argument for paternalism); Cass Sunstein, *Legal Interference with Private Preferences,* 53 U. CHI. L. REV. 1129, 1148-50 (1986) (endorsing Sagoff's form of paternalism but cautioning against the risk of abuse). Moreover, Sagoff's argument also fails to explain why we should reject the workers' present preferences in favor of greater safety. If we reduced safety levels, workers might put a lower premium on safety, shifting their preferences in precisely the opposite direction. Thus, the fact that workers' preferences might respond to government intervention does nothing to justify intervening in one direction rather than the other. It leaves unanswered the question why we should overturn the workers' current preferences.

71. This research is summarized in Ames Tversky & Daniel Kahneman, *Rational Choice and the Framing of Decisions,* in RATIONAL CHOICE: THE CONTRAST BETWEEN ECONOMICS AND PSYCHOLOGY 67 (R. Hogarth & M. Reder eds. 1987).

72. *See* E.J. Mishan, *Consistency in the Valuation of Life: A Wild Goose Chase?,* in ETHICS & ECONOMICS 152, 160-61 (E. Paul, F. Miller, & J. Paul eds. 1985); Pierce, *supra* note 54, at 1312.

B. *How Much Safety is Enough?*

Eliminating the paternalism problem still leaves us with the ultimate question of how much safety society should seek. Unfortunately, Sagoff does not really address this problem, apparently because he considers safety to be a moral imperative. Evaluating both the benefits of safety and the appropriate social burden turns out to be quite difficult.

In the previous section, we assumed the only relevant risk information was the level of risk, that is, in the simplest terms, the mortality rate. This risk information is often difficult to obtain, given the limits of scientific knowledge about toxic chemicals. But the problem is even more complex because most people consider other factors in evaluating the seriousness of risks.[73] The cause of death is important. People quite reasonably think that slowly dying of cancer is worse than a sudden heart attack or accidental death. Age is another factor. Accelerating the death of an elderly person is not considered to be as horrible as causing the death of a child. This, too, seems reasonable, not because the elderly have less intrinsic moral worth than the young, but because death does not deprive them of so many of the major experiences of human life. Moreover, because death in old age is an expected part of the life cycle, it does not have the same traumatic effect on survivors as early death. Clusters of deaths are also taken more seriously. While it is bad to kill three people in the general population, it is worse to kill three in the same community, and worse still to kill three in the same family. This aspect of risk preferences also seems reasonable, both because concentrated deaths have more traumatic effects on survivors and because it seems fairer to distribute risks broadly.

I have more qualms about two other factors that people seem to find important to assessing risk. One is the unfamiliarity of the risk. Familiar risks are given less weight than those involving mysterious technology or esoteric scientific principles. This is a factor that should not be wholly discounted. It is important that people be able to make sense of the major events in their lives, particularly something as important as their own impending death or the death of someone they love. It is easier to make sense of and accept the familiar than the exotic. Still, people's fear of novel technological risks at times seems almost hysterical, leading to burdensome regulations on extraordinarily small risks.

The other major factor in risk assessment is voluntariness. Like unfamiliarity, this too has some reasonable basis. Regulation of voluntary risks raises greater problems of paternalism. Voluntary risks are also less socially traumatic because the resulting deaths fit more easily into a

73. Much of the discussion in the text is purely impressionistic, but it does find some support in empirical studies of risk perception. *See* Paul Slovic, *Perception of Risk*, 236 SCIENCE 280 (1987). *See also* Mark Machina, *Decision-Making in the Presence of Risk*, 236 SCIENCE 537 (1987).

coherent narrative of the person's life. Nevertheless, perceptions of voluntariness seem to play an exaggerated role in risk assessment.

The most dramatic example is cigarette smoking.[74] Cigarettes pose the most serious public health threat of any known toxic substance. They kill approximately 350,000 people per year. They are known to be addictive and most smokers start before the age of 16, so the voluntariness argument itself is somewhat dubious.[75] Nevertheless, because smoking at least appears voluntary, most people think government intervention is much less warranted than for hazardous waste sites or drinking water contamination.[76] The result is that we spend vast sums of money dealing with relatively minute health hazards,[77] but very little on controlling cigarettes, even though cutting smoking in half would undoubtedly save more lives than every environmental statute ever passed.[78] Voluntariness is important, but it becomes something of a fetish when it leads to such perverse results.

Obviously, deciding how seriously to take various risks is neither straightforward nor uncontroversial. Evaluating the costs of regulation is more than a matter of mechanical computation. The weight society should place on costs depends greatly on their incidence. It may well be reasonable to require a million people to pay a dollar each to save one life, but unreasonable to require ten people to sacrifice $100,000 each, or to impose the entire cost on a small town whose economic foundation is destroyed by a plant closing. It may also matter whether the beneficiaries of the regulation are poorer or wealthier than those incurring the costs. Moreover, the type of product may be relevant. Decreased output may not be a serious concern for luxury goods, but may be much more important for necessities or for innovative products that promise important social benefits.

Given the difficulty of assigning values to the costs and benefits of health regulations, regulatory decisions clearly cannot be made by any mechanical formula or test. Sagoff argues, correctly I think, that we must rely heavily on such political virtues as dialogue, open-mindedness, clarity, participation, and intelligence. Some of the best passages

---

74. Smoking also involves two of the other factors: It mostly kills the old, and it is a familiar risk.

75. For a summary of the doleful facts about smoking, see Daniel Hays Lowenstein, *"Too Much Puff": Persuasion, Paternalism and Commercial Speech*, 56 U. CIN. L. REV. 1205, 1208-13 (1988).

76. When I teach environmental law, this is always the answer I get when I ask why it is worth spending hundreds of millions of dollars to clean up toxic waste sites based on speculative health risks, while the government does virtually nothing about cigarettes.

77. The scientific trend has been toward downplaying many toxics risks. *See, e.g.*, Philip Shabecoff, *Estimate of Risk of Dioxin Is Cut in Cancer Study*, N.Y. Times, Dec. 9, 1987, at A1, col. 1.

78. Outlawing cigarettes would be impractical, but an increased tax would be useful, as would greater investment in public education. *See* Peter Passell, *Who Should Pay Smoking's Cost?*, N.Y. Times, June 22, 1988, at D2, col. 1. As Lowenstein points out, a ban on cigarette advertising might well be warranted. *See* Lowenstein, *supra* note 75. A ban on vending machines would also reduce cigarette availability, particularly to children.

in the book are devoted to this theme, and to the dangers of attempting to replace these virtues with technocratic formulas like cost-benefit analysis.[79]

Although mechanical formulas cannot solve tough regulatory problems, we can still search for guidelines to aid in risk assessment. For example, it seems reasonable to say that the workplace would be sufficiently safe if going to work was as safe as staying home. This is almost true for the average worker,[80] but not for those in unusually hazardous occupations. This gives us some notion of the boundary of acceptable risk. There are also risks that we would clearly regard as insubstantial, such as the increased cancer risk from eating peanut butter or drinking a beer (both of which contain natural carcinogens).[81] On the cost side, we can look for existing public health projects that seem clearly justified to provide a benchmark for appropriate expenditures.

Politics being what it is, we can never expect an entirely coherent public policy on risk management. But we could move considerably farther in that direction. If we were to apply in this way the political virtues that Sagoff rightly praises, I suspect we would find that we are currently spending far too much money on reducing some kinds of risks, and far too little on others.

III. Environmentalism and the Public Interest

As the previous section indicates, I think Sagoff's fundamental thesis is correct: Environmental regulation is an essentially political rather than economic affair. This makes it crucial to have some clear understanding of the nature of government. Sagoff is a firm supporter of the recent revival of republicanism, a philosophy that stresses the communitarian nature of government.[82] Like that of others in this camp, Sagoff's view of politics is in some ways realistic, but in other respects gives politics too exalted a position.

79. *See* pp. 11-14, 17, 68, 77, 221-22. While Sagoff is not only right but importantly so in his praise of "practical reason," he may be wrong in his suggestion that these intellectual virtues can only be applied at the "micro-level," that is, on an ad hoc basis when administrators deal with particular problems. *See* pp. 212-15. Such micro-rationality may lead to grossly disparate regulatory solutions to risks that most people would regard as quite similar. Moreover, confining policymaking to the micro-level might reduce the political visibility of the regulatory process, thereby limiting public participation and giving undue power to bureaucrats and special interest groups. Consequently, we need to have at least some general rules of thumb about what risks to take seriously and how much we are willing to pay to eliminate them.

80. *See* W. Kip Viscusi, Risk by Choice: Regulating Health and Safety in the Workplace 47-49 (1983).

81. *See* Bruce Ames, Rene Magaw & Lois Swirsky Gold, *Ranking Possible Carcinogenic Hazards*, 236 Science 271, 273 (1987).

82. *See* pp. 10-11, 16-17. For an excellent survey of the republicanism literature, see Frank Michelman, *Foreword: Traces of Self-Government*, 100 Harv. L. Rev. 4, 17-36, 58-65 (1986).

A. *Private Preferences and the Public Forum*

Sagoff draws a sharp distinction between the interests people have as private consumers and those they possess as citizens.[83] His thesis "is that social regulation expresses what we believe, what we are, what we stand for as a nation, not simply what we wish to buy as individuals."[84] Frank Michelman, similarly, has argued that in the republican vision we must be able to imagine that someone would vote for the Endangered Species Act even though she had no private interest in environmental matters.[85] As Sagoff explains it, "[s]ocial regulation reflects public values we choose collectively, and these may conflict with wants and interests we pursue individually."[86]

This conflict doesn't trouble Sagoff, because he takes such a dim view of private life. "The pursuit of private satisfactions, except for the committed hedonist, soon becomes disappointing or boring, and we look for some public cause, like saving the whales, that does not benefit us personally but appeals to our conscience."[87] Sagoff's identification of hedonism and private satisfactions is telling. Only a frivolous pleasure-seeker, one gathers, would derive satisfaction from writing novels, practicing medicine, or raising children. As we saw in Part I, this casual dismissal of private life is at best thoughtless, at worst a denial of important moral values.

Indeed, Sagoff makes it clear that even minimal morality is not to be expected in private life. He tells us, with no evident embarrassment, that he bribed a judge to fix some traffic tickets, but then at election time helped to vote the corrupt judge out of office.[88] He speeds but wants the police to enforce laws against speeding.[89] From an economist's point of view, these are not irrational decisions, but typical behavior regarding public goods like honest government and highway safety. It is economically rational to vote for strong pollution laws while continuing to pollute in the meantime. But a moral philosopher might be expected to endorse a somewhat loftier precept for personal conduct than "Look Out for Number One."

Besides viewing private preferences as being morally valueless, Sagoff also seems to share the common belief that the government can readily modify private preferences.[90] There is certainly reason to

83. *See* pp. 27, 50-51, 69, 94, 171.

84. Pp. 16-17.

85. *See* Frank Michelman, *Politics and Values or What's Really Wrong With Rationality Review?*, 13 CREIGHTON L. REV. 487, 495-96 (1979).

86. P. 17.

87. P. 116. His earlier writings were harsher: "Beauty . . . is valued because it is a source of pleasure. But pleasure is merely contemptible." Sagoff, *supra* note 1, at 209.

88. P. 52.

89. P. 52. He also recounts that he has an "Ecology Now" sticker on a car that drips oil everywhere. P. 53.

90. *See* pp. 115-16, 63-64, 93; *see also* Sunstein, *supra* note 70, at 1154 ("the role of government is to shape preferences"). For a more guarded statement of this position, see MARK

doubt this belief. Despite decades of effort, the Soviet government seems to have been unable to motivate workers on collective farms to become productive. Equally stringent efforts to suppress religion have also been unsuccessful. If dictatorships cannot readily remold preferences, despite having complete control over the media and the educational system, it seems unlikely that democracies will have greater success. The government sometimes succeeds in changing private attitudes, but cultural traditions do seem to have tremendous inertia.[91]

Like private preferences, private customs often have considerable force of their own.[92] We are creatures of the legal system to a lesser extent than some scholars would like to admit. Fortunately, contrary to Sagoff's beliefs, public life is not the only arena for the exercise of virtue.[93]

B. *Defining the Public Interest*

Perhaps the most intriguing aspect of Sagoff's book is his attempt to

---

KELMAN, A GUIDE TO CRITICAL LEGAL STUDIES 131-37 (1987). For a powerful argument against ascribing such a central role to government, see Robert Ellickson, *A Critique of Economic and Sociological Theories of Social Control,* 16 J. LEGAL STUD. 67, 84-90 (1987).

91. When values do change, the causes are quite obscure. Environmentalism is a good example. Sagoff seems to think that environmental values are inculcated either by government action or by exposure to the environment itself. Thus, he says, if we leave our descendants dumps to live in, they will find dumps aesthetically attractive. *See* p. 63. Based on this theory, we would expect to find that environmentalism was strongest when the continent was mostly wilderness and progressively weakened as most people came to live in cities. We would also expect to find that the government's environmental programs preceded popular environmentalist attitudes. But the exact reverse of both of these expectations is true.

92. In general, like some other contemporary believers in republicanism, Sagoff underestimates the resiliency and autonomy of nongovernmental institutions. He argues, for example, that property is entirely a creation of the legal system. *See* pp. 188, 191-92. Obviously, the legal system conditioned much of the institution of property, but it is clear that property is not simply a creature of legal rules. People develop their own expectations about property with or without legal sanctions. As Professor Ellickson has pointed out, whalers developed elaborate rules about property rights during the hunt, even though ships from many different nations were involved in these events on the high seas. *See* Robert Ellickson, *A Hypothesis of Wealth Maximizing Norms: Evidence from the Whaling Industry,* 5 J.L. ECON. & ORG. — (1989) (forthcoming).

Closer to home, I recall that after a major Chicago blizzard, people who dug out parking spaces regarded them as their own property, often using signs to announce their property claims and sometimes resorting to force against "trespassers." Often, when the government does get around to giving legal recognition to new forms of property, it simply adopts the private understandings that already exist. *See* Ellickson, *supra*; Leo Raskind, *Reverse Engineering, Unfair Competition, and Fair Use,* 70 MINN. L. REV. 385, 397, 407-11 (1985) (Congress adopting semi-conductor industry custom as standard).

93. If Sagoff is too cynical about private life, he may be too romantic about politics. An opposing school of thought, often identified with public choice theory, takes the opposite perspective. It portrays politics as an arena of venality where self-serving special interests "belly up to the trough." So far as empirical evidence can settle such issues, the truth seems to be somewhere in between. No observer of contemporary politics can ignore the role of special interest groups. Statistical evidence confirms that campaign contributions and constituent pressure often explain legislative votes. But they are not the whole story. Sophisticated empirical studies also indicate that legislative votes are often determined by the legislator's own view of public policy. For a survey of the empirical literature, see Daniel Farber & Philip Frickey, *The Jurisprudence of Public Choice,* 65 TEX. L. REV. 873, 883-901 (1987).

explain what is meant by the "public interest." We know from Arrow's Theorem that the public interest cannot be defined as simply an agglomeration of private interests because an arbitrary collection of private interests cannot be combined into a coherent scheme of public preferences. On the other hand, Rousseau's talk of the "general will" seems to suggest a dangerous invitation to totalitarianism.[94] Anyway, it is hard to understand in what sense a group can have a separate existence with beliefs or desires completely distinct from those of its members. Imagine someone announcing: "No one in our group likes anchovies on pizza, but the group's general will is that anchovies are great!"

Sagoff is none too clear on the location of the "intersubjective entity" he calls the public. The bulk of his discussion seems to suggest that this entity represents the cultural identity of a group.[95] As members of the group, individuals learn group norms: Americans, as he says, learn to venerate rivers the same way that Catholics learn to venerate the pope.[96] Early American literature, a subject to which he devotes considerable space, is part of the tradition that constitutes American culture. By becoming members of the group, individuals accept the ongoing culture of the group as part of their identities, so that they say: "We Americans feel strongly about the environment." Sagoff's idea seems to be that values which are part of this heritage have a special status, which entitle them to greater governmental support than mere personal preferences. Thus, for Sagoff, environmental protection becomes a part of preserving the national identity.[97]

Clearly, appeals to "the American tradition" do carry special rhetorical weight. Yet, this understanding of what constitutes "the public interest" seems insufficient. The American tradition—like any living culture—contains too many conflicts to be reified as the contents of a unified group mind. Conflicting groups can all too easily proselytize their version of the American dream while denouncing their opponents as un-American.[98] Such difficulties seem to inhere in any attempt to view the "public interest" or "public values" as being descriptive terms for existing entities. If all members of the public agreed, there would be no need to distinguish private from public interests. If the members of the public disagree, there seems to be no way for an outsider to de-

94. *See* Suzanna Sherry, *Republican Citizenship in a Democratic Society* (Book Review), 66 TEX. L. REV. 1229, 1243-44 (1988) (reviewing AMY GUTMANN, DEMOCRATIC EDUCATION (1987)). For an insightful critique of the new "communitarians," see C. Edwin Baker, *Sandel on Rawls*, 133 U. PA. L. REV. 895 (1985).

95. *See* ch. 6.

96. P. 127.

97. *See* pp. 124-45.

98. Sagoff's theory also seems to make environmentalism too localized, almost as if it were just another quaint national trait: Americans love the environment, Germans drink beer, the British go nuts at soccer matches, etc. If Sagoff were correct, Japanese environmentalism could not possibly have anything in common with the American variety, since the two countries have radically different cultural traditions.

termine which preferences should be attributed to the group as a whole.

If determining the public interest were a matter of attaching the right philosophical label to existing preferences, we would do better to turn the government over to professional philosophers. As Sagoff points out, this is the antithesis of liberalism.[99] And yet pure pluralism, which rejects the notion of the public interest, seems to convert government into an unsavory exercise in self-aggrandizement. How can we speak of the "public interest," when all that we can observe at any one moment are individual preferences, and no *a priori* method exists for determining which of them can properly claim to be public values?

Perhaps the best answer, as Sagoff sometimes hints,[100] is that the public interest (or "general will") is not something that exists independently of the political process itself. Rather, in a democracy, the political process creates the public interest in the process of searching for it. The public interest can best emerge from a political process possessing the liberal virtues of broad participation, tolerance, and intelligent deliberation.[101] After such a political decision has been reached, everyone present can say: "*We* have decided such and such." The "we" is at once a reference to every member of the group, and a new dramatic persona in its own right. Thus, the democratic process earns the government the right to speak for "the Public."[102]

If I can be excused for perhaps trivializing an important idea, the "general will" can even be found in the pizza parlor. It is not simply a summary of the pizza tastes that people brought in the door. But it also does not exist separately from their individual views. Rather, the "general will" springs into being when, after the issue has been fully dis-

---

99. *See* pp. 155-62.

100. *See* pp. 119-21. The following passage comes closest to this idea:

> Suppose, for example, we are married to each other and have a child who we both intend shall have the best education possible. . . .
>
> Now suppose that in some matters we determine our intentions not individually but together. We ask ourselves what *we* shall do about Jared's education. We discuss what *our* policy should be and then set out tasks for each of us to accomplish. We might decide that you should earn the money while I help with the homework, or some such thing.
>
> We might then express our shared intention by each saying, "*We* intend Jared to have the best education possible." Wilfrid Sellars points out that statements of this kind "in the first person *plural* have the interesting properties that (a) they express the speaker's intention, yet (b) the intentions expressed are in the strongest sense the same." The *acts* of intending are subjective and therefore two in number, but the *content*, what is *intended*, is the same. In these circumstances, intention may be as intersubjective as perception and belief.

P. 120 (emphasis in original).

101. It is not essential that these virtues be found within the law-making body itself. For example, the electoral process could be deliberative, while legislative votes would be governed by strict party discipline.

102. I am putting aside the question of the role of courts as advocates for public values, since they have not typically served that function in environmental law. Tentatively, I would suggest that courts can propose public values but that these values do not become fully legitimate until the political process accedes to them.

cussed within the group, someone turns to the server and says, "*We'd* like to order a large pizza with mushrooms, but hold the anchovies."

In this review, I have criticized many aspects of Sagoff's argument. He is wrong, I think, in dismissing private preferences and the virtues of ordinary life. He makes claims of philosophical validity for moralism like environmental protection, but then makes no attempt to support those claims. He is too inattentive to problems of paternalism, and too simplistic in his analysis of risk management.

Nevertheless, his main argument, that cost-benefit analysis is misused to provide technocratic solutions to fundamentally political questions, is profoundly correct. There is no magic formula for determining how much whales are worth or how safe our drinking water should be. These issues can only be resolved through a political process which is always imperfect, but which at least aspires to identify the public interest.

Part II
Common Law Remedies and the Environment

[4]

CORNELL
LAW REVIEW

Volume 64 June 1979 Number 5

MOSSES FROM AN OLD MANSE: ANOTHER LOOK AT SOME HISTORIC PROPERTY CASES ABOUT THE ENVIRONMENT*

Daniel R. Coquillette†

> And now it was moved in arrest of judgment, that the building of the house for hogs was necessary for the sustenance of man: and one ought not to have so delicate a nose, that he cannot bear the smell of hogs; for *lex non favet delicatorum votis*: but it was resolved that the action for it is (as this case is) well maintainable; for in a house four things are desired [habitation of man, pleasure of the inhabitant, necessity of light, and cleanliness of air], and for nusance done to three of them an action lies . . . .
>
> —*Sir Edward Coke*[1]

* An earlier version of this Article was presented on March 10, 1977, at the Advanced Law and Economics Seminar, University of California, Berkeley. The author is particularly grateful to the Boston University School of Law for a research grant, to his students and research assistants for their help, and to Professor Milton Katz for his encouragement of the first version of this paper.

† Member of the Massachusetts Bar. B.A. 1966, Williams College; B.A. (Juris.) 1969, Oxford University; J.D. 1971, Harvard University.

[1] William Aldred's Case, 9 Coke 57b, 58a, 77 Eng. Rep. 816, 817 (K.B. 1611).

> If a man lives in a town, it is necessary that he should subject himself to the consequences of those operations of trade which may be carried on in his immediate locality, which are actually necessary for trade and commerce, and also for the enjoyment of property, and for the benefit of the inhabitants of the town and of the public at large.
>
> —*Lord Westbury*[2]

> [T]he wisdom of a lawmaker consisteth not only in a platform of justice, but in the application thereof; taking into consideration . . . what influence laws touching private right of *meum* and *tuum* have into the public state, and how they may be made apt and agreeable . . . .
>
> —*Francis Bacon*[3]

TABLE OF CONTENTS

---

[2] St. Helen's Smelting Co. v. Tipping, 11 Eng. Rep. 1483, 1486 (H.L. 1865).

[3] F. BACON, *Of the Advancement of Learning*, in 6 THE WORKS OF FRANCIS BACON 390 (J. Spedding ed. 1870).

INTRODUCTION
PROPERTY DOCTRINE AND JUSTICE

One of the oldest tasks of Anglo-American law has been the resolution of disputes involving conflicting uses of property. Security of property historically has been regarded as a paramount legal need, perhaps *the* paramount legal need.[4] Such security meant not merely the bare right to title or possession, but also the right to free use of the property.[5]

Thus legal history abounds with environmental litigation concerning rights to property use. *Commonwealth v. Sisson*[6] is one example. Acting pursuant to a state statute, the Massachusetts Board of Fish and Game Commissioners ordered the defendant sawmill owners to take measures to stop the pollution of an adjoining trout brook with saw dust. The sawmill owners contended that this deprived them of property without compensation or due process.[7] In *Morgan v. High Penn Oil Co.*,[8] the parties' roles were reversed. The plaintiff, owner of a trailer park, argued that gases and odors from the defendant's nearby oil refinery wrongfully deprived him of the use and enjoyment of his property.[9] In each case, a property owner sought court protection from a perceived threat to his right to the use of his property.[10]

---

[4] For example, the Magna Carta provided that "[n]o free man shall be . . . disseised . . . except by the lawful judgement of his peers or by the law of the land." MAGNA CARTA cap. 39 ("1215 Charter"), *reprinted and translated in* J. HOLT, MAGNA CARTA 327 (1965). Neo-Marxists and others long debated whether property rights have been treated as paramount to rights of personal liberty. During much of English history, a man's liberty and his relationship to property were interrelated. *See generally* P. VINOGRADOFF, THE GROWTH OF THE MANOR 332-65 (2d ed. 1911).

[5] *See generally* Honoré, *Ownership*, in OXFORD ESSAYS IN JURISPRUDENCE 112-24 (A. Guest ed. 1961).

[6] 189 Mass. 247, 75 N.E. 619 (1905).

[7] *Id.* at 249-50, 75 N.E. at 620. The court rejected the defendants' argument, holding that the legislature has the power to prohibit the pollution of waterways in order to "protect and preserve edible fish." The legislature can delegate this power to the Board of Fish and Game Commissioners, and the Board need not base its order on sworn evidence or afford a hearing to the persons affected. *Id.* at 251-53, 75 N.E. at 621-22.

[8] 238 N.C. 185, 77 S.E.2d 682 (1953).

[9] *Id.* at 187-89, 77 S.E.2d at 684-86. The court held the plaintiff had established that the defendant's actions constituted an actionable private nuisance. The evidence supported a finding that the defendant "intentionally and unreasonably caused noxious gases and odors to escape onto the nine acres of the plaintiffs to such a degree as to impair in a substantial manner the plaintiffs' use and enjoyment of their land." *Id.* at 194-95, 77 S.E.2d at 690.

[10] For a discussion of what can be "property," see note 228 and accompanying text *infra*.

But growth of population and industry has necessarily jeopardized the unencumbered use of property.[11] English cities felt this tension at least as early as the sixteenth century.[12] The demand on the legal system, then and now, has been to develop consistent doctrines that both satisfy the needs of society and justify the curtailment of property owners' and possessors' rights. Property rights are too fundamental to be determined on an ad hoc basis.[13] Outcomes must be rationalized to winners and losers alike in terms of a universal property doctrine that society as a whole accepts as just. This perception of distributive justice can be almost as important as the actual allocation of resources.[14] And legal historians, particularly Maitland, have long recognized that "known general laws" are at least perceived to "interfere less with freedom."[15]

With this in mind, this Article will exhume, yet again, three famous cases on Anglo-American property doctrine: *William Aldred's Case*,[16] *St. Helen's Smelting Co. v. Tipping*,[17] and *Illinois Central Railroad v. Illinois*.[18] These cases are remarkable for their multitudinous progeny and commentaries. But they are most remarkable as sources of ideas about history, justice, and the human environment.

---

[11] *See, e.g.*, Cohen, *Property and Sovereignty*, 13 CORNELL L.Q. 8 (1927). Cohen noted:

> To permit anyone to do absolutely what he likes with his property in creating noise, smells, or danger of fire, would be to make property in general valueless. To be really effective, therefore, the right of property must be supported by restrictions or positive duties on the part of owners, enforced by the state as much as the right to exclude others which is the essence of property.

Id. at 21.

[12] *See* notes 86-90 and accompanying text *infra*.

[13] The need for a general property doctrine to legitimate both court action and government policy concerned scholars at the dawn of English legal history. The first comprehensive book on English law, written by several hands between 1220 and 1256, was very much concerned with conceptualized, universal property doctrine. *See generally* 2 BRACTON ON THE LAW AND CUSTOMS OF ENGLAND 39-48 (S. Thorne trans. 1968) [hereinafter cited as BRACTON].

[14] *See generally* E. MISHAN, COST-BENEFIT ANALYSIS 127-44 (1976); Calabresi & Melamed, *Property Rules, Liability Rules, and Inalienability: One View of the Cathedral*, 85 HARV. L. REV. 1089, 1093-1105 (1972).

[15] F. MAITLAND, *A Historical Sketch of Liberty and Equality as Ideals of English Political Philosophy from the Time of Hobbes to the Time of Coleridge*, in 1 THE COLLECTED PAPERS OF FREDERIC WILLIAM MAITLAND 81 (H. Fisher ed. 1911).

[16] 9 Coke 57b, 77 Eng. Rep. 816 (K.B. 1611).

[17] 11 Eng. Rep. 1483 (H.L. 1865).

[18] 146 U.S. 387 (1892).

I

THE NATURAL RIGHTS OF SEISIN DOCTRINE AND WILLIAM ALDRED'S CASE (1611)

A. *Early Private Nuisance Law*

The early common law took the position that "[n]o plot of land [was] 'intire of itselfe.'"[19] In addition to the wrong of wholly depriving a man of possession of his land, *disseisina,* the common law recognized the wrong of interfering with property rights by entering on the land, *transgressio.* Beginning at least as early as the twelfth and thirteenth centuries, the law also remedied interference with the use of land from outside that land.[20] This last kind of interference was eventually to be called *nocumentum* or nuisance.

Both "nuisance" and "trespass" "began life as ordinary English, or rather French, words with no inherent technical significance."[21] Nuisance comprises an "annoyance" as opposed to a

---

[19] C. HAAR, LAND-USE PLANNING 124 (3d ed. 1976) (quoting JOHN DONNE, *Devotions Upon Emergent Occasions XVII,* in JOHN DONNE: COMPLETE POETRY AND SELECTED PROSE 538 (J. Hayward ed. 1929)); *see* Cohen, *supra* note 11, at 21; Newark, *The Boundaries of Nuisance,* 65 L.Q. REV. 480, 481-82 (1949).

[20] *See* Loengard, *The Assize of Nuisance: Origins of an Action at Common Law,* 37 CAMBRIDGE L.J. 144, 144-47 (1978); Newark, *supra* note 19, at 481-82. The earliest surviving Roman law texts also contain the idea that property was not "intire of itselfe." Gaius, who wrote in the mid-second century A.D., stated that ownership rights existed beyond tangible "corporeal" things "such as land, a slave, a garment." INSTITUTES OF GAIUS 2.13.

> Incorporeal are things that are intangible, such as exist merely in law. . . . Incorporeal also are rights attached to urban and rural lands. Examples of the former are the right to raise one's building and so obstruct a neighbour's lights, or that of preventing a building from being raised lest neighbouring lights be obstructed, also the right that a neighbour shall suffer rain-water to pass into his courtyard . . . in a channel or by dripping; also the right to introduce a sewer into a neighbour's property or to open lights over it.

Id. at 2.14.

[21] J. BAKER, AN INTRODUCTION TO ENGLISH LEGAL HISTORY 351 (2d ed. 1979). *See* C. FIFOOT, HISTORY AND SOURCES OF THE COMMON LAW 3-4 (1949); Loengard, *supra* note 20, at 158 n.44. In Latin, *nocumentum* simply meant "harm." Newark, *supra* note 19, at 481. *See also* W. PROSSER, HANDBOOK OF THE LAW OF TORTS § 89, at 571 n.7 (4th ed. 1971). The multifarious uses of the term "nuisance" have obscured its history as a private wrong against land. For instance, "nuisance" could also refer to various forms of petty crimes and public nuisances actionable only by government officials. Newark, *supra* note 19, at 481-83. *See generally* 2 F. POLLOCK & F. MAITLAND, THE HISTORY OF ENGLISH LAW 520 (2d ed. 1898). The confusion between public and private nuisance apparently dates from Y.B. Mich. 27 Hen. 8, f. 27, pl. 10 (1535), *reprinted in* C. FIFOOT, *supra,* at 89. In this action for blocking a highway, "[i]nstead of restating the rule that the existence of the remedy of a criminal presentment barred the action [one judge] attempted to rationalise it by saying that to allow the action to one would be to allow it to a hundred." Newark, *supra* note 19,

"direct physical harm."[22] At first, such annoyances were probably remedied on an ad hoc basis by the many local courts of medieval England. But eventually some remedies for such harms to another's free tenement developed into a royal *praecipe* ("command") writ, a simple but formal legal remedy. This writ commanded a defendant to permit (*quod permittat*) a plaintiff to exercise a right, or to abate by self-help a hindrance, which interfered with the plaintiff's *seisin* of land, but fell short of actually interfering directly with full land ownership.[23]

With the ordinance called the Assize of Novel Disseisin of 1166, Henry II replaced the older "writs of right" by simple, expeditious possessory assizes, with an attractive and novel right to jury trial. Just as these possessory assizes began to replace the older remedies for absolute interference with land, the use of *praecipe* writs for nuisance was also replaced by a new possessory remedy.[24] This remedy for nuisance was obtained by using a writ very similar to, and perhaps a kind of subgroup of, that employed to bring an action in *novel disseisin* for the possession of the land itself.[25] The plea rolls of John and Henry III show a frequent

at 483. Thus the peculiar private action in public nuisance was born as an action on the case that lies only when the plaintiff suffers "a particular damage . . . which is not common to others." E. COKE, THE FIRST PART OF THE INSTITUTES OF THE LAWS OF ENGLAND *56a. This confusion was then picked up in a 16th century case digest. R. BROOKE, LA GRAUNDE ABRIDGEMENT (Tottell ed. 1576) (1st ed. London 1573). Following the judicial language, the editor listed the above *Year Book* case under both "nuisance" and "action sur le case," compounding the confusion between public and private nuisance actions.

[22] J. BAKER, *supra* note 21, at 351.

[23] "[T]he writs themselves have an *ad hoc* quality which makes categorisation difficult and frustrates attempts at tracing evolution of a form . . . ." Loengard, *supra* note 20, at 147. For typical *praecipe* writs defending rights of access to wood, pasture, and proper use of common pasture short of full ownership, see THE TREATISE ON THE LAW AND CUSTOMS OF THE REALM OF ENGLAND COMMONLY CALLED GLANVILL, bk. 12, chs. 13, 14, at 142-43 (G. Hall ed. 1965) [hereinafter cited as GLANVILL]. *Glanvill* was written between 1187 and 1189. *Introduction* to GLANVILL at xi. *See generally* C. FIFOOT, *supra* note 21, at 3-23; 3 W. HOLDSWORTH, A HISTORY OF ENGLISH LAW 15, 128-30 (1909); F. MAITLAND, THE FORMS OF ACTION AT COMMON LAW 23-29 (A. Claytor & W. Whittaker eds. 1936).

[24] According to a new and penetrating analysis by Professor Loengard, the use of a possessory assize to remedy nuisance was part of the original scheme behind the ordinance of the assize of *novel disseisin*, and not a mere judicial interpretation or extension of the ordinance. Loengard, *supra* note 20, at 164-66. *But see* H. RICHARDSON & G. SAYLES, LAW AND LEGISLATION 109 (1966). *See* J. BAKER, *supra* note 21, at 352. *See also* C. FLOWER, INTRODUCTION TO THE CURIA ROLLS, 1199-1230 A.D., 62 SELDEN SOC'Y 13, 325-34 (1943); Chew & Kellaway, *Introduction* to LONDON ASSIZE OF NUISANCE 1301-1431 at xii-xx (London Record Society repr. 1973); Milsom, *Legal Introduction* to NOVAE NARRATIONES, *reprinted in* 80 SELDEN SOC'Y at xcvi-civ (1963).

[25] For the early forms of such writs, see GLANVILL, *supra* note 23, at 167-69; EARLY REGISTERS OF WRITS, *reprinted in* 87 SELDEN SOC'Y 3, 32 (viscontiel), 70-74, 85, 98, 214-15,

use of this type of writ, called *questus est,* in seeking relief from wrongs to property not amounting to a threat to total possession of *disseisin,* but merely to an interference with the enjoyment of a free tenement.[26] The writ required a jury of "twelve free and lawful men of that neighbourhood to view [the disputed area] . . . [a]nd summon[ed] them . . . to be before our justices at the first session."[27] The entire action, writ and jury proceeding, became known as the assize of nuisance.[28] Only a private party with a "freehold estate" could obtain its relief.[29]

219, 260-62, 271-72 (1970). By the time of *Bracton*, which was written between 1220 and 1256 (Thorne, *Translator's Preface* to 3 BRACTON, *supra* note 13, at v), there was a conscious comparison of the assize of nuisance with that of *novel disseisin*. In essence, if a wrong arose entirely on the defendant's land, the assize of nuisance was the appropriate remedy, as it "extends to another's estate." *Id.* at 197. But if the wrong was perpetrated on the plaintiff's land or deprived the plaintiff of his "free tenement" absolutely, the proper remedy was the assize of *novel disseisin*. *Id.* at 197. The writ of nuisance and the writ of *novel disseisin* were framed at the same time, if not originally both established, as Loengard suggests, in the ordinance called the Assize of Novel Disseisin. *See* note 24 *supra*. *See also* D. STENTON, ENGLISH JUSTICE BETWEEN THE NORMAN CONQUEST AND THE GREAT CHARTER, 1066-1215, at 42 n.59 (1964); Turner, *Introduction to* BREVIA PLACITATA, 66 SELDEN SOC'Y at cxix (1947).

[26] *See, e.g.*, 3 BRACTON, *supra* note 13, at 192-93; C. FIFOOT, *supra* note 21, at 20. The writ ran "[*q*]*uestus est nobis talis quod talis iniuste et sine iudicio levavit quendam murum . . . quandum domum, quandam portam . . . in tali villa ad nocumentum liberi tenementi.*" It translates as "[s]uch a one has complained to us that such a one wrongfully and without judgment constructed a certain wall (. . . 'house,' 'gate,' . . .) in such a vill to the nuisance of his free tenement." 3 BRACTON, *supra* note 13, at 192. For a list of cases involving this writ for injuries less than *disseisin*, or total dispossession, see notes 44-45 *infra*.

[27] 3 BRACTON, *supra* note 13, at 194.

[28] The word "assize" derives from the Latin word "assidere," "to set together," as in a "legislative enactment." 1 JOWITT'S DICTIONARY OF ENGLISH LAW 148 (2d ed. 1977). As Plucknett stated that:

> From this time onwards the word "assize" takes several new meanings; it began by signifying a solemn session of a council or a court, and soon came to mean an enactment made at such a meeting; among the most important of these assizes were those establishing trial by inquisition, and so it soon became customary to describe the inquisition of twelve men as an assize, while the various procedures leading up to this form of trial (which we should now call forms of action [including the assize of nuisance]) were likewise called assizes. Finally, travelling justices were established in the thirteenth century in order to try these assizes more speedily, and these justices were naturally called justices of assize, and their sessions in the provinces were called the assizes [later synonymous with local English trial courts, *i.e.*, "Norfolk Assizes"].

T. PLUCKNETT, A CONCISE HISTORY OF THE COMMON LAW 112 (5th ed. 1956).

[29] C. FIFOOT, *supra* note 21, at 93. This situation existed before the rise of the action on the case afforded tort relief, even for direct trespass, to plaintiffs who had no property interests. *See* 3 W. HOLDSWORTH, *supra* note 23, at 11 & n.3. Prosser stated that "the assize of nuisance" was "a criminal writ affording incidental civil relief." W. PROSSER, *supra* note 21, at 572. Legal scholarship other than that cited by Prosser contradicts this view. In particular, see C. FIFOOT, *supra* note 21, at 5-11, 93-96. The assize of nuisance was never a Plea of the Crown, a criminal action in which the King is a party.

The earliest cases of *novel disseisin ad nocumentum liberi tenementi* ("of nuisance to a free hold tenement"), fell into four classes: (1) interference with a variety of "agricultural diversions falling short of total disseisin," such as interference with pasture for cattle or pannage for pigs, (2) obstruction to rights of way, (3) interference arising from the operation of watermills, and (4) interference with rights to hold fairs or markets.[30] *Bracton* did contain the notion that the variety of nuisances was infinite.[31] But the examples given were still strictly tied to servitudes and freehold ownership, and the assizes of both *novel disseisin* and nuisance were thus denied to one who held only in wardship or for a term of years or who was in possession only in another's name.[32]

Even during its early development, nuisance, as a wrong against rights in rem, received special treatment relative to wrongs against legal rights in personam. For example, interference with

---

The ancient, alternative remedy of self-abatement of nuisance illustrates Prosser's error. *See, e.g.*, Crakehall v. Anon., Y.B. Trin. 6 Edw. 2 (1313), *reprinted in* 36 SELDEN SOCIETY 76 (1918). If the injury was flagrant, the complaining property owner could resort to self-help to eliminate the nuisance. *See* C. FIFOOT, *supra* note 21, at 9. The period of self-abatement, during which recourse to the judicial system was unnecessary, was limited. *Id.* *See* 3 BRACTON, *supra* note 13, at 189, 192 (party must take action while "misdeed is still fresh"). If the time period elapsed without any action by the complainant, he had to seek an assize of *novel disseisin* or an assize of nuisance, depending upon the location of the injury. *Id.* But even under the writs of *questus est* and *quod permittat*, the injured party, not the sheriff, abated the nuisance. *See* 3 W. BLACKSTONE, COMMENTARIES *221-22; 3 W. HOLDSWORTH, *supra* note 23, at 244.

[30] C. FIFOOT, *supra* note 21, at 5-7.

[31] "*Nocumenta vero infinita sunt, secundum quod inferius dicetur, quae omnino servitutes tollunt vel saltem dant impedimentum quo minus commode uti possit servitutibus*" ("nuisances which destroy servitudes completely or, at the least, keep them from being used effectively, are infinite"). 3 BRACTON, *supra* note 13, at 189. *Cf.* Chew & Kellaway, *supra* note 24, at xxxii ("although not infinite, the nuisances on our rolls are undoubtedly varied").

[32] The plaint and remedy by assise does not lie for anyone who is in possession in the name of another, because he does not possess though he is in possession; he possesses in whose name the thing is possessed. To possess is very different from being in possession. These are in possession though they do not possess: a guardian (sometimes) who holds in demesne though not in fee. A procurator. A household. A bondsman, one's own or another's possessed in good faith. A farmer or fructuary, though not one who holds in fee farm. A usuary and a guest. And he who holds at will, from day to day [or] from year to year, though he may vouch a warrantor, according to some, as a usufructuary who holds for a term of years. Such persons will have neither the plaint nor the remedy by assise, because they have no action; the owner has it, and thus, if they sue, the exception of property and free tenement lies against them, no matter by what kind of disseisor it is raised, whether he has the right to eject or not.

3 BRACTON, *supra* note 13, at 33 (footnotes omitted).

rights in rem did not constitute a single wrong but a continuous wrong which lasted until the status quo was restored.[33] As a result, at least theoretically, an injured party could institute an unlimited number of assizes of nuisance until the wrong had ceased, with damages awarded at each assize.[34] This doctrine formed the historical basis of a later and most potent remedy for private nuisance, the equitable injunction.[35]

To be actionable, a nuisance had to result in both *injuria* (legal injury) and *damnum* (material damage).[36] These concepts were distinguished in *Bracton*: If you built a mill on your land, taking customers from my mill, there was *damnum* to me, but no *injuria.*[37] A necessary element of *injuria* was *omne id quod non iure fit* ("anything wrongfully done").[38] The meaning of this crucial phrase was unclear for centuries;[39] perhaps there was no uniform definition. The *Year Book* cases treat these wrongs as interferences with the "natural rights" of the property owner or possessor.[40] Such "natural rights" arose solely through the operation of the

---

[33] *See* Beswick v. Cunden, Cro. Eliz. 402, 402, 78 Eng. Rep. 646, 647 (Q.B. 1592) ("the case in 14 & 15 Eliz. Dyer, 319. is good law; for there the Lady Brown made a new nusance by every turning of the cock, for which she was punishable, although she made it not at the first"); F. MAITLAND, *supra* note 23, at 77-78. This rule was later modified in Penruddock's Case, 5 Coke 100b, 77 Eng. Rep. 210 (C.P. 1598), which held that an action may lie directly against the person beginning a nuisance and continue as long as the wrong persists, but that a request to remedy is necessary before the right of action continues against a new neighbor who continues a nuisance begun by another.

[34] *See* F. MAITLAND, *supra* note 23, at 77-78.

[35] Occasionally, an early common law court would grant specific performance or issue a writ of prohibition that had almost the same effect as an injunction. *See* T. PLUCKNETT, *supra* note 28, at 678. Whether these were ever used for a *nocumentum* is apparently unknown. For discussions of the modern use of the injunction as a nuisance remedy, see Chafee, *The Progress of the Law, 1919-1920: Equitable Relief Against Torts,* 34 HARV. L. REV. 388, 392-400 (1921); Note, *Injunctions against Private Nuisances,* 22 HARV. L. REV. 596, 596-97 (1909). For a discussion of the standards for injunctive relief, see Riter v. Keokuk Electro-Metals Co., 248 Iowa 710, 82 N.W.2d 151 (1957); Elliot Nursery Co. v. Duquesne Light Co., 281 Pa. 166, 126 A. 345 (1924).

[36] 2 F. POLLOCK & F. MAITLAND, *supra* note 21, at 534.

[37] 3 BRACTON, *supra* note 13, at 164, 189, 195-96, 199; 2 F. POLLOCK & F. MAITLAND, *supra* note 21, at 534. *See also* 2 BRACTON, *supra* note 13, at 140, 267.

[38] 2 BRACTON, *supra* note 13, at 140.

[39] *See generally* McRae, *The Development of Nuisance in the Early Common Law,* 1 U. FLA. L. REV. 27 (1948); Winfield, *Nuisance as a Tort,* 4 CAMBRIDGE L.J. 189 (1931).

[40] For what Holdsworth called "natural rights incident to ownership," see Y.B. Trin. 18 Edw. 3 (1344), *reprinted in* ROLL SERIES 210 (1904); Y.B. Pasch. 12 Edw. 3 (1338), *reprinted in* ROLL SERIES 464 (1883); Y.B. Hil. 35 Edw. 1 (1307), *reprinted in* ROLL SERIES 456 (1879); Y.B. Mich. 30 Edw. 1 (1302), *reprinted in* ROLL SERIES 40 (1863); 3 W. HOLDSWORTH, *supra* note 23, at 129. *See also* J. BAKER, *supra* note 21, at 356-60; C. FIFOOT, *supra* note 21, at 8, 95; Newark, *supra* note 19, at 482.

property law and did not depend on an express grant or prescription.[41] Furthermore, they could not be taken away by express grant or prescription.[42] For example, there could be no easement of "foul smell" over another's property.[43]

In 1444, Judge Markham said "[i]f a man builds a house and stops up the light coming to my house, or causes the rain to fall from his house and so undermines my house, or does anything which injures my free tenement, I shall have the assize of nuisance."[44] The "natural rights" of *seisin* apparently included protection against interference with the owner's residential use or enjoyment of the property together with direct interference with any economic use of the land that was an exclusive legal right of the owner.[45]

Such interference with residential use was enough to constitute an *injuria,* and any resulting *damnum* gave rise to a right of action. The requisite interference could be extremely indirect. For example, *injuria* could result from foul smells, uncomfortable temperature, excessive noise, or the cutting off of light. Moreover,

---

[41] 3 BRACTON, *supra* note 13, at 163, 189-90. *See* F. POLLOCK, JURISPRUDENCE AND LEGAL ESSAYS 108 (A. Goodhart ed. 1961); A. SIMPSON, AN INTRODUCTION TO THE HISTORY OF THE LAND LAW 101, 246 (1961).

[42] Fowler v. Sanders, Cro. Jac. 446, 446, 79 Eng. Rep. 382, 382 (K.B. 1617).

[43] A. SIMPSON, *supra* note 41, at 246.

[44] 3 W. HOLDSWORTH, *supra* note 23, at 129 (quoting Y.B. Mich. 22 Hen. 6, pl. 23 (1443)). *See* Y.B. Mich. 30 Edw. 1 (1301), *reprinted in* ROLL SERIES 22 (1863). *But cf.* Bowry and Popes Case, 1 Leon. 168, 74 Eng. Rep. 155 (C.P. 1588) (stopping up recently built window not actionable).

[45] *See* Y.B. Trin. 18 Edw. 3, f. 22, pl. 1 (1344), *reprinted in* ROLL SERIES 210 (1904) (construction of house so that rain fell on plaintiff's house); Y.B. Trin. 18 Edw. 3, f. 22, pl. 2 (1344), *reprinted in* ROLL SERIES 210 (1904) (construction of house so that drainage of plaintiff's house impaired); Y.B. Pasch. 12 Edw. 3 (1338), *reprinted in* ROLL SERIES 468 (1883) (construction of wall so that rain fell on plaintiff's house); Y.B. Pasch. 12 Edw. 3 (1338), *reprinted in* ROLL SERIES 466 (1883) (construction of weir downstream from another); Y.B. Pasch. 12 Edw. 3 (1331), *reprinted in* ROLL SERIES 464 (1883) (diversion of stream from plaintiff's land); Grave v. Shorne, Y.B. Hil. 8 Edw. 2, pl. 2 (1315), *reprinted in* 41 SELDEN SOCIETY 1 (1924) (*disseisin* of common pasture); Crakehall v. Anonymous, Y.B. Trin. 6 Edw. 2, pl. 21 (1313), *reprinted in* 36 SELDEN SOCIETY 76 (1918) (diversion of stream from one mill to another); Burnhill v. Ringtherose, Y.B. Trin. 3 Edw. 2, pl. 30 (1310), *reprinted in* 20 SELDEN SOCIETY 200 (1905) (failure to have corn from certain land ground at plaintiff's mill); Y.B. Mich. 31 Edw. 1 (1303), *reprinted in* ROLL SERIES 404 (1863) (construction of weir upstream from mill); Y.B. 22 Edw. 1 (1294), *reprinted in* ROLL SERIES 568 (1873) (holding of market in same town as existing market); Y.B. 21 Edw. 1 (1293), *reprinted in* ROLL SERIES 414 (1866) (construction of pool on adjoining land); Wildeker v. Ros, Bracton's Note Book, pl. 685 (1232), *reprinted in* C. FIFOOT, *supra* note 21, at 16 (*disseisin* of estovers); Abbot of Meaux's Case, Assize Roll 1040, mem. 4, pl. 91 (1219), *reprinted in* 56 SELDEN SOCIETY 39 (1937) (obstruction of right of way).

it was argued that the *damnum* could be to simple enjoyment.[46] But, as discussed before, no amount of harm gave rise to actionable damages unless the injury was of a type legally recognized as giving a right of action.

---

[46] The issue of "whether the law took any notice of 'things of pleasure' as opposed to things of profit" was a repeatedly contested issue through the sixteenth century. *See* Baker, *Introduction* to 2 THE REPORTS OF SIR JOHN SPELMAN, *reprinted in* 94 SELDEN SOC'Y 35-36, 234-36 (1977). In 1530 one judge argued that "it is necessary for every man of ability to have pleasures; and when this pleasure is destroyed, is it not reason that he should have damages therefor? (As if to say yes)." Y.B. 21 Hen. 8, Keil. 203, pl. 1 (1530), *translation quoted in* Baker, *supra,* at 36. Temperature, light, smell and reasonable quiet unquestionably were protected.

> [I]f a man makes an oven for making chalk or pots . . . and by the heat of the fire my house becomes so hot that I cannot live there . . . this is nuisance. . . . In the same way, if one makes a forge so near my house that I cannot hear in my house because of the striking of the hammer, it is nuisance. In the same way, if one makes a common slaughterhouse which proves so bad that on account of the evil smell I cannot live in my house, it is nuisance. It is the same of a latrine . . . .

Treherne, *Lincoln's Inn Reading on Forest Laws* (1520), *conflated and quoted in* Baker, *supra,* at 235.

> [B]y the Common law, one shall not hurt the Freehold of another, and no greater hurt, greivance, or dammage can be done to any mans Freehold, then to take away the light and ayre thereof, which is comfortable, & commodious for him, for when this light, and ayre are taken from him, his house remaineth as a dungeon.

Hales' Case, [unreported] (c. 1560) (argument, Wraye), *printed in* A BRIEFE DECLARATION FOR WHAT MANNER OF SPECIALL NUSANCE CONCERNING PRIVATE DWELLING HOUSES, A MAN MAY HAVE HIS REMEDY BY ASSISE, OR OTHER ACTION AS THE CASE REQUIRES 11 (London 1636) [hereinafter cited as DECLARATION]; *see also* J. BAKER, *supra* note 21, at 357 n.13. But in the same case a contrary argument was made by Manwood:

> I will agree with you, that if all your windowes were stopped, that an action will lie, and where you say *sic utere tuo ut alienum non ladas,* this is not meant of things of pleasure, but of things of profit. And here is not any part of your house consumed, but herein a let of your pleasure onely, for which your action is not maintaineable.

DECLARATION, *supra,* at 20-21.

The debate on aesthetics continued into the 18th century in the context of indictment for public nuisance. Lord Mansfield, while reviewing a case in which the defendants had been convicted of a public nuisance "for erecting and continuing their works at Twickenham, for making acid spirit of sulphur, oil of vitriol, and oil of aqua fortis," stated that "it is not necessary that the smell [caused by defendants' operations] should be unwholesome: it is enough, if it renders the enjoyment of life and property uncomfortable." Rex v. White, 1 Burr. 333, 337, 97 Eng. Rep. 338, 340 (K.B. 1757). Indeed, in one case mere storage of "great quantities of gun powder" was held to be, *ipso facto,* a public nuisance, without any physical damage at all. Rex v. Taylor, 2 Strange 1167, 1167, 93 Eng. Rep. 1104, 1104 (K.B. 1741). Apparently, the anxiety alone was actionable. "So also it will be a nuisance, if life is made uncomfortable by the apprehension of danger . . . ." 3 W. BLACKSTONE, COMMENTARIES 171 n.3 (19th ed. J. Chitty ed. 1857).

It is unclear whether American nuisance law ever historically accepted purely "mental discomfort" or damage to aesthetics as actionable per se. *See* Chafee, *supra* note 35, at 393. *Cf.* Larremore, *Public Aesthetics,* 20 HARV. L. REV. 35, 42-45 (1906) (advocating such acceptance).

> If [the defendant] cannot be prohibited by law from doing it, though he creates a nuisance and causes damage it will not be wrongful, for each may do on his own property [whatever he wishes if] wrongful damages does not accrue to a neighbour, as where one erects a mill on his own land and takes from his neighbour his own suit and that of others; he does his neighbour damages but no *injuria* since he is not prohibited by law or a constitution from having or erecting a mill.[47]

Cutting off a neighbor's light, however, was argued to be actionable even though the *damnum* could be characterized as interfering with enjoyment and not profit.[48]

Anything, therefore, "erected, made, or done not on the soil possessed by the complainant"[49] that interfered with the "free enjoyment" guaranteed by *seisin* was a wrong that could be remedied by the assize of nuisance.[50] As *Bracton* stated, there was a "servitude . . . imposed on another's land by law, not by man . . . by which one is prohibited from doing on his own land what may damage a neighbor."[51] The "natural rights" incident to *seisin* were among the earliest legally protected rights, and courts vigorously debated the limitations of *damnum* and *injuria*.

B. *Sic Utere Tuo Doctrine*

Even in 1600 it was still unclear exactly what constituted these "natural rights" of *seisin*.[52] As in many other areas of the common law, the task of clarification fell to Sir Edward Coke. He undertook this task, like many others, by writing a report of a "case in point," a report which may or may not have accurately reflected the actual case.[53]

---

[47] 3 BRACTON, *supra* note 13, at 164 (footnotes omitted).

[48] *See* note 46 *supra*. Substantial blockage of light was actionable, but probably not just some interference with a view. *See* William Aldred's Case, 9 Coke 57b, 58a-58b, 77 Eng. Rep. 816, 817-21 (K.B. 1611) (quoting Bland v. Moseley, [unreported] (K.B. 1587) (Wray, C.J.)); J. BAKER, *supra* note 21, at 357-58. *But see* Bury v. Pope, Cro. Eliz. 118, 118, 78 Eng. Rep. 375, 375 (Ex. Ch. 1588) (interference with windows not actionable "for it was [the plaintiff's] folly to build his house so near to the other's land"). "[T]he right to clean air, undiverted and unpolluted water, light, and quiet, seems to have been incident to house ownership in general." Baker, *supra* note 46, at 235.

[49] 2 F. POLLOCK & F. MAITLAND, *supra* note 21, at 53.

[50] 3 W. HOLDSWORTH, *supra* note 23, at 11. *Novel disseisin*, on the other hand, protected "undisturbed possession" of property. *Id.*

[51] 3 BRACTON, *supra* note 13, at 189-90. *See also id.* at 163-64, 191.

[52] *See* C. FIFOOT, *supra* note 21, at 95.

[53] Plucknett explained Coke's case-reporting philosophy. "There was no clear boundary in [Coke's] mind between what a case said and what he thought it ought to say . . . . A case

The case was *William Aldred's Case*.[54] The pleadings were simple. The plaintiff brought an action on the case against the defendant for erecting a hog sty near the plaintiff's house. The sty allegedly fouled the air in the house and cut off the plaintiff's light. These allegations were found to be true at the Norfolk Assizes, and damages were assessed.[55] The defendant appealed to the King's Bench, arguing:

> (1) That there was no *damnum* to the plaintiff in the "corrupted air"—because the law should not favor delicate wishes, "one ought not to have so delicate a nose, that he cannot bear the smell of hogs";[56]
> (2) that the blocking of windows was permitted by a local custom;[57] and
> (3) "that the building of the house for hogs was necessary for the sustenance of man."[58]

The pleadings present two points of great interest. First, the plaintiff brought an action on the case rather than the older assize of nuisance. As indicated before, the assize of nuisance had from its inception been carefully restricted to plaintiffs seized of a freehold estate. This excluded some important potential plaintiffs, including leaseholders, copyholders, guardians, and holders of rights of commons.[59] But by 1500, plaintiffs were frequently bringing nuisance actions by use of the new action on the case, which permitted an action on a "case stated" where a remedy was not already available through an older form of action.[60] This de-

---

in Coke's *Reports* . . . . is dominated by Coke's personality, and derives its authority from him." T. PLUCKNETT, *supra* note 28, at 281. Coke's *Reports* contained other cases that clarified nuisance doctrine. *See, e.g.*, Robert Marys's Case, 9 Coke 111b, 77 Eng. Rep. 895 (K.B. 1613) (interference with commons, action on case by commoner, distinction from public nuisance); Baten's Case, 9 Coke 53b, 77 Eng. Rep. 810 (K.B. 1611) (overhang, abatement, pleading); Williams's Case, 5 Coke 72b, 77 Eng. Rep. 163 (K.B. 1592) (public "common" nuisance); Penruddock's Case, 5 Coke 100b, 77 Eng. Rep. 210 (C.P. 1598) (proper party, continuing wrong, abatement).

[54] 9 Coke 57b, 77 Eng. Rep 816 (K.B. 1611).

[55] *Id.* at 58a, 77 Eng. Rep. at 817.

[56] *Id.*, 77 Eng. Rep. at 817.

[57] *Id.* at 58b, 77 Eng. Rep. at 820.

[58] *Id.* at 58a, 77 Eng. Rep. at 817.

[59] *See* note 29 and accompanying text *supra*. *See also* C. FIFOOT, *supra* note 21, at 93; Baker, *supra* note 46, at 233.

[60] *See* Baker, *supra* note 46, at 232-33. At least one school of thought has traced the origins of the action on the case to the *in consimili casu* section of the Statute of Westminster II, 13 Edw. 1, Stat. 1, c. 24 (1285), *reprinted in* A. KIRALFY, A SOURCE BOOK OF ENGLISH LAW 138-39 (1957). *See* C. FIFOOT, *supra* note 21, at 66-68. This section specifically declared

velopment made a nuisance remedy available to lessees for years and tenants in common, and also confirmed that remedies could be obtained for nuisances caused by nonfeasance or by persons other than the adjacent freeholder.[61] Indeed, the advantages of case, including simplified pleading, damages, and greater expedition, led even those plaintiffs whose cause of action lay within the traditional assize to attempt to use the new form.[62]

These attempts were resisted on the grounds that the new "case" remedy should never be available if the older assize were appropriate.[63] Not long before *William Aldred's Case,* however, all the common law judges, meeting as the Exchequer Chamber, decided in *Cantrel v. Church*[64] that any nuisance plaintiff could have his election of case or the assize.[65] Obviously a careful plaintiff

---

that a *quod permittat* writ for a nuisance "shall not be denied" if the offending "House, Wall, or such" was "aliened to another." A. KIRALFY, *supra,* at 138. The statute provided that "[b]ut from henceforth, where in one Case a Writ is granted, in like Case, requiring like Remedies, the Writ shall be made as hath been used before." *Id. See* E. COKE, THE SECOND PART OF THE INSTITUTES OF THE LAWS OF ENGLAND *404-05. It is now doubted that the flexible, adaptive action on the case really originated in the statute, but the use of nuisance as a key illustrative example in the Statute of Westminster II remains of interest. *See* C. FIFOOT, *supra* note 21, at 68.

[61] And if a man levy a nusance unto the house of another who hath therein an estate but for term of years, then he shall not have an assize of nusance, but an action upon the case against him, because he hath no freehold: but yet it seemeth, he may enter and abate the nusance.

A. FITZ-HERBERT, THE NEW NATURA BREVIUM *185. "The function of the Assize was to abate the nuisance; action on the case lay only for damages." McRae, *supra* note 39, at 39. *See* Baker, *supra* note 46, at 233.

[62] *See id.* at 233-36. *See* Yevance v. Holcomb, 2 Dyer 250b, 250b n.88, 73 Eng. Rep. 553, 553 n.88 (K.B. 1566). Before 1600 plaintiffs enjoyed only spotty success in alleging case when the assize would have sufficed. *See* C. FIFOOT, *supra* note 21, at 94-95. *Compare* Beswick v. Cunden, Cro. Eliz. 520, 78 Eng. Rep. 768 (C.P. 1596) *with* Alston v. Pamphyn, Cro. Eliz. 466, 78 Eng. Rep. 719 (Q.B. 1596). *See also* Leverett v. Townsend, Cro. Eliz. 198, 78 Eng. Rep. 454 (Q.B. 1590).

[63] "The exercise of a nice discrimination would thus keep the Register tidy; but litigants might be forgiven if they felt the purchase of an archaic writ too heavy a price to pay for the preservation of juristic elegance." C. FIFOOT, *supra* note 21, at 94.

[64] Cro. Eliz. 845, 78 Eng. Rep. 1072 (Ex. Ch. 1601).

[65] [The judges] resolved, that the action was well brought, for [the plaintiff] hath election to bring either the one or the other: for although there had a difference been taken, where the way is so stopped up, that he loseth the use thereof altogether, and thereby his common, there an assise shall lie; but where it is estopped but in part, and not totally, that there an action upon the case lies, and not an assise; they conceived it not to be any difference, for he hath election to have either the one or the other action; especially as this case is, where it appears not that the stopping was made by him who is the tenant of the freehold; but it might be done by a stranger who hath nothing to do with the

would always allege in case, so that lack of a free tenement could not be argued at bar. Thus the assize of nuisance, although it historically preceded all actions on the case, was assimilated into the action on the case after 1601. Following the decision in *Cantrel v. Church,* a person with any possessory interest in land inherited the "natural rights" of *seisin* protected by the historic assize of nuisance, and perhaps more, but under the new guise of action on the case in nuisance. The plaintiff in *William Aldred's Case,* clearly well advised by his lawyer, used the new, safer form of nuisance action.[66]

The second remarkable pleading in *William Aldred's Case*—the defendant's pleading that "the building of the house for hogs was necessary for the sustenance of man"[67]—marks an even greater milestone in the law of nuisance. Never before had a defendant so clearly claimed social utility as a defense to a nuisance action. This pleading in itself makes *William Aldred's Case* a landmark in the law.

Nevertheless, the case has been most famous for its holding. Confronted with these pleadings, the court, according to Coke, dismissed all of the defendant's objections and upheld the award of the Norfolk Assizes. In doing so it made two major statements on the law of nuisance. First, the court stated that any injury to the plaintiff's enjoyment of his land was actionable so long as the injury pertained to a matter of necessity such as wholesome air or light.[68] Purely aesthetic damage, however, was beyond the scope of the action.

> [F]or prospect, which is a matter only of delight, and not of necessity, no action lies for stopping thereof, and yet it is a great commendation of a house if it has a long and large prospect . . . But the law does not give an action for such things of delight.[69]

> land, or by one who hath but a term therein. Wherefore they all resolved, that the action was well brought; thereupon the judgment was affirmed.

Id. at 845, 78 Eng. Rep. at 1072 (footnote omitted).

[66] The court in *William Aldred's Case* stated that: "The plaintiff in this as in all other possessory actions, may declare upon his possession without alledging the precise estate of which he is seised . . . ." 9 Coke at 57b n.(A), 77 Eng. Rep. at 816 n.(A).

[67] *Id.* at 58a, 77 Eng. Rep. at 817.

[68] *Id.* at 58b, 77 Eng. Rep. at 821.

[69] *Id.*, 77 Eng. Rep. at 821 (citing Bland v. Moseley, [unreported] (K.B. 1587) (Wray, C.J.), *summarized in* 2 W. HUGHES, THE GRAND ABRIDGMENT OF THE LAW 1369 (London 1662)). For another early precedent, see Hales' Case, [unreported] (c. 1560), *printed in* DECLARATION, *supra* note 46, *discussed in* notes 94-96 and accompanying text *infra*.

This rule placed a clear limitation on the "natural rights" of *seisin*. Courts could insist not only on a legal wrong, but also on damage to a thing of necessity. The question of what constituted such a necessity would be subject to demurrer, a question of law to be decided by the court.[70]

Having accorded itself this much discretion, the court drew the line. In its second major statement, the court in *William Aldred's Case* delineated the rule of *sic utere tuo ut alienum non laedas* (so use your own property as not to injure your neighbors).[71] This rule responded directly to the defendant's allegation in the pleadings that social utility justified some interferences. The court explicitly rejected this defense.

> [T]he building of a lime-kiln is good and profitable; but if it be built so near a house, that when it burns the smoke thereof enters into the house, so that none can dwell there, an action lies for it. So if a man has a watercourse running in a ditch from the river to his house, for his necessary use; if a glover sets up a lime-pit for calve skins and sheep skins so near the said watercourse that the corruption of the lime-pit has corrupted it, for which cause his tenants leave the said house, an action on the case lies for it, . . . and this stands with the rule of law and reason, . . . *sic utere tuo ut alienum non laedas.*[72]

The decision in *William Aldred's Case* was, therefore, a two-part ruling which, while finding an absolute right to enjoyment of certain property rights, gave the court some discretion to determine the nature of those rights. The necessity rule meant that the court could disallow some kinds of nuisance damages as a matter of law. The stench of the hogs and the cutting off of the light in *William Aldred's Case* interfered with such things of necessity as light ("*necessitas luminis*") and clean air ("*salubritas aeris*"), and the action was good.[73]

Given actionable damage, the defendant could not, however, ask the courts to balance social utilities. The court did not quarrel with the defendant's argument that a hog building was "necessary

---

[70] 9 Coke at 58b, 77 Eng. Rep. at 820-21.

[71] This famous Latin maxim was derived from Ulpian and is related to the general Roman principle "*expedit reipublicae ne sua re quis male utatur.*" INSTITUTES 1.8.2 (it is for the public good that no one should misuse his own property). *See* J. BAKER, *supra* note 21, at 354.

[72] 9 Coke at 58b-59a, 77 Eng. Rep. at 821 (citing the Prior of Southwark's Case, Y.B. Trin. 13 Hen. 7, f. 26, pl. 4 (1498), *reprinted in* C. FIFOOT, *supra* note 21, at 87).

[73] 9 Coke at 58a, 77 Eng. Rep. at 817.

for the sustenance of man," and it called a lime-kiln "good and profitable."[74] It simply said that once the defendant's activities threatened something necessary for the enjoyment of another's property, these arguments could not avail at law. To this extent, *William Aldred's Case* forcefully ratified the old "natural rights" of *seisin*.

Two minor points in the decision remain. First, the court did not discuss the hog-keeper's argument that the smell was de minimis: "one ought not to have so delicate a nose that he cannot bear the smell of hogs."[75] The defense of de minimis was inherent in the original definition of nuisance as one's "doing on his own land what may damage a neighbour."[76] Even today, one conceptual difficulty of private nuisance is that some significant degree of damage is inherent in the definition of injury. Thus, the classical *Year Book* distinction between *damnum* and *injuria* was somewhat artificial. The court in *William Aldred's Case* evidently considered the requisite degree of damage as a matter of fact already determined by the Norfolk jury's finding that the *injuria* of nuisance existed,[77] and saw as its task merely to determine, as a matter of law, whether the *damnum* was actionable.

Second, the declaration alleged that the defendant built the sty "maliciously intending to deprive the plaintiff of the use and profit of his house."[78] The court and parties ignored this pleading probably because the words "maliciously intending" were only words of art, or non-transversable pleadings, carried over into action on the case from its ancestor, the writ of trespass. By 1611, the words were recited as an empty formality, with no apparent connection to the kind of action on the case that was involved or to any other point of law, and they did not mean that an action

---

[74] *Id.* at 59a, 77 Eng. Rep. at 821.

[75] *Id.* at 58a, 77 Eng. Rep. at 817.

[76] 3 BRACTON, *supra* note 13, at 190. *See* Amphitheaters, Inc. v. Portland Meadows, 184 Or. 336, 198 P.2d 847 (1948); Bridlington Relay, Ltd. v. Yorkshire Elec. Bd., [1965] Ch. 436; Eastern & S. African Tel. Co. v. Cape Town Tramways Cos., [1902] A.C. 381; 62 HARV. L. REV. 704, 705 (1949).

For a discussion of what constitutes "damage" in England today and a critique of the extension of the de minimis defense in *Bridlington Relay*, see G. FRIDMAN, MODERN TORT CASES 182-84 (1968). Fridman warns that a too strict view of what constitutes actionable nuisance damage may "lead to a restriction of the utility of that tort as a means of protecting lawful interests in the use of land. That would be to stultify the idea, and reduce the value of liability in nuisance." *Id.* at 184.

[77] 9 Coke at 58a, 77 Eng. Rep. at 817.

[78] *Id.* at 59a, 77 Eng. Rep. at 821-22.

on the case in nuisance required malice, or even intent.[79] The older assize of nuisance, from which the new form of action on the case for nuisance took its substantive inspiration,[80] never involved questions of fault in the modern sense.[81] As in *William Aldred's Case,* English courts and lawyers, aware of the grafting of the substance of the nuisance assize to the action on the case, did not read the pleadings as requiring a fault element for private nuisance.[82] In a much later period, however, some American courts became confused by these words of art in the old pleadings and saw them as requiring fault or intent for an actionable nuisance.[83]

History provides two probable explanations for the *William Aldred's Case* court's decision to change the old *Year Book* rules and to take on more discretion as to actionable harm. First, plaintiffs of a middle-class, yeomen background were employing the action on the case in nuisance in the national courts.[84] Many of these men were probably tenants for years, or copyholders without the freehold estate or freehold tenure required for the assize of nuisance, but with enough possessory interest in land to satisfy the action on the case requirements of *Cantrel v. Church,* the 1601 case

[79] *See* C. FIFOOT, *supra* note 21, at 76-78. For the continuing juristic problem of legal "fault" in nuisance actions, see note 185 *infra.*

[80] *See* notes 63-66 and accompanying text *supra.*

[81] *See* 3 BRACTON, *supra* note 13, at 189-90; A. FITZ-HERBERT, THE NEW NATURA BREVIUM *183-85.

[82] *See* ÇLERK & LINDSELL ON TORTS ¶¶ 1393-95, at 781-85 (13th ed. 1969) [hereinafter cited as CLERK & LINDSELL].

[83] *See* 1 F. HARPER & F. JAMES, LAW OF TORTS § 1.24, at 67-70 (1956); Prosser, *Nuisance Without Fault,* 20 TEXAS L. REV. 399, 416-17 (1942). *See generally* M. HORWITZ, THE TRANSFORMATION OF AMERICAN LAW, 1780-1860, at 102 (1977). Benjamin Cardozo recognized the confusion arising from the old forms of action. *See* McFarlane v. City of Niagara Falls, 247 N.Y. 340, 343-44, 160 N.E. 391, 391-92 (1928). He recognized that traditional nuisance doctrine contained no fault requirement; harmful acts amounting to a nuisance were absolutely prohibited.

> The primary meaning [of nuisance] does not involve the element of negligence as one of its essential factors .... One acts sometimes at one's peril. In such circumstances, the duty to desist is absolute whenever conduct, if persisted in, brings damages to another .... Illustrations are abundant. One who emits noxious fumes or gases day by day in the running of his factory may be liable to his neighbor though he has taken all available precautions .... He is not to do such things at all, whether he is negligent or careful.

Id. at 343, 160 N.E. at 391-93. *See also* United Elec. Light Co. v. Deliso Constr. Co., 315 Mass. 313, 52 N.E.2d 553 (1943) ("A nuisance might exist in the absence of negligence."). For a modern formulation of the American view, see Seavey, *Nuisance: Contributory Negligence and Other Mysteries,* 65 HARV. L. REV. 984, 986-88, 995-96 (1952). Seavey challenged Judge Cardozo's analysis in part, and suggested that the *McFarlane* opinion has been misunderstood and that Judge Cardozo's language has caused confusion. *Id.* at 990-95.

[84] *See* C. FIFOOT, *supra* note 21, at 94-95; notes 59-66 and accompanying text *supra.*

that significantly opened the courthouse doors.[85] Before these plaintiffs had access to the national courts, they apparently had brought their cases before local presentment juries which decided cases informally and probably used rules of thumb similar to the necessity test.[86] These parties contrast sharply with the priors and "lords of the vill" who fill the *Year Book* cases,[87] and their property conflicts defy resolution in terms of the aesthetic privileges discussed in older English cases.[88]

The second reason for the new rule probably was the increasing population of British cities and the struggle for space within those cities. For example, between 1400 and 1600, open space in London disappeared dramatically. The population grew from nearly 100,000 in 1554, to 200,000 in 1602.[89]

This combination of new parties with new needs and the increasing population density of the cities prompted a more restrictive rule of nuisance harm than that found in the *Year Books*.[90] Coke's analysis of *William Aldred's Case* was an attempt to meet these social conditions with a rule that preserved reasonable property rights. Such leading seventeenth century cases as *Jones v. Powell*,[91] *Morley v. Pragnel*,[92] and even *Turberville v. Stamp*,[93] fol-

---

[85] Cro. Eliz. 845, 78 Eng. Rep. 1072 (Ex. Ch. 1601). *See* notes 59-66 and accompanying text *supra*.

[86] *See* J. DAWSON, A HISTORY OF LAY JUDGES 268-69 (1960). Professor Dawson notes that a major cause of complaints was, as in *William Aldred's Case*, pigs. *Id.* at 269. Dawson further notes that " 'hundreds of folio pages of Jury orders relate to swine alone and their numerous misdeeds and nuisances.' " *Id.* at 270 n.210 (quoting S. WEBB & B. WEBB, ENGLISH LOCAL GOVERNMENT FROM THE REVOLUTION TO THE MUNICIPAL CORPORATIONS ACT 104 (1908)). The jurors in Southampton, in despair at the number of pig offenses, declared that: " 'we thinck yt mete' that every man in town should keep pigs 'so that when the thinge is as the worste shame may redresse yt.' " *Id.* at 270 (quoting SOUTHAMPTON COURT LEET RECORDS 1, 7, 17 (1550)).

[87] *See* note 45 *supra*.

[88] *See* note 69 *supra*.

[89] 2 G. TREVELYAN, ILLUSTRATED ENGLISH SOCIAL HISTORY 4 (1949). The population is also thought to have increased by one-fifth between 1525 and 1545. *See* Baker, *supra* note 46, at 47.

[90] Even the pig problems became worse in the cities. *See* J. DAWSON, *supra* note 86, at 269; *see generally* DECLARATION, *supra* note 46, at 15 ("Swine are beasts that may cause diseases to be in a City").

[91] Hut. 135, 123 Eng. Rep. 1155 (C.P. 1628).

[92] Cro. Car. 510, 79 Eng. Rep. 1039 (K.B. 1638). In *Morley*, the plaintiff was an innkeeper. His business was threatened by the "stench" of a neighboring tallow furnace, and he brought an action upon the case. After a jury verdict for the innkeeper, the defendant appealed on the grounds that "he, being a tallow-chandler, ought to use his trade, which cannot be said to be a nusance." *Id.* at 510, 79 Eng. Rep. at 1040. The King's Bench dismissed the defense. *See also* H. ROLLE, UN ABRIDGMENT DES PLUSIEURS CASES ET RESOLUTIONS DEL COMMON LEY 89, 140-41 (London 1668) (case rejecting utility defence for lead smelting operation).

[93] 12 Mod. 151, 88 Eng. Rep. 1228 (K.B. 1697). *Turberville*, however, was an excellent

lowed this *sic utere tuo* rule carefully. In 1636 a book appeared that was directed precisely at the doctrine. This book, entitled *A Briefe Declaration For What manner of speciall Nusance concerning private dwelling Houses, a man may have his remedy by Assise, or other Action as the Case requires,*[94] collected four much earlier arguments by Mounson, Plowden, Wray, and Manwood,[95] and strongly reemphasized the basic issues set out in *William Aldred's Case.*[96]

Critics of the *sic utere tuo* doctrine have rarely appreciated *William Aldred's Case* and the court's careful attempt to preserve an absolute standard of property security, while disqualifying unreasonable damages.[97] For example, Lord Wright, in the leading

---

example of the gray area between nuisance law and a developing fault doctrine in negligence. The *Turberville* court stated:

> Every man must so use his own as not to injure another. The law is general; the fire which a man makes in the fields is as much his fire as his fire in his house . . . and he must at his peril take care that it does not, through his neglect, injure his neighbour: if he kindle it at a proper time and place, and the violence of the wind carry it into his neighbour's ground, . . . this is fit to be given in evidence. But now here it is found to have been by his negligence . . . .

Id. at 152, 88 Eng. Rep. at 1228-29. *See* C. FIFOOT, *supra* note 21, at 156. Problems of fault in "escape" cases finally led to the complex *Rylands v. Fletcher* doctrine. *See* note 185 and accompanying text *infra*. *See also* Rex v. Rosewell, 2 Salk. 459, 91 Eng. Rep. 397 (K.B. 1699) (self help for wrongfully stopped lights or escaping water).

[94] DECLARATION, *supra* note 46.

[95] The arguments were originally set forth in Hales' Case, [unreported] (c. 1560), *printed in* DECLARATION, *supra* note 46. *Hales' Case* involved windows blocked by city building, and city customs similar to those at issue in Bland v. Moseley, [unreported] (K.B. 1587), *discussed in* note 69 *supra*. Whereas *Bland* arose in York, *Hales' Case* arose in London, "the greatest City, and most populous in this Realme, and the more populous the more honourable, & the more buildings, the more populous and honourable will it be." DECLARATION, *supra* note 46, at 23. The four arguments, two on each side of the case, essentially assume the basic necessity test, later incorporated into the rationale of *William Aldred's Case*.

[96] Mounson stated that: "Therefore who so taketh from man so great a commodity as that which preserveth mans health in his castle, or house, doth in a manner as great wrong as if he deseised him altogether of his Free-hold." DECLARATION, *supra* note 46, at 1-2. Mounson further noted that an owner of property may put his land to productive use subject to the condition that the use not harm anyone else: "The soyle is his owne . . . though it be his owne, he must so use it, that hee hurt not his Neighbour." *Id.* at 2-3. Wray summarized the old rule when he said:

> [F]or by the Common law, one shall not hurt the Freehold of another, and no greater hurt, grievance, or dammage can be done to any mans Freehold, then to take away the light and ayre thereof, which is comfortable & commodious for him, for when this light, and ayre are taken from him, his house remaineth as a dungeon.

Id. at 11.

[97] Courts have made various disparaging comments on the doctrine. *See, e.g.*, Auburn & Cato Plank Rd. Co. v. Douglass, 9 N.Y. 444, 446 (1854) (doctrine only a moral precept

case of *Sedleigh-Denfield v. O'Callaghan,*[98] said of the *sic utere tuo* rule:

> This, like most maxims, is not only lacking in definiteness but is also inaccurate. An occupier may make in many ways a use of his land which causes damage to the neighboring landowners and yet be free from liability. . . . Even where he is liable for a nuisance, the redress may fall short of the damage . . . .[99]

Wright failed to understand that the *sic utere tuo* doctrine was not an isolated maxim meaning that all harms were actionable. It meant that once the plaintiff had established actionable damages (the necessity rule), no injury could be excused by balancing social utilities (the *sic utere tuo* rule).[100] Modern English and American courts forgot this compromise and its rationale.[101]

Blackstone, however, understood the *sic utere tuo* doctrine and used *William Aldred's Case* as authority.[102]

> [I]f one erects a smelting-house for lead so near the land of another that the vapor and smoke kills his corn and grass, and damages his cattle therein, this is held to be a nuisance. . . . [I]f one does any other act, in itself lawful, which yet being done in that place necessarily tends to the damage of another's property, it is a nuisance: for it is incumbent on him to find some other place to do that act where it will be less offensive.[103]

The authoritativeness of Coke's *Reports* and Blackstone's *Commentaries* made the *sic utere tuo* rule almost unquestioned law in England and America for more than two hundred and fifty years after *William Aldred's Case.*[104]

---

and "utterly useless as a legal maxim"); Brand v. Hammersmith & City Ry., L.R. 2 Q.B. 223, 247 (1867) (maxim is "no help to decision, as it cannot be applied till the decision is made"); Bonomi v. Backhouse, E1l.Bl.&E1l. 622, 643, 120 Eng. Rep. 643, 651 (Q.B. 1858) (maxim is "mere verbiage"), *rev'd,* E1l.Bl.&E1l. 646, 120 Eng. Rep. 652 (Ex. Ch. 1859), *aff'd,* 9 H.L.C. 503, 11 Eng. Rep. 825 (1861).

[98] [1940] A.C. 880.

[99] *Id.* at 903.

[100] *See* notes 71-74 and accompanying text *supra.*

[101] *See* notes 105-82 and accompanying text *infra.*

[102] *See, e.g.,* 3 W. BLACKSTONE, COMMENTARIES *216-19.

[103] *Id.* at *217-18.

[104] Authorities generally accorded the rule respect. *See, e.g.,* Tenant v. Goldwin, 2 Ld. Raym. 1089, 1092, 92 Eng. Rep. 222, 224 (K.B. 1705) (Holt, C.J.) ("every one must so use his own, as not to do damage to another"); 8 W. HOLDSWORTH, *supra* note 23, at 470-72.

II

THE BALANCING OF UTILITIES DOCTRINE AND ST. HELEN'S SMELTING CO. v. TIPPING (1865)

The *sic utere tuo* rule prohibiting courts from balancing the social utility of an alleged nuisance against the injury to the plaintiff was not seriously challenged in England until the middle of the nineteenth century.[105] A few American cases adopted a balancing approach, but these decisions were not greatly influential.[106] Indeed, some American jurisdictions retained the *sic utere tuo* rule until as late as 1890.[107] Yet today, the balancing of utilities doctrine is found in nearly every American jurisdiction.[108]

---

[105] *See* M. HORWITZ, *supra* note 83, at 74-78; Brenner, *Nuisance Law and the Industrial Revolution,* 3 J. LEGAL STUD. 403 (1974). According to Brenner, the "case that introduced the change" was Hole v. Barlow, 4 Com.B.(n.s.) 334, 140 Eng. Rep. 1113 (C.P. 1858). Brenner, *supra,* at 410. Brenner expresses his indebtedness to Horwitz for the observation that "[p]art of the decision's logic may have lain in the modern association of nuisance with the action on the case, which was being transformed into an action for negligence." *Id.* at 411 & n.21a. According to Horwitz, it was only after *St. Helen's Smelting* "that the courts began to acknowledge that a process of weighing utilities and not the mere existence of an injury for deciding whether a particular use of land constituted a nuisance." M. HORWITZ, *supra* note 83, at 75.

[106] Horwitz cites Lexington & Ohio R.R. v. Applegate, 38 Ky. (8 Dana) 289 (1839), as an early example of a court balancing utilities. M. HORWITZ, *supra* note 83, at 74-75. But this American case is not cited in 1 F. HARPER & F. JAMES, *supra* note 83, although *St. Helen's Smelting* is so cited. 1 F. HARPER & F. JAMES, *supra* note 83, § 1.24, at 72 n.34.

[107] In that year, the Maryland Court of Appeals stated:

> [The location of the fertilizer factory] may be convenient to the public, but, in the eye of the law, no place can be convenient for the carrying on of a business which is a nuisance, and which causes substantial injury to the property of another. Nor can any use of one's own land be said to be a reasonable use, which deprives an adjoining owner of the lawful use and enjoyment of his property.

Susquehanna Fertilizer Co. v. Malone, 73 Md. 268, 277, 20 A. 900, 901 (1890). The court refused to consider possible loss to the defendant's business.

> The law, in cases of this kind, will not undertake to balance the conveniences, or estimate the difference between the injury sustained by the plaintiff and the loss that may result to the defendant from having its trade and business, as now carried on, found to be a nuisance.

Id. at 282, 20 A. at 902.

[108] *See* 1 F. HARPER & F. JAMES, *supra* note 83, at 73-74; W. PROSSER, *supra* note 21, at 582, 596-602; RESTATEMENT (SECOND) OF TORTS §§ 822 & Comments, 826 & Comment b, 827, 828 (1977). In deciding whether an action is a nuisance and whether it should be enjoined, courts consider many factors. Those usually given the most weight in balancing utilities are the social value of the interests involved, the suitability of the conduct to the locality, and the relative hardship resulting from granting or denying an injunction. *Id.* §§ 826, 936. The social value of the conduct is measured by its benefit to the public. Thus a court may not enjoin the operations of a major defense plant (*see, e.g.,* Pritchett v. Wade, 261 Ala. 156, 73 So. 2d 533 (1954); Heppenstall Co. v. Berkshire Chemical Co., 130 Conn.

The dominance of the balancing of utilities doctrine owes much, both in England and America, to the authority of *St. Helen's Smelting Co. v. Tipping*,[109] the reputed origin of the balancing of utilities rule.[110] Although *St. Helen's Smelting* is cited frequently in English cases[111] and by eminent American authorities[112] as establishing the balancing of utilities rule in the common law doctrine of nuisance, these citations were apparently

---

485, 35 A.2d 845 (1944)) or an industry of great economic importance to the community (*see, e.g.*, Koseris v. J.R. Simplot Co., 82 Idaho 263, 352 P.2d 235 (1960); Riter v. Keokuk Electro-Metals Co., 248 Iowa 710, 82 N.W.2d 151 (1957)).

The factor most often considered decisive by the courts is probably the suitability of the conduct to the locality. *See* Riter v. Keokuk Electro-Metals Co., 248 Iowa 710, 82 N.W.2d 151 (1957) (factory in industrial district not enjoined); Pendoley v. Ferreira, 345 Mass. 309, 187 N.E.2d 142 (1963) (piggery in residential neighborhood enjoined); Mahoney v. Walter, 205 S.E.2d 692 (W. Va. 1974) (auto junkyard in residential neighborhood enjoined). The Iowa court in *Riter* explained that:

> [T]he right of a person to pure air may be surrendered in part by his election to live in a city where the atmosphere is impregnated with smoke, soot and other impurities. These statements are especially applicable to one who elects to live in or adjacent to an industrial district. Moreover, the operation of a lawful industry which would be considered a nuisance in a residential section might not be considered such when conducted in an industrial locality . . . . A fair test as to whether the operation of such industry constitutes a nuisance has been said to be the reasonableness of conducting it in the manner, at the place and under the circumstances in question.

Id. at 721-22, 82 N.W.2d at 158.

The most potentially far-reaching grounds for denying an injunction are the economic burdens placed on the defendant. *See* Koseris v. J.R. Simplot Co., 82 Idaho 263, 352 P.2d 235 (1960); Riter v. Keokuk Electro-Metals Co., 248 Iowa 710, 82 N.W.2d 151 (1957). The strength and importance of this approach today is revealed in the leading case of Boomer v. Atlantic Cement Co., 26 N.Y.2d 219, 257 N.E.2d 870, 309 N.Y.S.2d 312 (1970). The plaintiffs had suffered property damages in excess of $185,000, caused by dust from the defendant's plant. The cement plant was worth $45,000,000 and employed over 300 workers. In relegating the plaintiffs' relief to damages, the court overruled over 80 years of precedent that, given a nuisance, had granted injunctions as a matter of right. The court explained this departure from prior law when it stated that "[t]he ground for the denial of injunction, notwithstanding the finding both that there is a nuisance and that plaintiffs have been damaged substantially, is the large disparity in economic consequences of the nuisance and of the injunction." *Id.* at 223, 257 N.E.2d at 872, 309 N.Y.S.2d at 315. *See also* Spur Indus., Inc. v. Del. E. Webb Dev. Co., 108 Ariz. 178, 494 P.2d 700 (1972).

[109] 11 Eng. Rep. 1483 (H.L. 1865).

[110] *See* J. Fleming, The Law of Torts 404 (5th ed. 1977); G. Fridman, *supra* note 76, at 182-83; 1 F. Harper & F. James, *supra* note 83, § 1.24, at 72 n.34; 3 J. Kent, Commentaries on American Law 595 n.b (12th ed. O.W. Holmes ed. 1873); H. Street, The Law of Torts 216-17, 226-27 (5th ed. 1972).

[111] *See, e.g.*, Halsey v. Esso Petroleum Co., [1961] 1 W.L.R. 683, 689-92 (Q.B.); Salvin v. North Brancepeth Coal Co., [1874] L.R. 9 Ch. 705, 708-10 (Ch. App.); Crossley & Sons, Ltd. v. Lightowler, L.R. 3 Eq. 277, 289 (V.C. 1866).

[112] 1 F. Harper & F. James, *supra* note 83, § 1.24, at 72 n.34; 3 J. Kent, *supra* note 110, at 595 n.b.

made without a careful analysis of the precise holding or peculiar circumstances of the case. Because the premises and value judgments behind *St. Helen's Smelting* have remained largely unexamined, the case bears fresh scrutiny.

A. *Balancing of Utilities Doctrine as Dictum in St. Helen's Smelting*

William Tipping, the owner of Bold Hall Estate, brought the action in August 1863.[113] The plaintiff's pleaded declaration paralleled William Aldred's complaint: the declaration was (1) an action on the case for nuisance,[114] (2) the requested remedy was damages for injury to the beneficial use of land and premises,[115] and (3) the alleged injurious act was the release by the defendants of "noxious vapours" which diffused on to the plaintiff's neighboring land.[116] As in *William Aldred's Case*, the plaintiff initially brought the declaration before the local assizes court for trial by jury.[117] Moreover, the House of Lords faced a similar record on appeal: the jury had found for the plaintiff, the local court had denied a motion for a new trial, and the trial court granted leave to appeal on a point of law.[118]

The facts, however, reflected the passage of the centuries since *William Aldred's Case*, centuries which included the Industrial Revolution. The noxious fumes came not from pigs, but from a major copper smelting works owned by the St. Helen's Smelting Company.[119] The plaintiff's complaint did not focus on the proximity of the defendants' operation, an important factor in *William Aldred's Case*. In fact, the factory was one and a half miles from the plaintiff's estate.[120] William Tipping was also a different kind of plaintiff than William Aldred. Aldred apparently owned a house and a small plot of land.[121] Tipping owned a

---

[113] 11 Eng. Rep. at 1483.

[114] *Id.* Since the introduction of the famous Hilary rules of 1832, new judicial rules written under legislative authority had regulated the main forms of action. However, the final dissolution of the forms came only after the Supreme Court of Judicature Act, 1873, 36 & 37 Vict., c. 66. As *St. Helen's Smelting* shows, courts and practitioners still thought in terms of the old forms of action in 1863.

[115] 11 Eng. Rep. at 1483.

[116] *Id.*

[117] *Id.* at 1483-84.

[118] *Id.* at 1484. The Exchequer Chamber affirmed the jury instructions of Justice Mellor before the defendants appealed to the House of Lords. *Id.*

[119] *Id.* at 1483.

[120] *Id.* at 1486.

[121] 9 Coke at 57b, 77 Eng. Rep. at 816.

manor house and 1,300 acres, described by the judges as "an estate of great value."[122] To Tipping, the awarded damages, £ 361 18s 4 1/2 d, were probably of little financial significance, especially in light of the potential legal fees.[123] Tipping, however, was wealthy enough to pursue economically unreasonable ends. The apparent increase in the cost of legal proceedings between 1611 and 1863 for the average litigant[124] may be one reason why the more modest plaintiffs of the nineteenth century would not usually challenge the Industrial Revolution in the high courts, but would leave it to the Tippings.

The question of law on appeal in *St. Helen's Smelting* concerned a special finding of fact required by the jury instructions given at trial by Justice Mellor. Tipping testified that the vapors from the smelting company extensively damaged his trees and shrubs and bothered occupants on his estate.[125] The defense introduced evidence that its copper works was in business at the time Tipping purchased his property, and that several factories operated in the area so that the defendants' factory did not necessarily cause the damage.[126]

With this evidence before the court, Justice Mellor directed the jury that:

> [E]very man . . . was bound to use his own property *in such a manner as not to injure the property of his neighbors*; . . . that the law did not regard trifling inconveniences; that everything must be looked at from a reasonable point of view; and therefore, in an action for nuisance to property, arising from noxious vapours, the injury to be actionable must be such as *visibly to diminish the value of the property and the comfort and enjoyment of it*. . . . [I]t was

---

[122] 11 Eng. Rep. at 1483, 1486.

[123] *Id.* at 1484. Two years passed between the trial and final disposition on appeal. *Id.* at 1483. Furthermore, for the appeal, Tipping hired at least four lawyers. Three barristers' names appeared in the record. 11 Eng. Rep. at 1486. In addition, Tipping needed at least one solicitor, because only a solicitor could engage a barrister for a client. St. Helen's Smelting Company had hired the Attorney-General as their barrister. 11 Eng. Rep. at 1484.

[124] The cost of legal proceedings appears to have risen significantly over this period, although a scientific study has not been done. *See* H. Kirk, Portrait of a Profession 155-67 (1976); R. Robson, The Attorney in Eighteenth-Century England 28, 41-42 (1959); Prest, *Counsellors' Fees and Earnings in the Age of Sir Edward Coke*, Legal Records and the Historian 165, 174-75 (J. Baker ed. 1978) (fees and earnings for lawyers in Coke's day uncertain and modest). One of the causes was the abolition of local courts in many areas. *See* B. Abel-Smith & R. Stevens, Lawyers and the Courts 12-14 (1967).

[125] 11 Eng. Rep. at 1483, 1484.

[126] *Id.* at 1484.

> clear that in counties where great works had been erected . . . persons must not stand on their extreme rights . . . for if so, the business of the whole country would be seriously interfered with.[127]

Justice Mellor's direction essentially restated the law applied in *William Aldred's Case.* He reiterated the *sic utere tuo* doctrine of injury while limiting damages to what Lord Coke might have called "things of necessity." Yet Justice Mellor's emphasis on concerns over "reasonableness," standing on "extreme rights," and interference with "the business of the whole country" suggests a new judicial mood, a new willingness to compromise absolute principles.

The jury then answered three questions in a special verdict.

> The learned judge . . . did ask the jury whether the enjoyment of the Plaintiff's property was sensibly diminished, and the answer was in the affirmative. Whether the business there carried on was an ordinary business for smelting copper, and the answer was, "We consider it an ordinary business, and conducted in a proper manner, in as good a manner as possible." But to the question whether the jurors thought that it was carried on in a proper place, the answer was "We do not."[128]

The trial court entered judgment, with damages, for Tipping. The defendants unsuccessfully appealed to the Exchequer Chamber, alleging that Justice Mellor had incorrectly instructed the jury,[129] and then sought review in the House of Lords on identical grounds.[130]

The defendants' argument on appeal was simple: the court had misinstructed the jury by failing to instruct that, when a neighborhood is "denaturalised" by industry, "a person who comes into that neighbourhood cannot complain that what was done before he came there is continued."[131] In so arguing, the defendants cited *Hole v. Barlow,*[132] a lower court case, in which Justice Willes had said:

---

[127] *Id.* (emphasis added).

[128] *Id.*

[129] *Id.* In 1865, the Exchequer Chamber was an appellate court and consisted of at least five judges from the Common Pleas and the Exchequer. *See* 1 JOWITT'S DICTIONARY OF ENGLISH LAW 738-39 (2d ed. 1977). It heard important appeals from the Assize Courts regarding alleged errors of law. *See* Law Terms Act, 1830, 1 Will. 4, c. 70, § 8. Appeal lay directly to the House of Lords. The court was abolished by the Supreme Court of Judicature Act, 1873, 36 & 37 Vict., c. 66, pt. 2, § 18(4).

[130] 11 Eng. Rep. at 1484.

[131] *Id.* at 1485.

[132] 4 Com.B.(n.s.) 334, 140 Eng. Rep. 1113 (C.P. 1858).

> The common-law right which every proprietor of a dwelling-house has to have the air uncontaminated and unpolluted, is subject to this qualification, that necessities may arise for an interference with that right pro bono publico, to this extent, that such interference be in respect of a matter essential to the business of life, and be conducted in a reasonable and proper manner, and in a reasonable and proper place.[133]

According to the defendants, because the jury found that the smelting company conducted its business in "as good a manner as possible," the court should have asked the jury whether the surrounding neighborhood had been "denaturalised." By failing to submit such a question to the jury, the defendants argued that the court committed reversible error.[134]

The House of Lords, recognizing the importance of the case, had requested the presence of six "learned judges" from the lower courts.[135] After hearing the defendants' argument, Lord Chancellor Westbury asked the judges if they wished to hear further argument, including that of Tipping's counsel, or if they were ready to answer the Lords' questions regarding the correctness of the jury instructions.[136] The experts and the Lords agreed that the argument for the defendants misstated the law, and that the lower court decision should be upheld.[137]

This was the true holding of *St. Helen's Smelting*. The case explicitly rejected the balancing of utilities doctrine argued by the defendants on appeal. The House of Lords upheld a direction to the jury which, apart from Justice Mellor's casual remarks about standing on "extreme rights," essentially restated the *sic utere tuo* test of *William Aldred's Case*.[138] Undoubtedly, *William Aldred's Case* remained uncited on appeal only because the defendants' lawyers alone submitted argument; the House of Lords did not call for argument by the plaintiff's lawyers.[139]

---

[133] *Id.* at 345, 140 Eng. Rep. at 1118.

[134] 11 Eng. Rep. at 1485-86.

[135] They were Baron Martin, Justice Willes, Justice Blackburn, Justice Keating, Baron Pigott, and Justice Shee. *Id.* at 1484.

[136] *Id.* at 1486.

[137] *Id.*

[138] *See* note 127 and accompanying text *supra*.

[139] The result of *St. Helen's Smelting* disfavored industrial polluters in another way. At trial, defendants' counsel argued that it was impossible to tell how much of the damage to plaintiff's property was caused by its fumes, rather than by fumes produced by other neighboring factories. 11 Eng. Rep. at 1484. Justice Mellor, however, did not instruct the jury to determine how much of the damage was caused by the defendants' plant. Rather he

Many leading authorities have mistakenly cited *St. Helen's Smelting* as supporting the balancing of utilities doctrine,[140] apparently because of the confusing dicta of the case. Lord Westbury was partly to blame for this confusion. He accurately paraphrased the *sic utere tuo* rule and the de minimis limits to damage—found both in Justice Mellor's directions and in *William Aldred's Case*—when he summarized the grounds for the decision in *St. Helen's Smelting*:

> [T]he jurors have found the existence of the injury; and the only ground upon which your Lordships are asked to set aside that verdict, and to direct a new trial, is this, that the whole neighbourhood where these copper smelting works were carried on, is a neighbourhood more or less devoted to manufacturing purposes . . . and therefore it is said, that inasmuch as this copper smelting is carried on in what the Appellant contends is a fit place, it may be carried on with impunity, although the result may be the utter destruction, or the very considerable diminution, of the value of the Plaintiff's property. . . . I apprehend that that is not the meaning of the word "suitable," or the meaning of the word "convenient," which has been used as applicable to the subject. The word "suitable" unquestionably cannot carry with it this consequence, that a trade may be carried on in a particular locality, the consequence of which trade may be injury and destruction to the neighbouring property. Of course . . . I except cases where any prescriptive right has been acquired by a lengthened user of the place.[141]

---

only asked the jury if the use of the plaintiff's land was "sensibly diminished" (11 Eng. Rep. at 1485, 1488), or in the words of an unofficial account of the case, he only required that "the effect of the noxious vapors to a sensible extent can be traced to have come from the [defendants'] works" (12 L.T.R.(n.s.) at 777). The court thus did not force the plaintiff to show "a basis for apportionment of the damage among the various causative factors" as a prerequisite for recovery. *See generally* Katz, *The Function of Tort Liability in Technology Assessment,* 38 U. CIN. L. REV. 587, 619 (1969). Once the *St. Helen's Smelting* jury had found some substantive damage caused by the defendant, it was allowed to assess the amount of damages at its own discretion. The plaintiff apparently satisfied his burden of proof as to causation simply by showing that the defendants' plant produced a significant amount of "vapors" and that the winds commonly blew them across the plaintiff's land. 11 Eng. Rep. at 1183-84. This rule is in harmony with one recent scholarly suggestion. *See* Katz, *supra,* at 618. *Cf.* Ybarra v. Spangard, 25 Cal. 2d 486, 154 P.2d 687 (1944) (application of similar standard of proof of causation to negligence action). This rule essentially forces a defendant to demonstrate the presence of contributory causes once a plaintiff has shown some causation related to that defendant. *See* Katz, *supra,* at 618-20. These rules, if followed today, could significantly aid plaintiffs in pollution cases. *See id.*

[140] *See* notes 110-12 and accompanying text *supra.*

[141] 11 Eng. Rep. at 1487. Lord Westbury's assumption that prescriptive use can legalize a nuisance marks a significant change in nuisance law from the days of the *Year Books. See*

But Lord Westbury then introduced, as pure dictum, a new rule for claims of injury only amounting to mere sensible personal discomfort.[142] He essentially stated that personal sensibilities could never constitute strictly protected "natural rights" of *seisin*, but could be subjected to a balancing of utilities by courts. This qualification severely restricted the necessity test of *William Aldred's Case*, which protected such "personal sensibilities" as sensibility to foul smell.

Lord Wensleydale, in his opinion, did not discuss this distinction between personal sensibilities and material damage. He simply voiced his agreement with the decision below, and quoted Justice Mellor's direction that "the law does not regard trifling and small inconveniences, but only regards sensible inconveniences, injuries which sensibly diminish the comfort, enjoyment, or value of the property which is affected."[143] This was the old and accepted de minimis rule which Justice Mellor emphasized when he said that business could not survive if everyone stood on "extreme rights."[144] But Justice Mellor's directions to the jury were consistent with the necessity test set forth in *William Aldred's Case*. He did not advocate a balancing of utilities rule for either material damage to property or significant discomfort to the senses.

Lord Cranworth's opinion is more ambiguous. He stated that Justice Mellor "could [not] . . . have stated the law . . . better than he has done in this case."[145] Yet he gave a now famous example of an unreported case which he may have intended to support a balancing of utilities test.

---

note 43 and accompanying text *supra* (no easement of "foul smell" obtainable over another's land). According to Simpson, the law of property on this issue was, at some point, confused with the law of torts. A. SIMPSON, *supra* note 41, at 246.

[142] Lord Westbury stated that:

> With regard to . . . personal inconvenience and interference with one's enjoyment, one's quiet, one's personal freedom, anything that discomposes or injuriously affects the senses or the nerves, whether that may or may not be denominated a nuisance, must undoubtedly depend greatly on the circumstances of the place where the thing complained of actually occurs. If a man lives in a town, it is necessary that he should subject himself to the consequences of those operations of trade which may be carried on in his immediate locality, which are actually necessary for trade and commerce, and also for the enjoyment of property, and for the benefit of the inhabitants of the town and of the public at large. . . . But when an occupation . . . [causes] a material injury to property, then there unquestionably arises a very different consideration.

11 Eng. Rep. at 1486.

[143] *Id.* at 1488.

[144] *Id.* at 1484.

[145] *Id.* at 1487.

> [T]here was an action for injury arising from smoke in the town of Shields. It was proved incontestibly that smoke did come and in some degree interfere with a certain person; but I said, "You must look at it not with a view to the question whether, abstractedly, that quantity of smoke was a nuisance, but whether it was a nuisance to a person living in the town of Shields;" because, if it only added in an infinitesimal degree to the quantity of smoke, I held that the state of the town rendered it altogether impossible to call that an actionable nuisance.[146]

It is not clear whether Lord Cranworth found for the defendant in that unreported case because of: (1) the balancing of utilities doctrine, (2) a de minimis amount of damage caused by the defendants' acts, or (3) the difficulty in allocation of damages.[147] Lord Cranworth did not explain why the "state of the town" made it "altogether impossible" to find an actionable nuisance. Only the de minimis defense was consistent with the terms of Justice Mellor's jury instructions, which Lord Cranworth voted to uphold.[148]

Lord Cranworth never mentioned Lord Westbury's distinction between "personal sensibility" and "material injury." Only by making that distinction could Lord Westbury uphold the jury direction in the case at hand, while advocating a balancing of utilities doctrine for different situations. Since Lord Cranworth's opinion lacked this distinction, his approval of Justice Mellor's instructions gives no support to a balancing of utilities doctrine.

Thus, the balancing of utilities doctrine, for which *St. Helen's Smelting* is considered "authority," was:

---

[146] *Id.*

[147] For a discussion of the problem posed by "a defendant whose conduct by itself would cause too slight an interference with the plaintiff's use and enjoyment of his property to amount to nuisance, but whose conduct in fact combines with that of others to constitute a nuisance," see Katz, *supra* note 139, at 618 n.66; W. PROSSER, *supra* note 21, §§ 52, 91, at 322-23, 607-08.

[148] *See* notes 127-39 and accompanying text *supra*. But in Lord Cranworth's day, many courts refused to recognize the de minimis defense for acts harmless on an individual basis when it was clear that the product or conduct of the defendant combined with others to produce a nuisance. *See, e.g.*, Hill v. Smith, 32 Cal. 166, 167-68 (1867) (where defendant contributed to pollution of stream, no defense that his acts alone did not cause material injury); Woodyear v. Schaefer, 57 Md. 1, 9-10 (1881) (defendant-butcher liable for dumping blood into stream, even if his acts were only minor contribution to nuisance); Francis v. Alexander Cowan & Sons, [1866] 5 M. 214, 228-29 (Sess.) (each defendant who materially contributes to pollution of stream liable for nuisance created by all); Lambton v. Mellish, [1894] 3 Ch. 163 (where two or more persons make enough noise to create a nuisance, each individually liable for entire nuisance); W. PROSSER, *supra* note 21, § 52, at 322-23; Katz, *supra* note 139, at 618 n.66.

(1) clearly advocated by only one judge out of three;
(2) restricted even by that judge to "personal sensibilities" with a strict *sic utere tuo* rule retained for "material injury" to property;
(3) not a basis for the decision in the case, because material injury to property was involved; and
(4) absent from the lower court's jury instructions which all three Lords upheld.

In short, the holding of *St. Helen's Smelting* is not precedent for a balancing of utilities doctrine. Except for Lord Westbury's dictum and Lord Cranworth's ambiguous remarks, all of the opinions were clearly consistent with *William Aldred's Case.* Had Tipping's victorious lawyers presented their case, they undoubtedly would have pressed for a ringing and explicit reaffirmance of the *sic utere tuo* rule. But even without such a reaffirmance, *St. Helen's Smelting* did not bury the old rule.

B. *Assessing the Balancing of Utilities Doctrine*

St. Helen's Smelting was the last major House of Lords case to face directly the balancing of utilities issue. Its true holding remains the law of England.[149] In 1961, however, in *Halsey v. Esso Petroleum Co.,*[150] an English court again treated Lord Westbury's dictum as if it were the holding of *St. Helen's Smelting.*[151] This suggests that there might be merit, quite apart from authority, in Lord Westbury's doctrine. But serious analysis can also lead to the conclusion that Lord Westbury's balancing of utilities test reflected social values unacceptable in a modern democracy, and that Lord Westbury's doctrine, in practice, has protected the sensibilities of the wealthy Tippings of the world, while condemning the poor to damned cities like Lord Cranworth's Shields.

The unfairness of Lord Westbury's doctrine becomes clear when contrasted with *William Aldred's Case.* The *sic utere tuo* rule, unlike the balancing of utilities doctrine, assured the little man that he had inalienable rights of property. While these rights did

---

[149] *See* CLERK & LINDSELL, *supra* note 82, ¶ 1433, at 809.

[150] [1961] 1 W.L.R. 683 (Q.B.).

[151] *Id.* at 689-90. In holding the defendants liable, the court applied Lord Westbury's distinction between injury to property and damage to personal sensibilities. *Id.* at 691. In considering the issue of liability, the court considered the character of the neighborhood and balanced the rights of the plaintiff and the defendant. *Id.* at 691-93. Balancing, however, played no role in the court's computation of damages following its finding of liability. *Id.* at 702-03.

not include protection from every inconvenience to use of property, they did extend to those things necessary for a decent existence on his property. Such necessities included not only the integrity of his physical premises, but of his basic sensibilities as well. Under the traditional common law *sic utere tuo* doctrine, a man with some stake in property, even just a lease, had individual rights which neither big industrial users nor pig keepers could violate without lawful compensation.

This old common law doctrine was decent and humane compared to the hardened attitudes of the nineteenth century. The balancing of utilities doctrine advocated by Lord Westbury permitted the industrial user to externalize the costs of his pollution. Such a legal doctrine offered no economic incentive for the active user of property to develop technology that would prevent such side effects. This doctrine, combined with the inaccessibility and cost of legal remedy, left industry free to ravage the northern English cities, including Tipping's Liverpool.[152] It was an unjust way of forcing public investment in industrial growth, regardless of how desirable that investment might have seemed.

C. *Return of the Sic Utere Tuo Rule*

The balancing of utilities doctrine remains the established law in America.[153] But there have been faint signs of a return to the *sic utere tuo* rule. In *Morgan v. High Penn Oil Co.*,[154] the North Carolina Supreme Court confronted a situation similar to those in *William Aldred's Case* and *St. Helen's Smelting*. The defendant's refinery emitted "noxious gases and odors," which restricted the use of the plaintiff's land.[155] The defendant argued that it operated a lawful, socially useful enterprise which should not be subject to liability if "operated properly."[156]

Judge Ervin, writing for the court, rejected the defendant's argument of social utility and supported his decision with the ancient doctrine.

[152] The placement of liability for pollution and other social costs will influence wealth distribution and allocational efficiency. *See* Baker, *The Ideology of the Economic Analysis of Law*, 5 PHILOSOPHY & PUB. AFF. 3 (1975); Calabresi & Melamed, *Property Rules, Liability Rules, and Inalienability: One View of the Cathedral*, 85 HARV. L. REV. 1089, 1093-96 (1972). Horwitz emphasized this point in his analysis of American legal history. *See Introduction* to M. HORWITZ, *supra* note 83, at xvi-xvii.

[153] *See* RESTATEMENT (SECOND) OF TORTS §§ 822, 828-31 (1977); 1 F. HARPER & F. JAMES, *supra* note 83, § 1.25, at 75.

[154] 238 N.C. 185, 77 S.E.2d 682 (1953).

[155] *Id.* at 194-95, 77 S.E.2d at 690.

[156] *Id.* at 191, 77 S.E.2d at 687.

> The law of private nuisance rests on the concept embodied in the ancient legal maxim *Sic utere tuo ut alienum non laedas,* meaning, in essence, that every person should so use his own property as not to injure that of another. . . . As a consequence, a private nuisance exists in a legal sense when one makes an improper use of his own property and in that way injures the land or some incorporeal right of one's neighbor. . . .
>
> . . . [A]ny substantial non-trespassory invasion of another's interest in the private use and enjoyment of land by any type of liability forming conduct is a private nuisance.[157]

Judge Ervin qualified this accurate restatement of the *sic utere tuo* doctrine by adding a "reasonableness" test:

> [T]he invasion which subjects a person to liability for private nuisance may be either intentional or unintentional; . . . a person is subject to liability for an intentional invasion when his conduct is unreasonable under the circumstances of the particular case; and . . . a person is subject to liability for an unintentional invasion when his conduct is negligent, reckless or ultrahazardous.[158]

Judge Ervin never clarified this reasonableness test. Although it might merely be a disguised balancing of utilities test, it could also comprise a modern version of Coke's doctrine. Coke limited liability to circumstances where the defendant's actions damaged things of necessity.[159] Whether a nuisance was actionable turned on the presence of such damage. Judge Ervin's statements in *Morgan* could support a similar test which focuses, not on the social utility of the defendant's activities, but rather on the nature of the defendant's interference with his neighbor's property. Under such a test, any act that damages a thing of necessity to a neighbor would be unreasonable and comprise an actionable nuisance.

Judge Ervin also encountered a pitfall unique to American nuisance law—a requirement of negligent or intentional damage.[160] English courts never required fault for nuisances because

---

[157] *Id.* at 193, 77 S.E.2d at 689.

[158] *Id.*, 77 S.E.2d at 689.

[159] *See* notes 68-77 and accompanying text *supra.*

[160] *See generally* note 83 and accompanying text *supra.* In addition to a possible misunderstanding of the imported English pleadings (*see* note 83 and accompanying text *supra*), the American requirement of fault may have arisen because of a desire to promote industry in the nineteenth century (*see* M. HORWITZ, *supra* note 83, at 74-78, 102), or the influence of Bentham's concepts of individualism (*see* R. POUND, THE FORMATIVE ERA OF AMERICAN LAW 50-57 (1938)) or a combination of these factors.

they historically used nuisance law to allocate property rights between two persons engaged in lawful pursuits.[161] The American requirement of fault ignored the history of and the rationale for nuisance as a distinct action. Trespass or negligence can redress intentional or negligent injuries to property.[162] To retain a separate function, nuisance must offer specific guidelines of property protection when all of the conflicting parties are acting in good faith and with reasonable care.[163]

Judge Ervin attempted to solve this problem by eliminating the fault test from intentional nuisance, and then defining "intentional" so broadly as to cover almost any continuous invasion of property rights.

> An invasion of another's interest in the use and enjoyment of land is intentional in the law of private nuisance when the person whose conduct is in question as a basis for liability acts for the purpose of causing it, or knows that it is resulting from his conduct, or knows that it is substantially certain to result from his conduct. . . . A person who intentionally creates or maintains a private nuisance is liable for the resulting injury to others regardless of the degree of care or skill exercised by him to avoid such injury.[164]

His formulation minimizes the role of fault when private ownership interests conflict.[165] Judge Ervin chose this course because only a *sic utere tuo* standard, based objectively on the type and degree of property interference, avoids arbitrariness where one legitimate business conflicts with the operation of another legitimate business. In such cases, the judge's discretion should be lim-

---

[161] CLERK & LINDSELL, *supra* note 82, ¶¶ 1393-94, at 781-84. English courts originally adopted this position because the assize of nuisance was fully developed as a legal remedy long before fault first began to appear as a requirement in any part of the law including trespass to the person. *See* Weaver v. Ward, 1 Hob. 134, 80 Eng. Rep. 284 (K.B. 1616); W. PROSSER, *supra* note 21, § 29, at 141-42; W. PROSSER, J. WADE & V. SCHWARTZ, CASES AND MATERIALS ON TORTS 5 (6th ed. 1976).

[162] All that would be required is an extension of trespass to include intangible invasions as well as tangible physical invasions. *See generally* 1 F. HARPER & F. JAMES, *supra* note 83, § 1.23, at 67.

[163] *See generally* C. HAAR, *supra* note 19, at 124-25; Beuscher & Morrison, *Judicial Zoning Through Recent Nuisance Cases*, 1955 WIS. L. REV. 440.

[164] 238 N.C. at 194, 77 S.E.2d at 689. *See* RESTATEMENT (SECOND) OF TORTS § 825 (1977).

[165] In addition, Judge Ervin classified some nuisances as actionable per se even without proof of damages to things of necessity. 238 N.C. at 191, 77 S.E.2d at 687. His classification extends to only a few public nuisances, such as houses of prostitution. *See* Tedescki v. Berger, 150 Ala. 649, 43 So. 960 (1907).

ited to the question of substantial damage to things of necessity. This limitation gives precision to Judge Ervin's otherwise circular definition. This reading also coincides with the clear historical meaning of the *sic utere tuo* doctrine which Judge Ervin cites as his authority.

Such a rule leaves the defendant with several options after a court finds that a nuisance exists. He can, unless the court issues an injunction, continue his operations following payment of damages.[166] He can, in any event, buy the plaintiff's property or acquire the plaintiff's permission to continue his operations. He can always move elsewhere. If a plaintiff demands too great a price and the defendant does not wish to move, he may request eminent domain power from the legislature.[167] But the defendant

---

[166] *See* Boomer v. Atlantic Cement Co., 26 N.Y.2d 219, 257 N.E.2d 870, 309 N.Y.S.2d 312 (1970) (where defendant has investment of over $45,000,000, employs over 300 persons, and cannot correct dust pollution, injunction will be stayed upon payment of permanent damages).

[167] Many nuisances are active, continuing interferences with land use. The wrong continues day-to-day. That earlier tortfeasors may have avoided the cost of such active interference with property use is no reason why the present victim should have no remedy at all, at least for continuing physical interferences with property. This is particularly true because, by the historical development of delegated eminent domain powers, passive property users may be forced to sell out to a socially important, private enterprise at a "fair price" if a legislature agrees, and if the price can survive a court challenge. *See* Berman v. Parker, 348 U.S. 26 (1954); Strickley v. Highland Boy Gold Mining Co., 200 U.S. 527 (1906). *See also* Sax, *Takings and the Police Power*, 74 YALE L.J. 36 (1964); Scheiber, *The Road to* Munn: *Eminent Domain and the Concept of Public Purpose in the State Courts*, 5 PERSPECTIVES IN AMERICAN HISTORY 329 (1971); Comment, *Land Use Regulation and the Concept of Takings in Nineteenth Century America*, 40 U. CHI. L. REV. 854 (1973). *Cf.* M. HORWITZ, *supra* note 83, at 63-66 (eminent domain power used to promote cheap economic development prior to the establishment of the principle of fair compensation). In determining this price, actual purchase prices are always considered, although other factors, including the owner's rights to prevent wrongful interferences with his property, are also considered.

> The ultimate evil of a deprivation of property, or better, a frustration of property rights . . . is that it forces the owner to assume the cost of providing a benefit to the public without recoupment. There is no attempt to share the cost of the benefit among those benefited, that is, society at large. Instead, the accident of ownership determines who shall bear the cost initially. Of course, as further consequence, the ultimate economic cost of providing the benefit is hidden from those who in a democratic society are given the power of deciding whether or not they wish to obtain the benefit despite the ultimate economic cost, however initially distributed. . . . When [the cost is] successfully concealed, the public is not likely to have objection to the "cost-free" benefit.

Fred. F. French Investing Co. v. City of New York, 39 N.Y.2d 587, 596-97, 350 N.E.2d 381, 387, 385 N.Y.S.2d 5, 11 (1976) (citation omitted).

With appropriate "fair price" safeguards, windfall profits will be uncommon. For a discussion of windfall profits, see Comment, *Internalizing Externalities: Nuisance Law and Economic Efficiency*, 53 N.Y.U. L. REV. 219, 230 (1978). What is unacceptable is de facto expropriation of property rights without any attempt to compensate or to obtain legislative

cannot substantially deprive other property owners of things necessary to the enjoyment of their land without compensation. The *sic utere tuo* rule assures the passive property owner that changes in surrounding land and environment, including those that are beyond his control will not erode his rights. Before *St. Helen's Smelting*, all property owners, including small leaseholders, possessed such rights. Even accepting Lord Westbury's dictum as to personal sensibility, this position remains good law in England when material damage to property occurs.[168]

D. *Extension of the Balancing of Utilities Doctrine*

The common misunderstanding of the *St. Helen's Smelting* holding may be extended further. Professor Street has implied that nuisance law requires a balancing of utilities even for cases of physical injury.[169] Street observed that the other judges in *St. Helen's Smelting* did not support Westbury's dictum distinguishing between physical injuries and harms to only the sensibilities.[170] From this lack of support Street draws his conclusion that a balancing test was meant to apply to both types of damages. A more logical conclusion, however, is that the majority favored the old *sic utere tuo* rule. Moreover, Street's analysis is contradicted by the words of the other judges,[171] and is also entirely inconsistent with Justice Mellor's directions to the jury,[172] the very directions the Lords approved.[173] In addition, none of the lords or judges, except Lord Westbury in his isolated dictum concerning personal sensibility,[174] indicated that he was modifying prior doctrine—a

approval; that is a legacy inherent in the "balancing of utilities." Legal tests turning on economic welfare maximization are legacies that favor "the claimant of the right whose use is productive over one whose use is consumptive" and "the rich claimant whose use is consumptive over the poor claimant whose use is consumptive." Baker, *supra* note 152, at 9 (emphasis omitted). For extensive discussions, see Rice, *Pollution as a Nuisance: Problems, Prospects, and Proposals*, 34 J. AM. TRIAL LAW. A. 202 (1972); Note, *Nuisance Damages as an Alternative to Compensation of Land Use Restrictions in Eminent Domain*, 47 S. CAL. L. REV. 998 (1974); Note, *An Economic Analysis of Land Use Conflicts*, 21 STAN. L. REV. 293 (1969); Note, *The Cost-Internalization Case for Class Actions*, 21 STAN. L. REV. 383 (1969); Michelman, Book Review, 80 YALE L.J. 647 (1971).

[168] *See* Halsey v. Esso Petroleum Co., [1961] 1 W.L.R. 683, 691 (Q.B.); CLERK & LINDSELL, *supra* note 82, ¶ 1394, at 783-84.

[169] H. STREET, *supra* note 110, at 221-27.

[170] *Id.* at 226.

[171] *See* text accompanying notes 143-46 *supra*.

[172] *See* text accompanying note 128 *supra*.

[173] *See* text accompanying notes 127-39 *supra*.

[174] *See* text accompanying note 142 *supra*.

course of conduct that normally accompanies a major change in the law, such as the introduction of a balancing of utilities test to nineteenth century England.[175] Extending the balancing test would not only frustrate the true holding of *St. Helen's Smelting*, but also would ignore the long and rational development of the *sic utere tuo* doctrine.

E. *Future of the Sic Utere Tuo Rule*

In light of the predominance of the balancing of utilities test, the future of the *sic utere tuo* rule seems dim.[176] Although *William Aldred's Case* is still widely cited, courts often focus on its limitation of damage to things of necessity, and ignore its most important holding—its refusal to balance utilities.[177] This unwarranted rejection of the *sic utere tuo* rule shows an unwillingness to go behind the confusion of *St. Helen's Smelting* and reconsider afresh the

---

[175] *See* text accompanying notes 143-48 *supra*.

[176] Indeed, the spirit of Lord Cranworth's Shields, the "denaturalised" neighborhood, lives on. Thus in Riter v. Keokuk Electro-Metals Co., 248 Iowa 710, 82 N.W.2d 151 (1957), the court stated:

> Many authorities point out that the right of a person to pure air may be surrendered in part by his election to live in a city where the atmosphere is impregnated with smoke, soot and other impurities. These statements are especially applicable to one who elects to live in or adjacent to an industrial district. Moreover, the operation of a lawful industry which would be considered a nuisance in a residential section might not be considered such when conducted in an industrial locality.

Id. at 721, 82 N.W.2d at 158.

[177] *See, e.g.*, J. FLEMING, *supra* note 110, at 400 & n.6, 592 & n.20. *But see* CLERK & LINDSELL, *supra* note 82, ¶ 1434, at 809 & n.34. *William Aldred's Case* is also cited widely for the proposition that an odor can constitute a nuisance. *See* CLERK & LINDSELL, *supra* note 82, ¶¶ 1393, 1402, at 783 & n.21, 788 & n.59; 1 F. HARPER & F. JAMES, *supra* note 83, § 1.26, at 78; W. PROSSER, *supra* note 21, § 89, at 592 & n.22.

Unfortunately, many modern courts have exhibited only a very general understanding of the *sic utere tuo* principle. Often courts mention it in support of a duty to exercise ordinary care. *See, e.g.*, Reynolds Metals Co. v. Thompson, 381 S.W.2d 536 (Ky. 1964) (duty to use ordinary care in performance of any dangerous act which might endanger others); Hayes v. Malkan, 26 N.Y.2d 295, 258 N.E.2d 695, 310 N.Y.S.2d 281 (1970) (dissenting opinion, Fuld, C.J.) (duty to use reasonable care prohibits utility from placing utility pole dangerously close to highway). One court has stretched the maxim's concept of responsibility to others so far as to find that it contains the basis for no-fault insurance legislation. *See* Shavers v. Attorney General, 402 Mich. 554, 267 N.W.2d 72 (1978). Another court has extended the meaning of the maxim even further in using it to support the notion that a property owner does not have the right to prevent entry on to his land by an entrant seeking to contact the owner's employees for their benefit. *See* State v. Shack, 58 N.J. 297, 277 A.2d 369 (1971). Such loose uses of the maxim only confuse the law. Used as a general rule, the maxim is nearly devoid of content. The *sic utere tuo* doctrine's fullest utility can be realized only if courts understand that its meaning is largely tied to its historical context and origins.

merits of the original doctrine. Only within the context of *William Aldred's Case* does the *sic utere tuo* doctrine become more than an empty maxim.

More courts faced with cases like *Morgan v. High Penn Oil Co.* should give the experience of their own past a fair hearing.[178] They would do well to compare the wise formula set forth in *William Aldred's Case*[179] with the unspoken economic assumptions of

---

[178] The requirement of damage to things of necessity combines objectivity with limited judicial discretion. *See* notes 68-70 and accompanying text *supra*. In Walter v. Selfe, 4 De G. & Sm. 315, 64 Eng. Rep. 849 (Ch. 1851), Vice Chancellor Bruce described the standard:

> [T]his inconvenience [ought] to be considered in fact as more than fanciful, more than one of mere delicacy of fastidiousness, as an inconvenience materially interfering with the ordinary comfort physically of human existence, not merely according to elegant or dainty modes and habits of living, but according to plain and sober and simple notions among the English people?

Id. at 322, 64 Eng. Rep. at 852. *Accord*, Fleming v. Hislop, 11 App. Cas. 686, 691, 697 (1886).

[179] Indeed some jurisdictions explicitly reject the balancing of utilities test. *See*, Jost v. Dairyland Power Coop., 45 Wis.2d 164, 172 N.W.2d 647 (1969).

> While there are some jurisdictions that permit the balancing of the utility of the offending conduct against the gravity of the injury inflicted, it is clear that the rule, permitting such balancing, is not approved in Wisconsin where the action is for damages. We said in Pennoyer v. Allen . . . :
>
> "When such comfort and enjoyment are so impaired, and compensation is demanded, it is no defense to show that such business was conducted in a reasonable and proper manner, and with more than ordinary cleanliness, and that the odors so sent over and upon such adjacent premises were only such as were incident to the business when properly conducted. It is the interruption of such enjoyment and the destruction of such comfort that furnishes the ground of action, and it is no satisfaction to the injured party to be informed that it might have been done with more aggravation. The business is lawful; but such interruption and destruction is an invasion of private rights, and to that extent unlawful. It is not so much the manner of doing as the proximity of such a business to the adjacent occupant which causes the annoyance. A business necessarily contaminating the atmosphere to the extent indicated should be located where it will not necessarily deprive others of the enjoyment of their property, or lessen their comfort while occupying the same."
>
> In Dolata v. Berthelet Fuel & Supply Co. . . ., relying on *Pennoyer*, this court concluded that even though a coal yard was operated properly, nevertheless, it, a socially and economically useful business, would be abated if it caused substantial damage to the adjoining plaintiff.

Id. at 174, 172 N.W.2d at 652 (citations omitted). The *Jost* court continued:

> We adhere to the rule of *Pennoyer v. Allen*. Although written in 1883, we believe it remains completely applicable under modern conditions. We conclude that injuries caused by air pollution or other nuisance must be compensated irrespective of the utility of the offending conduct as compared to the injury. Nor do we imply that a different rule should apply where the remedy sought is abatement rather than damages. That point is not considered herein. We consider that the rule of *Dolata* continues to be the law in Wisconsin where the action is for abatement.

Id. at 177, 172 N.W.2d at 654.

the balancing of utilities doctrine. The *sic utere tuo* doctrine has never had a record of obstructing economic growth.[180] Furthermore, the judicial discretion favored by the balancing of utilities doctrine has the potential of being equally obstructionist and, in certain instances, has actually been used to block socially desirable developments solely on aesthetic or psychological grounds.[181] Balancing utilities gives the courts too much discretion to evade the democratic process and principles of fair compensation. The rule in *William Aldred's Case* most fully protects these values, while encouraging economic rationality.[182]

III
THE RES COMMUNES DOCTRINE: ILLINOIS CENTRAL RAILROAD V. ILLINOIS (1892)

The greatest historical limit on the *sic utere tuo* rule's operation has been the requirement that the plaintiff possess an injured private real property interest.[183] This prerequisite severely curtails the doctrine's modern utility.[184] Many persons have no in-

---

[180] Rather, it has never been given a fair trial in modern society. "Only in the twentieth century did official and formal nuisance doctrine incorporate a balancing test." M. HORWITZ, *supra* note 83, at 293 n.73. But, as Horwitz points out, the *sic utere tuo* doctrine was substantially evaded earlier, leaving the question of its true effects, if rigorously applied, unanswered and unanswerable. *See id.* at 74-78. *See also* Brenner, *Nuisance Law and the Industrial Revolution,* 3 J. LEGAL STUD. 403, 431-33 (1974); Kurtz, *Nineteenth Century Anti-Enterpreneurial Nuisance Injunctions—Avoiding the Chancellor,* 17 WM. & MARY L. REV. 621, 670 (1976); Laitos, *The Social and Economic Roots of Judge-Made Air Pollution Policy in Wisconsin,* 58 MARQ. L. REV. 465, 466-74, 514-15 (1975).

[181] *See* Everett v. Paschall, 61 Wash. 47, 111 P. 879 (1910) (injunction granted against tuberculosis sanitarium which depressed land values); Managers of the Metro. Asylum Dist. v. Hill, 6 App. Cas. 193 (1881) (injunction granted against hospital for smallpox and other contagious diseases). *But see* Shuttleworth v. Vancouver Gen. Hosp., [1927] 2 D.L.R. 573 (Can.) (damages denied landowner near hospital even though presence of communicable diseases decreased land values).

[182] *See* note 167 *supra.*

[183] *See* text accompanying notes 40-41 *supra.*

[184] It is beyond the scope of this Article to discuss the limitations of modern private nuisance doctrine. A substantial body of literature on the subject exists. *See, e.g.*, Chaffee, *supra* note 35, at 394-400; Ellickson, *Alternatives to Zoning: Convenants, Nuisance Rules, and Fines as Land Use Controls,* 40 U. CHI. L. REV. 681 (1973); Juergensmeyer, *Control of Air Pollution Through the Assertion of Private Rights,* 1967 DUKE L.J. 1126; Katz, *supra* note 139, at 606-22, 641-45; Laitos, *The Social and Economic Roots of Judge-Made Air Pollution Policy in Wisconsin,* 58 MARQ. L. REV. 465 (1975); Larremore, *Public Aesthetics,* 20 HARV. L. REV. 35, 40-45 (1906); McCormick, *Damages for Anticipated Injury to Land,* 37 HARV. L. REV. 574 (1924); Newark, *supra* note 19, at 485-90; Rheingold, *Civil Cause of Action for Lung Damage Due to Pollution of Urban Atmosphere,* 33 BROOKLYN L. REV. 17, 24-26 (1966); Rice, *supra* note 167; Warren, *Nuisance Law as an Environmental Tool,* 7 WAKE FOREST L. REV. 211 (1971);

terest in real property other than short term leases, and almost everyone spends considerable time at work or leisure away from his property in which he has an interest. Traditional private nuisance law offers no protection in these situations. Furthermore, the alternative tort doctrines—negligence, public nuisance, trespass, and the rule of *Rylands v. Fletcher*—cannot by themselves protect against all wrongful infliction of injury through the use of property, particularly by air and water pollution.[185] But a fifth common law doctrine can assist private citizens in solving these problems, and that is the ancient property law doctrine of *res communes*.

The *res communes* doctrine provides that some forms of property are legally incapable of exclusive ownership. Instead, the commonalty[186]—the people collectively—own them. Such owner-

---

Winfield, *supra* note 39 (private nuisance, negligence, and trespass compared and contrasted); Note, *Exemplary Damages in the Law of Torts*, 70 HARV. L. REV. 517, 517-24 (1957) (limitation on damages as remedy); Note, *Nuisance Damages as an Alternative to Compensation of Land Use Restrictions in Eminent Domain*, 47 S. CAL. L. REV. 998 (1974).

[185] Negligence, of course, requires proof of carelessness (*see* 2 F. HARPER & F. JAMES, *supra* note 83, § 16.1, at 896-902), and trespass, in most jurisdictions, requires an element of intent or fault (*see* 1 *id.* § 1.4, at 11-16). But the damaging infliction of external costs can be unintentional and unavoidable, despite due care. *See* Wright v. Masonite Corp. 368 F.2d 661 (4th Cir. 1966) ("no negligence" and "invasion . . . unintentional" in harmful release of formaldehyde gas); Juergensmeyer, *supra* note 184, at 1138-48; 62 HARV. L. REV. 704, 704-06 (1949).

Public nuisance requires proof of "special damage" in the use of a public right, a very serious historical hurdle. *See* Bryson & Macbeth, *Public Nuisance, the Restatement (Second) of Torts, and Environmental Law*, 2 ECOLOGY L.Q. 241, 250-64 (1972). For an analysis of the use of public nuisance doctrine in nineteenth century American law to defeat private damage remedies and "to extend to private companies virtually the same immunity from law suits that the state received under the theory of consequential damages," see M. HORWITZ, *supra* note 83, at 76-78.

The *Rylands v. Fletcher* doctrine, if it ever really was relevant to injury beyond private real property interests, is now being brought back "closer to [private] nuisance." H. STREET, *supra* note 110, at 255.

> The doctrine of *Rylands v. Fletcher* . . . derives from . . . [the] mutual duties of . . . neighbouring landowners and its congeners are trespass and nuisance. If its foundation is to be found in the injunction sic utere tuo ut alienum non laedas, then it is manifest that it has nothing to do with personal injuries.

Read v. Lyons, [1947] A.C. 156, 173. For a discussion of the development of §§ 519 and 520 of the RESTATEMENT (SECOND) OF TORTS (Tent. Draft No. 10, 1964) (abnormally dangerous activities), see Katz, *supra* note 139, at 643-44. That author wisely saw the role of strict liability for abnormal activities in technology assessment as being more limited than that of historical private nuisance doctrine. *Id.* at 645.

[186] In the common law, the "commune" or the "commonalty" meant "the people of the whole realm" or "all the Kings subjects," as opposed to the King, the nobles, or the "commons" in Parliament. E. COKE, THE SECOND PART OF THE INSTITUTES OF THE LAWS OF ENGLAND *539.

ship differs from state sovereignty and state ownership in fee, although the state often holds the title in trust for the beneficial ownership interests of the people. In Rome, England, and America, the doctrine has regulated the use of property by both state and private owners. Although not a theory of tort liability, *res communes* as a doctrine of ownership allows for an extension of tort theory to protect commonly-owned property and property rights.

A. *Roman Law and English Law*

The doctrine of *res communes* originated in Roman law. Although the concept of nonexclusive ownership is found scattered among the writings of several classical Roman jurists, as preserved in the great *Digest*,[187] the fame of *res communes* among English lawyers probably derived from a passage in Justinian's *Institutes*:[188] "By natural law, these things are the common property of all: air, running water, the sea, and with it the shores of the sea."[189]

The common definition of *res communes* today is "[t]hose things which, though a separate share of them can be enjoyed and used by everyone, cannot be exclusively and wholly appropriated;

> [F]or this word *commune* and *comminaltie:* so as [*a le commune*] here signifieth not to the commons of the realm, but to the people of the whole realm; and herewith agreeth our books, that for a common nusance, which concerns *Le commune, ou le comminaltie, le suit serr' done au roy,* where [commune] and [comminaltie] include all the kings subjects.

Id. See 1 JOWITT'S DICTIONARY OF ENGLISH LAW 394 (2d ed. 1977). The expression was later used to describe, rationally enough, the body of any society or corporation, as distinguished from its officers. *See* BLACK'S LAW DICTIONARY 347 (4th ed. 1951).

[187] *See* DIGEST 1.8.2, 1.8.4, 1.8.5, 1.8.6, 18.1.6, 41.1.14, 41.1.15, 41.1.50, 43.7.1, 43.7.2, 43.8.1, 43.8.2, 43.8.3, 43.8.4, 43.8.5, 43.8.6, 43.8.7, 43.12.1, 43.12.3, 43.13.1, 43.14.1, 43.15.1. One of the earliest Roman references to nonexclusive ownership is in the INSTITUTES OF GAIUS 2.1, 2.10, 2.11. Gaius' treatment of ownership doctrine was, however, in this respect simplistic. "All he does is to divide *res humani iuris* [things subject to human right] into *publicae* and *privatae.* He fails to mention the interesting category of *res communes.*" F. DE ZULUETA, THE INSTITUTES OF GAIUS pt. 2, at 56 (1953) (footnote omitted). Cebus and Pomponius, writing even before Gaius, in the period 80-129 (*id.* at x), also had distinguished between things which could be subject to private ownership and things which, because of their "permanent appropriation to public uses," were not so subject (*id.* at 56). This included property and places "such as are not the object of commerce, but are public property, which, while they do not absolutely belong to the people, are used for public purposes, as, for instance, the Campus Martius." DIGEST 18.1.6 (Pomponius).

[188] H. JOLOWICZ, HISTORICAL INTRODUCTION TO THE STUDY OF ROMAN LAW 502-03 (2d ed. 1954). Although the *Institutes* were designed to be an "introductory text-book" for students, "they have themselves the validity of an imperial statute." *Id.* at 502.

[189] INSTITUTES 2.1.1 (author's translation).

as, light, air, running water."[190] The words as originally used in Roman law referred to any common property, "[t]hings belonging to two or more owners (co-owners, co-heirs) as a common property."[191] Things which were " 'by natural law . . . the common property of all men' " were called, by the Romans, *res communes omnium*.[192]

In fact, the Roman texts, as transmitted and editorialized by the Byzantine compilers of the Emperor Justinian, never defined *res communes omnium* as clearly as the modern usage. The fertile Roman juristic intelligence had created four other conceptual categories of "things" capable of nonexclusive ownership or incapable of ownership: *res universitatis*,[193] *res sacrae* or *religiosae*,[194]

---

[190] 3 BOUVIER'S LAW DICTIONARY 2905 (3d rev. 8th ed. 1914). *See* BLACK'S LAW DICTIONARY 1469 (4th ed. 1951); 2 C. SHERMAN, ROMAN LAW IN THE MODERN WORLD 140-41 (3d ed. 1937). In recent American cases the concept is usually discussed in the context of the residual Spanish civil law ideas in Texas and California. *See, e.g.*, Luttes v. State, 159 Tex. 500, 525-26, 324 S.W.2d 167, 182 (1958).

[191] A. BERGER, ENCYCLOPEDIC DICTIONARY OF ROMAN LAW 677 (1953). *See also* CODE 4.52, 8.20.

[192] A. BERGER, *supra* note 191, at 677 (quoting DIGEST 1.8.2.pr., 1.8.2.1 (Marcianus)). According to Buckland, "[t]he conception of *res communes omnium* is late. It may be due to Marcian, but is sometimes held to be Byzantine." W. BUCKLAND, A TEXT-BOOK OF ROMAN LAW FROM AUGUSTUS TO JUSTINIAN 182 n.9 (3d ed. P. Stein rev. 1963). Marcian, a good deal of whose writing was preserved in the *Digest*, lived in the first half of the third century A.D. *See* A. BERGER, *supra* note 191, at 578; H. ROBY, AN INTRODUCTION TO THE STUDY OF JUSTINIAN'S DIGEST at cciv-ccv (1884).

[193] *Res universitatis* were things "belonging to a corporate body, not to individuals" such as "theatres, race-courses, and other similar places belonging in common to a whole city." INSTITUTES 2.1.6. *See also* DIGEST 1.8.6.1. The concept of *res universitatis* is the closest Roman analogy to ordinary modern ownership by a state or state entity. *See generally* T. SANDARS, THE INSTITUTES OF JUSTINIAN 160 (1876).

[194] *Res sacrae* or *religiosae* were "duly consecrated by pontiffs, as sacred buildings and offerings, properly dedicated to the service of God, which we have forbidden by our constitution to be sold or mortgaged, except for the purpose of purchasing the freedom of captives." INSTITUTES 2.1.8. *See* DIGEST 1.8.1, 1.8.8, 1.8.9, 18.1.6, 43.8.2.19. *See also* W. BUCKLAND, *supra* note 192, at 183-84. The walls and gates of a city were also subject to special protection and called *res sanctae*. *See* DIGEST 1.8.11; INSTITUTES 2.1.10; INSTITUTES OF GAIUS 2.8; W. BUCKLAND, *supra* note 192, at 184.

[195] *Res publicae* were things "common to all men" such as rivers and ports. INSTITUTES 2.1.2. *See* DIGEST 1.8.6.1, 18.1.6, 43.7.1, 43.8.2, 43.8.5, 43.8.6, 43.8.7, 43.12.1, 43.12.3, 43.13.1, 43.14.1, 43.15.1. "The word *publicus* is sometimes used as equivalent to *communis*, but is properly used, as here, for what belongs to. . . . a particular people, but may be used and enjoyed by all men." T. SANDARS, *supra* note 193, at 158. The concepts of *res communes* and *res publicae* actually were very similar. W. BUCKLAND, *supra* note 192, at 184-85. But *res publicae* carried the additional implication of state ownership of the concerned property. *See id.* at 183, 185 n.1. *Res publicae* constituted "[p]ublic property such as theatres, market places, rivers, harbors, etc. . . . On the contrary RES COMMUNES OMNIUM were not considered property of the Roman people although their use was accessible to all citizens." A. BERGER, *supra* note 191, at 679. Perhaps another commentator gave the best articulation

res publicae,[195] and *res nullius.*[196] There was also an extensive law of city hygiene and cleanliness, similar to modern public nuisance law, enforceable by the aediles, a kind of Roman magistrate.[197] Scholars have long debated the nature of the ownership rights in *res communes* and *res publicae.*[198] Although much of this debate centered on whether individuals could sue for damages or an injunction if a *res communes* was damaged,[199] the Romans clearly conceived of a "middle ground" between absolute individual ownership and ownership by the state that was not limited to property owned by no one. It was, in the words of Pomponius, public property "not the object of commerce" and did "not absolutely belong to the people" but was "used for public purposes."[200] In modern terms, Roman ownership doctrine permitted more alternatives than state communism, individual private ownership, and anarchy.

---

of the concept: "[*Res publicae*] were in the ownership of the State, but this was not . . . private ownership at all, but public ownership, subject to special rules . . . . " F. Schulz, Classical Roman Law 340 (1951).

[196] *Res nullius* were things which "belong to no one" (Institutes 2.1.7), either because they were unappropriated by anyone, such as unoccupied lands or wild animals, or things similar to *res sacrae* or *res religiosae* "to which a religious character prevents any human right of property attaching" (T. Sandars, *supra* note 193 at 160). *See* Digest 1.8.1, 1.8.2. *See also* W. Buckland, *supra* note 192, at 184.

[197] *See* Digest 43.10.1, 43.11.1.

[198] Vegting, Domaine Public et Res Extra Commercium 36-51 (1950). *Compare* R. Lee, The Elements of Roman Law at 109-11 (4th ed. 1956) *with* W. Buckland, *supra* note 192, at 182-85 *and* W. Hunter, Introduction to Roman Law 65-66 (9th ed. rev. 1965). *See* Sax, *The Public Trust Doctrine in Natural Resource Law: Effective Judicial Intervention,* 68 Mich. L. Rev. 471, 475 (1970); Note, *State Citizen Rights Respecting Greater Resource Allocation: From Rome to New Jersey,* 25 Rutgers L. Rev. 571, 576 (1971). These debates cast doubt on the credibility of one commentator's remarks that: "Where subsequent law is found to differ, proponents of the public trust can hold the original Roman law up as a useful model of doctrinal purity to which we should return." Note, *The Public Trust in Tidal Areas: A Sometime Submerged Traditional Doctrine,* 79 Yale L.J. 762, 764 (1970).

[199] *See* W. Hunter, A Systematic and Historical Exposition of Roman Law in the Order of a Code 165 (1876); Note, *supra* note 198, 79 Yale L.J. at 788 n.124. *But see* Sax, *supra* note 198, at 475. The classical texts that have survived simply do not answer the question conclusively, but there is some evidence that a private reparation of injury was possible. According to Ulpian,

> [w]here anyone is prevented from fishing in, or sailing upon the sea, he will not be entitled to this interdict, just as in the case of a person who is prevented from taking part in games in a public field, or bathing in a public bath, or being present in a theater; but in all these cases an action for reparation of injury must be employed.

Digest 43.8.2.9. *See also id.* 43.8.5, 43.8.6, 43.13.1.9, 43.13.1.10, 43.15.1.3, 43.15.1.5 (evidence of legal relief, both prohibitive and reparative, for individual injury in use of *res communes* or *res publicae*).

[200] Digest 18.1.6.

The *res communes* doctrine entered English law early. The most important vehicle was probably the treatise called *Bracton*,[201] which was completed in 1256 or 1257.[202] That work clearly reflects the influence of the Romans.[203] *Bracton* preserved the Roman distinctions between public property, property belonging to no one, property belonging to individuals, and property of a common nature.[204] *Bracton*'s definition of *res communes* included the sea and its shores, air, and running water.[205] *Res publicae* included the right to fish in ports or rivers and to use river banks.[206] City buildings belonged to the civic corporations as *res universitatis*.[207] In various forms, *Bracton*'s description found its way into many other great treatises of the common law.[208]

Although it is not absolutely clear that the Romans had a privately enforceable legal remedy for disturbing the enjoyment of *res communes*,[209] the English by the sixteenth century had almost created such a remedy in the laws of the forest.[210] Obviously, no

---

201 *See* 2 BRACTON, *supra* note 13, at 39-41.

202 Thorne, *Translator's Preface* to 3 BRACTON, *supra* note 13, at v.

203 T. PLUCKNETT, *supra* note 28, at 261-62.

204 2 BRACTON, *supra* note 13, at 39-41.

205 *Id.*

206 *Id.* at 40.

207 *Id.*

208 *See* 2 W. BLACKSTONE, COMMENTARIES *14, 18, 395; 1 BRITTON bk. 2, ch. 2, § 1, at *84b; R. CALLIS, UPON THE STATUTE OF 23 H. 8 CAP. 5 OF SEWERS 78 (2d ed. London 1685) (1st ed. London 1647); J. COWELL, THE INSTITUTES OF THE LAWES OF ENGLAND 54-55 (London 1651); FLETA bk. 3, ch. 1, *reprinted in* 89 SELDEN SOC'Y 1-2 (1972); 2 J. KENT, COMMENTARIES ON AMERICAN LAW *347-48; J. SELDEN, MARE CLAUSUM ch. 2 (London 1635). *See also* Wiel, *Natural Communism: Air, Water, Oil, Sea, and Seashore*, 47 HARV. L. REV. 425, 425 n.2 (1934). Wiel, however, viewed the *res communes* theory differently from the earlier writers. *See* note 273 *infra*.

209 For incomplete evidence that such an action did exist, see note 199 *supra*. The Romans certainly did possess enforceable rights called praedial servitudes that protected private property owners' enjoyment of light within city bounds, and other common rights. B. NICHOLAS, AN INTRODUCTION TO ROMAN LAW 141-44 (1962).

210 Ironically, the lust of medieval English monarchs for the hunt led to these first conservation laws, elaborate rules that defined and protected the royal forests. These laws, enforced by an elaborate structure of wardens, foresters, agisters, and a chief justice of the forest, not only punished poaching and exploitation of the royal forests but also exerted a wide authority over the many Englishmen who lived in or next to the royal forests. Under the forests laws, these persons had limited, but valuable, rights to pasture animals in the forest, to cut some kinds of wood, to hunt animals defined as vermin, and to travel in the forest. *See* Turner, *Introduction* to SELECT PLEAS OF THE FOREST, 13 SELDEN SOCIETY (1899); Young, *The Forest Eyre in England During the Thirteenth Century*, 18 AM. J. LEGAL HIST. 321 (1974). For the classic treatise on the forest laws, see J. MANWOOD, A TREATISE AND DISCOURSE OF THE LAWES OF THE FORREST (London 1598), *cited in* United States v. New Mexico, 438 U.S. 696, 721 (1978) (dissenting opinion, Powell, J.).

private person had a freehold interest in the forest except the King, but injury to those who had rights to use the forest was subject to three nuisance actions, *nocumentum commune, nocumentum speciale,* and *nocumentum generale.*[211] The first action protected against "a general hurt and annoyance, as wel unto all the Inhabitants and dwellers within the Forest, as also unto the wild beastes of the same."[212]

Neither the common law nor the forest law would normally permit an individual to bring a private action for relief. It was argued that this would lead to limitless actions, each alleging no damage greater than that suffered by all of the King's subjects.[213] But if a nuisance specifically affected a local community,

---

The forest laws were technically distinct from the common law. Although Coke stated that "the law of the forest is allowed, and bounded by the common laws of this realm" (E. COKE, THE FOURTH PART OF THE INSTITUTES OF THE LAWS OF ENGLAND *290), he later acknowledged that "the forest laws differ in many cases from the common laws of England" (*id.* at *315). But the common law courts "exercised a sort of superintendence." *See* 1 W. HOLDSWORTH, *supra* note 23, at 348-49. In practice, "there was some intermingling of forest law and common law," including an intermingling of "pleas of the forest and common law pleas." Young, *supra*, at 329-30. One obvious reason for this fact was that "[i]mportant officials were involved in the operations of both kinds of courts" and the cooperation of the sheriff was required to make the forest laws effective. *Id.* at 329-30.

[211] J. MANWOOD, *supra* note 210, fol. 102-03.

[212] *Id.* fol. 102. *Nocumentum speciale* was a nuisance that "tendeth specially *ad nocumentum ferarum*, to the hurt of the wild beastes of the Forrest." *Id. Nocumentum generale* was basically a nuisance to the "Vert" or the trees and plants of the forest, although it also included

> all Surchargers of the commons, and Agistors of their owne pastures and landes, which by eating up of their pastures and commons so bare, that the Deare can have no feede there left. . . . and all manner of trespasses, that do tend to the hurt or distruction of any herbage of pasture within The Forest.

Id.

This action was brought before the Lord Chief Justice in Eyre of the Forest through procedure similar to the prosecution of a public nuisance.

[213] A contemporary case described the law that may have included the forest courts:

> A man shall not have an action on the case for a nuisance done in the highway, for it is a common nuisance, and then it is not reasonable that a particular person should have the action; for by the same reason that one person might have an action for it, by the same reason every one might have an action, and then he would be punished 100 times for one and the same cause. But if any particular person afterwards by the nuisance done has more particular damage than any other, there for that particular injury, he shall have a particular action on the case: and for common nuisances [*i.e.*, public nuisances], which are equal to all the King's liege people, the common law has appointed other Courts for the correction and reforming of them, *scil.* tourns, leets, &c.

Williams's Case, 5 Coke 72b, 73a, 77 Eng. Rep. 163, 164-65 (K.B. 1592). *See* T. BLOUNT, NOMO-ΛΕΞΙΚΟΝ (London 1670) (definition of "nusance"); G. JACOB, A NEW LAW-DICTIONARY (3d ed. London 1736) (1st ed. London 1729) (definition of "nusance").

adjoining inhabitants could bring a private action.[214] For example, a private nuisance action may have been allowed for disturbing a common watering place because the injury specially affected the local users of the water more than the public at large.[215]

Actions to protect a mere right to use property, even when that right was not one of exclusive possession, were very old in England, even in Coke's day. Early *praecipe* and *questus est* writs, and others, protected mere rights of use, when the plaintiffs had no right to exclusive possession of the land or water involved, and the assize of *novel disseisin* could lie to protect any kind of common appurtenant to a free tenement.[216] Examples included rights of common pasture, rights of fishery, rights of estovers, and rights of way.[217] Most of these rights, however, required that the plaintiff possess a freehold tenement to which the rights attached, in

---

[214] *See* Fowler v. Sanders, Cro. Jac. 446, 79 Eng. Rep. 382 (K.B. 1617); Robert Marys's Case, 9 Coke 111b, 113a, 77 Eng. Rep. 895, 898-99 (K.B. 1613). *See also* notes 59-62 and accompanying text *supra*.

[215] But though action may not be brought for a common nusance, but indictment or presentment; yet where the inhabitants of a town had by custom a watering place for their cattle which was stopped by another, it has been held, that any inhabitant might have an action against him, otherwise they would be without remedy, because such a nusance is not common to all the King's subjects.

G. JACOB, *supra* note 213 (definition of "nusance"). Such a nuisance could not be justified by prescription. Fowler v. Sanders, Cro. Jac. 446, 79 Eng. Rep. 382 (K.B. 1617). *Bracton* suggested that in certain cases, particularly in the context of running water, a wrongful nuisance may arise because of the "common and public welfare" despite a lack of *injuria* to any particular individual. 3 BRACTON, *supra* note 13, at 191. *See id.* at 191-93, 196. *See also* 3 FLETA, *reprinted in* 89 SELDEN SOC'Y 112 (1972). Of course, *Bracton* was written before there was a clear delineation between public and private nuisance doctrines, but these statements appear in the sections on possessory assizes.

[216] *See* 3 BRACTON, *supra* note 13, at 188-89; GLANVILL, *supra* note 23, at 168-69. As the translation of *Bracton* noted, "[a] nuisance of this kind does not differ substantially from a disseisin, and ought therefore to be removed by the assise, when it is wrongful." *Id.* at 190. Because the assize of *novel disseisin* also lay for an invasion of rights in common land, an injury to common rights appendant to a freehold was also an actionable nuisance. *Id.* at 190-91. *See* EARLY REGISTERS OF WRITS, *reprinted in* 87 SELDEN SOC'Y 71-74 (1970).

[217] Common pasture, for example, was very important before the enclosure of feudal lands. *See* 1 E. LIPSON, THE ECONOMIC HISTORY OF ENGLAND 78-84, 159 (12th ed. 1959). Enclosure later ensured exclusive private property as the major modern form of property holding, but it was not fully established by 1600. For discussions of enclosure generally, see G. DAVIES, THE EARLY STUARTS, 1603-1660, at 279-82 (2d ed. 1959); A. HARDING, A SOCIAL HISTORY OF ENGLISH LAW 325 (1966); 1 E. LIPSON, *supra*, at 136-50, 159-64; J. MACKIE, THE EARLIER TUDORS 1485-1558, at 448-53, 504-06 (1952). Early land radicals, the "Diggers" or "True Levellers," bitterly fought enclosure and possessed a fickle ally in Oliver Cromwell. *See* C. HILL, GOD'S ENGLISHMAN 18, 61, 260-61 (1970). For contemporary views on enclosure, see R. POWELL, DEPOPULATION ARRAIGNED, CONVICTED AND CONDEMNED BY THE LAWES OF GOD AND MAN 55-56 (London 1636).

the manner of modern easements appurtenant. The assize of nuisance always recited the free tenement of the plaintiff.[218]

To circumvent this free tenement barrier, plaintiffs began to experiment with action on the case pleadings in the sixteenth century. By *William Aldred's Case,* the action on the case in nuisance had become an acceptable alternative, and a preferable pleading, to the assize of nuisance.[219] Although the case form demanded some interest in land, the exact nature of the requisite interest remains unclear.[220] Rights of way and similar easements appeared sufficient.[221]

Had the concept of *res communes* endured in English courts after the widespread adoption of case pleadings, nuisance on the case could conceivably have protected rights to *res communes* just as it protected rights of tenants. Mere undivided ownership, consisting only of a right to use rather than a right to exclusive possession, would not have barred a potential plaintiff. After the development of case, the courts dropped the requirement of a free tenement. The proprietary right to use the *res communes* might have generally sufficed to give standing, as it did for common watering places.[222]

But the development of the *res communes* doctrine halted soon after the writings of Manwood and Coke, probably because ownership theory changed. The success of the enclosure movement hastened the transition to equating true ownership with exclusivity.[223] Grotius said that *res communes,* being unbounded, could not constitute property,[224] and others made similar statements.[225]

---

[218] *See* text accompanying notes 29, 59 *supra.*

[219] *See* text accompanying note 60 *supra.* A plaintiff could have an action on the case to recover damages to his rights of common pasture from a defendant whose cattle escaped and ate the grass. Robert Marys's Case, 9 Coke 111b, 113a-136, 77 Eng. Rep. 895, 898-900 (K.B. 1613).

[220] *See* C. FIFOOT, *supra* note 21, at 95.

[221] *See id.*

[222] *See* text accompanying notes 213-15 *supra.*

[223] *See* 3 J. KENT, COMMENTARIES ON AMERICAN LAW *403-05. Kent noted that "the change of manners and property, and the condition of society in this country, is so great, that the whole of this law of commonage is descending fast into oblivion." *Id.* at *405. *See also* note 217 *supra.*

[224] H. GROTIUS, DE JURE BELLI AC PACIS, bk. 2, ch. 2, § 3, at 190-91 (F. Kelsey trans. 1925) (1st ed. Paris 1625).

[225] "[P]roprietorship or dominion is a right whereby the substance, as it were, of something belongs to a person in such a way that it does not belong in its entirety to another person in the same manner." S. PUFENDORF, DE JURE NATURAE ET GENTIUM LIBRI OCTO 533 (C. Oldfather & W. Oldfather trans. 1934) (1st ed. Lund 1672). *But see* E. DE VATTEL, LE DROIT DES GENS bk. 1, ch. 20 (C. Fenwick trans. 1916) (1st ed. London 1758).

The exclusive ownership theory became dominant in America,[226] where Louisiana and California incorporated it into their civil codes[227] and Oliver Wendell Holmes endorsed it.[228] This trend

---

[226] In the later eighteenth century, Justice James Wilson wrote:

> Exclusive property multiplies the productions of the earth, and the means of subsistence. . . .
>
> By exclusive property, the productions of the earth and the means of subsistence are secured and preserved, as well as multiplied. What belongs to no one is wasted by every one. What belongs to one man in particular is the object of his economy and care.
>
> Exclusive property prevents disorder, and promotes peace. . . .
>
> The conveniences of life depend much on an exclusive property.

J. WILSON, *On the History of Property*, in 2 THE WORKS OF JAMES WILSON 719 (R. McCloskey ed. 1967).

[227] *See* LA. CIV. CODE ANN. art. 488 (West 1952) (ownership is "the right by which a thing belongs to some one in particular, to the exclusion of all other persons"); CAL. CIV. CODE ANN. § 654 (West 1954) (ownership of thing is "the right of one or more persons to possess and use it to the exclusion of others").

[228] O.W. HOLMES, THE COMMON LAW 246 (1881). Holmes concluded that an "owner is allowed to exclude all, and is accountable to no one." *Id.* Other legal writers offer similar definitions. *See, e.g.*, K. DIGBY, AN INTRODUCTION TO THE HISTORY OF THE LAW OF REAL PROPERTY 305 (5th ed. 1897); H. TIFFANY, THE LAW OF REAL PROPERTY 2-3 (3d ed. abr. R. Berman ed. 1970). Calling "exclusive control" the "very center of the concept of private property," Professor Brown concluded that "certain physical things, such as air, light, and running water are by their very nature incapable of being owned" because no one can control them exclusively. R. BROWN, THE LAW OF PERSONAL PROPERTY 7 (2d ed. 1955).

The exclusivity test of ownership remains alive in modern America. One court recently stated that " '[a]n essential element of individual property is the legal right to exclude others from enjoying it.' " Blaustein v. Burton, 9 Cal. App. 3d 161, 177, 88 Cal. Rptr. 319, 329 (1970) (quoting International News Serv. v. Associated Press, 248 U.S. 215, 250 (1918) (dissenting opinion, Brandeis, J.)). Another court has said that "the traditional test of ownership is the power to exclude others." Dairy Queen, Inc. v. Commissioner, 250 F.2d 503, 506 (10th Cir. 1957).

But this test might be yielding to a more flexible standard that would possibly permit the ownership of *res communes*. For example, one court has declared that " 'the meaning to be given to the word [property] depends upon the sense in which it is used, as gathered from the context and the nature of the things which it was intended to refer to and include.' " Fields v. Michael, 91 Cal. App. 2d 443, 449, 205 P.2d 402, 407 (1949) (quoting Franklin v. Franklin, 67 Cal. App. 2d 717, 725, 155 P.2d 637, 641 (1945)). A second court has stated that

> [t]he word [owner] usually signifies one who has the legal or rightful title, but this is not always the sense in which it is employed. It is not rigid in meaning, especially in ordinances and statutes. . . . The meaning usually depends, in great measures, upon the context and the subject matter to which it is applied.

Robinson v. Walker, 63 Ill. App. 2d 204, 209, 211 N.E.2d 488, 491 (1965).

This relative test of ownership approaches the original English and Roman concept in which the term "owner" included anyone with an ownership right, such as right to use. Max Rheinstein remarked on the late development of the concept of title in English law: "Only in recent times have the terms 'fee' and, more recently, 'title' assumed a meaning which comes near to that of the Roman *dominium*, which indicates the sum total of all rights and benefits which may be derived from a piece of land (as well as from a chattel)." MAX WEBER ON LAW IN ECONOMY AND SOCIETY 221 n.77 (M. Rheinstein ed. 1954). For Weber's own discussion, see *id.* at 221-22.

overwhelmed the law protecting common areas,[229] and many cities sold such areas in fee.[230] The cities assumed that they could pass good title, free of commonalty claims.

The exclusive ownership theory encouraged developing American industries to exploit the air, running water, sea, and seashores.[231] Owned by "no one," these things were theoretically free to all comers, and vulnerable to overuse.[232] Because states hesitated to discourage industry by use of public nuisance powers,[233] and special damages limitations precluded private suits to protect public users,[234] the overuse continued. Even where special damage to private property occurred, difficulties in determining causation, in apportioning damages, and in overcoming the balancing of utilities test could effectively bar private remedy.[235]

B. *American Law*

Ironically, excessive generosity by a state toward industry led to the surprising American resurrection of the *res communes* doctrine in 1892. In *Illinois Central Railroad v. Illinois*,[236] the Supreme

---

[229] For example, Massachusetts enacted statutes that provided for the partition of common areas. *See* 1786 Mass. Acts and Laws ch. 53, at 171-72; 1783 Mass. Acts and Laws ch. 39, at 599.

[230] For example, the present Cambridge Common represents just the tip of a much larger seventeenth century common. The original common extended far to the northwest. *See* CAMBRIDGE HISTORICAL COMMISSION, SURVEY OF ARCHITECTURAL HISTORY IN CAMBRIDGE, REPORT FOUR: OLD CAMBRIDGE 12-19 (1973).

English commons and manorial wastes suffered a similar fate. *See* The Commons Act, 1876, 39 & 40 Vict., c. 56, § 2; The Commons Act, 1899, 62 & 63 Vict., ch. 30, §§ 1-3; The Commons Act, 1908, 8 Edw. 7, ch. 44, § 1; The Law of Property Act, 1925, 15 & 16 Geo. 5, ch. 20, §§ 193-94. *See also* 7 W. HOLDSWORTH, *supra* note 23, at 315.

[231] Riparian rights were of course important in early America and "gave rise to the first important legal questions bearing on the relationship of property law to private economic development." M. HORWITZ, *supra* note 83, at 34.

[232] *Cf.* Demsetz, *Toward A Theory of Property Rights*, 57 AM. ECON. REV., PAPERS AND PROCEEDING 347, 354 (1967) (common property subject to overuse). Demsetz's argument that communal property was generally subject to exploitation has been proven false. Full freedom to exploit communal property rarely existed in any culture, even primitive societies. *See* Ciriacy-Wantrup & Bishop, *"Common Property" as a Concept in Natural Resources Policy*, 15 NAT. RESOURCES J. 713, 714-21 (1975). Early English commons were regulated by community customs. *See* 2 W. HOLDSWORTH, *supra* note 23, at 57-58. Abusing one's share of a common pasture, for example, was remedied by a writ of ad measurement of pasture. 3 BRACTON, *supra* note 13, at 182-89; 1 BRITTON bk. 2, ch. 27, §§ 1-9 at *148b-50. *See generally* THE LAW OF COMMONS AND COMMONERS (London 1698).

[233] *See* note 160 *supra*.

[234] *See* text accompanying note 185 *supra*.

[235] *See* Hartquist & King, *A Reprint from Capitol Hill*, 22 HARV. L. SCH. B., Dec. 1970, at 20-22; Katz, *supra* note 139, at 616-18.

[236] 146 U.S. 387 (1892).

Court voided the state's grant in fee to a railroad of a large section of land submerged beneath Lake Michigan in the Chicago harbor. The decision held that the people of the state, not the state itself, were the land's beneficial owners. Justice Field, writing for the majority, declared that the state held the title to the submerged land, but the state held it "in trust for the people of the State."[237] He added that "[t]he State can no more abdicate its trust over property in which the whole people are interested . . . than it can abdicate its police powers."[238] In analyzing the property interests, Justice Field followed the argument of John Miller, counsel for the City of Chicago. Miller had argued that:

> The bed of Lake Michigan . . . is held by the people of the State of Illinois in their sovereign capacity, and *de communi jure,* and wholly in trust for the public, and for the public uses, for which it is adapted. And the same was not held by the State in any proprietary or private right or as its demesne, and was not as to a large tract, extending a mile into the deep water of the open lake, and composing the outer harbor, and entrance to the inner harbor of a great commercial city, the subject of a private grant or contract.[239]

Miller restated precisely the traditional *res communes* doctrine. Both the Romans and *Bracton* recognized that the state could sell ordinary real property to private parties. But certain things remained incapable of exclusive ownership in fee by the state or by any individual. A private grant that ignored the public interest in the *res* could never dispose of such things because they belonged to the commonalty. For Miller, the Chicago harbor was a *res communes,* and the Supreme Court agreed.

A complete discussion of either the full political background of *Illinois Central*[240] or its effect on American property law is beyond the scope of this Article. The debate over the case has raged for nearly ninety years. Recently, Professor Sax, in a lead-

---

[237] *Id.* at 452. Justice Field clearly saw a trust in the true property sense, because he distinguished between lands the state owned in fee and lands in which the state held legal title in trust for the people as beneficial owners. *Id.* This statement reflects the traditional view that the commonalty, not the state, owns property of a *res communes* nature. Justice Field himself stated that "[the holding of this case] follows necessarily from the public character of the property, being held by the whole people for purposes in which the whole people are interested." *Id.* at 456.

[238] *Id.* at 453.

[239] *Id.* at 421.

[240] One commentator has hinted at the potential corruption behind the case. *See* Sax, *supra* note 198, at 490-91.

ing article, attempted to separate the public trust rationale of *Illinois Central* from traditional property doctrine, including *res communes*, by transforming it into a principle of administrative law.[241] The Supreme Court of Illinois, in *Paepcke v. Public Building Commission,*[242] cited Sax's article,[243] but continued to find the basis of a public trust in a public ownership interest in a *res communes.*[244] The Illinois Supreme Court chose the right course. The use of a *res communes* property doctrine in defending the environment will bear more fruit than Professor Sax's approach.

Contrary to Professor Sax's view, the property doctrine of *Illinois Central* is inseparable from the remainder of the case. Not only did the arguments[245] and the majority opinion[246] focus on the property question, but the Court's use of property doctrine was the primary target of the dissenters' attack. Justice Shiras, dissenting, wrote:

> That the ownership of a State in the lands underlying its navigable waters is as complete, and its power to make them the subject of conveyance and grant is as full, as such ownership and power to grant in the case of the other public lands of the State, I have supposed to be well settled.[247]

Sax argued against viewing the public trust in *Illinois Central* as a true property trust because the Court refused to prohibit absolutely conveying title to such property.[248] Instead, the Court instructed lower courts to determine a grant's validity in light of the circumstances.[249] Sax reasoned that the public trust doctrine tests the validity of government action as a matter of administrative law, rather than as a question of *res communes* property doctrine.[250]

---

[241] Sax, *supra* note 198.

[242] 46 Ill. 2d 330, 263 N.E.2d 11 (1970).

[243] *Id.* at 336-38, 263 N.E.2d at 15-16.

[244] *Id.* at 341, 263 N.E.2d at 18.

[245] In reference to other lake front land owned by the city, Miller described the City of Chicago as "owner in fee, in trust for public uses." 146 U.S. at 419.

[246] *See* text accompanying notes 236-39 *supra.*

[247] 146 U.S. at 465.

[248] Sax, *supra* note 198, at 489.

[249] *Id.* at 489-91.

[250] *Id.* Sax stated:

> When a state holds a resource which is available for the free use of the general public, a court will look with considerable skepticism upon *any* governmental conduct which is calculated *either* to reallocate that resource to more restricted uses *or* to subject public uses to the self-interest of private parties.

Id. at 490 (emphasis in original).

This argument rests on the false notion that the state cannot alienate the title to a *res communes.* As Justice Field explained, the state can dispose of the *res* under circumstances that protect any beneficial interests of the public.[251] The public trust vests legal title to *res communes* in the state as a convenience in most cases, but other groups can also hold the title. Indeed, private boards held titles to many New England commons, subject to the public trust for the commonalty.[252]

Sax's argument is close to the position taken by Professor Trelease in an earlier article[253] on *Ivanhoe Irrigation District v. All Parties and Persons.*[254] Following *Illinois Central,* the California Supreme Court in *Ivanhoe Irrigation* used property doctrine to support a public trust. The court said:

> [T]he state is not the owner of the domestic water of the state in the sense that it has absolute power and dominion over it to the exclusion of the rights of those who have the beneficial interest therein. The title is an equitable one residing in the water users of the state. The state as an entity is the holder of the legal title as trustee for the benefit of the people of the state, all of whom in the last analysis, are the water users of the state.[255]

In *Ivanhoe Irrigation,* as in the *Illinois Central,* the dissenting judges explicitly opposed the majority's knowing use of a property doctrine.[256] To explain such language while avoiding a *res communes* property doctrine, Trelease argued that the courts called something a "trust" merely to "put across the thought more forcefully" when they only meant it was "*like* a trust."[257] Sax and Trelease,

---

But the *Illinois Central* Court's holding rests on completely different ground. The Court never held the government's conduct questionable in the abstract. Instead, the case turned on the nature of the property interest involved. In addition, Sax never clearly explains what he means by "considerable skepticism." Professor Jaffe implies that Sax really has no clear meaning. *See* Jaffe, Book Review, 84 HARV. L. REV. 1562, 1566-68 (1971) (reviewing J. SAX, DEFENDING THE ENVIRONMENT (1971)).

The Court in *Illinois Central* set out to determine title, and it did. 146 U.S. at 433, 463. It did not exercise judicial review, but determined where the property interests lay as a matter of law. The Court never scrutinized the government's actual conduct in deciding the ownership issue.

[251] 146 U.S. at 452-53.

[252] *See* note 229 *supra.*

[253] Trelease, *Government Ownership and Trusteeship of Water,* 45 CALIF. L. REV. 638 (1957).

[254] 47 Cal. 2d 597, 306 P.2d 824 (1957), *rev'd sub nom.* Ivanhoe Irrigation Dist. v. McCracken, 357 U.S. 275 (1958). The Supreme Court found it unnecessary to deal with the question of ownership. 357 U.S. at 290-91.

[255] 47 Cal. 2d at 625, 306 P.2d at 840.

[256] *Id.* at 648, 306 P.2d at 855.

[257] Trelease, *supra* note 253, at 648 (emphasis in original).

in their eagerness to avoid a property basis for the public trust doctrine, had to rewrite the courts' clear language.

Sax offered two reasons for discarding the property background to the public trust doctrine. First, Sax noted:

> At most, the government may resolve that certain resources will be used for specific purposes—for instance, that land is to be set aside as a park. But it is reasonable to assume that such decisions imply that the specified uses shall be available only until the legislature decides to devote the land to some other public purpose.[258]

He reasoned that it is fruitless to try to demonstrate whether the government conveys a complete title or merely designates a specific, if transitory, purpose when the government grants a resource to the general public. Second, Sax believed that "[i]t makes economic sense to prevent the government from taking the property of an individual owner, but it is difficult to understand why the government should be prevented from taking property which is owned by the public as a whole."[259] He concluded that the use of the government's condemnation power is not an appropriate way to rededicate public land to a new use. Basically, Sax believed that governments should not be bound to irrevocable commitments through the *res communes* doctrine.

Sax's arguments are unpersuasive. The first argument begs the question of whether the state or the commonalty initially owned the *res*. But this question is exactly what courts must decide. The second argument assumes that the state can never convey title to *res communes* and that every act of the government which distributes costs equally over the entire commonalty is fair. But states can alienate *res communes*, and courts must often serve as the ultimate arbitrators of the fairness of such transactions even when the public shares the costs equally. In fact, courts played just that role under the public trust doctrine in *Illinois Central* and *Ivanhoe Irrigation*.[260]

Professor Jaffe has also criticized Sax's concept of the public trust doctrine as being so vague as to introduce virtual de novo court review into all administrative matters.[261] This result could be prevented by restricting the public trust doctrine to its original

[258] Sax, *supra* note 198, at 479.

[259] *Id.*

[260] *See* text accompanying notes 236-52 *supra*.

[261] Jaffe, *supra* note 250, at 1566-68.

base of property concepts and thus focusing on the clear and well-established rules of property law. Jaffe's criticism helps to reveal what may be the real reason Sax and Trelease have attempted to separate the public trust doctrine from its original property background—to make it more palatable to the courts. But Sax himself admits that "[t]he most common theory advanced in support of a special trust obligation is a property notion."[262] Jaffe correctly points out that a vague, apparently limitless doctrine of public trust, neither clearly nor historically based, stands far less chance of court acceptance than one firmly founded on ancient property notions.[263]

The recent *Paepcke* case[264] illustrates that a public trust doctrine tied to property concepts is more acceptable. The central question in this case was whether Chicago taxpayers had standing to challenge the decision of the city to build schools in two city parks.[265] The court held that such taxpayers had an "equitable interest . . . in the public property" sufficient for standing because of the public trust doctrine.[266] Like the courts in *Ivanhoe Irrigation* and *Illinois Central,* the Illinois court explained its decision in terms of property doctrine:

> Upon serious reconsideration of this question we now believe that portion of the opinion in *Droste* dealing with the right and standing of the plaintiff to sue should be overruled, as should any other former decisions of this court holding that a citizen and taxpayer has no right, in the absence of statute, to bring an action to *enforce the trust upon which public property is held* unless he is able to allege and prove special damage to his property. If the "public trust" doctrine is to have any meaning or vitality at all, the members of the public, at least taxpayers who are the beneficiaries of that trust, must have the right and standing to enforce it.[267]

The adoption of a public trust theory did not restrict the flexibility of the court's review. In fact, the court ultimately approved the building of the schools. In so doing, it cited Sax's article, not for the proposition that a property-based public trust doctrine was infeasible but to support the proposition that no property doc-

262 *See* Sax, *supra* note 198, at 478.
263 *See* Jaffe, *supra* note 250, at 1567-68.
264 46 Ill. 2d 330, 263 N.E.2d 11 (1970).
265 *Id.* at 340-41, 263 N.E.2d at 18.
266 *Id.* at 341, 263 N.E.2d at 18.
267 *Id.*, 263 N.E.2d at 18 (emphasis added).

trine which "prohibit[s] the government from ever accommodating new public needs by reallocating resources" could be supported.[268] The public trust doctrine did not prevent the state from changing a *res communes* from one beneficial use to another.[269] The state reallocated the property in a way which, as a practical matter, attempted to protect the collective interests of the public beneficial owners,[270] with judicial review available as a further safeguard.

The *Paepcke* court decided that the change in property use was made "in good faith and for the public good," and was thus within the state's discretion as trustee of the public trust property held for the public's benefit.[271] The decision, therefore, rested upon a strong foundation of traditional property trust doctrine. The court found that this *res communes* property doctrine provided standing for members of the public who possessed no private ownership interests and also a basis for careful judicial review of a state's decision with regard to the parks in question. The case reveals that a *res communes* property basis for public trust review is both palatable to courts and useful to environmentalists.

But change-in-use and alienation cases do not provide the only possibilities for the constructive use of this ancient doctrine. First, it could give standing for citizens or users to sue for pollution injuries to a *res communes*. Second, it might cause a shift in the burden of proof required to prevent the use of *res communes* in ways contrary to the public's beneficial ownership interest.

Public nuisance doctrine has long blocked the standing of private citizens to bring pollution suits. Unless an individual can show special damages, only the state, at its discretion, can sue for public nuisance.[272] But beneficial owners of a *res communes* under a state public trust should have standing to bring a mandamus suit against the state to force a public nuisance suit to protect the trust because "[a] trust imposes an affirmative duty upon the trustee to hold and use the property for the exclusive benefit of the beneficiary, and where that benefit involves conservation objectives, the government must act affirmatively to achieve its realization."[273] This approach would reduce the discretion enjoyed

---

[268] *Id.* at 337, 263 N.E.2d at 16 (quoting Sax, *supra* note 198, at 482).

[269] *See* text accompanying notes 251-52 *supra*.

[270] *See* Illinois C.R.R. v. Illinois, 146 U.S. 387, 453 (1892).

[271] 46 Ill. 2d at 347, 263 N.E.2d at 21.

[272] *See* W. PROSSER, *supra* note 21, § 88, at 586-87.

[273] Berlin, Kessler & Roisman, *Law in Action: The Trust Doctrine*, in LAW AND THE ENVIRONMENT 171 (M. Baldwin & J. Page eds. 1970).

by some state attorneys general. At present, they can choose not to bring a public nuisance suit, even where the facts would support one.[274] Under the *res communes* doctrine, a member of the public should at least have standing to bring a mandamus action to demand such a suit when a *res communes* is threatened.

Despite the advantages of the doctrine, several natural limitations would prevent it from resulting in excessive litigation. First, a *res communes* must be at stake. Whether the particular property in question constitutes a *res communes* would be a question of law for the court's determination. Samuel Wiel provided some guidance in defining the characteristics of a *res communes* by comparing the lists of items considered to be *res communes* in various American and English jurisdictions.[275] Even radio and television airwaves may be described as *res communes*, and efforts to buy them in fee, despite any interest of the commonalty, have been rejected.[276] Second, the expense of bringing a mandamus action

---

[274] *See* Jaffe, *Standing to Sue in Conservation Suits*, in LAW AND THE ENVIRONMENT 131 (M. Baldwin & J. Page eds. 1970). *See also* Katz, *supra* note 139, at 622. Statutes in Wisconsin and Florida allow private citizens to sue in the name of the state to enjoin a nuisance. FLA. STAT. ANN. § 60.05 (West 1969 & West Supp. 1979); WIS. STAT. ANN. § 823.02 (West 1977).

[275] Wiel, *supra* note 208. Wiel's article, however, is limited to the "four natural communisms" (air, running water, sea, and seashore), and does not attempt a general analysis of ownership rights. Wiel also summarily rejected ownership ideas such as a public trust because the theory would turn "negatives into some resembled positive." *Id.* at 426. His rejection of ownership by the commonalty results in no ownership of res communes. *Id.* at 426. *See* Wiel, *Running Water*, 22 HARV. L. REV. 190, 190-96 (1909). But Wiel's own copious examples, particularly those regarding rights to light, airport access, and radio waves, show that equitable interests recognized by property law do accurately describe the public's interest in *res communes.*

Other authorities disagree with the proposition that no one owns *res communes.* The Supreme Court discussed *res communes* in Geer v. Connecticut, 161 U.S. 519, 525 (1896). Justice White cited the Napoleonic Code as summing up an "unbroken line of law and precedent" on *res communes. Id.* at 526. The passage cited from the Napoleonic Code states that " '[t]here are things which belong to no one, and the use of which is common to all.' " *Id.* In the next paragraph, Justice White refers to this as "the principle of common ownership." *Id.* Importantly, Justice White recognized that although *res communes* belong to *no one*, this does not mean that they are ownerless or owned by the state, but rather it means that they are owned in common. Just because *res communes* "cannot be exclusively and wholly appropriated" does not mean they cannot be owned in common, unless one assumes the exclusivity test discussed earlier. *See* text accompanying notes 223-30 *supra.*

[276] *See* Wiel, *supra* note 208, at 429-30. Wiel concluded that, at any time, "about the closest to common right in *Air* is Radio." *Id.* at 456 (emphasis in original). The concept of radio waves as *res communes* is consistent with federal legislation and recent Supreme Court decisions. *See* 47 U.S.C. § 301 (1976) (United States shall "control" such waves and shall permit "use" but not "ownership" by persons for limited periods of time). The Supreme Court has indicated on several occasions that such control is to be governed by the public interest. *See* Red Lion Broadcasting Co. v. FCC, 395 U.S. 367, 394 (1969); Ashbacker

would inhibit litigants from undertaking an action for trivial reasons.[277] In addition, if the state had undertaken other affirmative action to protect the *res communes* in question, the courts could find a public nuisance suit unnecessary to enforce the public trust. Like any trustee, the state would be liable for abuse of discretion.[278] Finally, even a successful mandamus action would not spell ultimate victory, but only access to a trial on the merits.

Beyond opening courts to environmental litigants, using *res communes* property doctrine may furnish plaintiffs with another significant advantage—a favorable burden of proof. When private property is condemned, the owner normally bears the burden of showing that the government acted arbitrarily. Although no cases have established a different rule for the reallocation of *res communes,* the recent New Jersey decision of *Texas Eastern Transmission Corp. v. Wildlife Preserves, Inc.* forecasts a shift in the burden in favor of environmental plaintiffs.[279] In that case, the court instituted a special burden of proof rule when the state attempted to condemn a pipeline right of way through a privately owned wetland wildlife preserve.[280] The court distinguished this situation from "that of an ordinary property owner"[281] because "defendant's devotion of its land to a purpose which is encouraged and often engaged in by government itself gives it a somewhat more potent claim to judicial protection against taking . . . by arbitrary action of a condemnor."[282] The more favorable burden of proof rule may have tacitly reflected the public *res communes* interest in the unique environmental value of the preserve's wetland,[283] without discriminating unfairly between private owners. Favoring

Radio Co. v. FCC, 326 U.S. 327, 333 (1945); FCC v. Sanders Radio Station, 309 U.S. 470, 475 (1940). These statutes and cases are consistent with the concept of common beneficial ownership of the airwaves by the public with the title held in trust by the national government, which controls the use of the *res communes* for the public benefit. If this is true, sales of airwaves to private concerns by the government would have to meet the standards of *Illinois Central. See* text accompanying note 239 *supra.*

[277] *See* Scenic Hudson Preservation Conf. v. Federal Power Comm'n, 354 F.2d 608, 617 (2d Cir. 1965) ("experience with public actions confirms the view that the expense and vexation of legal proceedings is not lightly undertaken"), *cert. denied,* 384 U.S. 941 (1966).

[278] *See* G.G. Bogert & G.T. Bogert, Handbook of the Law of Trusts 322-24 (5th ed. 1973).

[279] 48 N.J. 261, 225 A.2d 130 (1966).

[280] *Id.* at 275, 225 A.2d at 138.

[281] *Id.* at 268, 225 A.2d at 134.

[282] *Id.* at 273, 225 A.2d at 137.

[283] The preserve had been described by expert witnesses as "'the finest inland, natural fresh water wetland in the entire Northeastern United States.'" *Id.* at 270, 225 A.2d at 135.

the preserve in this case could easily end in unfair results if the preserve's owners used its position to defeat the condemnation proceedings and then sold the wetland to the pipeline company at a higher price. In any event, if such a private owner merits a special burden of proof rule, a *res communes* case, which more clearly involves public ownership interests, would certainly deserve at least this advantage.[284]

Res communes doctrine may soon enter the public spotlight. Ralph Nader's *Study Group Report on Water Pollution* has alleged that a major polluter of water is the government itself.[285] Nader, in a press conference preceding the report's release, denounced federal and state government agencies for treating water resources as "their private sewers." Nader asserted: "water belongs to no one—except the people."[286] This is the spirit of the *res communes* doctrine. *Res communes* interests would serve as a disincentive to governmental as well as private misbehavior.

In a 1979 landmark decision, *Boston Waterfront Development Corp. v. Commonwealth*,[287] the Supreme Judicial Court of Massachusetts made a bold return to the spirit of *Illinois Central*. At issue was the ownership of land "covered by the seaward end of a wharf constructed over filled land, partly occupied by the corner of an ancient granite building now renovated into modern shops, offices, restaurants, and condominiums."[288] Holding that the title to the land was not an ordinary fee simple but was "subject to the condition that it be used for a public purpose related to the 'promot[ion of] trade and commerce'"[289] the court stated:

> The essential import of this holding is that the land in question is not, like ordinary private land held in fee simple absolute, subject to development at the sole whim of the owner, but it is impressed with a public trust, which gives the public's representatives an interest and responsibility in its development. This concept is difficult to describe in language in complete harmony with the language of the law ordinarily applied to privately owned property. We are not dealing with the allocation

---

[284] The court implied as much when it compared the wildlife preserve with more public enterprises. *Id.* at 268, 225 A.2d at 134.

[285] *See* D. Zwick & M. Benstock, Water Wasteland 340-65 (1971).

[286] Boston Evening Globe, Apr. 12, 1971, at 5, col. 1.

[287] [1979] Mass. Adv. Sh. 1992.

[288] *Id.* at 1993.

[289] *Id.* at 2023.

> of property rights between private individuals when we are concerned with a public resource such as Boston Harbor.[290]

In support of this holding, the court specifically referred to the Roman property doctrine of *res communes,*[291] the property doctrine of *Illinois Central,*[292] and the English law of jus privatum and jus publicum in relation to the shoreland.[293] According to the court:

> Legislative awareness of this historical background is evident, for example, in an 1850 report of the Senate Joint Committee on Mercantile Affairs and Insurance concerning the flats in Boston Harbor, in which the committee stated: "By the law of all civilized Europe, before the feudal system obtained in England, there was no such thing as property in tide waters. Tide waters were res omnium, that is, they were for the common use, like air and light .... In England, the fiction of a fee in the Crown, and the control of the trust in Parliament, we understand to have been a mode, suited to the times and the

---

[290] *Id.* at 2017.

[291] The court stated that:

> Throughout history, the shores of the sea have been recognized as a special form of property of unusual value; and therefore subject to different legal rules from those which apply to inland property. At Roman law, all citizens held and had access to the seashore as a resource in common; in the words of Justinian, "they [the shores] cannot be said to belong to anyone as private property." Institutes of Justinian, 2.1.1-2.1.6 cited in Note, The Public Trust in Tidal Areas: A Sometime Submerged Traditional Doctrine, 79 Yale L.J. 762, 763 (1970), see David A. Rice, Final Report: A Study of the Law Pertaining to the Tidelands of Massachusetts, 1971 House No. 4932, at 17-18.

Id. at 1994.

[292] Extensively quoting *Illinois Central,* the court stated that:

> This requirement, that such lands be granted only for public purposes, was held by the Court to be central to the notion of governmental power. "The State can no more abdicate its trust over property in which the whole people are interested," the Court stated, "so as to leave them entirely under the use and control of private parties, except in the instance of parcels mentioned for the improvement of the navigation and use of the waters, or when parcels can be disposed of without impairment of the public interest in what remains, than it can abdicate its police powers in the administration of government and the preservation of the peace."

[1979] Mass. Adv. Sh. at 2014 (quoting Illinois Central R.R. v. Illinois, 146 U.S. 387, 453 (1892)).

[293] The jus privatum/jus publicum distinction in regard to shoreland property was carried over to the new world, so that the company's ownership was understood to consist of a jus privatum which could be "parcelled out to corporation and individuals ... as private property" and a jus publicum "in trust for public use of all those who should become inhabitants of said territory .... "

[1979] Mass. Adv. Sh. at 1997 (quoting Commonwealth v. City of Roxbury, 75 Mass. (9 Gray) 451, 483-84 (1857)) (footnote omitted). The same distinction was made regarding

> genius of the feudal law, for insuring to the State the control over tide-waters. The Commonwealth succeeds to this right of control."[294]

The court concluded that "[t]he land below low water line can be granted by the State only to fulfill a public purpose, and the rights of the grantee to that land are ended when that purpose is extinguished."[295] This is close to the classic *res communes* property doctrine.[296]

CONCLUSION

Honoré observed that "a mature system of law" limits uses of property that cause harm to others because "without them, 'ownership' would be a destructive force."[297] During the nineteenth century, however, the law "hewed to an ideal of competitive self-assertion."[298] As Morton Horwitz has established, both English and American courts relaxed their protection of the more passive uses of property, and, in effect, subsidized developing industry by forcing the cost of its by-products on society in general.[299] In this atmosphere, the rationale of *St. Helen's Smelting* was misconstrued as establishing a balancing of utilities doctrine that overrode the previous absolute *sic utere tuo* guarantees of the common law to the passive property holder.[300] In addition, the relaxation of the *sic utere tuo* guarantee removed an important incentive for industrial control of pollution by improved technology.

The older common law, in contrast, constantly concerned itself with the concrete relations between individuals, especially in its development of property doctrine. Lime kilns, tallow furnaces, pig sties, and dyeing vats, although important to the social well-being of seventeenth century England,[301] were viewed by the

---

the ownership of shorelands in colonial New Jersey. *See* Martin v. Waddell, 41 U.S. (16 Pet.) 367, 411-13 (1842).

[294] [1979] Mass. Adv. Sh. at 1996-97.

[295] *Id.* at 2013.

[296] All the more remarkable is that the *res communes* issues were arguably not raised below, and that the relevant Massachusetts statute contained no explicit conditions for making the grant in question. *Id.* at 2024-25 (dissenting opinion, Braucher, J.).

[297] Honoré, *supra* note 5, at 123.

[298] Pound, *A Comparison of Ideals of Law*, 47 HARV. L. REV. 1, 15 (1933).

[299] M. HORWITZ, *supra* note 83, at 63, 74-78.

[300] *See* notes 105-182 and accompanying text *supra*.

[301] J. DAWSON, *supra* note 86, at 269-70.

courts in the context of the costs they inflicted on neighboring property owners and not as isolated under ideal conditions.[302] Similarly, the earlier common law protected certain things of importance to the entire community from private exploitation by individual owners.[303] These *res communes,* in theory, gave even the humblest person a legal interest in a part of his environment. The realization that the nineteenth century laissez faire ideals are not inextricably a part of our civilization or our rule of law is an important lesson that legal history can teach well.

In 1894, Professor John T. Dillon of Yale predicted that American property law would see "important changes of substance and form" as it adapted to the new values in American society.[304] Appropriately, the *res communes* doctrine, one of property law's oldest elements, may assist in this change. The courts can use it to clarify the protectable interests in things once considered freely exploitable, thus preventing social conflict by fairly identifying and allocating the costs of life in a crowded world.

The *sic utere tuo* or the *res communes* doctrines should not necessarily be restored to the present law in their old forms, or in any form. But a historical perspective on law can often give "a more significant perspective on legal reality than the logician's analytic intelligence."[305] When looking out on those neighborhoods that, in nineteenth century balancing of utilities terms, have become "denaturalised,"[306] the politician, the economist, the engineer, and the lawyer can find inspiration in the roots of our legal heritage.

> The reason and spirit of cases make law; not the letter of particular precedents.
>
> —*Lord Mansfield*[307]

---

[302] *See* text accompanying notes 67, 71-72 *supra*.

[303] *See* text accompanying notes 183-235 *supra*.

[304] J. DILLON, THE LAWS AND JURISPRUDENCE OF ENGLAND AND AMERICA 385 (1894).

[305] Howe, *Introduction* to O.W. HOLMES, THE COMMON LAW at xix (M. Howe ed. 1968).

[306] St. Helen's Smelting Co. v. Tipping, 11 Eng. Rep. 1483, 1485 (H.L. 1865).

[307] Fisher v. Prince, 3 Burr. 1363, 1364, 97 Eng. Rep. 876, 876 (K.B. 1762).

[5]

PRINCIPAL PAPERS

Liberating the Public Trust Doctrine from Its Historical Shackles

By Joseph L. Sax*

At a superficial level, the shape of the public trust doctrine is easy enough to discern. It draws upon the Roman Law idea of common properties (*res communis*)[1] and on certain provisions of Magna Carta.[2] It deals with lands beneath navigable waters, with constraints on alienation by the sovereign and with an affirmative protective duty of government—a fiduciary obligation—in dealing with certain properties held publicly.[3] Yet to restate these commonplace observations is not to begin to penetrate the core of this unusual legal doctrine.

Taken at face value, the public trust appears simply to limit public alienation of certain properties. Yet when so narrowly interpreted, it generates some rather peculiar responses. One example is the California Supreme Court's solemn examination of the intentions of the California Legislature in 1870 to ascertain whether grants made more than a century ago were meant to be free of the public trust, a question that the legislature gave no evidence of having considered.[4] And only last year the Supreme

---

* Professor of Law, University of Michigan. A.B. 1957, Harvard University; J.D. 1959, University of Chicago.

[1] Justinian, Institutes, 2.1.1-2.1.6.

[2] *See* Comment, *The Public Trust in Tidal Areas: A Sometimes Submerged Traditional Doctrine*, 79 Yale L.J. 762, 765-68 (1970).

[3] For reference to traditional cases, *see* Sax, *The Public Trust Doctrine in Natural Resource Law: Effective Judicial Intervention*, 68 Mich. L. Rev. 471 (1970).

[4] City of Berkeley v. Superior Court, 26 Cal. 3d 515, 606 P.2d 362, 162 Cal. Rptr. 327, *cert. denied*, 101 S. Ct. 119 (1980).

Court of Oregon permitted an airport to be extended into Coos Bay on the theory that bridges are routinely built over navigable waters, and that the autos that go over the water on bridges are indistinguishable from airplanes that traverse navigable waters on runways.[5] One must ask whether the destiny of San Francisco Bay or the ocean shoreline should turn upon such historical or analytical oddities.

It is unreasonable to view the public trust as simply a problem of alienation of publicly owned property into private hands, since many—if not most—of the depredations of public resources are brought about by public authorities who have received the permission of the state to proceed with their schemes. On the other hand, it is inconceivable that the trust doctrine should be viewed as a rigid prohibition, preventing all dispositions of trust property or utterly freezing as of a given moment the uses to which those properties have traditionally been put. It can hardly be the basis for any sensible legal doctrine that change itself is illegitimate.

At its heart, the public trust doctrine is not just a set of rules about tidelands, a restraint on alienation by the government or an historical inquiry into the circumstances of long-forgotten grants. And neither Roman Law nor the English experience with lands underlying tidal waters is the place to search for the core of the trust idea.[6]

The essence of property law is respect for reasonable expecta-

---

[5] Morse v. Oregon Div. of State Lands, 285 Or. 197, 590 P.2d 709 (1979).

[6] Roman Law most likely reflects an effort at rational classification. The Romans began by classifying as conventional private property those things which were amenable to ordinary purchase, sale or inheritance. Then the Romans classified everything that could not be so categorized, *i.e.*, temples, which were said to belong to the gods, public buildings, which belonged to the State, and a number of other things, called *res communis* or *res nullius*—like the seashore and wildlife—which could not be said to belong to anyone.

In all probability, categories like *res communis* were a response to what the Romans conceived to be the physical nature of certain properties—things that were abundant and not amenable to private possession, and therefore not the subject of purchase, sale, exclusion or possession. While some of these things can be physically and economically privatized, in fact they were not privately owned in Roman times, and probably were not subject to demands for private ownership. The Romans did, however, grant certain persons some exclusive rights to fishery in the sea. They also removed small farmers from their lands and instituted larger-scale, slave-operated farms which were owned by rich persons. *See* note 1 *supra*.

tions.[7] The idea of justice at the root of private property protection calls for identification of those expectations which the legal system ought to recognize. We all appreciate the importance of expectations as an idea of justice, but our concern for expectations has traditionally been confined to private owners. We have tied the *legal* concern with expectations to private proprietorship and to formal title; and while we recognize that mere title is not enough to sustain every claim of expectation that is made under it, it is hard to imagine legally enforceable expectations unconnected to formal title.[8] At the same time we know that, insofar as expectations underlie strong and deeply held legal-ethical ideals, they are not limited to title ownership.

In "*The New Property*," Professor Charles Reich[9] introduced the notion that many things lacking traditional status as formal property—things like television or liquor licenses—in fact generate expectations quite like those that attach to traditional forms of property.[10] Even interests that don't at all resemble ordinary property give rise to important values and expectations that cry for recognition, and sometimes get it. Much of the recent controversy over the federal highway program, and over urban renewal, was engendered by the prospect of the destruction of established communities.[11] Similar problems are arising today with the inundation of established western communities by energy development projects. The root values that inhere in the maintenance of an established community have much in common with the established expectations that underlie the recognition of private property rights.

To put the idea of expectations in a broader context, one

---

[7] *See, e.g.*, Michelman, *Property, Utility and Fairness: Comments on the Ethical Foundations of "Just Compensation Law,"* 80 HARV. L. REV. 1165 (1967).

[8] The courts are defining "property interests" more broadly than was traditional as a trigger for constitutionally protected *procedural* rights. *E.g.*, Goldberg v. Kelly, 397 U.S. 254 (1970). *See* Bishop v. Wood, 426 U.S. 341 (1976); Mathews v. Eldridge, 424 U.S. 319 (1976); Monaghan, *Of "Liberty" and "Property,"* 62 CORNELL L. REV. 405 (1977).

[9] 73 YALE L.J. 733 (1964).

[10] *See* note 8 *supra*. For a recent case demonstrating the traditional view in full bloom, *see* United States v. Fuller, 409 U.S. 488 (1973) (condemnation of land adjacent to Taylor Grazing Act "permit" lands did not require compensation for any value added to lands by permits).

[11] *E.g.*, A. LUPO, F. COLCORD & P. FOWLER, RITES OF WAY: THE POLITICS OF TRANSPORTATION IN BOSTON AND THE U.S. CITY (1971).

might say that stability, and the protection of stable relationships, is one of the most basic and persistent concerns of the legal system. Stability in ownership is what we protect with property rights; stability within a community is a major part of the business of the criminal law. Of course, stability does not mean the absence of change, nor does it mean political or legal reaction. It does mean a commitment to evolutionary rather than revolutionary change, for the rate of change and the capacity it provides for transition are precisely what separate continuity and adaptation from crisis and collapse.

Precisely the same point might be made from a biological perspective. The focus of environmental problems is *not*, as is sometimes suggested, the mere *fact* of change, which it is said environmental zealots cannot accommodate, but rather a rate of change so destabilizing as to provoke crises—social, biological and (as we see in the context of energy prices) economic. The disappearance of various species from the earth in the natural, evolutionary process is totally different from the disappearance of species over a short time. The key difference is not the *fact* of change, but the *rate* of change. The essence of the problem raised by public trust litigation is the imposition of destabilizing forces that prevent effective adaptation.

The central idea of the public trust is preventing the destabilizing disappointment of expectations held in common but without formal recognition such as title.[12] The function of the public trust as a legal doctrine is to protect such public expectations against destabilizing changes, just as we protect conventional private property from such changes.[13] So conceived, the trust

---

[12] Land-use regulation, whether effectuated by private covenant or by public zoning, reflects a recognition of values common to the community. The regulation most often is a joint effort to protect values diffused among all property owners within the regulated area.

[13] I am persuaded that the *absence* of perceived destabilizing change is the underlying rationale for the recent decisions in Penn Cent. Transp. Co. v. New York City, 438 U.S. 104 (1978), and Agins v. Tiburon, 100 S. Ct. 2138 (1980). By the time those proposals were initiated, sensible land owners knew, or should have known, that historical protection and open-space preservation were important public values and that they were increasingly being protected to the detriment of landowners. While it is impossible to specify exactly when owners will be charged with such knowledge, there comes a point at which courts simply cease to be sympathetic to owners' claims that their reasonable expectations are being sharply disappointed. That is, at some point the imposition of such restraints is no longer seen as sharply destabilizing for the land-

doctrine would serve not only to embrace a much wider range of things than private ownership, but would also make clear that the legal system is pursuing a substantive goal identical to that for the management of natural resources. Concepts like renewability and sustained yield, so familiar to us in fisheries and forest management, are designed precisely to prevent the sort of sudden decline in stocks that is destabilizing and crisis-provoking. The legal system incorporates parallel concerns in protecting expectations, and it remains only to assure the legal principle's application more comprehensively.

I can put some flesh on these bare bones by referring to the historical experience that most clearly reveals the proper sources for the legal public trust doctrine today: the tradition of the commons in medieval Europe. A statement of regional French law in the 11th century declared that "the public highways and byways, running water and springs, meadows, pastures, forests, heaths and rocks . . . are not to be held by lords, . . . nor are they to be maintained . . . in any other way than that their people may always be able to use them."[14] The wild places abundant in early settlements were commonly resorted to by members of nearby communities to cut wood and catch fish, to hunt and graze animals, to obtain peat and rushes from marshes, and brush and broom from the heaths. It was only natural that these places should be commonly available, since their common use was necessary for the maintenance of the feudal economy.

Feudal law was, of course, customary law. As the common use of uncultivated areas became customary, it was natural for these customary uses to be described as legally compelled and required by justice, since ideas of custom, justice and law were inextricably intertwined in medieval thought. To be sure, custom was not unchanging. Lords frequently imposed new demands on their people and thus created new customs. Nor was it unknown for new rights to be asserted and then described (fictionally) as if they were customary.

But as resources became scarce, objections by the lords to common rights were heard and were often the source of agrarian

---

development industry. One might say the same about the long line of wetland-protection cases. As such laws become more and more commonplace, wetlands owners will not be able to claim an expectational right to develop as they did in the past.

[14] M. Bloch, French Rural History 183 (1966).

revolts. The peasants responded to these incursions with indignation: "Let the knights then feel our strength," one writer said. "[W]e can go to the woods as we will—to cut the trees and take our pick—to catch the fish as they swim—to chase the deer through the forests—to do there what we please—in the clearings, waters and trees."[15] The claims did not ordinarily deny the legal or ethical possibility of private ownership. Rather, they asserted long-standing customary use and treated that assertion as a fact to be determined.[16]

It should be noted that not every attack on customary rights was deplored. Some traditional uses of the commons were condemned by agronomists as wasteful of good land which, with intelligent exploitation, might yield a richer harvest or support more livestock than it had in the past.[17] There was real merit to some of these claims, since traditional practices were often wasteful and sometimes highly destructive. The traditional customs were also an impediment to the aristocrats and entrepreneurs who stood ready to bring emergent capitalism to flower. They objected not only to inefficiency and waste, but also to

> the fact that the existence of commons and grazing rights made it too easy for small holders and manual laborers to eke out a meagre living, encouraged them to live in "idleness" when they might have been hiring themselves out to work on the great estates. In the eyes of men with a keen appreciation of individual effort, such people were a disgrace to "property."[18]

The agrarian economy of the forest, with its common uses and customary rights, was a pre-capitalist phenomenon. It was inefficient from the perspective of rising economic rationalism, and irresistible forces of economic change were washing over it.

---

[15] *Id.* at 182.

[16] In an English case of the 13th century, for example, men of the Archbishop of Canterbury of Maidstone complained that the Lord of Rochester stopped their ships going down the river and demanded a toll from them. It was argued that "they ought to give no toll . . . and ought to sail freely . . . and thus it was accustomed in the time of Archbishop Hubert Walter [in the past]." In response, it was said by Rochester, who sought to collect the toll, "that always from of old it has been used that, whether they were the ships of the archbishop [of Canterbury] or anyone else's, they were always accustomed and ought . . . to give tolls." Issue was thus joined, and the case was put to a jury for decision. Curia Regis Rolls, 15, No. 1079 (1234-1235).

[17] E. Thompson, Whigs and Hunters 109, 239-40 (1975); M. Bloch, *supra* note 13, at 213-18.

[18] M. Bloch, *supra* note 13, at 220.

Privatization of the bounty of nature was also a perfect symbol for emphasizing class distinctions.[19] Since nature's bounty obviously does not belong to anyone by common principles of justice—not being the product of anyone's labor, cultivation or discovery—to define it as the exclusive property of someone was to deem that person more important or more worthy than others. Nowhere was the point more tellingly made than in the rules about hunting. The events in early 18th-century England that led to the notorious Black Act—whereby deer poaching was made a capital offense—were perhaps the most extreme case. Terrible impositions were made on the traditional forest economy so that a newly rising class of London sportsmen could enjoy fashionable deer-hunting parties. The consumption of venison became a sign of status, "and the gift of game was one of the most delicate means by which the gentry expressed influence and solicited favor."[20]

Privatization and class separation were not the only pressures felt by the commons. The commons were also very valuable resources. In times of economic stringency, they became a battleground for sustenance between lords and peasants, a fertile source of controversy because their legal status was so often buried in a shadowy history of competing claims of title and custom.

This history of the commons does not demonstrate any absolute restraint upon the alienation of things comprising nature's bounty, for such things were frequently alienated away from community use. At the same time, despite alienation and formal ownership, *mere* title was not always sufficient to settle the controversies. One might have been able to trace a grant back a long time, but if common uses incompatible with the grant had developed, those uses had to be reckoned with. The more necessary the uses, the stronger the claims of justice that attached to the custom. By the same token, even long-standing uses could be attacked—sometimes for good and sometimes for base reasons—by appeal to claims of ownership right.

What brought disputes over the commons to crisis was neither

---

[19] "The absence of compact billages, and the dispersal of foresters, made social discipline impossible. . . . The gentry had decided . . . that enclosure was the best resource for agrarian class control." E. THOMPSON, *supra* note 7, at 239-40.

[20] *Id. See also* T. LUND, AMERICAN WILDLIFE LAW 8 (1980).

title nor custom, taken alone, but the sharp disappointment of expectations, continuance of which was perceived as a necessity. A stable equilibrium was being disrupted by the rigorous application of laws and claims of title unjustified by any social or economic necessity.

The medieval customary law had the striking advantage of putting developed expectations, rather than formalities such as title ownership, at the center of attention. While such established uses were not determinative, the significance of the established uses to the sustenance of the community as a stable entity was, in one way or another, factored into the ultimate result. The powerful reaction which the English Black Act engendered—precisely because its enforcement *was* so destabilizing and the advantages from its enforcement so largely trivial—suggests how claims of custom versus title worked themselves out.

To put these considerations into modern guise, consider the recent case of *City of Berkeley v. Superior Court of Alameda County*.[21] Although the grantee's chain of title extended back more than 100 years, there was no claim of private use during that period. Thus the potential destabilizing effect of disappointing the grantee's expectations should carry less weight than traditional analysis would give it. At the same time, there was a long-standing public or common use. The court took actual use into account in fashioning a remedy, to be sure, but there is no established doctrinal basis for recognizing these values. The same notions may be influential in the Mono Lake controversy, where it is the recent destabilizing action of Los Angeles which is really critical, rather than the formalities of arrangements made decades ago.[22]

I do not mean to suggest that the medieval doctrine of custom should be revived in the late 20th century under the name of the public trust.[23] I do believe, however, that the public trust doctrine should be employed to help us reach the real is-

[21] 26 Cal. 3d 515, 606 P.2d 362, 162 Cal. Rptr. 327, *cert. denied*, 101 S. Ct. 119 (1980).

[22] *See* National Audubon Soc'y v. Department of Water & Power, Civ. No. 566 (Alpine County Sup. Ct., Cal. filed 1979), *removed*, No. 80-127 (E.D. Cal. Feb. 20, 1980).

[23] The celebrated modern American custom case is State *ex rel.* Thornton v. Hay, 254 Or. 584, 462 P.2d 671 (1969).

sues—expectations and destabilization—whether the expectations are those of private property ownership, of a diffuse public benefit from ecosystem protection or of a community's water supply. The historical lesson of customary law is that the *fact* of expectations rather than some formality is central. Of course, title is not irrelevant where ownership is actually a surrogate for reliance and expectation and where non-recognition of title would in fact be destabilizing. Conversely, where title and expectations are not congruent, title should carry less weight. We do sometimes overtly recognize this point, as in the California cases of 1970 dealing with implied dedication of land permitting access to the sea.[24]

Our task is to identify the trustee's obligation with an eye toward insulating those expectations that support social, economic and ecological systems from avoidable destablization and disruption. Less acute intrusions should be selected where feasible. In dealing with projects proposed for bottomlands, for example, the trustee should ask whether they need to be water-based. Where the alternatives include a solution which will sustain yields and support long-established human uses or biological communities, that approach should be required. Where traditional expectations must give way to new techniques or new needs, the transition should be as evolutionary—rather than revolutionary—as the new needs permit.

In our legal system there is always a question of separation of powers underlying substantive questions. In considering the rights of private property owners and their rightful expectations, we endow the courts with the final word. Since expectations so diffusely held are not explicitly recognized in the Constitution, courts have been less willing to take ultimate responsibility for public trust claims. Some courts have nonetheless found the trust responsibility to be a constitutional mandate to legislatures, based on the requirement that legislative acts be for a public purpose.[25] For these courts, a failure to recognize, or at least to consider and deal with, expectations in ways that minimize destabilization of expectations could represent a failure to act for a public purpose.

---

[24] Gion v. Santa Cruz, 2 Cal. 3d 29, 465 P.2d 50, 84 Cal. Rptr. 162 (1970).

[25] People *ex rel.* Scott v. Chicago Park Dist., 66 Ill. 2d 65, 360 N.E.2d 773 (1976). *Cf.* P. Riesenberg, Inalienability of Sovereignty in Medieval Political Thought (1956).

But however appealing such interpretations may be, sharp confrontations between courts and legislatures should be avoided wherever possible. The courts can do much to provoke a search for less disruptive alternatives below the constitutional level. They can assure that decisions made by mere administrative bodies are not allowed to impair trust interests in the absence of explicit, fully considered legislative judgments. Under the rubric of the legislative remand,[26] courts can also press a legislature to fortify its decisions with a full consideration of less disruptive solutions. Finally, the courts can reduce the pressures that claims of private ownership put on public trust resources by looking to the history of common rights. The courts should recognize that mere unutilized title, however ancient, does not generate the sort of expectations central to the justness of property claims, and that long-standing public uses have an important place in the analysis.

With such an approach fully in operation, we could integrate legal doctrine and fundamental principles of intelligent resource management, instead of treating basic social decisions as if they were merely the province of a title examiner. We could draw sustenance from history, rather than viewing it as a sterile, manipulative game.

---

[26] *See* J. Sax, Defending the Environment 113-14 (1971).

Part III
Environmental Regulation

[6]

THE POLLUTION PROBLEM AND LEGAL INSTITUTIONS: A CONCEPTUAL OVERVIEW

James E. Krier*

INTRODUCTION

Even the staunchest of government-hands-off conservatives agree that some type of government intervention is generally called for in the case of pollution. Most environmental problems, pollution among them, must be solved by government action if they are to be solved at all. This is so simply because there are no viable alternative mechanisms to government control to restrain pollution and other environment-debilitating activities.[1] Without the imposition of governmental restraints, firms and individuals could pollute with utter abandon, because imperfections in the market mechanism would in most cases permit them to do so without taking account of the costs imposed upon others by their polluting activities.[2]

---

* B.S. 1961, J.D. 1966, University of Wisconsin. Acting Professor of Law, University of California at Los Angeles; Member, Wisconsin Bar. An earlier draft of this paper was prepared as a literature review for Project Clean Air, an interdisciplinary applied research project within the University of California. Many of the footnotes in that original paper served primarily a bibliographical function; I have kept them largely intact in the pages that follow with the thought that an organized and at least implicitly descriptive collection of the literature would be of value to others. I express my appreciation to Project Clean Air for the research support it made available.

1 One could argue, of course, that both public opinion and a sense of responsibility work as restraints on socially undesirable conduct, but in the case of pollution these usually cannot be considered "viable alternative mechanisms" to some form of governmental restraint. The reasons for this conclusion are suggested at various points in this article.

2 When I speak of governmental restraints or governmental intervention, I refer to restraints on or intervention in regard to a specific problem, such as pollution. In a pervasive way government always intervenes in social affairs by holding a monopoly on the legitimate use of force. But for this monopoly, pollution could disappear even without specific government intervention. One unhappy person could, for example, simply blow up all the polluters without fear of government reprisals. (Unhappy people occasionally act in spite of possible government reprisals. Consider, for example, the activities of "The Fox," "sort of an antipollution Zorro, who has been harassing various companies" to make them cut down on polluting activities. The Fox has been doing such things as plugging up the drainage systems and sealing the chimneys of firms in the Chicago area. "'Nothing seemed to make them stop. So I decided that even if I was only one man, I'd do something. I don't believe in hurting people or in destroying things, but I do believe in stopping things that are hurting our environment,'" the Fox has said. *See* Royko, *"The Fox" Stalks the Polluters . . . and Strikes*, L.A. Times, Sept. 23, 1970, pt. I, at 1, col. 1. *See also "The Fox,"* NEWSWEEK, Oct. 5, 1970, at 90.) The government monopoly of force under-

Take the case of air pollution. The air, when used as a garbage dump, becomes a factor of production because, once used in this way, it is less suitable for other uses. Like other factors (such as raw materials and labor), it should be purchased, and its "cost" should ultimately be reflected in the price the manufacturer charges for his product. But the market cannot function by itself to bring about this result in the case of air pollution. The market mechanism alone cannot force the polluter to pay for the right to use the air as a dump because there is no way the market can withhold air from the polluter; the air does not come in marketable packages. All of the receptors of pollution could, in theory, get together and pay polluters to stop, but as a practical matter this will never come about. In the first place, each receptor would be prone to take the position that he would be a fool to pay because the payments made by others would benefit him whether he paid or not. No person who paid a polluter could exclude these freeriders from the benefits of his payment. As a result, those few who might be willing to make payments to polluters would find it necessary to spend enormous sums, more or less equivalent to the sum a polluter would demand if all receptors were paying. Moreover, payments would have to be made to all polluters. A payment to one would obligate it to change its ways, but it would have no bearing on the conduct of others; they could continue to exploit the same air. (Indeed, it might encourage the appearance of new polluters who would demand similar payments in exchange for giving up the power to pollute.) Since the market would not function to charge for the right to pollute or the right to breathe, there would be no prices paid or payments foregone by pollution manufacturers which would convey to them information about the social utility of their conduct or give them an incentive to change their ways.[3] If quality improvements are to be realized, government intervention is called for.[4]

---

scores the inaccuracy often implicit in the position that government should do nothing. In not acting but in foreclosing others from a last resort to necessary physical force, government takes a position giving clear advantage to those who can realize their ends without force. In this sense, government cannot "do nothing." On the government monopoly of force, see J.W. HURST, LAW AND SOCIAL PROCESS IN UNITED STATES HISTORY (1960).

3 For some clear and excellent writing by economists on these points generally, see J.H. DALES, POLLUTION, PROPERTY, AND PRICES (1968); Goldman, *Pollution: The Mess Around Us*, in CONTROLLING POLLUTION: THE ECONOMICS OF A CLEANER AMERICA 3 (M. Goldman ed. 1967); Ruff, *The Economic Common Sense of Pollution*, PUBLIC INTEREST, Spring 1970, at 69.

4 *See, e.g.*, Mills, *Economic Incentives in Air-Pollution Control*, in THE ECONOMICS OF AIR POLLUTION 40-41 (H. Wolozin ed. 1966). One must always consider, of course, whether the benefits realized by quality improvements are worth the costs (the costs of government intervention, the value of opportunities foregone) involved in achieving them. *See* notes 19, 22-23 & accompanying text *infra*.

For those concerned with the form and function of legal institutions, there is little comfort in the advice that government must take a hand in solving pollution problems. Because government can only intervene through its agencies—through its executive, administrative, legislative and judicial bodies—important questions remain, including these: Which government or governments—federal, state, local or regional—should intervene, and in each case, through which of its institutions, and when, and in what manner? How has government intervened in the past, and with what success or failure? What indications are there of the need for change, and what direction should change take, and what risk is there that any change will, in solving the perceived problem, create other problems of greater dimensions?

These are the sorts of questions which must be confronted by those concerned with the role of legal institutions in society's response to pollution or any other problem. The purpose of this paper is to bring together and canvass knowledge about questions such as these and, in the process, to construct a framework for thinking about pollution problems which has meaning for legal institutions—in the sense of suggesting directions for fruitful change and research. While the focus of the discussion is primarily on the problem of air pollution, most of what follows applies to all pollution problems and, indeed, to the bulk of the other ills which plague the environment.

I. Legal Perspectives on the Pollution Problem

As a beginning, it may be worthwhile to return to a consideration of the nature of the air pollution problem, both to examine it in greater detail and to consider the role of political processes in the function of problem definition.

A. *The Nature of the Problem*

Lawyers and legal scholars have been far too ready to accept shallow definitions of the cause of air pollution. They have too often seen the essence of the problem as the presence of gases and particulates in the air or as their escape from smokestacks and other sources.[5] Of course, these are causes of the problem at one level of analysis. In another sense, however, they are only symptoms of underlying causes, the results of patterns of human behavior. While

[5] *See, e.g.*, Cowan, *Air Pollution Control in New Jersey*, 9 Rutgers L. Rev. 609, 610-11 (1955); Note, *Air Pollution: Causes, Sources and Abatement*, 1968 Wash. U.L.Q. 205.

this is all to some extent a matter of definition, it is not a matter to be settled arbitrarily, for one's perspective affects the action he takes. The smokestack viewed as a cause calls for an attack on the smokestack—put a control on it. This is very often the engineer's or technologist's response to the problem of pollution. The difficulty with this view is that it overlooks the possibility of attacking the underlying cause, of changing the incentives that lead to smoke production. Not all legal scholars have taken the perspective just described. There has recently appeared a good deal of legal research which discusses the sorts of market breakdowns which produce environmental problems,[6] and that discussion has led to valuable suggestions for dealing with social cost problems akin to the air pollution problem. For example, with regard to the sonic boom, Professor Baxter has concluded that the external costs imposed by the SST and its ear-cracking boom could be most efficiently internalized (that is, imposed on the SST) through the creation of a statutory fund supported by contributions from SST operators. This fund would be subject to damage suits and strict liability would be imposed upon it; moreover, social costs estimated by the government not to have been recovered in the damage suits would be assessed against the fund and made payable to the United States Treasury.[7]

Professor Baxter's analysis is interesting both because it illustrates the creative and constructive institutional mechanisms which can be built upon an understanding of social problems and because it is based upon a view of the social cost problem with which some scholars have taken issue. Professor Baxter's view of the problem of social cost is plainly reflected in two sentences taken from his article:

> Whenever a business activity imposes costs for which it is not required to pay, or bestows a benefit for which it is unable to charge, the price mechanism will not ensure a proper allocation of resources, even in a world of perfect competition.
>
> One of the primary functions of a legal system should be, then, to ensure that costs such as these do not remain external to the enterprise that creates them.[8]

---

[6] Several notable papers appear in one volume of the *Stanford Law Review*: Baxter, *The SST: From Watts to Harlem in Two Hours*, 21 STAN. L. REV. 1 (1968) [hereinafter cited as Baxter]; Note, *An Economic Analysis of Land Use Conflicts*, 21 STAN. L. REV. 293 (1969); Note, *The Cost-Internalization Case for Class Actions*, 21 STAN. L. REV. 383 (1969) [hereinafter cited as *The Cost-Internalization Case for Class Actions*]. *See also* Delogu, *Effluent Charges: A Method of Enforcing Stream Standards*, 19 ME. L. REV. 29 (1967); Hagevik, *Legislating for Air Quality Management: Reducing Theory to Practice*, 33 LAW & CONTEMP. PROB. 369 (1968).

[7] Baxter, *supra* note 6, at 53-57.

[8] *Id.* at 39.

But, which is the enterprise that "creates" the social cost? Professor Baxter's answer is consistent with the Pigovian tradition emphasizing the divergence between social and private cost. The private costs of the SST are less than the uncompensated costs its boom imposes on society, and unless that difference in cost is brought to bear on SST operators, resource misallocation will most likely result: too many SSTs will fly, and too many booms will crack. Similarly, in the case of the factory producing smoke, the same analysis would suggest that, since there is a divergence between the private and social product of the factory, it would be desirable from the standpoint of resource allocation to make the factory liable for smoke damage or impose on it a tax equal to the damage it causes or, finally, exclude it from areas in which the smoke is likely to cause harm to others.[9]

Professor Ronald Coase, an economist, has taken issue with both this analysis and the conclusions it suggests. He argues:

> The traditional approach has tended to obscure the nature of the choice that has to be made. The question is commonly thought of as one in which *A* inflicts harm on *B* and what has to be decided is: how should we restrain *A*? But this is wrong. We are dealing with a problem of a reciprocal nature. To avoid the harm to *B* would inflict harm on *A*. The real question that has to be decided is: should *A* be allowed to harm *B* or should *B* be allowed to harm *A*? The problem is to avoid the more serious harm.[10]

Professor Coase demonstrates that a pricing system operating without cost will automatically produce results which avoid the more serious harm—that is, results which reflect optimal resource allocation. These results will follow, if the pricing system operates without cost, whether or not polluters are liable for the damages they

---

[9] *See* Coase, *The Problem of Social Cost*, 3 J. LAW & ECON. 1-2 (1960) [hereinafter cited as Coase].

[10] *Id.* at 2. One case mentioned by Coase, *id.* at 11-13, Bryant v. Lefever, 4 C.P.D. 172 (1878-79), illustrates beautifully the reciprocal nature of the social cost problem. In *Bryant*, the plaintiff and the defendants occupied adjoining houses. Before 1876, the plaintiff could light fires in his house without the chimney smoking. But in that year the defendants rebuilt their house to a new height, cutting off the circulation of air over plaintiff's chimney and causing his house to fill with smoke whenever the plaintiff lit fires. The trial court found the defendants' activities had created a nuisance and awarded plaintiff damages. The appellate court reversed, holding that plaintiff's activity in lighting fires caused the nuisance. Coase says of these opinions, "Who caused the smoke nuisance? The answer seems fairly clear. The smoke nuisance was caused both by the man who built the wall *and* by the man who lit the fires. Given the fires, there would have been no smoke nuisance without the wall; given the wall, there would have been no smoke nuisance without the fires. Eliminate the wall *or* the fires and the smoke nuisance would disappear." Coase, *supra* note 9, at 13.

cause.[11] In other words, in a world with a frictionless market, liability rules are neutral from the standpoint of resource allocation.

A simple example will clarify this point (which is so contrary to most of the assumptions of law-trained people). Assume that a house on a plot of land is let by its owner at an annual rent of one thousand dollars. A factory buys an adjacent piece of land and begins production activity which sends sooty and unpleasant smelling smoke over and into the house during most of the year. Suppose that the factory makes a profit of two thousand dollars per year as conditions stand, but to abate its pollution (with control equipment or by changing fuels or production methods or by moving to a different area) would reduce the profit to fifteen hundred dollars. Suppose too that under the changed conditions the landlord can get only eight hundred dollars rent, and that putting his property to a different use or abandoning it altogether would leave him even worse off.

In a system in which the factory's activities do not give the landlord a right of action for damages, the landlord would bear the annual rent loss of two hundred dollars and the factory would continue to pollute. The landlord might offer to pay the factory up to two hundred dollars to abate its pollution. That offer, however, would be refused by the factory since abatement would cost five hundred dollars. The landlord would not rationally put his property to a different use or abandon it, for that would leave him even worse off than settling for the decreased rent payments.

Suppose, however, that the law makes the factory liable for damages to the landlord. The damages in this case would be two hundred dollars (loss of rent) and a rational factory owner would pay that amount, since any other means of avoiding liability would cost him at least an additional three hundred dollars. Presumably, landlord (and tenant) and a factory carrying on operations as usual would have been satisfied. And, just as with the case where the factory was not liable, the same amount of pollution would exist. There would be a different distribution of wealth between the landlord and the factory owner under one scheme than the other,[12] but resource allocation would be the same in either case.

Of course, liability rules are neutral only in a world which does not exist, a world where people are rational; where they have or can obtain without the cost of time, effort or money all the information

---

[11] *Id.* at 2-15.

[12] The question of wealth distribution is by no means unimportant. *See* note 23 & accompanying text *infra*.

they need to exercise their rationality; and where they can freely bargain without any effort or expense (other than the consideration exchanged in the bargaining process) with those whose activities bear on their interests. Obviously, these suppositions which underlie the assumption of costless market transactions make that assumption "a very unrealistic" one.[13] For, as Professor Coase says:

> In order to carry out a market transaction it is necessary to discover who it is that one wishes to deal with, to inform people that one wishes to deal and on what terms, to conduct negotiations leading up to a bargain, to draw up the contract, to undertake the inspection needed to make sure that the terms of the contract are being observed, and so on. These operations are often extremely costly, sufficiently costly at any rate to prevent many transactions that would be carried out in a world in which the pricing system worked without cost.[14]

When all of these information and transaction costs are taken into account, the sorts of bargains or market transactions which would efficiently allocate resources are unlikely to come about, for the costs of the bargaining process might well outweigh the benefits of the bargain. The landlord and factory owner in our illustration, for example, might not bargain if that process required substantial legal fees.

Under these circumstances the initial delimitation of rights and liabilities by the legal system does make a difference. When the costs of bargaining are greater than the benefits of the bargain

> the granting of an injunction (or the knowledge that it would be granted) or the liability to pay damages may result in an activity being discontinued (or may prevent its being started) which would be undertaken if market transactions were costless. In these conditions the initial delimitation of legal rights does have an effect on the efficiency with which the economic system operates. One arrangement of rights may bring about a greater value of production than any other. But unless this is the arrangement of rights established by the legal system, the costs of reaching the same result by altering and combining rights through the market may be so great that this optimal arrangement of rights, and the greater value of production which it would bring, may never be achieved.[15]

---

13 *Id.* at 15. Economics is often attacked for its unrealistic assumptions. *See, e.g.*, Hamill, *The Process of Making Good Decisions About the Use of the Environment of Man*, 8 NATURAL RESOURCES J. 279, 280 (1968): "All economic theories make general assumptions about the economic behavior of individuals, firms, and governments. These assumptions seldom are realistic. . . ." Professor Hamill, of course, asumes that unrealistic assumptions are not helpful. While this is in some cases undoubtedly true, in other cases it clearly is not. The unrealistic assumptions in Coase's model, for example, have great utility. They help identify the ways in which the real world diverges from the economist's ideal model, thus in turn helping to identify targets for government action designed to change the world (if that is what we wish to do).

14 Coase, *supra* note 9, at 15.

15 *Id.* at 16.

The bearing of Professor Coase's analysis on the form and function of legal institutions has been recently outlined in a cogent essay by Professor Calabresi.[16] The balance of this section will sketch Calabresi's ideas so that reference may be made to them in subsequent discussion.

Bear in mind that the central concern here is optimal allocation of the air resource to competing (polluting and nonpolluting) uses. Resource misallocation exists when a change in resource use would produce a situation where those who gained from the reallocation could fully compensate those who lost and, after this compensation process, some persons would be better off than before. Only when no reallocation could benefit someone at no necessary cost to anyone does an optimal allocation exist. The costless and rational bargaining described by Coase would obviously produce optimal resource allocation because a misallocation would exist whenever the situation could be improved by bargains and, with no costs attached to the process, rational people would always bargain under such circumstances to the optimal point. From this it follows that all resource misallocations can be corrected by the market except insofar as information and transaction costs and other impediments (like criminal sanctions which do not permit one to buy his way out) create bargaining obstacles. The resource allocation goal is to produce, as closely and as cheaply as possible, that allocation which would result if the market worked costlessly.[17] The relevant issues then become: Is this best accomplished by government intervention, by reliance on the market, or by some combination of these? If government intervention is required to achieve the resource allocation goal, what mix of institutional forms and means should be used?[18] Government can intervene at the federal, the state, the local and the regional level. At each of these levels, it can intervene through (or through any combination of) executive, legislative, judicial and administrative bodies; moreover, each of these bodies can intervene in a variety of ways. The legislature, for example, can regulate, it can subsidize, it can tax, it can simply gather and disseminate information. Each of these means probably brings with it different costs. Some means may bring with them higher relative chances of reaching wrong results. The problem is to pick, largely by guesswork, the institutional response which will likely bring with it the minimal mix of risk and cost and then to decide whether those

16 Calabresi, *Transaction Costs, Resource Allocation and Liability Rules—A Comment*, 11 J. LAW & ECON. 67 (1968) [hereinafter cited as Calabresi].
17 *Id.* at 67-69.
18 *Id.* at 69.

risks and costs are worth the benefits which will hopefully flow from the reallocation of resources.[19]

Of course, there is not a great amount of knowledge about what allocation of resources is optimal, nor is there much information in any rigorous sense about the benefits resulting from incremental steps toward that allocation.[20] Take once again the case of the air pollution problem. While more than an occasional voice can be heard to cry for absolutely clean air at any cost whatsoever,[21] most sensible people have come to realize that there is a point where the benefits from a further percentage increase in air quality are outweighed by what must be given up elsewhere to achieve that increase (as well as a point where information bearing on further possible benefits and costs is not itself worth the expense of acquisition). As a practical matter, however, we shall never know, in anything approaching rigorous quantified terms, just what that point is.[22] For one thing, there is no way to quantify all of the variables required by the calculus involved. Even if there were, the expense of reducing all of them to quantitative terms would probably be overwhelming. As a result, it is necessary to make collective guesses about whether the benefits of further increases in air quality are worth the costs of attaining them. Is action appropriate or should the market be left to work things out as best it can?

In facing this question, two guidelines should be considered. The first is to respond in ways which, if wrong, can be most cheaply corrected by unassisted market action. This guideline gives us insights into *whether* government should intervene (could the market more cheaply correct an error resulting from government action or from government inaction?) and *how* it should intervene (could the market more cheaply correct an error resulting from some form of regulation or from liability rules?). The second guideline is to take actions and forms of action which serve other goals with, at worst, no predictably unfavorable impact on resource allocation.

---

19 *Id.*

20 *Id.* at 69-70.

21 For example, Louis Fuller, former head of the Los Angeles Air Pollution Control District, has said, "No cost concerns me. As far as health and well-being is concerned, no cost." *The Advocates*, KCET Television, Los Angeles, Oct. 5, 1969 (transcript).

22 *See generally* Ayres, *Air Pollution in Cities*, 9 NATURAL RESOURCES J. 1, 12-18 (1969). On the imperfections of our present cost and benefit data, see Kneese, *How Much is Air Pollution Costing Us in the United States?*, in PROCEEDINGS, THIRD NATIONAL CONFERENCE ON AIR POLLUTION 529 (Public Health Service Pub. No. 1649, 1966).

Government action (or government action of a particular sort) may produce a favored distribution of income, for example, with no discernible adverse effect on resource allocation.[23] Indeed, with respect to the air pollution problem, the income distribution and resource allocation goals often appear to be very compatible.[24]

All of the above remarks have great bearing on the sorts of institutional responses which should be made to pollution problems. Before considering them in that context, however, it may be worthwhile to discuss briefly their implications for the environmental quality decision process again by focusing on the problem of air pollution.

B. *The Problem and the Political Process*

The air quality decision necessarily depends upon collectively made hunches about relative costs and benefits.[25] These hunches are loaded with subjective value judgments (which undoubtedly explains why the central point of most arguments over environmental quality questions is coming to be, at least implicitly and unconsciously, an analysis of costs and benefits at the margin). Consider, for example, the case of a big factory planned for a depressed city in the Deep South. The factory might foul the air for the people living there, but at least it will give them jobs. Most people sense that the issue is whether the new prosperity is worth the loss in good breathing; as one would expect, however, that issue tends to be resolved differently by the different classes of people involved in the decision. Low-income groups quite uniformly weigh the gains and losses in such a way as to make the factory a worthwhile addition to the local economy; the more affluent use accounting methods and measures that yield the opposite result.[26] This divergence in viewpoint illustrates the nature of the air quality decision.

The relevant inquiry then becomes a quite typical one. How should the institutions of political process be shaped to bring them most democratically to bear on these value questions of air quality? Consider the machinery of federal air pollution control legislation as it functioned before the recent amendments. With respect to fixed-source emissions, the law required that the Department of Health, Education and Welfare develop air quality criteria describing the nature of various pollutants and their effects at different

---

[23] Calabresi, *supra* note 16, at 70. Or, indeed, we may in some cases prefer to have the resulting distribution of income *even if* an adverse effect on resource allocation comes with it.

[24] *See* notes 43-44 & subsequent text *infra*.

[25] *See* text accompanying note 22 *supra*.

[26] *See, e.g.*, Simon, *Battle of Beaufort*, New Republic, May 23, 1970, at 11.

levels, and the states were then to translate these criteria into air quality standards (ambient air standards) and implementation programs (such as emission standards) designed to achieve the desired level of air quality.[27] Where should the value judgments which are an essential ingredient in the air quality decision have come to appear in this flow chart of decision making? More particularly, how should all the dirty and practical, but nevertheless unavoidable, considerations of politics have come to bear on the decision process? One would think not at the criteria stage:

> Air quality criteria, expressed in terms of pollutant concentration and duration of exposure, describe relationships between air pollutants and effects on health and welfare. Such criteria summarize what is known about the effects of pollutants in the atmosphere to provide a realistic base for selecting air quality standards.[28]

Thus, the criteria stage would at first appear to be a pure, and a purely scientific, phase of the decision process, based on objective and quantifiable standards, such as health considerations, damage to plants and animals, visibility, and metal corrosion,[29] which appear to admit of no room for "political" or value considerations.

Yet the "relationships between air pollutants and effects on health and welfare"[30] described by the federal criteria are loaded with aesthetic and physical and mental comfort factors which are difficult if not impossible to objectify. As a result, the extent to which criteria reflect them is a matter of judgment to be decided on the basis of principles or values—on a subjective rather than a totally scientific, or technical, or objective basis. But decided on the basis of *whose* values, and through the channels of what value-gathering processes? With regard to these questions, consider the statement of two Washington, D.C. lawyers:

> Before HEW . . . issues criteria, it must obtain the requisite advice. It was intended that HEW obtain the best advice available. Industry members should be prepared to do all they can to help develop sound criteria and accurate control information. Individuals invited by HEW to be a consultant or to work with an advisory committee in

---

27 *See generally* Air Quality Act of 1967 §§ 101-10, 42 U.S.C. §§ 1857-57e (Supp. V, 1970); Middleton, *Summary of the Air Quality Act of 1967*, 10 ARIZ. L. REV. 25 (1968). The Air Quality Act was recently amended by the Clean Air Amendments of 1970, Pub. L. No. 91-604 (Dec. 31, 1970). The amendments made some changes in the pattern described in the text; for example, federal air quality standards and some federal emission standards are now provided for. But the amendments do not make obsolete the questions of process described above or elsewhere in the text; indeed, they simply raise them in a new context.

28 U.S. DEP'T OF HEALTH, EDUCATION AND WELFARE, NATIONAL CENTER FOR AIR POLLUTION CONTROL, AIR QUALITY CRITERIA OF SULFUR OXIDES iv (1967).

29 *Id.* at vi-vii.

30 *Id.* at iv.

either of these areas will not be acting as industry representatives as much as experts in their fields. Therefore, other members of industry not serving on such committees must also seek an opportunity to present their points of view and information. This may be done by contacting members of an advisory committee after they have been announced or in consultation with state and local officials who will confer with the federal government on the local problems.[31]

The statement underscores the distinctly political (or "value-loaded") nature of the criteria decision process. Indeed, that process may be as much a political one as the later steps bearing on the setting of air quality standards, which were explicitly politicized by a statutory requirement of that great instrument of participatory democracy, the public hearing.[32]

---

[31] Martin & Symington, *A Guide to the Air Quality Act of 1967*, 33 LAW & CONTEMP. PROB. 239, 244-45 (1968) (emphasis omitted). The lawyers who wrote this article are members of a firm which acts as general counsel to the National Coal Policy Conference, Inc., and the article was "adapted from a pamphlet bearing the same title which was prepared by the authors for and distributed by the National Coal Policy Conference, Inc." *Id.* at 239 (introductory footnotes). What was originally conjecture about the pressure of politics on the criteria-setting stage can be stated as reported fact after the Nader task force report on the National Air Pollution Control Association. *See* J. ESPOSITO, VANISHING AIR 280-87 (1970).

[32] *See* Air Quality Act of 1967 § 108(c)(1), 42 U.S.C. § 1857d(c)(1) (Supp. V 1970). The hearings may in some instances have resulted in more *actual* participatory democracy than the draftsmen of the Air Quality Act anticipated. The following items are from an account of recent events in Pennsylvania, reported in the Wall Street Journal, Oct. 21, 1969, at 1, col. 1:

> Yesterday the breather's lobby won a victory that may have repercussions in many other states. Meeting in Harrisburg, the capital, the commission recommended that Pennsylvania's air pollution limits be made the most stringent in the nation.
>
> If public agitation seems to have had a striking effect in the Harrisburg decision, it is due to a national law—the Federal Air Quality Act of 1967—that specifically leaves the establishment of pollution limits up to the states.
>
> . . . .
>
> An unusual, key role for the public was written into the law. States are required to hold public hearings while setting standards and are urged to do so while drafting plans for implementation. Transcripts of such hearings must go to HEW along with the proposed standards. Whether HEW accepts or rejects standards "will be based in part on examination of the transcripts," according to the agency's official guidelines.
>
> . . . .
>
> Yesterday the commission heeded public sentiment. It decided to recommend a maximum standard of 65 micrograms per cubic meter of air for suspended particulates, far below the initial recommendation of 100 micrograms. And it proposed stiff controls on sulfur dioxide. . . .
>
> Chairman Brandt says the commission was influenced chiefly in its decision by two factors. One was "the many, many comments at the public hearings plus the many, many comments and letters we got in the mail."
>
> . . . .
>
> Mr. Brandt isn't happy with the commission's action. He thinks such strict controls aren't feasible. "The (state) health department had made a study in Philadelphia," he says, "and they don't think these numbers can be reached in that area with current technology."
>
> Major industrial companies in the state offered no comment on the commission's decision. Indeed, they have withheld public comment on the dispute throughout the hearing period. However, William B. Tipton, a state

This last observation suggests a number of questions, these among them: What bearing might the conclusions reached in the criteria-formulation process have on the decision processes of later stages (whether undertaken by legislative or administrative bodies), such as those relating to standard setting and the design and implementation of enforcement programs? What might the answers to this question suggest about the degree to which the criteria-formulation process should or should not be politicized (or open to competing values and interests)? If it should not be politicized, what adjustments are necessary? If it should remain politicized, to what extent does the present structure provide unequal access to various interests, and how do we go about constructing fairer procedures? Do the answers to these questions suggest alterations which should be made in later stages of the decision process and, if so, what are those changes, and where should they be made, and how? How can the invasion of nonpolitical stages by political forces and considerations be prevented? How can the dominance of political stages by intense and often overzealous interest groups, whether they speak for industry or "the public," be avoided?[33]

So long as the plain and simple question of how much pollution will be allowed remains one of values, answerable only by balancing subjective considerations, questions like these are crucial ones. And they are also questions to which the lawyer, with his insights into the reach and limitations of process and procedure, and his knowledge of the ways of negotiation and compromise, can contribute much, if not by himself, then along with others from such disciplines as economics, sociology and political science.[34]

Chamber of Commerce official who testified at the hearings, said, "The standards are much too stringent."

Joseph Mullen, an air pollution control expert for the coal industry, had this comment: "It will be interesting to see how they implement these things. I wish them well, but I don't see how they're going to make 65." Mr. Mullen argues that the quality of low-sulphur coal needed to meet such tight standards simply isn't available.

In a sense, yesterday's events are only a preliminary triumph for the breathers' lobby. Now the proposed standards must be forwarded to the HEW, which must pass on them. Then comes the massive task of devising plans to implement the standards and setting a timetable for action.

Since passage of the 1970 amendments, standard setting is now a federal job, and public hearings are not provided for. However, the states must hold public hearings before adopting implementation plans. *See* Clean Air Amendments of 1970, Pub. L. No. 91-604, § 4(a) (1970).

[33] Surely it would not be unfair to conclude that it was a small and intense interest group which captured the hearing described in note 32 *supra*, and—just as surely, it would seem—there is no reason to suppose that the fact that that group was composed of "just plain citizens" tends to assure that the result of the hearing was more in the actual public interest than if the hearing had been dominated and captured by industry lobbyists.

[34] For a valuable interdisciplinary study, undertaken by students, documenting the extent to which the public can be excluded from participation in the environ-

Unfortunately, lawyers and law-trained people have devoted very little attention to the issues springing from the distinctly subjective nature of environmental quality questions. As a result, there have been few insights into the processes by which those questions should be decided or the role legal institutions should play in problem definition. Some observers apparently believe there is agreement about quality goals and that only the mechanics (lawsuits, legislation, and so forth) of how to achieve them need be decided.[35] Others recognize the judgmental dimensions of environmental problems but are satisfied to stop there, to point out that much of our present problem "is due largely to the lack of any consensus to effectuate the necessary change," but to suggest only that we need a concept of living "in harmony with nature" which "can only be created through education and persuasion."[36] But it might be fair to ask a lawyer: Education and persuasion of whom, and by whom, through what specific means and to what specific ends? Questions like these have seldom been asked, let alone answered.

It should be clear that I am not downplaying the function of problem identification as opposed to problem solution; one of the great and necessary tasks of legal process is to help define the dimensions of social problems (for example, as lawsuits have done in the case of poverty and racial injustice and as the congressional hearing has done in the case of national malnutrition). But it is time to begin identifying in a more specific way problems which are not so obvious. Yes, the environment is polluted, but how clean do we want it, and how do we go about deciding that? Yes, the public has been indifferent, but why, and how do we turn indifference into constructive concern? And, more particularly, at which level of government

mental quality decision process (in this case, in the course of decisions by an air pollution control agency) and making constructive suggestions for change, see STANFORD WORKSHOP ON AIR POLLUTION, AIR POLLUTION IN THE SAN FRANCISCO BAY AREA, pt. III (1970). For other examples of the sorts of product which interdisciplinary research in the area of air pollution decision making could yield, see the article of a planner, Hagevik, *Legislating for Air Quality Management: Reducing Theory to Practice*, 33 LAW & CONTEMP. PROB. 369 (1968) and the comments thereon of a lawyer, Mandelker, *Quality Standards for the Control of Air Pollution*, in DEVELOPMENT OF AIR QUALITY STANDARDS 207, 209-12 (A. Atkinson & R. Gaines eds. 1970). For an example of the sort of rigorous and valuable interdisciplinary research to which law-trained people can contribute, see De Vany, Eckert, Meyers, O'Hara, & Scott, *A Property System for Market Allocation of the Electro Magnetic Spectrum: A Legal-Economic-Engineering Study*, 21 STAN. L. REV. 1499 (1969).

35 *See, e.g.*, Yannacone, *A Lawyer Answers the Technocrats*, TRIAL, Aug./Sept. 1969, at 14: "The basic priority is recognition by our courts that the public has a right to a salubrious environment. . . ."

36 Reitze, *Pollution Control: Why Has it Failed?*, 55 A.B.A.J. 923, 926-27 (1969). Compare the treatment in Hardin, *The Tragedy of the Commons*, 162 SCIENCE 1243 (1968).

should decisions about environmental quality be made? Which branch of government (for example, the administrative or the legislative) should bear the responsibility for the ultimate operative decisions about quality? At what stage and where should hearings be held, and what sorts of questions should they be concerned about? Does local control of hearings result in more citizen participation, but parochial decisions? What sorts of practical tradeoffs can be identified and evaluated in confronting these questions? I am not suggesting that the time and resources are available to explore all of these and similar issues, or that the answers would in each instance be worthwhile. However, some inquiries like these must be made by law-trained people. Only when questions become more specific will answers become less diffuse and more relevant.[37]

II. Pollution and the Courts

A striking feature of legal scholarship, reflected in the body of knowledge about pollution and the courts, is its preoccupation with judicial process. We have much more insight into the role of the courts, actual and potential, in pollution problems than we do, for example, into the legislature's role. There is an irony here, for one of our clearest and most significant insights is that the courts can play only a relatively small, although important, part in the environmental drama.

The discussion which follows focuses primarily on the courts in the context of private lawsuits seeking damages or injunctive relief against a polluter, and citizen suits challenging the pollution planning and enforcement activities of public officials.[38] Two other media of judicial intervention—the adjudication of criminal and civil charges against alleged violators of pollution control statutes and the policing of legislative programs under the constitutional requirements of due process and equal protection, are so much a part of the process of legislation and administration that they will be considered (albeit briefly) in that context in the next section. The main concern of this section is with the courts acting out the common-law tradition of rule origination, development and application.

---

[37] *See, e.g.*, Murphy, *A Law for Life*, 1969 Wis. L. Rev. 773. The interesting paper by Professor Murphy suggests many of the specific sorts of questions into which lawyers may fruitfully begin inquiry. For a constructive inquiry into specifics —into the role a specific legal institution (the courts) can play in regard to a specific problem (that of democratizing the process of decision making about environmental quality) through a specific legal doctrine (that of the public trust), see Sax, *The Public Trust Doctrine in Natural Resource Law: Effective Judicial Intervention*, 68 Mich. L. Rev. 471 (1970). *See also* J. Sax, Defending the Environment (1970).

[38] The latter is currently an area of exciting development. *See* text accompanying notes 53-59 *infra*.

A. *The Objectives of Environmental Litigation*

By assigning specific objectives to litigation arising out of environmental problems such as pollution, the strengths and weaknesses of the courts as a medium of pollution control can be assessed more systematically and areas that need change or at least further investigation can be isolated. Objectives in this context are not those of individual litigants, whose primary aim is usually to win either a judgment or some sort of moral victory, but rather the sorts of objectives litigation as an institution should serve. For example, an individual litigant's objective may be to exert pressure on an adversary by bringing a spurious but expensive lawsuit; but this is most surely not an institutional objective of litigation and, accordingly, barriers are erected to guard against such suits and various penalties may be imposed if they are discovered. The discussion which follows assigns three institutional objectives to pollution litigation; while the list is not all-inclusive, it represents the primary aims of importance here.

1. Internalization of Costs

A common analysis of the pollution problem is that it represents a case where certain costs are imposed on society at large by the activities of polluters, and because of failures in the market mechanism those costs remain external to their source—that is, they are not taken into account by polluters in deciding whether or not their activites are worthwhile to them or society at large. Recently some legal scholars have begun to make a constructive examination of private litigation as a means of internalizing these costs (for example, through the award of damages against polluters), thus bringing them to bear on private production decisions.[39]

Not all of the work thus far has considered the relevance of Professor Coase's article on *The Problem of Social Cost*;[40] rather, it has proceeded on the basis of the traditional Pigovian analysis upon which Coase cast doubt and has, accordingly, assumed that polluters should be required to pay receptors for pollution damage. Coase's analysis, on the other hand, would ask which group, polluters or receptors, is the cheapest cost avoider. (That is, in a costless market would receptors end up adjusting in some way to the presence of pollution, or would polluters end up taking abatement steps?) If it was known which group was generally the cheapest cost avoider,

39 *See* Katz, *The Function of Tort Liability in Technology Assessment*, 38 U. Cin. L. Rev. 587 (1969); and the three papers from volume 21 of the *Stanford Law Review* cited in note 6 *supra*.

40 Coase, *supra* note 9.

the appropriate action from the standpoint of resource allocation would be to put liability on it. Lacking this information, Coasian analysis would suggest asking whether transaction and information costs would be lower with the initial right in receptors (that is, with liability on polluters) or in polluters (that is, with no liability on polluters). This analysis would envision "bargains" (perhaps instigated by lawsuits) or an exchange of rights between polluters and receptors and would argue for that arrangement of rights which would minimize bargaining (transaction and information) costs, thus giving the market the best chance to correct any resource allocation errors which might result from the initial assignment of rights. The analysis would also suggest consideration of other means, such as programs of government regulation, which might permit errors to be corrected even more cheaply than under a regime of liability rules.[41]

While it may be that some economists have grasped the full significance of Coase's thesis for liability rules, most lawyers surely have not.[42] Indeed, it is not at all clear that law-trained people are even confident that they can formulate relevant questions. In some limited senses, this may not be a significant shortcoming. The few commentators who appear to have considered the question have concluded that a Coasian analysis suggests that bargaining costs are lowest when liability rests on polluters.[43] The reasoning underlying this conclusion can be illustrated as follows:[44] Assume that there is a single polluter, *P*, and a class, *C*, of pollution-receptor citizens. If no liability were placed on *P* (in other words, if *P* were given the right

---

41 *See* Calabresi, *supra* note 16; Calabresi, *Does the Fault System Optimally Control Primary Accident Costs?*, 33 LAW & CONTEMP. PROB. 429 (1968).

42 *But see* articles cited note 41 *supra*; Calabresi, *The Decision for Accidents: An Approach to Nonfault Allocation of Costs*, 78 HARV. L. REV. 713 (1965); Calabresi, *Fault, Accidents and the Wonderful World of Blum and Kalven*, 75 YALE L.J. 216 (1965); *The Cost-Internalization Case for Class Actions*, *supra* note 6; Note, *An Economic Analysis of Land Use Conflicts*, 21 STAN. L. REV. 293 (1969).

43 *See* Calabresi, *supra* note 16, at 69 n.7; Calabresi, *Does the Fault System Optimally Control Primary Accident Costs?*, 33 LAW & CONTEMP. PROB. 429, 447 (1968); *The Cost-Internalization Case for Class Actions*, *supra* note 6, at 383, 385-98, 403-04 (1969). (The ideas expressed in Professor Calabresi's series of articles have recently been collected in the valuable book, G. CALABRESI, THE COSTS OF ACCIDENTS (1970).)

Of course, many people would simply take the position that Coase's theorem is irrelevant to the liability decision in any event, that pollution is bad and should be forbidden or penalized on purely moral grounds. In principle, there is nothing wrong with this position, so long as one recognizes that he may be sacrificing the gains of an efficient resource allocation for the gains of moral satisfaction. In practice, the issue may turn on discovering the basis for a moral judgment that pollution is bad, or at least that it is morally worse than some alternatives to pollution activity, such as decreasing industrial production at the cost of fewer jobs for poor people.

44 The example is drawn from *The Cost-Internalization Case for Class Actions*, *supra* note 6, at 403-04.

to pollute), the members of *C* would face the expenses of getting together, holding meetings, negotiating among themselves and deciding what sum it was worth to all of them (and in what proportion) to offer *P* in an effort to induce *P* to stop polluting. These would be expensive transaction costs, and they would be increased by the fact that there will almost always be a large group of receptors (for example, all of the citizens living downwind of a polluting factory). Each member of the group would be likely to feel that he need not contribute anything, since any offer to *P* would benefit him (as a member of the downwind group) whether he paid or not. He could be a freerider, for no member could be excluded from the benefits of the group's offer to *P*. Because of the high transaction costs, voluntary bargains between *P* and *C* would be unlikely to occur if *P* had the enforceable right. Moreover, forced bargains in the frame of a lawsuit would also be unlikely to occur. *P* could enforce his right simply by polluting. *C* would have no basis for a suit (*P* would be within his rights) and, as explained above, no other bargain would likely occur; even if such a bargain did occur, it would be only after heavy bargaining expenditures. In short, with the right vested in *P*, internalization would probably never come about.

Many of these difficulties disappear or are minimized, however, if *P* is liable for polluting. Members of *C* would have an incentive to sue because they could recover damages—there would be far less freeriding. Members of *C* would not have to meet and negotiate among themselves, for each one could bargain with or sue *P*. Bargains in some form would be encouraged. *P* would know it faced a forced bargain in court and would thus be motivated to take steps to avoid pollution damage or to make voluntary offers to members of *C*, in order to avoid the costs of a lawsuit. It would also be likely that *P* would have lower information costs than members of *C*. *P*, for example, would have the best information about its own capability for pollution control and might see technological changes as its cheapest alternative. If *P* were potentially liable, it would make those changes rather than suffer lawsuit damages. If, on the other hand, *P* had pollution rights, it could in effect "hold up" members of *C* by extracting from them payments that represented to *C* members what it was worth to them to stop pollution or keep from moving to new homes, even if those payments were higher than the cost to *P* of pollution control.

This analysis would appear to hold even if there were more than one polluter, as long as there were significantly fewer pollution producers than pollution receptors. Assuming an absence of information about who is the cheapest cost-avoider, it seems almost axiomatic that in the case of pollution the polluter is the proper target for liability rules—essentially because of the typically high ratio of receptors to polluters, the polluter's greater command of relevant information and technology, and the fact that the problem centers around a common property resource, such as air, from the enjoyment of which freeriders cannot be excluded without prohibitive policing costs.[45]

To the extent that the fact assumptions about pollution problems which lead to this axiom are realistic ones, it appears to matter little whether liability is assigned to polluters on the basis of Coasian analysis, on the basis of traditional Pigovian analysis, or on the basis of some moral judgment about the "badness" of pollution-causing activity. But what of the case where at least some of these assumptions do not apply? What of the case, for example, in which the receptor is a unique firm which requires absolutely dust-free conditions in order to engage in its speciality of assembling precision equipment? Here there are millions of polluters (for almost all of us and all of industry engage in activities which cause dust, like cutting lawns or doing the wash), but only one suffering receptor. To eliminate the pollution at its source might be relatively inefficient, inconvenient, and generally undesirable in its impact, but the application of a rule against "polluters" under these circumstances would probably compel these results. There may be many similar kinds of situations of which we are unaware. Since liability has been traditionally assigned on bases—moral or otherwise—which have paid no heed to the way one situation differs from another in terms of transaction costs, information costs, and so forth, those differences do not tend to stand out. In short, we are not sensitized to them; yet they may be very relevant to our policy decisions.[46]

This seems to suggest that it would be worthwhile to inquire about the variety of pollution problems (problems where there are many polluters and many receptors, as with the case of the automobile; problems where there are many polluters and few receptors, as with the case of the assembly firm above; problems

---

[45] *See* Krier, *Environmental Litigation and the Burden of Proof*, in LAW AND THE ENVIRONMENT 105, 117 n.38a (M. Baldwin & J. Page eds. 1970). Since most persons would probably consider liability on polluters as the most desirable outcome from the standpoint of income distribution (not to mention moral judgment), the situation presents a set of goals which are quite compatible and reinforcing.

[46] I owe these observations and the assembly firm example to Professor Michael E. Levine of the University of Southern California Law Center.

For an example of the sorts of contrariness which can be discovered in assignments of liability if one is sensitive to other than the traditional and moral considerations, see Note, *An Economic Analysis of Land Use Conflicts*, 21 STAN. L. REV. 293 (1969) (discussing nuisance law). Both this Note, *id.* at 298 n.13, and *The Cost-Internalization Case for Class Actions*, *supra* note 6, at 383, 388-98 (1969) take issue with portions of Coase's analysis.

where there are few polluters and few receptors, as with the case of the factory in remote farm land) and about the variety of cost-avoiding techniques of receptors and polluters as to each strain of the problem, as well as to ask about how the findings bear on the decision about imposition of liability rules. Moreover, this is an inquiry which should be undertaken not simply by lawyers, and not simply by economists, but by lawyers and economists working in concert. And, as should become clear, this can be said of much of the research which needs to be done in the case of pollution problems and legal process.

Once it is decided, however, that liability should be imposed on the polluter in a specific type of case, there is a whole store of information about how to achieve that goal. One result of the long preoccupation with judicial process has been an industrious gathering up of kernels of knowledge about how to make polluters pay. The basic causes of action for relief by damages or injunction against polluting activity—negligence, nuisance, trespass, and strict liability—have received considerable attention[47] and the developing theories, especially strict products liability, are coming to be both tried out in lawsuits and discussed in the literature.[48] One theory of recovery—the inverse condemnation action—has been almost entirely ignored by the lawyer and legal scholar alike, yet it deserves the attention of each.[49] Theories of strict liability call for the greatest proportion of scholarly energy, both because they are in stages of rapid development and because they best serve the end of cost internalization by abolishing or at least largely avoiding the necessity of proving fault, a concept which ordinarily ignores the

---

[47] *See, e.g.*, Baxter, *supra* note 6, at 47-53; Bellis, Kolsby & Wolf, *Legal Approach to Industrial Pollution*, TRIAL, June/July 1968, at 29; Juergensmeyer, *Control of Air Pollution Through the Assertion of Private Rights*, 1967 DUKE L.J. 1126; Katz, *supra* note 39; Kennedy & Porter, *Air Pollution: Its Control and Abatement*, 8 VAND. L. REV. 854-64 (1955); Morse & Juergensmeyer, *Air Pollution Control in Indiana in 1968: A Comment*, 2 VALPARAISO U.L. REV. 296, 299-306 (1968); Rheingold, *Civil Cause of Action for Lung Damage Due to Pollution of Urban Atmosphere*, 33 BROOKLYN L. REV. 17 (1966); Seamans, *Tort Liability for Pollution of Air and Water*, 3 NATURAL RESOURCES LAWYER 146 (1970); Schuck, *Air Pollution as a Private Nuisance*, *id.* at 475; Steinberg, *Rights Under California Law of the Individual Injured by Air Pollution*, 27 S. CAL. L. REV. 405 (1954); Comment, *Equity and the Eco-System: Can Injunctions Clear the Air?*, 68 MICH. L. REV. 1254 (1970); Note, *The Role of Private Nuisance Law in the Control of Air Pollution*, 10 ARIZ. L. REV. 107 (1968); Note, *State Air Pollution Control Legislation*, 9 B.C. IND. & COM. L. REV. 712, 716-20 (1968); Note, *Air Pollution as a Private Nuisance*, 24 WASH. & LEE L. REV. 314 (1967); Note, *A Trend Toward Coalescence of Trespass and Nuisance: Remedy for Invasion of Particulates*, 1961 WASH. U.L.Q. 62.

[48] *See* Esposito, *Air and Water Pollution: What To Do While Waiting for Washington*, 5 HARV. CIV. RIGHTS-CIV. LIB. L. REV. 32, 38-40 (1970); Juergensmeyer, *supra* note 47, at 1128 n.7; Katz, *supra* note 39, at 623-41. *See also* McCarthy, *Recent Legal Developments in Environmental Defense*, 19 BUFF. L. REV. 195 (1970).

[49] *See* Juergensmeyer, *supra* note 47, at 1128 n.7.

relevant considerations. Whether or not a polluter is at fault, for example, reveals nothing about whether he has the lowest transaction costs and seldom indicates anything about whether he is the cheapest cost avoider.

2. Improvement of Private and Public Decision-Making

Private litigation should function to encourage better private and public environmental quality decisions. To some extent, cost internalization serves this end, especially in regard to private decisions: If rules of liability are fairly clear and an enterprise can anticipate that it will be liable for damages done to the environment by its activities, the enterprise will have some incentive to evaluate alternatives that might reduce or avoid environmental damage, such as choosing a different location for its activities or developing new technology. This theoretical model often breaks down in practice,[50] and even when working smoothly, the cost internalization function does not always serve to improve private decisions simply because, under present law, the liability question will often be decided without much regard to the quality of the defendant's decision-making processes.[51] Take the favorite liability theory in air pollution litigation—that of nuisance—as an example. Many courts will decide the issue of nuisance without considering the underlying management decisions which led to pollution production: Has the company done research and development in air pollution control technology? Has it considered alternative means of production, or a different location? As a result, many companies probably ignore the expensive process of thinking about how their activities bear on air quality simply because, unless the thought process itself leads to a new and cheaper means of avoiding damage liability, there is no payoff in worrying about the environment.

A larger problem is the company which escapes liability because its emissions are held not to constitute a nuisance even though the company could, through the application of knowledge within its command (but not, under present law, within the command of the court) reduce emissions even more at a cost lower than the resulting gains in air quality. Largely because of considerations such as these, it has been suggested that "the balance of considerations in nuisance cases may yet be broadened to include an appraisal of the defendant's search for possible new scientific discoveries or engineering designs."[52] I see this not as a possible doctrinal develop-

---

50 *See* text accompanying note 71 *infra*.

51 But this is not universally true. *See* Renken v. Harvey Aluminum, Inc., 226 F. Supp. 169 (D. Ore. 1963).

52 Katz, *supra* note 39, at 615.

ment which would allow an escape from liability under nuisance law as presently applied, but as a rationale for extending nuisance to situations which it might not reach at present. To what extent could such a doctrine effectively be applied in a way consistent with protection of trade secrets? Would the doctrine be wise in making the trial judge (or the jury) an arbiter of the "best" or "sufficient" research and development? Would application of the doctrine be inconsistent with the objective of cost internalization, since it might tend to free the cheapest cost avoider or the cheapest bargainer simply because he did all the research one could expect, or would losses in incentives here be balanced by the fact that while damages might not be present to work as a stimulant, the research requirements of the doctrine would? The point is, then, that while the cost internalization function of private litigation goes part of the way toward improving private decision-making processes about the impact of activities on environmental quality, it does not perform the further useful function of ventilating the decision process, of exposing it to public view and thus bringing both more pressure and more information to bear on decision-making.

The discussion thus far has focused on private decision makers. The decisions and activities of public agencies also bear heavily on environmental quality, most notably in regard to the *enforcement* of control regulations and the *planning* of resource allocations (for example, planning the size, number and location of power plants in the area under the planning agency's jurisdiction). Here, too, privately initiated litigation can contribute much to the improvement of public decisions as they bear on environmental quality.[53] Investigation and development of plausible legal theories is especially needed with regard to enforcement suits. Citizens dissatisfied with laxity in the enforcement activities of, say, air pollution control officers have little effective judicial recourse under present law. They might seek recovery against the allegedly nonfeasant official for negligent failure to abate a public nuisance or they might ask for a writ of mandamus compelling the enforcement of abatement statutes, but with the law as it now stands either strategy is likely to fail. It has been argued, however, that the law in each of these areas is ripe for change.[54]

---

[53] Professor Jaffe has termed this sort of privately initiated suit a "public action," in light of the suit's focus on the vindication of the public interest rather than the individual rights of particular plaintiffs. *See* Jaffe, *The Citizen as Litigant in Public Actions: The Non-Hohfeldian or Ideological Plaintiff*, 116 U. PA. L. REV. 1033 (1968); Jaffe, *Standing to Secure Judicial Review: Public Actions*, 74 HARV. L. REV. 1265 (1961).

[54] Esposito, *supra* note 48, at 41-45. The Clean Air Amendments of 1970, Pub. L. No. 91-604, § 12(a) (1970) provide for civil actions by citizens against the Adminis-

As an alternative strategy, the private citizen might opt to bypass the public enforcement official by attempting to clothe himself with that official's unexercised authority to abate public nuisances. Here, too, the plaintiff is likely to fail, for he must not only allege but prove that he has suffered "special damage" above and beyond that suffered by the public at large, and this is often difficult to show. In several states, however, statutes specifically provide for special proceedings by private citizens to abate nuisances in the name of the state.[55] Professor Jaffe has suggested that the concepts developing in recent standing decisions might play some part in a revision of the law of mandamus and public nuisance.[56]

Citizens dissatisfied with public agencies' *planning* activities might seek participation in proceedings incident to the planning function (such as administrative hearings) or seek judicial review of agency planning decisions which allegedly fail to comply with statutory guidelines. An important body of law is rapidly developing to the effect that private citizens have standing to participate in and seek judicial review of many such planning decisions if their past activities and conduct demonstrate that they have a special interest in the subject and outcome of the proceedings.[57] This de-

---

trator of the Environmental Protection Agency (charged with the federal enforcement responsibility of federal air pollution legislation) "where there is alleged a failure of the Administrator to perform any act or duty under this Act *which is not discretionary with the Administrator.*" (Emphasis added.) The legislation as originally proposed did not contain the italicized language. *See* S. REP. No. 1196, 91st Cong., 2d Sess. 122-23 (1970). Query the extent to which the present provision eases the citizen's problems.

55 *See* Katz, *supra* note 39, at 622. *See also* Michigan's Environmental Protection Act, Pub. Act No. 127 of 1970, MICH. STAT. ANN. §§ 14.528 (201)-(207) (1970).

56 Jaffe, *Standing to Sue in Conservation Suits*, in LAW AND THE ENVIRONMENT 123, 131 (M. Baldwin & J. Page eds. 1970).

57 For valuable discussions tracing judicial developments in the law of standing up to the time of this article, see Hanks & Hanks, *An Environmental Bill of Rights: The Citizen Suit and the National Environmental Policy Act of 1969*, 24 RUTGERS L. REV. 230, 231-51 (1970); Jaffe, *supra* note 56; Sax, *Public Rights in Public Resources: The Citizen's Role in Conservation and Development*, in CONTEMPORARY DEVELOPMENTS IN WATER LAW 136 (C. Johnson & S. Lewis eds. 1970).

For discussion of the bearing of the National Environmental Policy Act of 1969, 42 U.S.C. §§ 4331-35 (Supp. V, 1970) on judicial review, standing to sue, and an "environmental cause of action," see Coleman, *Possible Repercussions of the National Environmental Policy Act of 1969 on the Private Law Governing Pollution Abatement Suits*, 3 NAT. RESOURCES LAW. 647 (1970); Grad & Rockett, *Environmental Litigation—Where the Action Is?*, 10 NATURAL RESOURCES J. 742, 761 (1970); Hanks & Hanks, *supra*; Sive, *Some Thoughts of an Environmental Lawyer in the Wilderness of Administrative Law*, 70 COLUM. L. REV. 612, 643-50 (1970); Comment, *The Role of the Judiciary in the Confrontation with the Problems of Environmental Quality*, 17 U.C.L.A. L. REV. 1070, 1093 (1970). Hanks & Hanks, *supra*, argue that the National Environmental Policy Act creates a judicially protectible environmental interest capable of being asserted by citizen groups—an environmental cause of action. For a holding to the contrary, see Bucklein v. Volpe, No. C-70 700 RFR (N.D. Cal., Oct. 29, 1970), *reprinted in* 1 ENVIRON. L. REP. 20043 (1971) (stating

velopment is probably of more importance with regard to federal than to state planning agencies, simply for the reason that state courts have exhibited a liberal attitude with respect to the issue of standing to sue.[58] As Professor Jaffe has pointed out, however, the impact of these federal decisions might be most felt at the state level in the liberalization of public nuisance and mandamus law.[59]

3. Defining New Issues

Environmentalists in the trial bar have become quite sensitive to the fact that litigation might serve the objective of spotlighting areas which need further thought and attention from the public and lawmakers. One finds this attitude reflected in the following excerpt from an article in the *Christian Science Monitor*:

> Court actions now draw the most attention. Citizen groups go to the courts as a last resort when legislation, governmental executive decisions, and public opinion have failed to halt actions which they believe are endangering the environment. . . .
>
> One of the nation's leading trial lawyers in the environmental field, Victor J. Yannocone, Jr., has stated:
>
> "Every piece of enlightened social legislation that has come down in the past 50 or 60 years has been preceded by a history of litigation in which lawyers around the country have focused forcibly the attention of the legislature on the inadequacies of existing legislation."[60]

Litigation can uncover administrative abuses, gather together hard evidence about previously unknown or poorly understood problems, pinpoint shortcomings in present laws and suggest the shape and direction of new laws. Often these functions are merely tolerated as incidental to settlement of the particular controversy before the court; that they may also have an impact on larger questions is not (at least formally) considered as a justification for their operation. Accordingly, the rules of evidence will usually confine within narrow boundaries the amount and kinds of information which may be introduced. In some circumstances, however, the

---

that it is doubtful that the Act can serve as the basis for a cause of action, that the Act is simply a declaration of congressional policy and that the Act would as such not seem to create any rights or duties of which a court can take cognizance).

58 Jaffe, supra note 56. *See also* Davis, *The Liberalized Law of Standing*, 37 U. CHI. L. REV. 450, 468 (1970). For a suggestion that the public trust doctrine could be expanded into an effective instrument for judicial review of agency planning and enforcement decisions, see Sax, *supra* note 37.

59 Jaffe, *supra* note 56. *See* Michigan's Environmental Protection Act, Pub. Act No. 127 of 1970, MICH. STAT. ANN. §§ 14.528 (201)-(207) (1970).

60 Cahn, *Environmentalists Blaze Legal Trail to Preserve Nature*, Christian Science Monitor, Oct. 2, 1969, at 3, col. 1. *See also* Yannocone, *supra* note 35; Carter, *Conservation Law I: Seeking a Breakthrough in the Courts*, 166 SCIENCE 1487 (1969); *Conservation Law II: Scientists Play a Key Role in Court Suits*, *id.* at 1601.

function of providing information bearing on interests and ends larger than those immediately before the court is accepted as legitimate.[61]

But a judicial hearing is not a legislative hearing; under the most permissive of circumstances it is a more restricted system, both less searching and open to fewer points of view. As a result, there are dangers of distortion if litigation-generated facts are translated too literally into information which shapes broad public policy decisions. Consider the following taken from an account of a recent environmental conference:

> "We have been using the lawsuit as a device to teach people that they can demand environmental controls and get them," [Professor Sax] said.
>
> Professor Sax's educational tactic did not meet with complete favor at the table, particularly among the economists. Professor Breton remarked that he thought it wise to differentiate between the situations "where in one case the pollution is serious enough to arouse the public, and where in another we have to 'educate public opinion.'" He then warned "We should be careful not to engage in calling something education which, when other people try to sell us soap, we call advertising."[62]

B. *Shortcomings and Palliatives*

The discussion thus far has made at least implicit some of the shortcomings of litigation and the courts as an institution for effective pollution control and some possibly desirable directions for investigation and change. What follows is a more systematic critique of those shortcomings and of the sorts of palliatives that exist or might be produced to contribute to a more effective institution. For purposes of discussion, two classes of problems can be identified: (1) problems of proof and (2) problems inherent in the judicial process.

1. Problems of Proof

The problems of proof confronted by the plaintiff in environmental litigation have been catalogued; it is enough to capsulize

---

[61] See Professor Davis' discussion of legislative facts in Davis, *Judicial Notice*, 55 COLUM. L. REV. 945 (1955). Legislative facts are those which bear on the court's job of creating law and policy, as opposed to adjudicative facts which define the circumstances of the parties to the litigation. For example, whether marijuana causes broad harm to public interests might be a legislative fact (can the legislature constitutionally outlaw marijuana?); whether the defendant was smoking it or something else would be an adjudicative fact. Legislative facts are not subject to some of the usual evidentiary rules. *See id.* at 952-53.

[62] Shapiro, *Our Far-Flung Correspondents, E.D.* [*Environmental Disruption*], NEW YORKER, May 23, 1970, at 93, 102.

them here.[63] The problems arise from the plaintiff's burden to establish intentional or unreasonable conduct as a basis for liability under many of the theories common to pollution litigation and, even when that burden does not exist (as in the case of strict liability theories), to prove the causal link between the allegedly wrongful conduct and the injury of which plaintiff complains. There are, of course, well-known doctrines which lighten these burdens in some respects, but they by no means do a systematic job. *Res ipsa loquitur*, for example, permits an inference of negligence upon a showing that the event causing damage is of a kind that ordinarily does not occur in the absence of negligence, that the event was caused by an instrumentality within the exclusive control of the defendant, and that the damage was not due to voluntary action of the plaintiff. The doctrine has found application in pollution lawsuits,[64] but hardly on an across-the-board basis.

Similarly, the doctrine of negligence per se can be a valuable aid to the plaintiff in proving liability. According to this doctrine, the provisions of a statute, ordinance or administrative regulation may be taken to establish the standard of required conduct if the purpose of the provisions is exclusively or in part to protect a class of persons which includes the plaintiff, to protect the particular interest of the plaintiff which was invaded by the defendant's conduct and to protect that interest against the harm which resulted and against the hazard which produced that harm.[65] Most courts hold that when the above conditions are met, an unexcused violation of the provisions is conclusive on the question of negligence, but in some jurisdictions the violation is treated only as evidence of negligence. Which of these views is applied might turn on whether a statute or an ordinance (or administrative regulation) is involved, for there are courts which follow the majority rule in the case of

[63] *See, e.g.*, COMMITTEE ON POLLUTION, NAT'L ACADEMY OF SCIENCES-NAT'L RESEARCH COUNCIL, WASTE MANAGEMENT AND CONTROL 231-33 (1966); Baxter, *supra* note 6, at 44-53; Hines, *Nor Any Drop to Drink: Public Regulation of Water Quality*, 52 IOWA L. REV. 186, 196-200 (1966); Note, *State Air Pollution Control Legislation*, 9 B.C. IND. & COM. L. REV. 712, 716-20 (1968). These papers and the discussion in the text focus on proof problems in the context of private suits for damages or injunctive relief. Proof problems can also arise, of course, in the process of participation in administrative proceedings and suits seeking judicial review of them. On some promising developments with respect to the burden of developing the record in administrative proceedings, see Hanks & Hanks, *supra* note 57, at 265-68.

[64] *See, e.g.*, Reynolds Metals Co. v. Yturbide, 258 F.2d 321 (9th Cir.), *cert. denied*, 358 U.S. 840 (1958). *See generally* W. PROSSER, HANDBOOK OF THE LAW OF TORTS 218 (3d ed. 1964); Comment, *The Application of Res Ipsa Loquitur in Suits Against Multiple Defendants*, 34 ALBANY L. REV. 106 (1969).

[65] RESTATEMENT (SECOND) OF TORTS § 286 (1965). The *Restatement* states that statutory provisions have been accepted by the courts as a basis for civil liability in actions based on theories other than negligence, such as trespass, nuisance, and even strict liability. *Id.* at 26-27, comment *d.*

violations of the former but regard violations of the latter as evidence only.[66]

The value to the plaintiff of the doctrine of negligence per se will obviously grow as more, and more detailed, pollution control legislation is adopted.[67] But neither this doctrine nor *res ipsa loquitur* nor theories of strict liability remove all the obstacles to successful litigation. Cause and effect must still be established, and the problems of proof here can be intractable. It will often be the case, for example, that multiple emission sources contribute to a locality's air pollution problem, or that the type of injury involved in the lawsuit (for example, damage to plaintiff's health) could have been produced by conditions other than foul air. Even for problems such as these there are palliatives, but they are at best a mild tonic.[68]

The tendency of the courts has been to reallocate the burden of proof regarding liability in roundabout ways, rather than directly. The result has been doctrines—such as *res ipsa loquitur*, negligence per se, and so forth—which have been less than systematically applied. The air pollution case in which *res ipsa loquitur* applies, and the one in which it does not, for example, often will not differ in any way so fundamental as to call for different judicial approaches to problems of conserving the air resource. Indeed, conservation litigation has a fundamental constant which the legal system has been slow to recognize; once its implications are seen and understood, it should be possible to consider a more broad-based and systematic reallocation of the burden of proof.

The constant in resource conservation litigation is this: The person or enterprise whose activities deteriorate a resource will always be the defendant. This is because in the absence of legal constraints, conducting a resource-deteriorating activity can foreclose the conduct of non-deteriorating activities, while the converse is never true. The polluter's conduct can stop people from breathing

---

66 W. PROSSER, *supra* note 64, at 202-03.

67 *See* Miller & Borchers, *Private Lawsuits and Air Pollution Control*, 56 A.B.A.J. 465 (1970) (suggesting a variety of ways in which plaintiffs' attorneys can take advantage of air pollution control legislation); Note, *Water Quality Standards in Private Nuisance Actions*, 79 YALE L.J. 102 (1969).

68 On the problems raised by multiple causes and the judicial responses to them, see generally 2 F. HARPER & F. JAMES, JR., THE LAW OF TORTS § 20.3 (1956); RESTATEMENT (SECOND) OF TORTS § 433B(3). *See also* Katz, *supra* note 39, at 616-21. On the question whether multiple polluting activities might give rise to liability even though the acts of each individual polluter are independent and, considered alone, would not be tortious, see W. PROSSER, *supra* note 64, at 257. For a discussion of the bearing of federal air quality criteria documents on proof of injury, see Miller & Borchers, *supra* note 67.

clean air, but the breather's conduct cannot stop the polluter from going about his dirty business. To obtain relief, the breather ***must*** go to court, and it is one of the plain facts of the judicial system that plaintiffs carry the burden of proof on most of the important issues in a lawsuit, not to mention the financial burden of initiating litigation. Thus, even when substantive rules express a policy in favor of resource conservation, basic procedural mechanics tend to bias the system in the opposite direction. It is important to begin considering ways to make systematic reallocations of the burden of proof in resource conservation litigation to counteract the present discrimination against conservation.[69]

2. Problems Inherent in the Judicial Process

Some of the reasons why judicial process can never be a completely satisfactory institution for pollution control are inherent in the process itself. I shall sketch a few of the most fundamental of these and briefly discuss some existing and possible palliatives.[70]

Lawsuits are expensive and ordinarily culminate when someone is seriously injured in pocket, person or principle. Pollution damage, on the other hand, is often diffuse; a huge number of persons may be injured, but each to only a small extent. Though social costs may be high, individual damage will ordinarily be so low as to discourage an individual from hiring a lawyer to prosecute a suit. As a result, costs are internalized to only the most modest degree; litigation

---

69 For an elaboration on the bias against resource conservation and some suggestions about how to implement this conclusion, see Krier, *supra* note 45.

70 For a more thorough discussion, see Baxter, *supra* note 6, at 44-53; Hines, *supra* note 63, at 200-01 (listing the fortuity of litigation, lack of judicial expertise and administrative capability, and nonrepresentation of the public interest). *See* WASTE MANAGEMENT AND CONTROL, *supra* note 63, at 233-34, suggesting that the judicial process as a means of alleviating the worst effects of pollution, and as a means of shifting some costs of pollution back on to the polluter, can be made more efficient for these purposes by reforms that would do the following: (1) Establish an office of Ombudsman to receive private complaints and sue, at the discretion of the Ombudsman and at public expense, on behalf of private complainants. The various foundation-funded, public-interest law firms being established around the country could serve the same purpose to a limited extent. For a study of an agency which assumed the roles of environmental ombudsman and advocate and for a proposal that each role be formalized, see Krier, *Environmental Watchdogs: Some Lessons from a "Study" Council*, 23 STAN.'L. REV. 623 (1971). *See also* H.R. 18242, 91st Cong., 2d Sess. (1970) (proposing, among other things, an environmental ombudsman and an environmental legal services office). (2) Designate one or more courts in a jurisdiction to hear all pollution cases, so as to develop specialized judges. The courts should be authorized to appoint an appropriate pollution control agency as a master in chancery to aid in technical aspects of litigation. The latter is a common practice with respect to water rights adjudication and deserves careful consideration. (3) Authorize the court, when appropriate, to broaden the area coverage of an action so as to include, if necessary, all polluters in a problem shed.

thus fails to realize one of the primary objectives we have assigned to it.[71]

The class action is an obvious, though limited, solution.[72] The *Federal Rules of Civil Procedure* provide a liberal class action rule,[73] but its value as an internalization device has been severely limited by a recent ruling of the United States Supreme Court that class members may aggregate individual claims to reach the jurisdictional minimum of the federal courts (over $10,000) only when they share a common and undivided interest—an unlikely occurrence in pollution litigation.[74] While litigants may still resort to state class action rules, some commentators find these "even less viable than was the federal provision" before the Supreme Court's decision.[75] Moreover, it may well be that the class form of action itself is not a sufficient spur to effective litigation.[76] Much of the promising experience with class actions under the *Federal Rules* has been built upon the anti-trust laws, which provide for treble damages to those injured. Perhaps the analogue to triple recovery in pollution suits will be punitive damages. At least one court has expanded that concept of late to apply to a polluter who conducts activities knowing that there was a probability or at least a danger of harm yet failed to take appropriate measures to minimize dam-

---

71 One possible (and probably impracticable) way to guard against this failure is to have the judge attempt to total *all* the damages caused by an activity and, in those cases where it is perfectly clear that if all these damages were internalized the enterprise engaging in the activity could not pay them and survive, grant an injunction. *See* Calabresi, *Some Thoughts on Risk Distribution and the Law of Torts*, 70 YALE L.J. 499, 535 (1961). Too often, however, judges probably grant injunctive relief when relief by way of damages would be more efficient. *Id.* At times, too, they grant injunctive relief in a theoretically undesirable form. For example, in Renken v. Harvey Aluminum, Inc., 226 F. Supp. 169 (D. Ore. 1963), the court ordered Harvey to install the same type of pollution control equipment which had been used by Reynolds Aluminum, apparently on the theory that what was good for Reynolds was good for the industry. If Harvey had simply been ordered to reduce its emissions to the desired maximum, it might have found equipment which did that job at less cost than the Reynolds equipment.

72 *See The Cost-Internalization Case for Class Actions, supra* note 6.

73 FED. R. CIV. P. 23.

74 Snyder v. Harris, 394 U.S. 332 (1969). Legislation introduced in the Ninety-first Congress would have provided for environmental class actions without regard to the amount in controversy. *See* S. 3575, 91st Cong., 2d Sess. (1970); H.R. 19321, 91st Cong., 2d Sess. (1970). Similar legislation will probably be introduced in the course of the present Congress.

75 Esposito, *supra* note 48, at 36.

76 For example, in Riter v. Keokuk Electro Metals Company, 248 Iowa 710, 82 N.W. 2d 151 (1957), plaintiff filed a pollution class action which was never joined in by any potential class members. *But see* Conti, *Conservationists Press Suits to Assert Right to a Clean Environment*, Wall Street Journal, March 26, 1970, at 1, col. 6 (report on recent filings of pollution class actions). "There's ample evidence that the suits filed so far are just a start." *Id.*

age.[77] The potential reach of punitive damages as a therapeutic device subject to judicial development should be explored. The existence of federal records can also serve as an independent incentive to bring a class action, as has been the case with regard to such actions by small investors in the securities markets.[78] Attorneys can make valuable use of federal pollution documents in a variety of ways.[79]

But the most fundamental restraint on the future expansion of the class action in pollution litigation might be that class actions at the breadth of their potential would bring to the court more than the judge could handle. A recent class action in Los Angeles was filed in behalf of essentially all the people in Los Angeles County against two hundred ninety-one corporations allegedly responsible for air pollution in the area. The court dismissed the action for several reasons, one of them being that "a court of equity lacks facilities or competency to undertake the problem of abating air pollution within the Los Angeles Basin . . . ."[80] Expanding on this point, the court stated:

> It is readily apparent that the control of the emission of air pollutants is a highly complex problem. . . . The court does not have the facilities to undertake the balancing of the interests of the inhabitants of the Los Angeles Basin against the needs of productive industry in this same area.[81]

It is difficult to fault the judge for this view (certainly his candor is admirable). As we have seen, the question of air quality is an essentially political one, ideally to be decided by democratic political processes. The judicial process is not one of these. Moreover, the courts lack the purse power and jurisdictional base needed to ferret out the facts and balance the considerations essential to a reasoned decision and to police that decision once made.[82] Surely the

---

77 McElwain v. Georgia-Pacific, 245 Ore. 247, 421 P.2d 957 (1967). *Contra*, Fairview Farms, Inc. v. Reynolds Metals Co., 176 F. Supp. 178 (D. Ore. 1959).

78 *See The Cost-Internalization Case for Class Actions*, *supra* note 6, at 418.

79 *See* note 67 & accompanying text *supra*. It has been suggested that the right of individuals to enforce the federal pollution laws in private suits is ripe for judicial recognition. *See* Currie, *Trail Blazer-at-Law*, TRIAL, Aug./Sept. 1969, at 23. The citizen suit provision of the Clean Air Amendments of 1970, Pub. L. No. 91-604, § 12(a) (1970), makes such suits possible. Subject to certain notice provisions (or the commencement of a suit by state or federal officials), a citizen may bring a civil action against any person (including the United States and any other governmental "agency" to the extent permitted by the eleventh amendment) who is alleged to be in violation of applicable emission standards under the Act or orders issued with respect to such standards by federal or state officials.

80 Diamond v. General Motors Corp., No. 947429 (Super. Ct. Cal., Aug. 20, 1969), *appeal docketed* Civ. No. 36600, 2d Dist. Ct. App., Oct. 15, 1969.

81 *Id.*

82 On the polycentric nature of resource allocation problems and their insus-

courts can adjudicate *some* class actions, but not those which seek solutions to the most serious problem—multiple emitter pollution in large urban areas. As to this problem, the courts will serve best to the extent that they vigorously insist on reasoned and neutral processes of decision and enforcement by other agencies of government. To even hope for much more on the part of the courts would require the most fundamental changes in judicial process—changes which would take much in time and trouble and which might result in an institution far less desirable from other than the perspective of pollution problems. It is often easier to turn to other institutions than to change deeply rooted traits in the character of the courts, and this seems true in the case of pollution. Surely the courts have a role to play, but it is not an exclusive and probably not a major one. The bulk of the burden must be carried by other agencies of government.

III. Pollution Control Legislation and Its Administration

One way to begin a survey of pollution control legislation and administration in the United States is simply to note that, at least with regard to the air pollution problem, government at all

---

ceptibility to satisfactory resolution through the process of adjudication, see Fuller, *Adjudication and the Rule of Law*, in 1960 Proceedings of American Society of International Law 1, 3-5 (1960). There is some evidence that the courts themselves sense the problem; contrast the judicial responses in Diamond v. General Motors Corp., No. 947429 (Super. Ct. Cal., Aug. 20, 1969) and the standing cases, discussed in the literature cited note 57 *supra*, in light of Professor Fuller's remarks that courts run into trouble not when their decisions affect and enter into polycentric problems, but when they attempt to solve the problems rather than lay down rules governing solution of the problems by more appropriate decision-making bodies. *See also* Comment, *The Role of the Judiciary in the Confrontation with the Problems of Environmental Quality*, 17 U.C.L.A. L. Rev. 1070 (1970). These comments should caution those who argue that the United States Constitution should be either read or amended to include a right to a "clean" environment. *See, e.g.*, Roberts, *The Right to a Decent Environment: Progress Along a Constitutional Avenue*, in Law and the Environment 134 (M. Baldwin & J. Page eds. 1970); Note, *Toward a Constitutionally Protected Environment*, 56 Va. L. Rev. 458 (1970). *See also* Environmental Defense Fund v. Hoerner Waldorf Corp., Civil No. 1694 (D. Mont., Aug. 25, 1970) (suggesting that the fifth and fourteenth amendments contain a constitutional right to a clean environment, inasmuch as they protect life, liberty, and property; finding an absence of the requisite federal or state action). Even those who champion an expansion of the judicial role in environmental problems express much skepticism about the wisdom or utility of constitutional recognition of the right to a decent environment. *See, e.g.*, J. Sax, Defending the Environment 234-39 (1970) (constitutional right would lack substantive content and would give the courts ultimate authority and make them "environmental czars" with the power to ignore the wishes of the public and its elected representatives). One commentator has summarized quite cogently the objections to the recognition of a constitutional right to a clean environment: "Simply stated, a constitutional right requires the court to shoulder responsibility for decision-making which is more properly assumed by representative bodies." Comment, *The Role of the Judiciary in the Confrontation with the Problems of Environmental Quality*, 17 U.C.L.A. L. Rev. 1070, 1077 (1970).

levels has had an almost neurotic fixation on regulation. As discussed below, government can attack pollution in essentially three ways: (1) by regulation (proscriptions and prescriptions backed up by punitive measures); (2) by subsidies or awards; (3) by charges, or prices, or effluent fees.[83] There has been an incredible amount of regulation, a touch of subsidization, and virtually no pricing.[84] And it is fair to say that most of the significant gaps in knowledge about what government can and should do with regard to pollution problems are the direct result of this regulation imbalance. There is little empirical information about the merits and demerits of subsidies and awards and virtually none about pricing. Because there has been little in the way of a comparative institutional approach to solving pollution problems, systematic studies about the advantages and disadvantages of various control patterns are scarce.[85] Our approach has been monolithic—and barren.

---

83 *See, e.g.*, J.H. DALES, POLLUTION, PROPERTY AND PRICES 81-88 (1968); Mills, *Economic Incentives in Air-Pollution Control*, in THE ECONOMICS OF AIR POLLUTION 40, 43-44 (H. Wolozin ed. 1966).

84 For a catalog of air pollution legislation on the state and local level, see U.S. DEP'T OF HEALTH, EDUCATION AND WELFARE, A COMPILATION OF SELECTED AIR POLLUTION EMISSION CONTROL REGULATIONS AND ORDINANCES (Public Health Service Pub. No. 999-AP-43, rev. ed. 1968); U.S. DEP'T OF HEALTH, EDUCATION AND WELFARE, DIGEST OF STATE AIR POLLUTION LAWS (Public Health Service Pub. No. 711, 1967). On the federal level, see, e.g., Muskie, *Role of the Federal Government in Air Pollution Control*, 10 ARIZ. L. REV. 17 (1968); Comment, *A History of Federal Air Pollution Control*, 30 OHIO ST. L.J. 516 (1969).

85 There are, on the other hand, a mass of descriptive studies of federal, state and local regulatory programs in the legal literature. For the most part, these studies simply discuss the provisions of a particular program; at times, however, they engage in some valuable analysis and criticism. The following list is not all-inclusive:

A. *Federal Legislation.* Borchers, *The Practice of Regional Regulation Under the Clean Air Act*, 3 NATURAL RESOURCES LAWYER 59 (1970); Edelman, *Air Pollution Abatement Procedures Under the Clean Air Act*, 10 ARIZ. L. REV. 30 (1968); Edelman, *The Law of Federal Air Pollution Control*, 16 J. AIR POLLUTION CONTROL ASS'N 523 (1966); Kennedy & Weekes, *Control of Automobile Emissions—California Experience and the Federal Legislation*, 33 LAW & CONTEMP. PROB. 297 (1968); Martin & Symington, *A Guide to the Air Quality Act of 1967*, 33 LAW & CONTEMP. PROB. 239 (1968); Middleton, *Summary of the Air Quality Act of 1967*, 10 ARIZ. L. REV. 25 (1968); O'Fallon, *Deficiencies in the Air Quality Act of 1967*, 33 LAW & CONTEMP. PROB. 275 (1968); Reitze, *The Role of the "Region" in Air Pollution Control*, 20 CASE W. RES. L. REV. 809 (1969); Welch, *Federal Air Quality Act of 1967*, 3 NATURAL RESOURCES LAWYER 52 (1970); Note, *The Air Quality Act of 1967*, 54 IOWA L. REV. 115 (1968); Note, *The Federal Air Pollution Program*, 1968 WASH. U.L.Q. 283; Note, *The Expanding Scope of Air Pollution Abatement*, 70 W. VA. L. REV. 195 (1968).

B. *State and Local Legislation.* Chass & Feldman, *Tears for John Doe*, 27 S. CAL. L. REV. 349 (1954); Cowan, *Air Pollution Control in New Jersey*, 9 RUTGERS L. REV. 609 (1955); German, *Regulation of Smoke and Air Pollution in Pennsylvania*, 10 U. PITT. L. REV. 493 (1949); Kennedy, *The Legal Aspects of Air Pollution Control with Particular Reference to the County of Los Angeles*, 27 S. CAL. L. REV. 373 (1954); Moran, *The Air Pollution Control Act and Its Administration [New Jersey]*, 9 RUTGERS L. REV. 640 (1955); Morse & Juergensmeyer, *Air Pollution Control in Indiana in 1968: A Comment*, 2 VALPARAISO U.L. REV. 296 (1968); Pollack, *Legal*

What accounts for this Great American Regulatory Tradition? A few answers seem at least plausible. It has been suggested that the history of air pollution control in the United States illustrates the "catastrophe theory of planning"—the direct and immediate response by government to dramatic incidents, such as the disastrous Donora episode.[86] Such a theory may expose the roots of the regulatory tradition. Governmental response to crisis is often typified by quick and, therefore, generally crude measures aimed at preconceived "wrongdoers" like industrial polluters.[87] It is designed to punish those wrongdoers and placate intense public concern. The goal is immediate relief and clear results. The prohibitions and penalties of regulatory programs best suit all of these ends. With time and experience, it may become clear that an existing program, conceived out of crisis, is unsatisfactory, and that more subtle measures are necessary. But the path of least resistance—and, often, least short-run cost, a matter of importance to politicians—is to improve the old, rather than abandon it for an entirely new ap-

---

Boundaries of Air Pollution Control—State and Local Legislative Purpose and Techniques, 33 LAW & CONTEMP. PROB. 331 (1968); Warren, *State and Local Regulation of Air Pollution*, POPULAR GOVERNMENT, Feb. 1967, at 1; Comment, *Legal Methods for Control of Air Pollution in New York State: An Evaluation*, 34 ALBANY L. REV. 563 (1970); Note, *State Air Pollution Control Legislation*, 9 B.C. IND. & COM. L. REV. 712 (1968); Comment, *The California Motor Vehicle Pollution Control Law*, 50 CALIF. L. REV. 121 (1962); Note, *Air Pollution-Automobile Smog: A Proposed Solution*, 14 DEPAUL L. REV. 436 (1965); Comment, *Legislative Limitation on Air Pollution-Enforcement*, 9 HASTINGS L.J. 191 (1958); Comment, *The Wyoming Air Quality Act*, 4 LAND & WATER L. REV. 159 (1969); Note, *The Peril of Air Pollution in North Dakota*, 46 N.D.L. REV. 217 (1970); Comment, *Air Pollution Control in Texas*, 47 TEXAS L. REV. 1086 (1969); Note, *Local Regulation of Air Pollution*, 1968 WASH. U.L.Q. 232; Note, *State Regulation of Air Pollution*, 1968 WASH. U.L.Q. 249.

C. *General*. AMERICAN ASSOCIATION FOR ADVANCEMENT OF SCIENCE, AIR CONSERVATION COMM'N, AIR CONSERVATION 212-33 (1965); STAFF OF SENATE COMM. ON PUBLIC WORKS, 88TH CONG., 1ST SESS., A STUDY OF POLLUTION—AIR 23-37 (Comm. Print 1963); Edelman, *Air Pollution Control Legislation*, in 3 AIR POLLUTION 553-99 (A. Stern ed., 2d ed. 1968); Schueneman, *Air Pollution Control Administration*, in 3 AIR POLLUTION 719-96 (A. Stern ed., 2d ed. 1968); Note, *Smog—Can Legislation Clear the Air*, 1 STAN. L. REV. 452 (1949).

[86] *See* C. HAAR, LAND-USE PLANNING 130 n.6 (1959). Almost 6,000 persons were made ill and twenty died as a result of a three-day period of excessive air pollution in Donora, Pennsylvania. H. SCHRENK, AIR POLLUTION IN DONORA, PENNSYLVANIA, EPIDEMIOLOGY OF THE UNUSUAL SMOG EPISODE OF OCTOBER, 1948 (Public Health Bull. No. 306, 1949).

[87] Consider the following comment by a Vice President of the Boston Edison Company, reported in Goldner, *Air Pollution Control in the Metropolitan Boston Area: A Case Study in Public Policy Formation*, in THE ECONOMICS OF AIR POLLUTION 127, 150 (H. Wolozin ed. 1966): "What people fail to understand, he said, is that a utility merely represents one large power-generating operation in lieu of each home having its own power-generating and heating devices. The small quantitites of smoke which would be given off by each of the multitudes of homes if they used their own power-generating devices are now consolidated into emissions from a few plants and so become a noticeable target for attack."

proach to government intervention. It may be, too, that the roots of the regulatory tradition lie in the fact that most people, including most public decision makers, probably do not understand either the ways in which social and economic systems function to produce pollution problems or the programs of control offered by theoreticians and sophisticated experts. Then too, people—including many theoreticians and experts—may simply have concluded that regulation is the best approach.[88]

Whatever the reasons, the regulatory tradition is ours; it has been with us for years and it will probably continue well into the future.[89] It has provided some valuable lessons. The most beneficial application of the fruits of those lessons, however, may call for quite new responses by government. And the regulatory tradition is the constant which the force for change must overcome.[90] To the extent that this rigid tradition is the product of crisis, it suggests that at least some of the energy of crisis should be harnessed and directed toward the establishment of low-visibility study bodies whose job it would be to do research and prepare alternative programs of government control. Those programs should be introduced into the legislatures only when the panic of the moment has passed. Perhaps, in short, it would be best to adopt a tactic of striking not when the iron is hot, but when it is cool.

It is beyond the purpose of this paper to discuss all the varieties found in the jungle of legislative control programs. I propose rather to outline the main themes of regulation, subsidies, and pricing in a broad and comparative fashion in order to suggest what is known and to consider the research implications of what is not.

A. *Regulation*

Regulatory programs have appeared in a variety of styles and, when carefully drafted, have almost uniformly withstood constitutional attack.[91] This does not mean, of course, that constitutional

---

88 *See* Hagevik, *Legislating for Air Quality Management: Reducing Theory to Practice*, 33 LAW & CONTEMP. PROB. 369, 376-78 (1968) [hereinafter cited as Hagevik].

89 *Id.*

90 For illustrations of the point that enchantment with regulation is a real barrier to constructive change with respect to air pollution control, see Letter to the Editor from Seymour Schwartz, then a doctoral fellow, National Air Pollution Control Administration, University of Southern California, L.A. Times, Dec. 20, 1969, pt. II, at 4, col. 6; Hill, *Objections to a Tax on Pollution*, N.Y. Times, Dec. 10, 1969, at 38, col. 3.

91 There is a raft of literature on these points. *See, e.g.*, H. KENNEDY, LEGAL SUPPORT FOR LOS ANGELES COUNTY'S STRICT AIR POLLUTION CONTROL PROGRAM (Report to L.A. County Bd. of Supervisors, Sept. 1957); H. Kennedy, The Formulation

and other legal constraints have no impact on legislative design and the style and success of enforcement. As the following discussion illustrates, quite the contrary is true.

Regulatory techniques for controlling problems like air pollution can be placed into two broad categories—performance standards and specification standards.[92] In essence, performance standards allow polluters to act as they wish, so long as their emissions do not exceed specified limits for particular pollutants. Early legislation of this sort was aimed at the density and opacity of smoke

---

and Adoption of Reasonable Rules and Regulations, May 24, 1962 (unpublished manuscript in UCLA Law School Library); H. Kennedy, Legal Aspects of Community Air Quality Standards, June 14, 1962 (unpublished manuscript in UCLA Law School Library); H. Kennedy, Legal Aspects of Human Exposure to Atmospheric Pollutants, Dec. 4, 1961 (unpublished manuscript in UCLA Law School Library); H. Kennedy, Some Legal and Public Policy Problems in Air Conservation, Dec. 9, 1962 (unpublished manuscript in UCLA Law School Library); Delogu, *Legal Aspects of Air Pollution Control and Proposed State Legislation for Such Control*, 1969 WIS. L. REV. 884; Edelman, *Federal Air and Water Control: The Application of the Commerce Power To Abate Interstate and Intrastate Pollution*, 33 GEO. WASH. L. REV. 1067 (1965); Kennedy & Porter, *Air Pollution: Its Control and Abatement*, 8 VAND. L. REV. 854 (1955); Kennedy, *Legal Aspects of Air Pollution Control*, 79 PUBLIC HEALTH REPTS. 689 (1964); Kennedy, *Legislation and Environmental Health*, 12 ARCHIVES OF ENVIRONMENTAL HEALTH 129 (1966); Kennedy, *The Mechanics of Legislative and Regulatory Action*, in PROCEEDINGS, NATIONAL CONFERENCE ON AIR POLLUTION 306 (Public Health Service Pub. No. 1022, 1963); Pollack, *Legal Boundaries of Air Pollution Control—State and Local Legislative Purpose and Techniques*, 33 LAW & CONTEMP. PROB. 331 (1968); 8 BAYLOR L. REV. 249 (1956).

92 For more detailed discussion, see Pollack, *supra* note 91; Walker, *Enforcement of Performance Requirements With Injunctive Procedure*, 10 ARIZ. L. REV. 81 (1968); Note, *Local Regulation of Air Pollution*, 1968 WASH. U.L.Q. 232. Zoning, by itself or in conjunction with other regulatory techniques, has been used as a means of pollution control. In essence, of course, zoning puts the air pollution source "downwind." It has been suggested that to be effective, zoning constraints "should be couched in terms of emission royalties or license fees graduated by location rather than by black-and-white prohibitions here and permissions there" and should be combined with a program of property taxes designed to encourage optimum use of downwind and upwind land. AMERICAN ASSOC. FOR ADVANCEMENT OF SCIENCE, AIR CONSERVATION COMM'N, AIR CONSERVATION 295 (1965). *See also* J.H. DALES, *supra* note 83, at 88-92 (1968).

Some have argued that zoning has "served to exacerbate pollution problems rather than to isolate residential areas from environmental fallout." The argument is based, first on the point that "those who reside within the industrial area [are] often deemed to have foregone any nuisance claims" and, second, on the contention that "those who live outside the area are subjected to increasing amounts of pollution in the aggregate, but from increasingly numerous, remote, and unidentified sources." Esposito, *Air and Water Pollution: What To Do While Waiting for Washington*, 5 HARV. CIV. RIGHTS-CIV. LIB. L. REV. 32, 48, n.73 (1970). Residents within an industrial area might lose a nuisance claim either on the theory that they had "come to the nuisance"—that is, moved into the area knowing of its conditions—or on the theory that no nuisance exists because the area has been devoted to activities which inevitably cause pollution. *See, e.g.*, W. PROSSER, *supra* note 64, at 620-21, 632-33. In light of the fact that it is generally relatively poor people who "choose" to reside in industrial areas, the implications of either of these theories are painfully obvious. Compare Ross v. Butler, 19 N.J. Eq. 294, 306 (1868).

(measured against a visual chart—the almost proverbial Ringelmann Scale),[93] but modern statutes commonly contain further limitations on particular pollutants, such as particulate matter, sulfur dioxide and nitrogen oxides. Specification standards decree not what goal must be accomplished but how it must be accomplished. Most commonly they require pollution control equipment which meets certain design requirements, but they may go further and require particular makes and models of equipment.[94] Laws forbidding certain activities, such as open burning or the use of certain fuels, can be considered types of specification standards, since they go beyond simply establishing an emission goal.

Regulatory programs can, and at times do, employ both performance and specification standards. They might, for example, set an emission (performance) standard for smoke, prohibit fuels which produce inordinate amounts of smoke, and establish specification standards to control other types of pollutants. Some control programs blend the two approaches in another manner. They establish performance standards but require that operations cannot begin until the control agency is satisfied that the source is designed in such a way that it can be expected to meet the specified emission standards.[95] Programs of vehicle emission control have employed both specification and performance approaches. Some, that is, insist on the installation of certified devices capable of achieving given standards; others (most notably the federal program) simply instruct automobile manufacturers that the given standards must be met, then provide a means for assembly line or on-the-road testing.[96]

Performance standards have one distinct theoretical advantage over specification standards: by leaving to the owner of a pollution source the decision how best to comply with the law, they tend to induce him to do so in the most efficient manner (that which is cheapest for him), because it is in his interest to develop and employ least-cost solutions.[97] This observation, however, applies in only a very limited way to the case of controls aimed at many small pol-

---

[93] The Ringelmann Scale contains six blocks of graduated gray going from near white to near black. The inspector simply eyeballs the smoke plume and makes a judgment. Though primitive, the method is widely used; most laws specify that any shade darker than Ringelmann 2 (the third block on the scale) is a violation. The method has tremendous shortcomings. Since it measures density, not volume, one can simply build a larger-mouthed stack and avoid violation. The Ringelmann test cannot be used at night, nor during times of high wind, rain or humidity.

[94] *See Local Regulation of Air Pollution*, *supra* note 92, at 241.

[95] *See, e.g.*, Los Angeles County Air Pollution Control District, Rules and Regulations, R. 10, 20 (1969).

[96] *See, e.g.*, Cal. Health & Safety Code §§ 39100, 39107, 39129 (West Supp., 1970); Clean Air Amendments of 1970, Pub. L. No. 91-604, §§ 6-8 (1970).

[97] *See* Walker, *supra* note 92, at 85.

luters, such as people using backyard incinerators or driving automobiles. Small polluters have little capability to discover and design the devices best for themselves; they can, of course, save by purchasing on the market the cheapest effective control equipment, but the administrative costs of policing a large number of small operators to see if their emissions meet specified limits would probably be higher than the total of individual savings. In cases like these, if a regulatory approach is to be used at all, then some sort of specification program seems justified.

This last point makes it clear that the efficiency of a control program cannot be judged from the perspective of the regulated class alone. Relative costs of administration and enforcement must also be considered. While the question is a complex one, performance programs are probably more efficient from this perspective as well (with the exception of the small polluter). Specification programs are ordinarily administered through permit systems which require submission of specification data to an authority before operations begin.[98] Activity cannot lawfully begin without a permit, and no permit will be issued until the authority is satisfied that the required standards are met. The permit system itself requires a large staff which must engage in time-consuming appraisals and negotiation (sometimes ending in the granting of a variance, which is often nothing more than an arbitrary escape hatch for the most persistent or powerful of the regulated class).[99] Moreover, there is some opinion that staff work under a permit system tends to be overcautious, resulting in unnecessarily expensive over-engineering of control equipment.[100] The analogue of a permit for equipment already in operation is a certificate. Sources of pollution are periodically tested during operation to see that they meet design and operational standards; if they do not, a certificate of operation will be withheld. Administration of a certification program requires an even larger staff than permits and has the additional inefficiency of lost time and labor brought about by interruptions in business activity while machinery is being tested and evaluated.[101]

Of course, against these inefficiences of specification programs, there must be weighed those created by a performance program's need for policing emissions at the source. In most cases, however, only spot checking is necessary, and it is unlikely that the costs of

---

98 *Id.* at 84.

99 *Id.* at 85. This is not to say, of course, that variance provisions in a performance program are not subject to similar dangers of abuse. *See* STANFORD WORKSHOP ON AIR POLLUTION, *supra* note 34, at 226-30.

100 Walker, *supra* note 92, at 85.

101 *Local Regulation of Air Pollution*, *supra* note 92, at 242.

this procedure are significantly higher than annual certification costs. Even specification systems call for policing measures; control equipment can, after all, break down or be ignored. Reasonable conjecture and some evidence suggest that performance programs require no more inspectors than specification programs and relatively fewer engineers and other personnel.[102]

The relative inefficiencies apparently inherent in a program of specification standards are compounded by the fact that, ordinarily, such standards are enforced by criminal process,[103] probably the most cumbersome coercive tool available. The alleged violator is protected by all the constitutional protections which apply to any criminal trial. A study of Boston concluded that the criminal enforcement scheme "has not been of much help for since its inception, there has been an average per year of 700 to 800 complaints, four prosecutions, only one conviction, and no noticeable improvement in air quality."[104]

In terms, then, of both administrative costs and compliance costs, performance programs appear to be relatively more efficient than specification programs in reaching a collectively established environmental quality goal. Neither system appears to leave much room for market correction; neither system, that is, appears to leave much room for bargaining in any ordinary sense.[105] To some extent, the existence of a mixed system of regulation and liability rules might tend to correct for this rigidity. So long as the quality level required or achieved by a regulatory program is *lower* than that which would

---

[102] For example, Los Angeles, which uses essentially a specification system, has twice the sources of the San Francisco Bay Area Air Pollution Control District, which employs essentially a performance program. Los Angeles has 78 engineers, and the Bay Area 12; on the other hand, the Bay Area has 28 inspectors as compared to 71 in Los Angeles (about the same two-to-one ratio which exists as to sources). *But see Local Regulation of Air Pollution*, *supra* note 92, at 242 (suggesting that a specification program requires fewer inspectors than a performance program).

[103] Walker, *supra* note 92, at 84. Walker suggests that this pattern results because performance standards are insufficiently precise to support criminal convictions without fear of sound constitutional attack. This, of course, goes more to explain why a performance program *might not* use criminal sanctions than why specification programs ordinarily do. The real explanation probably lies in the forces behind the regulatory tradition coupled with the fact that those forces are least restrained in the context of a specification program.

[104] Kovel, *A Case for Civil Penalties: Air Pollution Control*, 46 J. Urban L. 153, 154 (1969). *But see* Mix, *The Misdemeanor Approach to Pollution Control*, 10 Ariz. L. Rev. 90 (1968).

[105] *But see* Hagevik, *supra* note 88, at 369 (suggesting a regulatory scheme which would provide for bargaining between polluters and the control agency and would, it is argued, tend to produce optimal results in terms of resource allocation). For some arguments against Hagevik's plan see Mandelker, *Quality Standards for the Control of Air Pollution*, in Development of Air Quality Standards 207, 209-10 (A. Atkisson & R. Gaines eds. 1970).

be established in a costless market, the present system of liability rules might function, in a small way, to raise it.[106] But it is difficult to conceive of similar "market" corrections if the legislatively established level is too high and is rigorously enforced. Insofar as *regulatory* programs are concerned, all of the above remarks suggest the wisdom of opting for the relative efficiencies of performance standards, since in general terms they bring no apparent disadvantages. This reveals very little, however, about just what such a program should look like and how it should be administered, and it is here that much work remains to be done. As Professor Mandelker has said, "From the administrative side, it would seem clear that we need a prescriptive model of an effective method of administration before we can decide on what standards to choose." Yet "lawyers . . . do very little work on the theoretic problems of modeling different types of legal controls, whether in a descriptive, predictive, or prescriptive sense."[107] This is the frontier of research for those concerned with the relations between pollution problems and legal process. What practical, political and legal constraints bear on program administration, and what do they indicate about the shape a program should take? Which constraints are most important in their impact, and which are most pliable? What are the net gains and losses from various approaches? Very little work has been done with regard to questions such as these. It must be interdisciplinary work and, most surely, it must have the input of lawyers.

B. *Subsidies*

This and the next section discuss two fiscal alternatives to regulatory programs—subsidies and pricing. Both share with regu-

---

106 For example, in some circumstances individuals injured by polluting activity can recover damages from a polluter even though the latter is in compliance with applicable regulations. *Cf.* Urie v. Franconia Paper Corp., 107 N.H. 131, 218 A.2d 360 (1966) (what is authorized by law cannot be a public nuisance, but this does not affect any claim of a private citizen for damages for injuries caused by the authorized act but not experienced by the public at large). Assuming perfect compliance with regulatory standards and assuming further that perfect compliance produces the air quality desired by the legislative body, application of the rule stated in *Urie* would tend over time to result in a higher level of quality than the legislative standard. One could thus argue that the function of the rule is to correct standards clearly below public desires, especially since its application would increase as more and more people became less and less satisfied with present standards and more willing to take on the burdens of lawsuits in which the rule might govern. Of course, no control program enjoys perfect compliance, nor is any likely to achieve precisely the desired level of air quality. Thus the rule stated in *Urie* might be more understandably viewed as a way of filling gaps in program design and administration (as well as a way of compensating those who suffer most directly and seriously from legitimate polluting activity—something a regulatory program does not achieve).

107 Mandelker, *supra* note 105, at 207, 209.

latory programs the feature that they are intended as means to reach a collectively determined quality goal. Both, as a matter of theory, are almost identical from the standpoint of efficient resource allocation; the only difference is in the initial locus of the right to use of the resource. For example, a subsidy to polluters would recognize this right in the polluter, and work as a payment to the polluter to give it up. A pricing system, on the other hand, would in essence recognize the initial right in receptors and would require a payment by polluters to use the receptors' rights in the resource. As we shall see, however, subsidy and pricing systems differ when theory is reduced to practice.

The principal subsidy programs in the case of air pollution control have taken the form of tax incentives—investment credits and accelerated depreciation.[108] The idea, of course, is that incentives such as these encourage efforts to achieve a higher level of air quality. The idea breaks down when applied. In many cases, the incentives merely reduce the cost of unprofitable equipment and reducing the cost of such equipment does not induce a firm to install it.[109] (Arguably, however, the tax breaks might have some desirable effect by reducing a firm's costs of achieving an image as a nonpolluter.[110]) Tax incentives also tend to be ineffective in that, at least in their present form, they subsidize only the capital costs of pollution control, which may be only a fraction of a firm's total pollution control costs.[111] A system of award payments—direct cash subsidies as opposed to tax relief—could avoid this problem. Payments could be geared either to the amount of abatement achieved by a firm or to the achievement of a certain standard of quality, with graduated payments for various levels of performance. However, the measurement devices needed for a reliable program of award payments probably do not exist.

Incentive programs are also difficult to justify on grounds of economic efficiency. First, it is difficult to determine from an administrative standpoint just how much of a plant's investment should be charged to pollution control and how much to capital improvements which would have been made in any event—for example, to

---

108 Except for certain taxpayers with prior commitments, federal investment credit was repealed for purchasers after April 18, 1969. INT. REV. CODE OF 1954, § 49. On accelerated depreciation, see INT. REV. CODE OF 1954, § 169.

109 Mills, *Federal Fiscal Policy in Air Pollution Control*, in PROCEEDINGS: THIRD NATIONAL CONFERENCE ON AIR POLLUTION 574, 575-76 (Public Health Service Pub. No. 1669, 1967).

110 *But see* Roberts, *River Basin Authorities: A National Solution to Water Pollution*, 83 HARV. L. REV. 1527, 1532 (1970).

111 FEDERAL COORDINATING COMM. ON THE ECONOMIC IMPACT OF POLLUTION ABATEMENT, COST SHARING WITH INDUSTRY? 27 (1967).

expand production capacity. A program that rewarded and underwrote improvements which would be made in any event (and which, indeed, might actually work toward undesired ends) would be most inefficient. Inefficiencies would also result if the incentive program encouraged capital improvements when undiscovered lower-cost approaches (such as the use of different fuel) existed.[112] Cash awards would not cure the problem. They might encourage a firm to search for the most efficient means of improvement, but the firm would still pocket the whole award, even if it were greater than the cost of improvements. Indeed, pollution abatement might itself tend to become a profitable business, encouraging the formation of firms which would engage in the wonderful business of getting paid not to pollute.[113] A related problem grows from those cases where pollution control might yield valuable by-products which could be sold at a profit by the polluter. Do we wish to subsidize profit-making ventures?[114] Neither award payments nor tax incentives function to internalize the social costs of pollution on polluting firms and their consumers. The cost of both forms of subsidy are borne by taxpayers, thus discouraging a shift in the market away from goods whose production involves high pollution costs. As a result, more of such goods might be produced than would be the case if the market were allowed to function.[115]

Award payment *would* avoid another set of problems peculiar to tax incentive programs. The tax system exists primarily to raise revenues in a fair way, and tax incentives erode the tax base, often in an unfair way. Moreover, once embodied in the tax laws (which are already badly pocked with scars of past subsidies), tax incentives tend to remain there. This is both worrisome and likely, inasmuch as tax subsidies do not receive the periodic review and approval of legislative bodies given to direct expenditures and, in any event, cannot be evaluated with precision since they consist of incalcuable amounts of revenue foregone.[116]

---

112 *See* Gerhardt, *Incentives to Air Pollution Control*, 33 LAW & CONTEMP. PROB. 358, 361-62 (1968).

113 *See* J.H. DALES, *supra* note 83, at 87. This problem could be avoided, but only by policies creating other inefficiencies. *Id.*

114 Gerhardt, *supra* note 112, at 362.

115 *See* Roberts, *supra* note 110, at 1535-36. Professor Ruff has put this point in another way: "[A] subsidy on waste *treatment* is a subsidy on waste *production*, and leads to far too many resources devoted to the production of pollution-intensive goods in pollution intensive ways; a badly structured subsidy (and they all are) may actually increase pollution at great cost." Letter to the author from Larry Ruff, Assistant Professor, Department of Economics, University of California at San Diego, Oct. 15, 1970.

116 Gerhardt, *supra* note 112, at 363. *See* Note, *Government Programs to Encourage Private Investment in Low Income Housing*, 81 HARV. L. REV. 1295, 1309-11, (1968). For discussion in a broader setting, see Surrey, *Tax Incentives as a Device*

Most people would also find subsidies hard to justify in terms of other goals, namely income distribution and general grounds of equity and morality. Not only do subsidies acknowledge a right to pollute which is repugnant to most of society, they also tend in many cases to transfer wealth to relatively affluent groups. All in all, subsidy programs seem unattractive from the standpoint of central objectives (although they tend to be politically attractive to the extent that big business, which has carried on a long love affair with subsidies, has influence over the legislative body).[117]

C. *Pricing*

Like subsidies, pricing programs are a fiscal means designed to achieve a desired state of environmental quality. Rather than positively award polluters for reducing emissions, they charge (or tax) the polluter for each unit of emission. Pricing is thus a direct attack on the external diseconomies of pollution resulting from breakdowns in the market system. The underlying principle of pricing is clear: "If you charge a person for disposing of his wastes he will find ways to reduce the amount of wastes he disposes of, and . . . the more you charge him the stronger the incentive he will have to find some less damaging method of disposing of his waste."[118]

To put the matter very simply, an air pollution pricing system might work roughly as follows.[119] An administrative agency would be given the responsibility of identifying pollutants and their sources and establishing methods of estimating emission outputs at the source. With this information in hand, the agency would designate schedules of prices for the various pollutants. Ideally, prices would vary depending upon how dangerous ("costly") a particular pollutant might be, the location of the source (emissions in a desert would probably cause less total damage than in a city),[120] the

---

for Implementing Government Policy: A Comparison with Direct Government Expenditures, 83 HARV. L. REV. 705 (1970) (arguing "that the tax incentive is generally inferior to the direct subsidy as a means of achieving social goals").

117 Although subsidy programs seem generally undesirable in terms of the resource allocation goal, the arguments leading to this conclusion may be diluted, or outweighed by other considerations, in certain cases—for example, payment of subsidies to low-income persons to enable them to afford the costs of installation of pollution control devices on their automobiles.

118 J.H. DALES, *supra* note 83, at 81-82.

119 The model is based on the discussion in Ruff, *The Economic Common Sense of Pollution*, PUBLIC INTEREST, Spring 1970, at 69. While the discussion in the text focuses on the fixed-source pollution problem, its application to the automobile is obvious. Fuel consumption, for example, could be taxed (and the tax rate could increase with the "dirtiness" of the fuel consumed).

120 For a convincing argument that prices should *not* be lower in remote, thinly populated areas, see J.H. DALES, *supra* note 83, at 88-93. Professor Dales argues that

season of the year, daily meteorological conditions, and so forth. The prices would be based on units of emission and would be uniform as to all polluters sharing identical circumstances.

Pollution producers would be free to adjust as they choose to the prices imposed upon them: a government regulator would not be looking over management's shoulder and giving (often ill-conceived) advice. This drastic decentralization is considered one of the great advantages of a pricing system.[121] Polluters could change fuels or production methods, move to a different area, install pollution control devices, pollute only during certain seasons, pay the price, or mix all of these alternatives in the way most advantageous to them. Consumers, of course, would tend to switch their purchases away from goods to the extent those goods increased in price, and it is this shift in demand which would encourage each firm to act in the way most efficient for it, in light of its presumed objective of profit maximization. The same phenomenon would mean higher consumption of goods the production of which involves little pollution and less consumption (and, thus, production) of those which involve relatively great amounts of pollution. Some firms might find it cheapest simply to pollute and pay, passing the cost on to their customers or shareholders. If this were common, it would probably suggest that prices were not set high enough to begin with; they could always be adjusted (up or down) in light of experience. A willingness upon the part of customers to pay the price might also suggest that society values certain services and products so highly that it is willing to take the pollution that goes with them. This information could be valuable to policy makers.

---

to accept the position that, of two factories producing the same amount of emissions, the one that does less damage (because, for example, it is located in a barren desert) should pay less in taxes would tend to push polluters into lower tax areas and thus to even out pollution geographically and make levels the same everywhere. He believes that people want separate facilities—areas of high concentration and areas which are virtually pollution free. He fears that with pollution levels the same everywhere, no area will be good; he believes there should be good and bad areas, among which people could choose based on their individual assessments of the advantages and disadvantages of each area (for example, lower versus higher pollution levels, lower versus higher land costs, lower versus higher wages). Accordingly, he argues that the authorities should adopt either a polluter-locationally neutral pricing policy (that they should, that is, set equal prices throughout a region) or a policy of relatively *lower* prices within highly polluted areas of a region. He argues that as a result of either policy business would tend to concentrate in highly polluted locations, rather than spread to clean areas.

121 *See, e.g.*, Hagevik, *supra* note 88, at 371-72. Pricing is said to maximize the incentive to discover technological improvements. As we have seen, subsidies can create the same incentive, but only in a less efficient manner (higher payment costs or higher administrative costs). A performance regulatory system can also create the incentive, but only on a discontinuous basis; the incentive ceases once the imposed emission standard is met. To surmount this discontinuity would entail tremendous administrative costs.

Some economists appear to believe that a pricing system would have lower administrative costs than alternative approaches,[122] but others conclude that these would be about the same in any sophisticated program.[123] Neither argument can go very far. Since there has been very little practical experience with pricing, reliable judgments about comparative administrative costs cannot be made. Even if costs are about equal, theory would seem to suggest that pricing would be relatively more efficient for essentially two reasons. First, assuming that firms are profit maximizers, each will act to keep its costs at a minimum. Second, emission prices can be raised until the collectively determined quality standard is reached. Putting these two points together, the desired quality can be achieved at the lowest cost.

A variation of the pricing model would establish a pollution ceiling, but would then translate that maximum figure into a number of pollution rights (very much like shares of stock).[124] Anyone would be permitted to purchase these rights at auction; conservation groups, for example, could buy and "bank" the rights in order to diminish pollution. An important advantage of this auction model as compared to a system of emission fees is that it requires no governmental decision about the set of prices needed to attain the desired level of quality. That decision is an exceedingly complex one, open to much room for error and perhaps not as subject to easy correction as some proponents of emission fees seem to assume. The auction model depends only upon the simpler calculation of the number of pollution rights to be issued. The market sets the prices. Moreover, the auction model would appear to be more capable of dealing with firms which do not strive to maximize profits, with firms which enjoy a monopoly position in the market, and with regulated industries—such as public power utilities—which are guaranteed an annual rate of return. Under a system of emission fees, firms and industries such as these might simply absorb or pass on the added costs of the fees without changing in any significant way activities which contribute to the pollution problem. Emission levels could remain high. Under the auction model, the number of rights issued would set absolute limits on the total amount of pollution. Once all the rights were purchased, pollution levels could not increase no matter how the costs of the rights were distributed. Finally, the auction model also appears to bring market

122 *Cf.* Ruff, *supra* note 119, at 78-79.

123 J.H. DALES, *supra* note 83, at 87-88. *But see id.* at 92-93, where Dales argues that an additional advantage of his separate facilities proposal is that it would bring with it lower administrative costs than other approaches.

124 *See generally id.* at 93-97.

forces to bear on the problem of error correction more than does the method of emission fees, since rights could be more easily transferred between polluting and nonpolluting interests. The appearance might be largely illusory, however, since nonpolluting interests such as conservation groups would have difficulty raising the necessary cash to compete for the rights. Even people who desired less pollution would tend to take the position that they need not contribute to the cause in the hope or belief that others would purchase and bank the rights—an act that would benefit contributors and noncontributors equally.[125] In any event, market forces could only work to correct an error setting the quality level too low, not one setting it too high. Proponents of all pricing models, however, contemplate that periodic adjustments, based on experience, would be made in the level of prices or the number of rights. They argue that this relative flexibility in any pricing model is one of its chief advantages.[126]

There are among economists a number of arguments waging over the subject of pricing, most of them growing from disagreements about economic theory.[127] Lawyers, on the other hand, have paid very little attention to a price system as a means of pollution control. From time to time, references are made to the difficulty one would face in drafting a program which could pass constitutional muster, but they are unconvincing.[128] Why, for example, would arguments urging vagueness or denial of equal protection based on the deficiencies of measuring equipment have any more force as to a pricing program than they do with respect to regulatory programs which depend upon, and lawfully use, the same imprecise equipment?

Various pricing models have apparently not been compared on the basis of legal, administrative and other policy considerations.

---

[125] This point was suggested to me by my colleague, Professor Kenneth Graham. *See also* Krutilla, *Conservation Reconsidered*, 57 AM. ECON. REV. 777, 782 (1967).

[126] *See, e.g.*, Ruff, *Price Pollution Out of Existence*, L.A. Times, Dec. 7, 1969, § G, at 7, col. 3. *But see* Roberts, *supra* note 110, at 1555.

[127] For summaries, see Hagevik, *supra* note 88, at 370-74; Wolozin, *The Economics of Air Pollution: Central Problems*, 33 LAW & CONTEMP. PROB. 227, 233-37 (1968); *The Cost-Internalization Case for Class Actions*, *supra* note 6, at 399-401 (1969).

[128] *E.g.*, Hagevik, *supra* note 88, at 373 (program would "have to survive legal attacks based on arguments of apparent discrimination and abuse of taxing power."). It has been suggested that the Federal Air Quality Act of 1967 contemplates only direct regulation. Havighurst, *Forward*, 33 LAW & CONTEMP. PROB. 195, 196 (1968). The language of the Act, however, does not appear to compel this conclusion. *See* Air Quality Act of 1967 § 108(c)(1), 42 U.S.C. § 1857d(c)(1) (Supp. V 1970). The same can be said of the 1970 amendments. *See* Clean Air Amendments of 1970, Pub. L. No. 91-604, § 4(a) (1970).

For example, it seems apparent that the auction model would involve lower policing costs than would emission fee models. The latter call for constant monitoring; the former would seem to require no more than spot checks by the authorities to ensure that pollution rights are not being abused.[129] Is this apparent advantage of the auction system a workable one? In another vein, how can a workable system be constructed to bring the price system to bear on receptors as well as polluters, so that they too have an incentive to avoid pollution damage? What is needed with regard to pricing as a means of control is some empirical data, some practical experience. We might find some of that experience to be already in existence if we once sat down and actually tried, after studying all the existing theoretical research, to draft a system and a means for its administration. For example, much of the practical experience under regimes of performance and specification standards would bear directly on the shape of a pricing program. That experience has yielded at least some knowledge about management behavior and administrative efficiencies with regard to pollution control. Actually implementing a program on a pilot basis would also generate empirical data. If that should sound far fetched, call to mind the fact that today's existing leased housing program grew directly from a pilot project and that there are currently underway the Office of Economic Opportunity's pilot programs on the negative income tax.[130]

Theoretical disagreements about the merits of pricing will probably go on forever and unless some concrete steps are taken such a system shall never be given a fair chance.[131] That would be a shame indeed, for in the few cases in which pricing has actually been used on a full-scale basis (for example, to control water quality in

---

129 The point is suggested by T. Crocker, On Air Pollution Instruments (unpublished, 1970).

130 *See* CALIF. ASSEMBLY SELECT COMMITTEE ON ENVIRONMENTAL QUALITY, ENVIRONMENTAL BILL OF RIGHTS 34 (1970) calling for legislation "to authorize demonstration areas in which test programs could be created to establish additional standards for improving environmental quality."

For an example of the value of empirical data, consider the implications of the studies which suggest that pollution control programs requiring simple equal-proportional reduction of waste loads on the part of all polluters would cost anywhere from 50 to 400 percent more than achieving the same quality standard by requiring firms to reduce waste loads in proportion to their harmful effects. *See* Hagevik, *supra* note 88, at 377.

131 It is fascinating to consider the background role to be played by the courts if a pricing system of control were to be adopted. Under a regulatory regime, parties injured by a polluter's activities always have a case for the recovery of damages (on such theories as nuisance, trespass, strict liability, negligence per se, etc.) if the polluter has violated applicable control regulations and may have a case even if the polluter has not. *See* note 106 *supra*. Should the same results hold under any of the possible pricing models? The problem seems quite simple in the case of the auction

the Ruhr Valley in Germany) it has met with success.[132] The Great American Regulatory Tradition, on the other hand, has been a disappointment at best.

IV. A Postscript

I have tried in the pages above to assess the state of our knowledge with regard to the role of legal institutions in coping with pollution problems and to suggest in some general terms areas badly in need of development and research.[133] There are several matters on which my discussion did not touch.

One concerns the question of international institutions to cope with the fact that pollution respects no political boundaries—a specialized inquiry beyond the scope of this paper.[134] Another concerns the environmental quality study and advisory councils being created, by either executive or legislative mandate, at the federal and state level.[135] These bodies are charged with the responsibility for determining and formulating environmental policy, and, to some extent, insisting on its pursuit. Among other things, the councils illustrate the function of government as a gatherer and disseminator of information; for the most part, their activities are just underway and there has been little opportunity to make inquiries into their work.[136] It is important that such inquiries begin as soon as possible, for the councils are likely to have a broad impact on environmental planning and to raise significant issues of legal process. For instance, what latent coercive powers do these study and advisory bodies

model, so long as the polluter has exceeded the pollution rights he has purchased. But suppose he has not? In the case of an emission fee, should the polluter ever be required to pay damages in a lawsuit so long as he has paid the appropriate tax? If he is required to pay, should he be given a credit against his tax in the amount of the damages? Or should the problem simply be resolved as it has been under a regulatory regime, and for the same policy reasons? *See* note 106 *supra*.

132 *See Hearings on Water Pollution Before a Special Subcomm. on Air and Water Pollution of the Senate Comm. on Public Works*, 89th Cong., 1st Sess., pt. 3, at 914 (1965) (statement of Allen Kneese).

133 For enlightening comments on research design and implementation, as well as on areas of needed research, see O. Herfindahl & A. Kneese, Quality of the Environment (1965). On a "research strategy," see especially *id.* at 81-96.

134 *See generally* Adinolfi, *First Steps Toward European Cooperation in Reducing Air Pollution Activities of the Council of Europe*, 33 Law & Contemp. Prob. 421 (1968); Kennan, *To Prevent a World Wasteland*, 48 Foreign Affairs 401 (1970); Comment, *International Air Pollution—United States and Canada—A Joint Approach*, 10 Ariz. L. Rev. 138 (1968).

135 Some examples are the Council on Environmental Quality created by the National Environmental Policy Act of 1969, 42 U.S.C. §§ 4341-47 (Supp. V, 1970) and California's Environmental Quality Study Council, Cal. Gov't. Code §§ 16000-80 (West 1970). *See generally* Muskie, *Environmental Jurisdiction in the Congress and the Executive*, 22 Me. L. Rev. 171 (1970).

136 For one study, see Krier, *supra* note 70. *See also* J. Sax, Defending the Environment 89-100 (1970).

have? How democratically do they function? How do they see and implement their missions?

I have also left virtually untouched two matters closely related to each other. The first concerns the roles of different levels of government—federal, state, local and regional—in environmental quality control. While regional programs are the subject of much current discussion, the operational meaning of the concept and the extent of our commitment to it are by no means clear. For example, federal law provides for air pollution control regions in the case of stationary sources, but program implementation and enforcement are left primarily to the independent acts of the states within any particular region; moreover, the states in turn delegate to local governments. More attention should be devoted to the optimal arrangement of responsibilities of different levels of government with regard to environmental quality control.[137] Specifically, there is a clear need to investigate the optimal mix of responsibility, not simply in general but for different sorts of control programs, be they direct regulation, subsidies, or pricing. Pricing systems, for example, may make regional programs politically more acceptable by reducing the number of details on which stubborn, independent sovereigns within a region must agree.[138] Any program of control should be assessed in light of alternative levels of government, and the role of any government should be assessed in light of alternative control mechanisms.

Proposals for regional control programs tend to come hand-in-hand with proposals for an integrated-agency approach to environmental management.[139] A mild movement in favor of such an approach appears to be underway,[140] but there is as yet very little in-

---

137 *See* Schueneman, *Air Pollution Control Administration*, in 3 AIR POLLUTION 719, 759-67 (A. Stern ed., 2d ed. 1968); Kennedy, *Legislation and Environmental Health*, *supra* note 91, at 131-33; Kennedy, *Levels of Responsibility for the Administration of Air Pollution Control Programs*, in PROCEEDINGS, NATIONAL CONFERENCE ON AIR POLLUTION 389 (Public Health Service Pub. No. 654, 1959); PROCEEDINGS, NATIONAL CONFERENCE ON AIR POLLUTION 317-38 (Public Health Service Pub. No. 1022, 1963); PROCEEDINGS: THIRD NATIONAL CONFERENCE ON AIR POLLUTION 462-524 (Public Health Service Pub. No. 1649, 1967).

138 Ruff, *supra* note 119, at 83. On political problems confronted in programs of regional control, see Lieber, *Controlling Metropolitan Pollution Through Regional Air-Sheds: Administrative Requirements and Political Problems*, 18 J. AIR POLLUTION CONTROL ASS'N 86 (1968). For interesting discussions of a regional air pollution control program, see J. MAGA, AIR RESOURCE MANAGEMENT IN THE SAN FRANCISCO BAY AREA (1965); Note, *Regional Control of Air and Water Pollution in the San Francisco Bay Area*, 55 CALIF. L. REV. 702-11 (1967).

139 *See, e.g.*, R. Roemer, J. Frink & C. Kramer, Environmental Health Services: Multiplicity of Jurisdictions and Comprehensive Environmental Management (to be published in the *Milbank Memorial Fund Quarterly*, Vol. 49, No. 3, July 1971).

140 *See, e.g.*, the Environmental Protection Agency (EPA) established by Reorganization Plan No. 3 of 1970, July 9, 1970. EPA has been assigned many of the

formation bearing on the design of integrated environmental agencies.[141] While I have put explicit consideration of this issue beyond the scope of this paper, it does seem clear that the discussion of pollution control legislation and its administration applies as much to the design of an integrated agency as it does to separate agencies concerned with distinct categories of environmental problems. In any event, disparate programs aimed only at individual problems will be with us for some time, and there is much that can be done while waiting for the grand approach.

---

duties of setting and enforcing environmental protection standards previously scattered among disparate federal agencies. Similar agencies exist in several states. *See, e.g.*, N.Y. ENVIRON. CONSERV. LAW § 1-129 (McKinney 1970); ORE. REV. STAT. §§ 449.001.855 (1970).

For thoughtful presentation of the case for an integrated, regional environmental quality control institution, see R. Roemer, J. Frink & C. Kramer, *supra* note 139.

141 *See* O. HERFINDAHL & A. KNEESE, *supra* note 133, at 91-92.

[7]

MEDIA-QUALITY, TECHNOLOGY, AND COST-BENEFIT BALANCING STRATEGIES FOR HEALTH AND ENVIRONMENTAL REGULATION*

THOMAS O. McGARITY†

I

INTRODUCTION

The new wave of "social" regulation that Congress enacted in the early 1970's struck the chemical industry with particular force. Untouched by the economic regulation that constrained the transportation, communications, and utilities industries, the chemical industry's contact with the federal regulatory establishment was limited to clearing products such as drugs and pesticides with old-line federal agencies. By the end of the 1970's, the chemical industry was laboring under a wide variety of regulatory constraints on its emissions of chemical by-products into the workplace and the environment, and further limitations on the ultimate disposal of hazardous chemicals were still germinating.[1] At the same time that Congress imposed substantial new requirements on the chemical industry, it created new regulatory agencies to administer the new statutes.[2] As a result, the chemical industry is rapidly becoming one of the most heavily regulated industries in the United States.

The new health and environmental statutes generally adopt one or both of two

---

* The author would like to express his appreciation to Professors Sidney A. Shapiro, Douglas Laycock, Richard Markovits, and Mr. William F. Pedersen, United States Environmental Protection Agency, for their comments on an earlier draft of this article and to Ms. Teresa Salamone, Class of 1983, University of Texas School of Law, and Ms. Jane Ellen Hamilton, Class of 1984, University of Texas School of Law, for research assistance in the preparation of this article.

† Professor or Law, University of Texas School of Law.

1. Congress also enacted the Toxic Substances Control Act, 15 U.S.C. §§ 2601-2629 (1982), in 1976. This comprehensive regulatory statute was aimed directly at the chemical industry. The Toxic Substances Control Act more closely resembles a more traditional product licensing statute than the other environmental statutes of the 1970's. In effect, the Environmental Protection Agency (EPA) is given limited powers to compel a product manufacturer to test its products and report to the EPA on their possible adverse effects. The EPA may then choose from among specified regulatory options when it finds that the risks for a particular use of the product outweigh the benefits. Since the regulatory section of this risk-benefit product licensing statute has not yet been implemented, it will therefore not be discussed further in this article.

2. This article will focus primarily upon two agencies, the Occupational Safety and Health Administration (OSHA) and EPA. The EPA was created pursuant to congressional authorizations by President Nixon in Reorganization Plan Number 3 of 1970, 5 U.S.C. app. 1132 (1982), and it is therefore not strictly a creature of Congress.

approaches toward the content of regulations that the implementing regulatory agencies must promulgate. The "media-quality-based" approach focuses upon the quality of the receiving media (usually air or water) and requires the agency to promulgate and enforce regulations capable of rendering the media acceptably "safe" or "clean" without regard to the costs or technological feasibility of reaching that goal. The "technology-based" approach focuses upon the control technologies that are available to industrial entities and requires the agency to promulgate and enforce regulations capable of ensuring that regulated firms adopt the appropriate cleanup technology without regard to the quality of the receiving media.[3] Between these two extremes is a "balancing" approach that weighs media-quality considerations against technological and economic considerations in determining the amount of pollutant a source may discharge into the environment or the workplace. The balancing approach is usually associated with product licensing statutes such as the Food, Drug and Cosmetic Act,[4] the Federal Insecticide, Fungicide and Rodenticide Act,[5] and the Toxic Substances Control Act,[6] that require an affirmative governmental decision before society can be exposed to the risks of a product or its by-products. Although the major environmental statutes do not often prescribe a balancing aproach, many policy analysts (especially from the economics profession) strongly advocate broadening the role of cost-benefit balancing beyond the product licensing context. Nevertheless, Congress has until now rejected the balancing approach in favor of media-quality-based and technology-based approaches, both of which reduce cost considerations to a secondary or even less consequential status.[7]

This article will examine these three fundamental regulatory techniques in the context of health and environmental regulation. The article will argue that Congress has wisely rejected the balancing approach for a host of practical reasons and because the approach, as applied by most practitioners, is fundamentally flawed as a theoretical matter. Briefly, when applied to matters of intense personal interest, such as credible risks to life or risks to very highly valued environmental entities, the Kaldor-Hicks formulation of the balancing approach, which is almost exclusively relied upon by balancing proponents, cannot yield a "correct" answer to the question how much risk is too much. The "willingness to purchase safety" test for

3. A statute can, of course, mandate a combination of approaches. For example, the Clean Water Act adopts a technology-based approach but backs it up with a media-quality-based approach. Under the first approach, the agency prescribes technologies without regard to the quality of the receiving media. States, however, may promulgate water quality-based standards that must be met in addition to the technology-based standards. Hence, if implementation of the technology-based standards does not produce water of sufficient quality, the media-quality-based standards take precedence.

4. 21 U.S.C. § 301 (1982).

5. 7 U.S.C. § 136 (1982).

6. 15 U.S.C. § 2601 (1982).

7. Similarly both approaches may be implemented by a variety of regulatory tools, including the traditional standard-setting tools and more esoteric tools such as effluent fees and marketable permits. This article will examine the comparative merits of the two approaches within the context of traditional standard-setting since that is the universal implementation tool adopted by Congress in the existing statutes. However, when one approach may be more effectively implemented through some alternative tool, such as marketable permits, it will be considered with the appropriate caveat concerning the political feasibility of enacting that tool into existing statutes.

the value of safety-enhancing technologies is not on theoretical grounds preferable to the "willingness to sell risks" test for the value of those technologies. Yet, policy analysts almost invariably adopt the former test, which is, as the article will show, biased strongly against the adoption of health and environmentally-oriented technologies.

While both the media-quality-based and technology-based alternatives to the balancing approach are heavily weighted with problems of their own, this article will suggest that the general preference of Congress and especially of implementing agencies for the technology-based approach in the context of the chemical industry is warranted by an almost universal recognition that citizens of this country have a "right" to a healthy environment and workplace, at least insofar as the societal pursuit of that right is not technologically impossible or prohibitively expensive. Finally, this article will suggest a mixed strategy that rejects the balancing approach but attempts to arrive at an acceptable (if not "optimal") level of health and environmental protection and to encourage research on protective control technologies.[8]

II

THE CHEMICAL INDUSTRY

For purposes of health and environmental regulation, three characteristics of the chemical industry distinguish it from other manufacturing industries. These three characteristics might impel the policymaker to treat the chemical industry differently from other industries in promulgating health and environmental regulations.[9]

The chemical industry is extraordinarily varied and complex. A glance at the Standard Industrial Classifications for the chemical industry reveals an enormous variety of finished products ranging from soap deodorizers to acetone.[10] Not surprisingly, the chemical industry produces an equally heterogeneous variety of unwanted by-products.[11] A given plant may manufacture dozens of different

8. This article will focus upon only one dimension of health and environmental regulation—*viz*, the nature of the immediate regulatory goal. It will examine some of the advantages and disadvantages of a regulatory focus on technology, media quality or some combination of these two considerations, in pursuing health and environmental objectives. The problem can be viewed along other dimensions as well. For example, one can focus on the nature of the regulatory statement. On one extreme of that dimension is the regulatory command; on the other extreme is the economic incentive. One could likewise focus upon whether the regulatory statement is source-oriented or receptor-oriented and whether it is promulgated on a generic or case-by-case basis. *See* McGarity & Bayer, *Federal Regulation of Emerging Genetic Technologies*, 36 VAND. L. REV. 461 (1983).

9. For example, some of the writers on "charges" as alternatives to standards seem to sidestep the problem of toxics, pointing out that strict prohibitions may be more appropriate for such discharges. *See* F. ANDERSON, A. KNEESE, P. REED, R. STEVENSON & S. TAYLOR, ENVIRONMENTAL IMPROVEMENTS THROUGH ECONOMIC INCENTIVES 17 (1977) [hereinafter cited as F. ANDERSON]. At other times, charge proponents have maintained that the toxic problem is solvable if the charge is merely set at a high enough level. *Id.* at 88-89; Ruff, *Federal Environmental Regulation*, in COMM. ON GOVERNMENTAL AFFAIRS, STUDY ON FEDERAL REGULATION, S. DOC. NO. 14, 96th Cong., 1st Sess. 251, 342-343 (1979). All charge proponents, however, acknowledge that toxic substances must be treated differently.

10. OFFICE OF MANAGEMENT AND BUDGET, STANDARD INDUSTRIAL CLASSIFICATION MANUAL 111-26 (1972).

11. *See, e.g.*, U.S. Environmental Protection Agency, Development Document for Proposed Effluent

products and generate hundreds of different by-products. This bewildering complexity can easily hamstring any strategy of health and environmental regulation that requires a detailed understanding of the industry being regulated.

Many of the products and by-products that the chemical industry produces are hazardous at relatively low exposure levels. While some chemical products, such as pesticides, are intended to be toxic to living organisms, toxicity is an undesirable but inevitable characteristic of most chemical products. Some chemical products and by-products are quite acutely toxic to man and environmental organisms, while others pose long term carcinogenic, mutagenic, or reproductive hazards. The toxicity of many by-products of the chemical industry is, therefore, quantitatively and often qualitatively different from the toxicity of conventional by-products given off by other manufacturing processes. Moreover, large uncertainties often cloud attempts to assess the long term risks that the products and by-products of the chemical industry pose to humans and the environment.[12] Thus, while the costs of regulatory mistakes are likely to be higher for the chemical industry, the probability of making mistakes is also higher.

Finally, the sources of any individual toxic product or by-product of the chemical industry are not likely to be ubiquitous. Most of the very toxic products and by-products of that industry come from very few sources at discrete locations. Hence, monitoring of complex waste streams is simplified by the fact that the waste stream for a particular toxic chemical from an individual plant will rarely overlap with the waste stream for the same chemical from another plant.[13] Like all generalizations, this characteristic has its limitations for some chemicals, such as the phenols, and some sites, such as hazardous waste disposal facilities serving heavily industrialized areas. But, nevertheless, it is a worthwhile simplifying generalization.

III

MEDIA-QUALITY, TECHNOLOGY, AND BALANCING

Nearly all of the regulatory provisions in the more recent occupational health and environmental statutes can be classified as media-quality-based, technology-based, or balancing approaches to pollution control. A media-quality-based approach focuses primarily upon the quality of the receiving media. Society first articulates some overall goal for the receiving media. This goal could be specified with great particularity (for example, no more than 150 dead fish or cases of human cancer per year), but more often it is expressed in more hortatory terms

---

Limitations Guidelines, New Source Performance Standards, and Pretreatment Standards for the Inorganic Chemicals Manufacturing Point Source Category 66-68 (1980) (characterizing waste streams of categories of the inorganic chemicals manufacturing industry).

12. *See infra* notes 37-39 and accompanying text.

13. *See* Rose-Ackerman, *Market Models for Water Pollution Control: Their Strengths and Weaknesses*, 25 PUBLIC POLICY 383, 401 (1977); *Implementation of the Federal Water Pollution Control Act: Summary of Hearings on the Regulation and Monitoring of Toxic and Hazardous Chemicals Under the Federal Water Pollution Control Act Before the Subcomm. on Investigations and Review of the House Comm. on Public Works and Transporation*, 95th Cong., 1st Sess. 599 (Comm. Print 1977) (testimony of Dr. Charles Schultze). This is, of course, always true of the workplace where waste streams from different plants never interact.

such as "fishable/swimmable water."[14] The regulatory entity then determines the level of pollutant in the receiving medium that will just meet the external goal by estimating the environmental and health effects of the pollutant at various concentrations in the receiving medium.[15] A pollution allocation load (for locations meeting the standard) or pollution reduction load (for locations not meeting the standard) can then be calculated with a model that relates discharges from individual facilities to overall media quality.[16] Finally, the regulatory entity must apportion the load among the existing sources, perhaps saving some portion of the available load for future sources.[17]

The allocation formula that the regulatory entity uses is of very little consequence to media quality, but it is of great importance to pollution sources. A reasonably comprehensive list of load allocation techniques includes first-come-first-served, a lottery, uniform percentage reduction for all sources, an auction and a subsequent market in pollution "rights," effluent charges set at a level that would induce the degree of control just adequate to use up the load, technology-based effluent limitations for all sources just adequate to use up the load, and allocation in accordance with other unspecified "political" factors. If the entire load in a relevant media-quality region is attributable to a single source, as is the case with many sources of toxic substance discharges into air and water and all discharges into workplaces, then no allocation is necessary. The regulatory entity can simply use its reduction model to work backwards from the desired level of media quality to an effluent or emission limitation for the source. After allocating the available load, the regulatory entity then monitors the sources and the receiving media to detect violations and to determine whether the model functioned properly.

Under the technology-based approach, the legislature specifies in vague terms, such as "best available technology," or "lowest achievable emissions rate," the degree of pollution control technology[18] that it expects regulated industries to implement.[19] The legislature typically distinguishes between new and old sources

---

14. Clean Water Act, 33 U.S.C. § 1313 (Supp. V 1981).

15. *See, e.g.*, 1 EPA Air Quality Criteria for Particulate Matter and Sulfur Oxides (External Review Draft No. 2, Feb. 1981); Air Quality Criteria for Lead (Dec. 1977) (EPA-600/8-77-017).

16. *See* Texas v. EPA, 499 F.2d 289, *cert. denied*, 427 U.S. 905 (1974); Clean Water Act, 33 U.S.C. § 1313 (Supp. V 1981); *cf.* G. GRIMSRUD, E. FINNEMORE & H. OWEN, EVALUATION OF WATER QUALITY MODELS: A MANAGEMENT GUIDE FOR PLANNERS (1976) (EPA Socioeconomic Environmental Studies Series, EPA-600/5-76-004).

17. *See* 33 U.S.C. § 1313 (Supp. V 1981); 42 U.S.C. § 7410 (Supp. V 1981); TEXAS AIR CONTROL BOARD, TEXAS STATE IMPLEMENTATION PLAN: CONTROL STRATEGIES (1979).

18. In using the term "pollution control technology," I do not intend to limit the discussion to "end-of-pipe" technologies aimed exclusively at pollution controls. Changes in the design and operation of the basic units of production and in the way that employees perform their tasks can reduce pollution as well as (and often more cheaply than) end-of-pipe technologies. *See* A. KNEESE & C. SCHULTZE, POLLUTION, PRICES AND PUBLIC POLICY 24 (1975).

19. Very often the statute will specify criteria that the agency must apply in identifying the specified level of pollution control technology. For example, the Clean Water Act specifies that:

> Factors relating to the assessment of best available technology shall take into account the age of equipment and facilities involved, the process employed, the engineering aspects of the application of various types of control techniques, process changes, the cost of achieving such effluent reduction, non-water quality environmental impact (including energy requirements), and such other factors as the Administrator deems appropriate . . . .

33 U.S.C. § 1314 (Supp. V 1981); *see* Sierra Club v. Costle, 657 F.2d 298 (D.C. Cir. 1981) (pointing out the

in articulating these broad requirements. The regulatory entity then divides the various regulated industries into categories and subcategories in accordance with the production processes they employ, the nature of the waste streams, the age of the facilities, the cost of pollution control, and other factors that appear to be relevant to the standard setter and its engineers.[20] The regulatory entity next surveys the pollution control technologies in use in the regulated industry and in industries with similar waste streams and searches for technologies that may be in use in pilot plants or that may be at even less mature developmental stages. It then picks the technology that best meets the statutory criteria. Since cost is invariably one of those criteria, the standard setter must consider economic feasibility as well as technological feasibility. Finally, the standard setter must specify the degree of effluent or emissions reduction achievable by the specified technology within each category and subcategory and write an effluent or emissions limitation expressed in units of pollution per unit of production, input, or discharge, that mandates that degree of reduction.[21]

Statutes nearly always allow an individual source the freedom to meet the promulgated limitation with any technology it desires; the standard setter is only very rarely given the authority to mandate the use of particular technologies.[22] A technology-based regime could, however, assume an even less direct approach by requiring the standard setter to establish a "charge" or "tax," rather than a limitation, that would induce the relevant sources to adopt the desired technology.[23] In either case, the regulatory entity would establish the limitation or charge without regard to the quality of the receiving media.

Congress has frequently adopted a mixture of both media-quality-based and technology-based approaches for regulating health and safety. The Clean Air Act, for example, takes a predominantly media-quality-based approach. The core of the Act is the primary and secondary national ambient air quality standards for ubiquitous pollutants, which must be set at a level which protects the public health and welfare with an adequate margin of safety.[24] Standards for less ubiquitous toxic air pollutants must protect public health with an "ample margin of

---

conflict between maximum technological feasibility and limiting criteria such as energy and other environmental requirements).

20. A technology-based standard need not be promulgated on an industry-wide or even a subcategory-wide basis. In principle a technology-based standard could be promulgated for each individual source of pollutant. The standard setter would then act very much like a court, adjudicating the economic and technological feasibility of various suggested pollution control alternatives for each source. This approach would, however, entail enormous administrative costs. Congress has required the EPA and the states to make case-by-case "best available technology" determinations in granting permits to major emitting facilities under Part C of Title I of the Clean Air Act, 42 U.S.C. §§ 7475(a)(4), 7479(3) (Supp. V 1981).

21. *E.g.*, 40 C.F.R. §§ 400-460 (1980).

22. *See* Clean Air Act § 112, 42 U.S.C. § 7412 (Supp. V 1981). OSHA gives the agency the flexibility to require the implementation of specific "practices, means, methods, operations or processes . . . ." Occupational Safety and Health Act § 3(8), 29 U.S.C. § 652(8) (Supp. V 1981).

23. Despite strong support among academicians, this approach has not been adopted in the United States. F. ANDERSON, *supra* note 9; W. IRWIN & R. LIROFF, ECONOMIC DISINCENTIVES FOR POLLUTION CONTROL: LEGAL, POLITICAL AND ADMINISTRATIVE DIMENSIONS (1974) (EPA Socioeconomic Environmental Studies Series, EPA 6005-74-026).

24. 42 U.S.C. § 7409 (Supp. V 1981).

safety."[25] In addition to these media-quality-based standards, however, the Environmental Protection Agency (EPA) must also promulgate technology-based new source performance standards that require the implementation of the "best available demonstrated" technology.[26]

The Clean Water Act also takes a mixed approach. The EPA has focused its efforts on promulgating technology-based standards for new and existing sources of ubiquitous "conventional" pollutants.[27] The Act does, however, provide for water-quality-based standards[28] and effluent limitations.[29] The Act, as amended in 1977, also provides for both technology-based effluent limitations[30] and media-quality-based effluent standards[31] for discharges of toxic substances.

The Occupational Safety and Health Act and the Safe Drinking Water Act prescribe a feasibility-limited media-quality-based approach. The Occupational Safety and Health Administration (OSHA) must promulgate occupational safety and health standards,[32] and the EPA must promulgate National Primary Drinking Water Standards[33] capable of protecting worker and public health (a media-quality-based approach) insofar as that is feasible (a technology-based concept).

As an alternative to focusing primarily upon media quality or upon technology, Congress occasionally requires the regulatory agency to combine both considerations in a balancing process. Typically, Congress mandates balancing in product licensing statutes that require a product's proponent to demonstrate that a product's benefit outweighs the risks that it poses to the public.[34] A balancing approach could with somewhat greater administrative difficulty be implemented for controlling process and by-product risks as well, although Congress has seldom done so. For example, Congress could mandate that the EPA set media-quality standards at precisely the level at which the costs of meeting the standards equalled the benefits of the standard. This would, of course, necessitate an inquiry into the availability and costs of pollution control technologies in addition to the risks of various levels of pollutant to humans and the environment and the value of the threatened consequences. Alternatively, Congress could require that the regulatory entity set technology-based standards at precisely the point at which the pollution reduction benefits derived from the standard equalled the cost of implementing the standard. Again this would require an examination of both media-quality and technology considerations. The balancing approach is therefore in the middle of a spectrum of pollution control approaches ranging from pure media-quality-based standards to strict technology-based standards.

---

25. 42 U.S.C. § 7412 (Supp. V 1981).
26. 42 U.S.C. § 7411 (Supp. V 1981).
27. 33 U.S.C. § § 1311, 1316 (Supp. V 1981).
28. 33 U.S.C. § 1312(e) (Supp. V 1981).
29. 33 U.S.C. § 1312 (Supp. V 1981).
30. 33 U.S.C. §§ 1311(b)(2)(A), 1317(a)(2) (Supp. V 1981).
31. 33 U.S.C. § 1317(a)(4) (Supp. V 1981).
32. 29 U.S.C. § 655(b) (1976).
33. 42 U.S.C. § 300(f)(1)(B)-(C) (Supp. V 1981).
34. *See* Environmental Defense Fund v. EPA, 548 F.2d 998, 1012-18 (D.C. Cir. 1976) (burden of proving pesticide's benefits outweighs its risks at all times on the proponent of the pesticide); Federal Insecticide, Fungicide and Rodenticide Act, 7 U.S.C. § 136 (Supp. IV 1982).

IV

BALANCING AND THE FAILURE OF THE MARKET PARADIGM

The weltanschauung of the policy-oriented economist has come to dominate the intellectual analysis of the pollution control and worker health policy problems.[35] At the heart of the policy-oriented economist's conceptual framework is a commitment to utilitarianism—society should strive to achieve the greatest good for the greatest number of its citizens.[36] From a pure utilitarian perspective, governments and markets should strive for Pareto efficiency—a policy or exchange should be undertaken if it makes a least one person better off and leaves no persons worse off. When this ideal cannot be achieved, a policy is still appropriate under the utilitarian analysis if the "good" (or utils) that it produces for its beneficiaries is greater than the "bad" (or loss of utils) that its victims suffer. Many utilitarians would stop the analysis here without attempting to reduce utils to a more common unit of exchange such as money. Others might attempt to measure gains and losses in monetary terms, but weigh those preferences in accordance with some function that recognizes that when wealth is unevenly distributed people do not convert utils to dollars at the same rate.[37]

To the policy-oriented economist and his fellow travellers in the legal profession, however, pure utilitarian analysis is viewed as impractical. The starting point for the analysis should not be a poll where persons are asked to hypothesize about the pain they would suffer or the satisfaction they would derive from the implementation of a public policy. Rather, the policy analyst should look to the real world for surrogate measures of the value that people attribute to goods and bads. The real world is, of course, the marketplace. Government policies, in this view, should strive to achieve that allocative result which the marketplace would itself reach were it not hindered by some unfortunate market defect. An ideological corollary to this "practical" application of utilitarianism is the proposition that the unregulated marketplace is the norm, and it should not be disturbed absent some demonstrable and correctable failure.[38]

---

35. In using the term "policy-oriented economist" I mean to identify a subcategory of neoclassical economists that are concerned with the practical applications of microeconomic theory in the public policy arena. The intellectual product of this group of economists is not highly mathematical or theoretical. Rather, the policy-oriented economist concerns himself with the application of various well-developed paradigms to concrete problems of private firm strategy or public policy. Examples are too numerous to mention but include R. DORFMAN & N. DORFMAN, ECONOMICS OF THE ENVIRONMENT: SELECTED READINGS (1977); A. KNEESE & C. SCHULTZE, *supra* note 18; D. NORTH & R. MILLER, THE ECONOMICS OF PUBLIC ISSUES (1976). While this approach to problem solving is predominant in the nation's business schools, it is by no means confined to those institutions. It also dominates many graduate schools of public policy and undergraduate economics courses. *See* E. STOKEY & R. ZECKHAUSER, A PRIMER FOR POLICY ANALYSIS (1978). Indeed, it has even achieved a strong foothold in the law schools. *See* R. MILLER, ECONOMICS TODAY: THE MICRO VIEW 355-75 (1982); R. POSNER, TORT LAW: CASES AND ECONOMIC ANALYSIS (1982); R. STEWART & J. KRIER, ENVIRONMENTAL LAW AND POLICY (1978);

36. *See, e.g.*, THE HARPER DICTIONARY OF MODERN THOUGHT (A. Bullock & O. Staslybrass eds. 1977).

37. It has been suggested, but by no means proven, that wealthy persons attach a lower value to an additional dollar of income than poor persons. *See, e.g.*, Markovits, *Legal Analysis and the Economic Analysis of Allocative Efficiency*, 8 HOFSTRA L. REV. 811, 815 (1980).

38. Professor Breyer's classic analysis of "regulatory failure," for example, "assumes that an unregulated marketplace is the norm and that those who advocate government intervention must justify it by

Market failure means that someone would be willing to pay more for a thing than the possessor of the thing would be willing to sell it for, but the transaction does not take place. There should be a market for the thing; for some reason or reasons (usually afforded the common label—"transaction costs"), however, the market does not exist. Adopting the Kalder-Hicks formulation of the problem, the policy-oriented economist argues that when markets fail, government should intervene when the beneficiaries would be willing to pay more for the resulting policy than the victims would be willing to sell it for. In simpler terms, a policy should be adopted if its beneficiaries could bribe its victims to accept it.[39] The transaction, however, need not occur; the policy is efficient in any event and should be adopted.[40]

---

showing that it is needed to achieve an important public objective that an unregulated market cannot provide." Breyer, *Analyzing Regulatory Failure: Mismatches, Less Restrictive Alternatives, and Reform,* 92 HARV. L. REV. 549, 552 (1979); *see also* Posner, *Some Uses and Abuses of Economics in Law,* 46 U. Chi. L. Rev. 281, 288-89 (1979).

39. *See* Markovits, *supra* note 37, at 815.

40. Professor Markovits has articulated an alternative (and in my opinion preferable) test for whether a policy is allocatively efficient. Under the Markovits test:

> [a] policy increases allocative efficiency if and to the extent that the number of dollars its beneficiaries would have to receive to leave them as well off as they would be if the policy were adopted exceeds the number of dollars its victims would have to lose to leave them as badly off as they would be if the policy were adopted, assuming no one's real income is affected either directly by the sequence of events which led to his receiving the money in question or indirectly by the payment (by any tendency of the finance payment to charge the prices he must pay for goods, the price or quantity of goods he sells, or the real income of other individuals whose welfare he values).

Markovits, *supra* note 37, at 817-18. This extremely careful definition more closely comports with the reality that money does not in fact flow from the beneficiaries of a government policy to its victims. In reality, the beneficiaries will be better off with the adoption of a non-Pareto efficient policy and the victims will be worse off. The Markovits test realistically acknowledges this.

The Markovits test as applied will more often support governmental intervention on behalf of the poor than the Kalder-Hicks test:

> Since the number of dollars that poor individuals would have to be paid to induce them to reject such a policy will tend to exceed the number of dollars they would be willing and able to pay to obtain the policy, the [Kalder-Hicks] approach will tend to make such policies seem less efficient than they are by measuring the gains they generate for their beneficiaries in an incorrect way—by measuring them according to the lower number of dollars they would be willing to pay for the policy rather than the higher number of dollars they would be willing to accept instead of the policy.

Markovits, *supra* note 37, at 821-22.

The Markovits test remedies some of the deficiencies of cost-benefit analysis that Professor Kennedy identifies. Kennedy, *Cost-Benefit Analysis of Entitlement Problems: A Critique,* 33 STAN. L. REV. 387 (1981); R. Markovits, Duncan's Do Nots (unpublished manuscript) (forthcoming in STAN. L. REV.). See text accompanying notes 57-64 *infra*. The test, however, is still incoherent or schizophrenic in cases involving large shifts of wealth (defined in utils rather than dollars), such as in the contexts of risks to health and destruction of highly valued natural entities.

The Markovits test is also difficult to apply as a practical matter, because in many cases it poses a difficult psychological question to the potential beneficiaries and victims of a policy. The beneficiary, for example, must tell the policymaker (or the policymaker must somehow otherwise ascertain) the amount of money that would satisfy him as much as a governmental policy without informing him of the direct link between the policy and the dollar gift. When the policy entails a direct transfer of dollars (for example, licensing taxicabs in New York City), this may be an easy operation. When the policy implements other values, it may be more difficult. Implementation of a policy that greatly reduces the risk of death that a person otherwise faces will generate a great feeling of relief. It is difficult, I suspect, to compare this feeling of relief with the feeling of satisfaction or joy that the same person would experience upon receiving a windfall gift of dollars.

It is not clear why the Kalder-Hicks test has historically carried the day. It is clear that the Markovits test has until now attracted few proponents.

A. The Market Paradigm and the Problem of Externalities

In the context of health and environmental risks, the policy-oriented economist would argue that governmental regulation should be strictly limited to the narrow goal of "internalizing externalities" or, phrased differently, "correcting for spill-overs." The spillover problem results from the fact that a firm is allowed to engage in conduct that causes harm to others or otherwise consumes a valuable common resource, and from the fact that these costs do not affect the firm's conduct because it does not have to pay them.[41] The market for health and environmental controls has failed.

If the legal system specified a rule that no effluent or emission from any plant could harm any interest of any person and gave any aggrieved party the right to enjoin such conduct, a firm would then be required to purchase the "right" to pollute from its neighbors.[42] The firm would expend resources on pollution controls up to the point at which it would be cheaper to purchase rights from the neighbors. Similarly, if the rule were the opposite—that any firm could pollute with impunity—then those damaged by a firm's conduct would band together and purchase the desired amount of pollution control devices up to the point at which the reduced pollution was no longer worth their resource outlays. Professor Coase has suggested that in a smoothly functioning system the amount expended upon pollution control and the level of pollution would be the same under either rule.[43] A "market" for pollution control would develop under both rules, and government intervention, except insofar as was necessary to enforce the contracts and the "property rights," would be unnecessary.[44] The market would allocate the resources in the optimum manner for society.

A smoothly functioning market would likewise efficiently allocate worker safety. Informed workers could bid up wages to the point at which income from increased wages matched their individual assessments of the disutility of exposure to additional risks. A rational employer would make health and safety related expenditures up to the point at which the cost of such measures equaled the sum of the reduced output due to work-related injury or illness and the increased wages it would have to pay to induce employees to accept more hazardous employment.[45]

---

41. *See* F. ANDERSON, *supra* note 9, at 3-6; A. KNEESE, & C. SCHULTZE, *supra* note 18, at 4-6; Breyer, *supra* note 38, at 555.

42. The legal system would also have to acknowledge the right of a person to alienate his "right" to enjoin a polluter, and it would have to be capable of enforcing the contract of alienation. This, of course, is "government intervention" into private conduct, but the economist would probably not consider it intervention into the marketplace because enforceable property "rights" and contracts *define* the marketplace. Without at least this much government intervention there can be no effective market, and the rule of the jungle would prevail.

43. *See* Coase, *The Problem of Social Cost,* 3 J. LAW & ECON. 1 (1960). This point is well-illustrated in the pollution control context in R. STEWART & J. KRIER, *supra* note 35, at 133-36.

44. This intervention is not insignificant. The legal system must be prepared to enjoin all emissions that were not bargained for under the first rule, and it must be prepared to protect the firms' facilities from attack by angry neighbors under the second rule.

45. R. SMITH, THE OCCUPATIONAL SAFETY AND HEALTH ACT, ITS GOALS AND ITS ACHIEVEMENTS 27-28 (1976); Zeckhauser & Nichols, *The Occupational Safety and Health Administration—An Overview* in COMM. ON GOVERNMENTAL AFFAIRS, STUDY ON FEDERAL REGULATION, S. DOC. NO. 14, 96th Cong., 1st Sess. 169, 172 (1978).

Again, society would produce the "optimal" amounts of health and other commodities, and government intervention would be necessary only to enforce contracts and "property rights."

Although the policy-oriented economist's goal is to reach that result which the parties themselves would have "freely" reached in a smoothly functioning marketplace,[46] he accepts the fact that the real world does not function ideally. First, the market paradigm requires that both parties to the transaction have perfect knowledge of the risks posed by the release of chemical substances and the incremental costs of reducing those releases.[47] In the case of toxic substances in the workplace or the environment, information on the chronic hazards posed by these substances is very expensive, and "perfect" knowledge is entirely unobtainable.[48] When large uncertainties dominate attempts to assess the risks posed by toxic substances, [49] both sides of the bargaining process are likely to underestimate the true long term costs of industrial illness and death.[50] Furthermore, in the case of two or more sources of pollution, the absence of perfect knowledge about which source contributes how much additional risk to the neighbors further complicates an already impossibly complex bargaining problem.[51]

Second, collective action in the environmental pollution context involves high "transaction" costs.[52] If, for example, the courts were to adopt a rule that polluters may pollute with impunity, then affected neighbors could pay them to reduce pollution. Yet, since each neighbor is damaged only a small amount, no individual

46. *Use of Cost-Benefit Analysis by Regulatory Agencies: Joint Hearings Before the Subcomm. on Oversight and Investigations and the Subcomm. on Consumer Protection and Finance of the House Comm. on Interstate and Foreign Commerce*, 96th Cong., lst Sess. 68-70 (1980) (statement of R.W. Crandall, Senior Fellow, Brookings Institute)[hereinafter cited as *Cost-Benefit Hearings*]; W. BAXTER, PEOPLE OR PENGUINS, THE CASE FOR OPTIMAL POLLUTION (1974); B. MITNICK, THE POLITICAL ECONOMY OF REGULATION 291-92 (1980).

47. F. ANDERSON, *supra* note 9, at 22; B. MITNICK, *supra* note 46, at 291.

48. *See* N. ASHFORD, CRISIS IN THE WORKPLACE 335-38 (1976); J. MENDELOFF, REGULATING SAFETY 7-8 (1979); Zeckhauser & Nichols, *supra* note 45, at 178-79.

49. *See generally* American Textile Mfrs. Inst. v. Donovan, 452 U.S. 490 (1981); Industrial Union Dep't, AFL-CIO v. American Petroleum Inst., 448 U.S. 607 (1980); N. ASHFORD, *supra* note 48, at 332-33; Cornell, Noll & Weingast, *Safety Regulation*, in SETTING NATIONAL PRIORITIES: THE NEXT TEN YEARS 458-70 (1976); McGarity, *Substantive and Procedural Discretion in Administrative Resolution of Science Policy Questions: Regulating Carcinogens in EPA and OSHA*, 67 GEO. L.J. 729 (1979).

50. Employers facing circumscribed planning horizons feel great pressures to emphasize short term production over long term risk reduction. *See generally* McGarity & Schroeder, *Risk-Oriented Employment Screening*, 59 TEX. L. REV. 999, 1016 (1981). Employers will therefore tend to place unrealistically low estimates on risks. Moreover, psychological studies in other low probability-high consequence contexts where risks can be more objectively assessed indicate that individuals who expose themselves to risks of death or serious bodily injury tend to underestimate the risks to themselves, perhaps in the belief that "those horrible things only happen to the other guy." *See, e.g.*, Arnold & Grabowski, *Auto Safety Regulation: An Analysis of Market Failure*, 12 BELL J. OF ECON. 27, 34-35 (1981); Zeckhauser & Nichols, *supra* note 45, at 178. Hence the short run tendency of both sides of the bargain is toward long run inefficiency and human loss. *See* McGarity, *Contending Approaches to Regulating Laboratory Safety*, 28 U. KAN. L. REV. 183, 200 (1980). Moreover, since greater information about workplace risks can only lead to a higher probability that workers will demand higher wages before encountering those risks, employers will have little incentive to produce information on those risks.

51. The problem of multiple sources of chemical pollutants is not as relevant to worker protection where the source of chemical contaminants is nearly always the employer's operations.

52. *See generally* R. STEWART & J. KRIER, *supra* note 35, at 140-42; Coase, *supra* note 43, at 15-19; Calabresi & Melamed, *Property Rules, Liability Rules, and Inalienability: One View of the Cathedral*, 85 HARV. L. REV. 1089 (1972).

would be willing to pay enough to reduce the pollution to a significant extent. All would benefit from a collection from all of the neighbors that would then be paid to the source of the pollution. Unfortunately, the cost of the collection system might be very high, especially if, as the market paradigm would require, the "fee" collected would vary with the amount of harm that each individual felt. Moreover, a "free rider" could reap the benefits of the others' efforts without contributing to the collection in the absence of an expensive legal mechanism to force contributions.[53] The problem is the same if the opposite liability rule applies. If any damaged party may acquire an injunction against the source, then the firm must seek out and pay off all possible plaintiffs. The seeking-out process alone could be very expensive. Moreover, since any plaintiff could "hold out" for more compensation than the harm actually felt, it would be impossible to tell whether the holdout was expressing his true disutility or merely being too greedy.

Third, the courts have not yet developed an adequate scheme of "rights" in environmental entities.[54] While the pollution source in a jurisdiction in which polluters must pay will have to strike an acceptable deal with all humans that consider themselves affected by its activities, it may damage nonhuman receptors with impunity to the extent that no human is willing to make the nonhuman's disutility his own.[55] The utilitarian ideal is thus anthropocentric—it considers only human utility.[56]

These practical limitations on the bargaining model have, with the possible exception of the third objection, been well accepted by proponents of the market paradigm. Few of the policy-oriented economists would suggest that the pollution problem should be left to the unregulated marketplace, and only a few more would leave the worker health problem to private negotiations between workers and employers. There is, however, in addition to these *practical* limitations to the bargaining model, a more serious and ultimately more damaging *theoretical* flaw in the model. This theoretical flaw stems from the fact that the Coase theorem, as applied to worker safety and pollution control problems where risks are relatively high, is demonstrably wrong.

It is not true that the same amount of resources will be invested in pollution control and worker safety under either liability rule. A neighbor might demand much more in payment per unit of pollution reduction under the first rule (the polluter must pay off neighbors) than he would pay to reduce pollution by the same amount under the second rule (the neighbor must buy off the polluter). The neighbor may not be able to afford the amount of pollution control that he would really like because he is not wealthy. His own financial status, however, will not

---

53. *See* J. GREGOR, INTRA-URBAN MORTALITY AND AIR QUALITY: AN ECONOMIC ANALYSIS OF THE COSTS OF POLLUTION INDUCED MORTALITY 7 (1977) (EPA Socioeconomic Environmental Studies Series, EPA 600/5-77-009); J. KRIER & E. URSIN, POLLUTION AND POLICY 29 (1977).

54. *Cf.* Hardin, *The Tragedy of the Commons,* 162 SCIENCE 1243 (1968).

55. *See* Stone, *Should Trees Have Standing?—Toward Legal Rights for Natural Objects,* 45 S. CAL. L. REV. 450 (1972).

56. *See* Tribe, *Ways Not to Think About Plastic Trees: New Foundations for Environmental Law,* 83 YALE L.J. 1315 (1974); *see also* Sagoff, *On Preserving the Natural Environment,* 84 YALE L.J. 205 (1974); Tribe, *From Environmental Foundations to Constitutional Structures: Learning from Nature's Future,* 84 YALE L.J. 545 (1975).

limit to the same extent the amount that he will request from the polluter if he has a right to stop the pollution. In the second case the neighbor suffers a lost opportunity to add resources to his existing steady-state stream of income and outgo. In the first case he suffers a disruption of that steady state, and as the "right" involved becomes increasingly more important, the neighbor suffers greater disruption. If the neighbor is very wealthy, this disruption may be relatively inconsequential. But if the neighbor is poor, then the price at which he is willing to buy a very valuable right will very quickly reach a limit dictated by his impecunious circumstances. There is no reason to believe that a poor person values money any less than a rich person when he has a valuable object to sell.[57] There is obviously good reason to believe that a poor person will pay less than a rich person for safety if they are both required to purchase that commodity. The practical end result is that more commodities are produced from more polluting plants located near low income neighborhoods under the first rule whereas fewer commodities are produced from less polluting plants more evenly distributed among the population under the second. The current distribution of industrial activity with respect to rich and poor should suggest which rule has often predominated in this country.

The same dichotomy applies to the workplace. The worker may demand more for the risk of an industrial disease if he had a "right" to a workplace free of disease-causing chemicals than he would be willing to pay to be rid of the risk. The fact that the employment relationship is regarded as consensual by the policy-oriented economists motivates them to argue that wage premiums for hazardous jobs would be the same under either rule. A worker has a "right" to as much safety as he wants because he can shop around for a safer job if he does not care to accept the wage premium that the employer is willing to offer. The fully informed worker is willing to sell his health at precisely the price (or wage premium) which the emloyer is willing to buy it. Laborers are laborers and not members of the Board of Directors because they prefer risking their health to risking their capital.[58]

To state this proposition is to declare its implausibility. The wage premium that an employer offers for hazardous work, if such a premium ever exists,[59] is not always determined by free parties in an open marketplace. For many low skill jobs it is set by the unemployment rate and the level of desperation of currently employed workers. The alternatives to a low skill, low income worker are too few to support the argument that he freely accepts the employer's tradeoff between safety and wages. The low skill worker "chooses" high risk employment in much the same sense that a robbery victim "chooses" to part with his money—in both

57. Indeed, the more plausible assumption is precisely the opposite—a wealthy person probably values an additional increment of wealth less highly than a poor person. Markovits makes much the same point when he suggests that the demand for a particular policy may be "wealth elastic." Markovits, *supra* note 37, at 819.

58. *See* F. KNIGHT, RISK, UNCERTAINTY AND PROFIT 301 (1921) (alluding to "the disposition of laboring people to gamble recklessly with life and limb as well as income").

59. *Compare* Chelius, *The Control of Industrial Accidents: Economic Theory and Empirical Evidence,* 38 LAW AND CONTEMP. PROBS. 700 (1974) *with* W. VISCUSI, EMPLOYMENT HAZARDS: AN INVESTIGATION OF MARKET PERFORMANCE ch. 12 (1979) *and* R. SMITH, THE OCCUPATIONAL HEALTH AND SAFETY ACT app. B (1976) (American Enterprises Inst., Wash., D.C.).

cases, given the alternatives, it is the intelligent thing to do. There would probably be higher wages, more safety, fewer manufactured commodities, and perhaps greater unemployment in a system under which workers have a realistic "right" to trade safety for wages.

In both the environmental and workplace contexts there are likely to be "ideological holdouts" who, under the "willingness to sell" rule, would be unwilling to be bribed by the polluting entity at any price. Even a large copper company, for example, might not have sufficient resources to meet the price that one of the leaders of Earth First,[60] a radical environmental organization, would demand for yielding up his right to stop the construction of a new copper smelter in an Idaho wilderness area. Indeed, for some kinds of transactions we are all probably ideological holdouts; there are some things that most of us are unwilling to sell at any price. Characteristic examples are our general reluctance to become prostitutes or to sell our votes.[61] Risks to health probably belong to this category of "not-for-sale" aspects of personhood. I am unwilling to sell you my arm because I will not be the same person after the transaction is completed. Not only would I be a one-armed person, I would also be a person who has sold my arm. The same analysis applies to the sale of a high risk to my arm or to the sale of a treasured environmental entity. In both cases the price I would demand for the sale would be higher than the amount that would compensate me if the arm or the entity were lost due to an act of God because there is an added cost attributable to the very act of selling something so intimately attached to self-identity.[62]

There is no reason to choose the "willingness to buy" or the "willingness to sell" liability rule on "efficiency" grounds.[63] Professor Kennedy explains that the efficiency criterion as applied to the externality problem is "incoherent."[64] If not incoherent, the market paradigm is at best schizophrenic. It has two very different personalities, and there is no "neutral" way to choose between the two. Yet, the

60. *Cf.* Kaufmann, *Earth Saving: Here Is a Gang of Real Environmental Extremists,* AUDOBON, July 1982, at 116.

61. *See* S. KELMAN, WHAT PRICE INCENTIVES? 54-77 (1981).

62. *See* Markovits, *supra* note 37, at 824 n.13.

63. Kennedy, *supra* note 40, at 388.

64. According to Professor Kennedy, "[T]he concept of efficiency is indeterminate—it cannot yield an answer—if we try to apply it to the whole system of private law rules." *Id.*

Professor Markovits disputes Professor Kennedy's assertion that cost-benefit analysis is incoherent. First, Markovits rejects the Kalder-Hicks "willingness to buy"—"willingness to sell" formulation of cost-benefit analysis. Instead, Markovits asserts that the proper question to ask is whether the amount of money required to make the "winners" as well off as the proposed policy exceeds the amount of money that would have to be taken away from the "losers" to make them suffer as much as the implementation of the proposed policy. *See* Markovits, *supra* note 37, at 815-18; R. Markovits, *supra* note 40. Interestingly none of the policy-oriented economists of which I am aware have used this formulation of cost-benefit analysis, even though it is, as Markovits demonstrates, a more realistic assessment of the real world.

Professor Markovits convincingly demonstrates that when his approach to cost-benefit analysis is employed, it is normally neither incoherent nor biased in favor of the status quo. Nevertheless, Professor Markovits concedes that cost-benefit analysis cannot yield a correct result (and is therefore, in my terms, schizophrenic) when it is applied to cases where dollar costs and benefits are significantly affected by the wealth of the winners and losers. This is precisely the case when the benefits of a regulation (or the costs of a failure to regulate) are life saving in nature. In these cases a proper "Markovitsian" cost-benefit analysis is likely to demonstrate that both the policy and its reversal are cost beneficial. The test is therefore indeterminate. When the policy merely reduces small risks to life, the test may be less indeterminate.

analyst cannot prescribe even a hypothetical "best answer" to the externality problem without first deciding which valuation rule should hold. This determination is quintessentially a political judgment. The "best answer" is therefore not scientific or objective but necessarily ideological and highly dependent on the analyst's view of the status quo allocation of resources.

Health and environmental amenities are valuable societal resources, as are the commodities that industrial processes produce. The market paradigm, if it functions properly, maximizes overall societal wealth or allocative efficiency, but the paradigm will yield different mixes of these two forms of wealth, depending upon how the political system allocates "rights."

This final defect in the "bargaining" model is more than merely a practical problem for which a "second best" solution can be hypothesized. Policy analysts have tools for factoring uncertainty, transaction costs, and incommensurables into a utilitarian equation with varying degrees of analytical validity. Each of these tools, however, ultimately depends upon the analyst's political choice between the "willingness to pay" and "willingness to sell" criteria for valuing health and environmental resources. Its dependency on this political choice is a fundamental theoretical flaw in the market paradigm with profound implications for any attempts to guide health and environmental regulation toward that ideal.

B. The Tort System and the Market Paradigm

Tort law is a form of indirect government intervention into the marketplace that has the potential to reinforce the bargaining model by ensuring that firms and their consumers compensate employees and neighbors for damage that their activities cause. In addition to compensating those actually harmed, the threat of future payouts can provide an immediate inducement to firms to invest in risk reduction technologies. Yet, despite this indirect incentive, the tort system in practice does not produce the results dictated by the market paradigm.

A variety of compensation systems are available to those who have been injured by industrial activities. Neighboring landowners and government entities may sue to abate private or public nuisances.[65] Similarly, those who suffer physical harm from exposure to toxic substances may sue, alleging negligence or strict liability for abnormally dangerous activities.[66] Employees, in addition, may press claims against employers in workers compensation proceedings.[67] All of these compensation systems, however, share one crucial element—they all require the claimant to establish a causal link between the defendant's conduct and the

65. *See generally* W. PROSSER, LAW OF TORTS ch. 15 (1971); W. RODGERS, ENVIRONMENTAL LAW ch. 2 (1977).

66. *See generally* W. PROSSER, *supra* note 65, chs. 5, 13. Employees faced severe obstacles at common law in establishing a cause of action based upon these two theories. At common law employers could raise the "unholy trinity" of defenses—contributory negligence, assumption of the risk, and the fellow servant rule. *See* Suter v. San Angelo Foundary & Machine Co., 81 N.J. 150, 406 A.2d 140 (1979); 1 A. LARSON, LARSON'S WORKMEN'S COMPENSATION LAW §§ 4.30-.50 (1978). Workers compensation statutes were enacted to reduce those barriers to employee recovery. However, it has been argued that the "unholy trinity" defenses reappear in different forms in workers compensation proceedings. *See, e.g.*, D. BERMAN, DEATH ON THE JOB 66-67 (1978).

67. *See* 1 A. LARSON, *supra* note 66, ch. 5.

claimant's harm.[68] This causation requirement poses the same practical problems as the "full knowledge" assumption of the bargaining model.

When the causal link between an individual's exposure to an acutely toxic substance and resulting harm can be established with an adequate degree of certainty to convince a judge or jury to compensate the injured party,[69] the threat of potential liability has been a strong inducement to polluters and employers to reduce or eliminate acute health risks.[70] Claimants have much greater difficulty, however, establishing a sufficient causal link between past exposure to a chemical substance and a present chronic ideopathic disease.[71] Even if adequate epidemiological or laboratory studies demonstrated a causal relationship between a substance and harm to human beings or environmental species, it would not follow that any individual plaintiff could establish that exposure to the chemical caused identifiable harm to his person or property.[72] Courts generally require the plaintiff to present expert testimony that the defendant's conduct "probably" caused the plaintiff's harm.[73] Only where the cause-effect relationship is especially well established—as in the case of acute damage, very rare chemically induced diseases,[74] and

68. *See* W. PROSSER, *supra* note 65, § 41; Calabresi, *Concerning Cause and the Law of Torts: An Essay for Harry Kalven, Jr.*, 43 U. CHI. L. REV. 69 (1975); Malone, *Ruminations on Cause-in-Fact*, 9 STAN. L. REV. 60 (1956).

69. *See, e.g.*, Borland v. Sanders Lead Co., 369 So. 2d 523 (Ala. 1979) (nuisance action for damage caused by lead and sulfur oxides); Luthringer v. Moore, 31 Cal. 2d 487, 190 P.2d 1 (1948) (strict liability for personal injuries due to hydrocyanic acid); Cities Serv. Co. v. State, 312 So. 2d 799 (Fla. 1979) (strict liability for fish kill); Roessler & Hasslacher Chem. Co. v. Doyle, 73 N.J.L. 521, 64 A. 156 (1906) (nuisance for personal injuries due to sodium cyanide).

70. Systematic worker exposure to acutely toxic chemicals that threaten immediate death or serious bodily injury is virtually nonexistent in the United States today. One important exception is the exposure of farmworkers to acutely toxic pesticides. *See* S. EPSTEIN, THE POLITICS OF CANCER 291-92 (1979). Although EPA ensures that the labels for acutely toxic pesticides specify appropriate field reentry times, these are not always observed in practice. OSHA has yet to promulgate effective farmworker protection standards. *See* Comment, *Farmworkers in Jeopardy: OSHA, EPA and Pesticides*, 5 ECOLOGY L. Q. 69 (1975).

Many kinds of workers are, however, systematically exposed to substances that pose high risks of low consequence harms, such as contact dermatitis. NATIONAL ASSOCIATIONS OF FARMWORKERS ORGANIZATIONS, PESTICIDE DESK REFERENCE (second draft 1980). The tort system apparently fails here not because of problems of establishing causation but because the high costs of entry into the compensation system preclude suits for the relatively small damage recoveries that can be had for such injuries.

Acute environmental risks have likewise been reduced, though not as much as human health risks. While incidences of large fish kills and air pollution-induced deforestation seem to be declining, air and water pollution still generate a large number of common law nuisance suits based upon easily established causal relationships.

71. *See* Gelpe & Tarlock, *The Uses of Scientific Information in Environmental Decisionmaking*, 48 S. CAL. L. REV. 371, 371-88 (1974); Comment, *Judicial Attitudes Towards Legal and Scientific Proof of Cancer Causation*, 3 COLUM. J. ENV. L. 344 (1977).

72. *See generally* Small, *Gaffing at a Thing Called Cause*, 31 TEX. L. REV. 630 (1953).

73. *See, e.g.*, Kramer Serv., Inc. v. Wilkins, 184 Miss. 483, 186 So. 625 (1939); Comment, *supra* note 71, at 367, 371.

Although the causation requirement in a workers compensation proceeding is somewhat less stringent, *see generally* 1 A. LARSON, *supra* note 66, § 1, workers must still show more than a mere possibility that their physical harm resulted from exposure to a particular industrial chemical unless the legislature has already recognized the statistical causal relationship and erected a statutory presumption of causation. *See* Miller v. National Cabinet Co., 8 N.Y.2d 277, 168 N.E.2d 811, 204 N.Y.S.2d 129 (1960); Miller v. Olin Mathieson Chem. Corp., 398 S.W.2d 472 (Ky. Ct. App. 1966). *See generally* Comment, *supra* note 71, at 355-68.

74. The courts are beginning to allow plaintiffs to attempt to convince the factfinder that exposure to asbestos causes mesothelioma. *See* Karjala v. Johns-Manville Prods. Corp., 523 F.2d 155 (8th Cir. 1975); Borel v. Fibreboard Paper Prods. Corp., 493 F.2d 1076 (5th Cir. 1973), *cert. denied*, 419 U.S. 869 (1974); *see also* Comment, *Asbestos Litigation: The Dust Has Yet to Settle*, 7 FORDHAM URB. L.J. 55 (1978-79).

extremely well studied chemicals that emanate from very few sources,[75]—will the courts be willing to allow the plaintiff's case to go to the factfinder.[76]

Even when causation can be established, the multiplaintiff lawsuit presents the same transaction costs problem that plagues the bargaining model. In many cases of acute and chronic exposure, no single person has suffered sufficient harm to make it worth his while to sue the defendant. Theoretically, all of the plaintiffs can join together in a single lawsuit, but the costs of bringing and keeping them together are sufficiently high that the lawsuit often never happens.[77] The class action lawsuit is a potential solution to this dilemma,[78] but the courts have not been receptive to innovative uses of the class action tool and have erected sufficient procedural barriers to render the device ineffectual.[79]

Another disadvantage of relying on the tort system to correct for spillovers is its passive character. A plaintiff can only with great difficulty persuade a court to enjoin risky conduct before the plaintiff has suffered actual injury. While the threat of future damage payouts should theoretically induce firms to reduce risks

---

75. *See, e.g.*, Pritchard v. Liggett & Myers Tobacco Co., 295 F.2d 292 (3d Cir. 1961) (smoking and lung cancer). Even when cause-effect relationships can be established for chronic diseases, statutes of limitations in some states may preclude recovery for diseases that manifest themselves many years after the disease-producing event. *See* Harwood, *Accrual Dilemma: Statute of Limitations in Hazardous Waste Cases*, 45 ALBANY L. REV. 717 (1981); Comment, *Occupational Carcinogenesis and Statutes of Limitations: Resolving Relevant Policy Goals*, 10 ENVTL. L. 113 (1979).

76. The causation problem is exacerbated in environmental pollution cases involving multiple defendants. Even when a cause-effect relationship between a particular chemical and a health or environmental effect is well established, the tort system may be unable adequately to sort out which of several firms emitting that substance into an airshed or watershed should be liable for how much damage. While modern courts will generally not allow one of the many polluters to escape liability on the ground that the plaintiff has failed to trace his or her harm directly back to that firm's discharge, *see, e.g.*, Michie v. Great Lakes Steel Div., Nat'l Steel Corp., 495 F.2d 213 (6th Cir. 1974); Landers v. East Texas Salt Water Disposal Co., 151 Tex. 251, 248 S.W.2d 731 (1952), they still have difficulty apportioning the damage among the various defendants. The most commonly applied rule is a simple equal division of the damages among the joint tortfeasors, even if one contributed a great deal more to the pollution than another. *See* W. PROSSER, J. WADE & V. SCHWARTZ, TORTS: CASES AND MATERIALS ON TORTS 385 (1976); UNIFORM CONTRIBUTION AMONG TORTFEASORS ACT §§ 1(b), 2, 12 U.L.A. 63 (1975). More recent cases in the product liability area divide up liability according to market share. *See* Sindell v. Abbott Labs., 26 Cal. 3d 588, 607 P.2d 924, 163 Cal. Rptr. 132, *cert. denied*, 449 U.S. 912 (1980). It is not clear that either of these approaches sends the correct signals to the polluters, although any signal is better than no signal at all.

77. H. NEWBERG, CLASS ACTIONS §§ 1010.1b, .2h (1977); R. POSNER, ECONOMIC ANALYSIS OF LAW 24-25, 349-350 (1972); Dewees, Prichard & Trebilcock, *An Economic Analysis of Cost and Fee Rules for Class Actions*, 10 J. LEGAL STUDIES 155 (1981); Note, *Notice Cost Problems Under Rule 23(b)(3) and (c)(2) after* Oppenheimer Fund Inc. v. Sanders, 1979 DUKE L.J. 882.

78. 7A C. WRIGHT & A. MILLER, FEDERAL PRACTICE AND PROCEDURE § 1782 (1969); Lamm & Davison, *Environmental Class Actions Seeking Damages*, 16 ROCKY MT. L. INST. 59 (1971); Parsons & Starr, *Environmental Litigation and Defendant Class Actions: The Unrealized Viability of Rule 23*, 4 ECOLOGY L.Q. 881 (1975); Comment, *The Federal Class Action in Environmental Litigation: Problems and Possibilities*, 51 N.C.L. REV. 1385 (1973).

79. Oppenheimer Fund Inc. v. Sanders, 437 U.S. 340 (1978) (plaintiff should normally bear the costs of identifying absentee class members); Zahn v. International Paper Co., 414 U.S. 291 (1973) (diversity suit may not proceed as a class action when the named plaintiffs meet the jurisdictional amount requirement but the unnamed members of the class do not); Note, *Class Actions—Failure of Unnamed Plaintiffs to Meet Jurisdictional Amount Requirement Bars Class Action*, 8 CREIGHTON L. REV. 497 (1974).

Even if the courts were willing to entertain huge class action lawsuits against multiple defendants, the kind of lawsuit necessary to internalize large externalities effectively could reach such gigantic proportions that it would exceed the capacity of a single judge. *See, e.g.*, Diamond v. General Motors Corp., 20 Cal. App. 3d 374, 97 Cal. Rptr. 639 (1971) (class action suit on behalf of all residents of Los Angeles County against 293 industrial corporations and municipalities accused of polluting the air).

up to the point at which current expenditures equal the present value of future payouts, the hit-or-miss nature of tort damage awards and the circumscribed planning horizons of today's corporate management combine to produce management decisions that underinvest in health and environmental controls. It is, in other words, very difficult to induce the tort system to administer that necessary ounce of prevention.[80]

The tort system thus faces numerous practical obstacles to bringing about the result that the bargaining model would reach in the ideal world.[81] In addition, tort *theory* does not necessarily impel the tort system toward that result. Except for the relatively rare case in which a court will enjoin a nuisance,[82] the tort system begins with the premise that the polluter or employer has a "right" to expose others to risks. Among its other goals, tort law seeks to encourage polluters and employers to optimize those risks.

In some cases of very hazardous conduct the tort rule is that the entrepreneur must pay for all damages caused by the enterprise.[83] The source will therefore expend money on pollution control or worker safety up to the point that the last dollar spent on controls brings about a dollar's worth of reduced future damage payouts, discounted to present value. The source will elect to pay future damages at this point rather than waste resources cleaning up pollution and the workplace more than it is worth.

The same result will be reached, in theory, under a negligence rationale.[84] Under the famous negligence formula first articulated by Judge Learned Hand, a defendant should be required to pay for a nonnegligent plaintiff's loss only when the risks posed by its conduct (the probability of harm multiplied by the consequences) exceed the cost of avoiding those risks.[85] This formula, of course, is simply the balancing test of the bargaining model written in tort law.[86] The pol-

80. The tort system also requires the judiciary as an institution to make difficult balancing decisions concerning the extent to which the costs of development should be borne by the sources and receptors of the unwanted by-products of industrial activities. To leave the entire matter to the tort system is to place a huge responsibility in the hands of persons who are ultimately unaccountable to the democratic process. Society might legitimately determine that these sensitive questions should not be decided on an ad hoc basis by unelected and unresponsible judges. Moreover, since many issues that would be expected to arise in most "toxic torts" suits will involve complicated questions of toxicology and ecology, judges and lay juries may not be in the best position to evaluate the competing scientific claims.

81. R. POSNER, *supra* note 77, ch. 23; A. STONE, REGULATION AND ITS ALTERNATIVES 102-03 (1982).

82. An injunction flatly prohibiting conduct causing a nuisance is an available remedy in a common law nuisance action, but in most cases the court will either award damages or "balance the equities" and order the defendant to implement technologically feasible abatement efforts. *See* W. RODGERS, *supra* note 65, at 143-50.

83. *See* W. PROSSER, *supra* note 65, § 78.

84. In practice the private nuisance action, which is generally more appropriate to environmental disruption, is similar. *See* Reserve Mining Co. v. EPA, 514 F.2d 492 (8th Cir. 1975); Spur Indus. Inc. v. Del E. Webb, 108 Ariz. 178, 494 P.2d 700 (1972); Boomer v. Atlantic Cement Co., 26 N.Y.2d 219, 257 N.E.2d 870, 309 N.Y.S.2d 312 (1970); W. RODGERS, *supra* note 65, at 107-12. The defendant is subject to abatement or damages only if its use of its property is unreasonable in the context of the surrounding activities. W. PROSSER, *supra* note 65, at 596-602; W. RODGERS *supra* note 65, at 117-21; *see supra* note 82.

85. United States v. Carroll Towing Co., 159 F.2d 169 (2d Cir. 1947).

86. Using the same utilitarian analysis, Professor Calabresi maintains that the goal of the tort system is to minimize the sum of accident costs and accident avoidance costs. This offers a mechanism for choosing among several alternative rules (or technologies), all of which meet the cost-benefit criterion. Calabresi would place all of the costs of a particular accident on that party who could best minimize the sum of

luter or employer will, under this rule, invest in cleanup equipment up to the point at which a court holds him to be nonnegligent. But this is precisely what he would have invested under a strict liability rule because the negligence formula cuts off liability at the precise point at which costs exceed risks. The only difference between the two rules is that the defendant must still compensate plaintiffs for the damages that occur despite its control efforts under the strict liability rule, whereas it may force plaintiffs to bear those losses under the negligence rule. The defendant only has to pay damages under the negligence rule when a court or jury later finds that it has made an error in its calculations.

As in the case of the pure bargaining model, the ideal tort model results in the optimum amount of resources spent on pollution control and worker health. Nevertheless, the crucial ambiguity that haunts the bargaining model likewise afflicts the tort model. The polluter's optimization decision (and the court's determination under the negligence formula) depends upon an accurate measurement of the damage caused by pollution discounted by the probability that the damage will occur at various levels of exposure. But what is the measure of the damage? Is it the amount the victims are willing to pay to be rid of the damage or is it the amount they would charge one who would inflict it upon them? The "willingness to buy"/"willingness to sell" ambiguity remains. Like the bargaining model, the ideal tort model is schizophrenic. Neither measure is logically more appropriate.

At first glance, the real world tort system appears to adopt the "willingness to pay" measure of damage. A wrongful death award is usually calculated by reference to the lost wages and services of the decedent. This amount is, of course, all that the decedent could possibly have paid for the right to remain alive had he been able to strike a deal with the defendant that would have prevented his death. The decedent, however, probably would have demanded a great deal more in return for his life had he the power to prevent the defendant from taking it.

Similarly, if the plaintiff is maimed, she may recover for medical expenses, out of pocket expenses such as lost wages, and permanent disability and disfigurement. Most plaintiffs who could afford it would pay at least this much to avoid the damage altogether, assuming (as we must) that the defendant had a "right" to inflict it upon him. Some plaintiffs, however, could not afford to pay the defendant this amount. Thus, to the extent that the tort system requires that it be paid anyway (and to the extent that it is included on the risk side of the negligence formula), then the tort model in practice is departing from the "willingness to pay" version of the bargaining model.

The real world tort system also allows a damaged plaintiff to recover for pain and suffering. This type of recovery goes far beyond the "value" of the plaintiff in any market-determined sense, except to the extent that a suffering person is not as productive as one who is not in pain. While we all are willing to pay dearly to avoid pain and suffering, some of us are able to afford less pain-avoidance than others. Once again, to the extent that this element enters into the risk side of the

---

accident costs and accident avoidance costs. G. CALABRESI, THE COST OF ACCIDENTS: A LEGAL AND ECONOMIC ANALYSIS 133-40 (1970).

calculation, the result reached by the tort system more closely resembles that reached by the "willingness to sell" version of the bargaining model.

In other subtle ways, the tort system in practice orients its outcome toward the "willingness to sell" criteria. The trial court delegates the balancing function in most negligence cases to a lay jury.[87] The court does not tell the jury to apply the knowledgeable buyer or the knowledgeable seller criterion to the hypothetical bargain between the plaintiff and the defendant; nor, in most cases, does it tell the jury to balance the utility of the defendant's conduct against the risks to the plaintiff or the class of potential plaintiffs.[88] The courts reject the market paradigm altogether. The jury is told only to measure the defendant's conduct against that of a reasonable person in the same or similar circumstances.[89] This instruction gives the jury a great deal of discretion to apply factors, such as the relative wealth of the parties, that the policy-oriented economist would condemn as irrelevant.

Moreover, the tort system allows the jury, within bounds set by the supervising judiciary, to evaluate the defendant's conduct under a moral, as well as a utilitarian, standard. Thus, we observe a jury assessing damages for a single plaintiff in the Pinto litigation against Ford Motor Company equal to the amount saved by the company in making its "cold blooded" decision to subject its customers to an increased probability of future deaths rather than expend fifty dollars per auto for additional protection. It will be a rare jury indeed that will accept an automobile manufacturer's a priori calculation of the costs and benefits of the preservation of human life when presented with a dead or severely maimed plaintiff. Furthermore, in cases of intentional or grossly negligent misconduct, the tort system in most states gives the jury the express option to "punish" the defendant for its moral fault by assessing punitive or exemplary damages against the defendant.[90] This is an explicit recognition of the decisionmaker's role as a moral faultfinder as well as a risk and benefit assessor.

While the policy-oriented economist might condemn all of this as irrational, it may very well represent a rough approximation of a "rational" assessment of the net utility and costs of the defendant's conduct under the market paradigm but applying the "willingness to sell" rather than "willingness to pay" criterion.[91]

---

87. Vaughan v. Menlove, 3 Bing. N.C. 468, 132 Eng. Rep. 490 (1837); F. HARPER, LAW OF TORTS 159 (1933); L. GREEN, JUDGE AND JURY 160-70 (1930); C. MORRIS & C.R. MORRIS, MORRIS ON TORTS 49 (1980); Reynolds, *The Reasonable Man of Negligence Law: A Health Report on the "Odious Creature"*, 23 OKLA. L. REV. 410 (1970).

88. In some formulations of the standard for strict product liability, juries are told explicitly to evaluate risks and benefits of the product at issue. *See, e.g.*, Mitchell v. Fruehauff Corp., 568 F.2d 1139, 1145 (5th Cir. 1978); Turner v. General Motors Corp., 584 S.W.2d 844, 846-47 (Tex. 1979); Green, *Strict Liability Under Sections 402A and 402B: A Decade of Litigation*, 54 TEX. L. REV. 1185 (1976).

89. W. PROSSER, *supra* note 65, at 206; RESTATEMENT (SECOND) OF TORTS § 464 (1965).

90. W. PROSSER, *supra* note 65, at 9.

91. A more common alternative explanation for the tort system's failure in practice to reach results dictated by the bargaining model is that most of us are willing to sacrifice allocative efficiency when it conflicts with justice. *See* R. DWARKIN, TAKING RIGHTS SERIOUSLY (1977); Dwarkin, *Why-Efficiency?*, 8 HOFSTRA L. REV. 563 (1980). The tort system should be aimed at achieving just results rather than efficient results. In suggesting that the tort system might be achieving an "efficient" result under the "willingness to sell" test, which recognizes the plaintiff's "right" not to be harmed, I do not mean to suggest that justice should play no role. Indeed, justice may in many cases not involving large physical loss dictate results different from those arrived at through application of the "willingness to sell" test. My intent here is

Since the economist is no better qualified than the rest of us to make this choice, disapproval of the current tort system may reflect political views about the relative statuses of industrial activity and other human activity. Thus, the current appeals from industry and some economists to reform the tort system[92] may not be motivated by a desire to implement a more rational system; rather, they may be viewed as calls for a different system in which manufacturers and other defendants do not pay as much to avoid damage to others.

C. Health and Environmental Regulation and the Market Paradigm

Government regulation can to some extent remedy the defects in the tort system and the pure bargaining model. A regulatory regime would not require the causal link between a chemical and a particular disease to be established with nearly the particularity of the tort system because the regulatory system addresses overall societal risks rather than individual damage. The regulatory entity can use broad epidemiological studies and animal experiments to draw conclusions about the nature and extent of the health and environmental harm attributable to the release of a substance into the workplace or the environment. The regulator can often anticipate potential problems in advance and attempt to remedy them before human beings and environmental entities are harmed, perhaps irreversibly. A regulatory regime can offer direct incentives that should considerably broaden societal and individual firm planning horizons. The regulator can also solve the multiplaintiff, multidefendant transaction costs problem by acting as a surrogate for all injured parties and by framing generic controls or incentives that affect all firms discharging harmful substances. A regulatory agency can acquire in-house expertise to aid it in resolving questions of scientific fact and separating resolvable questions of fact from policy or value questions. Finally, the regulatory entity can be placed closer to the political process than the courts, thus ensuring greater political accountability.

Many policy-oriented economists, agreeing that a regulatory system helps resolve many of the practical problems of the bargaining model and the tort system, still argue that the market paradigm should dictate the regulatory results.[93] Society is best off, according to these economists, when the marginal dollar expended on health and environmental control achieves exactly one dollar's worth of health and environmental benefit.[94] When more than one of many tech-

---

only to suggest that even those unwilling to ignore considerations of justice and/or fairness in prescribing a tort system are still making a political statement when they measure the existing system according to the "willingness to pay" test.

92. *See* H.R. 7921, 96th Cong., 2d Sess. (1980); *see also* O'Donnell, *Design Litigation and the State of the Art: Terminology, Practice and Reform,* 11 AKRON L. REV. 627 (1978).

93. *See, e.g.,* A. KNEESE & C. SCHULTZE, *supra* note 18, at 71; Comar, *SO_2 Regulation Ignores Costs, Poor Science Base,* 57 CHEM. & ENG'G NEWS, Apr. 23, 1979, at 42, 46; Lave & Seskin, *Neither Cynical nor Idealistic View is Sound Basis for Policy,* 57 CHEM. & ENG'G NEWS, Apr. 23, 1979, at 49.

94. *See* M. BAILEY, REDUCING RISKS TO LIFE 15 (1980); Breyer, *supra* note 38, at 570; Chelius, *supra* note 59, at 701-02; Freeman, *Air and Water Pollution Policy,* in CURRENT ISSUES IN U.S. ENVIRONMENTAL POLICY 12, 19-20 (P. Portney ed. 1978); Solow, *The Economist's Approach to Pollution and Its Control,* 173 SCIENCE 498 (1971).

Some economists would also add that the costs of imposing a control should include administrative or enforcement costs borne by the government as well as the costs that the regulated entities must pay to

nological solutions can meet this criterion, society should choose that solution which minimizes the sum total of the cost of the damages remaining after implementation of the technology and the cost of implementing the technology.[95] By carefully balancing control costs against health and environmental benefits, society maximizes the total output of goods and services and puts each resource to its best use.[96] Thus, in the context of health and environmental regulation, the policy-oriented economist suggests that immediate regulatory goals be determined by cost-benefit analysis.

This simple utilitarian notion has a firm foundation in plain common sense.[97] It is not sensible to spend more on pollution control than it is worth. Health and environmental quality, in this view, are collective economic commodities that society pays for just as it pays for streets, police protection, and fire prevention.[98] As with these other commodities, there is an optimum amount of industrial and pollution-induced disease, harm to environmental organisms, and damage to material that health and environmental regulators should attempt to achieve.[99] This optimum can be derived through a careful cost-benefit balancing process. To spend more than the optimal amount of resources on pollution control is, in the policy-oriented economist's engaging metaphor, to reduce the size of the total economic pie.

1. *Practical Limitations.* In the context of health and environmental regulation, one will discover once again that numerous practical difficulties hobble attempts to accommodate the bargaining paradigm to real world problems. Since these practical limitations are treated in great detail in the policy analysis literature,[100]

---

comply with the regulation. *Cost-Benefit Hearings, supra* note 46, at 326 (statement of M.L. Weidenbaum). Whether this is a legitimate component of the cost of regulatory intervention is as much a question of ideology as of analytical correctness. In the common law, the costs of maintaining the judiciary are generally borne by the state. In some cases, however, they are imposed on the polluting source. This would argue for putting the costs of the regulatory system on the benefits side of the ledger as one of the costs of controlling the harms which the source would otherwise freely impose on the rest of society.

95. *See* N. ASHFORD, *supra* note 48, at 328-29; Oi, *On the Economics of Industrial Safety,* 38 LAW & CONTEMP. PROBS. 669, 670 (1974).

96. Seskin & Lave, *Health Benefits Exceed by 70% Costs to Control Stationary Source Air Pollution,* 57 CHEM. & ENG'G NEWS, Apr. 23, 1979, at 38 ("In particular, when society's scarce resources are allocated among competing government programs or private production and consumption additional resources should go to those activities that will produce the greatest social benefits. There is no alternative to evaluating the additional benefits flowing from devoting additional resources to competing activities."); W. BAXTER, *supra* note 46, at 27 ("If individuals in a society are free to engage in whatever exchanges of resources are mutually satisfactory for themselves then, at least in theory, every resource in the society will be deployed in the way that yields the greatest possible human satisfaction."); *see also* J. KRIER & E. URSIN, *supra* note 53, at 31.

97. *See* Freeman, *supra* note 94, at 19; Sagoff, *Economic Theory and Environmental Law,* 79 Mich. L. Rev. 1393, 1394 (1981) (citing Ruff, *supra* note 9).

98. *See Cost-Benefit Hearings, supra* note 46, at 4 (statement of Rep. Lent: "The cost of this regulation hits the citizen in his capacity both as a taxpayer and a consumer. Its costs add to inflation and significantly cut back on the amount of disposable income every American earns."); A. KNEESE & C. SCHULTZE, *supra* note 18, at 69; Chelius, *supra* note 59, at 701; Leone & Jackson, *The Political Economy of Federal Regulatory Activity: The Case of Water Pollution Controls,* in STUDIES IN PUBLIC REGULATING 239 (G. Fromm ed. 1981).

99. *See* M. BAILEY, *supra* note 94, at 23.

100. *See, e.g.,* M. GREEN & N. WAITZMAN, BUSINESS WAR ON THE LAW: AN ANALYSIS OF THE BENEFITS OF FEDERAL HEALTH/SAFETY ENFORCEMENT (1979); Baram, *Cost-Benefit Analysis: An Inadequate Basis*

they can be briefly summarized here. The following discussion will pay particular attention to the practical problems of health and environmental regulation of the chemical industry. As it happens, the chemical industry poses some of the more intractable real world obstacles to the successful implementation of a balancing approach.

a. Quantifying Costs. Quantifying the costs of regulatory intervention is the simplest of the tasks facing the regulatory entity. It need only sum the forecasted costs of implementing various levels of pollution control. Numerous practical problems, however, plague even this conceptually simple operation. The information necessary to perform these forecasts is very costly, and large predictive uncertainties accompany the calculations. Engineers must estimate the costs of various pollution reduction technologies for all of the firms discharging a particular chemical substance into a relevant body of air or water. The engineers must further predict the effects of the installation of the alternative technologies on receiving media quality so that the regulatory entity can know the total cost of each level of media quality.[101] This operation requires both a prediction of the end-of-pipe pollution concentrations resulting from each technology and the development and application of a pollutant dispersion model capable of converting end-of-pipe concentrations to steady-state ambient concentrations. For some pollutants in some media, such models already exist,[102] but they are plagued by large uncertainties.[103] For other media, such as ground water, dispersion and fate models are still in relatively primitive stages of development,[104] and the huge uncertainties surrounding them make them virtually useless for relating the costs of pollution con-

---

for Health, Safety and Environmental Regulatory Decisionmaking, 8 ECOLOGY L.Q. 473 (1980); Rodgers, *Benefits, Costs, and Risks: Oversight of Health and Environmental Decisionmaking*, 4 HARV. ENVTL. L. REV. 191 (1980).

101. If more than one firm discharges a pollutant into the relevant media so that the discharges of all firms overlap, the informational costs of assessing the costs of various levels of media quality are further exacerbated. Fortunately, one characteristic of the chemical industry is that this condition is not often met. Hence, the assessment of pollution control costs for a given body of air or water reduces simply to an assessment of a single firm's costs. In cases of multiple polluters, however, the assessment of costs is vastly more difficult. Ruff, *The Economic Common Sense of Pollution,* 19 PUB. INTEREST 69, 76 (1970).

102. Requirements for Preparation, Adoption and Submittal of Implementation Plans, 40 C.F.R. § 51 (1980). Texas v. EPA, 499 F.2d 289 (5th Cir. 1974), illustrates some of the disputes that can occur over the accuracy of such models.

103. *See* U.S. Environmental Protection Agency, Cost and Economic Impact Assessment for Alternative Levels of the National Ambient Air Quality Standard for Ozone I-7 (Draft Report June 1978): "Depending on the [modeling] technique used, wide variations can result in allowable emission levels and the concomitant reduction in projected emissions that is required [to meet alternative ambient air quality standards for ozone]." Table I-1 in the Economic Impact Assessment Document for Ozone dramatically demonstrates the sensitivity of cost estimates to the choice of the reduction model. For example, the linear rollback dispersion model yields estimated costs of $6 billion to $8 billion for meeting a 0.08 ppm ozone standard while the empirical kinetic modeling approach yields estimated costs of $9 to 12.5 billion for the same standard. While both of these models are reasonably sophisticated, the choice between them depends upon one's assumptions about air dispersion modeling. Clearly, large uncertainties cloud the application of even those reasonably well accepted models. Even larger uncertainties can be expected with water quality modeling, which is at a more primitive stage of development. However, the fact that only one source need be considered for the discharge of toxic pollutants from chemical industry may simplify modeling assumptions.

104. Rose-Ackerman, *Effluent Charges: A Critique,* 6 CAN. J. OF ECON. 512, 518 (1973); A. KNEESE & C. SCHULTZE, *supra* note 18, at 17.

trol to levels of media quality.[105]

Another factor on the costs side of the equation that severely confounds any attempt at marginal analysis is the limited supply of pollution control technologies that are available to firms over relevant time periods. A particular source or category of sources may have only two or three realistic pollution control options, each of which yields a particular level of receiving media quality. "Turning down" the pollution control machine may be impossible or may not significantly reduce overall operating and maintenance costs. In other words, control technologies may often come in discrete and nontunable units.[106] Once a firm has installed a particular technology, any greater reduction in pollution may be achievable only by installing the next most effective equipment, and any lesser reduction may be impossible short of turning off the technology.[107]

If it is difficult to fine-tune pollution reduction systems to meet specific limitations, it may be impossible to set a limitation at precisely the point at which costs equal benefits. Figure 1 provides a hypothetical example of a costs-versus-pollution reduction curve and a benefits-versus-pollution-reduction curve. The benefits curve is a simplified linear curve. The costs curve illustrates the technological

105. "While reasonably adequate engineering models exist relating discharges to ambient water quality, cost data are generally weak and fragmentary." Rose-Ackerman, *supra* note 13, at 389.

In addition, the ability of a single technology to reduce concentrations of more than one chemical can be a benefit that is not accounted for in a proceeding involving the costs and benefits of reducing exposure to an individual pollutant. The regulatory entity may simultaneously or within a short period of time regulate several pollutants within a single firm's discharge. It is certainly possible (and for some pollutants likely) that a single technology is capable of reducing discharges or emissions of many pollutants at the same time. *See* Development Documents for Effluent Limitations Guidelines and Standards for the Inorganic Chemicals Manufacturing Point Source Category (Proposed), Environmental Protection Agency 137 (1980). For example, in the nickel sulfate subcategory, alkaline precipitation with dual media filtration will remove some nickel, copper, chromium, antimony, zinc, and lead. *Id.* at 771. Similarly, secondary treatment can apparently remove numerous organic toxics from effluent wastes. *Implementation of the Federal Water Pollution Control Act: Hearings on Regulation and Monitoring of Toxic and Hazardous Chemicals under the Federal Water Pollution Control Act Before the Subcomm. on Oversight and Review of the House Comm. on Public Works and Transportation*, 96th Cong., 2d Sess. XV (1980) (summary of hearings) [hereinafter cited as *Implementation Hearings*]; SUBCOMM. ON OVERSIGHT AND REVIEW OF THE HOUSE COMM. ON PUBLIC WORKS AND TRANSPORTATION, 96TH CONG., 2D SESS., IMPLEMENTATION OF THE FEDERAL WATER POLLUTION CONTROL ACT 49 (Comm. Print 1980) [hereafter cited as PROHLMAN REPORT]. If a single technology can remove more than one pollutant, that additional benefit may not be factored into the cost-benefit balance for a single pollutant. It would therefore be inappropriate to list the entire cost of installing the single technology (or perhaps minor modifications of a single technology) in the cost estimation for each of the individual pollutants.

106. "On the basis of what we already know, it is difficult to agree that the shapes of air pollution cost and abatement functions are linear, as implied by Kneese." Wolozin, *The Economics of Air Pollution: Central Problems*, 33 LAW & CONTEMP. PROBS. 227, 229 (1968). Some technologies, such as scrubbers, can be tuned to some extent to reach a spectrum of emission concentrations. *See* 1 U.S. Environmental Protection Agency, Proceedings: Symposium on Gas Desulfurization 43-58 (1978).

107. For example, it is becoming apparent that the "secondary treatment"—activated sludge, trickling filters, and other minor variations on this theme—which has been required for publicly owned treatment works and for many firms as part of EPA's "best practicable technology" effluent limitations, is capable of removing more than 90% of some toxic organics. *Implementation Hearings*, *supra* note 105, at 43 (statement of Walter E. Garrison, Chief Engineer and General Manager, County Sanitation District, Los Angeles County). Lesser technologies remove much lower percentages of these pollutants. Hence, assuming only a single source in a relevant body of water, the cost side of the cost-benefit equation will not vary from some high level of ambient water concentration to that much lower level reached by 90% removal. The choice for the regulatory entity is therefore "all or nothing," even if the benefits side of the equation warranted expenditures less than secondary treatment but greater than less effective treatments.

options available to a source on the assumption that technologies are discrete and nontunable. The broken curve is the curve that would presumably exist if technologies were nondiscrete and tunable. In the real world of discrete technologies, it would appear worthwhile to install technologies A and B but not technology C. The benefits of installing technology B are 6.5 million dollars while the cost is only five million dollars. Technology C is too expensive because thirteen million dollars in expenditures yields only ten million dollars in benefits. It would be ideal to install a technology that cost $8.75 million and produced $8.75 million in benefits, but unfortunately, that technology does not exist. The regulatory entity is therefore likely to settle for technology B. Since the costs of installing technologies capable of reducing pollution by a given amount rise dramatically with the overall amount of pollution reduction, the cost-benefit based approach may result in a systematic bias toward underprotection.[108]

Finally, an accurate assessment of the costs of a spectrum of possible regulatory controls would require some measurement of secondary economic effects such as anticompetitive and employment effects.[109] While it would be irresponsible for the regulatory entity to ignore these effects, their very amorphous nature will provide substantial leeway to hinge its cost estimates on untestable assumptions.[110] Moreover, any assessment of costs must depend heavily upon input from the regulated firms. It would be unrealistic to expect that a firm's cost projections will not be affected by the purpose for which the regulatory entity plans to use the projections.[111] Hence, both primary and secondary costs may be biased against regulatory intervention.

In sum, the estimates of the costs side of the cost-benefit equation will in most cases be highly dependent upon the scientific assumptions that underlie the dispersion model that the agency chooses and the economic assumptions behind cost predictions. The uncertainties inherent in these calculations provide great leeway for the regulatory entity. Since regulated firms can be expected to participate fully in the cost-assessment process, the regulatory entity must either vigilantly police industry-submitted cost estimates or independently produce its own. If it chooses the former alternative, it must acknowledge that its estimates are likely to gravitate toward the high side.

b. *Quantifying Risks.* The uncertainties that plague the regulatory entity's attempts to quantify costs pale into insignificance when measured against the uncertainties inherent in assessing the benefits side of the equation. The quantitative study of risks posed by human exposure to environmental contaminants is still

108. If a particular industry contained enough firms, many individual cost curves might aggregate into a single smooth upwardly sloping curve common to the economics literature. Nevertheless, the sources of a particular chemical within the chemical industry are likely to be sufficiently few that a smooth aggregate curve will not result. Indeed, since a given technology for removing particular pollutants has about the same capital costs for any firm, the only variability among firms is likely to be in installation and operation and maintenance costs. The aggregate curve for a small number of sources may therefore look much like the curve for an individual source.

109. *See* Leone & Jackson, *supra* note 98, at 232.

110. *Id.* at 233.

111. *See* Baram, *supra* note 100, at 483, 490.

FIGURE 1

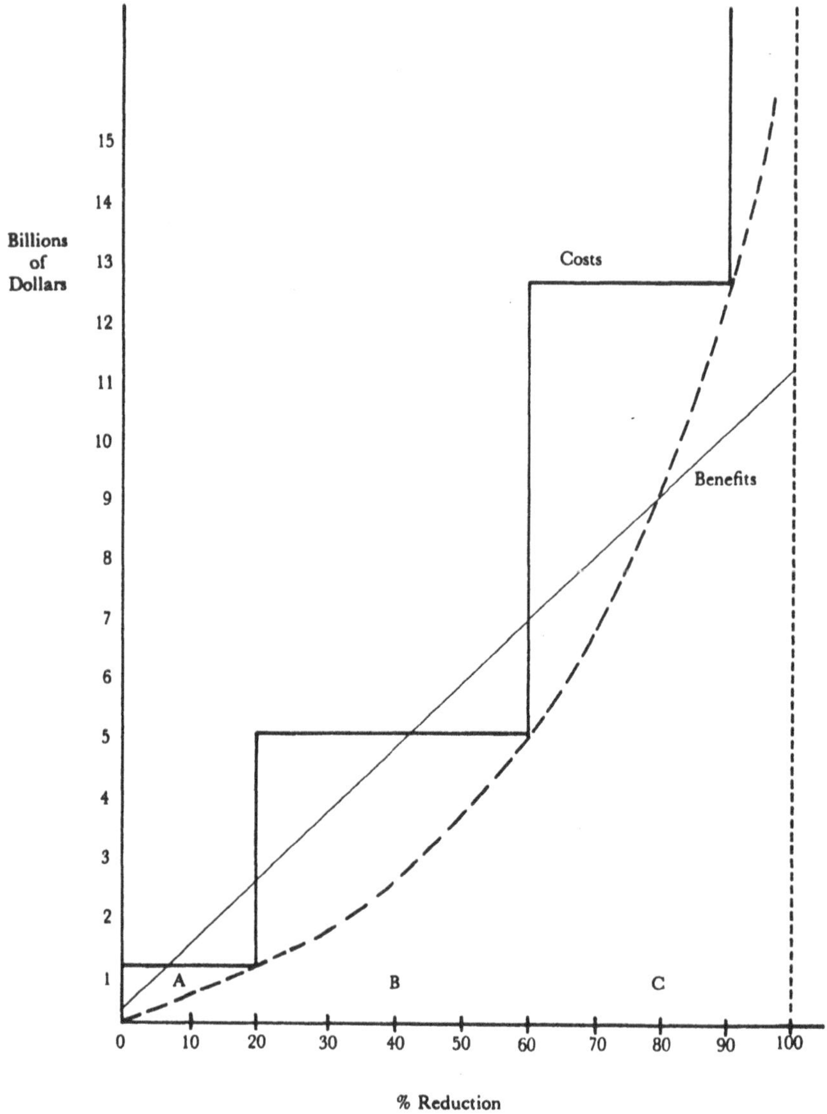
Billions of Dollars
15
14
13
12
11
10
9
8
7
6
5
4
3
2
1
Costs
Benefits
A
B
C
0
10
20
30
40
50
60
70
80
90
100
% Reduction

in a state of awkward infancy.[112] Even the comparatively straightforward assessment of the toxicological properties of a particular environmental contaminant is fraught with uncertainty. Epidemiological studies are notoriously inconclusive, as the continuing disputes over the health effects of beryllium and benzene amply demonstrate.[113] Animal studies can provide advance information on the toxicological effects of a chemical, but cost considerations usually preclude testing an adequate number of animals at environmentally relevant dose levels.[114] Hence attempts to extrapolate human risks from animal studies must make untestable assumptions about interspecies extrapolations[115] and about the shape of the dose-response curve for the chemical at low exposure levels.[116] Finally, uncertainties arise in attempts to ascertain actual human exposure to environmental contaminants.[117] The net result is that risk assessments can vary over nine orders of magnitude, depending upon the assumptions that fuel the models.[118]

The science of assessing the risks that pollutants pose to nonhuman species and materials is also imprecise and fraught with uncertainty.[119] Yet these effects, too, must be factored into any reasonable cost-benefit analysis of mandated pollution controls,[120] thus enlarging the overall margin of uncertainty. The National Environmental Policy Act has spurred a large number of commendable efforts to include small effects on ecosystems in the analysis of governmental activities, and this knowledge is now available to regulatory decisionmakers. Still, environmental

---

112. For the author's analysis of the scientific and policy debates surrounding "science/policy" issues arising out of carcinogen regulation see McGarity, *supra* note 49.

113. *See* McGarity, *supra* note 49, at 740-41; *see also* Scientific Bases for Identification of Potential Carcinogens and Estimation of Risks, 44 Fed. Reg. 39,858 (1979); 45 Fed. Reg. 5,009 (1980).

114. *See* McGarity, *supra* note 49, at 733-34; Schneiderman, Mantel & Brown, *From Mouse to Man—Or How to Get From the Laboratory to Park Avenue and 59th Street,* 246 ANNALS OF THE N.Y. ACAD. OF SCI. 237, 241 (1975).

115. *See* McGarity, *supra* note 49, at 743-45; Wood, *Interrelations of Humans, Dogs and Rodents,* 176 SCIENCE 437 (1972).

116. *See* Leape, *Qualitiative Risk Assessment in Regulation of Environmental Carcinogens,* 4 HARV. ENVTL. L. REV. 86, 100-01 (1980); McGarity, *supra* note 49, at 734-35. I have placed the issue of high dose-low dose extrapolation models in a category of science/policy questions that Dr. Alvin Weinberg calls "trans-scientific." These are questions which "hang on the answers to questions which can be asked of science and yet *which cannot be answered by science.*" Weinberg, *Science and Trans-Science,* 10 MINERVA 209 (1972).

117. McGarity, *supra* note 49, at 738; *see also supra* notes 102-05 and accompanying text. The problem of determining human exposure in the workplace is not an especially difficult one. In most cases, the chemical concentrations in the actual workplace can be monitored relatively easily. However, determining human exposure to environmental contaminants is much more difficult. For air pollutants the calculation requires at least an adequate dispersion model and, for chemicals like lead, an assessment of alternative pathways, such as ingestion or dermal exposure, in addition to the more usual inhalation exposure. For persistent water pollutants the calculation is extraordinarily complex, requiring an adequate dispersion model, an assessment that the contaminant will become part of a drinking water supply, an assessment of the exposure to various organisms as the chemical makes its way up the food chain, and a prediction of the amount that will ultimately find its way into the human food supply.

118. Comment, *The Significant Risk Requirement in OSHA Regulation of Carcinogens:* Industrial Union Department, AFL-CIO v. American Petroleum Institute, 33 STAN. L. REV. 551 (1981).

119. Baram, *supra* note 100, at 483; Gelpe & Tarlock, *supra* note 71, at 371.

120. For one extensive, though in many ways dissatisfying, effort to quantify the benefits of attaining alternative levels of sulfur dioxide and particulate controls see U.S. Environmental Protection Agency, Benefits Analysis of Alternative Secondary National Ambient Air Quality Standards for Sulfur Dioxide and Total Suspended Particulates (Draft Final Analysis July 1981) [hereinafter cited as EPA Sulfur Dioxide Standards]. *See generally* A. FREEMAN, THE BENEFITS OF ENVIRONMENTAL IMPROVEMENT (1979).

impact analysis is hardly a precise science, and agency policy analysts tend to belittle these "soft variables."[121]

The foregoing difficulties with quantitative risk assessment constitute a formidable threat to the rationality of cost-benefit analysis. How much useful knowledge has the regulatory decisionmaker gained when he is told, as the Administrator of the EPA was once told, that the risks posed by a polluting activity range from zero to 660,000 cancers over a seventy-year period?[122] Arguably, the decisionmaker can use this information in setting priorities;[123] he might decide to regulate this contaminant after he has regulated one that poses a risk of zero to 990,000 cancers over the same period. This information, however, cannot be of much utility in a marginal balancing analysis.

This branch of reductionist quantitative risk analysis can, however, work a positive harm when the decisionmaker (or, more likely, his or her technical underlings) masks the huge uncertainties inherent in the enterprise and presents to the public a "best estimate" that implies an accuracy that simply does not exist. The public is in a very real sense being deceived when it is told that the lifetime risks posed by a chemical are twenty-six cancers, rather than somewhere in the range between zero and 660,000 cancers. The public is also being deceived when it is told, without further elaboration, that the risks posed by a pesticide are about the same as smoking one cigarette per lifetime.[124] The regulator can choose from among a wide variety of proposed risk assessment models, some of which resolve uncertainties in favor of protecting the public and the environment and others of which resolve uncertainties in favor of maximizing industrial activity. Only rarely will the proponent of a model acknowledge the covert political considerations that motivate the choice among models.[125] Yet, until models are developed which can attract a reasonable scientific consensus, the choice between models is entirely policy dominated. Regulators who use such highly refined, but ultimately hollow,

---

121. Tribe, *Trial By Mathematics: Precision and Ritual in the Legal Process,* 84 HARV. L. REV. 1329, 1361-65 (1971).

122. This example comes from the author's personal experience in the Office of General Counsel of the EPA.

123. Identification, Classification, and Regulation of Potential Occupational Carcinogens, 45 Fed. Reg. 5,002, 5,256 (1980); *see infra* text accompanying note 340.

124. In August 1981, Dr. John Todhunter, EPA Assistant Administrator for Pesticides and Toxic Substances, determined that the cancer risk from one year's use of ethylene dibromide (EDB) to fumigate citrus crops was 100 times less than the risk of smoking one cigarette in a lifetime. PESTICIDE & TOXIC CHEM. NEWS, Aug. 26, 1981, at 19-20. One week later, Dr. Todhunter corrected this estimate of cancer risk to equal the risk of smoking between one and two cigarettes over a lifetime. PESTICIDE & TOXIC CHEM. NEWS, Sept. 2, 1981, at 14.

Dr. Adrian Gross, at that time chief scientist of EPA's hazards evaluation division, said that "Todhunter is trying to say that the risk is one in a million that someone will contract cancer whereas I find the data to show that the risk is one in a thousand and possibly 50 to 70 per thousand." Wash. Post, Oct. 8, 1981, at A29, col. 5. He continued that the chemical "is much more dangerous than Todhunter believes because it can find its way into food products as easily as it can be consumed" in fruit. *Id.* One staff member who worked on the Agency position document said he would not eat fruit treated in accordance with Dr. Todhunter's "minimum expectations for residue." *Id.*

125. *See* Mantel & Schneiderman, *Estimating "Safe" Levels, A Hazardous Undertaking,* 35 CANCER RESEARCH 1379, 1382 (1975) (choice of log-probit dose-response model over more conservative linear model justified on grounds that use of former ultimately would result in fewer products taken off the market).

techniques to "fine tune" benefits analyses are deceiving the public and perhaps themselves.

2. *Theoretical Limitations.* In addition to the foregoing practical limitations of cost-benefit analysis, it also has several important theoretical limitations. Some of these have already been suggested in the previous analysis of the "bargaining" and "tort" models.

a. *Valuing the Benefits.* While the adoption of a regulatory agency approach to the pollution problem remedies many of the practical defects of the "bargaining" and "tort" models, it fails to resolve the debilitating schizophrenia that afflicts the bargaining model. Even if scientists could precisely quantify all of the lives, organisms, and materials lost at all relevant levels of media quality, only some of these could be evaluated in any meaningful way[126] because the "willingness to pay" measure of health and environmental harm will in many cases diverge widely from the "willingness to sell" measure.

Past attempts by regulatory agencies and policy analysts to measure the benefits of health and environmental controls have invariably invoked the "willingness to pay" criterion.[127] The implicit, and often explicit, assumption of the economists who attempt to place a monetary value on the benefits of health and environmental controls is that the freely polluting market is the norm and any governmental intervention must be justified.[128] This is the equivalent of a rule of law that all polluters may freely pollute unless they have contracted not to. As we have seen, one can have an equally rational society in which the opposite rule holds. Translated to the regulatory sphere, the polluter in the latter society must justify its pollution by showing that the surrounding neighbors would be willing to accept it for the decrease in product price attributable to the amount that the firm saves from failing to control it. Yet, strangely, no economist of which I am aware has taken the "willingness to sell" criteria as the appropriate test for the benefits of pollution reduction. In the case of pollutants that cause only minor discomfort or property damage, the two measures are, as Coase suggests,[129] probably about the

126. There is a real, working market in most materials. The damage to materials can be evaluated by reference to the market costs of replacement or repair. For some materials, however, such as the Statute of Liberty, this valuation method may not be entirely adequate. Aesthetics as well as economics play a role in the valuation process, and the market paradigm once again becomes schizophrenic. *See infra* text accompanying notes 127-130.

127. *See, e.g.*, EPA Sulfur Dioxide Standards, *supra* note 120, at I-4; 5 U.S. Environmental Protection Agency, Methods of Development for Assessing Air Pollution Control Benefits 6 (1979) (EPA-60015-79-001); U.S. Environmental Protection Agency, Critical Review of Estimating Benefits of Air and Water Pollution Control I-5 (1978) (EPA-60015-78-014); Zeckhauser & Shepard, *Principles for Saving and Valuing Lives*, in THE BENEFITS OF HEALTH AND SAFETY REGULATION 91, 96-97 (1981).

Even the "willingness to pay" criteria is criticized by some economists as being unrealistic when the beneficiaries of health and environmental controls are not actually forced to pay for them. *See* Crandall, *Environmental Control is Out of Control*, CHEM. & ENG'G NEWS, Apr. 23, 1979, at 29, 31.

One instance in which the "willingness to sell" test has been invoked is in current proposals to compensate localities for siting hazardous waste facilities within their borders. *See* Bacow & Milkey, *Overcoming Local Opposition to Hazardous Waste Facilities: The Massachusetts Approach*, 6 HARV. ENVTL L. REV. 265, 275-79 (1982). The authors point out that this is efficient because it allows "projects to proceed only if their social benefits outweigh their social costs." *Id.* at 275.

128. *See* Breyer, *supra* note 38, at 552.

129. Coase, *The Problem of Social Cost*, 3 J.L. & ECON. 1 (1960).

same. But if willingness to sell were the measure of the benefits of controlling life-threatening industrial activities, the numbers that the various economic models produce, which are indeed quite large under the "willingness to pay" criterion,[130] would probably become significantly larger.

A second theoretical conundrum with benefits analysis is the value of reduced risks to persons not yet in existence.[131] Those persons, of course, are not consulted as to either their willingness to pay for or their willingness to sell additional risks to their health and well-being. The decisionmaker can make a very crude attempt to consider the interests of future generations by adjusting the "discount rate" of the benefits analysis in such a way that a dollar's worth of future benefit is worth more than the value given to it by a current investor.[132] Yet, the fact that future benefits are discounted at all connotes a bias of sorts against future inhabitants of the planet. One report on benefits analysis suggests that "in the future, one may very well value good health and a clean environment even more than one does today so that an individual might choose to use a negative, rather than a positive discount rate for certain future benefits."[133] Indeed, for harms like physical pain and suffering the entire discounting theory may be inappropriate. While a present dollar is clearly worth more than a future dollar, it is not clear that present pain is worth more or less than the promise of future pain.

Another infirmity that afflicts standard economic valuation of pollution control benefits is the disturbing tendency of the policy-oriented economist to "dwarf soft variables."[134] Policy analysts are often inclined to ignore unquantifiable variables, such as the psychic costs of knowing that a species has become extinct,[135] and to undervalue those "soft variables" that they can identify but cannot easily appraise.[136] Moreover, the analyst's assessment of the environmental benefits of

130. Crude estimates were made of the "willingness to pay" for improved air quality in the south coast air basin of southern California. Assuming approximately 30% improvement in ambient air quality, where a household is willing to pay $42 per month, the annual benefit to this area was predicted to be $950,000,000. 5 U.S. Environmental Protection Agency, Methods of Development for Assessing Air Pollution Control Benefits 16-17 (1979) (executive summary).

In determining health benefits derived from a 60% reduction of particulates and sulfur dioxide, the national urban benefits were estimated at $4.1 to $13.7 billion and $2.2 to $7 billion respectively. *Id.* at 7; *see also* 1 EPA Sulfur Dioxide Standards, *supra* note 120; M. Freeman, The Benefits of Air and Water Pollution Control: A Review and Synthesis of Recent Estimates (1979) (report prepared for the Council on Environmental Quality).

131. *See* Baram, *supra* note 100, at 486; Rodgers, *supra* note 100, at 196; Massachusetts Institute of Technology Center for Policy Alternatives, Benefits of Environmental, Health, and Safety Regulation, (1980) (prepared for the Senate Comm. on Govtl. Affairs, 96th Cong., 2d Sess.) [hereinafter cited as MIT Report].

132. The discount rate is a standard economic tool for taking into account the fact that a dollar in hand is worth more than the promise of a dollar in the future. *See* Baram, *supra* note 100, at 486-87. Benefits due to a present environmental improvement that accrue in the future must therefore be discounted to their present value.

133. MIT Report, *supra* note 131, at 18; *see also* Baram, *supra* note 100, at 486 n.47 (suggesting that analysts have chosen rates that tend to confirm the outcomes they desire); Rodgers, *supra* note 100, at 196 ("the decisionmaker who uses today's preferences to discount tomorrow's life is one whose impartiality might reasonably be questioned").

134. *See* Tribe, *Trial by Mathematics: Precision and Ritual in the Legal Process*, 84 HARV. L. REV. 1329, 1361-65 (1971).

135. *See supra* text accompanying notes 54-56.

136. The decisionmaking process fixates on the comparison of the monetary terms and fails to suffi-

environmental regulation is invariably anthropocentric. The value placed upon a segment of stream, for example, does not take into account the stream's value to the fish, deer, insects, and plant life that also use the stream, except insofar as these entities are valuable to humans.[137] Many policy-oriented economists therefore have little patience with statutes like the Endangered Species Act[138] that seem to give nonhuman entities greater intrinsic value than they have in any conceivable marketplace.[139]

b. *Distributional Considerations.* The policy-oriented economist does not directly concern himself with the distributional effects of the policies that he advocates.[140] He is more interested in maximizing the size of the economic pie than in suggesting how it should be sliced.[141] Yet, virtually any governmental action, including the definition of the property and contract rules that define the "free market," affects the distribution of wealth among its citizens. A property rule giving a polluter the right to pollute unless he has contracted otherwise makes polluters richer; a rule giving neighbors the right to enjoin polluters makes surrounding property owners wealthier.[142] Even if Professor Coase is correct in maintaining that the unimpeded market will ultimately maximize total wealth under either rule, it is clear that under the first rule polluters will receive a greater proportion of that total wealth than they will under the second.[143]

Regulatory intervention in the workplace and the environment will likewise shift wealth. If the regulatory entity follows the policy-oriented economist's approach, it must still elect the "willingness to sell" or the "willingness to pay" criterion for valuing the benefits of the intervention. A choice of the "willingness to pay" criteria will shift wealth from the poor to the rich because the poor have fewer resources to draw upon. A choice of the "willingness to sell" criteria will shift wealth from the rich to the poor because the poor can ask for as much in return for risks to their health as the rich.[144] Even if as an empirical matter poor

---

> ciently incorporate non-monetary terms in the decision. There is a strong tendency for a decisionmaker and for other parties critiquing the process to compare only the monetary terms apart from the non-monetary terms, and to introduce the non-monetary terms as a marginal adjusting factor, if at all.

MIT Report, *supra* note 131, at 19; *see also* Baram, *supra* note 100, at 484; Leape, *supra* note 116, at 96-97; Rodgers, *supra* note 100, at 197.

137. *See* Tribe, *supra* note 56.

138. 16 U.S.C. §§ 1531-1543 (Supp. VI 1982).

139. "I argue that environmental legislation, at least during the past twenty years, fails to make economic 'common sense', that is, it fails to maximize the satisfaction of consumer demand over the long run. Laws like the Endangered Species Act flaunt this concept of economic efficiency." Sagoff, *supra* note 97, at 1396.

140. A. KNEESE & C. SCHULTZE, *supra* note 18, at 28.

141. *See* A. FREEMAN, R. HAVEMAN & A. KNEESE, THE ECONOMICS OF ENVIRONMENTAL POLICY 81 (1973); Rodgers, *supra* note 100, at 194.

142. *See* Calabresi & Melamed, *supra* note 52, at 1095.

143. *See id.* at 1095-96. This point is different from the argument that "willingness to pay" will not always equal "willingness to sell." That argument relied upon the distribution of wealth (and perhaps of risk propensity) immediately prior to the time the property rule is determined. This argument, that regulatory intervention has distributional consequences, speaks to the distribution of wealth after the government decides to intervene or to fail to intervene. The earlier argument says that because of unequal wealth distribution it makes a difference which property rule is adopted. The argument here is that governmental intervention will redistribute wealth regardless of the property rule adopted.

144. This point assumes that the right to enjoin really exists. In the workplace, of course, it does not.

people do not generally demand as many dollars for health risks as wealthy people, they will almost certainly demand more than they can pay under the opposite test.

Irrespective of the valuation criteria, governmental intervention will shift wealth from polluters and consumers of their products to the beneficiaries of the regulatory intervention, and any intervention that does not completely eliminate risks will allow the polluters and their consumers to profit from the loss of others. Consumers of the polluter's products would be willing to pay the victims (under the "willingness to sell" rule) or the victims would be willing to pay the polluter (under the "willingness to buy" rule), but the failure of the "bargaining" and "tort" models means that these transactions never occur. The utilitarian regulator would allow the polluting activity to continue if the overall benefits of the activity outweigh its costs, but the regulator will not actually require the beneficiaries to compensate the losers. Any rule short of a complete prohibition of polluting activity or a perfectly enforced strict liability compensation system therefore creates an uncompensated minority of victims who must endure health risks and environmental harm so that the economy as a whole may expand.[145] On the other hand, a rule of complete prohibition forces consumers to pay more for risks than the victims would demand under the "willingness to sell" rule or pay under the "willingness to pay" rule (assuming transaction costs did not impede the transaction), and this would certainly seem inequitable to the beneficiaries of the polluting activity. These distributional concerns can be addressed, perhaps more efficiently, through direct transfers from the public treasury to the "victims" of the governmental policy through mechanisms like a large "superfund." Such transfer devices, however, face the same causation problems as the tort system, and they are often difficult to implement politically.[146]

The distributional concerns raised by regulatory application of the market paradigm are not limited to shifts of wealth between distinctive groups within society. To the extent that the regulatory entity neglects to measure the value of or undervalues future human beings or nonhuman inhabitants of the planet, the result will be a shift of the world's resources away from those neglected groups and toward present human consumers' manufactured products.

Finally, economists have recently postulated that regulatory controls can have

A worker cannot really insist that the employer eliminate toxic substances from the workplace; the worker can always be fired and replaced by a "less picky" worker. Under this sort of economic duress, the worker may be willing to sell his health for an unrealistically low price. Low income persons operating under economic duress may well sell their health for less than the rich. To a limited extent the same is true for environmental controls. Since a dollar means more to someone with very few of them, the poor may sell their right to a clean environment at a lower price than the rich.

145. Occasionally this minority of victims can be identified. For example, many forms of air pollution are more irritable at lower levels of exposure to persons afflicted with emphysema. *See, e.g.*, American Petroleum Inst. v. Costle, 609 F.2d 20 (D.C. Cir. 1979). Many pollutants affect children more dramatically and at lower exposure levels than adults. Lead Indus. Ass'n. v. EPA, 647 F.2d 1130, 1141 (D.C. Cir.), *cert. denied*, 449 U.S. 1042 (1980). For other pollutants a "susceptible" group is less easily identified, although some preliminary attempts have been made. *See generally* E. CALABRESE, POLLUTANTS AND HIGH RISK GROUPS (1978).

146. *See* Roberts & Stewart, *Energy and the Environment*, in SETTING NATIONAL PRIORITIES: THE NEXT TEN YEARS 411 (1976).

distributional impacts within the regulated industry itself.[147] Government-required capital investments in pollution controls can put some firms at a disadvantage with respect to their competitors.[148]

The fact that the economist *qua* economist is uninterested in the distributional impacts of the policies that he advocates does not mean that the rational policymaker is likewise free to ignore the distributional implications of her decisions. The response of some economists that inequities can be resolved through direct transfer payments to the victims of utilitarian policies presumes that a mechanism for this transfer exists and that it will be used. Moreover, this response also ignores the negative symbolic impact of a governmental action which allows some to profit from health risks imposed upon others. Finally, the advocate of transfer payments implicitly espouses the same presumptuous premise that afflicts policy-oriented economists' pursuit of the valuation problem—that all values can be reduced to coin. The policymaker must therefore directly address the distributional concerns that alternative policies raise. A sufficient reason for rejecting a wealth-maximizing policy is that too much wealth would change hands in the process.

D. Politics and the Rejection of the Market Paradigm

The policy-oriented economists often appear frustrated by politicians' persistent failure to heed their teaching with respect to the proper goals of health and environmental regulation,[149] and to select efficient tools for the pursuit of designated environmental goals. There is some justification for the frustration arising from the failure to select efficient *tools*.[150] The economist, however, should not feel slighted by the politician's failure to pursue the market paradigm in setting the *goals* for health and environmental regulation because that endeavor requires more than economic expertise. There are important reasons why the politician must reject that paradigm, not the least of which is its basic schizophrenia. The politician does not reject the discipline of economics; she merely seeks to accommodate a broader range of values than most policy-oriented economists are willing to address. The pollution problem is not merely an economic problem, as some policy-oriented economists maintain;[151] rather, it is primarily a *political* problem to be resolved by the political process.

---

147. *See, e.g.*, A. KNEESE & C. SCHULTZE, *supra* note 18, at 22-23; Leone & Jackson, *supra* note 98, ch. 5.

148. Relaxation of governmental controls can have similar intrafirm distributional effects, as illustrated by the recent dramatic changes in the airline industry. "Some firms, finding that they simply cannot afford the cleanup may have to go out of business." Leone & Jackson, *supra* note 98, at 27.

149.
> Over the past decade, the U.S. has made a major commitment to improving the quality of our air and water. During this entire period, economists who think about environmental policy have, virtually without dissent, accused the government of going about the task of environmental cleanup in the wrong way.

Kelman, *Economists and the Environmental Muddle*, 64 PUB. INTEREST 106 (1981); *see also* Freeman & Haveman, *Clean Rhetoric and Dirty Water*, 28 PUB. INTEREST 51, 52 (1972).

150. *See generally* F. ANDERSON, *supra* note 9; A. KNEESE & C. SCHULTZE, *supra* note 18; B. MITNICK, *supra* note 46; Lave, *Health and Environmental Regulations*, in SETTING NATIONAL PRIORITIES: AGENDA FOR THE 1980'S 131 (J. Pechman ed. 1980); Rose-Ackerman, *supra* note 13.

151. Chelius, *supra* note 59 ("For all the moral anguish associated with accidents, it must be remembered that safety is an economic commodity."); Freeman & Haveman, *supra* note 149, at 52 (referring to the basic economic nature of the problem); Ruff, *supra* note 101, at 69 ("We are going to make very

The fact that the market paradigm is only rarely invoked in the actual political debate that impels legislators to enact pollution control statutes is unsurprising to the student of the political process.[152] A politician stands to gain little political capital by announcing to her constituents: "I have identified an instance in which the tort system has failed adequately to internalize externalities, and I am today introducing legislation to minimize the sum of pollution and pollution avoidance costs." The politician is likely to attract much more attention if she announces: "I have discovered that a large chemical company is poisoning its neighbors and the environment, and I am today introducing legislation to protect the environment." The arguments opposed to pollution control legislation can likewise be translated into the language of politics. Rather than arguing that "the statute will require the regulatory agency to induce an inefficient allocation of resources by setting the marginal cleanup costs for most firms higher than the marginal benefits," the anti-interventionist politician assures her constituents that "the statute will create a self-serving bureaucracy that will drive small firms out of business, stifle innovation, contribute to galloping inflation, and send capital overseas."

When the focus of the debate is a subject as sensitive as toxic substances in the air and water and the threat of bankrupting small businesses, symbols play a large role.[153] Proponents of controls are likely to strive for absolutist symbolic legislative statements such as the proposition that "the discharge of toxic pollutants in toxic amounts be prohibited"[154] or that no new sources of pollution should be allowed to degrade media quality in pristine areas of the country.[155] Complex controversies about the extent to which media quality goals may be met through dispersion enhancement, intermittent controls, and flow augmentation reduce to slogans such as "dilution is not a solution to pollution,"[156] and "treatment for treatment's sake."[157]

As any smart advertising executive knows, much of our energies are directed toward symbolic and unachievable goals. We do not begin a mountain climb with the goal of scaling to the optimal height; we strive for the summit. The coach does

---

little real progress in solving the problem of pollution until we recognize it for what, primarily, it is: an economic problem, which must be understood in economic terms.").

152. *See* M. FIORINA, CONGRESS: KEYSTONE OF THE WASHINGTON ESTABLISHMENT (1977); Freeman & Haveman, *supra* note 149, at 59.

153. *See* Ingram, *The Political Rationality of Innovation, The Clean Air Act Amendments of 1970*, in APPROACHES TO CONTROLLING AIR POLLUTION 12, 20-23 (1978); Kelman, *supra* note 149. Even in those very rare cases in which Congress has considered a tool aimed solely at curing a defect in the market or the tort system, the language of the debate has been largely symbolic. For example, proponents of Senator Proxmire's sulfur dioxide tax stressed that it "makes polluters pay" while detractors contended that it would "force companies to pay twice" or argued that it would give companies a "license to pollute." *See* Busby, *Environment Report/White House Plans Push for Sulfur Tax Despite Strong Industry Opposition*, 4 NAT'L J. 1663 (1972); *Environment Report/White House Activists Debate Form of Sulfur Tax—Industry Shuns Both*, 4 NAT'L J. 1643 (1972); 118 CONG. REC. 833-35 (1972) (statement of Sen. Proxmire).

154. Clean Water Act § 101(a)(3), 33 U.S.C. § 1251(a)(3) (1976).

155. Clean Water Act § 101(a), 33 U.S.C. § 1251(a) (1976); Clean Air Act § 101(b)(1), 42 U.S.C. § 7401(b)(1) (Supp. V 1981).

156. *See* Hines, *A Decade of Nondegradation Policy in Congress and the Courts: The Erratic Pursuit of Clean Air and Clean Water*, 62 IOWA L. REV. 643 (1977).

157. *See, e.g., Implementation Hearings*, *supra* note 105, at 40 (statement of Walter E. Garrison, Chief Engineer and General Manager, County Sanitation District, Los Angeles County).

not direct his charges to fight for the alma mater up to the point at which marginal costs exceed marginal benefits; he exhorts them to give their all. We recognize that we will not always reach the summit and that we will not always win. But if we set our sights on the bland optimum, we will always set them too low. The advertising industry invokes this human characteristic in a cynical fashion when it urges us to expend more than the optimal amount of resources on products that are just beyond the material lifestyles that we can safely afford. Congress manifests the same motivation in a more idealistic way when it sets "inefficient" goals for the quality of life.

The political debate is the appropriate locus of that quintessentially political choice between the "willingness to buy" and "willingness to sell" measures of the value of health and environmental improvement in setting national goals. The policy-oriented economist cannot give an apolitical, scientific answer to the question of the appropriate level of pollution control. The economist can inform the political debate by calculating the probable costs of various pollution control measures, yet he can say very little about the benefits absent an *a priori* political value judgment. The politician must explicitly or implicitly choose between the two approaches—she must decide whether as a starting point companies have a "right" to pollute or citizens have a "right" not to be placed at risk by polluters. The basic political choice that renders the market paradigm impotent as a scientific tool is thus expressed succinctly in the politician's vernacular. The statutory standard that the legislature articulates to guide the implementing agency reflects that body's resolution of this question as well as its assessment of other issues, such as the respect due to future generations and the extent to which environmental controls should redistribute wealth, that are relevant to the political debate. The entire dialogue is, unfortunately, played out against a backdrop of huge uncertainties concerning the relationship between chemical pollutants and human and environmental well-being.

Historically, Congress has behaved as if it were following a "willingness to sell" approach.[158] There has been much talk in the political debate of a "right" to a healthy workplace and a clean environment.[159] Proponents of early occupational

---

158. The major exception to this proposition is the large construction grants program under the Clean Water Act where the federal government pays up to 80% of the cost of building publicly owned sewage treatment works. Here, it would appear that the federal government is, in a sense, determining its "willingness to pay" for pollution control. The same may be true of pollution control in public utilities, where virtually all citizens pay for the increased costs of controlling pollution that they themselves produce.

159. SUBCOMM. ON LABOR, COMM. ON LABOR AND PUBLIC WELFARE, 92D CONG., 1ST SESS., LEGISLATIVE HISTORY OF OCCUPATIONAL SAFETY AND HEALTH ACT OF 1970 432 (1971) [hereinafter cited as LEGISLATIVE HISTORY OF OSHA]. "The worker is entitled to know that standards in the workplace are geared to overcoming safety and health hazards that are shortening his life." *Id.* at 865 (statement of Sen. Williams); "The well being of every American working man and woman is an essential human right which we can no longer deny." *Id.* (statement of Rep. Perkins); "This bill represents a long overdue significant additional recognition that working men and women need Federal assistance to secure their inalienable right to earn their living free from the ravages of job-caused death, disease or injury." *Id.* at 891 (statement of Rep. Burton); "Mr. Speaker, our Nation has had a sad and frustrating history of weak-kneed inaction by those who have been charged with protecting the divine right of every citizen to breath clean air." COMM. ON PUBLIC WORKS, 93D CONG., 2D SESS., LEGISLATIVE HISTORY OF THE CLEAN AIR ACT AMENDMENTS OF 1970 116 (1974) (statement of Rep. Hechler) [hereinafter cited as HISTORY OF CAA AMENDMENTS OF 1970]; "Surely in a nation that has scaled the peaks of technological achievement where most people enjoy

and environmental legislation were anxious to enact measures that would successfully "clean up the environment and the workplace" and keep it clean. Since the states were not accomplishing those goals rapidly enough, the federal government had to intervene.[160] Congress therefore required that media-quality-based standards for exposure to pollutants be set at levels which would "protect public health" with an "adequate margin of safety"[161] or even an "ample margin of safety."[162] If feasible, workers were entitled to a "safe and healthful" place of employment.[163] The toxics control sections of the statutes are emphatic in their rejection of a narrow cost-benefit approach.[164] These absolutist legislative statements have great symbolic value. The lofty goals of the environmental statutes give us all a common sense of mission in the same nonutilitarian way that the goal of putting a man on the moon galvanized the American public for a decade in support of the space program. As consumers we may dislike paying more for automobiles, fuel, electricity, and products of the chemical industry, but as citizens we can rationally vote for extremely costly and, by the "willingness to pay" measure, inefficient goals.[165] The goals that we set as voters constantly remind us

---

unprecedented standards of personal property it is not asking too much to insist on the right to breathe decent air." *Air Pollution, 1967: Hearings on S. 780 Before the Subcomm. on Air and Water Pollution of the Senate Comm. on Public Works*, 90th Cong., 1st Sess. 759 (1967) (statement of Sec. Gardner of Health, Education and Welfare).

160. Prior to 1967, the states had the primary responsibility for air pollution control. The inadequacy of most state programs, however, soon attracted national attention. In the 1967 amendments to the Clean Air Act, Congress removed this sizable and complex burden from the states and substituted a strong national media-quality-based approach. The congressional debate was characterized by strong "cleanup" rhetoric:

> This bill . . . recognizes that control efforts considered acceptable just a few years ago are now clearly inadequate . . . . Developed in full awareness of the public's greatly increased support and demand for prompt and effective control action, the Air Quality Act of 1967 broadens control programs at all levels of government in an effort to protect and enhance the quality of the environment.

S. REP. NO. 403, 90th Cong., 1st Sess. 17 (1967).

By 1970 this sense of urgency increased as the compliance deadlines neared. Congress once again amended the statute and once again stressed cleanup and nondegradation goals: "Here we have learned that tests of economical and technological feasibility applied to those standards compromise the health of our people and lead to inadequate standards . . . . It is clear that enforcement must be toughtened [sic] if we are to meet the national deadlines." HISTORY OF CAA AMENDMENTS OF 1970, *supra* note 159, at 226 (statement of Sen. Muskie); *see also* Sierra Club v. Ruckelshaus, 344 F. Supp. 253 (D.D.C. 1972), *aff'd sub nom.* Fri v. Sierra Club, 412 U.S. 541 (1973); "The problem of assuring safe and healthful workplaces for our working men and women ranks in importance with any that engages the national attention today." S. REP. NO. 1281, 91st Cong., 2d Sess. (1970), *reprinted in* LEGISLATIVE HISTORY OF OSHA, *supra* note 159, at 141 (statement of Sen. Williams); "We surely owe it to the millions of working men and women whose health and lives are unnecessarily jeopardized by hazards of the workplace to pass the most effective measure we can devise." *Id.* at 141 (statement of Sen. Kennedy).

161. Clean Air Act § 109, 42 U.S.C. § 7409 (Supp. V 1981).

162. Clean Water Act § 307, 33 U.S.C. § 1317 (Supp. V 1981); Clean Air Act § 112, 42 U.S.C. § 7412 (Supp. V 1981).

163. Occupational Safety and Health Act § 6(b)(5), 29 U.S.C. § 655(b)(5) (1976).

164. Occupational Safety and Health Act § 56(b), 29 U.S.C. § 655(b) (1976); Clean Water Act § 307, 33 U.S.C. § 1317 (Supp. V 1980); Clean Air Act § 112, 42 U.S.C. § 7412 (Supp. V 1981). Indeed even the older health and environmental statutes, such as the Federal Insecticide, Fungicide and Rodenticide Act, 7 U.S.C. § 135 (1982), and the Food, Drug and Cosmetic Act, 21 U.S.C. § 301 (1976), that articulated a risk-benefit approach did so in the context of a product licensing scheme that placed the burden of demonstrating that the benefits of the *product* outweighed its costs. This surely represented a tacit conclusion that the public had a "right" to reasonably safe pesticides and food and drug products, and that it would exchange for the benefits of the products only upon a showing of reasonable safety.

165. *See* Sagoff, *supra* note 97, at 1399.

as we assume our role as consumers that there are things in life more important than the pursuit of material wealth.

In addition, environmental goals reflect society's nonutilitarian moral judgments. We may wish to reaffirm to ourselves that pollution is not merely inefficient—it is wrong.[166] We may desire to invoke the ritual of a civil or criminal trial to remind ourselves and the defendant of our determination that pollution is antisocial conduct. The tort system provides an avenue for a plaintiff to seek revenge as well as shift loss, and the tort alternative in theory operates as an inducement to forego self-help.[167] The failure of the tort system to shift loss is likewise a failure to assuage this strong human emotion. We may therefore legislatively set goals and prescribe implementation techniques that satisfy our collective desire for retribution.

The Supreme Court has recognized and reaffirmed this political judgment in the worker safety context in the *Cotton Dust* case.[168] This case dealt with the Occupational Safety and Health Act, which requires OSHA to establish standards that "require conditions, or the adoption or use of one or more practices, means, methods, operations, or processes, reasonably necessary and appropriate to provide safe or healthful employment or places of employment."[169] For toxic materials and harmful physical agents, the statute further requires the agency to set the standard "which most adequately assures, to the extent feasible . . . that no employee will suffer material impairment of health or functional capacity even if such employee has regular exposure to the hazard dealt with by such standard for the period of his working life."[170] OSHA read these provisions to require it to establish ambient standards for toxic substances at a "safe" level where feasible and at the lowest feasible level if safe levels were infeasible.[171] Since OSHA knew of no mechanism for establishing a "safe" level for carcinogens, it set standards for carcinogenic substances at the lowest feasible level without regard to the health effects at that level. In other words, for carcinogens and other nonthreshold pollutants, OSHA read the Act as requiring it to adopt a technology-based approach rather than a media-quality-based approach.

The petrochemical industy in the earlier *Benzene* case[172] and the textile industry in the *Cotton Dust* case[173] challenged OSHA's view. According to these industries, the statute commanded OSHA to adhere to a balancing approach for all chemicals; since section 3(8)'s definition of "standard" modified section 6(b)(5)'s feasibility requirement, OSHA could only promulgate media-quality-based standards that were reasonably necessary or appropriate. The industries further argued that since "reasonableness" connotes cost/benefit balancing,

---

166. *See* S. KELMAN, *supra* note 61, at 32-39; Kelman, *supra* note 149, at 114-15.

167. *See* W. PROSSER, *supra* note 65, at 23.

168. American Textile Mfrs. Inst. v. Donovan, 452 U.S. 490 (1981).

169. 29 U.S.C. § 652(8) (1976).

170. 29 U.S.C. § 655(b)(5) (1976).

171. Identification, Classification, and Regulation of Toxic Substances Posing a Potential Carcinogenic Risk, 42 Fed. Reg. 54,148 (1977).

172. Industrial Union Dep't, AFL-CIO v. American Petroleum Inst., 448 U.S. 607 (1980).

173. American Textile Mfrs. Inst. v. Donovan, 452 U.S. 490 (1981).

OSHA could only promulgate standards at ambient levels at which benefits outweighed costs.[174] The Fifth Circuit agreed with the industry's contentions in the *Benzene* case,[175] but the D.C. Circuit disagreed in the *Cotton Dust* case.[176]

The Supreme Court refused to decide the cost/benefit question in the *Benzene* case, but a plurality of the Court did find fault with OSHA's approach to carcinogens.[177] The Court held that OSHA could not promulgate a standard for a toxic substance, whether or not it was a carcinogen, unless it could sustain the affirmative burden of showing that the standard was "reasonably necessary and appropriate to remedy a *significant risk* of material health impairment."[178] In the *Cotton Dust* case, however, the Court squarely addressed industry's cost/benefit claims and rejected them. At the heart of the majority opinion was its conclusion that "cost-benefit analysis by OSHA is not required by the statute because feasibility analysis is."[179] The Court was persuaded that Congress had the power to mandate that the agency adopt a nonutilitarian technology-based approach and that it had done so.[180]

While the policy analyst should not be surprised or judgmental when the politician seems to ignore his appeals for more "rational" goals, he should be prepared to elaborate upon many of the disadvantages of adopting nonutilitarian goals. For example, the policy analyst might explain to the participants in the political debate who invoke symbolic and highly moral goals that they should not be surprised if those goals seem long in coming. They may in fact be gaining symbolic benefits at the expense of practical effectiveness.

Congressional articulation of health and environmental goals does not necessarily put the political forces to rest. Very often the locus of the political debate

---

174. *Id.* at 501; Industrial Union Dep't, AFL-CIO v. American Petroleum Inst., 448 U.S. 607, 634-40 (1980). Although it was not necessary to do so in either of the two cases, industry would presumably have argued further that OSHA could not promulgate infeasible standards even if the benefits of such standards would outweigh the costs because section 6(b)(5) places feasibility limits on section 3(8) standards. Section 6 of the Occupational Safety and Health Act empowers OSHA to promulgate occupational safety and health standards. 29 U.S.C. § 655 (1976). Section 3(8) defines "occupational safety and health standard" to be a standard that is "reasonable, necessary or appropriate to provide safe or healthful employment and places of employment." *Id.* § 652(8). Section 6(b)(5) specifies that in setting occupational safety and health standards for toxic materials and harmful physical agents, the agency must set the standard "which most adequately assures, to the extent feasible, . . . that no employee will suffer material impairment of health or functional capacity even if such employee has regular exposure to the hazard dealt with by such standard for the period of his working life." *Id.* § 655(b)(5).

175. American Petroleum Inst. v. OSHA, 581 F.2d 493 (5th Cir. 1978), *aff'd sub nom.* Industrial Union Dep't, AFL-CIO v. American Petroleum Inst., 448 U.S. 607 (1980).

176. AFL-CIO v. Marshall, 617 F.2d 636 (D.C. Cir. 1979), *aff'd sub nom.* American Textile Mfrs. Inst. v. Donovan, 452 U.S. 490 (1981).

177. Industrial Union Dep't, AFL-CIO v. American Petroleum Inst., 448 U.S. 607 (1980).

178. *Id.* at 607 (emphasis added). This holding has been criticized. *See* Rodgers, *Judicial Review of Risk Assessments: The Role of Decision Theory in Unscrambling the Benzene Decision,* 11 ENVTL. L. 301 (1981); *The Supreme Court, 1979 Term,* 94 HARV. L. REV. 75, 242-51 (1980).

179. American Textile Mfrs. Inst. v. Donovan, 452 U.S. 490, 509 (1981). The Court thus recognized the distinction between media-quality-based standards and technology-based standards and applied it in the context of the language of the OSHA Act.

180. Hence, it would appear that OSHA requires a technology-based approach. Yet, the Court reaffirmed the *Benzene* plurality's holding that OSHA may only promulgate standards that are necessary to remedy a significant risk. This approach would appear to be a media-quality-based one. The resulting mixed requirement can probably best be described as a technology-limited, media-quality-based strategy with a zero discharge goal.

merely shifts to the implementing agency. The implementation process often follows a familiar pattern. As the agency pursues the statute's inspiring goals through its typically hazy implementation instructions, the agency inevitably encounters strong opposition from those who argue that the agency is, in its unrestrained enthusiasm for those goals, ignoring the economic consequences of its activities. The losers of the Congressional debate, in other words, have a second chance to influence policy when the agency attempts to bring the statutory goals to earth.[181] After the agency has resolved the tensions in a more concrete fashion, the political battle is waged one further time before the reviewing courts.[182] Statutory deadlines are missed; administrative initiatives are constantly blunted by political and judicial review and the agency begins to lose its enthusiasm for its "mission." Indeed, it often begins to appear that the political system may have promised more than it could deliver.[183]

Economic factors must inevitably play an important role in the actual implementation of the goals that society sets for itself.[184] It is a simple economic reality

---

181. *See* Stewart, *The Reformation of American Administrative Law,* 88 HARV. L. REV. 1667 (1975).

182. *See* Currie, *Judicial Review Under the Federal Pollution Laws,* 62 IOWA L. REV. 1221 (1977); Stewart, *The Development of Administrative and Quasi-Constitutional Law in Judicial Review of Environmental Decisionmaking: Lessons from the Clean Air Act,* 62 IOWA L. REV. 713 (1977).

183. Another disadvantage of relying upon the political system to set health and environmental goals is the potential that such reliance offers for the insertion of other goals, or hidden agendas, that are only tangentially related to society's efforts to protect human health and the environment. A well-reported example of the insertion of a hidden agenda into an environmental statute is the provision in the 1977 amendments to the Clean Air Act that the EPA establish both an allowable emission limitation and a required "percentage reduction" of emissions for new fossil-fuel-fired stationary sources of pollutants. Clean Air Act § 111(a)(1), 42 U.S.C. § 7411 (Supp. V 1981). This provision was enacted at the behest of a bizarre coalition of environmentalists, who wanted to preserve pristine areas in the West where new sources would burn low sulfur coal, and eastern coal interests, who wanted to ensure that coal-fired power plants in the East were required to install scrubbers so that "dirty" eastern coal would not lose its competitive advantage over "clean" western coal. Whereas the environmentalists' concerns were clearly related to pollution problems, the provision owes its existence to the hidden agenda of the representatives in Congress of the eastern coal interests. *See* Ackerman & Hassler, *Beyond the New Deal: Coal and the Clean Air Act,* 89 YALE L.J. 1466, 1491-95 (1980). This ostensibly protective measure arguably left the eastern United States worse off than it was before enactment of the amendments. *See id.* at 1496. The lesson here is that when the political process is allowed to define nonutilitarian health and environmental goals, it may be expected to include an occasional red herring. Advocates of the political process are open to legitimate criticism on this score.

Similarly, the debate over the appropriate regulatory control technique can absorb other hidden agendas that are wholly unrelated to the primary goal of clean air or water. For example, the question whether decisions about individual sources of pollution should be made at a local or national level can be analyzed independently of the implications that the answer to the question has for the power relationships among the affected bureaucracies, but these latter otherwise irrelevant considerations are likely to motivate the bureaucratic participants in the debate more than the merits of the national versus local issue. Similarly, arguments concerning the likelihood that various regulatory techniques may result in "forum shopping" for "pollution havens" may be motivated more out of concern for a loss of a tax base than a concern that the media quality in pristine areas not be allowed to degrade. *See id.* at 1504-05. Finally, competitive concerns may motivate a company to favor a particular implementation technique that appears anomolous from the perspective of the environment versus economic growth. *See, e.g.,* Leone & Jackson, *supra* note 98, at 241.

184. Another independent reason for taking economic considerations into account in setting health and environmental goals is the possibility that large expenditures on pollution and workplace controls will put the United States at a competitive disadvantage with countries that have lower health and environmental goals. *See* SENATE COMM. ON PUBLIC WORKS, 93D CONG., 1ST SESS., LEGISLATIVE HISTORY OF THE WATER POLLUTION CONTROL ACT AMENDMENTS OF 1972 1133 (1973) (testimony of Paul V. McCracken) [hereinafter cited as HISTORY OF THE WPCA AMENDMENTS]. There is a great debate over

that the unlimited pursuit of the clean-up and nondegradation goals that emerge from the political system would cost an enormous sum. Indeed, it is probably impossible literally to meet the absolutist goals implicit in the "ample margin of safety" language of the toxics provisions of the Clean Air Act and Clean Water Act short of catastrophic economic disruption.[185] Cost is therefore an extremely important political consideration, and those with a strong economic interest in continued discharge can be depended upon to raise the question of economic and technological feasibility at every possible opportunity in the political debate before Congress, the agencies, and the courts.[186]

Congress has reacted to feasibility arguments in two ways. First, it has often simply ignored feasibility concerns and left absolutist media-quality-based goals in place. By adopting a stringent media-quality-based approach, Congress in effect has announced its decision to clean up dirty areas and maintain pristine areas "whatever the cost." The goals are established in the hope that the technology capable of reaching those goals either exists or will soon be developed[187] and that the implementing agency will have the political courage to resist the pressures generated by regulatees who must pay large sums to meet the goals.

In the alternative, Congress has explicitly acknowledged economic concerns by adopting a technology-based approach. Congress has incorporated feasibility considerations directly into health and environmental statutes through such language as "to the extent feasible,"[188] and "tak[ing] into account the age of equipment and facilities involved, the process employed, the engineering aspects of the application of various types of control techniques, process changes, [and] the cost of achieving

---

the reality of the threat that this poses for U.S. export markets. Indeed, it may well be that the retooling required by health and environmental controls will have the effect of enhancing the efficiency of production processes, thereby increasing the U.S. share of foreign markets. This may have been the effect of OSHA's cotton dust standard. Interview with Ray Marshall, Secretary of Labor, during promulgation of the standard (Apr. 25, 1982).

185. A. FREEMAN, R. HAVEMAN & A. KNEESE, *supra* note 141, ch. 2; Kneese, *Pollution and a Better Environment*, 10 ARIZ. L. REV. 10, 11-16 (1968).

186. Cost considerations have always been a part of the congressional debates. In arguing that cost considerations should be included in Clean Water Act standards, Senator Bentsen stressed that:

> If these programs cause too severe economic dislocations, if the economic and social benefits of pollution control programs bear no reasonable relationship to the costs involved in implementing them, then all of our best efforts to clean up the waterways could be defeated in a backlash against those of us who are working to clean up the environment.

HISTORY OF THE WPCA AMENDMENTS, *supra* note 184, at 1281. Senator Dominick succinctly argued that feasibility should be a consideration in promulgating standards under OSHA by suggesting that "[w]hat we are trying to do is put people to work, not put them out of work." LEGISLATIVE HISTORY OF OSHA, *supra* note 159, at 526.

187. *See* J. BONINE, THE EVOLUTION OF 'TECHNOLOGY-FORCING' IN THE CLEAN AIR ACT (BNA Env't Rep. Monograph No. 27, July 25, 1975); La Pierre, *Technology-Forcing and Federal Environmental Statutes*, 62 IOWA L. REV. 771, 776 (1977). Senator Muskie, the author of the 1970 Clean Air Act Amendments, was a strong proponent of this view:

> The first responsibility of Congress is not the making of technological or economical judgments—or even to be limited by what appears to be economically or technologically feasible. Our responsibility is to establish what the public interest requires to protect the health of persons. This may mean that people and industries will be asked to do what seems impossible at the present time, but if health is to be protected, these challenges must be met.

HISTORY OF THE WPCA AMENDMENTS, *supra* note 184, at 227.

188. Occupational Safety and Health Act § 6(b), 29 U.S.C. § 655(b)(5) (1976).

such [controls]."[189] The statutory language, however, rarely prescribes a finely tuned balancing of environmental considerations against feasibility considerations for setting technology-based standards. The language, rather, is aspirational. The agency is told to require the implementation of the "best available technology economically achievable,"[190] or the "best technological system of continuous emission reduction which . . . has been adequately demonstrated,"[191] or the technology capable of producing the "lowest achievable emission rate."[192] Economic considerations are relevant to the standard-setting process, but they are not meant to dominate it. The economic impact of achieving technology-based standards is to be considered along with a host of other factors that may legitimately affect the regulatory entity's decision.[193] By contrast, media-quality considerations play only a very small role in technology-based standard-setting. Congress has, in other words, announced to the world: "If we cannot have a perfectly clean workplace and environment, then we shall do the best that we can."[194]

While neither of these goals meets the policy-oriented economist's efficiency criterion, they are both rational *political* end points.[195] Society may rationally decide to make costs a relevant consideration to a media-quality approach only at the extremes and err on the side of overprotection. Similarly, a rational society might pledge itself to do the best that it can in pursuit of safe workplaces and a healthy environment even though it recognizes that even those efforts will not make those places safe or healthy in any absolute sense and even though they may, in the policy-oriented economist's opinion, cost too much.

If we acknowledge that it was rational for Congress to reject a narrow cost-benefit approach to pollution control and adopt either a media-quality-based approach or a technology-based approach to that problem, it is still necessary to ask which of the two alternative approaches (or, perhaps more appropriately, which combination of the two approaches) is best suited for health and environmental regulation of the chemical industry. This article now turns to a consideration of the factors that can enlighten that choice.

---

189. Clean Water Act § 304(b)(2)(B), 33 U.S.C. 1314(b)(2)(B) (Supp. V 1981).

190. Clean Water Act § 301(b)(2)(A), 33 U.S.C. § 1311(b)(2)(A) (Supp. V 1981).

191. Clean Air Act § 111(a), 42 U.S.C. § 7411 (Supp. V 1981).

192. Clean Air Act § 173(2), 42 U.S.C. § 7473 (Supp. V 1981).

193. EPA v. National Crushed Stone, 449 U.S. 64 (1980); American Paper Inst. v. Train, 543 F.2d 328, 346 (D.C. Cir.), *cert. dismissed,* 429 U.S. 967 (1976); Weyerhaeuser v. Costle, 590 F.2d 1011, 1012 (D.C. Cir. 1978).

194. Addressing the rationale for the technology-based effluent limitations of the 1972 amendments to the Clean Water Act, Senator Bayh explained: "The whole thrust of the bill is to force industry to do the best job it can do to clean up the nation's water and to keep making progress without incurring such massive costs that economic chaos would result." HISTORY OF WPCA AMENDMENTS, *supra* note 184, at 216.

195. Recently, Congress has expressed a keen interest in mandating that regulatory agencies balance costs and benefits in promulgating regulations. *See* S. REP. NO. 305, 97th Cong., 1st Sess. (1981) (discussing the Regulatory Reform Act (S. 1080)). None of the serious efforts, however, have sought to overturn the nonutilitarian approaches of the worker safety and environmental statutes.

V

THE CHOICE BETWEEN MEDIA-QUALITY-BASED AND TECHNOLOGY-BASED APPROACHES TO POLLUTION CONTROL

Congress has taken a variety of attitudes toward the choice between media-quality-based and technology-based approaches to pollution control. Only very rarely has Congress mandated one to the exclusion of the other.[196] More often, Congress has required agencies to implement both approaches simultaneously. For example, under the Clean Water Act the EPA must prescribe technology-based effluent limitations for new and existing sources[197] while the states with EPA approval must establish and enforce media-quality-based water quality standards.[198] The two approaches come together in the statute's prescription that every point source of water pollution have a discharge permit.[199] At the permit stage, the implementing agency must require implementation of the more stringent of the two requirements.[200] This strategy of mandating the more stringent of the two requirements typifies the statutes that adopt both approaches.[201] In practice, however, the implementing agency has a great deal of discretion in choosing which of the two approaches to emphasize.[202] Moreover, the statutes that exclusively require a media-quality-based approach often give the implementing agency the practical flexibility to transform the media-quality-based approach into a technology-based approach at the implementation stage.[203]

---

196. Standards under section 302 of the Clean Water Act are apparently intended to prescribe effluent limitations for point sources of water pollution strictly on the basis of media quality. 33 U.S.C. § 1312 (Supp. V 1981). However, the language, "can reasonably be expected to contribute to the attainment or maintenance of such water quality," *Id.* § 1312(a), leaves the door open for a technology-based approach, especially in light of the fact that the hearings on such standards are to "determine the relationship of the economic and social costs of achieving any such limitations . . . ." *Id.* § 1312(b)(1). This section has never been implemented by EPA.

Section 112 of the pre-1977 Clean Air Act prescribed a strictly media-quality-based approach to emissions limitations for hazardous pollutants. However, when faced with the practical impossibility of prescribing a media-quality-based standard for asbestos emissions from buildings being demolished, the EPA promulgated a technology-based standard. After this standard was overturned by the Supreme Court on the ground that it was not an "emission standard," Adamo Wrecking Co. v. United States, 434 U.S. 275 (1978), Congress amended the statute to allow the EPA to promulgate technology-based standards when "it is not feasible to prescribe or enforce" a media-quality-based emission standard. 42 U.S.C. § 7412(e)(1) (Supp. V 1981).

197. Clean Water Act §§ 301, 306, 33 U.S.C. §§ 1311, 1316 (1976).

198. *Id.* § 303(e), 33 U.S.C. § 1313(e)(1976).

199. *Id.* § 402(a), 33 U.S.C. § 1342(a)(1976).

200. *Id.*

201. *See Id.* § 307(a)(2), 33 U.S.C. § 1317(a)(2) (Supp. V 1981) (administrator may substitute media-quality-based toxic effluent *standard* for technology-based toxic effluent *limitation* if the standard "imposes more stringent requirements"); Clean Air Act § 165(a)(3), (4), 42 U.S.C. § 7475(a)(3), (4) (Supp. V 1981) (new major emitting facilities in prevention of significant deterioration areas must install "best available control technology" but may not be constructed at all if they will cause or contribute to a violation of a media-quality-based increment required by section 163, 42 U.S.C. § 7473 (Supp. V 1981), or a violation of a national ambient air quality standard).

202. The EPA has, for example, concentrated the bulk of its attention on promulgating technology-based effluent limitations under the Clean Water Act, even though it also has authority to implement a media-quality-based water quality standards approach under section 303. 33 U.S.C. § 1313 (1976).

203. *See infra* text accompanying notes 204-23.

A. The Transformation of the Media-Quality Approach into a Technology Approach

In the case of the primary ambient air quality standards, which are required to protect the public health with an "adequate margin of safety," the EPA has arguably adhered to the statute's absolutist goal without regard to the economic consequences.[204] The Clean Air Act leaves it up to the states to decide how the ambient air quality standards shall be reached and maintained within their borders. In theory, one would expect the states to determine a pollution load (for areas that currently meet the standard) or a pollution reduction load (for areas that do not currently meet the standard) and then parcel out this load among current and future emitters. The states could distribute the load according to historic use, emissions charges, marketable permits, or political clout as demonstrated in individual permitting proceedings.[205] In practice, however, the states rarely follow this logical progression. They do calculate pollution reduction loads for nonattainment areas because this is already required by the EPA.[206] They do not, however, always determine how much additional pollution it will take in attainment areas before the standards will be violated.[207] Instead, they often force individual sources in individual permitting proceedings to demonstrate no threat to the media-quality-based standards.[208] In neither case do the states allocate the pollution "pie" among sources according to any fixed formula. Rather, the states typically prescribe technology-based regulations for various categories of new and existing sources of pollutants, not unlike the EPA's technology-based standards for new sources,[209] and they hope that they can convince the EPA that the technology-based standards will not result in violations of the ambient air quality standards.[210] Occasionally, the states allow economic considerations to intrude still farther into the implementation process by providing for variances for individual sources upon a showing that the costs of the technology-based controls outweigh the benefits.[211]

---

204. There are at least two instances in which the EPA has apparently considered the costs of achieving the standard in establishing the "margin of safety." The agency did not require absolute safety for its lead standard; rather, it set the standard at the level that would, according to its statistical analysis, protect 99.5% of the most sensitive exposed human population. *See* Lead Indus. Ass'n v. EPA, 647 F.2d 1130, 1144 (D.C. Cir.), *cert. denied,* 449 U.S. 1042 (1980). Arguably, the fact that the EPA did not set the standard at the level that would protect 100% of the population constituted a bow to economic considerations.

In the EPA's decision to raise the national primary ambient air quality standard for photochemical oxidants, economic considerations allegedly played a role through the intervention of White House economic advisors. The Council on Wage and Price Stability "urged EPA to ignore the law—to consider costs, as well as medical information." *Executive Branch Review of Environmental Regulations: Hearings Before the Subcomm. on Environmental Pollution of the Senate Comm. on Environment and Public Works,* 96th Cong., 1st Sess. 28 (1979) (statement of Richard Ayres, Natural Resources Defense Council).

205. 40 C.F.R. § 52 (1980) (the EPA state implementation estimate pollution reduction load).

206. Clean Air Act § 172(a)(1), (b)(3), (8), 42 U.S.C. § 7503(a)(1), (b)(3), (8) (Supp. V 1981).

207. Interview with Terrel Kott, Permitting Officer, Texas Air Control Board (July 16, 1982).

208. *Id.*

209. Clean Air Act § 111, 42 U.S.C. § 7411 (Supp. V 1981).

210. This has been the pattern in Texas. Interview with Terrell Kott, Permitting Officer, Texas Air Control Board (July 8, 1982); *see also* Currie, *State Pollution Statutes,* 48 U. CHI. L. REV. 27, 65-69 (1981).

211. *See generally* Currie, *supra* note 210, at 53-62. The heavy reliance on this individual permitting process has two important practical consequences. First, in areas that currently meet the media-quality-

The conversion from a media-quality-based approach to a technology-based approach is even more dramatic in the case of toxic substances regulation under the Clean Air Act[212] and the pre-1977 Clean Water Act.[213] Both of these statutes mandate a stringently absolutist test regarding standards for the release of toxic substances. Yet, when pressed to set an air-quality-based standard for a carcinogenic substance, for which no "safe" level of exposure or "ample margin of safety" could realistically be established, the EPA ultimately considered economic feasibility and promulgated a technology-based standard.[214] Similarly, in light of the immense administrative difficulties that the EPA faced in promulgating water-quality-based effluent standards under the pre-1977 Clean Water Act, the EPA and several environmental groups compromised upon a process whereby the EPA would attempt to promulgate media-quality-based standards for a small number of very toxic pollutants and promulgate technology-based standards for categories of sources of sixty-five other pollutants.[215] Congress later amended the statute to incorporate this compromise retroactively.[216]

Finally, when many areas of the country failed to meet the media-quality-based national ambient air quality standards by the 1977 statutory deadline, Congress amended the Clean Air Act to address these "nonattainment" areas.[217] In addition to requiring the states to meet the standards "as expeditiously as practicable,"[218] the amendments require states to require major new stationary sources to install technology capable of achieving the "lowest achievable emission rate"[219] and existing sources to use "reasonably available control measures"[220] and "reasonably available control technology."[221] While not entirely superseding the former media-quality-based approach, the 1977 Amendments do significantly shift the focus from media-quality-based standards to technology-based standards. The

---

based standards the available load is in effect used up on a first-come-first-served basis. There is little opportunity for overall planning and few opportunities for a new source to "purchase" some emissions once the available increment has been allotted. Second, in areas that do not meet the media-quality-based standards, the failure to distribute the pollution reduction load in any explicit fashion means that deadlines will inevitably be missed as optimistic assumptions about the ability of technology-based standards to meet the media-quality-based standards are proven wrong. Federal law currently prevents the construction of major new sources of pollutants in areas that do not meet the national ambient air quality standards for those pollutants unless the new source achieves the "lowest achievable emission rate" (a technology-based standard) and procures an "offset" for its emissions so that total emissions are reduced. Clean Air Act § 173, 42 U.S.C. § 7503 (Supp. V 1981).

212. Clean Air Act § 112, 42 U.S.C. § 7412 (Supp. V 1981).

213. Clean Water Act § 307(a), 33 U.S.C. § 1317 (1976).

214. Occupational Safety and Health, Standard for Exposure to Vinyl Chloride, 39 Fed. Reg. 35,896 (1974) (codified at 29 C.F.R. § 1910.1017 (1982)). *See generally* Doniger, *Federal Regulation of Vinyl Chloride: A Short Course in the Law and Policy of Toxic Substances Control,* 7 ECOLOGY L.Q. 497, 563-64, 572 (1978).

215. Natural Resouces Defense Council v. Train, 8 Env't Rep. Cas. (BNA) 2120 (D.D.C. 1976), *rev'd in part on other grounds sub nom.* Natural Resources Defense Council v. Costle, 561 F.2d 904 (D.C. Cir. 1977); Hall, *The Control of Toxic Pollutants Under the Federal Water Pollution Control Act Amendments of 1972,* 63 IOWA L. REV. 609, 611-17 (1978).

216. Clean Water Act § 307(a), 33 U.S.C. § 1317(a) (Supp. V 1981).

217. Clean Air Act §§ 171-178, 42 U.S.C. §§ 7501-7508 (Supp. V 1981).

218. *Id.* § 7502(a). The statute sets a new attainment deadline of December 31, 1982, which may be extended for photochemical oxidants and carbon monoxide until December 31, 1987. *Id.*

219. *Id.* § 7503(2).

220. *Id.* § 7502(b)(2).

221. *Id.* § 7502(b)(3).

Texas Air Control Board, for example, has proposed to achieve the emissions reduction necessary to meet the new attainment deadline by simply incorporating the EPA guidelines for technology-based standards into the state's already existing technology-based regulations.[222]

The past decade has witnessed a fairly consistent trend toward transforming the pure media-quality-based approach into a technology-based approach. Sometimes this has been mandated explicitly by the legislature in amendments to the relevant statutes; at other times it has been accomplished *sub silentio* through administrative action. The following section of this article will examine many of the theoretical and practical advantages and disadvantages of both approaches in an attempt to explain this trend and to assess whether it is, by and large, a wholesome development for health and environmental regulation of the chemical industry.

B. A Critical Comparison

An adequate comparison of the media-quality-based and technology-based approaches to health and environmental regulation must begin with a set of criteria against which the two may be measured. This article adopts the following considerations as its list of evaluative criteria, recognizing that every policy analyst's list of evaluative criteria would probably differ in significant respects from that of any other analyst: (1) efficiency; (2) administrative feasibility; (3) survivability (under existing conditions of judicial and political review); (4) enforceability; (5) fairness and equity; and (6) ability to encourage technological advance.

1. *Efficiency.* While this article has argued that the "efficiency" criterion should not dictate health and environmental *goals,* efficiency is certainly an extremely important consideration in determining which *techniques* should be used to implement those goals. It does not profit even the most ardent environmentalist to waste valuable resources to achieve his goals. All other things being equal, if two approaches can reach the desired goal and the implementation of one costs more than the other, it is sensible to adopt the cheaper of the two approaches. The process of choosing the most efficient mechanism for achieving a given political goal is often referred to as "cost-effectiveness" analysis.[223]

Measured against only the efficiency criterion, the media-quality-based approach can theoretically be much more efficient than the technology-based approach. Media quality standards specify an ascertainable end point in the pursuit of which the implementing agency may choose from among many regulatory tools. Once the pollution reduction load is specified, the regulatory entity can implement positive incentives, such as emissions or effluent charges or marketable permits, that give the regulatees the maximum flexibility to achieve the media-

---

222. *See* TEXAS AIR CONTROL BOARD, TEXAS STATE IMPLEMENTATION PLAN: CONTROL STRATEGIES VI-33 & 34 (1979).

223. F. ANDERSON, *supra* note 9, at 9-12; M. GREEN & N. WAITZMAN, *supra* note 100, at 75; J. KRIER & E. URSIN, *supra* note 53, at 30-32; Baram, *supra* note 100, at 478.

quality goal at the least cost.[224] A regulatory scheme that simply divides up the pollution load on a pro rata basis or allocates the load according to historical use is justifiably condemned by economists as wasting societal resources that could be put to better use.[225]

The efficiency advantage of the media-quality-based approach may, however, be overstated in the context of the chemical industry. Unless two firms discharge the same substance into the same receiving medium, a relatively rare occurrence for the chemical industry, the marketable permits incentive approach is unavailable. When there is no market in which to bargain, the initial sale of the permit is the last, and the technique becomes indistinguishable from a one-time-only "charge." The "charge" approach still has efficiency advantages, but these too can be overstated. The regulatory entity under the "charge" approach must estimate what charge will induce the necessary cleanup to meet the predetermined media quality goal. Yet the regulatory entity cannot know how various charges will affect the conduct of the regulatees absent knowledge about the technologies available to the regulatee and the costs of implementing those technologies.[226] The agency may in effect set the charge at the level that will induce the adoption of a particular technology. If technologies come in discrete untunable units, the charge may in practice give the source as little choice as a technology-based command.[227]

---

224. Economists have for two decades urged policymakers to implement incentive-based schemes for achieving pollution control goals. *See Economic Analysis and the Efficiency of Government, Part 6—Economic Incentives to Control Pollution: Hearings Before the Subcomm. on Priorities and Economy in Government of the Joint Economic Comm.*, 92d Cong., 1st Sess. (1971) [hereinafter cited as *Economic Analysis Hearings*]; F. ANDERSON, *supra* note 9; A. KNEESE & C. SCHULTZE, *supra* note 18; Solow, *The Economist's Approach to Pollution and its Control*, 123 SCIENCE 498 (1971). Economists have also been uniformly critical of the technology-based approach for its failure to achieve adequate media quality efficiently. *See* Henderson & Pearson, *Implementing Federal Environmental Policies: The Limits of Aspirational Commands*, 78 COLUM. L. REV. 1429 (1978); Ruff, *supra* note 9, at 314-20; Comment, *Forcing Technology: The Clean Air Act Experience*, 88 YALE L.J. 1713, 1719 (1979). In theory both the media-quality-based approach and the technology-based approach could be implemented to accord with the market paradigm either through "command-and-control" style standards or through "charges." Although the "charges" technique is more commonly associated with a media-quality-based performance standard, the technique can be used to implement, presumably at less cost, a technology-based approach. *See* F. ANDERSON, *supra* note 9, at 33. The marketable permits technique, however, is not adaptable to the technology-based approach to pollution control.

225. HISTORY OF CAA AMENDMENTS of 1970, *supra* note 159, at 752 (letter from Manufacturing Chemists' Ass'n); A. KNEESE & C. SCHULTZE, *supra* note 18, at 26; Freeman & Haveman, *supra* note 149, at 62 n.16. Another possible advantage of a media-quality-based approach is that for some health and environmental effects it accepts a level of media quality at which there is no harm so that no pollution reduction is necessary. *See* R. STEWART & J. KRIER, *supra* note 35, at 570. Discharge into pristine waters, however, would violate the nondegradation policy and thus may be inconsistent with a stringent media-quality-based approach.

A similar response can be made to the argument that media-quality-based standards are superior because they can be met through more efficient techniques such as dispersion enhancement and flow augmentation. *See, e.g.*, A. KNEESE & C. SCHULTZE, *supra* note 18, at 86; Solow, *supra* note 224, at 501. The courts and Congress have frowned upon dispersion enhancement as a media-quality technique under the Clean Air Act. 42 U.S.C. § 7423 (Supp. V 1981); *see also* Kennecott Copper Corp. v. Train, 526 F.2d 1149 (9th Cir. 1975), *cert. denied*, 425 U.S. 935 (1976). The situation is more ambiguous under the Clean Water Act. *See* Ford Motor Co. v. EPA, 567 F.2d 661 (6th Cir. 1977) (flow augmentation not unlawful in absence of EPA regulations to the contrary).

226. *See* F. ANDERSON, *supra* note 9, at 175.

227. There is still a practical difference between the use of a charge in implementing a media-quality-based approach and a technology-based effluent limitation. The charge under the media-quality-based approach will require the implementation of that technology necessary to meet the media-quality-based standard. The effluent limitation under the technology-based approach will be set irrespective of media

The efficiency concept is generally less relevant to the technology-based approach than the media-quality-based approach. The regulatory entity under the technology-based approach searches about for technologies that are capable of reducing emissions or effluent from a given category of sources and then prescribes numerical limitations or reductions based on the capabilities of the "best" of these technologies. Cost is certainly a relevant consideration in determining which of a variety of available technologies is "best."[228] The "best efforts" goal itself, however, is ambiguous with respect to economic efficiency because media quality considerations are largely irrelevant.[229] Under the pure technology-based approach, the receiving media is never too dirty nor is it ever clean enough short of zero discharge. The marginal balancing analysis that the efficiency criterion demands is foreign to the technology-based approach.

In practice the regulatory entity examines the costs of the various available technologies, compares their efficacy, and looks for a point at which costs begin to escalate much more rapidly than efficacy.[230] Indeed, the agencies may simply establish a "rule of thumb" of X dollars per pound of removal and look for technologies that meet this rule of thumb in promulgating technology-based standards for several industries.[231] While these approaches may be equitable and in some sense cost-effective, they are not necessarily efficient ways of pursuing an overall societal goal of cleaning up the receiving media.[232] Moreover, the technology-based approach in practice can bias pollution control in favor of capital-intensive "white elephant" technologies which may be ineffective in the long run.[233]

There is a sense, however, in which the technology-based approach is efficient. The promulgation of an ambient media-quality-based standard does not tell an

---

quality. Even this distinction, however, narrows in the case of the discharge of toxics into pristine waters when the media-quality-oriented nondegradation policy would require the charge to be so high as to induce the implementation of the very best technology available. This would be largely indistinguishable from a technology-based effluent limitation based on the best available technology.

228. All of the federal statutes mandating a technology-based approach specify cost as a relevant consideration. *See supra* note 19.

229. *See Implementation Hearings, supra* note 105, at 58 (testimony of Jan Olson); HISTORY OF CAA AMENDMENTS of 1970, *supra* note 159, at 226 (statement of Sen. Edmund Muskie: "Emissions standards alone will not—and probably cannot—guarantee ambient air quality which will protect the public health."); B. MITNICK, *supra* note 46, at 405.

The efficiency of the technology-based approach can be enhanced by subdividing categories of industrial sources into smaller and smaller subcategories. As the categories became smaller, individual cost considerations play a larger role. *See* F. ANDERSON, *supra* note 9, at 10-11.

230. This was essential to the approach the EPA took in setting technology-based standards for vinyl chloride under section 112 of the Clean Air Act, 42 U.S.C. § 7412 (Supp. V 1981). *See* Doniger, *supra* note 214, at 575-76.

231. This is *sub silentio* the position that the Texas Air Control Board takes toward setting "best available technology" limitations for new sources of volatile organic compounds in its individual permitting proceedings. Interview with Terrell Kott, Permitting Officer, Texas Air Control Board (July 17, 1982).

232. *See* HISTORY OF THE WPCA AMENDMENTS, *supra* note 184, at 1117, 1144-45 (testimony of Russell E. Train: "the imposition of enormous incremental costs unsupported by water quality benefits attained will divert an inordinate amount of our resources from other environmental priorities, where they could be much more effectively utilized"); *Id.* at 1123 (testimony of Paul V. McCracken); *see also* Roberts & Farrell, *The Political Economy of Implementation*, in APPROACHES TO CONTROLLING AIR POLLUTION 152 (A. Friedlander ed. 1978); Letter from W.J. Driver, Manufacturing Chemists Ass'n., to Hon. Jennings Randolph (Sept. 1, 1970), *reprinted in* HISTORY OF CAA AMENDMENTS OF 1970, *supra* note 159, at 750.

233. *See* A. KNEESE & C. SCHULTZE, *supra* note 18, at 80.

individual source much about what is expected of it. Unless the media-quality-based standard is implemented through technology-based standards binding on individual sources or through a historically based allocation scheme, the source has little basis for planning for the future. The value of its marketable permit may rise or fall, and its charge may have to be raised or lowered to reflect the addition of new sources to the receiving media. The source may face constant uncertainty about the regulatory entity's future expectations. This uncertainty can hinder capital investment and precipitate economically wasteful investment decisions.[234] A technology-based new source performance standard tells the regulatee exactly what is expected and can therefore facilitate private planning.[235] This may be particularly valuable in the chemical industry where the regulatory entity cannot be expected to promulgate media-quality-based standards for all of the hundreds of toxic pollutants simultaneously. Technology-based standards can address all of a given plant's toxic discharges, thereby avoiding the "pollutant of the month syndrome" that often afflicts the media-quality-based approach.[236]

2. *Administrative Feasibility.* Whatever its theoretical advantages, a regulatory tool that cannot be implemented in the real world is useless. Practical considerations of administrative feasibility must therefore play a large role in the choice between the media-quality-based and technology-based approaches. Indeed, the history of the implementation of the federal pollution control statutes indicates that administrative feasibility has been the dominant consideration. The media-quality-based approach has been abandoned repeatedly because it proved to be, in the minds of the regulatory decisionmakers, administratively infeasible.

The media-quality-based approach demands huge quantities of detailed information about the effects of a discharger's wastes on the quality of the receiving medium, and uncertainties fill the inevitable informational voids. We have already seen that quantifying the effects of a particular plant's discharges on humans and environmental entities is a formidable informational challenge that is ultimately policy dominated.[237] The uncertainties that plague this process, when combined with the large unknowns inherent in modeling the fate of toxic substances in receiving media, should dampen the enthusiasm of even the most ardent instrumental rationalist.[238]

234. *See* Pierce, *The Choice Between Adjudicating and Rulemaking for Formulating and Implementing Energy Policy,* 31 HASTINGS L.J. 1, 21-27 (1979).

235. *See* H. R. REP. NO. 92-911, 92d Cong., 2d Sess. 397 (1972) (additional views of Reps. Abzug & Rangel); S. REP. NO. 403, 90th Cong., 1st Sess. 4 (1967); B. MITNICK, *supra* note 46, at 354.

236. If a mixed strategy is adopted by the regulatory entity, however, this planning advantage of the technology-based approach may disappear. If, for example, the agency requires sources to meet the more stringent of media-quality and technology standards, compliance with a technology-based new source performance standard will not necessarily protect the source from a later arriving more stringent media-quality-based standard. The Clean Water Act, which takes this mixed approach, however, cushions the harshness of this possibility by protecting the owner of a new source for up to 10 years from more stringent future standards. Clean Water Act § 306(d), 33 U.S.C. § 1317(d) (Supp. V 1981).

237. *See supra* notes 112-18 and accompanying text.

238. The absence of adequate models for tracing the effects of pollutants back to their sources was one of the primary factors that Congress relied upon in mandating the technology-based approach of section 301 of the Clean Water Act. *See* S. REP. NO. 92-414, 92d Cong., 1st Sess. 8 (1971) ("Water quality standards . . . often cannot be translated into effluent limitations—defendable in court tests, because of the

If the regulatory entity operates under a statute that requires a "margin of safety," the regulator's task under the media-quality-based approach may become downright impossible. For some pollutants the agency may be able to rely upon existing epidemiological studies to determine a "no-effect" level and add a margin of safety to that level to arrive at a media-quality standard. It could be argued, however, that even this level would result in harm to some very sensitive persons or environmental entities.[239] Moreover, the nature of the chronic effects of other pollutants is such that there may be no scientifically acceptable way to determine a "no-effect" level, and *a fortiori* no basis for specifying a margin of safety. For such chemicals the margin of safety requirement simply cannot be implemented in a straightforward media-quality-based fashion. When faced with this dilemma, the EPA has implemented the media-quality requirement through a technology-based approach. In explaining its toxics effluent standards under the Clean Water Act, for example, the agency made this conversion explicit. Referring to the "elastic" nature of the margin of safety concept, the agency suggested that:

> In any case where a discharge is allowed, on a spectrum ranging from certain safety (a prohibition) to that uncertain point where harmful effects are caused and safety ends, a logical break point is struck where the very best that control technology can do is required.[240]

The media-quality-based approach also requires economic and technical information about the regulated sources. If the implementing agency chooses any allocation technique other than a marketable permit approach,[241] it must have some idea of the costs faced by the various regulatees for various degrees of polution control.[242] This in turn requires at least a superficial knowledge of the technologies available to the sources of a given pollutant and the cost of implementing those technologies.

The technology-based approach, by contrast, requires the regulatory entity to struggle with only the latter sort of information, albeit perhaps in greater detail than under the media-quality-based approach.[243] Rather than resolve extremely

imprecision of models for water quality and the effects of effluents in most waters."); H. R. REP. NO. 92-911, 92d Cong., 2d Sess. 394 (1972) (additional views of Reps. Abzug and Rangel).

The problem of modeling the fate of toxic pollutants continues to dominate congressional consideration of the Clean Water Act, *see* PROHLMAN REPORT, *supra* note 105, at 48, despite optimistic projections in the early 1970's that adequate models would be forthcoming within five years. *See* HISTORY OF THE WPCA AMENDMENTS, *supra* note 184, at 1116-17 (testimony of Russell E. Train).

239. *See* Thompson, *Margin of Safety as a Risk-Management Concept in Environmental Legislation,* 6 COLUM. J. ENVTL. L. 1 (1979).

240. Proposed Toxic Pollutant Effluent Standards, 41 Fed. Reg. 12,576 (1976). Even though the statute required an "ample margin of safety," the D.C. Circuit upheld this approach in Environmental Defense Fund v. EPA, 598 F.2d 62 (D.C. Cir. 1978), and in Hercules, Inc. v. EPA, 598 F.2d 91 (D.C. Cir. 1978).

241. The marketable permit approach in theory requires no information about the economic and engineering problems of implementing various controls. The regulatory entity under this approach merely sells the pollution load to the highest bidder. Presumably those sources that face the greatest cleanup costs will bid higher for the right to pollute. *See* B. MITNICK, *supra* note 46, at 389-95.

The marketable permit allocation technique, however, is not likely to be very useful in health and environmental regulation of the chemical industry. *See supra* text accompanying notes 225-26.

242. *See* F. ANDERSON, *supra* note 9, at 5, 35-36; Rose-Ackerman, *supra* note 104, at 575; Roberts & Stewart, Book Review, 88 HARV. L. REV. 1644, 1653 (1975).

243. The media-quality-based approach in theory requires only marginal cost data from the relevant

complex and value-laden questions about the toxic effects of chemicals, the regulatory entity need only group the relevant industries into categories and subcategories, identify potentially applicable technologies, assess the implementation costs, and choose the technology that best fits the statutory standard. Although this is a formidable task in its own right, it is much simpler than assessing environmental risks in addition to the costs of cleanup technologies. Moreover, implementation of the technology-based approach is at least possible, whereas a strict application of the margin of safety version of the media-quality-based approach cannot be accomplished without a certain degree of administrative dissembling.

The technology-based approach also offers the path of least political resistance. Since this approach does not directly implicate important moral questions about the value of human lives and endangered environmental entities, the standard-setting process is less likely to precipitate the highly emotional controversy that can accompany the promulgation of media-quality-based standards. The important issues under the technology-based approach are unexciting questions of engineering and economics that generally appear better suited for expert resolution than for public debate. Moreover, since the technology-based approach focuses upon industrial categories rather than individual bodies of water or air, a proposed technology-based standard will almost certainly attract greater attention among the regulated industry than it will among the potentially affected public. Public participation will therefore be minimized, and matters can be quietly resolved between the regulator and the regulatees.

Finally, the technology-based approach gives the administrative decisionmaker greater discretion than the media-quality-based approach. Statutes mandating a media-quality-based approach are typically straightforward—"protect the public health with an ample margin of safety." While it may be impossible to implement this directive, it is not difficult to comprehend. Statutes mandating a technology-based approach, however, typically use more vague terms such as "best technology adequately demonstrated" and specify a host of factors that further cloud the meaning of the guiding phrase. This hint at the need for clarification through expertise greatly enhances the administrator's discretion. In practice, the agency has more leeway to bargain with the interested parties and to bend to such political pressures as the process generates.[244]

The technology-based approach is therefore likely to be more attractive to bureaucrats than the media-quality-based approach. Likewise, the regulated firms may feel more comfortable with a process that gives them room to bargain with the agency in low visibility proceedings that depend heavily on industry-supplied information, especially when the agency may be sympathetic toward their plight. Administrative convenience may go a long way toward explaining the historical

sources to estimate the effects of various levels of charges on the dischargers. F. ANDERSON, *supra* note 9, at 36. The pure technology-based approach requires the agency to survey all appropriate pollution control technologies for efficacy and expense and then choose among them. *See id.* at 12; A. KNEESE & C. SCHULTZE, *supra* note 18, at 1; R. STEWART & J. KRIER, *supra* note 35, at 557. In the not atypical case where there is only one source of a pollutant and only two or three alternative technologies, however, the amount of information needed for both approaches would seem to be roughly equivalent.

244. *See* F. ANDERSON, *supra* note 9, at 158, 164.

conversion of the media-quality-based approach to a technology-based approach. This historical development, while understandable, is not necessarily sound. Before embarking upon the technology-based approach toward setting effluent limitations for conventional pollutants under the Clean Water Act, Administrator Ruckelshaus warned that:

> [I]n completely obliterating the admittedly complex relationship between municipal and industrial effluent and water quality, the Senate may have sacrificed wisdom for simplicity. It is simpler to address the problem in terms of available technology than in terms of complex treatment and ambient water quality relationships. But it is my conviction that in the environment as elsewhere, the renunciation of known complexity on the altar of simplicity is the essence of bad government policy.[245]

3. *Enforceability.* No regulatory scheme can function properly if its requirements may be violated with impunity. The regulatory mechanisms that society establishes to influence the conduct of employers and polluters must ultimately be backed by a realistic threat of sanctions for cheaters.[246] Yet, before society can punish someone for cheating, it must specify with sufficient clarity the conduct that will bring forth government sanctions. While this can be done generically, it is often more effective to put each individual regulatee on notice of what is expected of it through a permit system.

At first glance it may appear that the media-quality-based approach is easier to enforce. When the regulatory entity allocates the pollution reduction load, it can simply assign a numerical effluent or emissions limitation to each permitholder[247] or, in the case of the workplace where no allocation is necessary, specify an ambient concentration for all workplaces. The enforcer then requires only an accurate mechanism for monitoring sources. Indeed, enforcement could be further simplified by requiring sources to monitor their own discharges with some acceptable monitoring device that is not subject to undetected tampering.[248]

245. HISTORY OF THE WPCA AMENDMENTS, *supra* note 184, at 1183.

246. It has been suggested that some regulatory techniques compatible with the media-quality-based approach, such as marketable permits and charges, do not require as much vigilance by the policy authority because compliance is in the self-interest of the polluter. *See* B. MITNICK, *supra* note 46, at 351-52. The regulatory entity, however, must still have an enforcement capacity to ensure that sources are not "cheating on their tax returns" or do not emit more than their marketable permits allow. *See Economic Analysis Hearings, supra* note 224, at 1284 (testimony of David R. Zwick); F. ANDERSON, *supra* note 9, at 93; Rose-Ackerman, *supra* note 13, at 396-97; Roberts & Stewart, *supra* note 242, 1652 n.34. This problem can be alleviated somewhat by requiring self-monitoring so that cheating can be easily detected. *See* F. ANDERSON, *supra* note 9, at 93. But even with self-monitoring, enforcement would be necessary to ensure that sources did not cheat by diverting emissions to unmonitored vents and outfalls or (in the case of air pollution) by expanding "fugitive" emissions at the expense of monitored emissions. *See* Wolozin, *supra* note 106, at 236.

247. The individual source emission or effluent limitation in the case of a political or historical allocation would be set by the regulatory entity according to its allocation formula. In the case of a marketable permit system, it would be the sum total of the source's permits. In the case of a charge system, a specific limitation would not be necessary. The enforcing authority would simply take note of the discharge for purposes of calculating the tax at some later time. Under all of the approaches, however, there must be a numerical measure of pollution and a mechanism for monitoring sources in accordance with that measure.

248. The major pollution control statutes have provisions allowing the regulatory agency to require self-monitoring. Occupational Safety and Health Act § 8(c), 29 U.S.C. § 657(c) (1976); Clean Water Act § 308(a)(4)(A)(iii), 33 U.S.C. § 1318(a)(4)(A)(iii) (1976); Clean Air Act §§ 114(a)(1)(C), 42 U.S.C. § 7414 (a)(1)(C) (Supp. V 1980).

The enforcement agency, however, faces numerous practical limitations that greatly reduce the ease with which it can police the media-quality-based approach.[249] Accurate monitoring devices do not exist for all toxic chemicals.[250] Such monitoring equipment as does exist is often very expensive to purchase and use.[251] Sampling a single stack for sulfur dioxide and particulates can consume two or three man-days and entail over two thousand dollars in equipment costs.[252] The monitoring costs for a source of many different chemical pollutants can be even higher.[253] Even when the EPA exercises its authority to require self-monitoring, the cost of installing the equipment can be so high as to be arbitrary and capricious.[254]

Enforcement costs for a technology-based aproach can run considerably less than media-quality monitoring costs. While technology-based standards normally specify numerical limitations for individual facilities, the limiations are based upon the pollution removal capacity of a particular technology or its equivalent. The enforcement officer can normally infer that the numerical limitations are being met from the fact that the technological components are running properly, without monitoring actual discharges. This greatly simplifies the enforcement process because the enforcement officer need only check to see if the pollution control equipment is being properly used and maintained and observe recorded evidence that the equipment was in fact turned on during the relevant enforcement period.[255]

---

249. For a thorough treatment of the problems of monitoring under a media-quality-based approach, see F. ANDERSON, *supra* note 9, ch. 4.

250. There is, for example, some question whether an accurate monitoring device exists for monitoring stack emissions of sulfur dioxide. *See* 40 Fed. Reg. 46,240 (1975); B. MITNICK, *supra* note 46, at 382; Roberts & Farrell, *supra* note 232, at 163.

251. *See* PROHLMAN REPORT, *supra* note 105, at 48; F. ANDERSON, *supra* note 9, at 91-101; B. MITNICK, *supra* note 46, at 382; Wolozin, *supra* note 104, at 235. Relatively inexpensive monitoring devices do exist. For example, environmental protection officials in the decades before the recent federal environmental legislation routinely used bioassays to monitor stream quality near an industrial outfall. *Implementation Hearings, supra* note 105, at XXV (testimony of Douglas Costle: "EPA soon will form rules to incorporate standardized bioassay tests in its testing regulations, anticipating that bio-testing will play a larger future in toxics control."); *id.* at 490 (testimony of John Convery); *id.* at 33 (testimony of W.E. Garrison). The bioassay directly measures the impact of water on living aquatic species by observing whether a member of a test species dies during the duration of the test. This monitoring device is inexpensive, but it is very crude. It does not reveal the amount of various pollutants in the waters which might cause chronic effects in aquatic organisms and humans who consume aquatic organisms. It is therefore especially inappropriate for monitoring discharges of toxic substances. Nevertheless, it has been suggested that the EPA be allowed to grant media-quality-based waivers from its technology-based standards for toxic water pollutants on the strength of bioassays demonstrating that the receiving water is not immediately toxic to test organisms. *Id.* at 22 (statement of Dr. John Hernandez).

252. *See* Roberts & Farrell, *supra* note 232, at 165.

253. A monitoring protocol now exists for measuring all 65 of the toxic pollutants listed in the NRDC consent decree. A complete scan for all of these chemicals costs approximately $2,000 per sample. Interview with Dr. Elinor Zimmerman, Office of Water Planning, U.S. Environmental Protection Agency (Mar. 18, 1982).

254. *See* Asarco, Inc. v. EPA, 14 Env't Rep. Cas. (BNA) 1340 (9th Cir. 1980) (EPA arbitrary and capricious in requiring smelter to install self-monitoring device at estimated cost of over $300,000); F. ANDERSON, *supra* note 9, at 97 (cost of installing continuous monitor for water discharges of total organic carbon and chemical oxygen demand estimated at $5,000-$10,000 plus maintenance).

255. *See* B. MITNICK, *supra* note 46, at 403. Recording devices for documenting that a machine is operating are very inexpensive. Since they can, of course, be tampered with, the enforcement officer may need to make surprise visits or take other action to discourage tampering. The difficulties with forging

While technology-based standards are probably easier to police, it may be more difficult to convince a judge or a jury to levy an effective penalty for a violation of a technology-based standard than for a media-quality-based standard. It may be more impressive to the fine setter that the defendant has violated a standard that is designed to protect human health than a standard designed only to compel the implementation of the best available technology. On the other hand, the fine setter may be swayed by the fact that a technology-based standard is usually set at a level that someone, perhaps a competitor, has been able to meet. Yet, even this may be unconvincing to a judge or juror when presented with the defendant's assertion that compliance with the technology-based standard will cause its financial demise, especially if the prosecutor can point to no definite environmental harm that will flow from the violation.[256]

Moreover, the overall ease of enforcement of technology-based standards may be offset somewhat by the diminished likelihood that any given enforcement action will result in penalties high enough to deter future violations.[257] Still, ease of detecting violations is a significant advantage, especially in a regime in which citizens are allowed to prosecute violations of the standards on their own initiative.[258]

4. *Survivability.* Any standard or requirement that an agency imposes upon regulatees must ultimately survive review by designated reviewing institutions. Health and environmental standards are no exception to the general presumption in American administrative law that agency actions are subject to judicial review. Under the current environment statutes, the agency must demonstrate that a standard is not "arbitrary and capricious";[259] OSHA must establish that its standards are supported by "substantial evidence on the record as a whole."[260] In addition, agency actions must survive less formal, but still very real, review by the political entities that have the power to influence and control the implementing agency's

---

chart recordings are sufficiently great, however, that this should not pose a great threat to the technology-based enforcement strategy.

256. *See* F. ANDERSON, *supra* note 9, at 12; A. KNEESE & C. SCHULTZE, *supra* note 18, at 402.

257. The agency can avoid the problem of low penalties if it has the authority to administer civil penalties and if it uses that power to assess penalties that roughly approximate the economic savings to the source that resulted from its failure to comply plus some additional "deterrent" penalty. The EPA at one time had promulgated a civil penalty policy to guide prosecutors in determining what to ask for in judicial enforcement actions. *See* U.S. Environmental Protection Agency, Civil Penalty Policy For Major Source Violations of Clean Air Act and Clean Water Act, 8 ENV'T REP. BNA 2011 (Apr. 11, 1978); *see also* Ohio *ex rel.* Brown v. Dayton Malleable, Inc., 13 Env't. Rep. Cas. (BNA) 2189 (Ohio C.P. Montgomery County 1979). This policy has since been repealed. Section 120 of the Clean Air Act, 42 U.S.C. § 7420 (Supp. V 1980), allows the EPA to assess noncompliance penalties in an amount sufficient to deter future violations. *See* Assessment and Collection of Noncompliance Penalties by EPA, 40 C.F.R. § 66.1 (1982); Orloff, *Buttressing the Traditional Approach to Enforcement of Environmental Requirements: Noncompliance Penalties Under the Clean Air Act,* 9 ENVTL. L. RPT. (ENVTL. L. INST.) 50,029 (1979); Zener & Olstein, *Pollution Regs: Problems for Lawyers, Accountants,* Legal Times of Wash., Sept. 22, 1980, at 11.

258. All of the major environmental statutes have citizen enforcement provisions. *See* Toxic Substances Control Act § 20, 15 U.S.C. § 2619 (1982); Clean Water Act § 505, 33 U.S.C. § 1365 (1976); Resource Conservation and Recovery Act § 7002, 42 U.S.C. § 6972 (1976 & Supp. V 1981); Clean Air Act § 304, 42 U.S.C. § 7604 (Supp. V 1980). OSHA does not, however, provide for citizen enforcement.

259. 33 U.S.C. § 1319 (Supp. V 1981); 42 U.S.C. § 7607 (1982).

260. 29 U.S.C. § 660(a) (1976).

conduct.[261] If the agency's actions do not satisfy the relevant Congressional committees, the agency head faces difficult oversight hearings and possible loss of funds or statutory authority. If those actions do not satisfy the President, the heads of OSHA and the EPA, which are not independent agencies, can lose their jobs. The political supervision described here is not usually the detailed case-by-case review of the judiciary, although it can be detailed and particularized at times; rather, it is the understanding that an agency official rapidly acquires that its actions must be explainable to the satisfaction of politicians whose constituents perceive themselves harmed by those actions.

The inevitability of judicial and political review may have an impact upon the choice of regulatory approaches. If one approach is likely to survive judicial and political review more readily than the other, then proponents of stringent health and environmental goals may prefer the first approach and regulated industries the second.

a. *Judicial Reivew.* The EPA's technology-based standards have taken a terrible beating in the courts of appeals. The agency's initial effort in the mid-1970's to promulgate national technology-based effluent limitations for new and existing sources under the Clean Water Act precipitated more than 250 court challenges.[262] After many of these cases were consolidated, the courts of appeals across the country decided sixteen appeals,[263] all but three of which resulted in remands to the agency on one or more substantive issues.[264] While many of the remands involved only minor components of much larger standards, the EPA has had difficulty in establishing virtually all of the engineering techniques that it has adopted for setting technology-based standards. The agency has been most successful when it can point to an existing source which currently meets its proposed effluent limitation.[265] Similarly, when the EPA can point to an existing pilot plant that can

---

261. *See* Pierce & Shapiro, *Political and Judicial Review of Agency Action,* 59 TEX. L. REV. 1185 (1981).

262. *See* Note, *Effective Regulation of Point Sources Under the 1972 Federal Water Pollution Control Act,* 10 GA. L. REV. 983, 1019 (1976).

263. There are sixteen written opinions involving appeals from EPA's BPT effluent limitation regulations under Clean Water Act §§ 301(b)(1)(A), 304(b)(1)(A), 33 U.S.C. §§ 1311, 1314 (1976): Consolidated Coal Co. v. Costle, 604 F.2d 239 (4th Cir. 1979), *rev'd,* 449 U.S. 64 (1980); National Crushed Stone Ass'n v. Costle, 601 F.2d 111 (4th Cir. 1979), *rev'd,* 449 U.S. 64 (1980); BASF Wyandotte Corp. v. Costle, 598 F.2d 637 (1st Cir. 1979); Weyerhaeuser Co. v. Costle, 590 F.2d 1011 (D.C. Cir 1978); American Iron & Steel Inst. v. EPA, 568 F.2d 284 (3rd Cir. 1977); Marathon Oil Co. v. EPA, 564 F.2d 1253 (9th Cir. 1977); Appalachian Power Co. v. Train, 545 F.2d 1351 (4th Cir. 1976); American Paper Inst. v. Train, 543 F.2d 328 (D.C. Cir.), *cert. dismissed,* 429 U.S. 967 (1976); National Renderers Ass'n v. EPA, 541 F.2d 1281 (8th Cir. 1976); E.I. du Pont de Nemours & Co. v. Train, 541 F.2d 1018 (4th Cir. 1976), *aff'd,* 430 U.S. 112 (1977); CPC Int'l, Inc. v. Train, 540 F.2d 1329 (8th Cir. 1976); Tanners' Council of Am. v. Train, 540 F.2d 1188 (4th Cir. 1976); American Petroleum Inst. v. EPA, 540 F.2d 1023 (10th Cir. 1976); FMC Corp. v. Train, 539 F.2d 973 (4th Cir. 1976); American Frozen Food Inst. v. Train, 539 F.2d 107 (D.C. Cir. 1976); Hooker Chemicals & Plastics v. Train, 537 F.2d 620 (2d Cir. 1976); CPC Int'l Inc. v. Train, 515 F.2d 1032 (8th Cir. 1975).

264. *See* Weyerhaeuser Co. v. Costle, 590 F.2d 1011 (D.C. Cir. 1978); California & Hawaiian Sugar Co. v. EPA, 553 F.2d 280 (2d Cir. 1977); American Paper Inst. v. Train, 543 F.2d 328 (D.C. Cir.), *cert. dismissed,* 429 U.S. 967 (1976).

265. *See* Weyerhaeuser Co. v. Costle, 590 F.2d 1011 (D.C. Cir. 1978); American Frozen Food Inst. v. Train, 539 F.2d 107 (D.C. Cir. 1976); American Meat Inst. v. EPA, 526 F.2d 442 (7th Cir. 1975). *But see* Tanners' Council of Am. v. Train, 540 F.2d 1188 (4th Cir. 1976); Hooker Chemicals & Plastics Corp. v. Train, 537 F.2d 620 (2d Cir. 1976).

meet its proposed limitation, the agency can usually survive judicial review.[266] However, when the EPA cannot point to an exemplary or pilot plant in the same industrial category or subcategory and therefore relies upon its prediction that an existing treatment technology will transfer from one industry to another, the courts are more skeptical, and the agency usually loses.[267] In the rare cases in which the EPA has gone beyond existing technology to project that the industry will be able to develop a technology capable of meeting the prescribed effluent limitations at some future date, the EPA has lost two out of three appeals.[268]

A large proportion of the many remands have resulted from the reviewing courts' dissatisfaction with the EPA's numerical calculation of the level of pollution removal that a given technology is capable of producing.[269] Even though the reviewing courts might agree with the EPA's identification of the "best available" or "best practicable" technology, it may be skeptical that the technology, when installed in most plants, can reduce pollution to the extent required by the effluent limitation.[270] This unfortunate impasse results from Congress's general failure to empower the EPA to prescribe the technologies itself; the agency may only promulgate limitations based upon the technologies that it has identified. While this limitation on the EPA's power has the salutary purpose of maximizing an individual source's freedom to develop different technologies capable of meeting the same limitation, the practical effect has been to hamstring the EPA's efforts to set any limitations at all.

The flood of remands ultimately deprived the EPA of the benefit of the Supreme Court's holding in *E.I. du Pont de Nemours, Inc. v. Train*[271] that the EPA

---

266. American Paper Inst. v. Train; 543 F.2d 328 (D.C. Cir.), *cert. dismissed,* 429 U.S. 967 (1976); CPC Int'l, Inc. v. Train, 540 F.2d 1329 (8th Cir. 1976); FMC Corp. v. Train, 539 F.2d 973 (4th Cir. 1976); American Iron & Steel Inst. v. Train, 526 F.2d 1027 (3d Cir. 1975).

267. *See* Tanners' Council of Am. v. Train, 540 F.2d 1188 (4th Cir. 1976); American Petroleum Inst. v. EPA, 540 F.2d 1023 (10th Cir. 1976), *cert. denied,* 430 U.S. 922 (1977); FMC Corp. v. Train, 539 F.2d 973 (4th Cir. 1976); Hooker Chemicals & Plastics Corp. v. Train, 537 F.2d 620 (2d Cir. 1976); American Iron & Steel Inst. v. Train, 526 F.2d 1027 (3d Cir. 1975); American Meat Inst. v. EPA, 526 F.2d 442 (7th Cir. 1975). *But see* Weyerhaeuser Co. v. Costle, 590 F.2d 1011 (D.C. Cir. 1978); California & Hawaiian Sugar Co. v. EPA, 553 F.2d 280 (2d Cir. 1977); American Frozen Food Inst. v. Train, 539 F.2d 107 (D.C. Cir. 1976).

268. *Compare* FMC Corp. v. Train, 539 F.2d 973 (4th Cir. 1976); American Iron & Steel Inst. v. Train, 526 F.2d 1027 (3d Cir. 1975) *with* American Paper Inst. v. Train, 543 F.2d 328 (D.C. Cir.), *cert. dismissed,* 429 U.S. 967 (1976).

269. *See* National Renderers Ass'n v. EPA, 541 F.2d 1281 (8th Cir. 1976); FMC Corp. v. Train, 539 F.2d 973 (4th Cir. 1976); Hooker Chemicals & Plastics Corp. v. Train, 537 F.2d 620 (2d Cir. 1976); American Iron & Steel Inst. v. Train, 526 F.2d 1027 (3d Cir. 1975); American Meat Inst. v. EPA, 526 F.2d 442 (7th Cir. 1975); CPC Int'l, Inc. v. Train, 515 F.2d 1032 (8th Cir. 1975).

270. Perhaps the most egregious example of judicial second-guessing in all of the appeals is CPC Int'l Inc. v. Train, 540 F.2d 1329 (8th Cir. 1976). The EPA established an effluent limitation for new sources in the Corn Wet Milling Industry of 10 pounds of total suspended solids per thousand standard bushels of corn. The Eighth Circuit held this action to be arbitrary and capricious in CPC Int'l Inc. v. Train, 515 F.2d 1032 (8th Cir. 1975). The EPA responded to the remand by attempting to provide greater record support for its limitation. The court, however, was unpersuaded. CPC Int'l, Inc. v. Train, 540 F.2d 1329 (8th Cir. 1976). The court allowed that a standard of 25 pounds per thousand standard bushels could be supported by the record, but not the original standard of 10 pounds per thousand standard bushels. The court therefore remanded to the EPA "with directions to it to revise the TSS standard to 25 pounds per MSBu or to compile additional evidence to support a lower standard." *Id.* at 1345. Not surprisingly, the EPA took the none-too-subtle hint. 40 C.F.R. § 406.15 (1982).

271. 430 U.S. 112 (1977).

had the power to promulgate national effluent limitations. The EPA responded to only a very few of the remands,[272] and even when it did, it could not always persuade the remanding court of the validity of its standards.[273]

The EPA's batting average in the courts of appeals is not much better for its technology-based new source performance standards (NSPS) under the Clean Air Act.[274] Even with the wisdom gained from its humiliating Clean Water Act experience, the EPA could not in 1977[275] draft a new source performance standard for lime manufacturing plants that could survive in the generally sympathetic D.C. Circuit.[276]

The EPA's technology-based standard setting under both the Clean Air and Clean Water Acts has been plagued by the intractable problem of excursions and upsets.[277] The agency readily acknowledges that even the best technologies do not perform flawlessly under strenuous real world conditions. Startups and upsets (such as those caused by unexpected rainfall or equipment breakdowns) can swamp the pollution control technology and cause a facility's discharge to exceed an effluent limitation that is predicated upon normal operating conditions.[278] The dilemma is initially attributable to the requirement that the EPA write effluent limitations rather than prescribe actual technologies. Yet even if the agency could prescribe technologies, it would face the enforcement problem of limiting the number of upsets to those actually required by bona fide production disruptions. The EPA initially proposed to address this conundrum by wisely exercising its enforcement discretion.[279] The regulated sources are, not surprisingly, invariably dubious about this "solution" in light of the fact that any citizen may sue to

---

272. *See* CPC Int'l, Inc. v. Train, 540 F.2d 1329 (8th Cir. 1976); *cf.* Appalachian Power Co. v. Train, 620 F.2d 1040 (4th Cir. 1980).

273. *See* CPC Int'l, Inc. v. Train, 540 F.2d 1329 (8th Cir. 1976) (discussed *supra* note 270).

274. Although many of the new source performance standards have gone into effect without challenge, industry has usually been successful in securing a remand when those standards have been challenged. *Compare* National Lime Ass'n v. EPA, 627 F.2d 416 (D.C. Cir. 1980); Essex Chem. Corp. v. Ruckelshaus, 486 F.2d 427 (D.C. Cir. 1973), *cert. denied,* 416 U.S. 969 (1974) (remand on two relatively minor issues); Portland Cement Ass'n v. Ruckelshaus, 486 F.2d 375 (D.C. Cir. 1973), *cert. denied,* 417 U.S. 921 (1974), *on hearing subsequent to remand sub nom.* Portland Cement Ass'n v. Train, 513 F.2d 506 (D.C. Cir.) (per curiam), *cert. denied,* 423 U.S. 1025 (1975) *with* Sierra Club v. Costle, 15 Env't Rep. Cas. (BNA) 2137 (D.C. Cir. 1981); National Asphalt Pavement Ass'n v. Train, 539 F.2d 775 (D.C. Cir. 1976).

275. The New Source Performance Standard (NSPS) for lime manufacturing plants was promulgated on May 3, 1977. Standards of Performance for New Stationary Sources: Lime Manufacturing Plants, 42 Fed. Reg. 22,506 (1977).

276. National Lime Ass'n v. EPA, 627 F.2d 416 (D.C. Cir. 1980).

277. *See* Corn Refiners Ass'n v. Costle, 594 F.2d 1223 (8th Cir. 1979); Weyerhaeuser v. Costle, 590 F.2d 1011 (D.C. Cir. 1978); Marathon Oil Co. v. EPA, 564 F.2d 1253 (9th Cir. 1977); United States Steel Corp. v. Train, 556 F.2d 822 (7th Cir. 1977); CPC Int'l, Inc. v. Train, 540 F.2d 1329 (8th Cir. 1976), *cert. denied,* 430 U.S. 966 (1977); American Petroleum Inst. v. EPA, 540 F.2d 1023 (10th Cir. 1976); FMC Corp. v. Train, 539 F.2d 973 (4th Cir. 1976); Essex Chem. Corp. v. Ruckelshaus, 486 F.2d 427, 432-33 (D.C. Cir. 1973), *cert. denied,* 416 U.S. 969 (1974); Portland Cement Ass'n v. Ruckelshaus, 486 F.2d 375, 398-99 n.91 (D.C. Cir. 1973), *cert. denied,* 417 U.S. 921 (1974).

278. *See* Weyerhaeuser v. Costle, 590 F.2d 1011, 1056-57 (D.C. Cir. 1978); FMC Corp. v. Train, 539 F.2d 973, 986 (4th Cir. 1976).

279. In Marathon Oil Co. v. EPA, 564 F.2d 1253, 1272 (9th Cir. 1977), the EPA refused to include a provision for upsets in the permit, preferring instead to "set a standard by using a 97.5 or 99 percent 'confidence interval,' and then to address the expected one percent or more of 'excursions' when they actually occur. If . . . a violation . . . was not the fault of the permit holder, EPA will informally exercise its discretion not to prosecute."

enforce an effluent limitation that is reflected in a discharge permit.[280] Yet, if the effluent limitation itself must provide for predictable upsets, a source might abuse its privilege to upset entitlements.[281] And if the EPA must set the limitation so high that it can be reached under upset conditions, as one court has apparently suggested,[282] then the limitation will be far too lenient. While the courts of appeals have split on the issue of whether to require the inclusion of upset conditions as a factor in setting the limitations, most have required the EPA to do more than allude to its enforcement discretion.[283] Most recently, the EPA has decided to write excursion and upset provisions into its general permitting regulations under § 402 of the Clean Water Act.[284] This merely delegates the problem to the permit writers and enforcers.

OSHA's experience with judicial review of technology-based standards has been less bleak. All of OSHA's standards for carcinogens and its standards for lead and cotton dust have been technology-based because the point of economic and technological infeasibility was reached before the level of toxic substance in the workplace was deemed safe.[285] In only one case did a court of appeals reject OSHA's conclusions concerning the feasibility of a standard.[286] In the only case in which the Supreme Court has considered the record's support for a technology-based standard, the Court upheld OSHA's cotton dust standard over vigorous industry objections that OSHA had made wholly unsupported assumptions and had manipulated the existing studies in an unreasonable way to support its conclusions.[287]

In sharp contrast to its mixed experience with technology-based standards, the EPA has been reasonably successful in securing judicial approval of its media-quality-based standards. Industrial firms challenged only one of the EPA's initial national ambient air quality standards. While that challenge was successful, it

---

280. Marathon Oil Co. v. EPA, 564 F.2d 1253, 1273 (9th Cir. 1977); Bethlehem Steel Corp. v. Train, 544 F.2d 657, 660 (3d Cir. 1976) ("There is no authorization to block a citizen's suit under section 505 even though the agency believes that the suit should not go forward.").

281. Weyerhaeuser v. Costle, 590 F.2d 1011 (D.C. Cir. 1978); CPC Int'l, Inc. v. Train, 540 F.2d 1320 (8th Cir. 1976); American Petroleum Inst. v. EPA, 540 F.2d 1023 (10th Cir. 1976), *cert. denied,* 430 U.S. 922 (1977) (court emphasizes the temptation to store pollutants for excess discharges).

282. National Lime Ass'n v. EPA, 627 F.2d 416 (D.C. Cir. 1980).

283. *Compare* Marathon Oil Co. v. EPA, 564 F.2d 1253 (9th Cir. 1977); Essex Chem. Corp. v. Ruckelshaus, 486 F.2d 427, 432-33 (D.C. Cir. 1973), *cert. denied,* 416 U.S. 969 (1974); Portland Cement Ass'n v. Ruckelshaus, 486 F.2d 375, 398-99 n.91 (D.C. Cir. 1973), *cert. denied,* 417 U.S. 921 (1974); Getty Oil v. Ruckelshaus, 467 F.2d 1349 (3d Cir. 1972), *cert. denied,* 409 U.S. 1125 (1973) *with* Corn Refiners Ass'n v. Costle, 594 F.2d 1223 (8th Cir. 1979); Weyerhaeuser Co. v. Costle, 590 F.2d 1011 (D.C. Cir. 1978).

284. American Petroleum Inst. v. EPA, 661 F.2d 340 (5th Cir. 1981).

285. *See* American Textile Mfrs. Inst., Inc. v. Donovan, 452 U.S. 490 (1981); American Iron & Steel Inst. v. OSHA, 6 O.S.H. Cas. (BNA) 1451 (3d Cir. 1978); Society of Plastics Indus., Inc. v. OSHA, 509 F.2d 1301 (2d Cir. 1975); Synthetic Organic Chem. Mfrs. Ass'n v. Brennan, 506 F.2d 385 (3d Cir. 1974), *cert. denied,* 423 U.S. 830 (1975); Industrial Union Dep't, AFL-CIO v. Hodgson, 499 F.2d 467 (D.C. Cir. 1974).

286. American Petroleum Inst. v. OSHA, 581 F.2d 493 (5th Cir. 1978), *aff'd sub nom.* Industrial Union Dep't, AFL-CIO v. American Petroleum Inst., 448 U.S. 607 (1980).

OSHA's emergency temporary standards for 14 carcinogens, 38 Fed. Reg. 20,074 (1973), were rejected for lack of support on the toxicity issue in Dry Color Mfrs. Ass'n v. Department of Labor, 486 F.2d 98 (3d Cir. 1973), and Synthetic Organic Chem. Mfrs. Ass'n v. Brennan, 503 F.2d 1155 (3d Cir. 1974), *cert. denied,* 420 U.S. 973 (1975). The permanent standards, however, were upheld in Synthetic Organic Chem. Mfrs. Ass'n v. Brennan, 506 F.2d 385 (3d Cir. 1974), *cert. denied,* 423 U.S. 830 (1975).

287. American Textile Mfrs. Inst., Inc. v. Donovan, 452 U.S. 490 (1981).

resulted in a relatively limited remand requiring the EPA to provide greater record support for one of its assertions.[288] The EPA apparently learned from this experience, and its revised standard for photochemical oxidants survived challenges from both environmentalists and industry.[289] The reduction models with which the EPA calculates pollution reduction loads have also easily survived judicial review, even when petitioners have pointed to other models that appear to depend upon fewer brash assumptions.[290] There have been no challenges to the EPA's hazardous emission standards under section 112 of the Clean Air Act,[291] and the EPA's media-quality-based toxics effluent standards, promulgated under section 307(a) of the Clean Water Act, easily survived judicial review in the D.C. Circuit.[292]

From a reading of the EPA's history, it would appear that the courts are inclined to review technology-based standards more carefully than media-quality-based standards. Judges may be less hesitant to substitute their judgment for that of the agency on questions of engineering and economics, or it may be that lawyers can characterize an agency action as erroneous and arbitrary more easily when those kinds of issues are involved. When the question before the court concerns the intricacies of toxicology and meteorology, the judges apparently feel uneasy with the conclusion that the agency's decision lacks support. Yet, this reasoning does not explain why most of OSHA's technology-based standards have survived so well, even though the standard of review for OSHA's technology-based standards has traditionally been viewed as more exacting.[293] One explanation for this apparent inconsistency is that OSHA's standards, like the EPA's media-quality-based standards (but unlike the EPA's technology-based standards), are directly tied to human health.[294] OSHA may only impose a technology-based standard when the workplace is already unsafe, and even after the standard is in place the workplace may still pose risks to workers. The direct link between a standard and worker health may make the courts more reluctant to overrule OSHA's standards. It is also possible that OSHA has simply done a better job than the EPA in justifying its standards.[295]

288. Kennecott Copper Corp. v. EPA, 462 F.2d 846 (D.C. Cir. 1972). Interestingly, the EPA did not respond to the remand. The agency may have read more into the court's opinion than was required. *See* McGarity, *Substantive and Procedural Direction in Administrative Resolution of Science Policy Questions: Regulating Carcinogens in EPA and OSHA,* 67 GEO. L. REV. 729 (1979).

289. American Petroleum Inst. v. Costle, 609 F.2d 20 (D.C. Cir. 1979).

290. *See* Republic Steel Corp. v. Costle, 621 F.2d 797 (6th Cir. 1980); Alabama Power Co. v. Costle, 13 Env't Rep. Cas. (BNA) 1993, 2032 (D.C. Cir. 1979); Cleveland Elec. Illuminating Co. v. EPA, 572 F.2d 1150 (6th Cir. 1978); Mission Indus., Inc. v. EPA, 547 F.2d 123 (1st Cir. 1976); Texas v. EPA, 499 F.2d 289 (5th Cir. 1974). *But see* Cincinnati Gas & Elec. Co. v. EPA, 578 F.2d 660 (6th Cir. 1978), *cert. denied,* 439 U.S. 1114 (1979).

291. There was a challenge to the section 112 standard for vinyl chloride, but it was not pursued. *See* Doniger, *supra* note 214, at 581-85.

292. Environmental Defense Fund, Inc. v. EPA, 636 F.2d 1267 (D.C. Cir. 1980); Hercules, Inc. v. EPA, 598 F.2d 91 (D.C. Cir. 1978).

293. *See* McGarity, *supra* note 288, at 791-92.

294. This explanation is even more true after Industrial Union Dep't, AFL-CIO v. American Petroleum Inst., 448 U.S. 607 (1980), because OSHA must first determine that current exposure levels pose a "significant risk" to workers before the agency may promulgate a feasibility-based standard.

295. OSHA may be aided in this by the fact that OSHA always allows opposing counsel to cross-examine witnesses and otherwise conducts its hearings in a relaxed trial-like fashion while the EPA's

One can perhaps draw the tentative conclusion that pure technology-based standards may have greater difficulty in surviving judicial review.[296] The evidence on this score, however, which is derived largely from a single agency's experience with two statutes mandating across-the-board technology-based standards, is not especially compelling. Nevertheless, the ability to survive judicial review would appear to be a factor that weighs in favor of media-quality-based standards.

b. *Political Review.* The evidence concerning political review of the two approaches is extremely sparse, and it supports few conclusions. Since OSHA's health standards usually have both media-quality and technology components, it is impossible to tell whether the considerable political attention that has surrounded many of those standards is directed toward the agency's scientific or engineering judgments. While the first round of the EPA's ambient air quality standards generated little political debate, the more recent revisions are causing intense political interest both in the White House and in Congress.[297] On the other hand, the EPA's recent technology-based standard for steam electric power plants has also received a great deal of political attention,[298] as did its recent regulation requiring that lead be phased out of gasoline.

While it seems reasonable to surmise that most technology-based standards, which are directed at narrow industrial categories, will not achieve the high political profile of media-quality-based standards for toxic substances that could affect the health of millions, it is impossible to draw that conclusion from the available evidence. In any event, one could equally plausibly argue that the most effective political review is the low-key suggestion by a member of the agency's appropriation committee at the behest of an important constituent who is lagging behind his competitors in installing the technology that the EPA proposes as the basis for a technology-based standard.[299]

5. *Equity.* In addition to its great concern for practicality and economic efficiency, this country has always exhibited an often countervailing concern for equity.[300] Although pollution control has not raised questions of fairness or equity with nearly the frequency and forcefulness of many other social programs, important equity issues do reside under the surface of the pollution control debate.

---

effluent limitations hearings are generally of the "paper hearing" variety. *See* Stewart, *supra* note 182, at 731.

296. This is apparently the conclusion of many of the commentators. *See* F. ANDERSON, *supra* note 9, at 12-13, 186; B. MITNICK, *supra* note 46, at 374, 406.

297. American Petroleum Inst. v. Costle, 609 F.2d 20 (D.C. Cir. 1979); *see* Verkuil, *Jawboning Administrative Agencies: Ex Parte Contacts by the White House,* 80 COLUM. L. REV. 943 (1980); Letter from Robert J. Ranch, Environmental Defense Fund attorney, to Douglas Costle, Legal Times of Washington (1979); *see also Iron and Steel Officials Object to EPA Draft Particulate Impact Analysis,* INSIDE E.P.A., Oct. 29, 1982, at 11-12.

298. *See* Ackerman & Hassler, *supra* note 183, at 1542-43; Banks, *EPA Bends to Industry Pressure on Coal New Source Performance Standards—And Breaks,* 9 ECOLOGY L.Q. 67, 83-91 (1980).

299. For an interesting example of very critical political review by a Congressman at the behest of constituents who were *ahead* of their competitors in installing pollution control technology and therefore wanted the EPA to enforce more stringent standards, see *Hearings on EPA Regulatory Delay Impact on Industry and State Environmental Programs: Connecticut Before a Subcomm. of the House Comm. on Government Operations,* 97th Cong., 1st Sess. (1981).

300. *See* A. OKUN, EQUALITY AND EFFICIENCY, THE BIG TRADEOFF (1975).

These concerns can also have an impact on the choice between the media-quality-based and technology-based approaches.

Any health and environmental standard that does not achieve very close to zero risk will over time shift wealth from those who are harmed by the discharge of hazardous substances to those who benefit thereby. As we have seen, the tort system rarely forces the beneficiaries to compensate the losers.[301] For many polluting activities, the class of beneficiaries—the consumers of manufactured products—overlaps with the class of losers. Much of the chemical industry probably fits within this category of activities for which the winners and losers are largely coterminous. There are, however, exceptions to this more-or-less equitable arrangement. Workers in the chemical industry generally receive higher exposures than other consumers.[302] Moreover, scientists are increasingly able to isolate groups of people who, because of genetic factors, are at a higher risk of contracting disease from low exposure to chemicals than the rest of the population.[303] The EPA has made an effort in promulgating its national ambient air quality standards to identify groups of unusually susceptible persons and to protect a large proportion of them from harm.[304] OSHA, too, has written special provisions into its standards to protect sensitive workers.[305]

The media-quality-based approach can address these inequities directly.[306] As the ambient standard is lowered the disparity weakens. The technology-based approach, however, does not address this equity concern at all because it does not dwell on the quality of the receiving media. In the workplace, the Occupational Safety and Health Act's combined media-quality-based and limited technology-based approach adequately addresses the worker/consumer inequity by requiring the receiving media to be free of significant risks, but it allows the inequity to creep back in when it is infeasible to protect susceptible populations.

Any health and environmental standard that directly or indirectly requires large capital expenditures can create interfirm inequities.[307] Professors Leone and Jackson have recently undertaken pathbreaking economic studies on the interfirm

301. *See supra* text accompanying notes 65-92.

302. There is a large literature on this particular inequity. *See, e.g.*, D. BERMAN, DEATH ON THE JOB (1978); C. GERSUNY, WORK HAZARDS AND INDUSTRIAL CONFLICT 143 (1981) ("If there can be no such thing as a riskless society then the distribution of these risks is a matter of grave importance. Are the risks faced by the Rockefellers of this world similar to the risks faced by the manual labor force?"); J. PAGE & M. O'BRIEN, BITTER WAGES (1973); R. SCOTT, MUSCLE AND BLOOD (1974).

303. *See* OFFICE OF TECHNOLOGY ASSESSMENT, THE ROLE OF GENETIC TESTING IN THE PREVENTION OF OCCUPATIONAL DISEASE (1982); McGarity & Schroeder, *supra* note 50, at 1010-12.

304. Lead Indus. Ass'n, Inc. v. EPA, 647 F.2d 1184 (D.C. Cir.), *cert. denied,* 449 U.S. 1042 (1980); National Ambient Air Quality Standard for Lead, 43 Fed. Reg. 46,246 (1978). There is less evidence that the EPA takes this approach in promulgating its hazardous emissions limitations under section 112 of the Clean Air Act, 42 U.S.C. § 7412 (Supp. V 1981).

305. 29 C.F.R. § 1910.1018 (1981) (arsenic); *id.* § 1910.1025 (lead); *id.* § 1910.1045 (acrylonitrile); *see* Rothstein, *Employee Selection Based on Susceptibility to Occupational Illness,* 81 MICH. L. REV. 1379 (1983).

306. Media-quality-based standards can also address interspecies inequities directly. The secondary ambient air quality standards are intended to do this, but the fact that harm to other species is encompassed within the term "human welfare" indicates that the standard-setter is to take an anthropocentric approach toward setting these standards.

307. *See* Small Refiners Lead Phase-Down Task Force v. EPA, 705 F.2d 506 (D.C. Cir. 1983) (small petroleum refiners and large petroleum refiners disagree over proper standard for lead gasoline additive).

impacts of capital-intensive health and environmental requirements.[308] From this standpoint the technology-based approach may be less "equitable" than the media-quality-based approach. The technology-based approach groups an industry into various categories and subcategories and prescribes the same effluent limitation for all firms within a given category or subcategory, many of whom compete with one another in product markets. While this approach may at first glance appear equitable because it treats equals equally,[309] it may appear inequitable from the standpoint of the individual sources within a given category. Some may have to undertake greater capital expenditures than others, and (perhaps more importantly) some will have to defer capital investments in production capacity to a greater extent than others.[310]

Technology-based standards for many industries are calculated with reference to the best performers in a given category. The best performers at the time that the standard is promulgated will necessarily face lower cleanup costs than the poorer performers. All of these factors will operate to the competitive advantage of some firms and to the detriment of others.[311] This shift in the relative positions of the competing firms may have very little effect on the product market. However, if the cost increase forces marginal firms out of the product market, the regulation will certainly appear inequitable to them,[312] and the net result could be less competition and artificially high prices. Moreover, if a substantial proportion of the "marginal"[313] firms are smaller firms with smaller income streams and less access to capital, the result may appear inequitable from a populist, small business-oriented perspective.[314]

A related interfirm inequity of the technology-based approach is the disparity

308. *See* Leone & Jackson, *supra* note 98.

309. This is not precisely true to the extent that an individual source may secure a variance. *See* E.I. du Pont de Nemours & Co. v. Train, 430 U.S. 112, 123 n.10 (1977); Clean Water Act § 301(c), 33 U.S.C § 1311(c) (1976).

310. For a detailed explanation of how regulation-induced deferral of capital investments in production capacity can disproportionately harm a firm in comparison to its competitors, see Leone & Jackson, *supra* note 98, at 234-39.

311. Leone and Jackson demonstrate the effect of the "best practicable technology" standards under section 301 of the Clean Water Act on the competitive positions of firms in the pulp and paper industry. *Id.* at 254.

312. The shutdown of marginal firms need not appear inequitable to the rest of society. In a sense, to the extent that such firms were surviving because they were able to put the costs of doing business off on others, their demise is well-deserved. They may have been forced out of business by the market in any event. *See id.* at 257; Letter from Alvin L. Alm to Joe G. Moore (Feb. 6, 1976), *reprinted in* National Commission on Water Quality, Final Report 44-45 (1976) ("Few industries face the threat of plant closures and many of those plants which are projected to close down rather than invest in pollution control equipment are those which could not remain economically viable over the next decade in the absence of water pollution control."); *see also Economic Analysis Hearings*, *supra* note 224, at 1220 (statement of Robert K. Davis).

313. In using the term "marginal" here, I mean marginal with respect to income flow and large and immediate regulation-induced capital expenditures. In this sense it is more likely that small firms fall into this category.

314. This argument has been raised in the political debates. *See* HISTORY OF THE WPCA AMENDMENTS, *supra* note 184, at 1355 (statement of Sen. Nelson); National Commission on Water Quality, Final Report 17 (1976). It probably also explains why Vice President Bush ordered the EPA to re-examine its lead phase-down rule immediately prior to the date that it became effective for both large and small refiners. *See* Small Refiner Lead Phase-Down Task Force v. EPA, 705 F.2d 506, 512 n.9 (D.C. Cir. 1983).

in treatment usually afforded to new firms and existing firms.[315] Virtually all true technology-based standards set separate requirements for new sources. This practice is justified to the extent that retrofit costs for existing plants are much larger than the costs of designing pollution control into a new plant.[316] The distinction also has greater political attractiveness because the potential owners of new sources are not always as well repesented in the political debates. It is easy for a political body to load the burden of pollution control onto sources that do not exist. The disparity will, however, appear inequitable to the new source owner after the standard has been promulgated. Moreover, the new source/old source distinction has the considerable practical disadvantage of discouraging existing firms from retiring inefficient and heavily polluting old plants and replacing them with newer and more efficient equipment.[317]

The media-quality-based approach can create similar interfirm inequities. To the extent that media-quality-based standards are implemented through technology-based implementation techniques, the same interfirm inequities exist. If the agency allocates the pollution reduction load in accordance with historical use, the interfirm inequities should be reduced because the pollution reduction required will not depend upon the performance of the best among a category of competitors. The historical allocation approach does, however, put new sources at a disadvantage relative to existing sources when the available increment of pollution has been consumed. A stringently implemented nondeterioration policy will create a similar new source/old source inequity.[318]

Implementing a media-quality-based approach through incentive-oriented techniques, such as charges and marketable permits, will also create inequities among existing sources in areas where the media-quality-based standards are exceeded, because *any* regulation-induced cleanup will have some impact on the relative competitive positions of the existing firms.[319] This should not, however, be equivalent to the impact of a technology-based standard because any particular source will have the flexibility to implement its own optimum pollution control technology. Moreover, a firm can cushion the impact of an incentive-based allocation scheme by paying the charge or purchasing pollution rights out of short term revenues and thereby avoiding the deferral of capital investments in production capacity. Finally, incentive-oriented techniques do not distinguish between new and old sources. Both classes pay the same for an equivalent amount of pollution.

---

315. *See* B. MITNICK, *supra* note 46, at 405.

316. *See generally* Huber, *The Old-New Division in Risk Regulation,* 69 VA. L. REV. 1025 (1983).

317. *See id.* at 1073. Ackerman and Hassler suggest that the large differential between the stringent new source performance standards for coal-fired steam electric power plants and the sulfur dioxide removal requirements for old sources under the state implementation plans had the net effect of increasing the amount of acid rain over that which would have resulted from a less stringent NSPS. *See* Ackerman & Hassler, *supra* note 183, at 1522-25.

318. A stringent PSD policy would preclude *any* construction of new sources in areas that are already clean. In practice, the PSD policy allows new sources if they can demonstrate that they are beneficial overall and if they implement the best available technology. *See* Hines, *A Decade of Nondegradation Policy in Congress and the Courts: The Erratic Pursuit of Clean Air and Clean Water,* 62 IOWA L. REV. 643, 645 (1977). This creates the same new source/old source inequity that exists in a technology-based system.

319. *See* Leone & Jackson, *supra* note 98, at 239.

6. *Technological Advance.* The policy-oriented economists are right to insist that policymakers recognize that health and environmental protection requires tradeoffs. We cannot have as much health and as many environmental amenities as we might like without sacrificing other important material resources. Nevertheless, the economy and technology are not static. Advances in technology can bring about changes that greatly diminish the agony of some tradeoffs. Pollution control problems that today appear intractable may disappear tomorrow with the advent of new technology. Indeed, the possibility of technological advance is itself a strong reason for abandoning the strict economic approach, which in practice often reduces to a static assessment of the costs and benefits of regulatory requirements under existing technological constraints. The government can, of course, encourage technological advance by directly funding engineering and environmental research. Government can also encourage technological progress by molding its regulatory requirements to give private firms, operating under competitive conditions, an incentive to conduct their own research and development efforts.[320] Congress might, for example, decide to "force" technology by prescribing requirements that are capable of being met only through the implementation of newly evolving or nonexistent technologies.[321] Alternatively, Congress might attempt to "nudge" technology by making it very expensive for sources to pollute. The ability of a regulatory approach to encourage technological advance might therefore influence the choice between the media-quality-based and technology-based approaches.

The technology-based approach, when it is functioning properly, can effectively force companies to install technologies that other companies with similar production processes and wastes already use. When the regulatory entity can point to a competitor that is using a technology, it can justifiably insist that the laggard install the same or equivalent technology.[322] Technology-based standards can thus bring all of the firms in an industrial category up to the level of its best performers, and this upgrading activity can in theory be initiated quite rapidly.[323] Technology-based standards are likely to be even more effective in forcing new sources to implement the best of existing technology, because it should be easier to design an existing technology into a new plant than to retrofit it into an existing plant.

When the regulatory entity cannot point to an existing plant that has successfully implemented a technological innovation, it can attempt to rely upon innova-

320. For a complete discussion of the choice between technology-based standards and media-quality-based standards and "technology-forcing," see RADIAN CORP., CASE STUDIES OF AIR POLLUTION CONTROL TECHNOLOGY INNOVATIONS (1980) (Final Task II Report to the National Commission on Air Quality); La Pierre, *supra* note 187; *see also* Comment, *supra* note 224.

321. *See supra* note 268 and accompanying text; *cf.* Renken v. Harvy Aluminum, 226 F. Supp. 169 (D. Or. 1963) (nuisance case in which court was impressed by the fact that competitor had installed existing technology).

322. Technology-based standards that are based upon technologies already in operation within the relevant category are much more likely to survive judicial review. *See* La Pierre, *supra* note 187, at 823.

323. *See* American Paper Inst. v. Train, 543 F.2d 328 (D.C.Cir.), *cert. dismissed,* 429 U.S. 967 (1976); CPC Int'l, Inc. v. Train, 540 F.2d 1329 (8th Cir. 1976); FMC Corp. v. Train, 539 F.2d 973 (4th Cir. 1976); American Iron & Steel Inst. v. Train, 526 F.2d 1027 (3d Cir. 1975).

tive technologies in the "pilot plant" or "demonstration" phase of development for new source standards and for standards that take effect in the future. Technology-based standards can also force the transfer of technologies from one industry to another with similar processes and wastes. We have seen, however, that the EPA has not been especially successful in persuading reviewing courts of the rationality of standards that are based upon innovative techniques and technology transfers.[324]

The technology-based approach has the further capacity to impel an entire industry forward by requiring firms to install or retrofit nonexistent technologies that are projected to be available in the near future. The courts, however, have been very reluctant to allow the EPA to impose technology-based requirements on the basis of this sort of "crystal ball" inquiry.[325]

Technology-based standards, in sum, can "press" existing firms toward existing technologies, and they can probably "force" new sources to implement the best of existing technologies and perhaps, if the agency is especially careful in preparing its support documents, force new sources to implement new technologies that are just on the horizon.[326] In theory this limited technological advance can be accomplished rapidly and with little risk of unsympathetic judicial review. In practice, however, the EPA's technology-based standards have not been rapidly implemented, and they have not fared well in the courts. This result may be curable with experience, but the EPA's recent mixed record in securing judicial approval of its new source performance standards under the Clean Air Act does not warrant optimism on this score.

It seems clear that the technology-based approach cannot induce real technological change. It can at best bring the laggards into line with the leaders; it cannot effectively force the leaders to innovate.[327] Indeed, the leaders have a positive disincentive to invest in research and development toward new pollution control technologies. If a more expensive but less polluting new technology is developed, that firm's own new sources may have to apply it.[328]

The media-quality-based approach has a greater potential to stimulate technological advance, but only if the right implementation techniques are adopted. If the regulatory entity implements the media-quality-based approach with technology-based standards, then little real innovation can be expected. The agency will make optimistic assumptions about the ability of existing technologies to meet

324. *See supra* notes 267-68 and accompanying text.

325. *See* International Harvester Co. v. Ruckelshaus, 478 F.2d 615, 629 (D.C. Cir. 1973).

326. Extensive case studies done for the National Commission on Air Quality have concluded that the EPA's new source performance standards have induced technological advance in several industries. *See* RADIAN CORP., *supra* note 320. Another study of sulfur dioxide removal from copper smelters and electric power plants has likewise concluded that technology-based standards have induced research and development investment in those industries with the largest investments being directed toward new sources. Comment, *supra* note 224.

327. *See* A. KNEESE & C. SCHULTZE, *supra* note 18, at 82; La Pierre, *supra* note 187, at 805; Comment, *supra* note 224, at 1727.

328. *See Economic Analysis Hearings, supra* note 224, at 1192 (testimony of Michael McClosky, Executive Director, Sierra Club); A. KNEESE & C. SCHULTZE, *supra* note 18, at 63; La Pierre, *supra* note 187, at 774; Comment, *supra* note 224, at 1727.

the ambient media-quality standards and the standards will continue to be exceeded or, at best, incremental progress toward attainment may result. The historical and political allocation techniques are also unlikely to stimulate innovation or even to push existing sources toward the best existing technology. Unfortunately, few, if any, health and environmental agencies go beyond these standard tools for implementing a media-quality-based approach.

Forceful implementation of the media-quality-based approach could stimulate innovation in geographical areas where media-quality-based standards are exceeded as long as there is a firm deadline for attainment of the standards. If the sources in those areas were assured that they in fact faced shutdown if the standards continued to be exceeded after a given period of time, then they would have a very large incentive to develop pollution control technology prior to the deadline. However, the incentive hinges entirely upon the credibility of the shutdown threat. In the past, the threat has not been credible. The threat is largely unavailable to OSHA because it cannot close down too many employers without undermining the purpose of the standard—that is, safe and healthful *employment*. The threat of shutdown from the EPA is in theory somewhat more credible, but historically it has proved just as empty. The EPA's vinyl chloride experience aptly demonstrates the agency's reluctance to promulgate media-quality-based limitations at near-zero levels if doing so threatens a substantial portion of a vital industry.[329] The states that are charged with implementing the national ambient air quality standards seldom prescribe emissions limitations that cannot be met by existing technology, even when failure to do so means that the ambient air quality standards will be exceeded past the relevant deadlines. Even if the EPA or a state adopted a hard line, it is not clear that a court would not accept an individual company's economic and technological feasibility claims in reviewing the reasonableness of the individual limitation[330] or in framing relief in an enforcement action.[331] Finally, footdragging industries know that failing all else, they can return to Congress and appeal for an extension of the deadline, as many industries successfully did in 1976 and may do again in 1984. With the threat of sanctions or shutdown thus reduced to low comedy, a firm has very little incentive to invest in new pollution control technologies. Indeed, a firm that took seriously its apparent obligations and invested in research and development would probably suffer real economic harm at the hands of its more cynical and less obedient competitors.

A pollution charge or marketable permit allocation technique, by contrast, can stimulate pollution control innovation beyond that necessary to rise to the performance level of the best in the industry. Since every unit of pollution under either of those allocation schemes is a costly item, every source has an incentive to

329. *See supra* text accompanying note 214; *see also* Doniger, *supra* note 214, at 563-64, 572; La Pierre, *supra* note 187, at 793-94.

330. In many states a source may challenge a state-ordered emissions limitation on economic and technological infeasibility grounds in state court. Courts have held individual requirements invalid on this basis, even though it means in practice that another source must face even more stringent limitations or, more likely, that the media-quality-based standard will not be met sufficiently rapidly. *See* Menzel v. County Util. Corp., 14 Env't Rep. Cas. (BNA) 1126, 1128 (E.D. Va. 1979).

331. Union Elec. Co. v. EPA, 427 U.S. 246 (1976).

develop pollution reduction technologies,[332] thus creating a market for innovative firms that develop pollution control devices.[333]

The incentive-oriented techniques are, however, no panacea. The charge must be set sufficiently high to provide a realistic incentive to innovate. Research and development is costly and risky; it will not be undertaken unless the firm is persuaded that it will ultimately pay for itself in reduced payments for fees or in sales of permits.[334] Unfortunately, the relationship between financial rewards and research and development decisions in a firm is not well understood. The implementing agency will therefore lack the ability to predict with much accuracy whether a particular charge will provide the threshold incentive to send research and development funds into pollution control rather than into style changes and new product lines.[335] In addition, a fee or permit that is sufficiently costly to send a clear signal to firms may be so expensive that it threatens the financial integrity of a large segment of the regulated industry, in which case the agency will face precisely the same pressure from the regulated firms to lower the fees that it now faces to lower its standards and extend its deadlines. Congress is unlikely to enact a fee or permit allocation scheme without a provision for judicial review. Judicial review of the level of the fee or the number of permits will involve many of the same issues that typify judicial review of technology-based standards, and the courts are likely to be equally sympathetic to claims of economic infeasibility.

If a sufficiently stringent charge or permit scheme can be put into place, it will probably be more efficient and effective in bringing about real technological innovation than the studied brinksmanship of the current technology-based techniques. Still, a media-quality-based incentives scheme would only operate until pollution reductions sufficient to reach the media-quality-based standard were implemented.[336] At that point the incentive to innovate should disappear, at least until a new source entered the area and forced the regulatory entity to inaugurate the charge mechanism once again. One remedy to this uneven incentive structure is to have the charge operate independently of media quality. This could be done on the moral premise that no one has a "license to pollute," or on the more realistic theory (in the context of the chemical industry) that thresholds for the effects of toxic substances are so difficult to identify, if they exist at all, that it is worth society's while to keep dischargers of such substances under constant pressure to develop new pollution control technology.

---

332. *Economic Analysis Hearings, supra* note 224, at 1193 (testimony of Michael McClosky); *id.* at 1188 (testimony of Robert Haveman); F. ANDERSON, *supra* note 9, at 34; A. KNEESE & C. SCHULTZE, *supra* note 18, at 24-25, 90-91; B. MITNICK, *supra* note 46, at 375.

333. *See* Burby, *White House Plans Push for Sulfur Tax Despite Strong Industry Opposition,* 4 NAT'L J. 1663, 1667 (1972); Rose-Ackerman, *supra* note 13, at 400.

334. *See* B. MITNICK, *supra* note 46, at 375; Rose-Ackerman, *supra* note 13, at 399-401.

335. *See* Rose-Ackerman, *supra* note 13, at 399-400.

336. The marketable permit scheme would continue to provide incentives to reduce pollution so long as a market existed for the permits. One obvious source for such a market, once the media-quality standard is met, is potential new sources. A firm that cleans up more will have more permits available to sell to new sources. Another source is existing sources that can save in maintenance and operating expenses by turning off their pollution control devices. However, it is entirely possible that this remote incentive will have little impact on a source in an area that meets the media-quality-based standards. In any event, this is an academic question for the chemical industry, where markets are unlikely to develop in the first place.

VI

A SUGGESTED SYNTHESIS

From the foregoing it would appear that neither the media-quality-based approach nor the technology-based approach has a clear advantage as a candidate for health and environmental regulation of the chemical industry. The media-quality-based approach stumbles on its inability to draw clear links between media quality and particular sources in the environmental context, and it is stymied in both the environmental and worker health contexts by the failure of the scientific community to predict with any reasonable degree of accuracy the health effects of low dose exposures to chemical substances. In any event, administrative bodies apparently face irresistible pressures to convert the media-quality-based approach into a technology-based approach in the context of nonthreshold pollutants and to implement media-quality-based standards through technology-based allocation techniques in other contexts.

The technology-based approach is attractive to implementing agencies because it maximizes their discretion in determining the regulatory targets and because it simplifies enforcement. The technology-based approach allows the regulator to motivate laggard companies without threatening the economic viability of whole industrial sectors. Yet, this approach is difficult to implement because reviewing courts seem somewhat less hesitant to search for the implementing agencies' analytical mistakes and to remand standards for corrections. The technology-based approach requires the regulatory entity to rely upon easily challengeable assumptions about the future of industrial and economic growth and the rate of technological development that are perhaps too facilely evaluated by judges. Furthermore, the agency and the public are placed at a great knowledge disadvantage with respect to the regulated industries. The technology-based approach requires the decisionmaker to acquire an extensive familiarity with the processes, products, and by-products of the regulated industry that must come, largely on faith, from the industry itself. Under the media-quality-based approach, which focuses more on toxicology than technology, the sides are more evenly matched. Additionally, the technology-based approach does not address inequities as effectively as the media-quality-based approach. Finally, the technology-based approach is incapable of inducing private investment into innovative technological solutions to pollution problems that can bypass some of the more difficult societal trade-offs and send society farther on its way toward its nonutilitarian health and environmental goals.

Since both approaches have important strengths and weaknesses, it is possible that the best overall regulatory strategy consists of some optimal combination of both approaches. The following section will offer some suggestions for a sensible combined strategy for regulating the chemical industry. These rather modest and somewhat tentative recommendations reflect the perhaps conservative viewpoint of one who is not especially dissatisfied with the current statutory arrangement and who is wary of untried proposals for radical change.

Congress was, in my opinion, wise to reject the narrow balancing approach to setting health and environmental goals. These goals are too important to be left to the manipulations of a cloistered corps of policy analysts stuck to a schizophrenic paradigm. The absolutist "cleanup" goal will never be achieved in the real world, but with adequate incentives for technological development we can increasingly approach it. As a society we are better for the effort. The balancing goal is set too low. We can become too easily satisfied with a "optimal" steady-state where lives and environmental amenities circulate into and out of the system and are compared to and replaced by electric toothbrushes, push button windows, and other frivolous commodities yet to be imagined. The same intellectual energy that produces thneeds[337] and creates markets for them can be channeled toward developing technologies capable of enhancing the workplace and of preserving the environment

I am convinced that the new source/existing source distinction is a good one. Installing pollution control technologies into new facilities is very often less expensive than retrofitting them into old ones.[338] Moreover, entire production processes can be designed for new plants that recycle wastes and thereby reduce overall discharges. The regulatory entity should be allowed to guide the future, even if it cannot correct all of the mistakes of the past.

The major disadvantage of stringent technology-based new source performance standards is the incentive that they provide to firms to extend the life of existing, more polluting sources. Stringent controls on existing sources can reduce this incentive, but the flexibility that agencies have to consider costs in prescribing standards for existing sources normally ensures that the incentive to delay remains alive. Another way to reduce this incentive is to require something less than the very best on-the-horizon technology for new sources. A somewhat lower technology-based standard for new sources would make the shift toward new technology less expensive, and it would provide the regulated firms with a greater degree of certainty that the pollution control technology identified by the regulatory entity would in fact work.

The regulatory entity could further reduce the disincentive to build new facilities by implementing a charge system for new and existing sources. If a firm must pay for every unit of pollution that it discharges and if it can reduce pollution by installing new production and pollution control technologies, then the reduced charge provides an incentive to make capital expenditures on new facilities. Indeed, the regulatory entity could go farther and set the charge at just the level that would induce the changeover to new facilities. In practice, however, such a technology-based charge would be even more difficult to implement than a technology-based effluent limitation, because it would require the regulatory entity to know the details of the investment decisions of the regulated sources as well as the economics of their production and pollution control processes. The regulatory

337. *See* DR. SEUSS (T. GEISEL), THE LORAX (1971).

338. Congress recognized the problems created by the technology-based new source performance standard: "It may be that in most instances, the technology for elimination of discharge of pollutants from new sources can be achieved on a considerably more reasonable basis than for existing sources." 118 CONG. REC. 33,697 (Oct. 4, 1972) (statement of Sen. Muskie). *But see* Ackerman & Hassler, *supra* note 183, at 1529-30 (arguing that a better course would be to design plants with possible modifications in mind instead of modifying existing plants).

entity would be even more at the mercy of the regulated firms for crucial information under a technology-based charge system. If the regulatory entity underestimated the charge necessary to induce the desired technology in a particular category, the new source opportunity would be lost, and the agency would in practice have to wait for the next generation of new sources for another change to induce pollution control technology in that category.

A better solution might lie in a combination of technology-based standards and stringent media-quality-based charges. Since the toxic products and by-products of the chemical industry are likely to lack accepted thresholds of toxicity and since our knowledge of environmentally caused diseases is in any event so weak, the overall media-quality goal should be to reduce exposure as much as possible. This charge would therefore be assessed for every unit of pollution. The charge would eliminate the need for the agency to undertake the almost impossibly difficult scientific and value judgments that are inherent in setting an acceptable level of media quality. The zero-discharge goal would rarely be reached, because at some point it will be cheaper to pay the charge than to reduce the discharge. But the incentive to reduce would always remain.

Since the effect of a charge on capital investment and research and development decisions is so indirect and so poorly understood, the charge standing alone may not be acceptable to proponents of a cleaner environment and workplace. The charge system could therefore be supplemented with a system of technology-based new source standards. The standards would ensure that when firms do shift to new production and pollution control technologies, they will implement the desired first-level technology. The standards need not, however, require untried, on-the-horizon technologies. Rather, the new source technology should be a technology that the implementing agency is confident can be implemented by new sources within the category. This would almost certainly enhance the agency's ability to survive judicial review, and it would avoid the risk, which must be in the minds of most reviewing courts, that the agency will mandate the implementation of a "white elephant" technology. Finally, the agency should have greater flexibility to prescribe technology and, if necessary, production processes and operating techniques for new sources, rather than relying exclusively upon effluent limitations based on the processes and techniques that its engineers identify. The minor degree of added flexibility that sources receive when the regulatory entity prescribes limitations rather than actual technologies is, in the opinion of the author, far outweighed by the distracting and ultimately senseless disputation that occurs over whether a particular technology is capable of producing a particular level of pollution control in the waste stream and over excursion and upset provisions in standards and permits.[339]

The new source standards/charge system proposed here would offer a contin-

339. Effluent limitations will still be necessary for enforcement purposes for discontinuous processes and for other technologies for which the knowledge that the installed pollution control technology is operational does not guarantee that it is not being circumvented. Effluent limitations will also be useful when a new source proposes to install an innovative technology capable of even greater pollution reduction than the prescribed new source technology. To verify the greater efficacy of the proposed technology, the

uing incentive to develop pollution control process and technologies even after the firm complies with the technology-based standards. Under the mixed strategy suggested here, the charge must be paid for *every* unit of pollution, whether it comes from a new or an existing source. Owners of new sources can rest complacently upon compliance with new source standards only if they are willing to pay for such pollution as survives the installation of the new technology. Whereas the pure technology-based approach is inclined to push sources to the limits of today's technology and freeze it there, the mixed strategy suggested here would force new sources to meet a threshold technological burden and provide continuing incentives to do even better.

As a further refinement of the mixed strategy suggested here, the charge could vary from pollutant to pollutant depending upon the relative toxicity of and exposure to the pollutants, thus adding to the incentive to control the pollutants likely to do the most harm. This would require more information and necessitate higher administrative costs, but it would further the cleanup goal, and, to the extent that it could be validated, it would produce a more equitable system in which dischargers of more harmful pollutants must pay more than dischargers of less harmful pollutants. While current risk assessment techniques are thoroughly incapable of accurately quantifying the risks posed by individual chemicals in particular workplace and environmental contexts, they may be appropriate for the cruder task of segregating chemicals into a few distinct categories. Different charges could then be assessed for different categories.[340]

The chief disadvantage of a categorization approach is that it may precipitate sharp debates about the appropriate categorization of a particular chemical that may ultimately result in time consuming administrative and judicial proceedings. It is, in the author's opinion, a close question whether the advantages of a categorization scheme outweigh this significant disadvantage. While the scheme would seem to be a very sensible approach, it may in fact never get off the ground. If the regulatory entity were to delay implementation of the entire mixed approach until categorization disputes were resolved, the categorization attempt would probably not be worthwhile. The EPA's experience with regulating hazardous discharges into water under section 311 of the Clean Water Act[341] offers little comfort here.[342]

---

agency must know the performance capacity of the chosen technology. Otherwise, a source could propose as an innovative technology one that is really less effective than the prescribed technology.

The best solution is probably to allow the EPA to promulgate effluent limitations based upon identified technologies but eliminate from the standard-setting hearing the issue of whether the identified technology can achieve the prescribed emission limitation. At the individual permit hearing, the individual source could be allowed to demonstrate that the identified technology, installed in its plant, will not meet the prescribed limitation or that it has an innovative process that will do even better than the prescribed limitation. In either case, a new effluent limitation would be set for the individual plant.

340. *See, e.g.,* Ruff, *supra* note 9, at 342. Agencies have attempted to use risk assessment techniques to categorize chemicals according to toxicity in the past. *See* Identification, Classification, and Regulation of Potential Occupational Carcinogens, 45 Fed. Reg. 5205 (1980) (codified at 29 C.F.R. § 1990.112 (1982)); *see also* Manufacturing Chemists Ass'n v. Costle, 11 Env't Rep. Cas. (BNA) 2014 (W.D. La. 1978).

341. Clean Water Act § 311, 33 U.S.C. § 1321 (1976); *see* Manufacturing Chemists Ass'n v. Costle, 11 Env't Rep. Cas. (BNA) 2014 (W.D. La. 1978).

342. The EPA attempted an elaborate categorization scheme to characterize substances according to toxicity for purposes of defining "hazardous discharge." The listing and categorizing process itself consumed several years and a huge amount of agency resources. The standard was overturned by a federal

While the charge might be media-quality-based in the limited sense of varying from category to category, it should not be media-quality-limited. The charge setter should not seek to achieve any particular degree of media quality in the receiving waters short of zero exposure. The technology-based new source standards should ensure that reasonable efforts are being made to achieve clean receiving media; this is as much as the current media-quality-based approach seems capable of achieving in any event. The charge should be set at a level which will provide a strong inducement to clean up beyond what might be established as an "acceptable" level of media quality under a balancing approach. This attitude would implement the two strong policies underlying the prevention of significant deterioration approach to new sources. First, it recognizes the absolutist position that no pollution is really acceptable to society. All of it must be paid for. Second, it recognizes that the huge uncertainties involved in assessing the risks of toxic chemicals mean that we can never be sure that a given level of media quality is really safe enough. Sources should be under constant financial pressure to develop technologies for pollution reduction. The predictable response of some environmental purists that this response is merely a "license to pollute"[343] is elevating rhetoric over substance. It is a matter of practical politics that new sources of pollution will be allowed to discharge toxic substances into the workplace, the water, and the air, and that most old sources will not be forced out of business. We can strive toward justifiable absolutist cleanup goals by decrying the construction of new sources and thereby tacitly accepting the discharges of existing sources, or we can pursue those goals more sensibly through a mixed system of technology requirements and charges that insists upon the installation of some reasonably available control technology and that encourages the development of even better technology through a system of stringent charges.

The mixed strategy is also adaptable to existing sources. As previously discussed, the charge system should be implemented with respect to existing sources to encourage pollution reduction and to reduce the disincentive to convert to new production processes that technology-based new source standards provide. The question remains whether technology-based requirements should be imposed upon existing sources in addition to the charge. The case for technology-based requirements is somewhat weaker for existing sources for which any new technology requirements must be retrofitted. Nevertheless, a good case can be made for technology-based requirements in areas in which media quality is poor and for substances for which adequate media-quality-based standards are impossible to promulgate. In both cases the regulatory entity faces strong practical pressures to convert media-quality-based standards into a technology-based implementation

---

district court because the agency's rule was insufficiently detailed in its prescriptions, Manufacturing Chemists Ass'n v. Costle, 11 Env't Rep. Cas (BNA) 2014 (W.D. La. 1978), and Congress ultimately amended the statute to give the EPA authority to adopt its cruder approach.

343. *See* HISTORY OF WPCA AMENDMENTS, *supra* note 184, at 1322 (statement of Sen. Muskie: "if the degree of control achieved is adequate to implement effluent standards, the effluent fee is a useful means to implement existing public policy—if less control is achieved, then the fee is a license to pollute"); Burby, *supra* note 333, at 1665 ("The National Association of Manufacturers believes that taxes on effluents and emissions represent an unmanageable, uneconomic, and negative approach and in principle would allow polluters to continue to adversely sue our environment by payment of a tax.").

approach. It might be more straightforward to acknowledge this tendency forthrightly and prescribe technology-based requirements in the first place. The chemical industry meets the second of these two preconditions especially well. The large uncertainties that surround attempts to assess health and environmental effects of most chemical substances produced by the chemical industry argues against any media-quality-based standard other than zero. Since the societal cost of zero discharge for most existing sources is ultimately unacceptable, the next best regulatory alternative is to require existing sources to do the best that they can. This will, of course, entail all of the disadvantages of technology-based standards, including the likelihood that not all of them will survive stringent judicial review. However, society will at least assure that "best efforts" are being made toward its absolutist goals. Moreover, the charge will reinforce upon the existing sources society's conviction that any pollution is bad, and it should make the installation of retrofit technologies less painful.

The novel issue in the mixed technology-based standards/charge approach will be the level at which the regulatory entity sets the charge. The charge suggested here is not intended to induce any particular level of media quality; nor is it meant to induce the implementation of any particular degree of technological control. The purpose of the charge is twofold—(1) to reinforce in a very pragmatic way society's absolutist goals for worker health and the environment; and (2) to encourage the development of more sophisticated pollution control technologies. Neither of these purposes can be reduced to a concrete end point. Yet, if we cannot know when we have sufficient reinforcement or when we have provided adequate research and development incentives, how can we prescribe a dollar charge per unit of chemical discharged?[344]

Congress could simply articulate a broad goal for the charge, such as "sufficient to encourage significant pollution reduction efforts" and leave the matter to the discretion of the implementing agency and ultimately the reviewing courts. This would make matters extremely difficult for the agency. It would be required to resolve the contending forces generated by polluting sources who would rather pay nothing and environmental groups who would desire very large charges. The agency would then face the prospect of supporting its resolution of the question in a reviewing court, because it is highly unlikely that Congress would delegate such an important and open-ended question to an agency without providing aggrieved parties an avenue for judicial review. This approach toward setting the charge would thus rely heavily upon administrative and judicial discretion. Whether or not one supports this approach would largely depend upon the extent to which one has faith in the current agency and judicial personnel.

The questions of adequate goal reinforcement and research and development incentives are, however, not so much technical as political questions. Once society

344. Most charge proponents advocate fixing the charge per unit of pollution at the level of environmental harm caused by that unit of pollution. *See, e.g.*, Rosenthal, *The Federal Power to Protect the Environment: Available Devices to Compel or Induce Desired Conduct*, 45 S. CAL. L. REV. 397, 436-39 (1972). This is merely the utilitarian ideal as implemented through a charge system. We have seen how this goal is impractical and inappropriate.

has invested in up-to-date technologies for all existing sources and has ensured that new sources will likewise implement reasonable technological controls, the question of the additional expense that society will impose on polluting conduct is in a real sense the question of society's willingness to sell workplace disease and environmental harm at the margin. Once we have done all that we reasonably can to stop workplace and environmental harm with today's technologies, how much shall we charge polluters for the right to discharge toxic substances?

Congress may be the more appropriate institution to make this sensitive collective decision. Congress could therefore specify in advance a sum that the charges must produce on a yearly basis and leave it to the implementing agency to ensure that the charges for the discharge of various chemicals are set at the level capable of producing that sum by the end of the year.[345] This sum could be collected in a separate fund, called the "pollution control research and development fund," rather than made a part of general revenues. Under this approach workplace hazards and environmental insults would be allocated on the basis of the willingness of society to sell, rather than willingness of the employers and polluters to pay.[346] Moreover, in setting the amount of this sum, Congress could turn the inevitable industry complaint, that we should not regulate until we know more about the risks of pollution and the capabilities of technology, around on itself. If we need to know more, then we should raise the level of the fund, and hence the level of the charges, so that more research can be performed.

Unfortunately, the system does not compensate those members of society who are especially harmed by the remaining pollution. The fund could be expanded in concept to incorporate a compensation function as well as a research and development function, but this would entail the creation of a complex fact-finding and allocating mechanism that would largely duplicate tort and workers' compensation systems while not eliminating any of the practical difficulties, such as establishing causation, that befuddle those systems.

If the fund served only a research and development function, the strategy proposed here could be even further simplified by giving the regulatory entity the discretion to forego collecting the charge from any entity that could demonstrate that it was expending an equivalent amount on its own pollution control or worker safety research and development. The total annual amount of the fund would reflect this sum, but it would not actually be transferred to the fund. The entity would be required to show that the funds were in fact being spent on ways of reducing pollution. In some cases manufacturing design research would fit this description, especially if the research were directed toward minimizing raw mate-

345. Obviously, some flexibility will have to be designed into the system to take into account the large uncertainties concerning investment decisions of private firms and the impact of those decisions on the fund. In some years the charges set by the implementing agency may not reach the congressionally mandated target; in others it will exceed that target. The goal should be to reach the target over time.

346. To the extent that the benefits of a particular industrial activity are spread evenly throughout all of society, the willingness of society to sell may roughly equal the willingness of society to pay because the charge will be reflected in price increases. Yet, since very few products have price inelastic demand functions, a charge cannot be passed on entirely to consumers. Shareholders will bear a part of the charge as well. This should have the long term effect of moving both consumers and capital into less polluting technologies.

rial consumption and toward recycling technologies. The agency would have to examine the manufacturer's case with some care, however, to avoid having the fund sponsor product development or marketing research.

One objection that is continually raised to a charge system is that the government will become addicted to the revenue that the charge brings in and will not be willing to accept reductions in the charges as pollution is brought under control. For a charge system grounded in the market paradigm, this is indeed a disadvantage. For the nonmarket system proposed here, it is a less powerful objection. Congress could re-evaluate the fund periodically and thereby reestablish the price at which society is willing to sell worker, public health, and environmental amenities. Unless Congress agreed to lower the level of the fund, the agency would be required to maintain it at the prescribed level despite the shrinking payments attributable to the installation of pollution controls in existing sources.[347] Unless new sources filled the gap in payments, the charge for each unit of pollution would have to be increased as overall discharges are reduced.[348] The policy-oriented economist will argue that this will ensure that at some point society is paying too much per unit of pollution, and if the political representatives agree, the fund can be reduced accordingly. But the cleanup advocate can respond that, to the contrary, society is merely engaging in constant efforts to develop technological solutions to the worker health and pollution control problem. The incentive grows as we get nearer to the ultimate cleanup goal.

The charge system advocated here thus resembles a budget for pollution control research, except that it is financed by the polluters on a "worst first" basis. First priority upon the budget resources will go to the polluters themselves, so long as they can demonstrate that the resources will in fact be spent upon research relevant to workplace health or pollution control. The remaining funds will be disbursed by the regulatory entity to other research and development-oriented entities. There is, for example, a burgeoning mini-industry of pollution control vendors that could benefit substantially from grants from the agency or from the regulated companies.

The charge system would entail significant administrative costs, but it would probably not be as expensive as the current system. The agency would have to

347. If each assessment were required to be made on the record after a hearing with judicial review, the mixed technology-based-standard/charge strategy proposed here would have no hope of succeeding. However, there is no need to provide for hearings or judicial review of the annual charge reassessments because the risk of error is very small. While the probability of error in any given year is very high, any error in one year can be corrected in the next. The agency's goal is to maintain a fund at a more-or-less constant level over the years. There is no reason to make that level a talisman in any given year. Very little harm can come to regulatees if the agency is off the mark in one year so long as it corrects for its mistakes in the next year.

348. One important difficulty with the solution advocated here is the powerful incentive it offers to the polluting industry as a whole to conspire against the agency. If the tax per unit of pollution is merely raised as the total amount of effluent or emissions decreases, the industry as a whole has no incentive to curtail emissions. The gross payout is the same for the whole industry, regardless of the level of pollution abatement installed. Thus, the real incentive for an individual firm to install pollution controls is an incentive to get the jump on its competitors. The industry thus will find itself in a kind of reverse tragedy of the commons. By conspiring against the EPA, the industry could avoid this competition and avoid the installation of controls.

maintain a branch capable of constantly updating new source standards as technology evolves. The same branch could promulgate the initial existing source standards, which should not have to be revised in the future. The agency would also need an economics branch with the necessary expertise to establish the relevant charges. An enforcement branch would be necessary to monitor the technology-based standards and the charge system for cheating. Finally, a research and development branch would be necessary to allocate the fund. The agency would not need a large risk assessment capability, and its technology assessment capability could shrink after it promulgated its standards for existing sources and its first round of standards for new sources. In any event, the costs of administering the suggested system would certainly be no greater than the administrative costs of the present system.

The suggested strategy seems altogether fair and equitable from the standpoint of the regulated firms. Since any discharge of a nonthreshold pollutant may be regarded as harmful, it seems equitable to charge sources that discharge large amounts of a substance more than a source that is discharging smaller amounts. The fairness of the system is enhanced by its willingness to plow the charge directly back into the research that will help reduce discharges. The firm's resources are not necessarily expropriated; they are merely rechanneled into more beneficial uses for which the firm would not otherwise expend resources. The regulatory entity mandates "inefficient" technology-based standards in the first instance, but further pollution control is brought about by each individual firm in a cost-effective way using the results of fund-sponsored research as well as those of its own research.

VII

CONCLUSION

A society does not always achieve all of the goals that it sets for itself. But reaching El Dorado is not always as important as the attempt. The United States has set very high health and environmental goals for itself and it has launched on a decade-long quest to reach those goals. Not surprisingly, we have failed. We have failed in part because the goals were set too high and in part because some of us do not share those goals and have hampered the quest. In the process, however, we have learned a great deal about worker and environmental health and about ways to reduce risks to health and the environment.

Despite a significant change in the political climate that inaugurated the decade of the 1980's, there is little indication that Congress intends to retreat from the goals set in the early 1970's. This is, in the author's opinion, encouraging. Yet, while we should not abandon our ambitious goals, we can recognize the futility of the media-quality-based approach insofar as it applies to most producers of the chemical industry. The technology-based approach, while no panacea, can, in combination with the charge system described here, keep us on the right path toward the goals that we will probably never reach.

Part IV
Economic Incentives and Environmental Protection

[8]

COMMENT

Reforming Environmental Law†

Bruce A. Ackerman*
Richard B. Stewart**

In 1971, Ezra Mishan brilliantly satirized the views of a Dr. Pangloss, who argued that a world of largely unregulated pollution was "optimal" because cleanup would involve enormous transaction costs.[1] Less than 15 years later, Professor Latin uses the same Panglossian argument to rationalize the current regulatory status quo.[2] He not only accepts but endorses our extraordinarily crude, costly, litigious and counterproductive system of technology-based environmental controls. Like Mishan's Pangloss, he seems to believe that if it were possible to have a better world, it would exist. Since it does not, the transaction costs involved in regulatory improvement must exceed the benefits. Proposals for basic change accordingly are dismissed as naive utopianism.

What explains this celebration of the regulatory status quo? As critics of the present system, we believe this question to be of more than academic interest. The present regulatory system wastes tens of billions of dollars every year, misdirects resources, stifles innovation, and spawns massive and often counterproductive litigation. There is a variety of fundamental but practical changes that could be made to improve its environmental and economic performance. Why have such changes not been adopted? Powerful organized interests have a vested stake in the

---

† We are grateful to Errol Meidinger for his thoughtful comments on an earlier draft.

* Beekman Professor of Law & Philosophy, Columbia University.

** Byrne Professor of Administrative Law, Harvard University.

1. Mishan, *Pangloss on Pollution*, 73 SWED. J. ECON. 1 (1971). While tempted to emulate Mishan, we have (recognizing our comparative disadvantage) eschewed satire and have chosen to present an affirmative program for reform.

2. Latin, *Ideal Versus Real Regulatory Efficiency: Implementation of Uniform Standards and "Fine-Tuning" Regulatory Reform*, 37 STAN. L. REV. 1267 (1985).

status quo. The congressional committees, government bureaucracies, and industry and environmental groups that have helped to shape the present system want to see it perpetuated.[3] But the current system is also bolstered by an often inarticulate sense that, however cumbersome, it "works," and that complexity and limited information make major improvements infeasible.

Professor Latin has performed an important service in providing an articulate, informed, and sophisticated exposition of this view. By developing and making transparent the arguments that might justify the status quo, he has made it easier to assess their merits. If, as we believe, those arguments lack merit, his sophisticated defense of the status quo may ultimately serve to hasten its demise.

We will not respond to all of the groundless charges that Professor Latin levels at the critics of the current system, ourselves included. We focus instead on the major flaws in his defense of existing law and policy. First, Latin's view is based on a Panglossian interpretation of the status quo. The current system does not in fact "work" and its malfunctions, like those of Soviet-style central planning, will become progressively more serious as the economy grows and changes and our knowledge of environmental problems develops.

Second, Latin mistakenly treats economic incentive systems as a form of regulatory "fine-tuning," rather than recognizing them as fundamental alternatives to our current reliance on centralized regulatory commands to implement environmental goals. Moreover, he completely ignores experience showing that economic incentive systems are feasible and effective.

Third, Latin ignores the increasingly urgent need to improve the process by which Congress, the agencies, and the courts set environmental goals. He is mesmerized by decisionmaking costs, ignoring the great social benefits flowing from a more intelligent and democratically accountable dialogue on environmental policy. We deal with each of these points in turn.

I. The Existing System

The existing system of pollution regulation, which is the focus

3. *See generally* Stewart, *The Discontents of Legalism: Interest Group Relations in Administrative Regulation*, 1985 Wis. L. Rev. 655. The forces favoring as well as those opposing reform are examined in Weidinger, *On Explaining the Development of "Emissions Trading" in U.S. Air Pollution Policy*, 7 Law & Pol'y 457 (1985).

of Latin's defense, is primarily based on a Best Available Technology (BAT) strategy. If an industrial process or product generates some nontrivial risk, the responsible plant or industry must install whatever technology is available to reduce or eliminate this risk, so long as the costs of doing so will not cause a shutdown of the plant or industry. BAT requirements are largely determined through uniform federal regulations. Under the Clean Water Act's BAT strategy, the EPA adapts nationally uniform effluent limitations for some 500 different industries. A similar BAT strategy is deployed under the Clean Air Act for new industrial sources of air pollution, new automobiles, and industrial sources of toxic air pollutants.[4] BAT strategies are also widely used in many fields of environmental regulation other than air and water pollution, which are the focus of Latin's analysis.[5]

BAT was embraced by Congress and administrators in the early 1970s in order to impose immediate, readily enforceable federal controls on a relatively few widespread pollutants, while avoiding widespread industrial shutdowns. Subsequent experience and analysis has demonstrated:

1. Uniform BAT requirements waste many billions of dollars annually[6] by ignoring variations among plants and industries in the cost of reducing pollution and by ignoring geographic variations in pollution effects. A more cost-effective strategy of risk reduction could free enormous resources for additional pollution reduction or other purposes.

2. BAT controls, and the litigation they provoke, impose dis-

4. Clean Air Act, 42 U.S.C. §§ 7411(a)(1), 7412, 7521(a)(3)(A)(i) (1982) (amending 42 U.S.C. §§ 1857–58(a) (1976)). Under other portions of the Clean Air Act, regulation of existing industrial sources of certain widespread pollutants is based, in theory, on the achievement of uniform federal air quality standards, rather than available technology. *See id.* §§ 7409, 7410. In practice, however, the controls imposed on sources in regions that do not comply with the federal air quality standards are based on "reasonably available control measures"—a form of BAT. *See id.* § 7502(b)(2).

5. Examples include control of low-level radioactive emissions from normal operation of nuclear power plants and standards for treatment and disposal of toxic substances under the Resource Conservation and Recovery Act. Resource Conservation and Recovery Act, 42 U.S.C. §§ 6901–87 (1982). Rather than rely on uniform standards requiring that a category of plants or products meet BAT requirements, some environmental regulatory programs use case-by-case screening of particular products or development projects under open-ended criteria such as "unreasonable risk." *See* Stewart, *Regulation, Innovation and Administrative Law: A Conceptual Framework*, 69 CALIF. L. REV. 1259, 1263–66 (1981). While our proposals for reform focus on air and water pollution control, we consider briefly their possible application to these other areas of environmental law. *See* note 39 and text accompanying notes 63–64 *infra*.

6. *See* text accompanying notes 10–16, *infra*.

proportionate penalties on new products and processes. A BAT strategy typically imposes far more stringent controls on new sources because there is no risk of shutdown. Also, new plants and products must run the gauntlet of lengthy regulatory and legal proceedings to win approval; the resulting uncertainty and delay discourage new investment. By contrast, existing sources can use the delays and costs of the legal process to burden regulators and postpone or "water-down" compliance. BAT strategies also impose disproportionate burdens on more productive and profitable industries because these industries can "afford" more stringent controls. This "soak the rich" approach penalizes growth and international competitiveness.[7]

3. BAT controls can ensure that established control technologies are installed. They do not, however, provide strong incentives for the development of new, environmentally superior strategies, and may actually discourage their development. Such innovations are essential for maintaining long-term economic growth without simultaneously increasing pollution and other forms of environmental degradation.[8]

4. BAT involves the centralized determination of complex scientific, engineering, and economic issues regarding the feasibility of controls on hundreds of thousands of pollution sources.

---

7. On the differential treatment of old and new sources and resulting implications for investment and productivity, see Crandall, *The Political Economy of Clean Air: Practical Constraints on White House Review*, in ENVIRONMENTAL POLICY UNDER REAGAN'S EXECUTIVE ORDER 205, 215–21 (V. Smith ed. 1984); Huber, *The Old-New Division in Risk Regulation*, 69 VA. L. REV. 1025 (1983); Stewart, *supra* note 5. For the impact of domestic environmental regulatory policies on United States international competitiveness, see J. Kalt, The Impact of Domestic Environmental Regulatory Policies on U.S. International Competitiveness, in ENERGY AND ENVTL. POL'Y CENTER, JOHN F. KENNEDY SCH. OF GOV'T, HARV. U., DISCUSSION PAPER SERIES E-85–02, (1985). For suggestive evidence that the current BAT system gives a comparative competitive advantage to large plants within a regulated industry, see Pashigian, *The Effect of Environmental Regulation on Optimal Plant Size and Factor Shares*, 27 J.L. & ECON. 1 (1984).

8. *See* J. KRIER & E. URSIN, POLLUTION AND POLICY 24–27 (1977); Stewart, *supra* note 5. In attacking the treatment of innovation in the latter work, Latin wrongly suggests that it advocates sacrifice of environmental objectives in favor of market investment and productivity gains ("economic innovation"). As Stewart's article makes quite clear, economic incentives are also needed to promote innovation in the development and adoption of environmentally superior technologies ("social innovation"). In contrast to BAT, market incentives allow the two forms of innovation to complement each other, encouraging new investments that are at the same time environmentally and economically superior.

For a more optimistic view of the ability of a BAT approach to stimulate social innovation, see Ashford, Ayres & Stone, *Using Regulation to Change the Market for Innovation*, 9 HARV. ENVTL. L. REV. 419 (1985).

Such determinations impose massive information-gathering burdens on administrators, and provide a fertile ground for complex litigation in the form of massive adversary rulemaking proceedings and protracted judicial review. Given the high costs of regulatory compliance and the potential gains from litigation brought to defeat or delay regulatory requirements, it is often more cost-effective for industry to "invest" in such litigation rather than to comply.[9]

5. A BAT strategy is inconsistent with intelligent priority setting. Simply regulating to the hilt whatever pollutants happen to get on the regulatory agenda may preclude an agency from dealing adequately with more serious problems that come to scientific attention later. BAT also tends to reinforce regulatory inertia. Foreseeing that "all or nothing" regulation of a given substance under BAT will involve large administrative and compliance costs, and recognizing that resources are limited, agencies often seek to limit sharply the number of substances on the agenda for regulatory action.[10]

This indictment is not idle speculation, but the product of years of patient study by lawyers, economists, and political scientists.[11] There are, for example, no fewer than 15 careful efforts

9. *See* Stewart, *supra* note 5; R. MELNICK, REGULATION AND THE COURTS: THE CASE OF THE CLEAN AIR ACT 193–238 (1983).

10. *See* Harrison, Haig & Nichols, *Benefits Assessment and Environmental Regulation: Case Studies of Hazardous Pollutants*, in ENERGY AND ENVTL. POL'Y CENTER, JOHN F. KENNEDY SCH. OF GOV'T, HARV. U., DISCUSSION PAPER SERIES E-83–07 (1983); Dorfman, *The Lessons of Pesticide Regulation*, in REFORM OF ENVIRONMENTAL REGULATION 13 (W. Magat ed. 1982); Crandall & Portney, *Environmental Policy*, in NATURAL RESOURCES AND THE ENVIRONMENT: THE REAGAN APPROACH 48–49, 72–73 (R. Portney ed. 1984).

11. For an up-to-date review of relevant sources, see the bibliographies at the end of each chapter compiled by T. TIETENBERG, EMISSIONS TRADING: AN EXERCISE IN REFORMING POLLUTION POLICY (1985). The development of the reformist critique may be traced in ENVIRONMENTAL POLICY UNDER REAGAN'S EXECUTIVE ORDER, *supra* note 7; NATURAL RESOURCES AND THE ENVIRONMENT: THE REAGAN APPROACH, *supra* note 10; R. CRANDALL, CONTROLLING INDUSTRIAL POLLUTION: THE ECONOMICS AND POLITICS OF CLEAN AIR (1983); R. MELNICK, *supra* note 9; R. NOLL & B. OWEN, *supra* note 3; INCENTIVE ARRANGEMENTS FOR ENVIRONMENTAL PROTECTION: A CRITICAL EXAMINATION (T. Schelling ed. 1983); W. MAGAT, *supra* note 3; L. LAVE, STRATEGY OF SOCIAL REGULATION: DECISION FRAMEWORKS FOR POLICY (1981); B. ACKERMAN & W. HASSLER, CLEAN COAL/DIRTY AIR (1981); J. KRIER & E. URSIN, *supra* note 8; W. BAUMOL & W. OATES, THE THEORY OF ENVIRONMENTAL POLICY (1975); B. ACKERMAN, S. ROSE-ACKERMAN, J. SAWYER & D. HENDERSON, THE UNCERTAIN SEARCH FOR ENVIRONMENTAL QUALITY (1974); J. DALES, POLLUTION, PROPERTY AND PRICES (1968); A. KNEESE & B. BOWER, MANAGING WATER QUALITY: ECONOMICS, TECHNOLOGY AND INSTITUTIONS (1968); Stewart, *Economics, Environment, and the Limits of Legal Control*, 9 HARV. ENVTL. L. REV. 1, 7 (1985); Stewart, *supra* note 5; Krier, *The Irrational National Air Quality Standards: Macro-and Micro-Mistakes*,

to estimate the extra cost burden generated by a wide range of traditional legalistic BAT systems used to control a variety of air and water pollutants in different parts of the country. Of the twelve studies of different air pollutants[12]—ranging from particulates to chlorofluorocarbons—seven indicated that traditional forms of regulation were more than 400% more expensive than the least-cost solution; four revealed that they were about 75% more expensive; one suggested a modest cost-overrun of 7%.[13]

---

22 U.C.L.A. L. REV. 323 (1974); Rose-Ackerman, *Effluent Charges: A Critique*, 6 CAN. J. ECON. 512 (1973).

12. For an up-to-date review of empirical research, along with a table that usefully summarizes the results of eleven of the air pollution studies, see T. TIETENBERG, *supra* note 11, at 39–52.

In addition to the 11 studies summarized by Tietenberg, some excellent unpublished work by McGartland and Oates. *See* McGartland & Oates, *Marketable Permits for the Prevention of Environmental Deterioration*, — J. OF ENVTL. ECON. & MGMT. — (198—) (forthcoming). This study estimates that traditional regulation in the Baltimore area is at least twice as expensive as a least-cost approach. We have therefore counted it among the four studies we have placed in the second of the three crude categories presented in the text.

13. This was the study of sulfate pollution in Los Angeles. Hahn & Noll, *Designing a Market for Tradable Emission Permits*, in W. MAGAT, *supra* note 3, at 39–52. Two important factors help account for the anomalous character of the Hahn and Noll findings:

> First, in contrast to other areas, the command-and-control strategy in California did not include scrubbers, a very expensive approach. Had California required scrubbers, the potential cost savings would have been higher.
>
> Another reason, of more general applicability, is that the amount of control required [to reach air quality objectives in Los Angeles] is so great that every source is forced to control as much as is economically feasible. By definition, little further control can be undertaken. Therefore . . . the divergence between the command-and-control and least-cost allocation would be small.

T. TIETENBERG, *supra* note 11, at 45. It should be noted that existing federal law now requires the installation of scrubbers on all new coal-burning power plants in Los Angeles. *See* B. ACKERMAN & W. HASSLER, *supra* note 11, at 101–03. As a consequence, Tietenberg's first point emphasizes the limited power of Hahn and Noll's conclusions even in the extreme situation posed by Los Angeles.

A recent study by Anderson comes to a less certain conclusion. Anderson, *Marketable Pollution Permits and Acid Rain Externalities*, 16 CAN. J. ECON. 704 (1983). While it finds that marketable rights schemes could generate significant savings in reaching Cleveland's local sulfur dioxide goals, it reaches a more equivocal conclusion once Cleveland's contribution to the larger North American acid rain problem is taken into account. Given Cleveland's strategic geographic location in the Midwest, any plausible solution to acid rain would require all its polluters to treat at very high levels—so high that the cost difference between marketable rights and a more traditional system would be substantially reduced. In respect to its contribution to acid rain, then, Cleveland seems similar to the case of Los Angeles discussed by Hahn and Noll.

Of course, Cleveland is but one of the many sources of the acid rain problem experienced by Canada and the northeastern United States. Unfortunately, however, Anderson has not yet moved beyond Cleveland to study the cost-saving potential of an acid rain marketable rights scheme for the entire North American acid rain control region.

Three studies of water pollution control in five different watersheds also indicate the serious inefficiency of traditional forms of command-and-control regulation.[14] These careful studies of selected problems cannot be used to estimate precisely the total amount traditional forms of regulation are annually costing the American people.[15] Nonetheless, very large magnitudes are at stake. Even if a reformed system could cut costs by "only" one-third, it could save more than $15 billion *a year* from the nation's annual expenditure of $50 billion on air and water pollution con-

---

Telephone conversation (September 17, 1985). Thus, his study does not permit any firm conclusion on the cost-saving potential of a marketable rights scheme in the regulatory response to the acid rain problem. As a consequence, we have omitted it from the studies summarized in the text.

14. These water studies are somewhat less suggestive than are the air studies. They all have to do with the removal of a single (albeit important) water pollutant: biochemical oxygen demand. Moreover, they do not expressly deal with the precise form of BAT regulation actually used under the present Clean Water Act. Instead, the studies investigate a more primitive form of regulation that does not, like BAT, require different cutbacks from different industries depending on the best available technology in each economic sector. Instead, the traditional regulatory approach used as a benchmark in the water studies simply requires all dischargers, regardless of industry, to cut back wasteloads proportionally to reach water quality objectives. This proportionate reduction would be equivalent to BAT only if the best available technology in every industry permits all industries to cut back by the same percentage. While BAT often does lead to this result, the proportionality assumption invoked by all existing water pollution studies can only serve as a crude approximation of BAT's economic impact. Nonetheless, the existing data does suggest the possibility of substantial savings by abandoning BAT, though the overruns are somewhat less substantial than those suggested by the air studies. Four of the computer studies suggest that traditional regulation is more than twice as expensive as the least-cost program; six suggest an overrun in the 40–60% range; while four indicate extra costs of 12–40%. A summary of these studies appears in T. TIETENBERG, *supra* note 11, at 42–43.

15. Speaking broadly, the empirical estimates we have summarized in the text are generated by procedures that overestimate BAT's short-term costs, while underestimating its long-term costs. Thus, on the one hand, the computer models do not generally take into account that many polluters have already sunk capital into treatment facilities that would never have been required under a cost-minimizing regulatory scheme. This leads to an overestimate of the short-term savings of regulatory reform because it ignores that some existing equipment might be operated cheaply in the short run, however inefficient it was to install in the first place. On the other hand, existing cost estimates are generated by static models that do not take into account the BAT regime's depressive effect on the rate of pollution control innovation. *See* text accompanying notes 18–19 *infra*. As a consequence, even the very large cost-overruns presented in the text underestimate likely realities 10 or 20 years in the future. These and other useful interpretive points may be found in Professor Tietenberg's recent review of the evidence. *See* T. TIETENBERG, *supra* note 11, at 38–53. We do not think a lengthy elaboration of his discussion is necessary to make our basic point: By even the most conservative reckoning, the economic savings promised by a successful reform are substantial indeed.

trol alone.[16]

While Latin entirely fails to address this evidence, he does not seriously contest the economic wastefulness of the current system's excessive compliance costs and penalties on new investment. He simply ignores the last three points in our indictment, even though they have been well developed in the literature. Instead, Latin spends all his time castigating all reform proposals as unrealistic. In his view, reformers characteristically propose utopian efforts at administrative "fine-tuning" that would in practice lead to a bureaucratic nightmare, making the present system seem benign by comparison.

We do not accept this despairing view. To explain why, however, we must correct an analytic deficiency in Latin's critique. The various reforms rejected in his article have little in common with one another—except that they all represent departures from BAT. Indeed, it is a sign of Latin's deep commitment to the status quo that, simply because they depart from BAT, he thinks of them as if they were all variations on the problem of "fine-tuning" that he decries. But "fine-tuning" is much too diffuse a notion on which to base an analysis of the reform agenda. Some of our proposals involve reform of the criteria and procedures which Congress, agencies, and the courts use in *setting environmental goals*; others involve reform of the means by which the goals (whatever they may be) are *implemented* in the real world. Latin's indiscriminate condemnation of "fine-tuning" fails to distinguish systematically between these two types of proposals. In this, as in so much else, his critique is faithful to the BAT system, which also conflates means and ends, preventing the intelligent assessment of either. If, however, we are to move beyond the status quo, it is best to treat these two different kinds of structural reform separately, beginning with the implementation problem and concluding with the question of goal-setting.[17]

16. *See* OFFICE OF POLICY PLANNING AND EVALUATION, U.S. EPA, THE COST OF CLEAN AIR AND WATER (1984) (estimating expenditures to comply with federal air and water pollution control expenditures in the ten years 1981–1990 at $525 billion (in constant 1981 dollars)). Moreover, we also think that our reforms are applicable to many other kinds of pollution as well. *See* notes 39–40 *infra* and accompanying text.

17. While, as we hope to show, this simple means-end schema clarifies the reform agenda, it can lead to distortions of its own. In particular, it may be used to blind one to the complex ways in which a particular implementation scheme shapes the standard-setting process over time—and vice versa. *See* Roberts & Stewart, Book Review, 88 HARV. L. REV. 1644, 1661–62 (1975). We shall, however, try to be attentive to this very important factor in the ensuing discussion. *See* notes 44–47 *infra* and accompanying text.

II. Implementation

A BAT system has an implicit environmental goal: achievement of the environmental quality level that would result if all sources installed BAT controls on their discharges. The usual means for implementing this goal are centralized, industry-uniform regulations that command specific amounts of cleanup from specific polluters. When a polluter receives an air or water permit under existing law, the piece of paper does not content itself, in the manner of Polonius, with the vague advice that he "use the best available technology." Instead, the permit tries to be as quantitatively precise as possible, telling each discharger how much of the regulated pollutants he may discharge.[18]

Although Latin condemns us as unrealistic, our reforms build upon, rather than abandon, this basic permit system. Indeed, we have only two, albeit far-reaching, objections to the existing permit mechanism. First, existing permits are free. This is bad because it gives the polluter no incentive to reduce his wastes below the permitted amount. Second, they are non-transferable. This is bad because polluter A is obliged to cut back his own wastes even if it is cheaper for him to pay his neighbor B to undertake the extra cleanup instead.

Our basic reform would respond to these deficiencies by allowing polluters to buy and sell each other's permits—thereby creating a powerful financial incentive for those who can clean up most cheaply to sell their permits to those whose treatment costs are highest. This reform will, at one stroke, cure many of the basic flaws of the existing command-and-control regulatory systems discussed earlier.

A system of tradeable rights will tend to bring about a least-

---

18. While the text describes the existing system's implicit regulatory objective, in fact the process of writing, monitoring, and enforcing permits is the Achilles heel of the BAT strategy. *See* text accompanying notes 28–30 *infra*. While officials in Washington promulgate regulations that are supposed to govern the operation of every plant in an industry, such regulations must be adapted to the specific and varying conditions of different plants throughout the nation. Thus, the actual writing of permits is often accomplished by low-level state or federal field personnel. These permits are often vague and obsolescent. Pedersen, *Why the Clean Air Act Works Badly*, 129 U. Pa. L. Rev. 1059 (1981). Moreover, enforcement of permit conditions is often ineffective. *See* U.S. Gen. Acct. Off., Wastewater Dischargers Are Not Complying with EPA Control Permits (1983); Roberts & Farrell, *The Political Economy of Implementation: The Clean Air Act and Stationary Sources* in Approaches To Controlling Air Pollution 152 (A. Friedlander ed. 1978). See text accompanying notes 19–33 *infra* for the reasons we believe that a reformed system of transferable permits will tend to alleviate these problems.

cost allocation of control burdens, saving many billions of dollars annually.[19] It will eliminate the disproportionate burdens that BAT imposes on new and more productive industries by treating all sources of the same pollutant on the same basis.[20] It will provide positive economic rewards for polluters who develop environmentally superior products and processes.[21] It will, as we show below,[22] reduce the incentives for litigation, simplify the issues in controversy, and facilitate more intelligent setting of priorities.

Would allowing the sale of permits lead to a bureaucratic nightmare? Before proceeding to the new administrative burdens marketability will generate, it is wise to pause, as Latin does not, to consider marketability's great administrative advantages.

First, marketability would immediately eliminate most of the information-processing tasks that are presently overwhelming the federal and state bureaucracies. No longer would the EPA be required to conduct endless adversary proceedings to determine the best available control technologies in each major industry of the United States, and to defend its determinations before the courts; nor would federal and state officials be required to spend vast amounts of time and energy in adapting these changing na-

---

19. An emissions trading system tends to achieve a least-cost allocation of control for all sources by forcing them to pay the same price for pollution. In practice, a regulated emission trading market is likely to deviate somewhat from the perfect market ideal, but substantial cost savings will still be achieved. *See* T. TIETENBERG, *supra* note 11, at 50–56.

20. Equal treatment of old and new sources will not necessarily lead, as Latin apparently fears, to shutdowns of old plants. It is true, of course, that old plants may evade clean-up under BAT if their profits are too low to bear the expense. Because of concern over shutdown, they are often allowed to discharge large wasteloads that could otherwise be treated at low cost. The tradeable permits strategy, however, can provide the needed financing for cleanup by enabling the old plant to sell its pollution rights to others. Thus, a marketable rights system may allow old plants to stay in business *and* clean up. If shutdown does occur, it may be more readily accepted as the product of market forces rather than as a deliberate, isolated government decision.

If the unemployment and dislocation caused by plant shutdowns due to pollution control programs are judged unacceptable, the appropriate response is not, as Latin advocates, to weaken the program or impose disproportionate controls on new sources so as to throttle investment and productivity gains. The appropriate response is remedial: Compensation programs should be designed to deal with unemployment and dislocation.

21. *See* Levin, *Getting There: Implementing the "Bubble" Policy*, in SOCIAL REGULATION: STRATEGIES FOR REFORM 59 (E. Bardach & R. Kagan eds. 1982); Stewart, *supra* note 5, at 1309–11, 1332–37; REGULATORY REFORM STAFF, U.S. EPA, EMISSIONS TRADING REPORT (May 10, 1984).

22. *See* text accompanying notes 31–33 *infra*.

tional guidelines to the particular conditions of every important pollution source in the United States. Instead of giving the job of economic and technological assessment to bureaucrats, the marketable rights mechanism would put the information-processing burden precisely where it belongs: upon business managers and engineers who are in the best position to figure out how to cut back on their plants' pollution costs. If the managers operating plant A think they can clean up a pollutant more cheaply than those in charge of plant B, they should be expected to sell some of their pollution rights to B at a mutually advantageous price; cleanup will occur at the least cost without the need for constant bureaucratic decisions about the best available technology. Latin seriously misleads when he describes a marketable permit system as one involving administrative "fine-tuning." To the contrary, it is the existing system of command-and-control regulation that envisions inevitably ill-informed bureaucrats continually "fine-tuning" technological and economic decisions best made by the people operating the plants.

Second, marketable permits would open up enormous financial resources for effective and informed regulation. While polluters would have the right to trade their permits among themselves during the *n* years[23] they are valid, they would be obliged to buy new ones when their permits expired at an auction held by the EPA in each watershed and air quality control region. These auctions would raise substantial sums of money for the government on a continuing basis. While no study has yet attempted to make global estimates for the United States as a whole, existing work suggests that auction revenues could well *equal* the amount polluters would spend in cost-minimizing control activities.[24] Even if revenues turned out to be a third of this amount, the government would still be collecting more than $6–10 billion a year. Moreover, it seems reasonable to suppose that Congress would allow the EPA (and associated state agencies) to retain a substantial share of these revenues. Since the

23. All permits would not have to expire at the same time. For a discussion of systems that allow for variable time periods and differential privileges during emergency conditions, see T. TIETENBERG, *supra* note 11, at ch. 7; B. ACKERMAN, S. ROSE-ACKERMAN, J. SAWYER & D. HENDERSON, *supra* note 11, at 268; J. DALE, *supra* note 11, at 95.

24. T. TIETENBERG, *supra* note 11, at 102–13, contains a comprehensive discussion of existing data. He concludes: "Of the 39 numerical entries [in his summary tables] permit expenditures are at least as great as control costs in 22 cases. . . . Large permit expenditures are the normal, rather than the exceptional, outcome." *Id.* at 106.

current EPA operating budget is $1.3 billion,[25] using even a fraction of the auction fund to improve regulatory analyses, research, and monitoring would allow a great leap forward in the sophistication of the regulatory effort—something Latin says he supports, but is unable to find any practical way of achieving.[26] Given its revenue-raising potential, environmental reform is hardly a politically unrealistic pipe dream. To the contrary, it is only a matter of time before the enormous federal deficit forces Congress and the President to consider the revenue-raising potential of an auction scheme.[27]

Third, the auction system would help correct one of the worst weaknesses of the present system: the egregious failure of the EPA and associated state agencies to enforce the laws on the books in a timely and effective way. Part of the problem stems from the ability of existing polluters to delay regulatory implementation by using legal proceedings to challenge the economic and engineering bases of BAT regulations and permit conditions. But agencies also invest so little in monitoring[28] that they

25. *See* Davis, *Reagan Boosts EPA Funding, Slashes Interior Spending,* 43 CONG. WEEKLY REP. 255 (1985). This figure excludes municipal water treatment subsidies and Superfund cleanup, but includes all regulatory programs, including pesticides, hazardous waste, drinking water, and chemicals as well as air and water pollution regulation.

26. *See* Latin, *supra* note 1, at 1279.

27. Not that the political fight for an auction will be an easy one. Apart from thoughtful people like Latin, who are committed by conviction to the status quo, our market reform will be opposed by businesses who (despite their promarket rhetoric) will predictably resist the prospect of buying pollution rights after all these years of polluting for free. Nonetheless, we believe that the reformist claim that the air and water of America belong to the people, and that polluters should pay if they wish to use it for limited periods, has enormous popular appeal. While it is possible to design efficient auction systems that ameliorate, or eliminate entirely, the financial burdens imposed upon polluters, *see* T. TIETENBERG, *supra* note 11, at 100–13 (and sources cited therein), we would oppose these schemes on principle. We believe that just as firms are obliged to pay for other raw materials they require for their production process, they should be obliged to pay for the air and water they degrade. (Unlike current proposals to impose new taxes on all industries to finance toxic cleanup, tradeable permits would make sources pay in proportion to their contribution to pollution.)

The only exception we believe justified—for distributional and other reasons—is one for domestic waste processed by municipal sewage authorities. Congress could accommodate this interest by ordering the EPA to give each municipality *free* permits based on the normal domestic waste produced by the average American. Cities could, of course, then make money by selling these rights to firms if private cleanup is relatively more expensive than public. In addition, Congress might well accommodate individual polluter interests by allowing a transitional period of free use, *see* note 20 *supra*, in order to soften adjustment pains and reduce political opposition.

28. Total federal, state, and local expenditure on air quality monitoring averaged only $44 million a year during the four fiscal years between 1978 and 1981—.02% of the

must rely on polluters for the bulk of their data on discharges. Since polluters are predictably reluctant to report their own violations, the current system perpetuates a Panglossian view of regulatory reality. For example, a General Accounting Office investigation of 921 major air polluters officially considered to be in compliance revealed 200, or 22%, to be violating their permits; in one region, the number not complying was 52%.[29] Even when illegal polluters are identified, they are not effectively sanctioned: The EPA's Inspector General in 1984 found that it was a common practice for water pollution officials to respond to violations by issuing administrative orders that effectively legitimized excess discharges.[30] Thus, while the system may, after protracted litigation, eventually "work" to force the slow installation of expensive control machinery, there is no reason to think this machinery will run well when eventually installed. Although there are many reasons for this appalling weakness in enforcement, one stands out above all others: The present system does not put pressure on agency policymakers to make the large investments in monitoring and personnel that are required to make the tedious and unending work of credible enforcement a bureaucratic reality.

The auction system would change existing compliance incentives dramatically. It would reduce the opportunity and incentive of polluters to use the legal system for delay and obstruction by finessing the complex BAT issues, and it would limit dispute to the question of whether a source's discharges exceeded its permits. It would also eliminate the possibility of using the legal system to postpone implementation of regulatory requirements by requiring the polluter that lost its legal challenge to pay for the permits it would have been obliged to buy during the entire

---

estimated costs of air pollution control during this period. *See* Crandall, *supra* note 7, at 220. Crandall goes on to report:

> In 1979, the GAO reported that as many as 81 percent of all monitoring sites had one or more problems that could affect data reliability. In response, EPA developed a plan to assure that a total of more than five thousand monitors be sited and operated in a reliable fashion by federal, state, and local authorities. By the end of 1981, GAO reported that only about one-half of all monitors met EPA specifications.

Id.

29. U.S. Gen. Acct. Off., Improvements Needed in Controlling Major Air Pollution Sources 9 (1979) (Report CEP-78-165).

30. 5 Inside EPA Report No. 11, at 6 (March 16, 1984). For other critiques of agency implementation efforts, see Roberts & Farrell, *supra* note 18; Crandall & Portney, *supra* note 10 at 42–49, 69.

intervening period of noncompliance (plus interest).[31]

The marketable permit system would also provide much stronger incentives for effective monitoring and enforcement. If polluters did not expect rigorous enforcement during the term of their permits, this fact would show up at the auction in dramatically lower bids: Why pay a lot for the right to pollute legally when one can pollute illegally without serious risk of detection? Under a marketable permit approach, this problem would be at the center of bureaucratic attention. For if, as we envisage, the size of the budget available to the EPA and state agencies would depend on total auction revenues, the bureaucracy's failure to invest adequately in enforcement would soon show up in a potentially dramatic drop in auction income available for the next budgetary period. This is not a prospect that top EPA administrators will take lightly. Monitoring and enforcement will become agency priorities of the first importance. Moreover, permit holders may themselves support strong enforcement in order to ensure that cheating by others does not depreciate the value of the permit holders' investments.[32]

A system of marketable permits, then, not only promises to save Americans many billions of dollars a year, to reward innovative improvements in existing clean-up techniques, and to eliminate the BAT system's penalty on new, productive investment. It also offers formidable administrative advantages. It relieves agencies of the enormous information-processing burdens that overwhelm them under the BAT system; it greatly reduces litigation and delay; it offers a rich source of budgetary revenue in a period of general budgetary stringency; and it forces agencies to give new importance to the critical business of enforcing the law in a way that America's polluters will take seriously. Despite his emphasis on administrative realities, Latin has failed to take any of these advantages seriously.[33] Instead, he speaks forebodingly

31. In addition, of course, a fine should be imposed if a polluter's discharges exceeded the permits it has acquired. Such a fine should be based not only on the extent of the excess but also its duration: $X per unit of excess emission per day. While noncompliance penalties can be added on to a regulatory approach, see Drayton, *Economic Law Enforcement*, 4 HARV. ENVTL. L. REV. 1 (1980), they appear to have played a minor role to date.

32. The opposition of New York taxi companies to competition by gypsy cabs without medallions shows that this is by no means a fanciful prospect.

33. While he mentions the first perfunctorily, he completely ignores the other three.

of the dangers of "fine-tuning" that the market reform entails. What precisely *are* these dangers?

The reformed system we have described involves the execution of four bureaucratic tasks. First, the agency must estimate how much pollution presently is permitted by law in each watershed and air quality region. Second, it must run a system of fair and efficient auctions in which polluters can regularly buy rights for limited terms. Third, it must run an efficient title registry in each region that will allow buyers and sellers to transfer rights in a legally effective way. Fourth, it must consistently penalize polluters who discharge more than their permitted amounts.

And that's that. So far as the fourth bureaucratic task is concerned, we have already given reasons to believe that the EPA would enforce the law far more effectively under the new regime than it does at present. So far as the first three management functions are concerned, we think that they are, in the aggregate, far *less* demanding than those they displace under the BAT system.

Taking the three functions in reverse order, we assume that Professor Latin would agree that a system of title registration is within the range of bureaucratic possibility. In contrast, the second task—running fair and efficient auctions—is a complicated affair, and it is easy to imagine such a system run incompetently or corruptly. Nonetheless, other agencies seem to have done similar jobs in satisfactory fashions: If the Department of Interior can auction off oil and gas leases competently,[34] we see no reason the EPA could not do the same for pollution rights. Finally, there remains the task of estimating the total allowable wasteload permitted under existing law in each watershed and air control region. If the BAT system functioned properly, these numbers would be easy to obtain. EPA's regional administrators would simply have to add up the allowed amounts appearing in the permits that are in their filing cabinets. We have no illusions, however, about present realities: So much bureaucratic time and energy has been diverted into the counterproductive factfinding tasks generated by the BAT system, and so little attention has been paid to actual discharges, that even the data needed for these simple arithmetic operations may well be incomplete and inadequate. Nonetheless, total permitted emissions in a region

34. We are commenting here on the Department's technical success in running auctions, not on the substantive policies it has pursued in the past or present.

can be approximated in order to get a system of permits and auctions started. Surely this start-up effort would be less complex than the unending inquiries into available technologies required by the existing system.

We believe, in short, that Latin has confused the novel with the complex in his condemnation of the auction proposal. While it is true that the three new tasks involved in running the reformed system are novel, they seem, in the aggregate, a good deal easier to discharge than the bureaucratic functions they displace. Moreover, what little experience the EPA has had with market approaches supports this conclusion. While Latin completely ignores this important evidence, the fact is that the EPA has effectively discharged the bureaucratic tasks necessary to develop its market-based "bubble" and "tradeoff" control strategies under the Clean Air Act. These strategies create limited markets in pollution rights by: 1) allowing a new source to offset its new emissions by inducing an existing source to reduce its discharges (this is the so-called "tradeoff" policy); 2) allowing an existing source that is expanding to reallocate control burdens among its existing and new units (new source bubble); and 3) allowing existing sources in the same region to reallocate control burdens (state implementation plan bubble).[35] The use of these innovations was for many years clouded by legal uncertainties until the Supreme Court recently rejected challenges from some environmental groups.[36] Despite this uncertainty, the Clean Air Act bubble policy alone, in limited use for only a few years, has achieved compliance cost savings of over $700 million without any reduction (and in some cases an increase) in pollution control.[37]

More recently, the EPA has successfully instituted and managed a tradeable permit system among refiners in connection with an EPA-mandated phasedown of lead additives in gasoline.

35. *See* Stewart, *supra* note 11, at 13–14, and sources cited therein.

36. Chevron, U.S.A., Inc. v. Natural Resources Defense Council, Inc., 104 S. Ct. 2778 (1984).

37. *See* T. Tietenberg, *supra* note 11, at 52–56; sources cited *supra* note 12. Like any policy innovation, implementation of bubbles and tradeoffs raises numerous administrative and legal micro-problems. *See* Liroff, The Bubble Policy and Emissions Trading: The Toil and Trouble of Regulatory Reform (1985). As the Liroff study shows, many of these problems are caused by the effort to graft a limited system of tradeable pollution rights onto an existing regulatory system. Our proposal would entirely replace that system with tradeable rights, eliminating many of the complexities of a hybrid approach.

Refiners with higher lead-reduction costs buy lead rights from refiners with lower costs. All refiners file quarterly reports showing the lead content of their gasoline, as well as sales and purchases of rights with other refiners. Three-quarters of all refiners participate in purchases and sales of lead rights. The system will save hundreds of millions of dollars compared to uniform BAT commands.[38]

In ignoring this record, it is Latin, not the reformers, who is "short on empiricism." The time is ripe for a market reform of the kind we have just described. Rather than using tradeable emission rights as a limited modification of BAT strategies, the bubble and tradeoff approaches should be generalized to permit regional trading of all air and water pollution permits. Moreover, the tradeable permit strategy should be used to deal with pollution problems—such as acid rain—that are currently unregulated and could be handled efficiently and effectively through economic incentives.[39]

Would a system of marketable rights preclude improvement of environmental quality? By no means. The initial stock of rights can be amortized on a fixed schedule in order to reach a targeted goal, or the government may decide not to reissue existing rights after they expire.[40] Any such reductions will increase the price of rights by reducing supply. Prices will also automatically tend to rise over time as the economy grows and the demand for rights increases. Under a BAT approach, by contrast, regulators must consistently undertake new, difficult, and unpopular initiatives to impose ever more stringent BAT controls on existing sources in order to accommodate economic growth without increased pollution. The prospect of steady increases in the price of rights will be a powerful incentive— far more powerful than the patchwork efforts at "technology forc-

38. *See* Office of Policy Planning and Evaluation, U.S. EPA, Costs and Benefits of Reducing Lead in Gasoline: Final Regulatory Impact Analysis (1985).

39. *See* Stewart, *supra* note 11, at 14–15, and sources cited therein. Nor do we see any reason to limit the use of tradeable permits to air and water pollution problems. As we argue in the next section, hazards from toxic chemicals might appropriately be controlled through a system of "risk rights." Under this system, producers of new pesticides or other chemicals would purchase rights from existing producers or compete successfully for rights at one of the regular EPA auctions. Either way, the entry of new producers would force existing producers to reduce existing risk, thereby ensuring that the new product would not increase the total risk from chemicals faced by society.

40. *See* note 23 *supra*.

ing" under the BAT system—for businesses to develop cleaner products and processes.

A more serious objection to our proposal is that it ignores the problem of defining the region within which trades are permitted. The short answer is that the EPA and the States have already divided the nation into several hundred air quality control regions; similarly, the states have delineated the watershed boundaries for pollution control and other water management purposes.[41] Rather than starting from scratch, our proposal can proceed on the basis of these existing boundaries. Especially in the area of air pollution, however, we have no doubt that existing regional lines have been drawn in a way that is extremely insensitive to ecological realities.[42] We strongly recommend, therefore, that a reformed statute provide a mechanism for the orderly reexamination of existing regional boundaries—although it may well be wiser to defer this question for five or ten years to allow the EPA to concentrate on the challenges involved in managing the transition to a marketable permit system.

Latin is on stronger ground, we believe, in emphasizing that a reformed implementation system would not easily solve all foreseeable regulatory problems. In particular, the market system we have described could allow the creation of relatively high concentrations of particular pollutants in small areas within the larger pollution control region. In tolerating "hot spots," of course, our reform proposal shares the defects of the existing BAT system, which also generates risk of "hot spots" by imposing the same controls on sources regardless of their location, the size of the human population affected by their discharges, and the nature and vulnerability of affected ecosystems.[43] Nonetheless, the

41. Most major lake and river systems are the subject of intense water quantity and water quality management under watershed systems established under state law or interstate compacts. We would establish the geographic boundaries of water pollution permit markets by reference to these systems.

42. They typically follow state lines, for example, leading to extremely unwieldly efforts by courts to take interregional impacts into account. *See, e.g.*, Connecticut v. EPA, 656 F.2d 902 (2d Cir. 1981); New England Legal Found. v. Costle, 632 F.2d 936 (2d Cir. 1980) (per curiam).

43. Existing federal laws contain some provisions to prevent excessive local environmental damage from sources that already comply with BAT standards. But as Latin notes, these provisions have not been effectively implemented. We believe that an important reason for this failure is the diversion of bureaucratic energies into BAT determinations. Thus, even in our first-generation proposals for reform, it may be possible to design crude, but useful, mechanisms by which the EPA can realistically respond to "hot

blindness of both systems to intraregional variation is a serious source of concern. The extensive literature on marketable permits—almost entirely ignored by Latin—points to a variety of feasible means for dealing with the hot spot problem.[44] We believe that a long-run strategy for institutional reform should strive to take advantage of these more sophisticated market solutions to the problem of intraregional variation. For the present, it will be enough to emphasize our agreement with Latin's caution that administrative feasibility is an important constraint on the degree of sophistication that we may reasonably expect.[45]

The critical question here, however, is not whether our market reform fails to solve problems that the BAT system also fails to solve. It is whether the reformed implementation system will generate *new* problems that offset its great economic, environmental, and administrative advantages. Curiously, Latin fails to note one potential difficulty that may prove significant. We can foresee situations in which existing polluters might try to manipulate the rights market to deter entry by new firms in a way that is inconsistent with the antitrust laws, by either monopolizing the pollution rights market itself, or using it to block entry by competitors. There is, however, a considerable literature in which problems like this are discussed,[46] and we ourselves have worried about them.[47] Neither Latin nor anybody else, however, has offered a list of particular administrative problems that remotely offset the multiple advantages of a system reformed in the manner we have sketched here.

III. Goals

We now address reforms that have more to do with the way existing policy goals are established than with the way they are

---

spots" once it has been liberated from its BAT routines. All we can do here, however, is to flag this problem of statutory design as deserving high priority on the reform agenda.

44. *See* T. Tietenberg, *supra* note 11, at 64–86, and sources cited therein.

45. The need to strengthen regulatory institutions on the regional level is discussed further at text accompanying note 57 *infra*.

46. *See, e.g.*, T. Tietenberg, *supra* note 11, chs. 4, 6, & 7 and sources cited therein; Rose-Ackerman, *Market Models for Water Pollution Control: Their Strengths and Weaknesses*, 25 Pub. Pol'y 383 (1977).

47. B. Ackerman, S. Rose-Ackerman, J. Sawyer, & D. Henderson, *supra* note 11, at 275–81; Stewart, *supra* note 5, at 1336. Administrative authorities may also have to play a "market-maker" role in the rights market in order to ensure an adequate supply of rights at all times and smooth out price fluctuations, *see* J. Dales, *supra* note 11, at 94–95, although it is possible that private institutions could discharge these functions.

implemented. Latin writes as if our proposals aimed for a system in which "[d]ecisionmakers must evaluate all relevant ecological circumstances, human impacts, and regulatory costs to identify the "optimal" level of environmental protection in particular controversies or locations."[48] We have never advocated any such utopian scheme; our writings demonstrate that we have been well aware of the problems of limited information and excessive regulatory complexity.

Instead, it is Latin who has fallen into the trap of supposing that the only relevant alternative to the status quo is a fantastic rococo system in which every conceivable form of "fine-tuning" is institutionalized immediately. We reject this view. Rather than imagining reform as one extravagant "great leap forward," we envision a series of steps in an ongoing process of piecemeal improvement. Each element in the reform program can be implemented at a different time and should be evaluated on its own merits. Thus, the market implementation mechanism described in the preceding section was a piecemeal reform based on the allowable pollution loads *prevailing under existing law*. Even if Latin's critique of "fine-tuning" in the goal-setting process were entirely correct, the merits of the marketable rights program as an implementing mechanism would remain untouched. Similarly, we regard the policymaking proposals we make in this section as a series of discrete steps toward a more democratic, and more enlightened, dialogue on the nature of America's evolving environmental objectives. While some immediate reforms will lay the foundation for further advances, we hope that doubts about the institutional feasibility of some of our long-run proposals will not deflect attention from feasible short-term reforms that promise immediate and substantial improvements.

A. *A Short-Term Strategy: Redesigning Statutory Variables*

To focus first on the short-term prospect for clear and present improvement, we begin by provisionally accepting Latin's assertion that administrative and political difficulties in devising nonuniform standards dictate uniform federal environmental objectives throughout the nation, regardless of regional variations. Even if we accept this constraint, we can nonetheless build upon the preceding marketable rights proposal in a way that en-

48. Latin, *supra* note 1, at 1275.

hances the democratic quality of the policymaking process. At present, the BAT system focuses congressional debate, as well as administrative and judicial proceedings, upon arcane technological and definitional questions which rapidly outstrip the time and energy that most politicians and citizens are willing to spend on environmental matters. In contrast, the marketable permit system will allow the policymaking debate to take a far more intelligible shape. Rather than debating the difference between the "best available control technology" and "lowest achievable emission rate,"[49] citizens will be encouraged to focus on a different question when the environmental acts come up for revision: During the next *n* years, should we instruct the EPA gradually to decrease (or increase) the number of pollution rights by *x* percent? Environmentalists will, of course, argue for big reductions; others, who are more impressed with the costs of control, will argue for smaller reductions or even selective increases. But at least the congressional debate would be encouraged to focus upon the fundamental question: Speaking broadly, do the American people believe existing environmental objectives are too ambitious (in which case Congress should increase the number of rights), or do they think that Congress should cut back further on pollution by cutting back on the number of rights?

Rather than supposing—as Latin intimates—that such a question should be answered by a cost-benefit analysis, we believe that it is *the* quintessentially political question that should be answered by the legislative process. The great virtue of the marketable permit program is that it puts the question in an operational form accessible to the general public. An analogy from a very different policy area may be instructive. Imagine that the Department of Labor refused to report an unemployment rate each month. Instead, when it was asked about the employment situation, it inundated its audience with stories about how workers in one or another industry might be displaced or reemployed by one or another technology. While such stories *are* informative, wouldn't there be a great danger that the general public and Congress would miss the forest for the trees? The preeminent question that generalist decisionmakers can and should answer is

49. *See* Clean Air Act § 165(a)(4), 42 U.S.C. § 7475(a)(4) (BAT requirements applicable to new sources in prevention of significant deterioration areas); Clean Air Act § 171(3), 42 U.S.C. § 7501(3) (BAT requirements applicable to new sources in nonattainment areas).

how much overall unemployment is tolerable. And for this purpose, the unemployment rate functions as a key control variable. The same holds true in environmental policy: A vote on a proposal to change the overall number of pollution permits would be a vehicle for the democratic formulation of policy superior to any generated by the existing BAT regulatory system.

To put the point more broadly, we propose the use of a new statutory control variable in the design of our environmental statutes. Rather than speaking in *technology-based* terms, the key statutory variables would be *pollution-based*. More precisely, they would specify the *rate of change* in existing levels of pollution that Congress wishes to achieve during the period until the Clean Air Act once more comes up for congressional reconsideration. Under the revised system, Congress would no longer content itself with mouthing pieties about the need to achieve "reasonable further progress"[50] in environmental protection. It would instead specify, in quantitative terms, how much change is "reasonable" by voting for an *n* percent reduction (or increase) in the number of aggregate permits that the EPA would be allowed to auction off annually to the nation's polluters.[51] This single change, we believe, would vastly increase the degree to which the critical questions of environmental policy can be framed in a way that is more transparent to the general public.

This single change, however, can only serve as a first step toward more transparent decisionmaking. Because it is limited to upward or downward adjustment of the *aggregate* pollution levels permitted under federal standards, it does not allow for more discriminating regulation of particular pollution problems. We see no reason, though, for Congress to content itself with the crude uniformity that Latin commends. For example, within the general context of a 20% rights reduction, Congress might target certain pollutants for a 40% reduction, while allowing others to be reduced by only 5%. Similarly, Congress may announce principles concerning the way in which the reductions should be allocated across the nation: For example, should stricter cutbacks be scheduled in areas violating primary or secondary health standards? In ecologically sensitive areas? If so, by how much?

50. *See* Clean Air Act § 171(1), 42 U.S.C. § 7501(1).

51. *See* J. KRIER & E. URSIN, *supra* note 8 (authors proposed a similar reduction schedule to deal with noncompliance with federal air quality standards under the Clean Air Act).

Latin insists that such decisions would require Congress to guess about countless contestable matters involving both facts and values. And in this he is surely right. The fact is, however, that these uncertainties already exist, and it is precisely because they cannot be resolved technocratically that they should be framed in a way that invites *self-conscious* political decision by the Congress. In contrast, the BAT system fails to focus attention on the overall rate at which America should clean up the environment, leaving it to unguided and disjointed bureaucratic and judicial decision in an endless series of BAT inquiries into the "availability" of one or another cleanup technology.

B. *Long-Term Strategies: Toward Decentralization and Constrained Cost-Effectiveness Analysis*

While the piecemeal "first-generation" change described in the previous subsection stands on its own merits, it also lays the foundation for a "second-generation" reform in setting environmental goals: Congress would create a statutory foundation for *legally constrained cost-effectiveness analysis*. Like the first-generation approach, this second-generation statute would express itself in terms of a change-oriented, pollution-based command. Imagine, for example, that the reformed statute mandated a 20% reduction in allowable pollution levels over the next ten years. In contrast to our first-generation approach, however, the statute would not insist that the 20% cutback be obtained in each and every part of the country, or in those areas specified by Congress. Instead, the EPA, in conjunction with state and regional authorities, would be given discretion to allocate the cleanup effort. So long as an *average* 20% cutback was achieved, the statute would enable administrators to force some areas to cut back up to 30% while allowing others to cut back only 10%— provided that they could support these judgments with a thoughtful cost-effectiveness analysis indicating that such variations would lead to cutbacks where they would do the most good in reducing health risks and harm to the environment.

In allowing for limited regional variation, we would be making a final break with the BAT insistence upon nationwide uniformity. We believe that completely uniform goals are seriously dysfunctional, producing too much control in some regions, too little in others, and completely missing special problems in still other regions. A notorious example of mindless uniformity is the effluent limitations imposed by the present Clean Water Act, which have required the same level of cleanup by all plants in a given industry, regardless of whether a plant discharges into an ocean or large lake, where the discharges will have little or no effect, or into a pristine river.[52] This blindness to environmental reality—which is replicated in many other areas[53]—is a parody of the ecological consciousness that should motivate sound policymaking.

Latin, however, opposes every institutional step aimed to take regional variation into account. He attacks our advocacy of constrained cost-effectiveness analysis by supposing that we champion a slide rule determination of economically optimal controls for every source of every pollutant in every region. As we have already noted, we have never advocated such views. Our own study of particular problems, however, has convinced us that it *is* possible to conduct an intelligent debate about whether, for example, it makes more sense to clean up the Delaware River in the vicinity of Philadelphia or whether greater percentage cutbacks are warranted in the ecologically threatened regions of the Delaware Bay.[54] We fully agree that a narrow economic analysis can

52. *See, e.g.*, Appalachian Power Co. v. EPA, 671 F.2d 801 (4th Cir. 1982). The original system of nationally uniform ambient air quality standards in the Clean Air Act, § 109, 42 U.S.C. § 7409, have been transformed into a nonuniform system by subsequent amendments that recognize the difficulty of achieving the standards in nonattainment areas, *see* Clean Air Act §§ 171–78, 42 U.S.C. §§ 7501–08, and the desirability of prevention of significant deterioration (PSD) in clean air regions, *see* Clean Air Act §§ 160–69A, 42 U.S.C. §§ 7470–79, 7491. The nonattainment and PSD systems are not based, however, on ecological and health realities, but on the happenstance of BAT implementation and the historical accident that some regions have been less industrially developed, and therefore less polluted, than others.

53. Consider recent congressional proposals to deal with toxic pollution problems by mandatory uniform BAT controls on industrial sources. For example, H.R. 2576, 99th Cong., 1st Sess. (1985), introduced by Congressmen Wirth, Waxman, and Florio, would require the EPA to set stringent BAT standards for 85 named chemical substances, plus any additional substances that might contribute to serious illness. Any citizen could petition the EPA to designate a substance, and the EPA would be required to respond within 180 days. If the EPA failed to set stringent standards for any such substance within two years, the applicable standard would be "no detectable release." This is the use of an indiscriminate BAT strategy with a vengeance, ignoring evidence suggesting that many problems are localized ones in which nonindustrial sources play a major role. *See* E. Haemisegger, The Air Toxic Problem in the United States: An Analysis of Cancer Risks for Selected Pollutants (EPA–450/1–85–001 (1985)); U.S. Environmental Protection Agency, A Strategy to Reduce Risks to Public Health from Air Toxics (June 1985). *See also* Harrington, Krupnick & Peskin, *Policies for Nonpoint-source Water Pollution Control*, 40 J. SOIL & WATER CONSERVATION 27 (1985).

54. *See* B. ACKERMAN, S. ROSE-ACKERMAN, J. SAWYER & D. HENDERSON, *supra* note 11.

only serve as part of an answer to such questions; nonetheless, it is also wrong to imagine that these questions can be responsibly answered without taking costs, as well as benefits, into account. In the end, of course, there will be no escaping the inherently controversial nature of the particular administrative judgments in which cost-effectiveness analysis plays some role. So long as particular agency decisions are made within a larger framework of Congressional policy, however, we believe that they will generate an ongoing public discussion that will, over time, greatly enhance the insight with which the nation confronts its environmental dilemmas.[55]

Latin opposes ecologically and economically sensitive goal-setting exercises on the ground that our empirical understanding of the relevant factors is often rudimentary. But this falsely supposes that cost-effectiveness analysis is useful only when it delivers clear and decisive technocratic answers to policy problems. In our view, such analyses only serve to guide, and not displace, intelligent guesswork. The question is whether we operate under a system, like BAT, which tries to ignore or suppress uncertainty, or whether we operate in a world in which decisionmakers are encouraged to make their guesses as openly and intelligently as they can.[56] The goal for a second-generation statute is to create a system in which decisionmakers can make limited variations in national priorities in the light of their best guesses about the regional realities they confront.

We entirely agree with Latin, however, that an immediate

55. *See* Reich, *Public Administration and Public Deliberation: An Interpretive Essay,* 94 YALE L.J. 1617 (1985).

56. Agency officials may fear that more explicit acknowledgment of uncertainty will make agency decisions more vulnerable on judicial review. But the record suggests that this fear is, as a general matter, unfounded. Courts generally respect agency choices that explicitly acknowledge uncertainty. *See, e.g.*, Environmental Defense Fund v. EPA, 548 F.2d 998 (D.C. Cir. 1976), *cert. denied,* 431 U.S. 925 (1977); Lead Indus. Ass'n v. EPA, 647 F.2d 1130 (D.C. Cir.), *cert. denied,* 449 U.S. 1042 (1980); Chemical Mfrs. Ass'n v. EPA, 673 F.2d 507 (D.C. Cir. 1982). *But cf.* Motor Vehicle Mfrs. Ass'n v. State Farm Mut. Auto. Ins. Co., 463 U.S. 29 (1983) (agencies must provide explanations for their decisions and must have adequate studies to reduce key uncertainties. Where agencies suppress uncertainty and seek to base decisions on narrow economic or technological grounds—as the BAT strategy encourages them to do—their decisions are often more vulnerable because the agency's resolution of these technical issues can more readily be shown to be empirically or technically flawed. *See, e.g.*, Portland Cement Ass'n v. Ruckelshaus, 486 F.2d 375 (D.C. Cir. 1973), *cert. denied,* 417 U.S. 921 (1974); 513 F.2d 506 (D.C. Cir.), *cert. denied,* 423 U.S. 1025 (1975) (BAT air pollution standards); Weyerhaeuser Co. v. Costle, 590 F.2d 1011 (D.C. Cir. 1978) (BAT water pollution control standards).

statutory embrace of regional variation would be premature at the present time. Before taking such a step, we must first construct stronger regional institutions than now exist in the overcentralized federal system. We look forward to a day when we might go to any region in the country and find a serious professional staff that could both describe the existing environmental data and models and explain how they propose to improve them over the next five or ten years. Without such an ongoing system of data collection and analysis, there can be little hope of designing regulatory systems which are sensitive to regional ecological and economic realities. Rather than conceiving the construction of such ongoing regional centers as a bit of "fine-tuning," we think that their absence constitutes one of the principal failures of the present system.[57] Indeed, if an effort at regional institution-building had been inaugurated 15 years ago with the enactment of the Clean Air and Water Acts, Professor Latin's assertions about the abysmal state of our ignorance would, by now, have less justification.

It is wrong, moreover, to assume that our failure to construct the requisite regional infrastructure is simply a result of tight EPA budgets.[58] The agency, after all, has spent plenty of time and money engaging in factfinding inquiry regarding the state of the best available technology. The reason for the infrastructural failure is that ongoing careful region-by-region study is irrelevant to the regulatory effort as defined by the present BAT system. To change agency incentives, our reformed law would expressly contemplate a more sophisticated form of auction to commence at some future point in time, say 10 or 15 years after enactment. Under these second-generation actions, different regions of the country could be allowed to cut back permitted quantities by dif-

57. What we propose is the modern-day equivalent of the plan, aired but never pushed in Franklin Roosevelt's second term, for a series of regional TVAs throughout the nation. *See* B. KARL, THE UNEASY STATE: THE UNITED STATES FROM 1915 TO 1945, 164–67 (1983).

58. See note 28 *supra*, for the paltry sums that are presently invested in the effort to monitor environmental realities. It is, of course, no easy matter to create strong regional authorities within our political system. But the TVA experience suggests that the federal government can most readily promote such authorities by endowing them with economic resources and responsibility for their management. By contrast, it is far more difficult to create new authorities with the power, customarily reserved to the national and state governments, to issue and coercively enforce legally binding orders. Accordingly, the shift in tools from BAT commands to transferable pollution permits—the federally created resource which our proposed new authorities would manage—will facilitate the development of regional institutions.

ferent amounts on the basis of a thoughtful cost-effectiveness analysis; similarly, each regional authority would be allowed to vary cutbacks *within* its region to account for special conditions.[59] At no point, however, would we endorse unfettered technocratic cost-benefit analysis. Congress would continue to decide the overall magnitude of natural cleanup and to stipulate an allowable range of variation that could be justified through regional analysis and decision.

C. *Priority-Setting*

Our final set of proposals seeks to correct serious deficiencies in the process by which the current BAT system sets priorities in the light of changing information about environmental realities. BAT discourages intelligent priority-setting for two related reasons. First, the EPA is so overwhelmed by factfinding tasks required to implement a technology-based approach that it has relatively few resources left for exploration of risks posed by new pollutants. Second, BAT imposes heavy bureaucratic costs on the EPA every time it recognizes a new threat to the environment. Once a new pollutant has been identified, BAT requires the agency to exhaust itself with yet another series of never-ending inquiries into the state of control technology in each of the industries that have been discharging the "newly discovered" pollutant and to establish an elaborate set of new industry-by-industry standards. Finally, once a pollutant has been targeted for regulation, BAT automatically requires the imposition of controls to the full extent of available technology[60]—a potentially enormous commitment of compliance resources that may not be justified by the benefits achieved and that is likely to be strongly

59. Of course, if the agency did not exercise its discretion, or if its regional variances did not survive judicial review, the national average (in our example, 20 %) would apply in the regions affected. Given its long-run perspective, a second-generation statute could also provide a schedule that would contemplate a lengthy period for administrative rulemaking and judicial review.

60. "Available technology" is an elastic concept. In many instances, including most cases of water pollution, technology is available in an engineering sense to eliminate pollution entirely. If we were willing to spend hundreds of billions of dollars, we could have drinking water flowing from industrial waste discharge pipes (although disposing of the pollutants removed from waste streams could present serious problems). Accordingly, most decisions about "available" technology must—implicitly or explicitly— take costs into account. The vice of the BAT strategy is that it ignores this inevitable cost-benefit consideration, or at best buries it, by treating it as an engineering decision about technological feasibility.

opposed by industry through protracted litigation. It should be no surprise, then, that the EPA has, in fact, been reluctant to expand the number of its pollution targets.[61]

The administrative inertia generated by BAT was, perhaps, of secondary concern so long as one could believe that environmental degradation was the product of a few widespread pollutants, each of which should be controlled to the greatest extent feasible within a period of years. After a decade's practical experience with environmental regulation, however, it should be clear that there are thousands of substances that pose at least some risk and that we cannot deal with all of them simultaneously or impose BAT on all of them within the near future. The defect of the BAT system is that it tends to select, more or less arbitrarily, a relatively few pollutants and devotes enormous administrative and control resources to regulating them to the hilt.

The reforms we have already advocated will create new incentives for the innovative priority-setting that is needed in today's world. First, a statute whose control variables were pollution-based, rather than technology-based, would encourage a more focused discussion of whether the goals set for different pollutants reflect sensible priorities. Indeed, it is not fanciful to suppose that a risk portfolio strategy eventually might emerge that would explicitly attempt to rank the comparative risks confronted by an EPA or an OSHA and then use cost-effectiveness analysis to determine how available administrative and control resources might best be devoted to minimizing overall risk in a given time period.[62] Such a strategy need not be limited to conventional air

61. Courts have empowered environmental plaintiffs to force agency action upon presentation of a prima facie case that a currently unregulated pollutant presents a substantial hazard, *see* Environmental Defense Fund, Inc. v. Ruckelshaus, 439 F.2d 584 (D.C. Cir. 1971), and Congress has codified these rulings in "action-forcing" statutory "citizen-suit" provisions. *See, e.g.*, Clean Air Act § 304, 42 U.S.C. § 7604; H.R. 2576, note 53 *supra*. While agency inaction is, as we have noted, a serious problem under a BAT regime, the reliance on "action-forcing" through litigation may well be a cure worse than the disease. Such a strategy invites a "pollutant of the month" approach to priority-setting. There is no assurance that the initiatives selected by different environmental groups will result in a sensible allocation of limited administrative and compliance resources. The Supreme Court's recent decision in Heckler v. Chaney, 105 S. Ct. 1649 (1985) may reduce "action-forcing" litigation in the context of regulatory statutes that do not contain citizen-suit provisions. *See generally* Sunstein, *Reviewing Agency Inaction After* Heckler v. Chaney, 52 U. CHI. L. REV. 653 (1985). But this would merely alleviate symptoms of the current BAT system without providing any positive incentives for intelligent priority-setting.

62. In order to reduce some of the administrative and other problems involved in

and water pollutants. It could also be used, for example, to manage the risks posed by pesticides, chemicals, or hazardous wastes.[63]

Second, the adoption of a marketable permit scheme would dramatically change bureaucratic incentives involved in a decision to target a new pollutant. Rather than ignoring new problems in an effort to avoid BAT burdens, the EPA may well gain additional bureaucratic resources by altering its regulatory priorities, since our proposed statutory reform would reward the agency with a share of any auction revenues that any newly regulated pollutant might generate. Indeed, given their budgetary rewards, a critic might fear that our proposals would generate an equal and opposite danger from the one prevailing under the current regime: Why wouldn't the EPA be transformed into a hyperactive agency, eager to maximize its budgetary revenues by expanding its concern to "pollutants" that do not in fact threaten any serious risk to ecological or human values?

While hyperactivity is a danger, its seriousness should not be exaggerated. After all, every large bureaucratic organization ex-

---

establishing separate permits and markets for many different pollutants, a "mutual fund" variant of the portfolio approach might be used, where appropriate, to control related pollutants through permits based on a weighted average of volume and risk.

63. Development of such strategies will take considerable time, and there will inevitably remain discrete sources of risk that must be dealt with through command-and-control standards or screening procedures. In these limited contexts, regulatory negotiation may be a promising mechanism for promoting more informed regulatory decisionmaking that is sensitive to the magnitude of various risks and the practical problems of managing them.

Latin devotes extensive energies to criticizing those portions of Stewart, note 5 *supra*, that favor increased experimentation with regulatory negotiation. While legitimately raising many real questions and doubts about the practicality and desirability of regulatory negotiation, Latin commits characteristic errors. First, he supposes that the author regards regulatory negotiation as one of a host of fungible "fine-tuning" mechanisms. The article in fact makes quite clear that regulatory negotiation is a "second best" ameliorative solution, and that economic incentive systems are a basic and preferred alternative to the existing command-and-control system. Second, Latin completely ignores recent practical experience that regulatory negotiation can work successfully to alleviate the worst features of the present adversary, legalistic regulatory system. Contrary to Latin's a priori predictions, the developing experience with regulatory negotiation shows that self-interested business, advocacy, and governmental groups and authorities in fact find negotiated solutions preferable to the expense and uncertainty of protracted legal proceedings. *See* Lempert, *Participants See Value in Reg-Neg's First Flight*, LEGAL TIMES, Oct. 10, 1983, at 2, col. 1 (partial success of regulatory negotiation at FAA); Miller, *Steel Effluent Limitations: Success at the Negotiating Table*, 13 ENVTL. L. REP. 10,094 (1983); L. Susskind & J. McMahon, Documentation of EPA's Nonconformance Penalties (NCP) Negotiated Rulemaking Demonstration (Report to U.S. EPA, Jan. 1985).

periences a great deal of difficulty redefining its priorities. Given the reality of bureaucratic inertia, and the fact that industry will continue to resist new initiatives (particularly when it must pay for the right to pollute),[64] we believe that it is wiser to offer budgetary rewards for innovative priority-setting rather than allow BAT to reinforce bureaucratic reluctance to take changing environmental realities into account.

Our proposed shift in bureaucratic incentives, however, does reinforce the need for a regulatory structure that endorses thoughtful cost-effectiveness analysis in the priority-setting process. Up to the present time, legislators have been able to indulge in apparently absolute statutory prohibitions of all harmful pollutants. This was possible because legislators could count on regulatory lethargy and covert consideration of costs by administrators in defining BAT to blunt statutory calls for an all-out war on pollution. Once a reformed statute has changed the balance of incentives for bureaucratic innovation, we should insist on thoughtful cost-effectiveness analysis before a new pollutant is made the subject of a marketable permit auction. The critical question, in each case, should be whether available administrative and compliance resources will achieve more reduction in environmental risks if they are used to control the new pollutant rather than being used to deal with other pollutants. (For these purposes, costs—like benefits— should not be measured in any mechanical way, and will inevitably involve major social judgments.) If so, the "new" pollutant should be regulated on the basis of the same pollution-based principles that we have elaborated previously; if not, it should not be regulated. Of course, even if an agency refused to list a new pollutant, Congress would be free to force the agency to change its mind the next time the governing statute is reappraised.[65] Once again, cost-benefit analysis would be subordinated to democratic decision.

Finally, we do not believe that all steps toward more intelli-

64. Industry pressure will also operate to offset potential EPA reluctance, for fiscal reasons, to increase the number of permits for a pollutant already being regulated when new evidence shows that the risks it poses are not nearly as great as originally believed.

65. Given the need for agency flexibility in priority-setting and the dangers of judicial inculcation of the "pollutant of the month" syndrome, we would exclude full-scale judicial review of decisions whether or not to initiate regulatory action against particular substances in all but extreme cases of arbitrariness, *provided* that a regulatory agency had developed an informed and reasonable process of priority-setting under which the refusal to act in a particular case can be justified.

gent priority-setting should be delayed until the adoption of some of the more far-reaching reforms we have advanced. It should be emphasized that analysis of costs and benefits is *not*, as some environmentalists too easily suppose, a code word for regulatory passivity. A stunning counterexample is the EPA's recent decision substantially to eliminate lead additives in gasoline. The key to this decision was an economic analysis performed in the EPA's Office of Planning and Policy Evaluation showing that the move would achieve major health benefits at little or no net cost.[66] Critics like Latin, moreover, underestimate the amount of information which *does* exist, but which is ignored by regulators who refuse to confront ecological and economic realities. The EPA, for example, routinely develops information relating each industry's costs of control to the amount of pollution or risk the industry's investment can be expected to eliminate.[67] It simply fails to use this available information to make the allocation of burdens among industries more cost-effective or to target enforcement resources to the highest-priority problems. Recent changes in the EPA's approach—again, ignored by Latin—show that such steps are feasible. For example, the EPA recently decided not to regulate emissions of acrylonitrile and other toxic emissions under section 112 of the Clean Air Act when analysis suggested that the risks involved were relatively low compared to the more serious problems posed by chromium emissions—which it did decide to regulate.[68] Such examples show that it is feasible to do a better job of goal-setting—by introducing cost-effectiveness considerations in evaluating control options for different risks and setting priorities more intelligently—even within the existing BAT system.

Steps such as these will not necessarily impose greater burdens on administrators than those that prevail under the BAT approach.[69] Even when they do involve additional burdens for

66. *See* note 38 *supra*.

67. *See, e.g.*, Crandall, *supra* note 7, at 214–15 (EPA data reproduced in table 8.1).

68. *See* "EPA to List Chromium Under Section 112, Decides Not to List Four Other Substances," 16 ENV'T REP. CURRENT DEVS. 236 (June 7, 1985); Harrison, Haig & Nichols, note 10 *supra*.

69. For example, in the 1972 Federal Water Pollution Control Amendments, Congress imposed uniform technology-based standards in order to avoid the transaction costs and implementation problems involved in policing environmental quality standards. In order to simplify decisionmaking, the 1972 Act ignored variations in water quality uses and goals. In implementing the Act, however, the EPA felt compelled to consider cost and other variables indirectly in setting BAT standards. This indirect ap-

administrators, however, this fact alone should not condemn them. The question is whether increased administrative costs are outweighed by greater benefits for society as a whole. The EPA's development of the bubble and tradeoff policies required additional information-gathering, analysis, and other effort. But the payoff has been enormous. The bubble alone has saved over $700 million[70] and stimulated new ways of cleaning up pollution. To focus on administrative costs, without considering the societal benefits of more intelligent regulation, produces penny-wise and pound-foolish public policies. Such myopia is understandable, if not excusable, in politicians. It should not be encouraged by academics who ignore solid evidence that reform can and has worked.

Conclusion

In urging the fundamental reform of environmental law, we do not mean to disparage the very great accomplishments of the generation that enacted sweeping federal legislation in the late 1960s and early 1970s. Apart from the many unambiguous achievements of this statutory revolution, even the embrace of a BAT approach made some sense as a crude first-generation strategy. During the early days of federal environmental concern, perhaps it was plausible for politicians and other policymakers to suppose that only a few pollution problems were out of hand and that these problems could be "solved" in a short time by an all-out war against "pollution." From this perspective, it could seem reasonable to try to force everyone to adopt the best available technology everywhere.

Our complaint is not with the statutory draftsmen of the early 1970s, but with lawyers of the 1980s who fail to put these early statutes in historical perspective.[71] Experience with more than a decade of intensive regulation emphasizes that the environmental risks we confront are numerous and vary widely in serious-

proach caused the EPA to set separate standards for over 500 different industry and subindustry standards, a majority of which were challenged in court. Long delays in implementing the statutory scheme resulted. *See also* R. Melnick, *supra* note 9, at 193–205 (chronicling problems in adjusting the uniform federal air quality standards to differing local and regional circumstances).

70. *See* note 37 *supra* and accompanying text.

71. For another effort to put these statutes in perspective, see Elliott, Ackerman & Millian, *Toward A Theory of Statutory Evolution: The Federalization of Environmental Law,* 1 J. Law, Econ., & Org. 313 (1985) (forthcoming).

ness. Our strategies for managing these risks must set intelligent priorities, make maximum use of the resources devoted to improving environmental quality, encourage environmentally superior technologies, and avoid unneeded penalties on innovation and investment. Rather than wringing our hands helplessly before these complexities, the challenge is to incorporate maturing perceptions about our regulatory problems into the evolving legal structure—and help our fellow Americans build a system that will not only save many billions of dollars a year, but make environmental law more democratically accountable and bureaucratically effective. It is time for environmental lawyers to stop celebrating the statutory revolution of the 1970s and to start building a statutory structure worthy of the year 2000.

[9]

ECONOMIC REFORM OF ENVIRONMENTAL PROTECTION: A BRIEF COMMENT ON A RECENT DEBATE

*Joel A. Mintz**

As environmental law neared and passed what is widely acknowledged to be its twentieth anniversary,[1] American scholars, lawyers, scientists and government officials have increasingly assayed the merits and practical implications of altering the fundamental thrust of federal environmental policy.[2] Rather than concentrate on particular statutes, administrative regulations, cases and other materials that constitute the corpus of the field, many of these writers have considered the federal law of pollution control as a whole. These writings suggest a plethora of differing

* Professor of Law, Nova University Shepard L. Broad Law Center. J.S.D. 1989, Columbia University; LL.M. 1982, Columbia University; J.D. 1974, New York University; B.A. 1970, Columbia University. I wish to acknowledge the research assistance of Leonard Berger in the preparation of this piece.

1. The precise "beginning date" of modern environmental law in the United States is controversial. Some observers trace the origins of the field to the publication of Rachel Carson's celebrated study of the ecological hazards posed by the pesticide DDT, R. CARSON, SILENT SPRING (1962). Others date its commencement to the landmark litigation in Scenic Hudson Preservation Conference v. Federal Power Comm'n, 354 F.2d 608 (2d Cir. 1965). The prevailing view, however, is that the current era in environmental regulation began in 1970 with the dramatic Earth Day celebration of that year and the passage of the National Environmental Policy Act of 1969, Pub. L. No. 91-190, 83 Stat. 852–56 (1970) (codified as amended at 42 U.S.C. §§ 4321–4370a (1988)), and the Clean Air Amendments of 1970, Pub. L. No. 91-604, 84 Stat. 1676 (1970) (codified as amended as part of Chapter 85—Air Pollution Prevention and Control, at 42 U.S.C. §§ 7401–7642 (1988)).

2. Among the more provocative and significant of these studies are: M. SAGOFF, THE ECONOMY OF THE EARTH, (1988); D. VOGEL, NATIONAL STYLES OF REGULATION: ENVIRONMENTAL POLICY IN GREAT BRITAIN AND THE UNITED STATES (1986); Babich, *Restructuring Environmental Law*, 19 Envtl. L. Rep. (Envtl. L. Inst.) 10,057 (1989); Blackwelder, *Environmental Benefits of Tax Reform*, 16 Envtl. L. Rep. (Envtl. L. Inst.) 10,322 (1986); Du Pont, *Environmental Law for the 1990's: Focus Private Initiative, Don't Stifle It*, 17 Envtl. L. Rep. (Envtl. L. Inst.) 10,353 (1987); Dwyer, *Contentiousness and Cooperation in Environmental Regulation*, 35 AM. J. COMP. L. 809 (1987); Portney, *Reforming Environmental Regulation: Three Modest Proposals*, 13 COLUM J. ENVTL. L. 201 (1988); Reilly, *The Future of Environmental Law*, 6 YALE J. ON REG. 351 (1989); Reitze, *Environmental Policy—It Is Time For A New Beginning*, 14 COLUM. J. ENVTL. L. 111 (1989); Rodgers, *The Lesson of the Owl and the Crows: The Role of Deception in the Evolution of the Environmental Statutes*, 4 J. LAND USE & ENVTL. L. 377 (1989); Rodgers, *The Lesson of the Red Squirrel: Consensus and Betrayal in the Environmental Statutes*, 5 J. CONTEMP. HEALTH L. & POL'Y 161 (1989); Russell, *Environmental Protection for the 1990's and Beyond*, 29 ENV'T 12 (1987); and Schoenbrod, *Environmental Law and Growing Up*, 6 YALE J. ON REG. 357 (1989).

"solutions" to the perceived shortcomings of a legal discipline whose extraordinary growth has paralleled its rising importance in our national political life.[3]

This Commentary is a critical review of one aspect of this literature. In Part I, I consider some of the claims of the "economic critique" of prevailing environmental policies. For example, I examine the notion that our current system of federal environmental regulation is unduly costly, litigious and stifling. These critics advocate economic incentive systems such as transferable pollution permits and pollution charges as desirable environmental reforms. In Part I, I also examine some criticisms that have been made of the economic critique and, in Part II, assess their validity. In Part III, I conclude by suggesting that, to the extent that economic reforms hold promise, these reforms of environmental programs should be implemented in selected communities on a "demonstration project" or trial basis, rather than fully substituted for existing regulatory programs.

I. Economic Approaches to Environmental Law Reform: A Summary of the Recent Debate

Economic criticism of environmental law is not a new phenomenon. Almost since the inception of the field, economists and legal scholars have argued that environmental requirements impose unnecessary costs and inhibit technological innovation.[4] In recent years, however, the pace of economic criticism of federal environmental regulation has increased.[5]

---

3. As Arnold Reitze has pointed out, the major federal environmental statutes now fill a 654-page book, and federal environmental regulations encompass 11 volumes and 8606 pages of the Code of Federal Regulations. Reitze, *supra* note 2, at 112.

4. *See, e.g.*, B. Ackerman, S. Rose-Ackerman, J. Sawyer & D. Henderson, The Uncertain Search for Environmental Quality (1974); F. Anderson, A. Kneese, P. Reed, S. Taylor & R. Stevenson, Environmental Improvement Through Economic Incentives (1977); A. Kneese & Schultze, Pollution, Prices and Public Policy (1975).

5. In addition to the articles discussed in this Commentary, see B. Ackerman & W. Hassler, Clean Coal/Dirty Air (1981); S. Breyer, Regulation and Its Reform (1982); R. Melnick, Regulation and the Courts: The Case of the Clean Air Act (1983); Stewart, *Regulation, Innovation and Administrative Law: A Conceptual Framework*, 69 Calif. L. Rev. 1256 (1981); and Breyer, *Analyzing Regulatory Failure: Mismatches, Less Restrictive Alternatives and Reform*, 92 Harv. L. Rev. 547 (1979). For a listing of further writings of this genre, see the bibliographies at the end of each chapter in T. Tietenberg, Emissions Trading, an Exercise in Reforming Pollution Policy (1985).

Richard Stewart has been a persistent critic of the present regime of environmental laws. His most recent law review article on the subject[6] provides a summary of many of the contentions and suggestions of scholars who take an economic approach to environmental policy. In forceful and eloquent prose, Stewart argues that the current system of federal environmental regulation is beset by several inevitable drawbacks: excessive bureaucratic centralization, rigidity, high cost, litigation, and delay.[7] According to Stewart:

> Our current environmental regulatory system . . . has grown to the point where it amounts to nothing less than a massive effort at Soviet-style central planning of the economy to achieve environmental goals. It strangles investment and innovation. It encourages costly and divisive litigation and delay. It unduly limits private initiative and choice.[8]

In response to these concerns, Stewart proposes that federal environmental laws be modified to incorporate economic incentive systems. These systems include waste deposit programs, refund programs, and charges on polluters which, for instance, impose a fee on each ton or other unit of pollution discharged. Stewart's most significant reforms would be a system of transferable pollution permits. This transferable permit system would operate by, first, limiting the total units of pollution permitted, second, issuing freely marketable permits equal in number to the emission units permitted, and third, requiring polluters to have permits equal to their discharges.[9]

While Stewart strongly advocates transferable permit systems, he concedes that such a system is not necessarily appropriate

6. Stewart, *Controlling Environmental Risks Through Economic Incentives*, 13 COLUM. J. ENVTL. L. 153 (1988).

7. *Id.* at 153.

8. *Id.* at 154. Professor Stewart also argues that "federal regulators have relied heavily on 'wholesale' standards that impose the same [technology-based] requirements on all sources in a given industry or other category. In order to simplify the decision process further, federal regulators have ignored local environmental variables and relied heavily on rationally uniform technology-based standards. This wholesale approach produced standards that require more control than necessary to achieve environmental quality objectives in some areas, and less control than is necessary in others." *Id.* at 156. Furthermore, he contends that "[c]entralized regulation tends to discourage technological innovation and investment in new products and plants, harming the international competitiveness of United States industry." *Id.* at 158.

9. *Id.* at 159.

for all pollution problems. For example, he indicates that such a system should not be applied to substances like pesticides that create risks which "elude workable quantification."[10] Similarly, he states that marketable permit systems may be inappropriate "in dealing with pollutants or chemical risks that have localized 'threshold' effects, causing serious damage only if they exceed a given concentration at a particular location."[11] Stewart further qualifies his position by stipulating that administrative feasibility should be taken into account, particularly given the lack of agency experience in administering these types of economic incentives. He states: "The lack of operational experience with economic incentives in many settings makes wholesale change undesirable. The problems of transition from the existing regulatory system to new incentive systems must also be carefully considered."[12]

Professor Stewart contends that the economic reforms he advocates will have a number of advantages for the private sector. They will, in his view, encourage flexibility in control technologies, achieve large cost savings and provide enterprises with an ongoing incentive to devise new products or production technologies to reduce environmental risk.[13] Government agencies also will benefit from economic reforms, since they no longer will have to acquire detailed information needed to determine the feasible and appropriate level of control for each plant or product, and since economic incentive systems can be used to provide the government with a new source of revenue.[14] Further, Stewart argues, economic approaches will enhance the democratic accountability of environmental policy decisions by moving public debate from complex technological issues to more fundamental questions of what environmental risks should be controlled and how extensive those controls should be.[15]

---

10. *Id.* at 161.
11. *Id.*
12. *Id.* at 165.
13. *Id.* at 160.
14. *Id.*
15. *Id. See also* Ackerman & Stewart, *Reforming Environmental Law: The Democratic Case for Market Incentives*, 13 COLUM. J. ENVTL. L. 171 (1988). Ackerman and Stewart write:

> BAT [referring to the Best Available Technology regimes under the Clean Air Act and the Clean Water Act] focuses Congressional debate, as well as administrative and judicial proceedings, upon arcane technological questions which rapidly exhaust the time and energy that most politicians, let alone the larger

The economic approach typified by Stewart's writing has not gone without criticism. One of its most trenchant critics is Howard Latin, whose writings have questioned some of the fundamental assumptions of the economic reformers.[16] Latin argues that the academic literature on regulatory reform reflects "an excessive preoccupation with theoretical efficiency," while placing inadequate emphasis on "actual decisionmaking costs and implementation constraints."[17] He contends that the inherent complexities of ecological systems, combined with a paucity of "adequate data and risk assessment methodologies for environmental dangers,"[18] would create delay and inconsistency in any economic incentive system. Such a system would, according to Latin, "increase decisionmaking costs . . . and [create] opportunities for manipulative behavior by regulated parties."[19]

Latin contends that the published work of Richard Stewart does not explain "why the asserted ability of economic incentive mechanisms to promote innovation should outweigh the propensity of those strategies to decrease environmental protection under conditions of uncertainty."[20] In his opinion, society's real choice, in many environmental protection contexts, may be to rely either on crude regulation or on no regulation. Under those circumstances, insistence upon particularized decisionmaking—as opposed to uniform pollution control standards—may be "not only intellectually misguided but politically naive."[21] Latin argues that fine-tuning environmental decisions is just as likely to result in net social harm as in net social benefit under conditions of uncertainty.

In a spirited rejoinder, published in the same issue of the *Stanford Law Review* in which Professor Latin's article appears,

---

> public, are willing to spend on environmental matters. In contrast, the marketable permit system will allow the policymaking debate to take a far more intelligible shape. Rather than debating the difference between the "best available control technology" and "lowest achievable emission rate", [sic] citizens may focus upon a different question when the environmental acts come up for revision: During the next *n* years, should we instruct the EPA gradually to decrease (or increase) the number of pollution rights by *x* percent?

Id. at 189.

16. *See, e.g.*, Latin, *Ideal Versus Real Regulatory Efficiency: Implementation of Uniform Standards and 'Fine-Tuning' Regulatory Reforms*, 37 STAN. L. REV. 1267 (1985).

17. *Id.* at 1270.

18. *Id.* at 1273–74.

19. *Id.* at 1332.

20. *Id.* at 1290.

21. *Id.* at 1332.

Bruce Ackerman and Richard Stewart take issue with many of Latin's conclusions.[22] Ackerman and Stewart contend that Latin uses "a Panglossian argument to rationalize the current regulatory status quo."[23] In their view:

> [T]o focus on administrative costs, without considering the societal benefits of more intelligent regulation, produces penny-wise and pound-foolish public policies. Such myopia . . . should not be encouraged by academics who ignore solid evidence that reform can and has worked.[24]

The authors defend their position by claiming that their earlier writings recognized the problems of limited information and regulatory complexity.[25] They concede that a reformed system of environmental regulation will "not easily solve all foreseeable regulatory problems"[26] and that "administrative feasibility is an important constraint on the degree of sophistication that we may reasonably expect."[27] However, rather than responding to the details of Latin's critique, they make a renewed attack on the existing system of pollution regulation, which they characterize as "primarily based upon a best available technology strategy."[28]

Ackerman and Stewart call for a system of transferable pollution permits similar to the economic incentive system advocated in the Stewart piece discussed above.[29] In response to Latin's concerns about implementation, they write:

> Rather than imagining reform as one extravagant great leap forward, we envision a series of steps in an ongoing process of piecemeal improvement . . . . Thus, the market implementation mechanism [that we advocate is] . . . based on the allowable pollution loads *prevailing under existing law* . . . . We hope that doubts about the institutional feasibility of some of our long run proposals will not deflect attention from feasible short

22. Ackerman & Stewart, *Reforming Environmental Law*, 37 STAN. L. REV. 1333 (1985).
23. *Id.* at 1333.
24. *Id.* at 1364.
25. *Id.* at 1352.
26. *Id.* at 1350.
27. *Id.* at 1351.
28. *Id.* at 1334–35.
29. *See supra* notes 6–15 and accompanying text.

term reforms that promise immediate and substantial improvements.[30]

The authors advocate the implementation of their proposals in two successive stages or "generations" of reform. In the "first generation," the United States Environmental Protection Agency ("EPA") would institute systems of marketable air and water pollution rights that both reflect and incorporate existing pollution control standards. To accomplish this, the EPA would first estimate how much pollution presently is permitted by law in each watershed and air quality control region. Next, the EPA would run a system of auctions, in which polluters could buy rights for a term, as well as establish regional title registries that would allow buyers and sellers to transfer pollution rights. Finally, the EPA would vigorously enforce existing standards so as to penalize polluters who discharge more than their permitted amounts.[31]

In the "second generation" of reform, to be implemented a number of years in the future, different regions of the country would be allowed to reduce permitted emissions on the basis of a cost-effectiveness analysis. Ackerman and Stewart contend that such variations would lead to emission cutbacks where those cutbacks would do the most good in reducing health risks and harm to the environment.[32] Similarly, each regional authority would be permitted to vary pollution cutbacks within its region "to account for special conditions."[33] Finally, unregulated pollutants would be made the subject of a marketable permit auction only after a cost-benefit analysis. This cost-benefit analysis would, in each case, determine whether available administrative and compliance resources would achieve more reduction in environmental risks if they were used to control the new pollutant, rather than being used to regulate other pollutants.[34]

---

30. Ackerman & Stewart, *supra* note 22, at 1352 (emphasis in original).

31. *Id.* at 1347.

32. *Id.* at 1355.

33. *Id.* at 1358–59.

34. Ackerman and Stewart believe that:

> The critical question, in each case, should be whether available administrative and compliance resources will achieve more reduction in environmental risks if they are used to deal with other pollutants. (For these purposes, costs—like benefits—should not be measured in any mechanical way, and will inevitably

II. Assessing the Debate: A Critical Review

How sound is this economic approach to environmental law reform that Bruce Ackerman and Richard Stewart have proposed?[35] How significant are the criticisms of their approach that Howard Latin has offered? How fully have Ackerman and Stewart responded to Latin's concerns? Contentions on both sides of this debate have merit. Nonetheless, I believe that Ackerman and Stewart's most recent suggestions fail to dispel all the doubts Latin's critique raises about administrative workability.

In the remainder of this Commentary, I shall contend that while certain of Ackerman and Stewart's proposals do, in fact, have sufficient promise to warrant their application on a limited basis, those authors have misconstrued or ignored certain aspects of Latin's analysis. Ackerman and Stewart's proposed "first generation" reforms—closely tied as they are to the pollution control standards established by the current Clean Air and Clean Water Acts[36]—will not result in all of the benefits those authors claim. Furthermore, their "second generation" proposals run squarely into the objections that Latin has raised concerning decisionmaking costs and implementation constraints.

At the outset, it seems useful to examine the contention, which is central to Ackerman and Stewart's economic critique, that the existing system of pollution regulation is "primarily based upon a best available technology strategy."[37] While this characterization is partially correct, it is a misleading oversimplification of

> involve major social judgments.) If so, the new pollutant should be regulated on the basis of the same pollution-based principles that we have elaborated previously; if not, it should not be regulated.

Id. at 1362. The benefits that Ackerman and Stewart argue this system will provide closely parallel those benefits discussed in Stewart, *Controlling Environmental Risks*, *supra* note 6. *See id.* at 1342–45. In addition, the authors claim that their proposal will improve the enforcement performance of the EPA and associated state agencies by pressuring agency policymakers to make large investments in monitoring and enforcement personnel. *Id.* at 1344–46.

35. Although the first article discussed in this Commentary was written by Stewart alone, *see supra* note 6, for the purposes of this discussion, I refer to the "economic approach" as shared by both Ackerman and Stewart.

36. The Clean Air Act Amendments of 1970, Pub. L. No. 91-604, 84 Stat. 1676 (codified as amended at 42 U.S.C. §§ 7401–7642 (1988)) and the Federal Water Pollution Control Act Amendments of 1972, Pub. L. No. 92-500, 86 Stat. 816 (codified as amended at 33 U.S.C. §§ 1251–1387 (1988).

37. Ackerman & Stewart, *supra* note 22, at 1335.

the complex regulatory scheme articulated by the Clean Air Act and other federal statutes.

Certainly some of the applicable standards of the statutes require that polluters utilize the best available control technology, as defined by the EPA on an industry-by-industry basis, to abate their discharges.[38] At the same time, however, the pollution control requirements that presently apply to existing sources of air and water pollution are, in the main, based upon a wide variety of other kinds of standards. The Clean Water Act, for example, requires application of the "best practicable technology currently available" for certain existing point source dischargers.[39] It further requires application of "best conventional pollutant control technology" to discharges of certain pollutants from point sources.[40] Similarly, the Clean Air Act calls for several kinds of pollution requirements which are based on standards not related to best available control technology.[41] Thus, it is incorrect to describe existing federal pollution control standards as "primarily" based upon best available technology.[42]

When one turns to Ackerman and Stewart's proposal for first generation reforms—grafting a system of transferable pollution permits over existing regulatory standards—other concerns arise. This set of proposals appears unlikely to engender several of the benefits that the authors have predicted. Under this phase of the proposal, the EPA will continue to have responsibility for establishing the pollution control standards under which aggregate "cutbacks" will be made.[43] Presumably, the procedural requirements

38. Perhaps the leading examples are the standards applicable to the regulation of new sources under § 111 of the Clean Air Act, 42 U.S.C. § 7411 (1988), and § 306 of the Clean Water Act, 33 U.S.C. § 1316 (1988), as well as the standards that apply to the discharge of toxic materials from existing point sources of water pollution under § 301(b)(2)(A) of the Clean Water Act, 33 U.S.C. § 1311(b)(2)(A) (1988).

39. Clean Water Act § 301(b)(1)(A), 33 U.S.C. § 1311(b)(1)(A) (1988).

40. Clean Water Act § 301(b)(1)(E), 33 U.S.C. § 1311(b)(2)(E) (1988).

41. Examples include the variable health and welfare based standards, applicable to existing stationary sources, that states must adopt and submit to the EPA as State Implementation Plans pursuant to § 110, 42 U.S.C. § 7410 (1988), and the emission standards the EPA is required to establish as to hazardous air pollutants by § 112, 42 U.S.C. § 7412 (1988).

42. In making this observation, I do *not* mean to suggest that *all* of Ackerman and Stewart's criticisms of the current regulatory system must be dismissed. I will later argue that some of their concerns are valid and should be added to future statutory reforms. *See infra* notes 59–64 and accompanying text. Similarly, my conclusion as to the present nature of federal environmental statutes should not be mistaken for "Panglossian rationalization" of the current regulatory system. I agree that there is need for change.

43. Ackerman & Stewart, *supra* note 22, at 1347.

established by the Administrative Procedure Act[44] and by various specific environmental statutes[45] would continue to apply with regard to those standards. Considering these facts, it is difficult to see how Ackerman and Stewart's first generation suggestions would do much to remedy identified problems of bureaucratic centralization, litigation, and delay. Although individual dischargers would, in fact, have greater flexibility in meeting their particular allocations of the overall cutbacks the EPA mandates, the size of those cutbacks would still be determined by central authority in this phase of the proposed scheme. Furthermore, because dischargers and environmental groups would continue to have vital and conflicting interests in the size, nature, and extent of aggregate emissions cutbacks, the prospect of further litigation and regulatory delay seems undiminished under the proposed economic approach.

It is difficult to credit Ackerman and Stewart's contention that their proposal—at least in its first stage—will relieve "bureaucrats" of the "information processing burden" of "economic and technological assessment."[46] Because the EPA would still be obligated to base its pollution cutback determinations on standards mandated by existing law, EPA decisionmakers would still be required to make numerous technical assessments as to the specific nature of the pollution control technology whose use would form the basis for the cutbacks. In certain instances, the EPA will also have a duty to consider economic costs and feasibility.[47]

Finally, Ackerman and Stewart's proposed first generation reforms may be less likely to improve EPA and state enforcement efforts than they contend.[48] In a recent review of EPA hazardous

44. *See, e.g.*, Administrative Procedure Act § 4, 5 U.S.C. § 553 (1988) (rulemaking).

45. *See, e.g.*, Clean Air Act § 110, 42 U.S.C. § 7410 (1988) (state implementation plans for primary and secondary ambient air quality standards); Clean Water Act § 301, 33 U.S.C. § 1311 (1988) (effluent limitations).

46. *Id.* at 1343.

47. *See, e.g.*, Clean Water Act § 306(b)(1)(B), 33 U.S.C. § 1316(b)(1)(B) (1988) (mandating that the EPA Administrator consider "the cost of achieving . . . effluent reduction" in setting new source performance standards); Clean Air Act § 111(a)(1)(C), 42 U.S.C. § 7411(a)(1)(C) (1988) (establishing an identical requirement as to new source emissions of air pollutants).

48. Ackerman and Stewart argue that their reformed system will improve EPA enforcement:

> If polluters did not expect rigorous enforcement during the term of their permits this fact would show up at the auction [of pollution rights] in dramatically lower bids . . . . If, as we envisage, the size of the budget available to the EPA

waste enforcement efforts,[49] I suggested that the potential success or failure of environmental enforcement programs is a function of several variables. The motivation of top administrators is one factor, as is the size of the enforcement staff.[50] However, other important considerations also have a critical bearing on the viability of environmental enforcement. These include the extent of enforcement staff turnover, the ability of top enforcement managers to communicate clearly their preference for a vigorous enforcement effort, and the extent to which intra-governmental rivalries on enforcement questions are kept within reasonable bounds.

Ackerman and Stewart's proposals may give EPA administrators more motivation to expand enforcement activity as a means of garnering more resources in a reformed budgeting arrangement. However, there is simply no evidence that their suggestions will have any impact on those managers' abilities to motivate or communicate with their staffs or to avoid the intra-governmental disputes that sometimes hamper the effectiveness of regulatory enforcement efforts. Thus, no matter how much these proposed reforms succeed in motivating top EPA enforcement managers to give enforcement a higher priority than it receives under current regulatory arrangements, a marketable permit approach would provide no assurance that managers would possess sufficient skill and tact to enhance enforcement success.[51] These reforms would also provide no guarantee that the Agency will be able to stem a continuing problem of turnover among its professional staff, a problem which has hampered enforcement efforts for some time.

> and state agencies would depend on total auction revenues, the bureaucracy's failure to invest adequately in enforcement would soon show up in a potentially dramatic drop in auction income available for the next budgetary period. This is not a prospect that top EPA administrators will take lightly. Monitoring and enforcement will become agency priorities of first importance.

Ackerman & Stewart, *supra* note 22, at 1346.

49. Mintz, *Agencies, Congress and Regulatory Enforcement: A Review of EPA's Hazardous Waste Enforcement Effort, 1970–1987*, 18 ENVTL. L. 683 (1988).

50. *Id.* at 758.

51. Notably, it is not clear that the leadership of EPA's enforcement program is currently as lacking in motivation as it was during the Gorsuch-Burford era. In a recent article, EPA's current administrator, William K. Reilly, stated: "The enforcement of environmental laws is absolutely essential. I intend to give enforcement a very high priority. I think it is at the very heart of the integrity and the commitment of our regulatory programs." Reilly, *The Future of Environmental Law*, 6 YALE J. ON REG. 351, 354 (1989).

The "second generation" environmental law reforms that Ackerman and Stewart advocate raise a somewhat different set of criticisms. As noted previously, Stewart argues that economic reform of environmental law will "enhance the democratic accountability of environmental policy decisions."[52] They contend, in effect, that their proposal will turn the attention of legislators and citizens away from technological questions and toward a more straighforward issue: whether the EPA should be instructed to decrease or increase the number of pollution rights to be permitted over a given time. In this way, they argue, environmental policy decisions will be more responsive to the popular will.

These contentions are unpersuasive. It is far from clear that Ackerman and Stewart's proposals will require Congress to make decisions any less technologically complex than the policy determinations that preceded enactment of existing environmental statutes. If Congress is going to make reasonable and balanced decisions concerning allowable levels of pollution rights, these decisions must necessarily take into account a broad array of complex matters, including the relative environmental impact of various levels of pollutant discharges, the implications of different alternatives with respect to energy consumption, and the relative economic costs of all options. Mere changes in the legal formulas by which the results of environmental policy are expressed are unlikely to alter the substantive content of the debate that produces such formulas. Nor are such changes less likely to exhaust the time and energy of politicians or the public.

Ackerman and Stewart's second generation reforms may, on balance, result in policymaking that is less democratic than current arrangements. Mark Sagoff, author of *The Economy of the Earth*, points out that environmental regulation is properly concerned with questions of public values and with the resolution of conflicts regarding their application on the basis of rational, open, and open-minded debate.[53] In contrast, economic analyses of the kind Ackerman and Stewart propose may resolve potential conflicts by application of a mechanical rule or decision procedure. If inappropriately applied, such public policy approaches may substitute themselves for the processes of democratic government. Ackerman and Stewart's proposed second generation reforms raise the

52. Stewart, *supra* note 6, at 160; *see also* Ackerman & Stewart, *supra* note 15.
53. M. Sagoff, The Economy of the Earth 96–97 (1989).

specter of cost-benefit analysis replacing democratic debate over what sort of goals federal and state environmental policies should pursue. It would be useful for them, in their future writings, to describe this aspect of their proposal with greater clarity.[54]

On another level, Ackerman and Stewart's proposed second generation reforms raise one of Latin's concerns. It is doubtful that enough knowledge currently exists about ecological systems or the effects of chemicals on human health to justify extensive reliance on cost-benefit analysis.[55] As several observers have noted, environmental risk assessment often relies on research data that is uncertain and difficult to interpret. Under these circumstances, it would be incorrect to describe regulatory policies that are based upon such an assessment as "neutral" or "objective."[56] Although environmental risk assessment may improve over time—perhaps within the ten to fifteen years preceding Ackerman and Stewart's second generation reforms[57]—it seems premature to rec-

---

54. Ackerman and Stewart do attempt to distinguish their proposal, which they describe as "legally constrained cost-effectiveness analysis," from "technocratic cost-benefit analysis," a technique they decline to endorse. Ackerman & Stewart, *supra* note 22, at 1358–59. These terms are nowhere defined. Thus, the nature of that distinction, as the authors understand it, is never explained. It is therefore difficult to predict with precision the extent to which this aspect of their second generation reforms actually will, in fact, result in democratically accountable policymaking procedures.

55. *See* Latin, *supra* note 16, at 1273–74 and *passim*.

56. *See* Grad, *Risk Assessment and The Tyranny of Numbers: A Brief Comment*, 1 J. Envtl. L. & Litig. 1 (1986); Baram, *Cost-Benefit Analysis: An Inadequate Basis for Health, Safety and Environmental Regulatory Decisionmaking*, 8 Ecology L.Q. 473 (1980); Lovins, *Cost-Risk Assessments in Energy Policy*, 45 Geo. Wash. L. Rev. 911 (1977); Uellin, *Judicial Review and Nuclear Power: Assessing the Risks of Environmental Catastrophe*, 45 Geo. Wash. L. Rev. 969 (1977). These conclusions are borne out in a recent EPA study of the comparative risks posed by a variety of environmental problems. Its authors write:

> The basic data on many subjects studied in this project are surprisingly poor. The general weakness of exposure data is a special problem because exposure is such an important determinant of risk. In addition, specific data on the specific types of risk and environmental problems are often lacking. More research would be very useful to clarify the issue of how serious various environmental problems are . . . .

U.S. Environmental Protection Agency, Unfinished Business: A Comparative Assessment of Environmental Problems 98 (1987).

57. According to Ackerman and Stewart, second generation reforms are to commence at some future time, "say 10 or 15 years," after enactment of first generation reforms. Ackerman & Stewart, *supra* note 22, at 1358. It should also be mentioned, however, that Ackerman and Stewart's response to Professor Latin's piece is unresponsive to several of his other concerns. The authors fail to address squarely Latin's point that economic critics of environmental law are "long on theory and short on empiricism." *See* Latin, *supra* note 16, at 1304. In addition, their characterization of Latin as a zealous defender of the status quo seems misplaced. Latin's attitude towards current environmental regulation is ambi-

ommend that they be given as central a role in environmental standard-setting as those authors would have them assume.[58]

In sum, Ackerman and Stewart's proposed reforms appear to be no panacea for the difficulties of environmental regulation. Their first generation reforms seem unlikely to result in less administrative centralization, fewer information-gathering costs, and lower levels of controversy and delay than do existing regulatory schemes. Their second generation proposal fails to consider the inherent complexity of ecological systems, the current difficulty of determining the impact of many chemical compounds on human health, and the inevitable intricacy of environmental policy discussions.

III. Toward a Middle Ground: A Suggested "Trial Run" for Economic Reform

Notwithstanding the shortcomings of some of Ackerman and Stewart's arguments, we should not dismiss their suggestions prematurely. While their criticisms are sometimes overstated, their concerns regarding the impact of environmental regulation on technological innovation may have merit, as may their observations with respect to the dilatory nature of the current regulatory system and the limited cost-effectiveness of some of its requirements. I am also unpersuaded by Howard Latin's suggestion that society's ultimate choice, in the environmental arena, is between "crude regulation" and "no regulation." Over the long term, thoughtful adjustments in our system of federal environmental regulation—perhaps including some of the measures Ackerman and Stewart endorse—may succeed in eliminating the regulatory Hobson's choices the current system creates.

If coupled with other reforms, a carefully limited system of transferrable pollution permits, based upon existing regulatory standards, may create useful incentives for technological innova-

---

valent: "In light of the inefficiencies associated with command-and-control standards, one could not conclude that uniform treatments are invariably superior to individualized decisionmaking, but that the opposite generalization is equally untenable." *See id.* at 1331.

58. This is not to gainsay Ackerman and Stewart's sound suggestion that it would be worthwhile for the EPA and other government agencies to make serious, systematic, and ongoing efforts to collect and analyze data with respect to the relative risks of environmental problems in different settings, as well as to the costs and feasibility of addressing those problems.

tion. Such a system may also enhance the cost-effectiveness of environmental regulation without diminishing the protections that such regulation affords. While this technique may not accomplish *all* of the goals its proponents endorse, it does appear to have sufficient merit to warrant serious consideration as a future regulatory tool.

However, some words of caution are in order. As noted earlier,[59] implementing Ackerman and Stewart's first generation reforms seems likely to maintain or even increase the information-gathering burdens on federal and state regulators.[60] They also carry the potential to dilute hard won environmental progress and to slow needed cleanups. While Ackerman and Stewart deny these contentions, they cite no careful, unbiased evaluations of previously instituted economic reform measures to support their optimism on this score. Furthermore, as Ackerman and Stewart have themselves observed, a regulatory system reformed along the lines they suggest will not easily resolve all foreseeable regulatory problems. Administrative feasibility is surely an important constraint on the degree of sophistication we may expect from such a system.[61]

In view of the administrative feasibility problem, it seems prudent to begin economic reform on a small scale. Rather than institute Ackerman and Stewart's first generation suggestions across the nation in one sweeping step, it would be more sensible to experiment with implementation in a limited number of localities for a defined period of time. Under such an approach, the EPA might be authorized to make grants to interested communities or sub-state regions—on a demonstration project basis—to implement a marketable permit scheme similar to that which Ackerman and Stewart recommend. The Agency, as well as interested parties from all perspectives, would have an opportunity to evaluate such a scheme in action and to determine its administrative feasibility as well as its larger implications for both environmental quality and economic prosperity. Following a demonstration project, the

59. *See supra* notes 46–47 and accompanying text.

60. In addition to amassing the body of information needed to meet current legal requirements regarding environmental standard-setting, "first generation" regulators would also be required to gather sufficient information to determine how much pollution is presently permitted in each watershed and air quality control region in the United States. This may well prove a time consuming, resource-intensive task.

61. Ackerman & Stewart, *supra* note 22, at 1350.

EPA might be required to report the results of its evaluation to Congress, which would then be better situated to make an informed and rational judgment about the ultimate role of marketable pollution rights programs in any reformed system of federal environmental regulation.[62]

A trial program of this type would involve some difficulties and risks. There may, for example, be inherent differences between local and national environmental regulation that preclude extrapolation of any results of local or regional marketable permit programs to the national level.[63] It may be difficult to find and study communities that might reasonably be viewed as controls. Marketable permit mechanisms may prove so infeasible to implement that the environmental quality of the communities that host demonstration projects may temporarily suffer. Despite these potential drawbacks, marketable permit mechanisms linked to existing environmental regulatory standards are worth trying on a small scale because they have sufficient potential for accomplishing cost savings and for spurring innovation in pollution control, without diminishing environmental quality.

Ackerman and Stewart incorrectly assert that their critics have ignored "solid evidence" that economic reform "can and has worked."[64] In fact, efforts by Congress and the EPA to implement such reforms have thus far escaped systematic, empirically-based evaluation. Nevertheless, Ackerman and Stewart's analysis justifies thoughtful and careful investigation into whether limited economic reform of environmental regulation can be practically accomplished—without delaying or defeating the vitally important purposes for which our existing environmental regulations have been instituted.

62. Congress may also wish to order the EPA to study and evaluate the environmental and economic results of economic reforms that have thus far been implemented on a national scale, including the "bubble policy," emission trading and banking, and other similar programs. *See, e.g.*, Comment, *EPA's Widening Embrace of the 'Bubble' Concept: The Legality and Availability of Intra-Source Trade-Offs*, 9 Envtl. L. Rep. (Envtl. L. Inst.) 10,027 (1979); Stewart, *Economics, Environment, and the Limits of Legal Control*, 9 Harv. Envtl. L. Rev. 1 (1985).

63. Technology-forcing strategies may be ineffective because firms which design and manufacture innovative pollution-control equipment will not have a national market for their products, and therefore, might not find such endeavors to be profitable.

64. Ackerman & Stewart, *supra* note 22, at 1364.

Part V
Beyond Environmental Regulation

[10]

UNDERSTANDING THE NEW ERA IN ENVIRONMENTAL LAW

ADAM BABICH*

TABLE OF CONTENTS

I. INTRODUCTION

The fundamental changes necessary to prevent wholesale destruction of the nation's (and the world's) natural resources will occur only if people have powerful incentives to rethink and reform their behavior toward the environment.[1] But because Congress either was supremely

---

* Adam Babich practices environmental law with the Denver, Colorado firm of Cornwell & Blakey. He is a graduate of Yale Law School. This Article is based in part on Babich, *Restructuring Environmental Law*, 19 Envtl. L. Rep. (Envtl. L. Inst.) 10057 (1989). Copyright: Adam Babich (1989).

1. According to former United States Environmental Protection Agency (EPA) administrator William D. Ruckelshaus, an adequate response to environmental problems will require "a modification of society comparable in scale to only two other changes: the agricultural revolution of the late Neolithic period and the Industrial Revolution of the past two centuries." Ruckelshaus, *Toward a Sustainable World*, 261 SCI. AM. 166, 167

confident in its ability to transform the nation by fiat or simply underestimated the problem at hand, the major federal antipollution statutes of the 1970s rest on the assumption that, if outlawed, harmful pollution will stop.[2] Of course, the threat of government enforcement provides one incentive for change, but the nation's exercise of its police power is neither certain nor efficient enough, and environmental regulations are not comprehensive enough, to force the expeditious, basic changes in attitude and behavior that are needed.[3] To be successful, environmental laws must move beyond command-and-control regulation and become largely *self*-enforcing.

In the 1980s, Congress—jolted into action by several highly publicized environmental disasters—began a fundamental restructuring of environmental law, creating persuasive new incentives for private action to prevent pollution.[4] For years, legal scholars had argued that

---

(1989). Mr. Ruckelshaus further notes that, because the required societal changes must be "a fully conscious operation, guided by the best foresight that science can provide," the undertaking would be "absolutely unique in humanity's stay on earth." *Id.*

2. The Clean Air Act, 42 U.S.C.A. §§ 7401-7642 (West 1983 & Supp. 1989), set the general pattern for the other major environmental statutes of the 1970s including: the Clean Water Act (also known as the Federal Water Pollution Control Act), 33 U.S.C.A. §§ 1251-1376 (West 1983 & Supp. 1989); the Solid Waste Disposal Act, as amended by the Resource Conservation and Recovery Act (RCRA), 42 U.S.C.A. 6901-6991i (West 1983 & Supp. 1989); the Safe Drinking Water Act (SDWA), 42 U.S.C. §§ 300f - 300j-11 (1982 & Supp. V 1987); the Toxic Substances Control Act (TSCA), 15 U.S.C. §§ 2601-2629 (1988); and the Federal Insecticide, Fungicide, and Rodenticide Act (FIFRA), 7 U.S.C. §§ 136-136y (1988).

An exception to the general pattern for 1970s environmental laws is the National Environmental Policy Act (NEPA), 42 U.S.C. §§ 4321-4370(a) (1982 & Supp. V 1987), which, rather than imposing substantive environmental quality standards, requires development of information to ensure that government agencies make decisions only after considering significant potential environmental impacts. Congress adopted an analogous information based approach to environmental protection in the Emergency Planning and Community Right-to-Know Act (EPCRA or SARA Title III), 42 U.S.C. §§ 11001-11050 (Supp. V 1987). EPCRA requires owners and operators of industrial facilities to report to public agencies about the kinds and quantities of dangerous chemicals they store, dispose of, and release from their facilities. The statute requires government agencies to use this information to develop plans for averting and responding to chemical emergencies.

3. Violators often receive economic benefits from their violations that exceed the fines that the EPA imposes, even assuming that the EPA discovers the violations. *See, e.g.*, *"Forceless Enforcement" Found by OMB at EPA; Inspector General Cites Millions in Reduced Fines*, 20 Env't Rep. (BNA) 1087, 1088 (Oct. 20, 1989). Arguably, the government might improve its enforcement record by increasing the use of the criminal provisions of environmental statutes to deter violators. *See* Starr, *Too Many Cooks . . .* , 6 ENVTL. F. 9 (Jan.-Feb. 1989). There are so many businesses subject to environmental regulation, however, that it is difficult to imagine an enforcement staff large enough to police the entire regulated community effectively.

4. *See United States v. Shell Oil Co.*, 605 F. Supp. 1064, 1071 (D. Colo. 1985) (Congress enacted the Comprehensive Environmental Response, Compensation, and Liability

traditional, command-and-control regulatory mechanisms were inadequate to control pollution and urged an overhaul of environmental legislation.[5] Rather than adopting the largely market-based schemes of these theorists, however, Congress turned for inspiration to a system that for centuries has used the threat of civil liability as a means of social control: the common law tort system.[6]

The resulting statutes—including the Comprehensive Environmental Response, Compensation, and Liability Act of 1980 (CERCLA),[7] the Hazardous and Solid Waste Amendments of 1984 (HSWA),[8] which amended the Resource Conservation and Recovery Act (RCRA),[9] and the Superfund Amendments and Reauthorization Act of 1986 (SARA),[10] which amended CERCLA and created the Emergency Planning and Community Right-to-Know Act (EPCRA or SARA Title III)[11]—herald a shift in the primary focus of environmental law from prospective regulation to retroactive liability.[12] The effect of these new, liability-based statutes is to assign much of the responsibility for planning for a dangerous and uncertain environmental future to that segment of society most capable of finding innovative and efficient solutions: the private sector. Congress's environmental initiatives of the 1980s disrupt the normal routines of businesses and consumers.

Act after concluding that existing prospective laws were inadequate to address environmental disasters such as Love Canal.).

5. *See, e.g.*, Ackerman & Stewart, *Reforming Environmental Law*, 37 STAN. L. REV. 1333 (1985); Breyer, *Analyzing Regulatory Failure: Mismatches, Less Restrictive Alternatives, and Reform*, 92 HARV. L. REV. 547 (1979); Hahn & Hester, *Marketable Permits: Lessons for Theory and Practice*, 16 ECOLOGY L.Q. 361 (1989).

6. Congress's focus on the common law tort system in enacting the Comprehensive Environmental Response, Liability, and Compensation Act (CERCLA), 42 U.S.C.A. §§ 9601-9675 (West 1983 & Supp. 1989), is clear from Congress's decision to allow significant issues to be determined by the courts as a matter of federal common law, *see, e.g.*, United States v. Aceto Agricultural Chem. Corp., 872 F.2d 1373, 1382 (8th Cir. 1989); Colorado v. Asarco, Inc., 608 F. Supp. 1484, 1486 (D. Colo. 1985); United States v. Chem-Dyne Corp., 572 F. Supp. 802, 808 (S.D. Ohio 1983), and from Congress's requirement for studies of the adequacy of common law remedies for injuries to the public not addressed in CERCLA. *See* 42 U.S.C. § 9651(e)(3) (1982).

7. Pub. L. No. 96-510, 94 Stat. 2767 (1980). Unless otherwise specified, "CERCLA," as used in this Article, refers to the Comprehensive Environmental Response, Compensation, and Liability Act, as amended by the Superfund Amendments and Reauthorization Act of 1986, and codified at 42 U.S.C. §§ 96019675.

8. Pub. L. No. 98-616, 98 Stat. 3221.

9. 42 U.S.C.A. §§ 6901-6991i (West 1983 & Supp. 1989).

10. Pub. L. No. 99-499, 100 Stat. 1613.

11. 42 U.S.C. §§ 11001-11050 (Supp. V 1987)

12. The courts uniformly have upheld the constitutionality of retroactive liability in this context. *See* United States v. Monsanto Co., 858 F.2d 160, 173-74 (4th Cir. 1988), *cert. denied* 109 S. Ct. 3156 (1989); United States v. Northeastern Pharmaceutical & Chem. Co., 810 F.2d 726, 733-734 (8th Cir. 1986), *cert. denied*, 484 U.S. 848 (1987).

Businesses now must analyze potential environmental liabilities not only for their waste disposal operations, but also for a vast array of other activities. Consumers ultimately may find familiar conveniences of the chemical era becoming unavailable or prohibitively expensive.[13] Nonetheless, a broad, liability-based approach to protecting the environment has the potential to bring about a quantum leap in the effectiveness of environmental laws. Whether short-term disruptions will cause Congress to retreat from this new approach before the long-term benefits are realized remains an open question.[14]

II. THE LIMITS OF PROSPECTIVE REGULATION

Most federal environmental laws, originally enacted during the 1970s, rely on a system known as command-and-control regulation.[15] Under these laws, the United States Environmental Protection Agency (EPA) and other government agencies try to control pollution by issuing detailed regulations and permits that prescribe the manner in which the regulated community may generate, transport, store, dispose of, and release chemicals that the government believes are dangerous.

Command-and-control regulation presupposes the government's ability to: (1) identify environmental problems and set rational priorities; (2) develop regulations that provide technologically workable and politically viable solutions; and (3) enforce those regulations effectively. Unfortunately, in the area of environmental protection none of these presuppositions has proven true.[16] The enormous scope and complexity of environmental problems and resulting scientific and political uncertainties explain much of this failure. Other problems result from

---

13. *See infra* note 102 and accompanying text (regarding the effect of liability-based statutes on business transactions); *see also* Davidoff, *Multiple Chemical Sensitivities*, 11 AMICUS J. 12, 23 (Winter, 1989) (consumers have become accustomed to the convenience of living with many of the chemicals that threaten public health and the environment).

14. *See Domenici Declares Superfund "Failure," Suggests Revamped Liability Scheme*, 10 Inside E.P.A. 4 (Sept. 22, 1989) Senator Pete Domenici has suggested that it might be time to consider a public-works rather than liability-based approach to cleaning up toxic waste sites. *Id.*

15. *See, e.g.*, Davis, *Approaches to the Regulation of Hazardous Wastes*, 18 ENVTL. L. 505 (1988); Stewart, *Regulation, Innovation, and Administrative Law: A Conceptual Framework*, 69 CALIF. L. REV. 1256 (1981); Hahn, Book Review, 4 YALE J. ON REG. 173 (1986) (review R. LIROFF, REFORMING AIR POLLUTION REGULATION: THE TOIL AND TROUBLE OF THE EPA'S BUBBLE).

16. *See* Stewart, *Controlling Environmental Risks Through Economic Incentives*, 13 COLUM. J. ENVTL. L. 153, 156-158 (1988); Commoner, *Failure of the Environmental Effort*, 18 Envtl. L. Rep. (Envtl. L. Inst.) 10195 (1988); Muskie, *Reflections on a Quarter Century of Environmental Activism: On Postponing Deadlines, Second-Guessing the Congress, and Ignoring Problems Until It is Too Late*, 18 Envtl. L. Rep. (Envtl. L. Inst.) 10081 (Mar. 1988).

deficiencies in various antipollution statutes and regulations. A more fundamental cause is rooted in the seemingly inherent inability of large government bureaucracies to accomplish their missions efficiently.

A. *Institutional Constraints*

The EPA bureaucracy's attempts to use command-and-control regulation to impose nationwide pollution control have been compared to the debacle of central economic planning in the Soviet Union.[17] No incentives are built into the regulatory process for the EPA to operate efficiently or creatively. Attempts to solve this problem through "regulatory reform" so far have only added paperwork (*e.g.*, Regulatory Impact and Regulatory Flexibility Analyses) and still another layer of bureaucracy (*i.e.*, the Office of Management and Budget) to an already bloated process.[18] Although bureaucratic inefficiencies provide no excuse for wholesale deregulation,[19] they do point to the need to augment the regulatory system to encourage private antipollution initiatives.

When faced with complex environmental issues, the EPA is much more capable of responding to immediate political pressures than of anticipating long-term environmental problems, setting priorities, or developing solutions. For example, despite Congressional enactment of RCRA—an ambitious law governing hazardous waste management—in 1976, the EPA did not even begin significant regulation of hazardous

---

17. *See* Ackerman & Stewart, *supra* note 5, at 1334.

18. Under Executive Order 12,291, the EPA must judge whether each regulation will cause sufficient economic impacts to qualify as a "major rule." The Agency generally must conduct a Regulatory Impact Analysis of major rules. Executive Order 12,291 also requires the EPA to submit proposed rules to the Office of Management and Budget (OMB) for review. Regulatory Flexibility Analyses are required by 5 U.S.C. § 603 (1988). Under the Paperwork Reduction Act, 44 U.S.C. § 3507 (1982 & Supp. V 1987), EPA information collection requirements must be approved by OMB. *See generally* Dole v. United Steelworkers of America, 110 S. Ct. 929 (1990).

OMB has imposed controversial delays on EPA promulgation of significant regulations. *See House Panel Democrats Release OMB/EPA Papers Showing Interference in Superfund Regulations*, 19 Env't Rep. (BNA) 2459 (Mar. 17, 1989); *House Subcommittee Denies OMB Funds for Rule Review Unit Pending Authorization*, 20 Env't Rep. (BNA) 604 (July 28, 1989); *OMB Rejects Proposed Incinerator Regs, Citing High Cost, Low Return*, 10 Inside E.P.A. 1 (March 10, 1989).

19. Damage to the nation's environment would have been worse if not for EPA regulation under the command-and-control environmental laws of the 1970s. Former EPA administrator Russell E. Train has stated that "[n]o nation in the world has grappled so successfully with those issues as the United States . . . . Without these accomplishments where would we be today? We would be like Mexico City or São Paulo." Shabecoff, *Minor Gains in Ecology and Major Challenges*, N.Y. Times, Nov. 30, 1988, at B10, col. 1.

waste until four years later, when required to do so by court order.[20] Congress's frustration with the EPA's consistent failure to implement environmental laws by statutory deadlines is reflected in the "hammer" provisions of HSWA, the 1984 amendments to RCRA.[21]

Congress itself, however, is no better than the EPA at responding to complex, and sometimes poorly understood, threats to the environment. This fact is highlighted by Congress's difficulties throughout the 1980s in reauthorizing the Clean Air Act.[22] Even when the EPA and Congress do act, powerful economic interests such as the oil and mining industries often persuade both institutions to grant broad exemptions from environmental laws, thus allowing vast quantities of dangerous materials to go unregulated.[23] Similarly, the United States Justice Department has convinced the EPA not to bring other federal agencies to court over pollution problems.[24] As a result, the federal government

---

20. *See* Illinois v. Costle, 9 Envtl. L. Rep. (Envtl. L. Inst.) 20243 (D.D.C. Jan. 3, 1979); *see also* Environmental Defense Fund, Inc. v. Gorsuch, 713 F.2d 802 (D.C. Cir. 1983) (court of appeals discussed district court's jurisdiction to review further actions of EPA after district court had ordered EPA to promulgate RCRA regulations). *See generally infra* note 132 (EPA's priorities may be more closely aligned with public opinion than with estimated risks).

21. As amended by HSWA, RCRA not only provides deadlines for EPA action, but also sets forth, in the so-called "hammer provisions," specific consequences for the EPA's failure to meet those deadlines. *See, e.g.*, 42 U.S.C. § 6921(d)(8) (Supp. V 1987) (unless EPA promulgates standards for small quantity generators by the statutory deadline, congressionally selected standards shall apply); 42 U.S.C. § 6924(g)(6)(c) (Supp. V 1987) (land disposal of certain hazardous wastes shall be banned if EPA fails to promulgate regulations under 42 U.S.C. § 6924(g)(5)). *See generally* Florio, *Congress as Reluctant Regulator: Hazardous Waste Policy in the 1980's*, 3 YALE J. ON REG. 351 (1986) (Congress has taken on role of regulator due to EPA's refusal to carry out congressional intent); Mugdan & Adler, *The 1984 RCRA Amendments: Congress as a Regulatory Agency*, 10 COLUM. J. ENVTL. L. 215 (1985) (amendments to RCRA indicate congressional distrust of EPA's implementation of regulations). Congress's frustration with EPA inaction is documented in Shapiro & Glicksman, *Congress, the Supreme Court, and the Quiet Revolution in Administrative Law*, 1988 DUKE L.J. 819, 826, n.34 (1988).

22. *See* Kilgore, *Muddling Through: Congressional Activity in 1988*, 19 Envtl. L. Rep. (Envtl. L. Inst.) 10016 (Jan. 1989); Ruckelshaus, *supra* note 1, at 169-70.

23. *See, e.g.*, 42 U.S.C. § 6921(b)(3)(A) (1982) (exempting, *inter alia*, waste from most mining and milling activities from RCRA regulation pending an EPA determination to be made after the completion of studies); 42 U.S.C. § 7419 (1982) (authorizing EPA to grant extra time for certain nonferrous smelters to comply with Clean Air Act regulations); 42 U.S.C. § 9601(14) (1982 & Supp. V 1987) (excluding "petroleum, including crude oil or any fraction thereof" from CERCLA's definition of "hazardous substance" unless specifically listed or designated); 42 U.S.C. § 9607(i) (1982 & Supp. V 1987) (exempting from CERCLA's liability provisions contamination caused by application of a registered pesticide product); 40 C.F.R. § 261.4(b)(5), (7) (exempting most mining wastes and wastes associated with exploration, development or production of crude oil from RCRA Subtitle C's definition of hazardous waste).

24. *See* EPA, FEDERAL FACILITIES COMPLIANCE STRATEGY VI-3 (Nov. 1988) (Pursuant

is one of the nation's most persistent violators of environmental laws.[25]

B. *Assessing the Risks*

Issues of EPA and Congressional competence aside, full regulation of the staggering number of dangerous chemicals in use and development is not a realistic possibility. Assessing the danger that even a single chemical poses to public health and the environment is a formidable task, clouded by scientific uncertainty.[26] Because scientists cannot ethically experiment on people to determine a chemical's toxicity, carcinogenicity, mutagenicity and teratogenicity, regulators must rely on relatively soft data in deciding which chemicals to regulate and how stringently to regulate them.

To determine the need for regulation, the government generally proceeds chemical by chemical, employing a risk assessment approach that is slow and resource intensive. Because industry constantly adds new chemicals to the thousands already on the market,[27] this chemical-by-chemical approach provides little assurance that the government has analyzed all or even most significant hazards.[28]

---

to the position of the U.S. Justice Department, the "EPA will not bring civil judicial suits against Executive Branch Agencies." (emphasis omitted)).

25. *See, e.g.*, UNITED STATES GENERAL ACCOUNTING OFFICE, WATER POLLUTION: STRONGER ENFORCEMENT IS NEEDED TO IMPROVE COMPLIANCE AT FEDERAL FACILITIES 3 (1988) (GAO/RCED-89-13) ("Federal facilities' rate of noncompliance with [Clean Water Act] priority program requirements is twice that of nonfederal industrial facilities."); Wald, *Waste Dumping that U.S. Banned Went on at Its Own Atom Plants*, N.Y. Times, Dec. 8, 1988, at A1, col. 1 (Extensive environmental damage at Federal nuclear weapon plants is largely a result of crude waste disposal practices that were banned in the private sector a decade ago.). Indeed, the United States Army's Rocky Mountain Arsenal reportedly is "the worst hazardous and toxic waste site in America." Colorado v. United States Dep't of the Army, 707 F. Supp. 1562, 1570 (D. Colo. 1989).

26. *See, e.g.*, Latin, *Good Science, Bad Regulation, and Toxic Risk Assessment*, 5 YALE J. ON REG. 89, 91 (1988). *See generally Risk Assessment in Environmental Law*, 14 COLUM. J. ENVTL. L. 289 (1989) (various symposium articles concerning risk assessment).

27. *See* Lave, *Risk Assessment and Regulatory Priorities*, 14 COLUM. J. ENVTL. L. 307, 308 (1989) (scientists have provided reasonably complete evidence on human toxicity on only about 1000 of the approximately 60,000 chemicals in common use).

28. One commentator stated:

> "[W]e may well find ourselves in the midst of a chemical holocaust brought upon ourselves by bureaucratic incrementalism and corporate tunnel vision. . . . After all, we are being asked to trust the same people who gave us DDT, Keypone, dioxin, PCBs, EDB in our foods, asbestos in our schools and houses and public buildings, DES to prevent miscarriages, UFFI, unvented gas heaters, tris flame retardant in children's sleepwear, hormones and antibiotics in our meat, pesticide residues in our food, and formaldehyde in our permanent press fabrics and paper towels. The list goes on and on. Those same folks who are supposed to be guarding the barn keep shutting the door after each horse

Generally, to assess the risks that a chemical poses to the public, government agencies must answer three questions:

- What types of risks does the chemical pose?
- At what dose is the chemical dangerous?
- How many people are exposed, or at risk of exposure, to how much of the chemical?[29]

Answering the first two questions, that is, performing the hazard identification and dose-response evaluation steps in a risk assessment, requires the agency to evaluate data from experiments on animals, epidemiological studies (generally of occupational exposures), if any, and theoretical analyses.[30] Essentially all of the techniques used to draw conclusions from these data, however, are controversial. For example, the fact that a chemical does or does not cause cancer in laboratory animals does not conclusively establish what dangers the chemical may pose to people. And it is not self-evident that chemicals that harm workers exposed to relatively large doses over long time periods will have similar effects on the population at large when those chemicals enter, and are diluted by, the environment.[31]

---

has been stolen."

Davidoff, *supra* note 13, at 23 (quoting Earon Davis).

Recently, Congress amended the Clean Water Act to authorize use of creative alternatives to a chemical-by-chemical approach. *See* 33 U.S.C. § 1314(a)(8) (1982 & Supp. V 1987) (EPA "shall develop and publish information on methods for establishing and measuring water quality criteria for toxic pollutants on other bases than pollutant-by-pollutant criteria, including biological monitoring and assessment methods."). Similarly, Congress's direction to the EPA to develop regulations under RCRA identifying measures or indicators of toxicity will reduce reliance on chemical-by-chemical analyses. *See* 42 U.S.C. § 6921(h) (1982 & Supp. 1987).

29. *See* 52 Fed. Reg. 12,870 (1987) (setting forth guidelines of the Agency for Toxic Substances and Disease Registry (ATSDR) for developing toxicological profiles under 42 U.S.C. § 9604(i)); *see also* Daggett, Hazen & Shaw, *Advancing Environmental Protection Through Risk Assessment*, 14 COLUM. J ENVTL. L. 315, 317 (1989); Gordis, *Epidemiologic Approaches for Studying Human Diseases in Relation to Hazardous Waste Disposal Sites*, 25 HOUS. L. REV. 837 (1988).

30. *See* F. CROSS, ENVIRONMENTALLY INDUCED CANCER AND THE LAW, 52-60 (1989); Lave, *supra* note 27, at 312.

31. As one commentator reports:

> Toxic risk assessment suffers from fundamental uncertainties about causal mechanisms for cancer and other hazards, extrapolative relationships between high-dose and low-dose responses and between animal test data and human risks, latent effects and latency periods, special sensitivities in exposed subpopulations, synergistic or co-carcinogenic effects of various substances, past and present exposure levels, dispersion patterns for contaminants, and virtually every other area of required knowledge. *These uncertainties generally preclude reliable assessments of relevant effects, and there is no scientific consensus on how they should be resolved.*

Latin, *supra* note 26, at 91 (emphasis added) (footnote omitted); *see also* Office of Sci-

To further complicate matters, dose-response relationships often differ between population groups. Children, fetuses, the aged and smokers are especially vulnerable to some chemicals.[32] Moreover, combinations of chemicals may have impacts greater than the sum of the effects of individual chemicals. Such synergistic effects are poorly understood and difficult to predict.[33]

Answering the third question accurately, that is, performing the exposure assessment step of a risk assessment, requires intensive data-gathering that is complicated and expensive.[34] Regulators who attempt to determine the quantities, types, and locations of chemicals present in the environment must rely on data, if any, from the monitoring of pollutants at the source or in the environment, estimates of chemical releases made in lieu of monitoring, and controversial attempts to model the dispersion of chemicals in air, water and soil.[35] To assess the extent to which people are exposed to these chemicals, regulators must have data—or make assumptions—about the behavior of the exposed population. For example, exposures will vary with the amount of contaminated soil ingested by children, or the extent to which people use polluted ground water to irrigate their gardens.[36]

Not surprisingly, scientists draw conclusions from risk assessment data that conflict wildly in their implications for environmental policy. Some scientists argue that we face an epidemic of cancer and other diseases caused by ubiquitous chemical contamination of our environment.[37] Others assert that environmental hazards are greatly exaggerated and that the government overregulates industry in a misguided

ence and Technology Policy, Chemical Carcinogens: A Review of the Science and Its Associated Principles, 50 Fed. Reg. 10,372 (1985) (adopting assumptions to resolve scientific uncertainties). *See generally*, F. CROSS, *supra* note 30, at 62-65 (discussing limitations of risk assessment). Indeed, even the definition of harm is controversial. *See, e.g.*, Lead Indus. Ass'n v. EPA, 647 F.2d 1130, 1156-61 (D.C. Cir.), *cert. denied*, 449 U.S. 1042 (1980) (affirming EPA's decision to set lead standard to protect against change in blood chemistry despite Lead Industries Association's claim that the change "is a mere 'sub-clinical effect'—a biological response to lead exposure—which is without health significance.").

32. Commoner, *The Hazards of Risk Assessment*, 14 COLUM. J. ENVTL. L. 365, 372 (1989); Latin, *supra* note 26, at 91.

33. S. EPSTEIN, THE POLITICS OF CANCER 58 (1978); Latin, *supra* note 26, at 91.

34. *See* Stanfield, *Problems with Data Collection Hinder Efforts on Pollution, Experts Say*, N.Y. Times, Nov. 8, 1988, at C4, col.1.

35. Finkel, *Is Risk Assessment Really Too Conservative?: Revising the Revisionists*, 14 COLUM. J. ENVTL. L. 427, 443-44 (1989).

36. Lave, *supra* note 27, at 311. *See generally* Paustenbach, *Health Risk Assessments: Opportunities and Pitfalls*, 14 COLUM. J. ENVTL. L. 379, 402-06 (1989) (detailing the exposure assessment phase of risk analysis).

37. *See, e.g.*, S. EPSTEIN, *supra* note 33.

effort to create a risk-free society.[38] Because scientists and others present these arguments to a public that lacks the scientific expertise to evaluate them, the debate is essentially political. Occasional chemical disasters such as the Bhopal incident,[39] and mounting evidence of the global effects of pollution, including ozone depletion, acid rain and the greenhouse effect,[40] make it unlikely that the public soon will be convinced that the government is being overprotective.

C. *Imposing Standards*

Once risks are assessed—however accurately or inaccurately—regulators face the difficult job of deciding how much danger to the public and environment to tolerate. Setting an "acceptable" level of risk involves the scientifically, legally and politically complex task of balancing, either implicitly or explicitly, public health and welfare con-

38. *See* M. DOUGLAS & A. WILDAVSKY, RISK AND CULTURE (1982); E. EFRON, THE APOCALYPTICS (1984). *See generally* F. CROSS, *supra* note 30; Elliott, *The Future of Toxic Torts: Of Chemophobia, Risk as a Compensable Injury and Hybrid Compensation Systems*, 25 HOUS. L. REV. 781, 785 nn.14-15 (1988).

39. In December 1984 methyl isocyanate released from a Union Carbide Corporation pesticide plant in Bhopal, India, killed more than 2,800 people and injured more than 300,000. *See All Claims from Bhopal Disaster Settled for $470 Million by India, Union Carbide*, 3 Toxics L. Rep. (BNA) 1157 (Feb. 22, 1989). One court called the Bhopal incident "the most tragic industrial disaster in history." *In re* Union Carbide Corp. Gas Plant Disaster at Bhopal, India 634 F. Supp. 842, 844 (S.D.N.Y. 1986), *aff'd*, 809 F.2d 195 (2d Cir.), *cert. denied*, 484 U.S. 871 (1987). The tragedy gave rise to fears that a similar disaster could occur in the United States, especially at Union Carbide's methyl isocyanate plant in West Virginia. Chern, *Union Carbide's Plant at Institute, W. Va.: Lessons from Bhopal*, 11 EPA J. No. 6 21 (July-Aug. 1985).

More recent incidents keep hazardous waste issues before the public. *See, e.g.*, *Chemical Disaster Spurs Doubts over EPA Chemical Awareness Program-Success*, 9 Inside E.P.A. 11 (May 1988) (discussing chemical explosion at Nevada manufacturing facility); Schmitt, *Leak Ends a Town's Idyllic Life*, N.Y. Times, Dec. 27, 1988, at A13, col. 6 (city ed.) (describing effects on public welfare and property values of an underground leak of one million gallons of leaded gasoline in Long Island, New York); Hanley, *Buried Chromium Poses a Threat to New Jersey*, N.Y. Times, June 28, 1989, at A12, col. 1 (nat'l ed.) (one person dead and tens of thousands face health risks from hexavalent chromium leaking from dump sites). Recent reports have publicized risks posed by storage of hazardous substances near population centers. For example, one such report states:

> [T]he water treatment plant for the District of Columbia keeps chlorine in tank cars stored on its premises. If one of those cars ruptured, it could send a plume of dense, highly poisonous chlorine gas 40 miles across the city and surrounding countryside. In all likelihood, the gas would pass directly over the Capitol and the White House.

Shabecoff, *The Early Returns of a Toxic Poll*, N.Y. Times, Nov. 20, 1988, at F10, col. 3.

40. *See* Graedel & Crutzen, *The Changing Atmosphere*, 261 SCI. AM. 58 (1989); Schneider, *The Changing Climate*, 261 SCI. AM. 70 (1989).

siderations against the economic costs of risk reduction. This balance necessarily depends on the value of the human life or environmental resource to be protected: a value that can be expressed, albeit controversially, in terms of dollars.[41]

Regulators can estimate (with questionable accuracy) the amount of money each regulation will require society to devote to risk reduction and the number of injuries, including deaths, that each regulation will avoid. As regulators attempt to save more and more lives, the cost of regulation per life saved generally increases. Presumably, at some point, the marginal cost of saving additional lives is too high to justify further regulation.[42]

Exactly how much money is too much to spend to save a life is a question that government officials avoid answering directly. Instead, the EPA tends to express risk management decisions in terms of a range of "acceptable risks," that the Agency purports to justify without reference to the cost of further risk reduction.[43] Alternatively, the EPA imposes regulatory limits based on the capabilities of reasonably available technology. The government usually does not justify these limitations (*e.g.*, Best Available Control Technology (BACT) and Lowest Achievable Emissions Rate (LAER)) in terms of risk.[44]

Arguably, the question of how many of society's dollars to spend

---

41. *See* C GILLETTE & T. HOPKINS, FEDERAL AGENCY VALUATIONS OF HUMAN LIFE: A REPORT TO THE ADMINISTRATIVE CONFERENCE OF THE UNITED STATES (July 7, 1988) at 1; F. CROSS, *supra* note 30, at 70-73.

42. C. GILLETTE & T HOPKINS, *supra* note 41, at 2 (Office of Management and Budget has documented "implicit" agency decisions that economic value of life is as low as $70,000 and as high as $312 million).

43. In setting a standard for benzene under the National Emission Standard for Hazardous Air Pollutants program, the EPA responded to the D.C. Circuit's holding that the Clean Air Act requires the Agency to determine an acceptable level of risk *before* considering cost. Natural Resources Defense Council, Inc. v. EPA, 824 F.2d 1146 (D.C. Cir. 1987). Rather than deciding that, if cost is not considered, only trivial risks are acceptable, the EPA compiled a "Survey of Societal Risk" and purported to base its decision on accepted risks "in the world in which we live." 54 Fed. Reg. 38,044, 38,046-47 (1989). The risk survey, set forth at 53 Fed. Reg. 28,496, 28,512-13 (1988), includes risks posed by car accidents, city air inhalation, home accidents, radon in homes, and pesticides. Because people presumably would reduce such risks if cost were not a factor, the EPA's use of its Survey of Societal Risk as the basis for a risk-acceptability decision allows cost to influence decisions through the back door.

44. *See, e.g.*, 42 U.S.C. § 7475(a)(4) (1982) (major air pollution sources in areas that have attained ambient air quality standards must use "the best available control technology" (BACT) to prevent significant deterioration of air quality); 42 U.S.C. § 7503(2) (Supp. V 1987) (major air pollution sources in areas that have *not* attained ambient standards must meet "the lowest achievable emission rate" (LAER)). For a general (and critical) description of technology-based standards, see Ackerman & Stewart, *supra* note 5, at 1335-38; *see also* B. ACKERMAN & W. HASSLER, CLEAN COAL/DIRTY AIR 94 & n.39 (1981).

protecting the environment is so fundamental that our democratically elected officials, rather than bureaucrats or courts, should answer it.[45] Congress, however, clearly is unwilling to face the issue squarely. Neither sacrificing environmental quality and public health for economic reasons nor bankrupting the economy to create a risk-free environment is acceptable politics.

Congress enacts environmental statutes that, on their face, call for virtual elimination of harmful pollution, but allows the EPA to promulgate regulations replete with explicit and implicit economic trade-offs.[46] For example:

- The Clean Water Act's stated goal is to *eliminate* discharge of pollutants into waters of the United States by 1985.[47] Yet the EPA ignores the Act's goal of pollution elimination in favor of a regulatory approach designed to protect designated uses of surface waters and to minimize further degradation.[48]
- The Clean Air Act requires the EPA to adopt National Ambient Air Quality Standards (NAAQS) and National Emission Standards for Hazardous Air Pollutants (NESHAP) that not only protect public health but also provide, respectively, "adequate" and "ample" margins of safety.[49] By defining the term "ambient air" to include only air to which the public has access, however, the EPA limits the applicability of NAAQS and thus avoids imposing stricter standards on polluters.[50] To obviate the need to

45. *See* B. ACKERMAN & W. HASSLER, *supra* note 44, at 122-26; Ackerman & Stewart, *Reforming Environmental Law: The Democratic Case for Market Incentives*, 13 COLUM. J. ENVT. L. 171, 188-90 (1988).

46. Dean Guido Calabresi explains such seemingly hypocritical government behavior as a response to an irreconcilable conflict between society's need to view each human life as priceless and the scarcity of resources available for actually treating each life as priceless. Thus, society tends to affirm the pricelessness of life in visible, symbolic ways (*e.g.*, spending a million dollars rescuing a single downed balloonist) while declining to spend money on projects that would prevent future deaths (*e.g.*, providing shore patrols). G. CALABRESI & P. BOBBIT, TRAGIC CHOICES (1978).

47. 33 U.S.C. § 1251(a)(1)(1982) ("[I]t is the national goal that the discharge of pollutants into the navigable waters be eliminated by 1985."); *see also* 33 U.S.C. § 1362(7) (1982) (defining "navigable waters" to mean "the waters of the United States").

48. *See* 40 C.F.R. § 131.11 (1989) (governing adoption of water quality criteria to protect designated uses); 40 C.F.R. § 131.12 (1989) (setting forth EPA's antidegradation policy).

49. 42 U.S.C. § 7409(b)(1) (1982) (Primary National Ambient Air Quality Standards); 42 U.S.C. § 7412(b)(1)(B) (1982) (National Emission Standards for Hazardous Air Pollutants).

50. *See* 40 C.F.R. § 50.1(e) (1989) (defining "[a]mbient air" as "that portion of the atmosphere . . . to which the general public has access"). By defining ambient air in terms of access, the EPA allows companies to avoid violating ambient standards by purchasing and fencing off the property where standards are exceeded. This technique of

require strict controls on most hazardous air pollutants, the Agency declines to regulate more than a handful of the myriad potentially carcinogenic and toxic air pollutants.[51]

- Congress intended RCRA to assure that hazardous waste is managed in a manner "so as to *minimize* the present and future threat to human health and the environment."[52] The EPA, however, avoids extensive regulation of various dangerous waste management practices by defining "hazardous waste" to exclude them.[53]
- CERCLA requires a level of cleanup of hazardous substances that, at a minimum, "*assures* protection of human health and the environment."[54] Nonetheless, the EPA interprets CERCLA to allow a wide "acceptable risk" range.[55]

Thus, Congress publicly—and largely symbolically—mandates that the environment be free of dangerous pollutants. But the EPA, rather than taking Congress at its word and imposing regulations that

---

achieving standards by limiting access enables businesses to avoid or minimize the need to reduce emissions. This result might make sense if Congress had intended *only* to require compliance with ambient standards. Congress, however, also intended ambient standards to lead to emission reductions. *See* 42 U.S.C. § 7423 (1982) (prohibiting businesses from avoiding the need to reduce emissions by building excessively tall smokestacks or adopting other techniques that use atmospheric conditions to disperse pollutants).

51. Graham, *The Failure of Agency Forcing: The Regulation of Airborne Carcinogens under Section 112 of the Clean Air Act*, 1985 DUKE L.J. 100 (1985).

52. 42 U.S.C. § 6902(b) (Supp. V 1987) (emphasis added).

53. RCRA Subtitle C regulations list hazardous wastes, *see* 40 C.F.R. § 261.30-.33 (1989), and also set forth characteristics that identify hazardous wastes even if they are not listed, *see* 40 C.F.R. § 261.20-.24 (1989). EPA regulations set forth only four characteristics for identifying hazardous wastes: (1) ignitibility; (2) corrosivity; (3) reactivity; and (4) toxicity. *Id.* In 1984, Congress ordered the EPA to identify "additional characteristics of hazardous waste, including measures or indicators of toxicity" by November 1986. *See* 42 U.S.C. § 6921(h) (1982). Perhaps because there is no "hammer provision" associated with section 6921(h), *see supra* note 21, the EPA did not revise its regulations governing the toxicity characteristic until 1990. *See* 55 Fed.Reg. 11,798 (1990).

Similarly, prior to enactment of HSWA, the EPA created out of whole cloth an exemption from RCRA requirements for "small quantity generators" (*i.e.*, businesses that generate less than 1,000 kilograms of hazardous waste in a month). *See* 45 Fed. Reg. 33,084, 33,102-05 (1980); 45 Fed. Reg. 76,620 (1980). Congress, with enactment of HSWA, adopted the concept of applying special rules to small-quantity generators, but sharply limited the EPA's approach. 42 U.S.C. § 6921(d) (Supp. V 1987). Additionally, the EPA will not regulate various wastes from mining operations under RCRA Subtitle C, despite the fact that the EPA "recognizes, as evidenced by the mining waste sites on the National Priorities List, the potential for problems from mining sites." 51 Fed. Reg. 24,496, 24,499 (1986).

54. 42 U.S.C. § 9621(d)(1) (Supp. V 1987) (emphasis added).

55. *See* 55 Fed. Reg. 8666, 8716-18 (1990) (discussing EPA's decision to set a range of acceptable risks for carcinogens in regulations promulgated under CERCLA).

would either force an economic restructuring or cause Congress to revise the laws,[56] makes *ad hoc*, painfully slow decisions as to how far to push congressional goals. Although Congress routinely lambastes the EPA for failing to implement the law as written, it rarely interferes with the Agency's actual decisions. Consequently, the system works well as a matter of politics, but does little to inspire confidence in command-and-control regulation as the sole means of protecting our environment.

D. *Implementation and Enforcement*

Once finally made, the EPA's regulatory decisions generally are questionable enough to allow special interests to tie up implementation and enforcement in months, if not years, of litigation.[57] Similarly, in recent years, the Office of Management and Budget has imposed long delays on the EPA's issuance of regulations while the Office pressures the Agency to reduce the economic impact of the regulations and accept greater environmental risks.[58]

Even after regulations are final, some environmental laws are extremely cumbersome to enforce. For example, to enforce many Clean Air Act requirements, the EPA must notify the violator of its violation and may file suit only if the violation persists over thirty days after the notice.[59] The regulatory structure of RCRA has become so byzantine that the prospect of explaining many of its provisions to a court can be quite daunting.[60] Overall, the EPA neither conducts nor requires sufficient monitoring of emissions or environmental quality to support a vigorous enforcement effort.[61] And as amply demonstrated during the early years of the Reagan administration, EPA enforcement often is complicated by the vagaries of politics.[62]

---

56. *Cf.* Tennessee Valley Auth. v. Hill, 437 U.S. 153 (1978) (the snail darter/Tellico dam case). In *Hill*, the Supreme Court declined to second-guess congressional policy decisions despite the fact that those decisions would lead to unintended economic impacts. *See id.* at 154. As Justice Powell noted in his dissent, if Congress is unhappy with the literal application of its statute, Congress may revise that statute. *Id.* at 195-96 (Powell, J., dissenting).

57. *See* Ackerman & Stewart, *supra* note 45, at 182; Stewart, *supra* note 16, at 157.

58. *See supra* note 18.

59. 42 U.S.C. § 7413(a) (1982).

60. For example, the definition of "hazardous waste" under RCRA covers more than ten pages in the Code of Federal Regulations. *See* 40 C.F.R. § 261.3-.33 (1989).

61. *See* Stanfield, *supra* note 34; *see also* Bethlehem Steel Corp. v. EPA, 782 F.2d 645, 657-65 (7th Cir. 1986) (Swygert, J., concurring in part and dissenting in part).

62. *See generally* Mintz, *Agencies, Congress and Regulatory Enforcement: A Review of EPA's Hazardous Waste Enforcement Effort, 1970-1987*, 18 ENVTL. L. 683 (1988).

The greatest weakness of command-and-control environmental statutes is that they are not self-enforcing. In other words, the laws fail to provide incentives for members of the regulated community to police themselves and one another. Moreover, under the command-and-control system, the regulated community's sole responsibility is to comply with government edicts. If a statute or regulation does not forbid a particular practice, industry may engage in that practice with impunity.[63] Thus, the risk that environmental hazards have escaped scientific scrutiny and regulatory control is borne by the public. Command-and-control regulation leaves the task of planning ahead to steer society through complex environmental problems solely to a government bureaucracy that simply is not up to the job.

III. THE MARKETABLE PERMIT MODEL

Several commentators argue that Congress should replace command-and-control regulation with a system that uses marketable permits to create economic incentives to reduce pollution in a more efficient manner.[64] In general, the current command-and-control system is designed to force each source of pollution to comply with specific emission limitations which, as a practical matter, require adoption of particular pollution control technologies.[65] In contrast, a marketable permit system would allow businesses to buy and sell rights to pollute within government designated areas, enabling businesses to make the same overall emission reductions less expensively. By regulating the amount of pollution rights available in each designated area, the EPA would protect the environment while eliminating some aspects of the central planning required under the current system.[66]

63. Of course, the possibility of tort actions may provide some deterrent. The tort system, however, as it has evolved to date, does not provide a consistent, credible threat that companies will have to pay for injuries that they cause. *See* F. CROSS, *supra* note 30, at 183-217.

64. *See supra* note 5 and accompanying text; *see also* Ackerman & Elliot, *Air Pollution "Rights,"* N.Y. Times, Sept. 11, 1982, at 23, col. 2.

65. *See supra* note 44 and accompanying text.

66. Professors Ackerman and Stewart argue that a marketable permit system would greatly reduce the EPA's information processing burden because the EPA would not need to determine the Best Available Technology (BAT) for limiting emissions. Similarly, Ackerman and Stewart suggest that their proposals would reduce the burden on the courts by eliminating appeals of BAT decisions. *See* Ackerman & Stewart, *supra* note 45, at 180. However, although a marketable permit system would reduce the government's involvement in assigning specific emission limitations to businesses, the EPA would continue to assign limits to pollution control regions (*i.e.*, determine the volume of pollution rights on the market). This decision necessarily would involve a determination of feasibility or risk—and the decision would be appealable. *See* 5 U.S.C. § 702 (Supp. V

Although ingenious, marketable permit schemes have yet to gain widespread acceptance. One reason is that the wholesale scrapping of command-and-control regulation, and replacement with a new system, would disrupt the status quo in favor of a theory that is largely untested.[67] Furthermore, a marketable permit program would not solve two of the most severe problems plaguing environmental protection programs: lack of adequate monitoring and insufficient enforcement.[68]

Unless carefully regulated, a system that allowed industry to redistribute pollution rights could result in excessive local impacts from individual facilities.[69] And although Congress presumably could use a marketable permit system to limit generation of hazardous materials,[70] it is unclear how marketable permits would enhance regulation of hazardous waste disposal facilities, since the regulatory goal generally is to prevent—rather than control—releases of pollutants.

The government continues to experiment with variations of the marketable permit idea to supplement existing programs.[71] In fact,

---

1987). Moreover, the EPA's chemical-by-chemical approach to risk identification and assessment presumably would continue unchanged.

67. *See* Ackerman & Stewart, *supra* note 5, at 1333-34.

68. Professors Ackerman and Stewart argue that a marketable permit system would motivate the EPA to enforce the law more effectively since poor enforcement would reduce the price of pollution rights, which, under the Ackerman/Stewart system would in turn reduce the Agency's funding. Ackerman & Stewart, *supra* note 45, at 183. Assertions that economic incentives will improve a huge federal bureaucracy's behavior, however, are unproven at best.

69. Professors Ackerman and Stewart nonetheless suggest that pollution rights could be traded freely for 5 to 10 years in existing air quality control regions and watershed boundaries. Ackerman & Stewart, *supra* note 5, at 1350. Stewart, however, acknowledges elsewhere that:

> [marketable permit systems] control aggregate pollution or risk levels, but not the levels produced by any one facility or at any one location. They are therefore best adapted to deal with environmental problems that are *not* local in character. . . . Local effects can, however, often be dealt with by a combination of regulation and economic incentives.

Stewart, *supra* note 16, at 167 (emphasis added).

In addition to the practical problem of local impacts, a marketable permit system could lead to political problems. A system that allows emissions to vary depending on the market for pollution rights may frustrate the desire of those who live or work near a pollution source to know, specifically, the amount of pollutants the source will emit and whether the source will employ state-of-the-art pollution control equipment.

70. Alternatively, generation of hazardous waste could be taxed. *See* Davis, *supra* note 15, at 521-22; *see also* Russell, *Economic Incentives in the Management of Hazardous Wastes*, 13 COLUM. J. ENVTL. L. 257 (1988) (advocating a "deposit-refund" system to control hazardous waste).

71. *See* Hahn & Hester, *supra* note 5, at 366-406 (describing experiments in marketable permits including emissions trading (*i.e.*, "offsets," "netting," "bubbles," and "banking") and inter-refinery averaging of lead in gasoline); *see also* 135 CONG. REC. H4450, H4451-52 (Daily ed. July 27, 1989) (remarks of Rep. Lent); Wicker, *Bush's Acid*

there are good reasons to conclude that, carefully applied, such a system could reduce some emission reduction costs.[72] But ultimately a program based on marketable permits depends—as does command-and-control regulation—on the EPA's ability to identify environmental hazards prospectively, determine acceptable levels of pollution, and enforce its decisions.[73] Like command-and-control regulations, marketable permits do not force the private sector to shoulder the risk that the level of regulation imposed by the government will be insufficient to protect the public.

IV. THE NEW LIABILITY-BASED INCENTIVES TO AVOID POLLUTION

Current regulatory programs, however flawed, result from years of legislative and administrative effort and comprise a system familiar to the regulated community, environmentalists, lawyers and politicians. And regardless of the shortcomings of command-and-control regulation, the environmental statutes of the 1970s did lead to some improvements, albeit in limited areas.[74] Nonetheless, even if the wisdom of attempting a massive overhaul of current regulatory programs remains unclear, by 1980 the need to supplement the system was obvious.[75]

In December 1980, during the final days of the Carter administration, Congress enacted the sweeping Superfund statute known as "CERCLA."[76] Public attention surrounding CERCLA focused on creation of the multi-billion dollar Superfund to pay for government cleanup of abandoned waste sites. But it is CERCLA's broad and retroactive liability provisions that fundamentally alter environmental law, imposing new planning and cleanup obligations on all segments of the economy.

Confounding those who considered CERCLA the last gasp of a liberal, lame-duck Congress and President, Congress enacted—and President Reagan signed—HSWA in 1984[77] and SARA in 1986,[78] increasing

---

Test, N.Y. Times, Oct. 31, 1989, at A19, col. 1 (President Bush proposed acid rain control program that depends, in part, on "market approach" to allocate emission reductions.).

72. Ackerman & Stewart, *supra* note 45, at 175-78.

73. *See* Latin, *Ideal Versus Real Regulatory Efficiency: Implementation of Uniform Standards and "Fine-Tuning" Regulatory Reforms*, 37 STAN. L. REV. 1267, 1301 nn.166 & 169 (1985).

74. Shabecoff, *supra* note 19.

75. *See supra* note 4.

76. For a legislative history of CERCLA, as enacted in 1980, see Grad, *A Legislative History of the Comprehensive Environmental Response, Compensation and Liability ("Superfund") Act of 1980*, 8 COLUM. J. ENVTL. L. 1 (1982).

77. *See supra* note 8.

the environmental liabilities of the business community still further. The use of retroactive, liability-based statutes to encourage private investment in environmentally sound practices clearly is an idea whose time has come.

A. The Creation of Strict, Joint and Several Liability

The liability-based statutes of the 1980s reflect a policy choice by Congress that those in some way responsible for the release of toxic chemicals, rather than the public at large, must bear the costs of environmental pollution.[79] Thus, Congress imposed strict, joint, several and retroactive liability for toxic contamination on broad categories of parties whom Congress deemed responsible for contaminated sites.[80] Furthermore, Congress authorized all citizens (in addition to the EPA, the states, local governments and Indian tribes) to enforce important provisions of the law.[81] By casting such a wide net of liability, and deputizing so many potential enforcers, Congress imposed a burden on the business community to anticipate, avoid and clean up environmental contamination that knows only ill-defined limits.

Congress designed CERCLA primarily to address inactive hazardous waste sites such as Love Canal—a problem that did not fall squarely within the ambit of previous environmental laws.[82] Nonetheless, CERCLA applies to essentially *any* actual or threatened release of a hazardous substance whether at an inactive or active site, regardless of the applicability of other statutes.[83] Under CERCLA, "responsible parties" are liable for investigation, cleanup and litigation costs, and natural resource damages. Such parties include current owners or oper-

---

78. *See* Atkeson, Goldberg, Elrod & Connors, *An Annotated Legislative History of the Superfund Amendments and Reauthorization Act of 1986 (SARA)*, 16 Envtl. L. Rep. (Envtl. L. Inst.) 10360 (Dec. 1986).

79. *See* United States v. Aceto Agricultural Chems. Corp., 872 F.2d 1373, 1380 (8th Cir. 1989); Walls v. Waste Resource Corp., 761 F.2d 311, 318 (6th Cir. 1985); United States v. Shell Oil Co., 605 F. Supp. 1064, 1072 (D. Colo. 1985); Ohio *ex rel.* Brown v. Georgeoff, 562 F. Supp. 1300, 1312 (N.D. Ohio 1983). *See generally* Grad, *supra* note 76.

80. Dedham Water Co. v. Cumberland Farms Dairy, Inc., 889 F.2d 1146 (1st Cir. 1989); *see also infra* notes 103-06 and accompanying text.

81. *See* CERCLA, 42 U.S.C. § 9659 (Supp. V 1987); RCRA, 42 U.S.C. § 6972(a)(1)(B) (Supp. V 1987); *see also* CERCLA, 42 U.S.C. § 9607(a)(1)-(4) (Supp. V 1987).

82. *See* United States v. Waste Indus., 556 F. Supp. 1301 (E.D.N.C. 1982) (district court holding, prior to HSWA, that RCRA applies to active conduct and *not* to leaching from waste disposed of before RCRA became effective), *rev'd*, 734 F.2d 159 (4th Cir. 1984). HSWA clarified that RCRA *does* apply retroactively to problems created before its enactment. *See, e.g.*, 42 U.S.C. § 6972(a)(1)(B) (Supp. V 1987).

83. *See, e.g.*, Colorado v. United States Dep't of the Army, 707 F. Supp. 1562 (D. Colo. 1989); Colorado v. Asarco, Inc., 616 F. Supp. 822 (D. Colo. 1985).

ators of pollution sources and contaminated sites, those who owned or operated such sites at the time of disposal of hazardous substances, those who "arranged for disposal" of hazardous substances, and those who transported the substances to disposal sites.[84]

The federal government, the states, Indian tribes and "any other person" may conduct CERCLA studies and cleanups (*i.e.*, "removal" and "remedial action") at contaminated sites and recover their costs from responsible parties.[85] In addition, the EPA may issue administrative orders requiring responsible parties to conduct removal or remedial action when "there may be an imminent and substantial endangerment to public health or welfare or the environment."[86] The United States, the states, Indian tribes and, arguably, local governments may recover damages for injuries to natural resources from those same parties.[87]

CERCLA cleanups must proceed in a manner "consistent" (or "not inconsistent") with the EPA's National Contingency Plan (NCP).[88] Before permanent cleanups ("remedial actions") are con-

---

84. 42 U.S.C. § 9607(a)(1)-(4) (Supp. V 1987). CERCLA's imposition of liability on those who "arranged for disposal" of hazardous substances encompasses generators whose hazardous substances arrive at contaminated sites in a variety of ways. *See e.g.*, Colorado v. Idarado Mining Co., 707 F. Supp. 1227, 1241 (D. Colo. 1989) (by allowing hazardous substances to erode into river, defendants "arranged for" disposal of hazardous substances at downstream site); O'Neil v. Picillo, 682 F. Supp. 706, 720, 731 (D.R.I. 1988) (waste generator is liable for releases from disposal site even though generator arranged for disposal of waste at different site and waste hauler took waste to site at issue without generator's authorization), *aff'd* 883 F.2d 176 (1st Cir. 1989), *cert. denied*, 110 S. Ct. 1115 (1990). *See generally* United States v. Aceto Agricultural Chems. Corp., 872 F.2d 1373, 1378-82 (8th Cir. 1989) (discussing CERCLA's "arranged for" language).

85. 42 U.S.C. § 9607(a)(1)-(4)(A), (B), (D) (Supp. V 1987). The terms "removal" and "remedial action" are defined at 42 U.S.C.A. § 9601(23)-(25) (West Supp. 1989).

86. 42 U.S.C. § 9606(a)(1982); United States v. Conservation Chem. Co., 619 F. Supp. 162, 191-97 (W.D. Mo. 1985); *see infra* note 97.

87. 42 U.S.C. § 9607(a)(1)-(4)(C) (1982). *See generally* Ohio v. United States Dep't of Interior, 880 F.2d 432 (D.C. Cir. 1989) (overturning U.S. Department of the Interior regulations regarding the measure of natural resource damages under CERCLA); Cross, *Natural Resource Damage Valuation*, 42 VAND. L. REV. 269 (1989); Kenison, Buchholz & Mulligan, *State Actions for Natural Resource Damages: Enforcement of the Public Trust*, 17 Envtl. L. Rep. (Envtl. L. Inst.) 10434 (1987); Landreth & Ward, *Natural Resource Damages: Recovery Under State Law Compared With Federal Laws*, 20 Envtl. L. Rep. (Envtl. L. Inst.) 10134 (1990). At least two courts have held that local governments are included within CERCLA's definition of "states" and, thus, may recover natural resource damages. *See* City of New York v. Exxon Corp., 697 F. Supp. 677, 683-86 (S.D.N.Y. 1988); Mayor of Boonton v. Drew Chem. Corp., 621 F. Supp. 663 (D.N.J. 1985). *But see* City of Philadelphia v. Stepan Chem. Co., 713 F. Supp. 1484 (E.D.Pa. 1989).

88. The National Contingency Plan (NCP) is codified at 40 C.F.R. §§ 300.1-.920. The EPA revised the plan effective April 9, 1990. 55 Fed. Reg. 8666 (1990); *see also* 53 Fed. Reg. 51,394 (1988) (the proposed revisions). Cleanups conducted by the United

ducted, the NCP requires an expensive array of studies for which responsible parties ultimately must foot the bill. The NCP mandates:

- Studies to identify the nature and extent of contamination at polluted sites ("the remedial investigation");
- Studies to evaluate cleanup or mitigation alternatives ("the feasibility study");
- Studies to evaluate the risks posed by the contamination ("the risk assessment");
- Identification of standards to be applied to the cleanup ("applicable or relevant and appropriate standards");
- Public education and participation; and
- Selection of a site-specific cleanup plan that complies with statutory and regulatory criteria ("the remedial action plan").[89]

States, a state, an Indian tribe, and, arguably, a local government (*see supra* note 87) must be "not inconsistent" with the NCP. 42 U.S.C. § 9607(a)(1)-(4)(A) (Supp. V 1987). In other words, government-conducted cleanups are presumed consistent with the NCP unless defendants in an enforcement action meet their burden of proving otherwise. United States v. Northeastern Pharmaceutical & Chem. Co., 810 F.2d 726, 747-48 (8th Cir. 1986), *cert. denied*, 484 U.S. 848 (1987). Private plaintiffs, however, must prove that their response actions were "necessary" and "consistent" with the NCP. 42 U.S.C. § 9607(a)(1)-(4)(B) (Supp. V 1987); New York v. Shore Realty Corp., 648 F. Supp. 255, 263 n.5 (E.D.N.Y. 1986).

89. Federally-financed remedial action is governed by 40 C.F.R. §§ 300.420-.435. (The Code of Federal Regulations citations contained in this footnote are the to-be-codified sections as they are set forth in the EPA's revised National Contingency Plan, 55 Fed. Reg. 8813-65 (1990)). Such action may be taken by federal agencies and—pursuant to EPA delegation—by states, Indian tribes or local governments. *See, e.g.*, 42 U.S.C. § 9604(d)(1) (Supp. V 1987); 40 C.F.R. Part 300, Subpart F (authorizing, *inter alia*, cooperative agreements and Superfund Memoranda of Agreement between EPA and other government bodies). The requirements of 40 C.F.R. §§ 300.420-.435 also serve as guidance for actions by states, Indian tribes or local governments that are not federally funded. *Id.* § 300.400(i)(2); *see also id.* § 300.515(e)(2)(ii) (EPA concurrence is not a prerequisite to state actions that are not federally-financed). Remedial action by private parties is governed by 40 C.F.R. § 300.700(c)(5)(vii)-(ix), (6), (7) & (8), which incorporates many of the standards of 40 C.F.R. §§ 300.420-.435.

If a "remedial site evaluation" (including a "remedial preliminary assessment" and a "remedial site inspection," 40 C.F.R. § 300.420), reveals the need for remedial action, the NCP requires the responding government or person to perform "scoping" to ensure that the response is appropriate to conditions at the contaminated site. *Id.* § 300.430(b). This step includes: evaluation of existing data; identification of potential cleanup alternatives; limited data collection (when appropriate); identification of the type, quality and quantity of data to be collected in future studies; preparation of health and safety plans (including an employee training plan); notification of appropriate natural resource trustees (so that they may begin steps to recover natural resource damages); development of a sampling and analysis plan (including a field sampling plan and a quality assurance plan); and preliminary identification of cleanup standards. *Id.* § 300.430(b)(1)-(8).

Next, the NCP requires a "remedial investigation" to determine the nature and extent of the threat posed by releases or threatened releases of hazardous substances. *Id.* §

In addition, the NCP specifies procedures for taking short-term

300.430(d)(1). The remedial investigation involves, as appropriate, data collection (including sampling, monitoring and treatability studies), a risk assessment study, and identification of applicable or relevant and appropriate requirements (ARARs). *Id.* § 300.430(d)(1)-(4). "Applicable" requirements specifically address the circumstances found at the site; "relevant and appropriate" requirements address problems sufficiently similar to those encountered at the site that their use is well-suited to the site. *Id.* § 300.5.

The NCP requires the responding government or person to perform a "feasibility study," more or less concurrently with the remedial investigation, to develop and evaluate alternative cleanup goals and technologies. *Id.* § 300.430(e). The feasibility study involves consideration of a broad range of options, including, as appropriate, recycling, treating, removing and containing hazardous substances, limiting public access, and taking no action. *Id.* § 300.430(e)(2)-(3). The NCP requires screening of these alternatives (as appropriate) to narrow the list of options and eliminate those that are ineffective, impractical or unduly expensive. *Id.* § 300.430(e)(7)(i)-(iii). Alternatives may be eliminated on the basis of cost when cheaper alternatives are available that are similarly effective and practical and that use similar technologies *or* when costs are grossly excessive compared to the overall effectiveness of the cleanup. *Id.* § 300.430(e)(7)(iii).

After the screening, each remaining alternative that represents a "viable" cleanup approach must be analyzed in detail, according to nine criteria for evaluation: (1) overall protection of the public and environment; (2) compliance with ARARs; (3) long-term effectiveness; (4) reduction of toxicity, mobility or volume through treatment; (5) short-term effectiveness and impact; (6) implementability; (7) cost; (8) acceptability to the affected state or Indian tribe; and (9) acceptability to the community. *Id.* § 300.430(e)(9).

Based on the remedial investigation/feasibility study, the NCP requires selection of a cleanup plan according to these same nine evaluation criteria. *Id.* § 300.430(f). Criteria 1 and 2 are "threshold criteria" that, subject to limited exceptions, must be met by any remedy. *Id.* § 300.430(f)(1)(i)(A), (ii)(A)-(C). Criteria 3 through 7 are "primary balancing criteria"—allowing for trade-offs between them. *Id.* § 300.430(f)(1)(i)(B), (ii)(D)-(E). Finally, criteria 8 and 9 are "modifying criteria" which must be considered, but cannot justify departure from threshold criteria. *Id.* § 300.430(f)(1)(i)(C), (ii)(E).

The NCP requires the responding agency or person to present its proposed selection of a cleanup plan to the public in conjunction with an ongoing community relations program. *Id.* § 300.430(f)(2)-(3); *see also id.* § 300.430(c) (setting forth community relations requirements). A final plan is selected after evaluation of public comment. *Id.* § 300.430(f)(4). The selected cleanup plan must (1) be protective of human health and the environment; (2) meet ARARs (subject to narrow exceptions); (3) be "cost-effective," providing that threshold criteria are met; and (4) provide the best balance of primary balancing criteria with an emphasis on long-term effectiveness and reduction of toxicity, mobility or volume through treatment. *Id.* § 300.430(f)(1)(ii).

To determine cost-effectiveness, the responding agency or person must compare cost with a balance of three of the five primary balancing criteria: long-term effectiveness; reduction of toxicity, mobility or volume through treatment; and short-term effectiveness and impact. *Id.* § 300.430(f)(1)(ii)(D). Under the NCP, an alternative is cost-effective if costs are "proportional" to overall effectiveness. *Id.* The cost-effectiveness requirement does not, however, require a cost-benefit study. *See* 55 Fed. Reg. 8666, 8726-30 (1990) (EPA's explanation of its approach to cost); *see also* HOUSE CONFERENCE COMM. REP., SUPERFUND AMENDMENTS AND REAUTHORIZATION ACT OF 1986, H.R. CONF. REP. NO. 962, 99th Cong., 2d Sess. 245 (1986), *reprinted in* 1986 U.S. CODE CONG. & ADMIN. NEWS 3276, 3338 (The term "cost-effective" means that the decision-maker "first determines the ap-

actions ("removal actions") to protect the public and environment from contamination pending selection, design and completion of permanent cleanups.[90]

Without changing this basic scheme, SARA—the 1986 amendments to CERCLA[91]—increases the cost of cleanups by requiring that remedial action provide "permanent solutions . . . to the maximum extent practicable."[92] SARA also enhances the states' ability to influence the EPA's remedy selection decisions, allows citizens to enforce standards that "have become effective" under CERCLA,[93] and authorizes states to obtain court-ordered cleanups.[94]

Under SARA, the Agency for Toxic Substances and Disease Registry (ATSDR) must prepare toxicological profiles of hazardous substances. Also, SARA Title III created the Emergency Planning and Community Right-to-Know Act (EPCRA), which requires businesses to submit reports to public agencies about the nature, quantity and location of dangerous chemicals that they use, store, dispose of and release.[95] Information provided by EPCRA and ATSDR's toxicological profiles may increase public pressure for additional government action and also may prove useful to plaintiffs using the tort system to respond to environmental risks.[96]

HSWA amended RCRA in 1984 by, among other things, authorizing any person (including states, local governments and Indian tribes) to bring suit against any transporter, generator, owner or operator who contributes or contributed to handling or disposal of any solid or hazardous waste that "may present an imminent and substantial endangerment to health or the environment."[97] This provision creates a fed-

---

propriate level of environmental and health protection to be achieved and then selects a cost-efficient means of achieving that goal.").

Selection of the cleanup plan is followed by documentation and design and by operation and maintenance. 40 C.F.R. §§ 300.430(f)(5), (6), .435.

90. *See* 55 Fed. Reg. 8842-44, 8858 (1990) (to be codified at 40 C.F.R. §§ 300.410-415, .700(c)(5)(v)-(vi), (6), (8)).

91. *See supra* notes 10 & 78.

92. 42 U.S.C. § 9621(b) (Supp. V 1987).

93. *See* 42 U.S.C. § 9621(f) (Supp. V 1987) (state participation); *id.* § 9659 (citizen enforcement).

94. *Id.* § 9621(e)(2); Colorado v. Idarado Mining Co., 707 F. Supp. 1227, 1232 (D. Colo. 1989); *see* Babich & Hanson, *State Enforcement of CERCLA: The* Idarado *Decision in Perspective*, 20 Env't Rep. (BNA) 735 (1989). *But see* United States v. Akzo Coatings of Am., Inc., 719 F. Supp. 571, 577-78 (E.D. Mich. 1989).

95. 42 U.S.C. § 9604(i) (Supp. V 1987) (ATSDR); *id.* §§ 11001-11050 (EPCRA).

96. *See* Sherwood & Fitzsimmons, *The ATSDR: A Plaintiff's Dream Come True?*, 2 Toxics L. Rep. (BNA) 1072 (Mar. 2, 1988).

97. 42 U.S.C. § 6972(a)(1)(B) (Supp. V 1987). The courts have interpreted the phrase "may present an imminent and substantial endangerment" to refer to a significant risk of eventual environmental harm. An "endangerment" (*i.e.*, threat) is "immi-

eral cause of action, as well as broad, strict, joint, several and retroactive liability, for public nuisances that pose a significant risk of eventual harm to the public or environment.[98]

HSWA also added provisions to RCRA to protect the public from leaking underground storage tanks,[99] mandate that the EPA and the states force parties regulated under RCRA to clean up past contamination,[100] and, generally increase the stringency, expense and complexity of RCRA compliance.[101]

In short, Congress's environmental initiatives of the 1980s impose strict, joint, several and retroactive liability for cleanup and for expensive federally-mandated studies on essentially every party who ever had significant involvement with hazardous waste or contaminated property.

B. *Creating Incentives to Clean Up*

Strict, joint and several liability directly threatens the profits of the countless businesses involved—directly or indirectly—with polluting activities, including businesses that acquire real estate polluted by

---

nent" even if the harm may not occur for many years. *See* United States v. Conservation Chem. Co., 619 F. Supp. 162, 194 (W.D. Mo. 1985). Thus, the situation need *not* present an emergency for RCRA to apply. *See* United States v. Waste Indus., 734 F.2d 159, 165 (4th Cir. 1984); *cf.* United States v. Midway Heights County Water Dist., 695 F. Supp. 1072, 1076 (E.D. Cal. 1988) (holding, under the Safe Drinking Water Act, that the court need not wait until actual harm occurs before acting under the "may present an imminent and substantial endangerment" standard).

Moreover, actions under 42 U.S.C. § 6972(a)(1)(B) are not limited by the EPA's regulatory definition of RCRA Subtitle C "hazardous waste". Instead, such actions may be based upon the broad, statutory definitions of "hazardous" and "solid" waste. *Cf.* 40 C.F.R. § 261.1(b)(2) (1989) (the regulatory definition does not limit EPA's authority to respond to potential imminent and substantial endangerments).

98. Middlesex County Board of Chosen Freeholders v. New Jersey, 645 F. Supp. 715, 722 (D.N.J. 1986) (Congress intended to codify public nuisance remedies). Persons who contribute or contributed to "the past or present handling, storage, treatment, transportation or disposal" of solid or hazardous waste are strictly liable for any resulting endangerment. Vermont v. Staco, Inc., 684 F. Supp. 822, 835 (D. Vt. 1988); *cf.* United States v. Northeastern Pharmaceutical & Chem. Co., 810 F.2d 726, 740 (8th Cir. 1986) (Congress intended 42 U.S.C. § 6973(a) to impose liability without fault or negligence), *cert. denied*, 484 U.S. 848 (1987). Moreover, 42 U.S.C. § 6972(a)(1)(B) authorizes courts to impose joint and several liability. *Cf.* United States v. Aceto Agricultural Chems. Corp., 872 F.2d 1373, 1382-84 (8th Cir. 1989); *Conservation Chem. Co.*, 619 F. Supp. at 199 (construing the substantially identical language of 42 U.S.C. § 6973).

99. 42 U.S.C. §§ 6991-6991i (Supp. V 1987).

100. *Id.* § 6924(u)-(v).

101. *See, e.g., id.* § 6924(c)-(k). *See generally* R. FORTUNA & D. LENNETT, HAZARDOUS WASTE REGULATION—THE NEW ERA (1987).

others.[102] Under strict liability statutes, responsible parties are liable for environmental contamination regardless of individual degrees of

---

102. *See generally* ABA Standing Committee on the Environment, *Burdens of Environmental Regulation on Private Property Ownership and Business Transactions: Reasonable or Unreasonable?* 18 Envtl. L. Rep. (Envtl. L. Inst.) 10348 (Sept. 1988); Evans, *Environmental Audits of Real Property*, 3 NAT. RESOURCES & ENV'T 20 (1988); Marcotte, *Toxic Blackacre: Unprecedented Liability for Landowners*, 73 A.B.A. J. 66 (Nov. 1, 1987); McNerney, McInnis & Towe, *Tilting at Windmills: Trying to be an Innocent Purchaser*, 4 Toxics L. Rep. (BNA) 135 (July 5, 1989); Leifer, *EPA's Innocent Landowner Policy: A Practical Approach to Liability Under Superfund*, 20 Env't Rep. (BNA) 646 (August 4, 1989).

Generally, the courts have read CERCLA's imposition of liability on "owners" and "operators" of contaminated property very broadly. *See, e.g.*, Colorado v. Idarado Mining Co., 18 Envtl. L. Rep. 20578 (Envtl. L. Inst.) (D. Colo. 1987) (parent corporation and subsidiary are liable as "owners" and "operators" of site owned by another subsidiary); United States v. Maryland Bank & Trust Co., 632 F. Supp. 573 (D. Md. 1986) (lender that took title to contaminated property at foreclosure sale is liable for cleanup costs.); United States v. Mirabile, 15 Envtl. L. Rep. (Envtl. L. Inst.) 20,994 (E.D. Pa. 1985) (lender who foreclosed on borrower's property may be liable for cleanup).

An owner or operator is *not* liable if he or she can prove that the act or omission of a third party (other than an employee or agent or one whose act occurs in connection with a "contractual relationship" with the defendant) was the sole cause of the contamination *and* that (1) the defendant exercised due care with respect to the hazardous substances at issue, *and* (2) the defendant took precautions against foreseeable acts or omissions of third parties. *See* 42 U.S.C. § 9607(b) (1982). As used in section 9607(b), the term "contractual relationship" includes contracts for sale or transfer of real property *unless* (1) the defendant acquired the property after contamination *and* (2) the defendant proves that he or she did not know and "had no reason to know" of the contamination, *or* the defendant is a government that acquired the property by escheat, by other involuntary transfer, or by eminent domain, *or* the defendant acquired the property by inheritance or bequest. *Id.* § 9601(35)(A) (Supp. V 1987).

To prove that he or she "had no reason to know" of the contamination, a defendant must have undertaken "all appropriate inquiry into the previous ownership and uses of the property consistent with good commercial or customary practice in an effort to minimize liability." *Id.* § 9601(35)(B). This "innocent landholder" exception to CERCLA liability is of uncertain scope, since the courts have yet to define "all appropriate inquiry." *See* United States v. Pacific Hide & Fur Depot, Inc., 716 F. Supp. 1341 (D. Idaho 1989) (under some circumstances, *no* inquiry may be sufficient). The exception does not apply to an innocent landholder who contributes to the release of hazardous substances or, after discovering the contamination, transfers the property to another without disclosure. 42 U.S.C. § 9601(35)(C)-(D). *See generally* Superfund Program: De Minimus Landowner Settlements and Prospective Purchaser Settlements, 54 Fed. Reg. 34,235 (1989).

Another exception to CERCLA liability, codified as an exception to the definition of "owner or operator," applies to a lender who "without participating in the management of a . . . facility holds indicia of ownership primarily to protect his security interest in the . . . facility." 42 U.S.C. § 9601(20)(A) (Supp. V 1987). A facility is "any site . . . where a hazardous substance has . . . come to be located." *Id.* § 9601(9). *See generally* United States v. Fleet Factors Corp., 724 F. Supp. 955 (S.D. Ga. 1988) (holding that a secured party was not an "owner or operator" under CERCLA).

fault.[103] In other words, it is unnecessary to prove that a responsible party negligently or intentionally caused contamination in order to force cleanup and recover costs and damages.

The doctrine of joint and several liability holds each responsible party at a contaminated site individually liable for the entire cleanup and the entire amount of damages.[104] Joint and several liability simplifies enforcement by making proof of each responsible party's specific contribution to the problem unnecessary. In many cases in which there are several responsible parties, such proof would be impossible, since chemicals in the environment rarely can be "fingerprinted" (*i.e.*, traced back to their original owners).[105] Congress provided liable parties with legal recourse against one another for contribution, to ensure that each pays its fair share of cleanup costs and damages.[106]

When liability for pollution threatens profits, businesses invest in reducing that threat until they judge it to be outweighed by the cost of taking further precautions.[107] Of course, in the short run, much of that investment consists of paying lawyers to find loopholes in the law and lobbyists to seek legislative changes. As it becomes clear, however, that Congress and the courts will not weaken the laws, the focus inevitably shifts to investment in more environmentally beneficial projects, such as early identification and management of pollution problems and min-

---

103. United States v. Bliss, 667 F. Supp. 1298, 1304 (E.D. Mo. 1987). The standard of liability under CERCLA is "the standard of liability which obtains under [the Clean Water Act, 33 U.S.C. §] 1321." 42 U.S.C. § 9601(32) (1982 & Supp. V 1987). The Clean Water Act, 33 U.S.C. § 1321, undoubtedly imposes strict liability. *See, e.g.*, United States v. Hollywood Marine, Inc., 625 F.2d 524 (5th Cir. 1980), *cert. denied*, 451 U.S. 994 (1981); United States v. Marathon Pipe Line Co., 589 F.2d 1305, 1309 (7th Cir. 1978). Thus, CERCLA also provides for strict liability. *See, e.g.*, New York v. Shore Realty Corp., 759 F.2d 1032, 1042 (2d Cir. 1985); Colorado v. ASARCO, Inc., 16 Envtl. L. Rep (Envtl. L. Inst.) 20,561 (D. Colo. 1985) (Carrigan, J.); United States v. Conservation Chem. Co., 589 F. Supp. 59, 62 (W.D. Mo. 1984); United States v. South Carolina Recycling & Disposal, Inc., 653 F. Supp. 984, 991 (D.S.C. 1984), *aff'd in part, vacated in part sub nom.* United States v. Monsanto Co., 858 F.2d 160 (4th Cir. 1988), *cert. denied*, 109 S. Ct. 3156 (1989); United States v. Chem-Dyne Corp., 572 F. Supp. 802, 805 (S.D. Ohio 1983); United States v. Price, 577 F. Supp. 1103, 1113-14 (D.N.J. 1983).

104. O'Neil v. Picillo, 883 F.2d 176, 178-79 (1st Cir. 1989), *cert. denied*, 110 S. Ct. 1115 (1990); United States v. Stringfellow, 661 F. Supp. 1053, 1059-61 (C.D. Cal. 1987); United States v. Chem-Dyne Corp., 572 F. Supp. 802, 810-11 (S.D. Ohio 1983).

105. *See* United States v. Wade, 577 F. Supp. 1326, 1332-33 (E.D. Pa. 1983).

106. 42 U.S.C. § 9613(f) (Supp. V 1987); *see also* Chemical Waste Management, Inc. v. Armstrong World Indus., 669 F. Supp. 1285 (E.D. Pa. 1987) (RCRA compliance costs may be recovered from other responsible parties under CERCLA). Colorado v. Asarco, Inc., 608 F. Supp. 1484 (D. Colo. 1985) (right to contribution is available under CERCLA as matter of federal common law).

107. *See* Dechert & Smith, *Environmental Liability and Economic Incentives for Hazardous Waste Management*, 25 HOUS. L. REV. 935 (1988); Frost, *Strict Liability as an Incentive for Cleanup of Contaminated Property*, 25 HOUS. L. REV. 951 (1988).

imization of toxic waste.[108]

C. Thy Brothers' (and Sisters') Keeper

Because the new environmental laws impose liability regardless of fault, potentially responsible parties must police not only their own conduct but also that of their peers. For example, a landowner—or a lender with an interest in property—may be liable for pollution that a tenant, borrower or even a prior owner has caused.[109] Thus, an increasing number of landowners, lenders, real estate investors and others with interests in property now insist on environmental audits to identify pollution problems before completing business transactions.[110] Similarly, because waste generators no longer may avoid liability by paying a waste hauler to take responsibility for disposal, generators have a powerful incentive to ensure that hazardous waste is handled properly by all involved.[111]

Liability-based laws empower parties facing potential liability due to contamination caused in whole or in part by others to bring private actions for cleanup and to recover their investigation, litigation and cleanup costs.[112] These private enforcement actions allow responsible parties to avoid liability to the EPA and the public by cleaning up problems at the expense of other, more culpable parties. Thus, strict, joint and several liability provisions inspire far more cleanups than could be achieved by the government acting alone.

D. Past Pollution, Future Liability

It is a commonplace that what the business community seeks most from government regulators is consistency and certainty. Yet just as the uncertainties of the market economy force industry to be creative and flexible in production activities, increasing the uncertainty of environmental liability can motivate businesses to approach environmental

---

108. *See* Hays, *Chemical Firms Press Campaigns to Dispel Their "Bad Guy" Image*, Wall St. J., Sept. 20, 1988, at 1, col. 6; Elkins, *Toxic Chemicals, The Right Response*, N.Y. Times, Nov. 13, 1988, at F3, col. 1.

109. *See supra* note 102.

110. *See, e.g.*, Evans, *supra* note 102. *See generally* Environmental Auditing Policy Statement, 51 Fed. Reg. 25,004 (1986).

111. *See* 42 U.S.C. 9607(a)(3) (Supp. V 1987); *see supra* note 84.

112. *E.g.*, Dedham Water Co. v. Cumberland Farms Dairy, Inc., 889 F.2d 1146, (1st Cir. 1989); Smith Land & Improvement Corp. v. Celotex Corp., 851 F.2d 86 (3rd Cir.), *cert. denied*, 109 S. Ct. 837 (1989); General Elec. Co. v. Litton Business Sys., Inc., 715 F. Supp. 949 (W.D. Mo. 1989); Chemical Waste Management, Inc. v. Armstrong World Indus., 669 F. Supp. 1285 (E.D. Pa. 1987).

issues with more care, creativity and flexibility. With its environmental legislation of the 1980s, Congress shattered industry's expectations of consistency by demonstrating a willingness to impose retroactive liability for pollution that was legal when caused.[113]

Following enactment of CERCLA, businesses are on notice that they can no longer rely on current EPA or Congressional decisions—whether based on risk assessments, cost or politics—to shield them from liability in the future.[114] To avoid future liability, *all* potential polluters must conduct independent assessments to anticipate and avoid the dangers their activities might otherwise create. Even industries that have convinced Congress to exempt them from requirements of today's regulatory and liability statutes (for example, the oil and gas industry) would be well-advised to minimize the damage they cause. Their exemptions may not last forever.[115]

Investors in property contaminated with substances not currently subject to CERCLA should carefully consider whether cleanup actions taken today can reduce the threat of liability for expensive EPA-directed cleanups in the future. By raising the spectre of retroactive liability, Congress has offered the business community compelling reasons to identify environmental problems as early as possible and to plan carefully to reduce risks.

E. The Role of Bureaucratic Waste

In an ironic twist, presumably unanticipated by Congress, the liability-based environmental statutes of the 1980s use the inherent inefficiency of the federal bureaucracy to motivate private businesses to conduct their own cleanups. Once a contaminated site comes to the EPA's attention and is placed on the National Priorities List,[116] the Agency generally will spend millions of dollars on studies, reports and community relations activities long before any actual cleanup takes

113. *See* United States v. Northeastern Pharmaceutical & Chem. Co., 810 F.2d 726, 732-37 (8th Cir. 1986), *cert. denied*, 484 U.S. 848 (1987); United States v. Shell Oil Co., 605 F. Supp 1064, 1068-79 (D. Colo. 1985).

114. Indeed, CERCLA settlements generally contain reopeners so that defendants are not released from liability if additional problems develop at the site. *See* 42 U.S.C. § 9622(f)(6) (Supp. V 1987).

115. *See* Eagle-Picher Indus. v. EPA, 759 F.2d 922 (D.C. Cir. 1985) (waste that is exempt from the definition of "hazardous waste" of RCRA Subtitle C nonetheless may be a "hazardous substance" under CERCLA).

116. The National Priorities List is an EPA-determined list of sites that present enough significant hazards to require federal action under CERCLA. 42 U.S.C. § 9605(a)(8)(B) (Supp. V 1987). The list is neither complete nor exclusive. *See* U.S. GENERAL ACCOUNTING OFFICE, SUPERFUND: EXTENT OF NATION'S POTENTIAL HAZARDOUS WASTE PROBLEM STILL UNKNOWN, (GAO/RCED-88-44) (Dec. 1987).

place.[117] When cleanup begins, it is unlikely to proceed in what members of the private sector would recognize as a cost-effective or efficient manner.[118] Thus, in assessing potential environmental liabilities, businesses must consider not only the potential for legitimate cleanup costs and natural resource damages, but also the probability that the EPA will waste a great deal of money that it will expect to recover from responsible parties.

The prospect of bureaucratic waste encourages responsible parties to organize and take responsibility for site investigations and cleanups.[119] If the EPA already has decided to address problems at the site under CERCLA, the Agency will require an expensive panoply of studies, no matter who performs them. But responsible parties can reduce costs by doing the studies themselves and in many cases can influence ultimate cleanup decisions.[120] Moreover, because strict compliance with the NCP is necessary only if the cleanup is directed or authorized by the EPA—or by another party who wishes to preserve the right to recover cleanup costs under CERCLA[121]—responsible parties who achieve a cleanup *before* a site receives the EPA's attention may save millions of dollars.

For these reasons, the relatively few—but highly publicized and alarmingly expensive—cleanups that the EPA actually has conducted have made a strong and constructive impression on the business community. In terms of inspiring private efforts to identify and clean up pollution problems and reduce waste generation, the EPA's inefficient Superfund program provides a great deal of bang for the buck.

F. Enhancing the Regulatory System

To reconcile its new, liability-based approach with existing regulatory programs, Congress carved an exception to liability under CERCLA for "federally permitted releases" of hazardous substances.[122]

---

117. *See supra* note 89.

118. *See, e.g.*, Lee, *EPA Response Action: Contracting and Cost Recovery Under CERCLA*, 4 Toxics L. Rep. (BNA) 216, 219 n.41 (1989) ("the government may spend from 100 percent to 500 percent more than a private client would spend to accomplish essentially the same site study or cleanup").

119. *See, e.g.*, INFORMATION NETWORK FOR SUPERFUND SETTLEMENTS, PRP ORGANIZATION HANDBOOK (1989).

120. *See* EPA, A MANAGEMENT REVIEW OF THE SUPERFUND PROGRAM 2-19 to -21 (1989) (discussing EPA oversight of cleanups conducted by potentially responsible parties).

121. *See* 55 Fed. Reg. 8835 (1990) (to be codified at 40 C.F.R. § 300.185(d)).

122. *See* 42 U.S.C. §§ 9607(j), 9601(10) (Supp. V 1987). An analogous provision precludes recovery of natural resource damages for an environmental injury that was "specifically identified as an irreversible and irretrievable commitment of natural resources in

Under this exception, responsible parties are not liable for contamination authorized by permits issued under federal, and some state, environmental laws. The provision encourages polluters to obtain and comply with permits, enhancing the effectiveness of the regulatory system. It also provides an incentive for those who discharge currently unregulated substances to encourage government regulation and provide information to aid the government in setting reasonable standards.

Nonetheless, the "federally permitted release" exception to CERCLA liability could work better. Currently, a permit based on inadequate or even false information could, arguably, insulate a polluter from liability. If the exception applied only to pollution for which the government had issued a permit after considering all potential environmental harm, it would encourage dischargers to provide complete, accurate, and detailed information to regulators during the permitting process.

G. *Continuing the Restructuring*

Because current liability-based statutes hold responsible parties liable for cleanup costs and damage to natural resources, but *not* for damage to the health of individuals, the laws create an incentive for reducing some risks of environmental contamination but not others. For example, pollution of ground water or soils with heavy metals is discouraged, since such pollution is long-lasting and expensive to clean up. No similar deterrent exists, however, to pollution of air with toxic chemicals, which, although dangerous, disperse in the atmosphere and, thus, often do not require expensive cleanup.[123] If polluters faced a realistic threat of liability for creating risks to public health, they would devote their efforts to reducing a greater variety of pollution problems.

The common law tort system, which governs most injuries to individuals, is not well-suited to problems of toxic pollution and, thus, fails to provide a credible threat of liability in many situations. In fact, the common law of many jurisdictions does not even recognize some of the injuries caused by exposure to toxic waste—such as increased risk of cancer or birth defects.[124]

---

an environmental impact statement" or comparable analysis. *Id.* § 9607(f)(1). *See generally* Idaho v. Hanna Mining Co., 882 F.2d 392 (9th Cir. 1989) (construing 42 U.S.C. § 9607(f)(1)).

123. *See Number of Air Pollution-Related Deaths in U.S., Canada, May be 50,000 Annually*, 19 Env't Rep. (BNA) 2629 (1989); Shabecroff, *Industrial Pollution Called Startling*, N.Y. Times, April 13, 1989, at D21, col. 4; Shabecroff, *U.S. Calls Poisoning of Air Far Worse than Expected and Threat to Public*, N.Y. Times, March 23, 1989, at B11, col. 1.

124. *See, e.g.*, Sterling v. Velsicol Chem. Corp., 855 F.2d 1188 (6th Cir. 1988). *See*

By the time a victim of toxic contamination actually develops cancer or has a child with a birth defect, years or even decades may have passed, making recovery of damages difficult. Often it is scientifically impossible to establish conclusively that a cancer or birth defect was caused by a particular chemical or pollution incident.[125] Thus, to provide an effective deterrent to polluters, victims' legal remedies for toxic contamination must be expanded and the burden of proof simplified.

One solution would be for Congress to create a legal remedy for those who suffer increased risks of cancer, birth defects or other injuries due to exposure to toxic chemicals.[126] The pollution victim's burden of proof could be set at a level that people who suffer such increased risks can practically achieve. Once a person who has been exposed to a dangerous pollutant makes a showing of an increased risk of harm, it would be the polluter's burden to show that the jury should not award damages. The polluter is in the best position to monitor and analyze his or her waste to rebut potential victims' claims of increased risk and to reduce exposures in the first place. By making polluters liable for risks to public health, and adjusting the requirements of proof appropriately, Congress can encourage polluters to study and control the risks that their activities create.

V. CONCLUSION

Some industry representatives contend that the strict, joint and several liability provisions of modern environmental laws are unfair and should be abolished.[127] Current liability-based statutes, however, embody a basic principle of American jurisprudence—long part of the common law tort system—that liability for harm should be assigned to those in the best position to prevent the harm from occurring.[128] Be-

---

generally Gluckstern, *In Support of a Uniform National Discovery Statute*, 4 Toxics L. Rep. (BNA) 551 (1989).

125. *See* Farber, *Toxic Causation*, 71 MINN. L. REV. 1219 (1987); Whitehead & Espel, *Legal Proof of Causation in Toxic Tort Litigation*, 2 Toxics L. Rep. (BNA) 1040 (1988).

126. *See* Robinson, *Probabilistic Causation and Compensation for Tortious Risk*, 14 J. LEGAL STUD. 779 (1985).

127. *See, e.g.*, Address by D.C. Thomas, Pollution Liability: The Tort System's Ticking Time Bomb (Feb. 16, 1988) (available in Oct. 1988 Inside Superfund Conference program).

128. *Cf.* Escola v. Coca-Cola Bottling Co., 24 Cal. 2d 453, 462, 150 P.2d 436, 440 (1944) (Traynor, J., concurring) ("Even if there is no negligence . . . public policy demands that responsibility be fixed wherever it will most effectively reduce the hazards to life and health . . . ."). *See generally* Special Committee on the Tort Liability System, *Towards a Jurisprudence of Injury: The Continuing Creation of a System of Substantive Justice in American Tort Law—Report to the American Bar Association* 4-3 to -8

cause problems of environmental pollution profoundly threaten the economic well-being and quality of life in every segment of society, the fairest solution is that which works best, most quickly, and least expensively.

A more sophisticated attack on current liability-based cleanup statutes is based on allegations that the EPA's Superfund program works poorly, slowly and is extremely expensive.[129] Citing the few, shockingly expensive cleanups obtained by the EPA and the tremendous amount of resources spent on litigation rather than cleanup, some businesses assert that a huge public works program to clean up existing sites would be preferable.[130] This argument, however, ignores the incentives that current statutes—regardless of EPA inefficiency—provide businesses to avoid creating pollution problems, clean up their own messes, and plan carefully to avoid future retroactive liability for chemicals that currently are not part of the federal statutory and regulatory scheme.[131]

Another argument for retreat from the environmental initiatives of the 1980s is grounded in an attack on EPA and congressional priorities. There is evidence—based on admittedly soft risk assessment data—that hazardous waste sites pose less of a day-to-day threat than other environmental problems, such as air pollution and pesticide contamination of food.[132] Arguably, if liability-based statutes divert soci-

---

(1984).

129. *See* OFFICE OF TECHNOLOGY ASSESSMENT, ARE WE CLEANING UP? 10 SUPERFUND CASE STUDIES: A SPECIAL REPORT OF OTA'S ASSESSMENT ON SUPERFUND IMPLEMENTATION (June 1988); SURVEY AND INVESTIGATIONS STAFF, A REPORT TO THE COMMITTEE ON APPROPRIATIONS, U.S. HOUSE OF REPRESENTATIVES, ON THE STATUS OF THE ENVIRONMENTAL PROTECTION AGENCY'S SUPERFUND PROGRAM (Mar. 1988).

130. Greenberg, *Opinion*, 18 Chem. Waste Litig. Rep. 192 (1989) (setting forth an insurance industry proposal for a public works program).

131. *See* EPA, *supra* note 120, at 4. The EPA states the following in partial answer to critics of its Superfund program:

> When all is said and done, few realize that the environmental benefits of Superfund go well beyond Superfund cleanups. Since the passage of CERCLA, many States have enacted their own hazardous waste site cleanup laws. The Superfund liability standard has also provided a powerful incentive for businesses, Federal facilities, and local governments to properly manage their wastes. Additionally, the threat of potential Superfund liability has spurred businesses, particularly during property transfers, to conduct environmental audits and remediate environmental problems, not only for hazardous wastes but for environmental problems in general.

Id.

132. *See* EPA, UNFINISHED BUSINESS: A COMPARATIVE ASSESSMENT OF ENVIRONMENTAL PROBLEMS—OVERVIEW REPORT (Feb. 1987). The EPA concluded that its rankings of environmental problems by risk do not correspond closely with the EPA's program priorities. *See id.* at xv. The EPA believes that criteria air pollutants, ozone depletion, and pesticide residues on food generally pose higher risks than active and inactive hazardous

ety's resources from more pressing problems to hazardous waste problems that can wait, Congress should revise the statutes. Nonetheless, until memories of environmental disasters and near misses involving hazardous substances fade, efforts to place hazardous waste problems on the back burner probably are doomed to failure.[133] Instead, Congress should seek ways of expanding its liability-based approach to address other significant risks.

The use of liability-based statutes to supplement regulatory programs and encourage the private sector to focus its energy, competence and creativity on protecting the environment is one of the most promising developments in the history of environmental law. Although the business community cannot be expected to shoulder its new environmental planning and cleanup responsibilities gladly, it is uniquely qualified to do so competently and efficiently. Continued reliance on strict, joint, several and retroactive liability is our surest means of achieving real progress in environmental protection.

waste sites. *See id.* at 95. Overall, "EPA's priorities appear more closely aligned with public opinion than with estimated risks." *Id.* at 96; *see also* Hanley, *New Jersey Questions Superfund Priority*, N.Y. Times, Nov. 7, 1989, at B1, col.2.

133. *See supra* note 39.

[11]

Environmental Policy—It Is Time for a New Beginning

Arnold W. Reitze, Jr.*

I. Introduction

Almost twenty years have passed since President Nixon signed the National Environmental Policy Act that began the "decade of the environment."[1] The Environmental Protection Agency (EPA) was also created in 1970 to centralize federal efforts to improve our environment.[2] Myriad environmental statutes and implementing regulations followed.[3] Today EPA employs over four-

* Professor of Law and Director, Environmental Law Program, The George Washington University, Washington, D.C. The author would like to express appreciation to Edna G. Reitze, Apphia Schley Esq., and Professor Joshua Schwartz for their valuable comments.

1. Pub. L. No. 91-190, 83 Stat. 852 (1970) (codified as amended at 42 U.S.C. §§ 4321-4370a (1982 & Supp. IV 1986)).

2. EPA was established December 2, 1970 by Reorganization No 3. Pub. L. No. 91-90, 83 Stat. 852 (1970) (codified at 42 U.S.C. § 4321 (1982)).

3. The major environmental statutes and the dates of their major amendments are:

a. Clean Air Act, Pub. L. No. 84-159, 69 Stat. 322 (1955); Clean Air Act Amendments of 1966, Pub. L. No. 89-675, 80 Stat. 954 (1966); Clean Air Amendments of 1970, Pub. L. No. 89-604, 84 Stat. 1976, (1970); Clean Air Amendments of 1977, Pub. L. No. 95-95, 91 Stat. 685 (1977) (codified at 42 U.S.C. §§ 7401-7642 (1982)).

b. Federal Water Pollution Control Act, 66 Stat. 755 (1952); Federal Water Pollution Act Amendments of 1961, Pub. L. No. 87-88, 75 Stat. 204 (1961); Federal Water Pollution Control Act Amendments of 1972, Pub. L. No. 92-500, 86 Stat. 816 (1972); as last amended by Pub. L. No. 100-4, 101 Stat. 60 (1987) (codified at 33 U.S.C.A. §§ 1251-1387 (West 1986 & 1987 Supp.)).

c. Toxic Substances Control Act, Pub. L. No. 94-469, 90 Stat. 2003 (1976); as last amended by Pub. L. No. 99-519, 100 Stat. 2989 (1986) (codified at 15 U.S.C. §§ 2601-2629 (1982 & Supp. IV 1986)).

d. Federal Insecticide, Fungicide and Rodenticide Act, c. 125 §§ 2-13, 61 Stat. 163 (1947); Pub. L. No. 92-516, 86 Stat. 975 (1972) as last amended by Pub. L. No. 98-620, 98 Stat. 3357 (1984) (codified at 7 U.S.C. §§ 136-136y (1982 & Supp IV 1986)).

e. Resource Conservation and Recovery Act of 1976, Pub. L. No. 94-580, 90 Stat. 2795 (1976), as last amended by Pub. L. No. 99-499, 100 Stat. 1613 (1986) (codified at 42 U.S.C. §§ 6901-6991i (1982 & Supp. IV 1986)).

f. Marine Protection, Research and Sanctuaries Act of 1972, Pub. L. No. 92-532, 86 Stat. 1052 (1972); as last amended by Pub. L. No. 99-499, 100 Stat. 1613 (1986) (codified at 33 U.S.C. §§ 1401-1445 (1982 & Supp. IV. 1986)).

teen thousand people.[4] Its major environmental statutes fill a 654 page book and the regulations encompass eleven volumes and 8608 pages of the Code of Federal Regulations. EPA's operating programs require about $2.7 billion and the Superfund and Leaking Underground Storage Tank (LUST) programs require an additional $1.6 billion.[5]

EPA's work and billions of dollars spent by the public and private sectors have given us cleaner air and water, but the approaches used for the past twenty years are about to run out of steam. New programs are becoming more expensive, more complex, and often provide only marginal benefits. The reason is not difficult to visualize. When a pioneer wanted to dispose of solid waste, it was thrown in the back yard. Small cities had to establish a municipal dump. Large cities today must ship wastes long distances, the wastes are much greater on a per capita basis (because of the increased use of packaging materials) and they must be disposed of in a manner that protects the public from nuisance, odor, and ground water contamination. The price per ton for proper disposal escalates. Similar patterns occur concerning discharges into the air and water.[6] Furthermore, when environmental problems receive governmental attention, not surprisingly, the inexpensive, quick payoff responses come first. For example, automobile air pollution control costs in 1981 dollars were $50 per vehicle for the 1970-1971 model year (MY), $370 for the 1972 MY, $700 for the 1977-1979 MY and $1400 for the 1981 MY. The 1979 to 1981 MY cars incurred marginal costs for pollution

g. Safe Drinking Water Act, Pub. L. No. 93-523, 88 Stat. 1660 (1974); as last amended by the Safe Drinking Water Amendments of 1986, Pub. L. No. 99-399, 100 Stat. 642 (1986) (codified at 42 U.S.C. §§ 300f-300j-11 (1982 & Supp. IV 1986)).

h. Comprehensive Environmental Response, Compensation and Liability Act of 1980, Pub. L. No. 96-510, 94 Stat. 2767 (1980), as amended by the Superfund Amendments and Reauthorization Act of 1986, Pub. L. No. 99-499, 100 Stat. 1613 (1986) (codified at 42 U.S.C. §§ 9601-9657 (1982 & Supp. IV 1986)).

i. Uranium Mill Tailings Radiation Control Act of 1978, Pub. L. No. 95-604, 92 Stat. 3021 (1978) (codified at 42 U.S.C. §§ 7901-7942 (1982)).

j. The National Environmental Policy Act, Pub. L. No. 91-190, 83 Stat. 852 (1970), as last amended by Pub. L. No. 94-83, 87 Stat. 424 (1975) (codified at 42 U.S.C. §§ 4321-4370a (1982)).

4. 14,323 work years are requested for fiscal year 1988, EPA 1988 Budget in Brief 3 (1987).

5. *Id.*

6. Steinhart, *Down In The Dumps*, AUDUBON, May 1986 at 102.

control of $700 (1981 dollars), yet, had only very modest marginal reduction in emissions.[7]

Since the mid 1960's the United States has seen a tremendous legal effort to deal with pollution. Our nation spent nearly $500 billion from 1972-1983 on pollution abatement—over $2000 for every person living in the United States.[8] The great output of laws and input of money have brought large programs and some measurable improvement in our environment. But the easy improvements have now been made and many of our programs are bogged down. In the past ten years there have been reductions in the levels of all six of the air pollutants for which health-based national ambient air quality standards have been established. However, three of the six showed no change between 1985 and 1986, while sulfur dioxide and ozone decreased only three and two percent respectively.[9] Increasingly, it is questionable whether the programs are worth their cost and hassle. Yet massive and more stringent programs are being developed that are aimed at truly marginal problems while serious issues are not addressed. This view is shared by EPA experts who believe that criteria air pollution including acid precipitation, stratospheric ozone depletion, and pesticide contamination are high priority subjects for control.[10] Yet all receive from modest to little attention. However, hazardous waste sites which are considered by EPA experts to be of medium/low risk, have the largest program budget in EPA devoted to their cleanups.[11] Environmental law programs ought to protect public health and/or the well being of ecosystems. Today they often seem to primarily produce billable hours for environmental consultants and lawyers.

7. L. WHITE, THE REGULATION OF AIR POLLUTANT EMISSIONS FROM MOTOR VEHICLES 85 (1982).

8. National expenditures are added from Table A-19, COUNCIL ON ENVIRONMENTAL QUALITY, ENVIRONMENTAL QUALITY, 15TH ANNUAL REPORT 614 (1984) [*hereinafter* CEQ, ANNUAL REPORT]. They are $499.371 billion in dollars of the year of expenditure (not adjusted for inflation). Population of the U.S. was 242.4 million in 1987.

9. EPA, NATIONAL AIR QUALITY AND EMISSION TRENDS REPORT, 1986 (1988).

10. Pesticide problems are generally unappreciated by a largely urban America. However, an estimated 300,000 farm workers suffer pesticide-related illnesses annually. This helps create a death rate in agriculture that in 1985 was 49 workers in 100,000 as compared with 11 in 100,000 for six other major occupational groupings. McCarthy, *Mysterious Maladies of Farm Workers*, Wash. Post, June 13, 1988 at A11, col. 4. These statistics, however, are challenged by the president of the American Farm Bureau Federation as being too high. Wash. Post, July 4, 1988 at A20, col. 3.

11. Allen, *The Situation: What The Public Believes; How The Experts See It*, 13 EPA J. November, 1987 at 9.

The following are some examples of the lack of focus in the system. In 1986, Congress enacted Title III of the Superfund Amendments and Reauthorization Act (SARA), known as the Emergency Planning And Community Right-To-Know Act of 1986.[12] This statute appears to require what EPA for years has had the authority to do under the Toxic Substance Control Act (TSCA).[13] Since EPA was unwilling to exercise its authority, Congress passed this legislation to mandate information gathering and direct the states to create another planning entity.[14] The private sector will incur substantial expense in generating the required data. Will the law prevent another accident such as the one in Bhopal, India?[15] It probably will not, if the recent chemical warehouse fire in Seabrook, New Hampshire is indicative.[16] Will the public benefit? Yes. But how much is it worth? Do states really have the resources to carry out effective planning? Could locally generated revenues be better spent housing the homeless, mentally ill, or dealing with some other locally pressing concern?

At the state level, examples of expensive marginally useful programs also exist. The most newsworthy is California's Proposition 65.[17] Beginning February 1988, this law bans the discharge of certain chemicals, designated by the state, into drinking water sources. It also requires companies using any substances on the list to post work place safety warnings and requires that warning labels be affixed to those consumer products containing such substances. Consumer warning requirements take effect one year af-

12. The Superfund Amendments And Reauthorization Act of 1986, Pub. L. No. 99-499, 100 Stat. 1613 (1986).

13. EPA's former director of the Office of Toxic Substances supports the concept of a broad TSCA authority to gather information. *See Issues in Toxic Control: An Interview With Don R. Clay*, EPA J. June, 1985 at 3.

14. EPA, TITLE III FACT SHEET, EMERGENCY PLANNING AND COMMUNITY RIGHT-TO-KNOW (1987); Elkins & Makris, *Emergency Planning and Community Right-to-Know*, 38 J. AIR POLLUTION CONTROL ASSOC. 243 (1988).

15. Galanter, *When Worlds Collide: Reflections on Bhopal, The Good Lawyer, and the American Law School*, 36 J. LEGAL ED. 292 (1986); D. KURZMAN, A KILLING WIND (1987).

16. On March 12, 1988 a fire at the Johnson Matthey chemical warehouse consumed 3000 or more chemicals and attracted national attention. The company was in full compliance with Title III of SARA, but problems existed in emergency response at the local, state and federal levels. *See* Burtis, *Title III Compliance May Not Be Enough: Lessons Learned from a Chemical Fire in Seabrook, NH*, ENVTL. MANAGER'S COMPLIANCE ADVISOR 11 (1988).

17. Proposition 65, The Safe Drinking Water and Toxic Enforcement Act of 1986. This law was passed as a water initiative and is codified at Cal. Health and Safety Code §§ 25249.5 - 25249.13 (West Supp. 1987).

ter they are added to the Governor's list.[18] Governor George Deukmejian submitted a list of only twenty-nine substances. This created an immediate outcry[19] which was followed by a law suit that resulted in 201 substances being added to the list.[20] Once a toxic substance is listed, "clear and reasonable" warnings must be provided. The burden of proving compliance is on the producer or seller, though, and there can be substantial uncertainty as to when there are "no significant risks" that would obviate the need for a warning.[21] As this law begins to be implemented, will notification of hazardous substances in consumer products provide benefits commensurate with the cost? Do we gain public health benefits from these required warnings that justify the costs—social and economic?

The nation is fixated on the dangers from hazardous substances. There is no question that they are undesirable. The right-to-know law and California's Proposition 65 each address a problem and will probably have some benefit.[22] But efforts aimed at control of hazardous substances seem imbalanced in a nation that casually accepts an estimated 314,000 deaths per year from cigarette smoking.[23] Our toxic cleanup program is giving increased attention to the protection of our underground water supply. EPA's operating plan for fiscal years 1986 and 1987 put the development of new standards in the drinking water program "among the highest priorities for the Agency."[24] Underground water protection programs have also expanded for waste management facilities under the Resource Conservation and Recovery

18. [Current Developments] Env't. Rep. (BNA) No. 2245 (Oct. 17, 1986).

19. Mathews, *Deukmejian Using Short List of Toxics*, Wash. Post, March 28, 1987, at A8, col. 1.

20. AFL-CIO v. Deukmejian, slip op. 348195 (Cal. Super. Ct. 1987).

21. Environmentalists would argue that the uncertainty over the "no significant risk" level gives industry a strong interest in having risk levels clearly established. California has set more numerical limits under this Act in one year than EPA has addressed under TSCA in 12 years. Roe, *Market Incentives for Toxic Chemical Protection*, 19 EDF LETTER 3:4 (1988).

22. Both of these statutory examples have strong proponents that see substantial public benefits from these laws. *See* Waisanen, *Management Systems Being Developed By OSHA And EPA*, [Current Developments] Env't Rep. (BNA) No. 231 (June 17, 1988) (emergency planning and community right to know); *Environmentalists and Industry Square Off Over California Toxics Law, The Fight For Prop 65*, 6 NRDC NEWSLINE 2:2, May/June 1988.

23. OFFICE OF TECHNOLOGICAL ASSESSMENT, U.S. CONGRESS, SMOKING-RELATED DEATHS AND FINANCIAL COSTS (Sept., 1985).

24. GENERAL ACCOUNTING OFFICE, GROUNDWATER STANDARDS STATES NEED MORE INFORMATION FROM EPA 5 (March, 1988).

Act (RCRA)[25] and remedial actions under "Superfund" which must attain the underground water Maximum Containment Level Goals established under the Safe Drinking Water Act.[26] Underground water protection is important, as it provides the water supply for half of our population.[27] But our efforts to protect this resource are offset by other governmental policies concerning underground water. We use seventy percent of this water for irrigation[28] that is often provided at government expense and is then used to produce low value crops such as hay.[29] We subsidize irrigation but use more than one third of the water from Western federal irrigation projects to grow crops that are eligible for federal subsidies because they are in oversupply.[30] We tolerate rapid exhaustion (mining)[31] of entire aquifers and the imminent regional economic collapse which will follow when the supply of underground water is gone or is effectively out of reach because of excessively high pumping costs.[32]

The most serious consequence of our lack of focus or perspective is the complete failure of our nation to grapple with the fact that environmental law brings arithmetic improvement to an exponentially worsening world pollution problem. Or, put another way, our population and consumption increases wipe out the benefits of environmental controls. This is the famous Malthusian theory now verifiable by real world data. But, we find our response is further limited by the law of diminishing returns. Pollution control programs usually bring further improvement at very high marginal cost, with continued environmental destruction oc-

25. WAGNER, THE COMPLETE HANDBOOK OF HAZARDOUS WASTE REGULATION 82 (1988).

26. ERT, INC. & SIDLEY AND AUSTIN LAW OFFICES, SUPERFUND HANDBOOK 73 (2d ed. 1987).

27. C. MEYERS, A. TARLOCK, J. CORBRIDGE & D. GETCHES, WATER RESOURCES MANAGEMENT 630 (3d ed. 1988).

28. *Id.* at 582.

29. Irrigation has been defined as: "The construction of vast works (dams, tunnels, canals, and so on) at public expense in order to produce surplus agricultural commodities, which are then purchased and stored at public expense. *Western Water Made Simple*, HIGH COUNTRY NEWS 192 (1987).

30. *First Waves in New Water Wars*, U.S. NEWS & WORLD REPORT, May 30, 1988 at 21.

31. Mining occurs when water withdrawal occurs faster than the aquifer can be renewed by rainfall percolating through the soil. The nation uses approximately 21 billion gallons per day of groundwater in excess of local recharge rates. *See* NATIONAL WATER COMMISSION, THE NATION'S WATER RESOURCES, 1975-2000, vol. 1 at 8 (1978).

32. Groundwater overdraft is more than 12,500 million gallons per day in the Texas-Oklahoma High Plains area, an amount about equal to the natural flow of the Colorado River. *Id.* at 18.

curring despite extraordinary efforts at control. No matter how stringent environmental controls become, the increase in population and consumption nullifies the effort, and the law of diminishing returns limits the effectiveness of new responses.

An example of this principle at work in water pollution is a large modern sewage treatment plant such as the Blue Plains Plant in Washington, D.C. After meeting EPA's effluent standards, such a facility can legally release the equivalent of forty-five million gallons of untreated sewage a day.[33] Our very expensive sewage treatment construction program reduces, but does not eliminate, adverse environmental impact. As more people enter the area and water consumption increase, benefits are further reduced. In the ten years prior to 1984, EPA reported that the population served by municipal treatment plants increased by eighteen million people but the total amount of pollutants entering the nation's rivers from these plants stayed constant. Water pollution did not worsen because the federal government spent $40 million, and state and local governments spent nearly as much, to build sewage treatment plants over a fifteen year period. The water pollution problems that did not receive substantial funding, such as non-point source discharge, worsened.[34] An example of this principle at work in air pollution would be a 1,000 Megawatt coal burning electric power plant which is subject to New Source Performance Standards (NSPS) under the Clean Air Act. If the plant utilizes particulate removal equipment with 99.4% efficiency, it will still release over 1200 tons per year of particulate pollution, *i.e.*, the equivalent of a major stationary source (as defined by the CAA) nearly ten times over.[35]

33. This is based on meeting 85% removal through "secondary treatment." EPA's effluent limitations for secondary treatment are found at 40 C.F.R. section 133.102. The 30-day removal shall not be less than 85% for BODs and suspended solids. More stringent requirements can be applied to meet stream quality standards, which is the situation with Blue Plains. *See* Montgomery Environmental Coalition, Inc. v. EPA, 19 ERC 1169, 1170 n.2 (D.C. Cir. 1983).

34. Houck, *Ending The War: A Strategy To Save America's Coastal Zone*, 47 MD. L. REV. 358, 379 (1988).

35. A major stationary source is defined in § 302(j) of the Clean Air Act (42 U.S.C. § 7602 (1982)) as a facility that has the potential to emit one hundred tons per year or more of any air pollutant. It is assumed here that a 1000 megawatt plant will burn 10,000 tons of bituminous coal per day. The coal produces 24 x 10 BTU/ton and is 8% ash. Thus 800 tons per day of ash is produced but since 70% is fly ash (30% is bottom ash) only 560 tons/day is released to the air. This is 3.36 tons/day after control or 1226.4 tons/year after controls.

We are exhausting our capacity to absorb high cost and marginally effective programs. At the present time, for example, Clean Air Amendments are pending in Congress. Our legislators are arguing over how stringent to make State Implementation Plans (SIPs) in order to reach ozone standards,[36] that are of modest importance to public health when compared, for example, to the problems posed by Acquired Immune Deficiency Syndrome (AIDS).[37] An Office of Technology Assessment study indicates that it would cost from $6 billion to $7 billion annually for ozone control to be implemented in cities that, under existing law, need further controls.[38] One aspect of this control program will be tighter standards on automobiles. Yet, it is not the tailpipe, but the front of vehicles that kills nearly 50,000 Americans per year.[39] Current regulatory efforts downplay airbags and other safety devices.[40] The chemical most in need of control, to protect public health from automobiles, is alcohol.[41] Instead, we press for costly programs to control marginal problems of air pollution.[42] The serious air pollution issues, such as acid rain[43] and carbon dioxide

36. Ozone standards of 0.12 parts per million, measured as a one-hour average, were to be achieved by the end of 1987. EPA states that 68 cities failed to meet the standard. On May 26, 1988, EPA expanded its definition of areas that violate ozone standards to include 345 counties or cities. [Current Developments] Env't Rep. (BNA) No. 171 (June 3, 1988).

37. Ozone in the lower atmosphere is a threat to health and is regulated under a complex federal/state program. Sixty-eight cities are ozone violators. Congress extended the December 31, 1987 attainment date to August 1988, and EPA has been developing a "Post-87 Ozone Attainment Policy." AIR POLLUTION CONTROL NEWS, March-April, 1988 at 2. Ozone in the stratosphere forms a band about six miles thick that protects humans from harmful ultraviolet solar radiation. This has received considerable attention, particularly concerning the "ozone hole" over Antarctica. This has led to laws and an international treaty (The Montreal Protocol, signed by President Reagan, April 5, 1988) restricting chloroflourocarbons (CFC's) that destroy stratospheric ozone. U.S. DEP'T OF STATE, THE OZONE TREATY: A TRIUMPH FOR ALL, UPDATE FROM STATE 3 (May-June 1988).

38. [Current Developments] Env't Rep. (BNA) No. 68 (May 20, 1988).

39. There were 47,900 deaths from motor vehicles in 1986. THE WORLD ALMANAC AND BOOK OF FACTS 810 (1988).

40. The Insurance Institute for Highway Safety estimates there would be 7,750 fewer deaths in 1990 if all cars were equipped with airbags. If airbags had been required since 1969, estimated lives saved could have exceeded 100,000. McCarthy, *Iacocca's Conversion*, Wash. Post, July 2, 1988 at A23, col. 3.

41. According to the U.S. National Highway Traffic Safety Administration, approximately 33% of fatal motor vehicle accidents in 1985 were alcohol-related. STATISTICAL ABSTRACT OF THE UNITED STATES 1987, 590. In 1986, approximately 34% of these fatalities were alcohol-related. STATISTICAL ABSTRACT OF THE UNITED STATES, 1988, 581.

42. LAVE & SESKIN, AIR POLLUTION AND HUMAN HEALTH 231, 245 (1977).

43. *See, e.g.* R. MELLO, LAST STAND OF THE RED SPRUCE (1987).

(CO_2) buildup (the greenhouse effect), receive little effective control efforts.[44]

In the 1960's, there was little federal environmental law.[45] Indeed there was little action by the legal profession. Much of the literature concerning the environment was being written by scientists acting as political activists. The consensus among these writers was that environmental degradation had reached crisis proportions, and that it was caused by the multiple effects of population, consumption, and social policies that allowed or even encouraged conduct that harmed ecosystems.[46] While some of the most outspoken of these environmental "gurus" differed as to whether population or consumption was the primary factor, they all agreed that these were the major factors.[47]

As the environmental programs began to evolve in the 1960's, the federal government took the dominant role. There was (and still is) no overall environmental program or goal. Each discreet problem competes for the attention of Congress and the Administration. Environmental protection measures compete for funds with other environmental programs and must also compete with all the other claimants seeking federal funds for their programs. The programs that survive and prosper are those that obtain the most political support and encounter the least effective opposition. In the environmental field this has meant that, from the beginning, the impacts of population and consumption have been ignored. These two problems lack well-organized constituencies and there is no consensus that they are problems, let alone problems in need of solution. So Congress focused on the obvious—the anti-environmental social conduct (pollution), which is

44. The first five months of 1988 were substantially warmer than any previous period in the past 100 years. The four warmest years in the last century have been in the 1980's. A NASA expert has testified before Congress that the agency has "99% confidence" that current temperatures represent a "real warming trend" rather than a chance fluctuation. Weisskopf, *Scientist Says Greenhouse Effect Is Setting In*, Wash. Post, June 24, 1988 at A4, col. 1.

45. Modern environmental law may have begun with the Federal Water Pollution Control Act of 1948 but the first federal laws with some enforcement powers were the Federal Water Pollution Control Act amendments of 1965 and the Clean Air Act of 1963.

46. Ehrlich & Holdren, The People Problem, THE SATURDAY REVIEW, July 4, 1970, at 2. Commoner, *The Causes of Pollution*, 13 ENVIRONMENT 2 (1971).

47. Dr. Paul Ehrlich was the leading proponent of population control as the most important measure of environmental control. Dr. Barry Commoner considered technology to be the major problem in the United States. A. REITZE, ENVIRONMENTAL LAW 23 (2d ed. 1972).

the least important of the three causes of ecosystem degradation. As the environmental law program developed, the sewage treatment construction program dominated the funding process.[48] Given the way the law evolves this was understandable, even if it was an irrational way to formulate environmental policy. Sewage treatment grants provided federal money to every congressional district; moreover, because the construction of sewage treatment plants is not a regulatory program, the program was not opposed by potential regulatees. Industry benefitted because waste producers were able to avoid capital costs associated with waste treatment by hooking into municipal treatment facilities.

As the nation congratulated itself on its environmental efforts, some professionals warned that these approaches would not work. But the nation was not listening. The environmental approaches that were adopted had developed a large constituency of beneficiaries that wanted to maintain the status quo. By the mid-1970's, the environmental program was largely in place. New laws were described as "mid-course corrections" or "fine tuning." When 1981 brought to power an administration that was committed to anti-environmental policies, the people interested in environmental protection fought to keep what they already had. Expansion of the field moved primarily in the direction of hazardous and toxic substance control. This subject had some support of the Reagan Administration, a national consensus that the problem needed attention, and a Congress that was very supportive. So like water seeking the easiest path, environmental law moved in the direction of least resistance.

The environmental field lacks any overall plan or direction. We can not continue indefinitely to create expensive programs. We can not continue to solely address the problem of environmental degradation through regulations to clean up the environment in which the twin problems of population and consumption are ignored. This nation needs a comprehensive environmental policy and that policy must be broad enough to include a population, material conservation, and energy policy. Included in this environmental policy should be a long range view of environmental

48. Between 1972 and 1984 federal, state, and local governments invested $56 billion in construction of municipal sewage treatment facilities. BNA U.S. ENVIRONMENTAL LAWS 475 (1986). In fiscal year 1987, a substantially reduced federal sewage treatment plant construction grants program was budgeted at $2.361 billion. OMB, BUDGET OF THE UNITED STATES GOVERNMENT, FY 1989, 5-47 (1988).

priorities and some consideration of costs and benefits. The focus of this article is the impact of population, material conservation and energy policies on environmental law, with recommendations concerning the integration of these subjects into environmental policy.

A broad view of the environment was taken by the 1972 Club of Rome study. It claimed that growth on this planet is ultimately limited by five basic factors—population, agricultural production, natural resources, industrial production, and pollution. The group's belief was that the problems facing mankind are of such complexity and are so interrelated that traditional institutions and policies are unable to cope with them.[49] Unfortunately, their pessimistic view of political institutions seems to be accurate, for despite the great publicity given to the study, little change has occurred.

II. Toward a Comprehensive Environmental Policy

A. *Population*

In 1977, President Carter instructed his Council on Environmental Quality (CEQ) and the Department of State to study the "probable changes in the world's population, resources and environment through the end of the century." The study would serve as the "foundation for our longer-term planning."[50] In 1980 the study, the Global 2000 Report, was released. It constituted the first attempt by the United States government to project long-term trends in population, resources and the environment.[51] The study predicted continued rapid growth in the world's population with the most growth in the poor, less-developed, nations. The projections were pessimistic, with per capita food supply declining in poor countries, especially in sub-Sahara Africa. The report predicted that oil prices would rise, which has not yet materialized, but the report accurately predicted a bleak outlook for lesser developed countries in terms of meeting their energy needs.

49. D.H. Meadows, D.L. Meadows, J. Randers & W. Behrens, The Limits to Growth (1972).

50. President's Message to Congress on the Environment, 13 Weekly Comp. Pres. Doc. 782 (May 23, 1977).

51. Council on Environmental Quality and U.S. Dep't. of State, The Global 2000 Report to the President: Entering the Twenty-First Century (1980).

While the picture painted by the report is depressing, overall it has not been inaccurate.[52]

When President Carter received the report, he established a Presidential Task Force on Global Resources and Environment to be headed by the Chairman of the CEQ. It was to include the Secretary of State, the Assistant to the President for Domestic Affairs and Policy, the Director of the Office of Science and Technology Policy, and the Director of the Office of Management and Budget. President Carter also directed the State Department to raise the issues identified in the Global 2000 Report in all appropriate international meetings.[53]

At approximately the same time as the Global 2000 Report was released, a study called the World Conservation Strategy was released by the United Nations Environment Programme (UNEP).[54] The UNEP report called attention to the 500 million people in developing countries that were malnourished and 800 million that were destitute. These people, in their struggle to subsist, were destroying the very resources that would be necessary to free them from poverty and starvation.[55] In the United States, the Presidential Commission on World Hunger stated that chronic undernutrition is a major world problem; some 800 million people outside the Communist countries exist in a state of chronic undernutrition.[56]

In 1969, President Nixon called for the creation of a commission on population growth.[57] Congress responded with legislation "to establish a Commission on Population Growth and the American Future."[58] This commission was to study population problems. Its report, *Population and the American Future*, was submitted on March 27, 1972.[59]

The major recommendations of the Commission were:

52. Brown & Flavin, *The Earth's Vital Signs*, STATE OF THE WORLD 1 (1988); Postel & Heise, *Reforesting the Earth*, STATE OF THE WORLD 83 (1988).

53. CEQ, 11TH ANNUAL REPORT 5 (1980).

54. International Union for the Conservation of Nature and Natural Resources (Morges, Switzerland), *World Conservation Strategy: Living Resource Conservation for Sustainable Development*, (1980).

55. CEQ, 11TH ANNUAL REPORT 5 (1980).

56. PRESIDENTIAL COMM'N ON WORLD HUNGER, OVERCOMING WORLD HUNGER: THE CHALLENGE AHEAD (1980).

57. H. R. Doc. No. 139, 91st Cong., 1st Sess. (1969).

58. Pub. L. No. 91-213, 84 Stat. 67-69 (1970).

59. COMMISSION ON POPULATION GROWTH AND THE AMERICAN FUTURE, POPULATION AND THE AMERICAN FUTURE (1972).

1) Schools should receive aid for population and sex education programs and such information should also be provided through the media and responsible community organizations. Information dissemination should strive to improve the quality of education for parenthood.
2) Discrimination based on sex should be fought through passage of the proposed Equal Rights (for men and women) Amendment to the Constitution. In addition, adequate child-care arrangements should be provided for parents who wish to use them.
3) Discrimination against children born out of wedlock should be eliminated and adoption laws reformed.
4) Investment should be increased in birth control research.
5) Access to abortion services should be liberalized, with the admonition that abortion not be considered a primary means of birth control.
6) Health services related to fertility, including prenatal and pediatric care, contraceptive services, voluntary sterilization, abortion, and the treatment of infertility, should be extended and improved through public and private financing mechanisms.
7) No increase in present levels of legal immigration should be permitted, and illegal immigration should be stopped.
8) To ease problems created by poor population distribution, programs for human resource development should be developed and assistance provided in relocating.
9) Comprehensive planning should be done on a metropolitan and regional scale, with greater public control over land use.
10) Genuine freedom of choice of housing within metropolitan areas should be promoted for minorities.
11) A National Institute of Population Sciences should be created within the National Institutes of Health, and an Office of Population Growth and Distribution should be created within the Executive Branch.

Although he stated, "I do not plan to comment extensively on the contents and recommendations"[60] of the Commission's report, President Nixon immediately rejected the main recommendations, and he did nothing to support any of the recommendations. President Nixon said that liberalizing abortion laws "would demean human life," and that he wished "to make it clear that I do not support the unrestricted distribution of family planning services and devices to minors. Such measures would do nothing to preserve and strengthen close family rela-

60. Rosenthal, *Nixon Rejects Population Panel Advice*, Wash. Post, May 6, 1972 at A1, col. 4.

tionships."[61] A mere glance at these recommendations demonstrates how little has been accomplished in achieving them. The major reason is that the development of a population policy has been engulfed by the concern over family planning, and the concern over family planning is dominated by the politics of abortion.[62]

In 1967, the Foreign Assistance Act was amended to require that a portion of United States foreign aid be spent for population planning.[63] Section 104(a)[64] of that Act states that "the Congress recognizes that poor health conditions and uncontrolled population growth can vitiate otherwise successful development efforts. . . ." However, Section 104 prohibits the use of United States population assistance funds to pay for research on abortion methods. It prohibits use of these funds to lobby for abortion. The Agency for International Development (AID) went further and prohibited use of AID funds for any abortion-related activities. According to AID, no funds were used for such activities.[65]

This law was further restricted by the Reagan Administration. The Administration policy is that no United States financial aid for population planning is to be given to any organization which provides information or services related to abortion, even if it does so in foreign nations with funds from other sources.[66] The irony is that this policy was announced in 1984 at the International Conference on Population sponsored by the United Nations in Mexico City, Mexico. Mexico has a very high birth rate and its impact on the nation's economy generates a constant flow of illegal immigrants to the United States. The Reagan policy led to the withdrawal in 1985 of United States funds for the International Planned Parenthood Federation (IPPF) and for the United Nations Fund for Population Activities (UNFPA). The UNFPA lost its funding because of presumed "indirect" support for "coercive" abortion in China, though, the charge concerning UNFPA appears to be untrue.[67] The policy of the Reagan Administration is that abortion is not an acceptable element of family planning

61. *Id.*
62. Reidinger, *Will Roe v. Wade Be Overruled?* 74 A.B.A.J. 66 (1988).
63. GUTTMACHER INSTITUTE, ISSUES IN BRIEF (Sept., 1987).
64. Pub. L. No. 95-424, 92 Stat. 945, (codified at 22 U.S.C. § 2151(a) (1982)).
65. PLANNED PARENTHOOD FEDERATION OF AMERICA, INC., FACT SHEET 2 (1988).
66. *Id.* at 2.
67. *Id.* at 3.

programs. The Agency for International Development (AID) rules that implemented this policy were challenged by a family planning organization in a federal court. In July 1988, the Federal District Court of the District of Columbia held that the AID rules violate First Amendment rights to free speech and association of the United States family planning groups. Spokesmen for the Justice Department and AID said the decision will be appealed.[68]

Domestic population policy is more ephemeral, but the most tangible expression is Title X of the Public Health Service Act.[69] This legislation was enacted in 1970 to make contraceptive services available to all.[70] This statute has remained controversial, for the Reagan Administration has attempted to promulgate regulations that would implement the agenda of anti-abortion groups. Under this law, the use of federal funds to perform abortions is forbidden. But anti-abortion groups do not want the subject mentioned. Under 1988 regulations,[71] family planning can not include any abortion-related information or abortion referral. A pregnant client must be referred for prenatal care services and must be provided with prenatal care information. These regulations have been challenged in three lawsuits.[72] In federal district courts in Massachusetts and Colorado, injunctions were issued against the anti-abortion regulations. In June 1988, a federal judge in New York upheld the Reagan Administration's prohibition on federally funded family planning clinics informing women that abortion is an option for handling an unintended pregnancy.[73] Within this arena is a sideshow of litigation concerning the Adolescent Family Life Act.[74] This law, enacted in 1981, is dubbed the "Chastity Act." It is aimed at dealing with the problem of teenage pregnancy, without the use of birth control or abortion. It seeks to educate adolescents to abstain from sex through counseling, frequently with the active and federally

68. Hockstader, *Funds Ban Rejected for Groups Performing Abortions Abroad*, Wash. Post, July 6, 1988 at A17, col. 4.

69. Pub. L. No. 97-35, (Title IX, § 3931(a)(1)), 95 Stat. 570, (codified at 42 U.S.C. § 300 (1982)).

70. GUTTMACHER INSTITUTE, *supra* note 63.

71. 53 Fed. Reg. 2,922 (1988) (to be codified at 42 C.F.R. Pt. 59) (proposed Feb. 2, 1988).

72. GUTTMACHER INSTITUTE, WASH. MEMO., (Feb. 8, 1988 and March 29, 1988).

73. Rich, *Judge Backs Ban on Abortion Advice*, Wash. Post July 2, 1988 at A5, col. 1.

74. Pub. L. No. 97-35, 95 Stat. 580 (codified at 42 U.S.C. § 300(z) (1982)).

funded involvement of religious groups. Part of this act was declared unconstitutional by the Federal District Court of the District of Columbia and was directly appealed to the United States Supreme Court.[75] The Supreme Court declined to strike down the law in a 5 to 4 decision written by Chief Justice William H. Rehnquist.[76] The Court suggested that the proper remedy was to withdraw funds from those grantees that were acting improperly.[77]

An important part of a population policy concerns the role that immigration should play in the increase in the size of the United States population. We must consider what measures to take to control legal and illegal immigration. The Immigration Reform and Control Act of 1986 is just beginning to be implemented.[78] More than 2.1 million illegal immigrants have filed for amnesty.[79] We do not yet know the environmental effects of this legislation.[80]

As the political and economic conditions in the Third World—particularly in Central and South America—continue to deteriorate, desperate individuals will try to immigrate to the United States. As immigrants become United States citizens and get involved in the political process, we can expect continued pressure to legalize larger immigration quotas. We can also expect illegal immigration to continue to increase because nothing is acting to diminish the desperate conditions which motivate migration. For much of the world, war, runaway inflation, and declining food supplies create intolerable conditions that cause people to illegally immigrate. The United States does not have a viable plan for dealing with an army of invaders from the south. This will be an unarmed army, composed largely of children who are merely seeking the American dream. Whether they are welcomed or rejected, the large numbers of immigrants pose a major policy

75. Reske, *The Abortion Counseling Case*, 74 A.B.A.J. 76 (1988).

76. Bowen v. Kendrick, 108 S.Ct. 2562 (1988).

77. Marcus, *Funding for Religious Groups To Promote Chastity Upheld*, Wash. Post, June 30, 1988 at A22, col. 5.

78. Hoffman, *The Immigration Reform and Control Act of 1986: What Does American Business Do Now?*, VIRGINIA BAR NEWS, April, 1988 at 17.

79. Barker, *2.1 Million Immigrants Beat Amnesty Deadline*, Wash. Post, May 6, 1988 at A9, col. 1.

80. One study, funded by the Ford Foundation, is to evaluate the Immigration Reform Act and its impact on American society and that of other countries. It is being done by the Urban Institute in Washington, D.C., *See* Rich, *Think Tank Survives Lean Times*, Wash. Post, May 16, 1988 at A13, col. 3.

problem for this nation. The most humane policies are those that deal with the underlying causes—energy prices, diminished natural resources, lowered agricultural production, and high birth rates.

The United States today is one of the fastest-growing industrialized nations.[81] The number of women of child-bearing age is at an all-time high. Immigration, legal and illegal, is a major contributor to our population growth. It is, therefore, imperative that citizenry in general, and not just the opponents of population planning, take an interest in the population growth impacts on our environment. The time has come to ask the question: What is the desirable size for the United States population (and for the world population)? The time has come to determine what steps might be taken to effectuate a population goal. Since about one-quarter of all births are unplanned or unwanted, the reduction in government support for family planning could result in population growth that few people desire.

The United States does not have an articulated population policy, but it does have a pro-natality tilt. The decision as to whether or not to have children is protected by the right to privacy, which is protected under the Constitution of the United States.[82] After that decision is made, however, the public pays to provide infrastructure for the child: government supplies education, health care, recreational facilities, and much more, to raise a newborn infant into an economically productive adult. This makes the public treasury an important subsidizer of the individual's private decision to have a child. The recent political proposals to provide subsidized child care for working parents is a further example of this shift in the costs from the parents to the public. Many of the public expenditures that benefit families are justified, but their indirect contribution to population growth remains unexamined. Private decisions, or careless indifference, concerning natality have a large societal impact. For every 100 children born today in the United States, thirteen will be born to teenage mothers, fif-

81. U.S. growth rate of .9% is low by developing world standards (3% for Sub-Saharan Africa) but it is nearly double the rate for Europe and the Soviet Union (.5%). Our growth rate, if continued, will result in the nation's population doubling during a human's lifetime and potentially occurring more rapidly with increased immigration. CEQ, 16TH ANNUAL REPORT 408 (1985).

82. *See, e.g.*, Griswold v. Conn., 381 U.S. 479 (1965); Eisenstadt v. Baird, 405 U.S. 438 (1971); Roe v. Wade, 410 U.S. 113 (1973).

teen will be born into households where no parent is employed, fifteen will be born into households with a working parent earning a below-poverty wage, and twenty-five children will be receiving welfare assistance at some time prior to their adulthood.[83]

Since 1960, the population of the United States has increased by about 60 million people[84] and the world population has increased by 2 billion.[85] Total energy consumption by the United States has increased sixty-nine percent and our population has increased by one-third.[86] These increases have nullified most of our efforts at pollution control. As a nation, it is time to recognize that the more rapidly we stabilize our population, the higher our per capita income will be. Conversely, the more our population grows, the poorer we will become and the greater the stress will be on our ecosystem and on our national security.[87] Merely feeding our expanding population will require large inputs of fertilizers, insecticides and agricultural machinery. All of the above are highly energy intensive inputs, but without such inputs, American agriculture is no more productive than the Third World agriculture and perhaps less. As energy costs rise, so will agricultural production costs, and production can be expected to decline, for purchasers will not be able to afford their present diet. Petroleum, as it becomes scarce and more costly, can only be used in agriculture by reducing consumption in other sectors of the economy. To maintain our standard of living over the next several decades will be difficult, if not impossible.

B. *Material Conservation*

In order to effectively deal with our environmental problems, we must develop a material conservation policy that can be implemented in conjunction with pollution controls. The material con-

83. Squires, *We Don't See Any National Agenda for Children*, WASH. POST HEALTH, May 24, 1988 at 9, col. 4.

84. THE WORLD ALMANAC AND BOOK OF FACTS 532, 535 (1988).

85. PLANNED PARENTHOOD FEDERATION OF AMERICA, INC., *supra* note 65.

86. THE WORLD ALMANAC AND BOOK OF FACTS 125 (1988).

87. Population increases also bring increases in domestic animal populations. World sheep and goat populations increased by about 250 million animals between 1955 and 1976. Grazing lands are under pressure from those seeking farm land and, thus, these lands are farmed and not allowed sufficient fallow time for soils to recover. Marginal lands are grazed and as the vegetative cover disappears so, too, does the soil to the effects of wind and rain. Desertification follows and has been especially serious in the arid areas south of the Sahara Desert. CEQ, 16TH ANNUAL REPORT 282-284 (1985).

servation policy must harmonize with the energy policy and, to the extent possible, with economic and environmental goals. However, it will be difficult to develop such a policy. Consumption is part of the American Dream. Each generation has expected to live better, *i.e.*, consume more, than their parents. If national consumption decreases, our natural environment might improve, but the economic and political implications would be profound. Consumption policy, therefore, must focus on certain aspects of consumption to be politically acceptable. This would include situations where recycling could be accomplished without objectionable adverse effects, the use and disposal of hazardous material, and the use and disposal of materials of strategic importance. Energy policy is the most important aspect of consumption, however, because energy use is so closely related to our major environmental problems, such as the large scale biosphere impacts of increased carbon dioxide,[88] acid rain[89] and pollution of the oceans.[90] In the longer term, conservation of material, *i.e.*, doing more with less, is the key to the United States staying wealthy. In the past, the resources of the world were easily available and inexpensive. Today, world population pressure, the increased consumption of other developed nations, and the diminishing resource base makes conservation imperative. We need to develop a sustainable economy within the carrying capacity of our resources. This is not only a economic and environmental necessity; it is also important in avoiding armed conflict as the world battles over who will get the last barrel of oil or the last ton of a rare mineral.

There have, in the recent past, been some limited efforts to develop a national materials policy. When the National Environmental Policy Act (NEPA) became law in 1970, it required the federal government to use all practicable means to "enhance the quality of renewable resources and approach the maximum attainable recycling of depletable resources."[91] In the fall of 1970, Congress established a National Commission on Materials Pol-

88. *See generally* Rotty & Reister, *Use of Energy Scenarios in Addressing the CO2 Question*, 36 J. Air Pollution Control Assoc. 1111 (1986).

89. *See generally* National Research Council, Acid Deposition, Long Term Trends (1986).

90. *See generally* National Advisory Committee on Oceans and Atmosphere, The Role of the Ocean in a Waste Management Strategy (Jan., 1981).

91. 42 U.S.C. § 4331(b)(6) (1982).

icy[92] under Title II of the Resource Recovery Act.[93] In 1973, the Commission produced a final report that called for a national materials policy to protect the environment and to conserve resources.[94] Needless to say, the report was ignored. In 1973, the National Academy of Sciences and the National Academy of Engineering held a symposium on materials policy. This meeting coincided with the renewal of the Arab-Israeli conflict and with a five month oil embargo against the United States.[95] Again nothing of substance developed from the report, despite the impact of oil cutoffs.

During the period from 1970 to 1975, state governments and Congress focused on a minor aspect of materials policy, the so called "bottle bills" aimed at reusing beverage containers.[96] A comprehensive solid waste statute was not enacted until 1976 when Congress passed RCRA.[97] RCRA has been amended several times since its enactment with the most important changes being the Hazardous and Solid Waste Amendments of 1984.[98]

RCRA as amended includes in Section 6901(c):

> (c) Materials
>
> The Congress finds with respect to materials, that—
>
> (1) millions of tons of recoverable material which could be used are needlessly buried each year;
>
> (2) methods are available to separate usable materials from solid waste; and
>
> (3) the recovery and conservation of such materials can reduce the dependence of the United States on foreign resources and reduce the deficit in its balance of payments.[99]

This finding has never resulted in serious efforts at implementation.

92. The subject had been studied earlier. In the 1950's President Truman, concerned about resource shortages experienced during and after World War II and the Korean War, established the Paley Commission to study the subject. U.S. PRESIDENTS MATERIALS POLICY COMM'N, RESOURCES FOR FREEDOM: A REPORT TO THE PRESIDENT (1952).

93. Pub. L. No. 91-512, 84 Stat. 1227 (1970).

94. FINAL REPORT OF THE NATIONAL COMM'N. ON MATERIALS POLICY, MATERIAL NEEDS AND THE ENVIRONMENT TODAY AND TOMORROW, (June, 1973).

95. NATIONAL ACADEMY OF SCIENCES, NATIONAL MATERIALS POLICY (1975); NATIONAL ACADEMY OF SCIENCES, MINERAL RESOURCES AND THE ENVIRONMENT (1975).

96. A. REITZE, ENVIRONMENTAL LAW 55 (1972); Note, *The Oregon Bottle Bill*, 54 OREGON L. REV. 175 (1975).

97. 42 U.S.C. §§ 6901 - 6991(i) (1982 & Supp. IV 1986).

98. Pub. L. No. 98-616, 98 Stat. 3221 (1984).

99. 42 U.S.C. § 6901(c) (1982).

RCRA as amended has developed into one of the major programs implemented by EPA. The statute is divided into nine subchapters or subtitles. The most significant is the subchapter III (or C) program dealing with hazardous waste management. The program for resource conservation and recovery has not gotten much past the use of the words in the Act's title. In the United States, we recycle only about ten percent of our waste; paper, glass and a few metals are the subject of most of the effort.[100] RCRA has had little effect on these dismal statistics. One small, tangible example of the federal program is the regulatory guidelines for federal procurement of recycled goods.[101] In addition EPA could use Section 6 of the Toxic Substances Control Act (TSCA)[102] to control the generation of wastes in specific industries, but it has not chosen to do so.

The RCRA subtitle C program encourages source reduction, recycling and waste minimization,[103] at least in regard to hazard-

100. Steinhart, *supra* note 6, at 102.

101. RCRA states that if a federal, state, or local procuring agency uses appropriated Federal funds to procure certain designated items, such items must be composed of the highest percentage of recovered materials practicable. EPA is required to designate these items and to prepare guidelines to assist procuring agencies in complying with these requirements. 42 U.S.C. § 6962 (1982 & Supp. IV 1986).

EPA issued the first of these guidelines for cement and concrete containing fly ash, on January 28, 1983, 40 C.F.R. §§ 249.01-249.33 (1987). EPA issued a second guideline for paper and paper products containing recovered materials, on October 6, 1987, 40 C.F.R. § 250.10 (1988).

A third guideline, for asphalt materials containing ground tire rubber, was proposed on February 20, 1986 (51 Fed. Reg. 6,202 (1986)). A fourth guideline, for engine lubricating oils, hydraulic fluids, and gear oils containing re-refined oils, was proposed on October 19, 1987 (52 Fed. Reg. 38,838 (1987)); this guideline is being finalized.

The most recent EPA effort is the EPA Proposed Guideline for Federal Procurement of Retread Tires under the Resource Conservation and Recovery Act (53 Fed. Reg. 15,624 (1988)). Other guidelines are to be issued pursuant to an agreement made in EDF v. EPA, DC, No. 87-CV-3212-SS, April 8, 1988. [Current Developments] Env't Rep. (BNA) No. 2451 (April 15, 1988).

102. 15 U.S.C. § 2605 (1982).

103. Source reduction reduces the amount of waste that exits from the process by changes in technology, process, plant operations and procedures and raw materials before the waste is generated. Recycling implies use, reuse or reclamation of the waste. If recycled on site the waste may be excluded from the reach of RCRA. American Mining Congress v. EPA, 824 F.2d 1177 (D.C. Cir. 1987). Waste minimization is defined at 42 U.S.C. § 6922(b) as the reduction in volume and toxicity of waste that has been generated. There is some inconsistency between EPA definitions and those used in pending legislation and others in the field. Note that waste minimization can be considered treatment that is subject to RCRA permitting requirements.

ous material.[104] There are three waste reduction provisions under RCRA: (1) section 3002(a)(6),[105] which requires generators to report efforts made to reduce the volume and toxicity of waste; (2) section 3002(b),[106] which requires that generators certify in their section 3002(a) manifests that they have a program to reduce the amount or toxicity of the wastes generated to the degree determined by the generator to be economically practicable; and (3) section 3005(h),[107] which requires the same certification for new permits issued for the treatment, storage, or disposal of hazardous waste.

These statutory provisions are more hortatory than regulatory. It is not surprising that a report by Congress' Office of Technology Assessment concluded that waste reduction efforts in industry have been minimal.[108] Current waste reduction is motivated by the increasing cost of land disposal. The high cost of land disposal prompts industry to reduce the creation of hazardous material and/or recycle the wastes[109] or burn them, sometimes in processes that utilize their energy.[110] A more important industry motivator is the "Superfund" legislation,[111] which makes generators liable for what they send to land disposal sites. Since this liability is joint and several and can extend far into the future, even a small amount of waste sent to a disposal site can expose the generator to substantial claims.[112]

EPA has taken the position that treatment and recovery should be the preferred methods for managing hazardous waste[113] and has formally adopted this policy.[114] Under RCRA, most untreated hazardous wastes will be banned from land disposal by

104. For an overview *see* Noll, Haas, Patterson, *Recovery, Recycle and Reuse of Hazardous Waste*, 36 J. AIR POLLUTION CONTROL ASSOC. 1163 (1986); EPA, THE NEW RCRA—A FACT BOOK 1 (Oct., 1985).

105. 42 U.S.C. § 6922(a)(6)(C) (1982 & Supp. IV 1986).

106. *Id.* at § 6922(b)(1).

107. *Id.* at § 6925(h).

108. OFFICE OF TECHNOLOGY ASSESSMENT, FROM POLLUTION TO PREVENTION (June, 1987).

109. Lehman, *Can Pollution Be Destroyed?* 12 EPA J. 10 (1986).

110. Skinner, *Research to Break the Land Disposal Habit*, 12 EPA J. 12 (1986).

111. Comprehensive Environmental Response, Compensation, and Liability Act of 1980, 42 U.S.C. §§ 9601-9657 (1982 & Supp. IV 1986).

112. ERT, INC. & SIDLEY & AUSTIN LAW OFFICES, SUPERFUND HANDBOOK (2d ed. 1987).

113. White, *EPA Program for Treatment Alternatives for Hazardous Waste*, 35 J. AIR POLLUTION CONTROL ASSOC. 369 (1985).

114. 41 C.F.R. § 35050, (1976). EPA created a waste minimization staff within the Office of Solid Waste to aid in efforts to encourage waste reduction and to release grant

1990. The major impetus for hazardous waste reduction is just beginning to be felt as EPA regulates to limit the land disposal of these hazardous substances. These regulations are causing disposal prices to rise sharply. In addition, facilities for disposal may not exist at any price due to public opposition to the presence of landfills,[115] as well as the waste industry's problems in dealing with uncertainty regarding regulatory requirements and the difficulties of obtaining affordable insurance.[116]

In the 1984 RCRA amendments,[117] Congress created a phased program for EPA to implement that would reduce the use of land disposal for hazardous waste. The Amendments state that "reliance on land disposal should be minimized or eliminated, and land disposal, particularly landfills and surface impoundments, should be the least favored method for managing hazardous wastes."[118] Under RCRA, EPA is required to set pretreatment requirements that reduce the toxicity of wastes.[119] The statute also prohibits storage of waste in excess of time and quantity limits.[120] The placement of hazardous wastes in salt formations or in caves is restricted and subject to permit requirements.[121] Bulk or non-containerized liquid wastes were prohibited from landfill disposal in May, 1985 and the rules were further strengthened in November, 1985.[122]

The first phase of the land disposal ban began November 7, 1986 when EPA set out the regulatory program for land disposal prohibitions and treatment standards for specified solvent and dioxin wastes.[123] The second phase is the ban on the "California list". These wastes were first banned by California and its pro-

monies that were approved by Congress. [Current Developments] Env't Rep. (BNA) No. 37 (May 13, 1988).

115. Tarlock, *Anywhere But Here: An Introduction to State Control of Hazardous Waste Facility Location*, 2 J. ENV. L. 1 (1981); Tarlock, *Siting New or Expanded Treatment, Storage, or Disposal Facilities: The Pigs in the Parlors of the 1980s*, 17 NAT. RES. L. 429 (1984).

116. COOKE, LAW OF HAZARDOUS WASTE: MANAGEMENT, CLEANUP, LIABILITY 189-190 (1988); *see generally* Abraham, *The Insurance Implications of Administrative Compensation Systems*, 25 HOUS. L. REV. 817 (1988).

117. Pub. L. No. 98-616, 98 Stat. 3221 (1984).

118. RCRA, § 1002(b)(7), 42 U.S.C. § 6901(b)(7). (1982 & Supp. IV 1986).

119. *Id.* at § 3004(m), 42 U.S.C. § 6924(m).

120. *Id.* at § 3004(j), 42 U.S.C. § 6924(j).

121. *Id.* at § 3004(b), 42 U.S.C. § 6924(b).

122. *Id.* at § 3004(c), 42 U.S.C. § 6924(c).

123. *Id.* at § 3004(e), 42 U.S.C. § 6924(e). Regulations are at 51 Fed. Reg. 40,572 (1986). *See also* 40 C.F.R. 261.31.

gram has been incorporated into RCRA.[124] These wastes include free liquids associated with sludge, heavy metals, acids with pH below two, polychlorinated biphenyls (PCB's), and halogenated organic compounds. A California waste, except halogenated organic waste, can be rendered into a solid and disposed of in a landfill.[125] The third phase is a schedule of disposal restrictions for wastes not dealt with in either phase one or phase two. The schedule is to be based on a ranking of the hazardous waste, with high volume, high toxicity wastes to be regulated first. EPA promulgated a schedule in 1986 that would regulate one-third of the ranked and listed hazardous waste by August 8, 1988, two-thirds by June 8, 1989, and the remaining waste by May 8, 1990.[126] In May, 1988, proposed regulations for restrictions on the first one-third of the list were promulgated.[127]

At the same time that restrictions on waste disposal have become more stringent, EPA has promulgated more restrictive technical and permitting standards for landfills and other disposal units. The basic regulations were issued in 1982.[128] In 1985, the rules were amended to reflect the statutory changes made in 1984.[129] These rules set standards for the required double liners and leachate collection systems.[130] In 1986, the rules were tightened again to further control and detect leachate.[131] The effect of these rules is to discourage land disposal of waste.

The impact of RCRA and CERCLA on hazardous waste disposal has resulted in a de facto policy that, however limited, is as close as we have come to a national material policy. A general consensus has developed that a hierarchy of waste management practices exist according to the ability to protect the environment. They are:[132]

- Waste reduction to produce fewer harmful residuals, including process changes and raw material substitutions.

124. RCRA, § 3004(d), 42 U.S.C. § 6924(d).

125. 51 Fed. Reg. 19,300 (1986).

126. RCRA, § 3004(g)(4), 42 U.S.C. § 6974(g)(4) (1982); *see also* 51 Fed. Reg. 44,713, 44,740 (1986).

127. 53 Fed. Reg. 17,578 (1988), [Current Developments] Env't Rep. (BNA) No. 106 (May 27, 1988).

128. 40 C.F.R. §§ 264.1-264.351 (1987).

129. 50 Fed. Reg. 28,702 (1985).

130. RCRA, § 3004(o), 42 U.S.C. § 6924(o) (1982 & Supp. IV 1986).

131. 52 Fed. Reg. 20,218 (1986).

132. Wolf, *Source Reduction and the Waste Management Hierarchy*, 38 J. AIR POLLUTION CONTROL ASSOC. 681 (1988).

- Waste recycling including resource recovery.
- Physical, chemical, and biological treatment that results in reduced volume and/or less toxicity.
- Incineration at high temperature.
- Solidification and/or stabilization before land disposal.

The disputes concerning this hierarchy usually involve the issue of when an option is no longer viable, so that a generator can move down the hierarchy to select another option. The extreme environmental position would demand source reduction in all, or nearly all, situations. The extreme industry position is to favor land disposal unless an alternative presently exists that would be cost effective in the short run, usually three years or less. Most people would occupy the middle ground, but areas of disagreement are many. Should requirements be eased for small quantity generators? How do you force decision makers to consider all disposal costs when many costs are masked by insurance or workmen's compensation, or can occur in the future on someone else's watch. Decision makers are often rewarded for being shortsighted.[133] This, however, is a problem that is pervasive in the environmental law field. The hazardous waste reduction program, with all its limitations and unresolved issues is, nevertheless, the best model of what will be involved in a materials policy and the problems that will arise in policy implementation.

One other aspect of materials policy that has received some attention is the subject of strategic materials. These are raw materials of significant importance to the nation's economy or defense. In 1985, the Office of Technology Assessment of the United States Congress (OTA) issued an assessment entitled *Strategic Materials: Technologies to Reduce U.S. Import Vulnerability*.[134] Among its findings were that the United States utilizes thirteen minerals and materials that are essential to the national economy and are subject to supply interruption. Four of these minerals, chromium, cobalt, manganese, and platinum are pervasively used in our industrial production and have no readily available substitute, and so are considered "first tier" strategic materials. The other nine materials are not as essential and are considered "second tier" strategic materials.[135] Chromium, cobalt and manganese

133. *Id.*

134. Office of Technology and Assessment (OTA), Strategic Materials: Technologies to Reduce U.S. Import Vulnerability (1985).

135. The nine are industrial diamonds, beryllium, vandium, graphite, rutile, bauxite, tin, tantalum, and columbium.

are essential to the production of high quality steels. Platinum group metals[136] are essential in catalytic applications in petroleum refining and chemical processing. Their major use, however, is in automobile catalytic converters, an important component of the Clean Air Program. The United States annually imports over $1 billion worth of these "first tier" materials. Three nations, South Africa, Zaire, and the U.S.S.R. produce over half the world's supply and therefore, we are vulnerable to supply disruption.

After the 1973-1974 oil embargo, the National Commission on Supplies and Shortages was established.[137] The Commission was to report on government policies affecting supply and economic stockpiling of natural resources. The Commission reported that the major threats to supply continuation were not foreign embargoes, but were military conflict, regional war or civil disorder. It recommended comprehensive strategic and economic stockpiling of essential resources. But, its report had no significant impact on government policy.[138]

Congress in 1980 enacted the National Materials and Minerals Policy, Research and Development Act.[139] This Act calls for material and mineral policy making to be coordinated in order to achieve a long-term balance between energy needs, a healthy environment, natural resources conservation, and social needs. The President is required to support research and development to include recycling, conservation, substitution, and new engineering designs for non-fuel minerals.[140] This Act, however, has not led to any structured mineral policy.[141] The National Critical Materials Act of 1984[142] establishes a Critical Materials Council reporting to the Executive Office of the President, but it has had minimal impact.[143]

136. Platinum, palladium, rhodium, iridium, osmium, and ruthenium.

137. 50 U.S.C. § 2169(d) (1982).

138. Jones, *United States Dependence On Imports Of Four Strategic And Critical Minerals: Implications And Policy Alternatives*, 15 B. C. ENVTL. AFF. L. REV. 217 (1988).

139. 30 U.S.C. §§ 1601-1605 (1982).

140. 30 U.S.C. § 1603 (1982).

141. Jones, *supra* note 137, at 253.

142. Pub. L. No. 98-373, 98 Stat. 242 (codified at 30 U.S.C. §§ 1801-1811 (1982 & Supp. IV 1986)).

143. OTA, *supra* note 133, at 44.

The Federal stockpiling law, amended in 1979 as the Strategic and Critical Materials Stock Piling Revision Act of 1979,[144] provides for acquisition of strategic and critical materials. However, it has been over thirty years since major additions to the stockpile have been made. The materials in the stockpile do not meet present industrial needs, and the law precludes their release for general economic or budgetary purposes. Thus, the stockpile has little to offer in the way of protection to the civilian economy and is very limited in its value for national defense.

Critical materials, by definition, are materials for which the United States can not develop self-sufficiency. To minimize the danger of dependency, we can use substitution, conservation, stockpiling, and seek more numerous foreign sources of supply. Substitutes for the first tier materials are unlikely in the foreseeable future. Stockpiling to meet basic defense goals would require an investment on the order of $6 billion.[145] Such investment is politically unrealistic. Improved sources of supply will be difficult to find, require substantial capital investment, and take many years to implement. For platinum metals, new sources are unknown.[146] Conservation through recycling, product life extension, lowering additions of alloys to the minimum, and improved processing techniques have potential in reducing foreign dependence. Platinum offers the best opportunity for successful material recovery if automobile catalysts can be recycled. Critical materials, thus, remains a subject that has been intensely studied but has not resulted in any coherent national policy.

The United States possesses five percent of the world's population, and yet, it consumes eleven times the world's average in energy, six times the steel, and four times the grain. Our consumption patterns, thus, have global impact, and are in turn affected by international events.[147] This is exemplified by the United States' expenditure of $15 million per month to maintain our military presence in the Persian Gulf, an expenditure that might create greater security if it were spent on energy conservation.[148] Our traditional consumption patterns can not continue.

144. 50 U.S.C. § 986 (1982 & Supp. IV 1986).

145. Jones, *supra* note 137, at 278.

146. *Id.* at 280.

147. Zero Population Growth, newsletter, May 1988.

148. Telephone conversation with Brian McCarten, Center for Defense Information, Washington, D.C., April, 1988.

As natural resources diminish and consequently become more expensive, the other industrialized, developed nations of the world will compete with us for these resources. This will increase prices and drive the lesser-developed nations further into poverty and debt. Increase in petroleum prices, for example, have increased the Third World's dependency on wood for fuel. More than one and a half billion people living in developing nations depend on wood as their only fuel for cooking and heating. This, in turn, has led to an increased rate of deforestation, followed by destructive wind and rain erosion, the silting of rivers and irrigation systems, and increasing severity of drought and floods.[149] In addition, multinational corporations, moving to the developing world, bring increased demand for resources to those countries. For example, the steel-making industry has expanded in Brazil, Korea, Taiwan, and elsewhere.[150] Thus powerful forces exist to deny the United States the right to continue its consumption of a disproportionate share of world resources. The more quickly we achieve a sustainable economy, the better the chance we have for a peaceful and environmentally sound world ecosystem.

C. *Energy*

In the 1950's, the United States was a net exporter of energy. But increased consumption changed the nation into a major importer of energy fuels. Between 1950 and 1965, United States energy consumption grew at an average annual rate of 3.5% and then increased to 4.5% per year until the 1973 oil embargo. Domestic production, however, grew at only three percent per year until 1970, and then growth essentially ceased.[151] Oil imports tripled from 1960 to 1973, with much of the increase coming from the Middle East and North Africa. Natural gas provided more than half the growth in energy consumption between 1950 and 1970. But artificially low natural gas prices, regulated by the government, served to encourage use and to discourage production. By the early 1970's, natural gas shortages were common.[152] Coal had been the dominant energy source from the late nineteenth century until 1910. After that year, the use of coal declined from over seventy-five percent of total United States

149. S. Pastel & L. Heise, *Reforesting the Earth*, STATE OF THE WORLD 1988 83 (1988).
150. J. GEVER, R. KAUFMAN D. SKOLE & C. VOROMARTY, BEYOND OIL 123 (1986).
151. CEQ, SIXTH ANNUAL REPORT 109 (1975).
152. *Id.* at 109-110.

energy consumption to about twenty percent in the early 1970's. Inexpensive oil and gas was the major reason for coal's loss of markets, combined with consumer preference for cleaner fuels. Beginning in the late 1960's, coal prices began to reflect the increased costs of meeting safety requirements and for air pollution controls in underground mines and reclamation requirements for surface mines. However, by that time, competing fuels also had pressures that increased their prices.[153]

After the Arab states cut off oil shipments to the United States in 1973, petroleum prices increased up to ten times the level of the previous year. President Nixon announced the start of "Project Independence" to move the nation to energy self-sufficiency by 1980.[154] On March 18, 1974, seven Arab oil-producing countries lifted the embargo. But the United States had been warned, and for at least a few years energy policy concerned the federal government. In May, 1974, the Federal Energy Administration was created to centralize and coordinate energy policy.[155] In October, 1974, energy research, as well as the military and production activities of the Atomic Energy Commission (AEC) were placed in the new independent agency, the Energy Research and Development Administration (ERDA).[156] The AEC was abolished.[157] The Energy Supply and Environmental Coordination Act was also enacted in 1974.[158] It was intended to encourage the use of coal, and the Act provided waivers from requirements of the Clean Air Act. It had little impact and has been largely repealed.

The blueprint for energy self-sufficiency was the Project Independence Report.[159] Released in November, 1974, it was the work of most federal agencies and of many private contractors acting under the direction of the Federal Energy Administration.

153. Dep't of Energy (DOE), Energy Security: A Report to the President of the United States 166, (March. 1987).

154. President's Address to the Nation Announcing Additional Action to Deal with the Energy Emergency, 1366 Weekly Comp. Pres. Doc. 9 (1973).

155. Federal Energy Administration Act of 1974, Pub. L. No. 93-275, 88 Stat. 196 (1974).

156. Energy Reorganization Act of 1974, Pub. L. No. 93-438, Oct. 11, 1974.

157. The regulatory functions of the AEC were given to the newly created NRC while the remaining functions went to ERDA. Title I of the Energy Reorganization Act of 1974 created ERDA; Title II created the NRC. Pub. L. No. 93-438, 88 Stat. 1233 (1974).

158. Energy Supply and Environmental Coordination Act of 1974, Pub. L. No. 93-319, 88 Stat. 246 (1974) (codified at 15 U.S.C. § 791 (1982)).

159. CEQ, Sixth Annual Report 111 (1975).

The report conveyed the message that there was no obvious or simple solution to the mess that we, as a nation, had created. Energy policy had to focus on virtually every aspect of the subject and seek improvements that were feasible. The report and its supporting studies were the roots of the energy policy recommendations made by President Ford in January, 1975. President Ford proposed the Energy Independence Act of 1975, which provided for (1) higher energy prices to encourage domestic production and to discourage consumption; and (2) a program of energy conservation through non-price measures. The 94th Congress responded to the President with its own proposals that included regulation of fuel inefficient automobiles. However, the Congress wanted mandatory, not voluntary, conservation and did not want substantial energy price increases.[160] Despite executive and legislative branch differences and jurisdiction battles among the key committees in Congress, many new energy laws were enacted.[161]

The Federal Non-Nuclear Energy Research and Development Act of 1974[162] directed the ERDA to conduct a comprehensive energy research and development program with particular emphasis on energy conservation, environmental protection and availability of water. The Solar Energy Research, Development, and Demonstration Act of 1974,[163] the Solar Heating and Cooling Demonstration Act of 1974[164] and the Geothermal Energy Research, Development and Demonstration Act of 1974[165] were all aimed at encouraging non-conventional energy technologies. Most of these programs were eventually budgeted out of existence in the 1980's.

Section 11 of the Federal Non-Nuclear Energy Research and Development Act of 1974[166] directed the CEQ to report annually on the probable environmental consequences of trends in the development and application of energy technologies. The first CEQ report appeared in its 1975 Annual Report.[167] It was based on a

160. DEMOCRATIC POLICY AND STEERING COMMITTEE OF THE HOUSE OF REPRESENTATIVES AND DEMOCRATIC POLICY COMMITTEE OF THE SENATE, THE CONGRESSIONAL PROBLEM OF ECONOMIC RECOVERY AND ENERGY SUFFICIENCY, (94th Cong., 1975).

161. CEQ, SIXTH ANNUAL REPORT 115 (1975).

162. 42 U.S.C. §§ 5902 and 5903 (1982 & Supp. IV 1986).

163. 42 U.S.C. § 5551 (1982).

164. 42 U.S.C. § 5501 (1982).

165. 30 U.S.C. § 1101 (1982 & Supp. IV 1986).

166. 42 U.S.C. §§ 5901-07 (1982 & Supp. IV 1986).

167. CEQ, SIXTH ANNUAL REPORT 427 (1975).

Stanford Research Institute (SRI) study of the economics of alternative energy scenarios for the year 2000. The report estimated that synthetic fuels from coal and oil shale would meet about sixteen percent of the nation's total energy demand, assuming prices of imported oil remained high.[168] But instead of becoming an important source of usable energy, the "synfuels" industry collapsed in the 1980's.

1. The Energy Policy and Conservation Act of 1975

In 1975, total United States energy consumption dropped by more than two percent for the second year in a row. However, imports of petroleum rose to about forty percent of United States oil consumption because domestic oil production continued to fall.[169] In late December, 1975 the Energy Policy and Conservation Act (EPCA) was enacted to address this problem.[170] The first title included a strategic petroleum reserve (SPR) to store 150 million to one billion barrels of oil to cushion the impact of future supply interruptions.[171] Title II provided for petroleum rationing and other emergency provisions.[172] Titles III and V included mandatory fuel economy standards for automobiles that required an average of 27.5 miles per gallon (m.p.g.) by 1985.[173] Title IV was a price control program for domestic oil that terminated after forty months.[174] The Act also mandated energy efficiency labeling requirements for consumer products[175] and provided financial assistance for federal, state, and industrial conservation programs.[176] There were also some minor provisions limiting the Clean Air Act and providing the Federal Energy Administration (FEA) with authority to order power plants and other major fuel-burning installations to convert from the use of oil to the use of coal.[177] The strategic petroleum reserve is considered to be a successful program by the Reagan Administration. In 1987 the

168. *Id.*

169. CEQ, SEVENTH ANNUAL REPORT 102 (1976).

170. Energy Policy and Conservation Act of 1975, Pub. L. No. 94-163, 89 Stat. 871 (codified at 42 U.S.C. §§ 6201-6422 (1982 & Supp. IV 1986)).

171. *Id.* at §§ 151-166, 42 U.S.C. §§ 6232-6247.

172. *Id.* at §§ 201-255, 42 U.S.C. §§ 6261-6275.

173. *Id.* at §§ 501-512, 15 U.S.C. §§ 2001-2012.

174. *Id.* at §§ 401-463.

175. *Id.* at §§ 321-339, 42 U.S.C. §§ 6291-6309.

176. *Id.* at § 361-367, 371-376, 42 U.S.C. §§ 6321-6363.

177. *Id.* at § 101, 106, 42 U.S.C. §§ 6211-6215.

SPR contained 500 million barrels of oil which is about the amount the nation imports in ninety-six days. President Reagan reaffirmed his commitment to the goal of 750 million barrels in the SPR in August, 1986.[178] Since we have not had occasion to use the SPR, it remains an insurance policy of unknown value.

Much of the EPCA has been a failure. Energy conservation took place largely because consumers were price sensitive, not because of legal mandates. The automobile fuel economy standards were initially not a major concern to American automobile manufacturers because consumer preferences and foreign competition assured that the fuel efficiency requirements would be met. When declining fuel prices began to affect the car-buying public, the manufacturers began to lobby for the corporate average fuel economy (CAFE) standards to be relaxed. The Ford Motor Company threatened to take advantage of a loophole in the law and turn its large cars into imports if the CAFE standards were not lowered.[179] The Reagan Administration, through the National Highway Traffic Safety Administration, responded to industry (over the objection of Chrysler Corporation) by lowering the fuel economy standard.[180] In 1986, a task force on governmental regulation chaired by Vice President Bush recommended abolishing the CAFE standards as they were squeezing the manufacturers out of the "muscle car" market.[181]

While the automotive fuel economy legislation could benefit from technical amendments to close loopholes, the law is both necessary and properly directed. The United States uses sixty-three percent of its oil for transportation, and its combustion releases more than 700 million tons of air-polluting carbon. The average American automobile generates its weight in carbon each year.[182] If the fleet fuel efficiency in the United States had remained at the 1973 level of 13 m.p.g., our gasoline consumption would have grown by one-third. Because fuel economy increased to 18 m.p.g. in 1985, fuel consumption growth was contained. This conservation effort was more important than the supply side

178. DOE, *supra* note 153, at 215.

179. Brown, *Ford Threatens U.S. Over Fuel Economy Rules*, Wash. Post, Nov. 2, 1985 at A1, col. 2.

180. [Current Developments] Env't Rep. (BNA) No. 24 at 858 (Oct. 10, 1986).

181. *Fuel Economy Standards Targeted by Task Force*, Wash. Post, Dec. 23, 1986 at A17, col. 5.

182. Flavin & Durning, *Raising Energy Efficiency*, STATE OF THE WORLD 1988 50 (1988).

efforts made to find more oil, and yet it has been almost without support by the government. If fuel efficiency were brought to the 50 m.p.g. level that is technically achievable by existing technology, global gasoline consumption could be cut by almost one-fourth (assuming no growth in vehicle miles traveled).[183] The vacuity of the supply side approach is obvious, for despite increases in oil prices and a 280% increase in drilling, the United States is producing less oil today than in 1973.[184]

Energy efficiency standards for consumer products have also fared poorly at the hands of the Reagan Administration. The EPCA was amended by the National Energy Conservation Policy Act (NECPA) of 1978.[185] This law authorized, but did not require, DOE to establish mandatory energy efficiency standards. It did require energy efficiency labeling.[186] By 1980, DOE had issued proposed standards for only eight classes of appliances.[187] In January, 1981, DOE reversed direction and declared that economics justified only a "no-standards" standard for household appliances.[188] This ended federal rulemaking but also precluded state regulation because of the preemption provisions of the EPCA.[189] Joined by one congressman and three states, the Natural Resources Defense Council (NRDC) challenged DOE's "no-standards." On July 16, 1985, the D.C. Circuit Court of Appeals overturned the DOE standards and remanded the case to the district court.[190] DOE then embarked on rulemaking. Before regulations could be promulgated, Congress enacted the National Appliance Energy Conservation Act of 1987 (NAECA)[191] to amend EPCA.[192] The law mandated that by 1993 household appliances be fifteen to twenty-five percent more efficient than 1985 models. It is estimated that the law will reduce electric power demand by an amount equal to the output of 22 large power plants.[193] NAECA was enacted by Congress to remove the discre-

183. Renner, *Car Crash*, 1 World Watch 35 (1988).

184. Gever et al, *supra* note 150, at 12.

185. 42 U.S.C. § 8201 (1982 & Supp. IV 1986).

186. 42 U.S.C. § 6272 (1982 & Supp. IV 1986).

187. National Appliance Energy Conservation Act of 1987, Pub. L. No. 100-12 § 1, 101 Stat. 103 (1987).

188. Pub. L. No. 100-12 § 5, 101 Stat. 107 (1987).

189. Pub. L. No. 100-12 § 7, 101 Stat. 118 (1987).

190. NRDC v. Herrington, 768 F.2d 1355 (D.C. Cir. 1985).

191. 42 U.S.C. § 6201 (1982 & Supp. IV 1986).

192. 42 U.S.C. §§ 6291-6309 (1982).

193. 133 Cong. Rec. § 2031 (daily ed. Feb. 17, 1987) (statement of Sen. Cranston).

tion of DOE and the Act passed with the support of industry, which wished to avoid regulation by the states that had found ways to regulate despite the Reagan Administration's "no-standard" approach.

In 1976, the United States economy was recovering and energy use increased again, rising 4.8%.[194] Another natural gas shortage arose in the winter of 1976-1977, leading to the Emergency Natural Gas Act of 1977.[195] That Act set up nationwide allocations of natural gas and provided for higher priced intrastate natural gas to be sold on the interstate market.

Despite renewed oil cutoffs the United States did not actually develop or implement a coherent energy policy. From November, 1978 through April, 1979, six million barrels a day of Iranian production were eliminated from the world market due to political turmoil. Part of this loss was made up by increased production elsewhere, but the net supply loss was over two million barrels per day and caused prices to increase by more than double the previous rate. The outbreak of war between Iraq and Iran in the fall of 1980 again removed from two to three million barrels a day from the world market, but worldwide surplus production capacity and high inventories limited the impact.[196]

In 1977 the Department of Energy was created.[197] Into this agency went the Federal Energy Regulatory Commission (the new name for the Federal Power Commission which regulates natural gas and licenses hydroelectric facilities) and the energy programs of numerous executive agencies. The most important transfers were the Federal Energy Administration and the Energy Research and Development Administration (ERDA).[198] ERDA contained the non-regulatory functions of the abolished Atomic Energy Commission as well as the more general energy research and development responsibilities.

2. The Carter Administration

In April 1977, President Carter submitted his National Energy Plan to Congress. The plan encouraged Congress to adopt seven goals to be achieved by 1985. They were to (1) reduce the rate of

194. CEQ, EIGHTH ANNUAL REPORT 61 (1977).
195. National Gas Act, 15 U.S.C. § 717 (1982).
196. DOE, *supra* note 153, at 16.
197. Department of Energy Organizaton Act, 42 U.S.C. § 7101 (1982).
198. 42 U.S.C. § 7151 (1982).

growth of energy consumption to below two percent per year; (2) reduce gasoline consumption by ten percent below its current level; (3) reduce oil imports from a projected level of sixteen million barrels per day to six million barrels per day; (4) establish a Strategic Petroleum Reserve of one billion barrels; (5) increase coal production by about two-thirds to more than one billion tons per year; (6) bring ninety percent of existing United States homes and all new buildings up to minimum energy efficiency standards; and (7) use solar energy in more than 2.5 million homes.[199]

The Carter Administration's energy policy primarily followed the "soft" energy path. Energy conservation was the cornerstone of Carter's plan, which built on the programs developed under Presidents Nixon and Ford. The "soft" energy path embodies the concept of natural limits to growth, with people striving to live within these limits. Conservation is important. This approach also emphasizes the development and use of energy sources that are relatively non-polluting, renewable, small-scale and often decentralized. The "hard" energy path seeks to develop all current energy sources, with a highly centralized, highly electrified energy future. It seeks to satisfy every possible consumption desire.[200] Governmental approaches have been stymied because neither approach has achieved a national consensus. The Carter Administration tried to appease both groups by supporting energy conservation and alternative energy development, as well as oil and gas leasing of the Continental Shelf, coal development on public lands, and other supply enhancement policies.[201] This dual approach was echoed in a February 1979, CEQ report—*The Good News About Energy*. It examined the contribution that increased energy production could make but concluded that the United States "can do well, indeed prosper, on much less energy than has been commonly supposed."[202] This fact, which CEQ gave half-hearted recognition to in its 1979 report, had been well-recognized by the private sector which had made intense efforts to conserve energy as energy costs soared. Since 1973, energy efficiency improvements have saved six times

199. CEQ, Eighth Annual Report 62 (1977).
200. *Id.* at 273.
201. CEQ, Ninth Annual Report 343 (1978).
202. CEQ, Tenth Annual Report 316 (1979).

more energy than the net capacity generated from all new sources.[203]

An error made by the "hard energy" advocates was to assume the nation needs, or benefits from, high consumption of fuels. It is the end use of power for heat, mechanical work, mobility, and other services that consumers desire. This is more easily supplied through increased efficiency of fuel utilization than by expanding the use of fuels. Thus, the private sector pushed energy conservation, while the misguided government leadership looked to increasing consumption.[204]

In November, 1978, five major energy laws were passed: (1) the National Energy Conservation Policy Act,[205] which established a variety of regulatory, grant, and loan programs to enhance conservation; (2) the Energy Tax Act,[206] which provided tax credits for conservation and solar energy; (3) the Natural Gas Policy Act,[207] (NGPA) which largely decontrolled the price of new natural gas and established measures to encourage production of natural gas; (4) the Public Utility Regulatory Policies Act,[208] (PURPA) which encouraged revisions in state public utility rate structures to price energy at, or near, its replacement cost; and (5) the Powerplant and Industrial Fuel Use Act,[209] (PIFUA) which was designed to increase the use of coal. The National Energy Conservation Policy Act and the Energy Tax Act, the two acts aimed at conservation, were phased out during the Reagan Administration. The NGPA created a myriad of gas categories by raising the price for "new" gas to a higher level than the ceiling price for old gas. Although this encouraged the production of natural gas, the NGPA price ceiling did not permit the marketplace to determine the price of natural gas. Thus, since present natural gas prices are higher than justified by market conditions, foreign oil is economically more attractive and oil imports continue to rise.[210]

203. Carothers, *Small Wonders: The Energy Efficiency Revolution*, 13 GREENPEACE, March/April 1988, at 11.

204. *Id.* at 13.

205. Pub. L. No. 95-619, 92 Stat. 3206 (1978).

206. Pub. L. No. 95-618, 92 Stat. 3174 (1978).

207. Pub. L. No. 95-621, 92 Stat. 3350 (1978).

208. Pub. L. No. 95-617, 92 Stat. 3117 (1978).

209. Pub. L. No. 95-620, 92 Stat. 3289 (1978).

210. DOE, *supra* note 153, at 115.

PURPA encourages electric cogeneration, in which waste heat from electric power generation is used beneficially, and where renewable resources such as wind, solar, biomass, and small hydroelectric generation (80 megawatts or less) are exploited. It provides favorable pricing provisions and exemptions from certain regulatory requirements. To qualify, the project must be designated a "qualifying facility" (QF) by FERC. PURPA has been enthusiastically received. Between 1980 and 1987, applications for more than 43,500 megawatts of generating capacity were filed with FERC. However, gas and oil-fueled cogenerators made up forty percent of this capacity,[211] thus continuing the use of nonrenewable fossil fuels.[212]

The PIFUA and other legislation aimed at increasing the use of coal and decreasing the use of petroleum had little effect, even though coal use increased by one quarter of a billion tons between 1974 and 1985. The reason for coal's resurgence was the great increase in oil and gas prices, combined with the reluctance of electric utilities to make further commitments to nuclear power.[213]

President Carter continued to push for energy conservation and production through hard and soft energy paths, but his efforts during the remainder of his term were largely in vain. The President pressed for an Energy Mobilization Board (EMB) that would accelerate the completion of important non-nuclear energy projects. In June, 1980 the House of Representatives unexpectedly voted down the EMB bill by a large margin.[214] The President did achieve passage of the Energy Security Act (ESA),[215] which established the Synthetic Fuels Corporation (SFC) to stimulate the production of two million barrels per day of synthetic fuels by 1992. That industry, as previously noted, collapsed economically in the 1980's. The Act also established a Solar Energy

211. *Id.* at 157.

212. *Id.* at 156. PURPA has been attractive to developers who qualify because prices to be paid for power produced by the projects are set before construction begins. If a developer keeps construction costs and operating efficiencies within projections the project can be profitable. Under conventional electric utility regulation, prices are determined after the project is completed and can be adjusted thereafter. Therefore, under conventional utility regulation, investment can be disallowed in whole or in part. Increasingly this is happening, thus, investment requires assuming the risk of regulatory change. This risk has made investors wary.

213. *Id.* at 162.

214. CEQ, Eleventh Annual Report 263 (1980).

215. Pub. L. No. 96-294, 94 Stat. 611 (1980).

and Conservation Bank, a biomass financial assistance program, a minimum rate for filling the Strategic Petroleum Reserve, and statutory support for electric and gas utility investments in energy conservation.[216] All but the last provision have fallen by the wayside.

3. The Reagan Administration

The Carter Administration was replaced by the Reagan Administration which was more comfortable with the "hard" energy path, but most comfortable with no government policy.[217] The Reagan Administration terminated investment in soft energy approaches, except under PURPA and in energy conservation. The Reagan Administration reverted to an energy policy which seeks to satisfy every consumptive desire by pursuing hard energy paths through the private sector. The Administration's rhetoric exalts the virtue of the free market, but the energy industry is highly concentrated, with fifteen companies accounting for two-thirds of the nation's production of crude oil.[218] These companies and their Organization of Petroleum-Exporting Countries (OPEC) petroleum suppliers have a vested interest in maintaining the *status quo*.

The Reagan Administration's program has avoided assisting renewable resource development. In fiscal year (FY) 1989, solar and renewable energy technology programs were funded at an estimated $123.090 million.[219] This is a little over one percent of the Department of Energy's (DOE) nuclear defense activities. The governments of Japan and West Germany consistently fund basic research in the solar area, particularly photovoltaic research. This may be the reason that Japan has moved ahead of the United States as the world's largest solar-cell producer.[220] Since the world of the present is often the result of the research and development efforts in the past, the future of renewable resources is being decided now. That future is bleak. Energy conservation was also downplayed by the Reagan Administration.

216. CEQ, ELEVENTH ANNUAL REPORT 264 (1980).

217. An important exception was the Carter Administration's synthetic fuel program. It was criticized by conservatives and dropped by the Reagan Administration. *See* BADEN, EARTH DAY RECONSIDERED 63 (1980).

218. J. GEVER ET AL., *supra* note 150, at 220-221.

219. OMB, *supra* note 48, at I-J4.

220. Best, *Solar Cells: Still A Tough Sell*, SIERRA, May/June, 1988 at 27.

Outlays for energy conservation research and development and grants in FY 1989 are an estimated $308 million compared with $2.2 billion for energy supply research and development.[221] Market forces responding to higher energy prices are the primary factor in stimulating energy technologies that are more efficient.

We are getting close to the post-petroleum age. If we are going to produce oil at the present level after the year 2000, it must be from fields which have not yet been discovered. Thus, the United States needs to confront its dependency on foreign petroleum by minimizing its demand and by attempting to change its energy fuel mix in an orderly way. The reason that conservation is so important is that OPEC can greatly increase prices when demand grows. Past experience demonstrates that OPEC increases prices when demand reaches eighty-five percent of its capacity.[222]

Minimizing demand, *i.e.*, conservation, is an indispensable part of the solution because of the low net energy of most of our energy options. As we drill deeper for oil, convert coal to liquid and gaseous fuels, or pursue alcohol fuel options, we must use energy to obtain fuels in a usable form. When direct and indirect energy inputs are considered, the net energy produced by many supply-side proposals is minimal or negative.[223] Consequently many of our energy resources can never be mined at a profit. When the price of energy rises and thereby makes production more attractive, the cost of production also increases. Only programs which increase efficiency in the use of energy and which emphasize non-petroleum energy supplies that have a net energy potential have a future in sustaining a viable ecosystem in a post-petroleum world.[224] The choice as to what energy fuel mix to adopt in the near future is complex. Coal use, for example, leads to acid rain and carbon dioxide buildup. Technologies which limit environmental damage, such as air pollution controls, also utilize energy and thereby decrease the net energy obtained from coal. Nuclear power, a potential alternative, has its associated adverse environmental and safety problems and it is of questionable economic viability. Nuclear energy's net energy production is low because of the large amount of energy used to produce the materials necessary to build the power plants and the supporting fuel cycle in-

221. OMB, The United States Budget In Brief, FY 1989 58 (1988).

222. DOE, National Energy Policy Plan Projections To 2010 2-3 (Dec., 1985).

223. *See generally*, H. Odum, Environment, Power, and Society (1971).

224. J. Gever et. al., *supra* note 150, at 20, 224.

frastructures, the energy intensive fuel production process, and the energy costs associated with the need to decommission obsolete plants and store the radioactive wastes. New energy production technologies involving oil shale, and coal gasification and liquefaction, have low net energy production because processing the fuel is energy-intensive. In addition, processing uses scarce water, precluding its use for agriculture, and can do considerable harm to human health and the environment because of its toxic chemical byproducts.[225]

The role of nuclear power in the United States is unclear. Since 1972, 117 nuclear plant orders have been cancelled; all projects on which construction began after 1973 have been canceled.[226] The Shoreham nuclear power plant in Long Island, for example, is likely to never produce power commercially even though it is completed.[227] Costs of construction, licensing delays, the public attitude since Three Mile Island and Chernobyl, high-level radioactive waste disposal problems, and insurance issues[228] have made investment in nuclear power very unattractive. The nuclear industry is dependent upon extensive government subsidies which makes its survival dependent upon political decisions.[229] But the attractiveness of nuclear power could change with a shortage or substantial price increase in oil. Even, in our antinuclear climate, 105 commercial nuclear power plants produce seventeen percent of the United States' electricity. This is the second largest source of electricity and is equal to the entire United States electricity demand in 1952.[230]

Outside of the United States, the picture is quite different. Nuclear power is expanding. More than 100 nuclear powerplants have been ordered since 1978, and more than 370 nuclear plants are operational. In France, over seventy percent of the electricity is nuclear-generated, and in Japan twenty-seven percent of the

225. MITRE CORPORATION, HEALTH AND ENVIRONMENTAL EFFECTS OF OIL SHALE TECHNOLOGY (1979); MITRE CORPORATION, HEALTH AND ENVIRONMENTAL EFFECTS OF COAL GASIFICATION AND LIQUEFACTION TECHNOLOGIES (1979). *See also* CEQ, TENTH ANNUAL REPORT 348 (1979).

226. DOE, *supra* note 153, at 189.

227. Kurtz, *Cuomo's Plan to Mothball Long Island Nuclear Plant Stalls*, Wash. Post, May 17, 1988 at C1, col. 2.

228. Reitze & Rowe, *The Price Anderson Act—Limited Liability For The Nuclear Industry*, 17 ENVTL. L. REP. 10185 (Envtl. L. Inst.) (1987).

229. One estimate of the U.S. government subsidy to the nuclear power industry is $15 billion per year. Carothers, *supra* note 202, at 17.

230. DOE, *supra* note 153, at 187.

electricity is nuclear-generated.[231] The disaster at Chernobyl has increased grass roots opposition to nuclear power, but, so far this has not led to a change in the many nations that are far more dependent upon nuclear power than the United States.

III. Conclusion

Since consumption-induced stress can seriously damage our environment, energy policy needs to be formulated as part of an environmental policy. We need to plan how much energy we should use and how it should be fueled. In addition, we must today consider that the Clean Air Act with its stringent environmental controls on new facilities provides a major incentive to keep aging dirty coal plants on line.[232] Expansion of the hydroelectric industry is largely precluded due to the lack of economically suitable sites for new plants and environmental opposition to dams.[233] Nuclear power expansion in the United States is dead primarily because of mismanagement by the industry.[234] The government seems content to see electrical power production expand and for such power to be generated from aging nuclear plants, the burning of dirty fossil fuels, and imported sources.[235] Solving the problem of acid rain is, we are told, precluded by considerations of employment and economic impacts.[236]

Environmental problems are not easy to solve, but we need to avoid focusing excessively upon narrow, isolated issues. We need to look at the important issues which were identified in the 1960's, but that seem to have been lost in the 1980's. The solution to our environmental problems does not lie in tirelessly regulating peripheral details; it lies in adopting basic, overall population, material conservation and energy policies. A great

231. *Id.* at 183.

232. Banks, *EPA Bends to Industry Pressure on Coal NSPS — and Breaks*, 9 Ecology L.Q. 67 (1980-81).

233. DOE, *supra* note 222, at B-6; Wild And Scenic Rivers, GAO/RCED-87-39, Dec., 1986. Small low-head hydro-projects do continue to be built over the opposition of many environmentalists. *See* Reisner, *Power, Profit, and Preservation*, Wilderness, Fall 1984 at 26 and *Small Hydroelectric Projects and State Water Rights*, 18 Pac. L.J. 1225 (1987).

234. Cook, *Nuclear Follies*, Forbes, Feb. 11, 1985 at 82; Komanoff & Van Loon, *"Too Cheap to Meter" or "Too Costly To Build"? (How Nuclear Power Has Priced Itself Out of the Market)* 4 Nucleus 3 1982; *but see*, Novak and Kaplan, *Power Politics, How the Nuclear Power Lobby Won Big on Capitol Hill*, Common Cause Magazine, Jan./Feb., 1988 at 20.

235. Huber, *Electricity And The Environment: In Search of Regulatory Authority*, 100 Harv. L. Rev. 1001 (1987).

236. CEQ, 16th Annual Report 202 (1987).

deal of research has already been done, but it has not resulted in policy development. Part of the reason is that the Department of Energy is not primarily an energy agency, for it commits about two-thirds of its budget to the production of nuclear weapons.[237] Its environmental mission is even more limited. Materials policy and population issues have been studied, also, but have not been integrated into environmental policy.

There are hard choices to be made. We must choose between an expanding population, an increased material standard of living, or continued high expenditures for national security. We can not simultaneously pursue all three. From 1980-1987 we spent $2 trillion trying to buy security,[238] in a world whose population has outstripped its resource base. In such a world, a wealthy well-armed population can not continue to consume a disproportionate share of the global resources. Our centralized and complex society is extremely vulnerable to disruption from terrorism, fuel and strategic material cut offs, and wars over access to natural resources.

Since the price at the pump for gasoline does not include the massive defense costs to assure its delivery, the price does not reflect the real cost. This encourages gasoline consumption and the continued growth of the national debt. We have created a runaway national debt that grew from $1 trillion in 1981 to $2.6 trillion in 1987 and now threatens the well being of our economy. A large chunk of this national debt was incurred to keep petroleum flowing to the United States. Thus our fuel consumption is a threat to our economy, security, and environment.

Developing the infrastructure to support a post-petroleum fuel mix will be difficult. Curbing consumption through increased efficiency and lifestyle changes will be even more difficult. But this environmental approach offers the best chance we have of sustaining our ecosystem, our economy, our national security, and our world. If the United States had a stabilized population, it could help other nations to do the same through technical, financial, and educational assistance. This proposed solution is simple, perhaps simplistic, but achieving it is very difficult.

237. Total federal funds for DOE in FY 1989 are $16,079,752,000 and are $12,529,893,000 after offsets. OMB, *supra* note 48 at 6f-72. Total obligations for atomic energy defense activities are $10.8 billion and $8.1 billion after offsets. OMB, APPENDIX BUDGET OF THE UNITED STATES GOVERNMENT, FY 1989, I-J1 (1988).

238. Center for Defense Information, 16 THE DEFENSE MONITOR 7 (1987).

Nevertheless, any success reduces the pressure on our environment and increases the time we have to protect our planet. At the same time, we should focus on lowering our dependency on natural resources, particularly petroleum. This can be accomplished by improved energy efficiency and by lifestyle changes, which would occur if we allow energy costs to slowly rise to reflect, as much as possible, the actual cost. Government efforts to provide a greater diversity of transportation options and a serious effort to reduce dependency on the automobile would assist in reducing the demand for petroleum. Diminished fuel use would be the way to lessen the onslaught of acid rain, the greenhouse effect, oil pollution of the oceans and other environmental problems which have not responded well to the existing regulatory approach. Reducing demand for oil would also slow the rate at which future petroleum prices increase and relieve some of the economic pressure on Third World nations.

A major effort by the United States should be made to reduce the energy used by agriculture. This will be absolutely necessary if we are to continue feeding our population and exporting food in an era of increasingly expensive petroleum. Post-petroleum agriculture could provide an opportunity to reverse the employment trend of this century by producing new opportunities for jobs; human labor would replace the current energy and petrochemical intensive American agriculture. Soil conservation efforts made to improve farm land could provide employment opportunities in reversing the declining fertility of the base of our farm economy. The nation's high paying, blue collar jobs that have been lost to foreign competition are unlikely to ever reappear.[239] But if we focus upon trying to build a sustainable economy, there will be plenty of meaningful work to do.

Investment must be made to develop viable technologies to replace petroleum. A mix is needed and no clear picture of what technologies will evolve is available. But the criteria for the technologies we should support should be: (1) technologies should be sustainable without serious harm to the ecosystem; (2) technologies should be decentralized rather than lead to economic concentration; (3) technologies should produce net energy. If this analysis had been performed in the 1950's, we would proba-

239. Rich, *Economic Fortunes Fading For America's Less Educated*, Wash. Post, June 2, 1988 at A1, col. A18.

bly not have sunk billions of dollars into nuclear technology and its limited payoff. Such an analysis would probably preclude development of an alcohol-fueled economy. Alcohol requires almost as much energy to produce as the product provides. Moreover, the removal of crop residues for alcohol production will increase soil erosion. If food crops or agricultural land is used for alcohol production then the amount of food diminishes.[240] Thus, solar, wind, and hydroelectric generation fit these criteria. However, the need for liquid fuels also requires efforts in the synfuel areas, but increased research and development is needed rather than moving environmentally dangerous present day technologies to the production stage.

We can not protect our environment with the approaches which we have vigorously pursued for the past twenty years. Many environmental regulations are requiring close to 100% control of pollution emissions, and the costs of such compliance are approaching infinity. Yet our ecosystems continue to decline in quality. Moreover, all of our problems are exacerbated by the sixty million people added to our population since 1960. Yet our population policy, or lack of one, receives little attention. We need a serious, sustained, interdisciplinary effort to develop and implement policy to resolve these problems. The policy we choose will determine what kind of world we leave our children. This choice is too important to be entrusted to a single mission agency, although many government agencies must be involved. The EPA, with its orientation largely determined by the statutes it implements, has sometimes become part of the problem rather than the source of solutions. The components of EPA lobby for more money to address their numerous existing mandates without much attention being given to the overall needs for ecosystem protection. The appropriate organization for broad environmental planning should be the Council on Environmental Quality (CEQ).

The CEQ has a national constituency and its placement in the Office of the President gives it a good location for carrying out planning functions that will affect many agencies and all levels of our government. Since it does not administer existing statutes or have many operational responsibilities, it is free to adopt new approaches to environmental protection. Its mission is simple; exe-

240. J. GEVER ET. AL., *supra* note 150, at 245.

cution is difficult. CEQ could generate information and create the plan to achieve a sustainable ecosystem that would offer a quality life to succeeding generations.

The CEQ engaged in broad spectrum environmental planning in its early years. Much of the work was valuable but unused. There was little leadership to explain the problem to the public and to move toward consensus. We need to develop environmental policy in a manner similar to the way economic policy evolves. Economic policy is very complex, but we have developed considerable proficiency in appointing qualified professionals to high level advisory groups within government. Political leaders use the work of skilled professionals to develop a political consensus followed by legislation and implementation. We have demonstrated in the economic sphere that we possess the ability to translate an admittedly imperfect, though complex discipline, into public policy within the framework of a democratic society. We need to do the same for environmental policy. We can not afford the *ad hoc* approach that has been used for twenty years. We can not pretend that ecosystem protection can be solved by a large intrusive bureaucracy generating endless regulations while ignoring the population and consumption elements of the equation.

The interest in serious broad spectrum environmental planning peaked in 1980. The anti-environmental agenda of the Reagan Administration began its work in 1981.[241] The CEQ was downgraded and its staff was significantly reduced. The exercise of leadership in the environmental field by the CEQ ended. In another agency, Surgeon General C. Everett Koop, with a comparably small staff, became a nationally recognized figure for his leadership and moral persuasion concerning AIDS and the dangers of smoking to the public health.[242] The CEQ, however, became unimportant. In the Reagan years the subjects of population and energy conservation have nearly disappeared from the annual reports of the CEQ except for a few pages in the 1984 report claiming that the anti-abortion policies espoused by

241. The Reagan Administration's efforts to stop pollution control are documented in Wood, *Principals, Bureaucrats, And Responsiveness In Clean Air Enforcements*, 82 AM. POLITICAL SCI. REV. 213 (1988).

242. Bean, *Surgeon General's Stature Is Likely to Add Force to Report on Smoking as Addiction*, Wall St. J., May 13, 1988 at 21.

the Administration at the International Conference on Population in Mexico City were an environmental policy.[243]

A primary responsibility of a new administration should be the rehabilitation of the CEQ. CEQ members should be chosen from the best minds on the subject—as close as we can come to philosopher kings. They should expand the concept of environment to include a long range view of environmental priorities. The CEQ will require a small, but professionally skilled, staff of at least the thirty-two of the pre-Reagan era.[244]

To bring our planet into harmony with its long term carrying capacity will not be easy. To even begin the task requires confronting and changing long established values of our society. Environmental law has become a technician's field. But this approach, while having value, will eventually lead to collapse. Our habitat can not be sustained by incrementally reducing pollution at extraordinary cost. Environmental law needs to become a revolutionary field that honestly confronts the physical and biological limits of our world and seeks to live within these limits. To do so, we all need to learn a lot more than we know today, but we know enough to now begin. We must start the dialogue that is necessary in a democratic society to produce change. Our problems of the present and the future are not separate individual problems of overpopulation, war, famine, and resource shortages. Our problems are interrelated problems for which harmful environmental impacts are often a symptom. Dealing with these problems requires simultaneous solutions in which the common theme is to cut down waste and to establish a stable and sustainable population. This requires a viable population, material conservation, and energy policy.

243. CEQ, 15TH ANNUAL REPORT 484 (1984).

244. ORLOFF & BROOKS, THE NATIONAL ENVIRONMENTAL POLICY ACT 40 (1980). For fiscal year 1987 the Council on Environmental Quality had 11 full-time permanent positions. OMB, *supra* note 237, at I-C4.

Part VI
The Future of Environmental Law

[12]

VOLUME 30, NUMBER 2, SPRING 1989

The Internationalization of Environmental Regulation

Robert W. Hahn*
Kenneth R. Richards**

I. INTRODUCTION

Historians will look back on the latter part of the twentieth century as a watershed in the history of environmental regulation, not so much because the world addressed problems in a particularly judicious manner, but rather because the configuration of forces driving environmental regulation changed dramatically. Where nations and states once viewed regulation of pollution and natural resources as a local or national issue, economic, political, and institutional forces have now pushed them to see many environmental problems as global in scope.

This new perception has changed the nature of the international environmental "game," Nation states remain major players in determining environmental policy, but formal and informal linkages across nations have become increasingly important.[1] International bodies, such as the United Nations Economic Committee for Europe (ECE), the United Nations Environment Programme (UNEP) and the World Meteorological Organization (WMO), are playing a larger role in environmental decisionmaking processes.[2] This "internationalization" of the field has led to many international agreements, including regulation of nitrogen oxides pollution and substances that deplete the ozone layer.

Although commentators have explored individual environmental agreements in some depth, few have constructed a framework to

---

* Senior staff member of the Council of Economic Advisers and associate professor of economics, Carnegie Mellon University. A grant from the National Science Foundation Decision, Risk and Management Science Program supported his research.

** Junior staff member of the Council of Economic Advisers, currently on leave from the Wharton School and the University of Pennsylvania Law School. The views in this Article represent those of the authors and do not necessarily reflect the views of the Council.

1. This is true more generally for economic patterns as well. Decreases in the cost of communication and transport have increased economic interdependence, giving rise to a highly interconnected global economy.

2. Jacobson & Kay; *A Framework for Analysis*, in ENVIRONMENTAL PROTECTION: THE INTERNATIONAL DIMENSION at 1, 10 (D. Kay & H. Jacobson eds. 1983).

explain the development of these agreements.[3] In this Article we shall attempt to create a framework capable of explaining the formation and shape of individual environmental agreements. We shall do so by shifting the emphasis from an individual or comparative case study approach to a generalized theory-building perspective. Specifically, we will derive theoretical tenets from a comprehensive review of multilateral environmental agreements on air pollution.[4] This analysis will demonstrate the strengths and limitations of international responses to global environmental issues. This study will also remedy current misunderstandings about the forces driving the form and scope of multilateral international agreements, particularly in the environmental arena.[5]

Three themes emerge from our framework. First, a small number of critical factors dictate the emergence, as well as the shape, of environmental agreements.[6] Second, decisionmaking about "internationalized" environmental agreements flows from the dynamic interaction among these factors. Finally, domestic politics plays a substantial, and perhaps dominant, role in forming and shaping international environmental agreements.

Section II of this Article provides a brief history of international environmental regulation, describing the recent increase in the number of international environmental agreements and reasons for this trend. Section III discusses relevant literature on environmental agreements. Section IV develops a general framework for understanding agreements, along with a series of testable hypotheses, concentrating on an explanation of the conditions under which environmental agreements emerge and take shape. Section V investigates the implications of our

---

3. *See* A. SPRINGER, THE INTERNATIONAL LAW OF POLLUTION: PROTECTING THE GLOBAL ENVIRONMENT IN A WORLD OF SOVEREIGN STATES (1983). Springer creates a legal framework within which one can systematically study questions of international environmental law. He does this through detailed analysis of the legal definitions of "pollution" and "reponsibility." This approach differs fundamentally from our analysis, which concentrates on the social, political, and scientific forces that drive the international environmental policy debate. *See also* Kindt, *International Environmental Law and Policy: An Overview of Transboundary Pollution*, 23 SAN DIEGO L. REV. 583 (1986).

4. In subsequent work, we plan to take a more detailed look at the factors leading to a variety of multilateral agreements, including agreements involving water pollution and species preservation.

5. Geographic circumstances essentially limit substantive United States bilateral environmental treaties to those with Canada and Mexico, although there are some agreements on migratory species with Japan and the Soviet Union. In addition to these substantive treaties, the United States has signed a number of agreements of varying formality involving cooperation in research and data gathering, equipment provisions and training.

6. In this regard, our analysis parallels that of Gerlach and Rayner. *See* L. Gerlach & S. Rayner, Managing Global Climate Change: A View from the Social and Decision Sciences (1988) (working paper ORNL/6390 available from Oak Ridge National Laboratories). However, we are interested in developing a more general theory of the shape of international environmental agreements that is, in principle, testable.

theory for national policy. We part company with those who attribute value to such agreements in and of themselves, and suggest that some consideration of economic costs and benefits should enter into decisions whether to sign particular accords. This section also includes an example of how the theory will work in an area of current environmental concern.

II. THE HISTORY OF MULTINATIONAL ENVIRONMENTAL AGREEMENTS

A. *The Internationalization of Environmental Issues*

Nations and states did little to regulate pollution and to explicitly promote the conservation of natural resources before the latter part of the twentieth century.[7] Legal intervention usually centered around issues associated with resource exploitation, such as defining property rights. The limited response to environmental problems that characterized the early stages of industrial development has recently given way to a concerted effort to place a variety of direct regulations on pollution and other hazards.[8] The international law response to environmental problems has mirrored domestic developments. Nations initially responded to environmental threats by developing regulations independent of efforts elsewhere in the world. Although nations certainly shared information and research findings, environmental controls were voluntary and local in nature.[9] As a consequence, environmental protection was limited to local goals.

However, the growing perception of the global nature of many environmental problems has revealed the shortcomings of voluntary and national responses. This growing awareness has stimulated the discussion of environmental issues in a number of bilateral and multilateral policy arenas. Nation states are still the principal players in environmental policy, but the tools employed to achieve state policy now depend more on international relations.[10] In addition, international bodies and nongovernmental organizations now play a major role in shaping the debate on important environmental issues.[11] This "internationalization" has fostered a series of pathbreaking formal and

7. *See, e.g.*, Elliott, Ackerman & Millian, *Toward a Theory of Statutory Evolution; The Federalization of Environmental Law*, 1 J. OF LAW, ECON. & ORGANIZATION 317 (1985).

8. *See, e.g.*, COUNCIL OF ECONOMIC ADVISERS, ECONOMIC REPORT OF THE PRESIDENT ch. 5 (1989).

9. On sharing of research findings, see generally R. BRICKMAN, S. JASANOFF, & T. ILGEN, CONTROLLING CHEMICALS: THE POLITICS OF REGULATION IN EUROPE AND THE UNITED STATES (1985).

10. *See supra* note 1.

11. Jacobson & Kay, *supra* note 2, at 10.

informal international agreements, prominent among them the Montreal Protocol, which calls for the control of substances leading to stratospheric ozone depletion.

B. *The Growing Use of Multinational Agreements*

Conventional wisdom suggests that the number and scope of international environmental agreements have increased dramatically in recent years as a result of the internationalization of the global environment. Interestingly, little factual analysis exists in support of this view, perhaps because it seems so self-evident. A review of the multilateral environmental treaties signed by the United States lends some support for the conventional wisdom.[12]

Table 1 provides information on how the number and type of these treaties have varied by decade. The last lines of Tables 1A and 1B reveal that the number of multilateral environmental treaties signed and entering into force has in fact increased over the last sixty years.[13] Interestingly, this growth occurred unevenly across categories. Indeed, some categories of treaties were signed primarily during particular periods of time. For example, the three whaling treaties were signed from the 1930's to the 1950's, and the five air pollution treaties in the last decade. The table also suggests that the scope of treaties has broadened somewhat over time, with treaties now covering a wider array of environmental problems.[14]

C. *The Forces Driving Internationalization*

The increase in the number of environmental agreements can be explained at several levels. For example, Kay and Jacobson studied the evolution of particular institutions that addressed environmental problems, while Morrisette examined the development of scientific understanding. In contrast, this Article will focus on more general trends that affect the emergence of international environmental agreements. The forces contributing to this growing use of international agreements fall into four broad categories — scientific, psychological,

12. Treaties may not be a good surrogate for the total number of agreements. At the same time, we find the frequency distribution of treaties an interesting number in and of itself.

13. A complete list of the treaties covered in this table is provided in the Appendix to this Article. We use the word "environmental" broadly here to cover agreements involving air and marine pollution, species preservation, fisheries management, and regional conservation. We are not sure that this list covers the universe of treaties, but we believe it does represent most of the multilateral environmental treaties during this time period that the United States has signed.

14. It would be desirable to measure the impact of these treaties using some objective variables. This is, in principal, possible to do, but beyond the scope of the present study.

Table 1. U.S. Multilateral Environmental Treaties

A. Treaties signed by U.S. per decade						
Category	1930–39	1940–49	1950–59	1960–69	1970–79	1980–89
1. Fur and feathers		1			4	
2. Whaling	1	1	1			
3. Fishing			1	1		2
4. Marine pollution			1	1	3	1
5. Air pollution					1	4
6. Miscellaneous	_	_	1	1	1	_
Totals	1	2	4	3	9	7

B. Treaties entering force for U.S. per decade						
Category	1930–39	1940–49	1950–59	1960–69	1970–79	1980–89
1. Fur and feathers		1			3	1
2. Whaling	1	1	1			
3. Fishing				2		2
4. Marine pollution				1	2	3
5. Air pollution						4
6. Miscellaneous	_	_	_	2	_	1
Totals	1	2	1	5	5	11

economic and political.[15] Scientific understanding of environmental problems has grown dramatically over the last few years. The world has become more polluted and our knowledge of pollution and its effects has increased. Researchers now have better measuring devices and mathematical models of pollution that embody an improved understanding of physics and chemistry. We now recognize, for example, that the cumulative production and use of chlorofluorocarbons and halons has contributed to worldwide depletion of stratospheric ozone. In addition, our understanding of how pollution affects human health has improved.[16] This increase in scientific understanding has helped to define the scope of problems and to promote internationalized solutions.

Public awareness and concern over environmental risks has heightened significantly during the last few decades. Public perceptions of risk, often engendered by these scientific discoveries, also play a role in the increased number of environmental agreements. The environ-

15. We have not included law here because we are unaware of major changes in legal thought or processes that have spurred the increase in environmental agreements.

16. *See, e.g.*, L. LAVE & E. SESKIN, AIR POLLUTION AND HUMAN HEALTH (1977). This work examines the relationship between air pollution and mortality. For an examination of the impact of better scientific understanding on the development of environmental law, see Elliott, Ackerman & Millian, *supra* note 7, at 316.

mental movement has catalyzed this change by bringing issues it considers important to public attention. Rachel Carson's *Silent Spring* sensitized people to the possible dangers associated with increased use of pesticides.[17] Polls show that people view the motives of the business community with greater suspicion. The public no longer perceives that what's good for General Motors is necessarily good for the country.[18] The change in public attitudes toward environmental issues has contributed to the greater demand for some form of action.[19]

This new sensitivity to environmental concerns has also changed the nature of the political landscape. Environmental groups in the United States now play an important role in shaping both domestic regulations and international agreements.[20] In fact, the growing influence of national environmental groups has helped shape the response to environmental needs throughout the world.[21] Many countries now have environmental control agencies. Bureaucrats within these agencies receive benefits from developing action-oriented regulatory programs and identifying new problem areas.[22] Politicians have learned that a concern for environmental problems can translate into strong popular support. They have capitalized on the demand for environmental preservation by politicizing ominous ecological developments.

The media has contributed to the efforts of environmental groups and politicians. News stories focusing on sensational environmental events that particularly alarm the public, such as medical waste washing up on beaches, have aroused the public's fears. We do not mean to suggest here that the media does not play a valuable role in bringing to light important environmental concerns. However, it is important to recognize that the approach the media uses in reporting sensitive issues, such as Times Beach, Love Canal or the Antarctic "hole in the pole," can have a dramatic effect on the public's attitudes towards

17. R. CARSON, SILENT SPRING (1962). For an alternative view of some of the issues raised in SILENT SPRING, see E. WHELAN, TOXIC TERROR (1985).

18. *See Is an Antibusiness Backlash Building?*, BUS. WEEK, July 20, 1987, at 71. *See also Backlash against Business*, ECONOMIST, April 15, 1989, at 11, 12.

19. *See, e.g.*, Lamm & Barron, *The Environmental Agenda for the Next President*, ENVIRONMENT, May 1988, at 6; Dunlap, *Polls, Pollution, and Politics Revisited, Public Opinion on the Environment in the Reagan Era*, ENVIRONMENT, July-Aug. 1987, at 7; Ladd, *Clearing the Air: Public Opinion and Public Policy on the Environment*, PUB. OPINION, Feb./Mar. 1982, at 16.

20. For an assessment of domestic impact, see for example, B. ACKERMAN & W. HASSLER, CLEAN COAL/DIRTY AIR (1981). For an overview of international influences, see Morrisette, *The Evolution of Policy Responses to Stratospheric Ozone Depletion*, 19 NAT. RESOURCES J. (1989) (forthcoming).

21. *See, e.g.*, Stanglin, *Seizing the Politics of Pollution*, U.S. NEWS AND WORLD REP., December 8, 1986; Mewes & Clark, *The Green Party Comes of Age*, ENVIRONMENT, June 1985.

22. R. Hahn, The Political Economy of Environmental Regulation: Towards a Unifying Framework, PUBLIC CHOICE (Working Paper 88-33, School of Urban and Public Affairs, Carnegie Mellon University) provides an overview of some of the bureaucratic and political forces that shape United States environmental policy.

environmental issues and the government's role in environmental regulation.

Several economic factors have also contributed to the number of recent agreements. Increased industrial activity has led to a general growth in economic welfare, as measured by standard income statistics.[23] As a consequence, the demand for a cleaner environment and related amenities has increased.[24] Another economic factor, the reduction in the cost of exchanging information, has also contributed to the increase in the number of agreements.[25]

III. THE STUDY OF MULTINATIONAL ENVIRONMENTAL AGREEMENTS

A. *Previous Studies on International Environmental Agreements*

Many scholars have analyzed the process by which nations reach international agreements. By and large, this research has used case studies to draw generalizations about the formation of international environmental agreements and to identify the factors leading to such agreements. For example, Wetstone and Rosencranz provide an account of the setting and negotiations that created the 1979 ECE Convention on Long-Range Transboundary Air Pollution.[26] Similarly, Morrisette describes the research and policy decisions leading up to the 1987 Montreal Protocol on Substances that Deplete the Ozone Layer.[27] Boxer recounts the role of the U.N. Environment Programme in the development of a series of agreements on pollution in the Mediterranean.[28]

While these studies provide valuable insights into the individual agreements, only Morrisette attempts to draw general conclusions regarding the internationalization of environmental regulation. He suggests that the process consists of two stages. In the first, governments take domestic action on the basis of a limited scientific consensus that a problem exists. As scientific consensus emerges and public concern grows, the second stage begins and the activities shift to international arenas.[29]

---

23. DIRECTORATE OF INTELLIGENCE, CPAS 87-10001, HANDBOOK OF ECONOMIC STATISTICS 34 (1987).

24. *See generally* A. WILDAVSKY, SEARCHING FOR SAFETY (1988). It is a general precept of economics that wealthier consumers demand more amenities, such as safety.

25. *See* R. BRICKMAN, S. JASANOFF, & T. ILGEN, *supra* note 9.

26. Wetstone & Rosencranz, *Transboundary Air Pollution: The Search for an International Response*, 8 HARV. ENVTL L. REV. 1, 100–05 (1984).

27. Morrisette, *supra* note 20.

28. Boxer, *The Mediterranean Sea: Preparing and Implementing a Regional Action Plan*, in ENVIRONMENTAL PROTECTION: THE INTERNATIONAL DIMENSION, *supra* note 2, at 267.

29. *See* Morrisette, *supra* note 20.

Other scholars have approached the issue of environmental agreement formation more systematically. Jacobson and Kay have examined eleven case studies of international environmental efforts and assessed the factors that contribute to the sponsoring organization's effectiveness.[30] They suggest two broad categories, general background variables and organization-specific variables, and identify three background variables of particular relevance to the development of a more general theory. These are: (1) the characteristics of the problem (such as the existence of consensus on the nature of the problem and the level of costs associated with environmental measures); (2) the characteristics of the individuals and organizations involved (such as individual states' willingness to assume a disproportionate share of the costs); and (3) the attitudes toward the problem (such as public perception of the immediacy of the threat and the visibility of the environmental problem's impact).

Our approach will resemble the one taken by Jacobson and Kay. However, their analysis differs from ours in two fundamental ways. First, they deal primarily with evaluating the effectiveness of international organizations engaged in environmental activities, whereas we will focus on identifying specific factors that affect the shape and emergence of multilateral environmental agreements.[31] Second, Jacobson and Kay place little emphasis on the impact of domestic politics on international environmental activities. In contrast, we argue that domestic political factors are critical to understanding the emergence of international environmental agreements.

B. *Contributing Ideas from Related Fields*

Scholarly literature describing general international agreements and public policymaking also applies to the specialized field of international environmental agreements. The analysis set forth in this Article will build on ideas borrowed from positive political theory, which attempts to show how political institutions affect political choices.[32] Related to this area of inquiry, theories about group formation lend

30. Jacobson & Kay, *Conclusions and Policy* in ENVIRONMENTAL PROTECTION: THE INTERNATIONAL DIMENSION, *supra* note 2, at 323–27.

31. *See* Jacobson & Kay, *supra* note 2, at 18–19, defining organizational effectiveness as a nontrivial task. Their criteria for effectiveness include: the realization of procedural and substantive goals, the attitude of program participants and observers, the performance of the program compared to other similar programs, and the environmental impact of the program. This definition of effectiveness has the advantage of being quite general, but the distinct drawback, as the authors note, of being difficult to measure. Moreover, programs can be effective in some dimensions and not others.

32. *See, e.g.*, A. DOWNS, AN ECONOMIC THEORY OF DEMOCRACY, (1957); Noll, *The Political Foundations of Regulatory Policy*, 139 ZEITSCHRIFT FUR DIE GESAMTE STAATSWISSENSCHAFT 377 (1983); P. ORDESHOOK, GAME THEORY AND POLITICAL THEORY: AN INTRODUCTION (1986).

themselves to the study of international environmental agreements, particularly those theories that explain group effectiveness within the political process.[33] The collective action literature teaches the important lesson that the distribution of benefits and costs from particular agreements will be a crucial factor in determining how individual countries respond to proposals.

Positive political analysis does not by itself sufficiently explain either the timing or the nature of the environmental agreements that we examine here. Several other factors, among them the public perceptions discussed above, also matter. A significant literature has documented the observation that "objective" or scientific measurements of risk do not necessarily coincide with personal or public concern with that risk.[34]

IV. TOWARD A GENERAL THEORY

A. *The Prisoner's Dilemma*

The area of game theory provides one approach to creating models of the cooperative and competitive dynamics of agreements. One of the more compelling ways of thinking about cooperative agreements is the classic prisoner's dilemma.[35] In this situation, each party will benefit more if all parties cooperate than if none do. At the same time, each benefits even more from not cooperating, regardless of what others do. Consequently, the individually rational outcome is that none of the parties cooperate. For example, the European countries might each be better off if pollution were reduced. However, each country has an incentive to attempt to develop a competitive advantage in industrial production by enjoying the benefits of the other countries' environmental protection activities, while taking limited action at home.[36] The chance of one country benefiting from the improved environment while refusing to enforce standards remains high. International agreements with enforcement powers can serve as a way out of the prisoner's

---

33. *See, e.g.*, R. HARDIN, COLLECTIVE ACTION (1975); M. OLSON, JR., THE LOGIC OF COLLECTIVE ACTION: PUBLIC GOODS AND THE THEORY OF GROUPS (1971); Becker, *A Theory of Competition Among Pressure Groups for Political Influence*, 98 Q.J. ECON. 371 (1983); Campos, *Legislative Institutions, Lobbying and the Endogenous Choice of Regulatory Instruments: A Political Economy Approach to Instrument Choice*, 5 J. L. ECON. & ORG. (1989) (forthcoming).

34. *See generally* Kraus & Slovic, *Taxonomic Analysis of Perceived Risk: Modeling Individual and Group Perceptions Within Homogenous Hazard Domains*, 8 RISK ANALYSIS 435 (1988).

35. *See, e.g.*, D. LUCE & H. RAIFFA, GAMES AND DECISIONS (1957).

36. It is important to recognize that for some pollution problems with local impact, for example sulfur oxides, countries might find it in their interest to take individual or unilateral action. For other problems, such as greenhouse gases, few if any countries would take unilateral action because of the highly dispersed nature of the benefits. This suggests that the prisoner's dilemma paradigm is not an adequate description of all international environmental problems.

dilemma, since theoretically all nations would be burdened with the increased costs.[37]

The prisoner's dilemma, however, cannot fully explain the dynamic within which international environmental agreements arise. The model makes a variety of simplifying assumptions about the unified interests of actors and the rationality of their decision making, and ignores the political climate within which they operate. In reality, environmental agreements flow from the combined pressure of numerous domestic interest groups, each with different interests. Domestic political considerations have driven most regulatory efforts in the past and will probably continue to do so in the future.[38] Moreover, a variety of decision makers, each operating within dissimilar spheres of power, affect environmental policy. Importantly, the prisoner's dilemma does not account for these forces because the model assumes unitary rational actors focusing on singular interests. Consequently, the model cannot explain the effect these factors have on the formation of international environmental agreements.[39]

The incentives and pressures influencing the formation of international environmental agreements bear a strong resemblance to the factors influencing other areas of international cooperation. In particular, numerous parallels exist with strategic defense issues. Analysts have fruitfully applied game theory to decision-making in armed conflict and arms control agreements.[40] Here too, the limitations of standard game theoretic approaches, including the prisoner's dilemma, have been noted. For example, Berkowitz shows how domestic political

---

37. The argument is similar to the case for setting uniform federal air quality standards as opposed to setting standards on a state-by-state basis. *See, e.g.*, Krier, *The Irrational National Air Quality Standards: Macro- and Micro-Mistakes*, 22 UCLA L. REV. 323 (1974). The limitations of this approach are examined in Kelman, *Competition Among the States: The Ethics of Regulatory Competition*, REGULATION, May-June 1982, at 39 and Olson, *Competition Among the States: A Response*, REGULATION, May-June 1982, at 44. Getting rid of uniform standards and allowing states to make these tradeoffs may actually increase welfare. *See* Oates & Schwab, *Economic Competition Among Jurisdictions: Efficiency Enhancing or Distortion Inducing?*, 35 J. PUB. ECON. 333, 334 (1988). The arguments for the desirability of more federal control depend crucially on political decisionmaking at various levels of government.

38. This is especially the case in industrialized nations and in the early stages of regulation. *See generally* J. DAVIES, THE POLITICS OF POLLUTION (1970). This early study of environmental regulation in the United States mentions international interests only in abstract terms.

39. For a cogent analysis of the prisoners' dilemma and its limitations in the context of arms reduction agreements see B. BERKOWITZ, CALCULATED RISKS: A CENTURY OF ARMS CONTROL, WHY IT HAS FAILED AND HOW IT CAN BE MADE TO WORK (1987). Berkowitz shows how domestic political forces render the standard prisoners' dilemma irrelevant for a large class of arms agreements. A similar argument can be made for environmental agreements. Moreover, many of the pollutants covered in international agreements are likely to have their most pronounced economic and environmental effects on domestic constituents.

40. *See generally* C. HITCH & R. MCKEAN, THE ECONOMICS OF DEFENSE IN THE NUCLEAR AGE (1960); T. SCHELLING, THE STRAGEGY OF CONFLICT (1960).

forces play an important role in shaping defense policy and strategic accords.[41]

B. *Identifying Key Factors*

In this section, as an alternative to the prisoner's dilemma, we outline a number of factors which form the beginning of a predictive theory about the emergence of environmental agreements. Though the analysis will focus primarily on treaty formation, the same factors can also be used to predict the likely shape of other international environmental agreements.

Table 2 summarizes observations from five agreements in the area of air pollution that can be used to develop a general theory.[42] The agreements and their provisions are:

(1) The Convention on Long-Range Transboundary Air Pollution ("LRTAP")[43] of 1979. This convention does not establish specific guidelines for air quality improvement, but signatories agree to research, monitor, and exchange information in order to develop policies for reducing air pollution.

(2) The Sulfur Emissions Protocol of 1985 ("Sulfur Protocol").[44] Signatories of this protocol to LRTAP agree to reduce sulfur emissions by thirty percent as part of an attempt to curb acid rain and to reduce air pollution.

(3) The Nitrogen Oxides Emissions Protocol of 1988 ("Nitrogen Oxides Protocol").[45] Starting in 1994 participating countries will limit nitrogen oxide levels to 1987 levels. Twelve West European countries agreed to roll back emissions by thirty percent over ten years.

(4) The Vienna Convention for the Protection of the Ozone Layer ("Vienna Ozone Convention").[46] The signatories agree to cooperate in research and to exchange information. The convention provides a

---

41. *See generally* B. BERKOWITZ, *supra* note 39.

42. Exploring the historical origins of these agreements may also provide insight, but we do not undertake to do so here in the interest of brevity and simplicity. For two insightful papers on the origins of recent air pollution agreements, the reader should consult Morrisette, *supra* note 20, and Wetstone & Rosencranz, *supra* note 26.

43. Convention on Long-Range Transboundary Air Pollution, Nov. 13, 1979, T.I.A.S. No. 10541, *reprinted in* 18 I.L.M. 1442 (1979) [hereinafter LRTAP].

44. Protocol to the 1979 Convention on Long-Range Transboundary Air Pollution on the Reduction of Sulfur Emissions or Their Transboundary Fluxes by at Least 30 Per Cent, *done* July 9, 1985, *reprinted in* EXECUTIVE BODY OF THE CONVENTION ON LONG-RANGE TRANSBOUNDARY AIR POLLUTION, ECONOMIC COMMISSION FOR EUROPE, REPORT OF THE THIRD SESSION OF THE EXECUTIVE BODY, U.N. ECE Doc. ECE/EB.AIR/7, Annex I [hereinafter Sulfur Protocol].

45. Protocol to the 1979 Convention on Long-Range Transboundary Air Pollution Concerning the Control of Emissions of Nitrogen Oxides or Their Transboundary Fluxes, *done* Nov. 1, 1988, *reprinted in* 28 I.L.M. 212 (1989) [hereinafter Nitrogen Oxides Protocol].

46. Vienna Convention for the Protection of the Ozone Layer, *opened for signature* March 22, 1985, *reprinted in* 26 I.L.M. 1516 (1987) [hereinafter Vienna Ozone Convention].

Table 2. Characteristics of Multilateral Air Pollution Aggrements[a]

	TREATIES				
Characteristics	LRTAP of 1979	SO_x Protocol of 1985	NO_x Protocol of 1988	Vienna Convention On Protection of the Ozone Layer, 1985	Montreal Protocol of 1987
1. Problem addressed	Reduction of transboundary air pollution	Reduction of SO_x[b]	Reduction of NO_x from mobile and stationary sources[c]	Protection of ozone layer from CFC's	Reduction of CFC use
2. No. of signatories[d]	34	21	25	41	46
3. Lag time from negotiation to need for action	4 years	8 years	2 years[e]	No significant action required	19 months
4. Type of action required	Monitoring, R&D, exchange of information	30% reduction in SO_x from 1980 level	Limitation of NO_x to 1987 (or earlier) levels	Research only	Restriction of CFC consumption
5. How monitored/ enforced	No enforcement	Self-monitored	Self-monitored with reports to executive body	No monitoring	Self-monitored with penalties to be determined at a later meeting
6. Scope of problem	Regional/global	Regional	Regional	Global	Global
7. Country-specific concerns addressed	Yes	No	Yes	No	Yes
8. Initiating body	UNECE	UNECE	UNECE	UNEP	UNEP

a The U.S. is a party to each of these agreements except the SO_x protocol. This list does not include the 1984 protocol to LRTAP for financing of the monitoring and evaluation of air pollutants in Europe.

b Sulfur oxides (SO_x) are considered a major contributor to acid rain.

c Nitrogen oxides (NO_x) contribute to both acid rain and ground level ozone.

d Number of signatories includes all countries that had signed the treaty, whether or not they had ratified, plus the number of countries that had deposited documents of accession, as reflected in U.S. State Department records as of February 15, 1989.

e It is unlikely that the U.S. will find the requirements of the Nitrogen Oxides Protocol binding until the mid- to late 1990's. Pending legislation on air pollution will likely become the binding constraint on nitrogen oxide emissions in the near term.

framework for negotiation of future protocols that would include regulatory measures.

(5) The Montreal Protocol on Substances that Deplete the Ozone Layer ("Montreal Protocol").[47] Signatories agree to freeze their use of chlorofluorocarbons at 1986 levels by the year 1989. They will then reduce use and production of chlorofluorocarbons to fifty percent of 1986 levels by 1999.

Based on the text of these agreements and the circumstances of their development, Table 3 provides a summary of how key variables affect the likelihood of reaching an agreement. Next to each variable in the column labeled "Effect" the table lists how an increase in that variable will affect the likelihood of reaching an agreement.[48]

Table 3. Variables Affecting the Likelihood of Signing International Environmental Agreements

Variable	Effect
Scientific Consensus	+
Public Perception of Risk	+
Costs of Control	−
Perception of Fairness	+
Short-term Political Benefits	+
Number of Participants	−
Previous Agreements	+
Monitoring/Enforcement	?
Forum of Negotiations	?
Scope of Impacts	?

Specifically, we argue that the likelihood of achieving an agreement increases with: (1) greater scientific consensus about the cause and seriousness of the problem; (2) increased public concern; (3) a perception on the part of the negotiating parties that other members are doing their "fair" share to address the problems; (4) an increase in short-term political benefits; and (5) the existence of previous, related

47. Montreal Protocol on Substances that Deplete the Ozone Layer, *opened for signature* Sept. 16, 1987, *reprinted in* 26 I.L.M. 1541 (1987) [hereinafter Montreal Protocol].

48. The likelihood or probability of reaching an agreement refers to the *ex ante* subjective probability that an agreement will be met. A "+" denotes an expected increase in the likelihood with an increase in the value of that variable; A "-" denotes an expected decrease; and a "?" denotes that the effect cannot be unambiguously predicted. Several other characteristics affect the formation of international environmental agreements in a less systematic manner. *See infra* notes 64–75 and accompanying text.

multilateral agreements. On the other hand, the likelihood of reaching an agreement should decrease as: (1) the costs of control increase; and (2) the number of parties to the agreement increases. The effect of the monitoring and enforcement scheme on the likelihood of agreement is more difficult to ascertain. After examining the factors with measurable effects on the likelihood of reaching agreement, we shall consider the effects of the other, less predictive considerations.

Scientific consensus: Scientific consensus on the severity of a problem is neither a necessary nor a sufficient condition for international agreement.[49] Nevertheless, agreements calling for significant changes in behavior will probably not emerge if scientists do not agree on the extent of the problem. For example, the 1985 Vienna Ozone Convention had little or no serious effect on the environment because the parties could not concur on a scientific model of the problem.[50] However, scientific evidence mounted from 1985 to 1987 regarding the damage to the ozone layer and the role of chlorofluorocarbons.[51] Increasing scientific certainty and public concern about adverse effects prompted the European delegations to shift their positions from one of encouraging only a freeze on the use of chlorofluorocarbons to one favoring a fifty percent reduction.[52] This growing scientific and political consensus contributed to the development of the Montreal Protocol.

Similarly, the evolving understanding of the damaging effects of sulfur oxides pollution and of the long-range spread of sulfates through the air induced countries to reconsider their negotiating positions. West German behavior in the period in which scientific consensus developed demonstrates this point. West Germany only reluctantly agreed to sign the essentially nonbinding LRTAP in 1979 after considerable pressure from France, Norway and Sweden.[53] Three years later West Germany provided active support for the 1982 Stockholm Conference, which drew strong conclusions regarding the need for action on transboundary air pollution abatement. The conference set the stage for the development of the Sulfur Protocol. This shift occurred in large part because of mounting scientific evidence that air pollution had seriously damaged West German forests.[54]

Public perception: A rise in public awareness and concern over the environmental problem in question also contributes to the conclusion of international environmental agreements. People generally consider new or unknown risks as more of a threat than old familiar concerns.[55]

49. *See supra* notes 43–45 and accompanying text.
50. *See* Morrisette, *supra* note 20.
51. *Id.* at 15–20.
52. *Id.* at 19.
53. Wetstone & Rosencranz, *supra* note 26, at 103.
54. *Id.* at 109.
55. *See* Kraus & Slovic, *supra* note 34, at 436.

Moreover, risks associated with catastrophic consequences attract greater attention and enhance public perception of risk, regardless of their likelihood. Taking all of these findings into account, studies conclude that the promulgation of regulations can depend more on these public perceptions than on scientific evidence of risk. For example, Morrisette notes how the so-called "hole in the pole," a break in the ozone layer over Antarctica detected in 1985, helped mobilize public and expert opinion.[56] The Montreal Protocol shows how this type of public pressure can force government officials to take action on issues they did not previously considered necessary or attractive.

Perceptions of fairness: Consideration accorded the special circumstances of different countries has also influenced the fate of individual agreements. For example, in 1985, the United States chose not to sign the agreement aimed at controlling sulfur oxide emissions, arguing that the agreement did not give it adequate credit for past actions taken to address the problem. In contrast, the United States ratified the subsequent Nitrogen Oxides Protocol, which provided it with special consideration for prior efforts to reduce nitrogen oxides emissions. Similarly, developing countries demanded concessions regarding chlorofluorocarbon use before they would sign the Montreal Protocol. The agreement allowed them to increase chlorofluorocarbon use up to 0.3 kilograms per capita annually. Other special provisions assured Soviet cooperation by allowing continued design and construction of new chlorofluorocarbon plants included in the Soviet Union's five-year plan.[57]

Perceptions of fairness become especially important when the agreement imposes large economic costs. A major part of the negotiations on the Montreal Protocol centered on devising a standard of fairness that would induce a large number of countries to participate. However, the standards advocated by parties often differ substantially, depending upon each party's particular interests and situation.[58] Developing countries tend to favor standards stated on a per capita basis because such rules provide more room for economic growth. Similarly, European and Scandinavian countries promote percentage reductions in emissions because such provisions deliver the largest net benefits to them. The United States generally frames issues either in terms of requiring all

56. *See* Morrisette, *supra* note 20.

57. Even with these provisions, some potentially major users of CFCs chose not to sign/ratify the Protocol — most notably India, China and Brazil. *See* Department of State, Department of State Treaty Record — Montreal Protocol on Substances that Deplete the Ozone Layer (unpublished document available from the HARV. INT'L L.J.).

58. Fairness applies to the distribution of both benefits and costs. In addition to problems presented by the high costs of addressing the global warming issue, there will be significant difficulties arising from the fact that benefits are likely to be very unevenly distributed, and in ways that are hard to predict. *See supra* note 37 and accompanying text.

parties to use state-of-the-art control technologies or granting parties credit for prior efforts to reduce pollution. This position stems from the fact that in all air pollution control negotiations, the United States had already imposed more stringent emissions reduction measures than most other parties involved.[59] Lack of prior credit provisions, as in the case of the Sulfur Protocol, may keep the United States from signing a treaty.[60]

Political impact: The effect that an agreement will have on a government's domestic political position also influences the probability of reaching agreement in a systematic fashion. One of the primary motives for countries' acceptance of these agreements lies in the benefits that signature confers on political leaders. The appearance of action may even outweigh the importance of actual progress; the mere act of signing often garners more political credit for leaders than efforts to eradicate the problem. If an agreement will lead to economic costs, politicians generally prefer to impose those costs in the future. This desire, in addition to the more explicit goal of avoiding disruption, gives impetus to the typical provision of a grace period before an agreement goes into effect.[61]

Economic cost: Substantive environmental treaties designed to meet specific goals or create solutions must impose substantive restrictions or requirements on their signatories. These regulations, to the extent that they are effective, create economic costs that represent powerful disincentives against treaty formation. Accordingly, lower economic burdens make agreement more probable. Agreements that do not require significant changes in behavior will more likely gain the adherence of several countries.[62] This dynamic appears to have aided the development and acceptance of the Nitrogen Oxides Protocol. The agreement allowed most countries to postpone implementation of new regulations until the 1990's by providing credits for past ameliorative efforts.[63]

---

59. U.S. Environmental Protection Agency, Briefing on International Comparison of Air Pollution Control, Aug. 5, 1988 (internal briefing document available from the Environmental Protection Agency).

60. Another reason is that the United States had a domestic program in place which it did not want to unduly disrupt. There was also a fear that the results of the United States research might be biased by participation in the Protocol.

61. *See* Table 2, *supra*, for data on time lags.

62. The Montreal Protocol, *supra* note 47, signed by 46 nations, represents an interesting case. While the number of participants is high, we think this resulted from widespread scientific consensus and public awareness of the problem, as well as the likely availability of substitutes over the time frame of the agreement.

63. *See* Nitrogen Oxides Protocol, *supra* note 45, at art. 2, para. 1. The protocol allows signatories to select any year as a basis against which to measure compliance, thereby accommodating reductions brought about by prior pollution control efforts.

Number of participants: The number of parties involved in an international environmental negotiation represents the last of the factors that systematically influence the likelihood of agreement. As more participants join the process, the difficulties associated with reaching agreement grow. Most importantly, each new party brings along a different agenda, interests and reservations that may conflict with other parties' plans. The window of potential agreement understandably narrows with the introduction of these additional issues. The transaction costs associated with reaching agreement also rise as the number of participants increases. The difficulties of coordinating increasingly complex negotiations accentuate existing administrative obstacles to agreement.

Previous agreements: Among the agreements we sampled, those calling for specific limitations of emissions all built on prior agreements. This fact may suggest that the probability of a substantive international agreement improves with prior consensus on the general nature of the issue. LRTAP, for example, represented an agreement to principles rather than to specific action. The Sulfur and Nitrogen Oxides protocols subsequently grew out of that convention. Similarly, while the 1985 Vienna Ozone Convention represented more of an agreement to agree than a commitment to action, it set the stage for the Montreal Protocol two years later.

C. *Other Considerations*

The preceding section dealt with factors that influence agreement formation and shape in a predictable or systematic manner. This section examines considerations that affect international environmental agreements in a less predictable manner.

Monitoring and enforcement: Noncompliance appears more attractive as the probability that signatories will have to pay the economic costs imposed by international environmental agreements increases. Strong monitoring and enforcement mechanisms could force all parties to bear their share of the costs. Because few countries desire to surrender such power, it is not surprising that international environmental agreements usually contain only weak enforcement mechanisms and that individual countries typically monitor their own compliance.[64]

This combination reinforces the incentives for treating international environmental agreements as tools of political rhetoric. Countries can reap the public image benefits of signature without bearing the cost of implementation. In short, signing weak agreements often makes

64. *See* Table 2, *supra*.

good political sense.[65] However, even weak agreements may have some environmental benefit by directing international attention on the issue, by laying the groundwork for future treaties, or by asserting moral pressure for voluntary compliance.

Of course some nations may desire substantive environmental agreements with actual bite, or strong enforcement of some issues with weak enforcement of others. A richer theory of agreements should take into account the interplay between parties' differing interests in assuring compliance and allowing noncompliance, and how that dynamic influences the development of the agreement.[66]

Forum: International environmental negotiations arise from or are conducted within a variety of international fora. Of the agreements we examine in Table 2, the first three—LRTAP, the Sulfur Protocol and the Nitrogen Oxides Protocol—came about under the aegis of the ECE.[67] The last two agreements—the Vienna Ozone Convention and the Montreal Protocol—were sponsored by the U.N. Environment Programme.[68]

Steering negotiations to a particular forum may have a great impact on the development of an international environmental agreement.[69] The negotiating and sponsoring forum is critical in two respects. First, international institutions often have special ties with specific groups of countries. Thus, LRTAP met under the aegis of the ECE because of that body's influence with the Eastern Bloc countries.[70] Similarly, the U.N. Environment Programme may provide the best forum for a global climate change agreement because of its influence with developing countries.[71] Second, the agency that sponsors an international environmental convention or negotiation generally becomes the sec-

---

65. *See infra* note 77 and accompanying text for a description of the role of environmental issues in presidential politics.

66. For problems that are truly global in scope, such as stratospheric ozone depletion, signatories would want to make sure that other signatories could not free-ride at their expense. For example, the Montreal Protocol included sanctions about not trading with parties that did not sign the accord. Article 4, titled Control of Trade with Non-Parties, provides for the ban of trade in controlled substances with non-parties, as well as restrictions on substances containing, produced with, or used in producing ozone-depleting materials. On the other hand, for problems that are primarily intrastate or localized, countries will focus less on international mechanisms for monitoring and enforcement. Countries seem reluctant to give up autonomy on monitoring and enforcement at this juncture in history.

67. *See supra* notes 43–45.

68. *See supra* notes 46–47.

69. Jacobson and Kay observe that disagreements about which international organization should perform certain tasks reflect differences of opinion over organizational competencies and international goals, as well as conflicts arising from bureaucratic politics. Jacobson & Kay, *supra* note 2, at 12.

70. Wetstone & Rosencranz, *supra* note 26, at 101.

71. Interview with Konrad Von Moltke, Dartmouth University and World Wildlife Fund, in Washington, D.C. (Jan. 12, 1989).

retariat of that agreement, so the choice of a forum affects who will manage an agreement and how they will enforce it.[72]

Scope of environmental impact: The breadth of the issues addressed by negotiations may also affect international environmental agreements. One might think that the existence of a worldwide or regional problem involving all potential signatories to an agreement is a necessary condition for achieving a multilateral international agreement. Interestingly, experience shows that this is *not* the case. For example, the Nitrogen Oxides Protocol, recently signed by the United States, concerns a pollutant that apparently causes harm primarily at a regional level.[73] However, the treaties discussed in this Article do not represent a large enough sample to fully assess the systematic influence of this factor.

This theory of predictive factors does have inherent limitations. The framework outlined here is static, in that the theory considers only the likelihood of reaching an agreement at a specific point in time. Because agreements develop over time from initial discussion to implementation, a test of the theory must include variables that would indicate how the passage of time affects the probability of reaching agreements. Many of the factors listed in Section II as determining the growth in the number of environmental agreements over the past six decades would also apply to a description of the development of individual agreements.[74]

The strength of the preceding formulation based on the variables in Table 3 lies in its generality. Such a formulation might with minor

72. Many commentators have suggested an alternative form of administration for multilateral agreements modeled on the more authoritative Intergovernmental Joint Commission (IJC). This is thought to insulate the science and policy evaluation functions of the administration from politics. However, even if this rather questionable assumption were true, we believe it would be unwise to grant authority to an organization untied to domestic considerations such as politics, fairness, and budget. *Id.*; *see also* Wetstone & Rosencranz, *supra* note 26.

73. Based on existing scientific evidence, nitrogen oxide causes concern primarily because it is a precursor to ground level ozone. It also contributes to the formation of nitric acid and nitrates, which represents part of the acid rain problem. Because nitrogen oxide is not a transatlantic or global pollutant, there is little reason for the United States to be signing a limitation agreement with the Europeans, particularly if doing so carries significant costs. At the same time, however, the Canadians, who also signed the Nitrogen Oxide Protocol, may be a logical group (on scientific grounds) with whom the United States would negotiate an international agreement.

74. If a regression or limited-dependent variable approach were used, a parameter for time could be introduced into the equation. Alternatively, variables that were thought to affect the increase in the number of agreements could be measured directly. Wealth is one example of such a variable. *See supra* notes 23–24 and accompanying text. In addition, we have considered only finalized agreements; a complete test would require samples drawn from agreements that failed.

Finally, it is important to note that several of the factors discussed, such as forum and number of participants, are not outside the control of the negotiating countries. As such they may interfere with the identification of cause and effect that the regression equation is designed to measure.

modifications apply to almost any international or domestic agreement involving important scientific questions and risks and a number of interested parties.[75]

To be sure, other considerations may also affect the formation of environmental agreements. For example, non-governmental interest groups have on occasion assumed a vital role in shaping environmental issues.[76] In terms of general theory, however, the factors and considerations outlined above represent the dominant variables accompanying international environmental agreements and together provide considerable predictive power.

V. IMPLICATIONS FOR UNITED STATES POLICY

A. *Domestic Pressures Leading to Environmental Agreements*

This analysis suggests that the domestic constraints discussed above structure international environmental policy and shape the agreements that countries can achieve. This is not to suggest that there is no role for leaders who wish to strive for improvements in international environmental policy. However, the individual should understand the forces that shape the policy arena and use those forces to effect change.

As indicated in the preceding discussion, two of the factors that drive United States international environmental policy are domestic electoral politics and the ability to postpone economic costs. International environmental agreements often permit the President to claim credit for a seemingly major policy initiative while incurring little political risk. When the immediate economic cost remains low, the President loses little and stands to gain much by supporting such agreements. Indeed, Presidents have found it difficult to veto environmental programs, even when they have had a substantial price tag and offered little in the way of environmental risk reduction.[77]

The President also does not exercise sole authority over international environmental policy. If the Executive Office does choose to exercise

---

75. Arms agreements are a case in point. *See* B. BERKOWITZ, *supra* note 39, for a cogent analysis of the incentives of individual countries and interest groups in fashioning such agreements.

76. *See* Caldwell, *Cooperation and Conflict : International Response to Environmental Issues*, ENVIRONMENT, Jan./Feb. 1985, at 6, 9. Caldwell notes a significant growth in the number of non-governmental environmental organizations, especially in the Third World countries. These organizations have taken advantage of economies of scale and scope through a world-wide networking process. Perry notes a similar trend among non-governmental organizations of scientists that arises from the need for international research collaboration. *See* Perry, *International Institutions: Managing the World Environment*, ENVIRONMENT, Jan./Feb. 1986, at 10, 13.

77. The Superfund program and legislation is an excellent example. *See, e.g.*, R. HAHN, A PRIMER ON ENVIRONMENTAL POLICY DESIGN (1989); Smith, *Superfund: A Hazardous Waste of Taxpayer Money*, HUM. EVENTS, Aug. 1986, at 2.

restraint and not to pursue an international agreement, Congress will attempt to fill the void. Indeed, even when the President tries to take the lead, members of Congress sometimes vie for the spotlight.[78] The case of global climate change presents a good example of this process. Congress passed the Global Climate Protection Act in 1987, which called for a series of studies to examine the effects of major changes in climate and to identify a range of policy options.[79] President Bush has recently stated his intention to expand "the leadership role of the United States in protecting our global environment."[80] These actions indicate the beginning of a battle between the legislative and executive branches to claim credit for any environmental breakthroughs.[81]

It is not only politicians and non-governmental organizations that promote international agreements. Bureaucrats in the State Department, Environmental Protection Agency and elsewhere directly benefit from promoting such agreements.[82] Pressure by parties harmed by environmental agreements, usually the affected industries, may influence the President and Congress.

The shape of the agreement also determines the economic impact on individual parties. Agreements are drafted in such a way as to apportion costs in response to basic political pressures. For instance, chlorofluorocarbon producers may actually benefit from the higher prices associated with restricted production mandated by the Montreal Protocol.[83] As is typical in such cases, consumers will bear the brunt of the economic costs in terms of higher prices.[84]

78. Elliott, Ackerman & Millian, *supra* note 7, argue that the competition among politicians in different branches of government can create a situation where legislation is adopted that is more stringent than any of the protagonists would have liked. The particular example the authors use was the passage of the Clean Air Act Amendments in the 1970's.

79. Global Climate Protection Act of 1987, Pub. L. 100-204, 101 Stat. 1407–09 (1987), *reprinted in* National Climate Program, 15 U.S.C.A. § 2901, notes (West 1987).

80. G. BUSH, BUILDING A BETTER AMERICA 84 (1989).

81. *E.g.*, *Scientist Says Budget Office Altered His Testimony*, N.Y. Times, May 8, 1989, at A1, col. 2. Sen. Albert Gore recently criticized the Office of Management and Budget for what he termed censorship of testimony in Senate Hearings. *See also*, *Bush Urged to Shift Stance on Global-Warmth Conference*, Wash. Post, May 10, 1989, at A2, col. 4. Sen. John Chaffee sent a highly publicized letter to President Bush stating that "[i]t is not to late to act" on global climate change.

82. The number of bureaucrats and political appointees running back and forth across the ocean to negotiate environmental agreements is not inconsequential. There are many private benefits from this travel and the personal networks that are formed as a result.

83. This will depend on how the property rights to produce and consume CFCs and halons are allocated. *See* Hahn & McGartland, The Political Economy of Instrument Choice: An Examination of the U.S. Role in Implementing the Montreal Protocol, NORTHWESTERN U. L. REV. (forthcoming) (Working Paper 88-34, School of Urban and Public Affairs, Carnegie Mellon University) for an analysis of this and related issues.

84. This analysis focuses solely on the distribution of economic costs. Presumably, the benefits from reduced rates of ozone depletion will be shared quite broadly. For an analysis of the costs and benefits associated with various levels of control, see generally OFFICE OF AIR AND REGULATION, U.S. ENVIRONMENTAL PROTECTION AGENCY, REGULATORY IMPACT ANALYSIS: PROTECTION OF STRATOSPHERIC OZONE (1987).

The President and the Congress will be under increasing pressure to reach environmental agreements that appear to address significant pollution problems.[85] Opponents of these agreements risk being identified as insensitive to environmental problems. For President Bush, who has promised to make the environment one of his top priorities, the pressures will be immense.[86] At the same time, the President has relatively few tools at his disposal to check the institutional forces promoting international environmental agreements. In the latter part of the Reagan Administration, officials at the Executive Office of the President made an attempt to require high level clearance within the White House before allowing participation in talks or establishing negotiating strategies for these agreements. This process would allow the President and interested agencies to study the possible domestic effects of an agreement before commencing negotiations solely for supposed foreign policy gains. To date, this proposal has met with only limited success.[87]

B. *The Need for Presidential Leadership*

The United States can only make rational decisions if policy makers examine the costs and benefits of participating in international environmental agreements. Because a number of the factors contributing to their formation and shape are substantially unrelated to the economic benefits of such agreements, the general theory predicts that many proposed agreements could have *negative* net economic effects. Public perception that a certain environmental problem poses a high level of risk, a factor vital in fostering an environmental agreement, does not in and of itself justify governmental action.[88] For many of the pollutants under consideration, the reduction in risk made possible by regulation does not offset the increased costs of control. If the government ignores this cost-benefit analysis, it may decide to sign

85. President Bush will have to make an early decision whether he wants to support an agreement related to the international transport of hazardous waste.

There may also be a proposal for an agreement on volatile organic compounds that follows in the footsteps of the sulfur and nitrogen oxide protocols. It is difficult to say how the United States will react toward this proposal until negotiators further develop the language for the agreement.

86. President Bush also may feel a need to change the view that Republicans have no interest in addressing environmental concerns. This will make it even more difficult not to sign agreements that enjoy the widespread support of other nations, particularly European nations or Canada.

87. Having played a part in this process, we conjecture that this limited success is due to the limited resources that the Executive Office of the President can use to control agency activities.

88. *See* ECONOMIC REPORT OF THE PRESIDENT, *supra* note 8, at 191–92.

environmental agreements that have significant adverse economic consequences.

A narrow economic calculation of costs and benefits, however, may neglect some important international political considerations. The State Department often argues that participating in and signing international environmental agreements enhances both the "leadership" role and the "credibility" of the United States.[89] In one sense, the State Department viewpoint is certainly correct. By participating in agreements, the United States negotiators can build up goodwill with other countries and this goodwill *may* increase their ability to obtain desired concessions in future agreements.[90]

Yet, these arguments about leadership and credibility are vulnerable to economic and political scrutiny. When the State Department pursues environmental agreements solely for goodwill or leadership purposes, it tends to neglect domestic economic costs that may outweigh foreign policy benefits.

In our view, the United States has little reason to base its policy on world environmental opinion. Instead, the President and other domestic politicians can shape domestic and world opinion by defining priorities.[91] President Bush should set priorities so as to ensure that the United States signs only effective and meaningful agreements. The President will be much less susceptible to criticism regarding the environment if he defines clearly articulated priorities that address the major environmental concerns of the American people and establishes policies accordingly.[92]

---

89. *See* Wetstone & Rosencranz, *supra* note 26, at 112. The United States refusal to sign a joint, nonbinding decision paper on sulfur dioxide abatement in 1983 was a "blow to the international credibility of President Reagan's . . . environmental awareness[.]" *Id. See also* Interview with Richard Mott, Environmental Law Institute, in Washington D.C. (Jan. 12, 1989). Mott argues that by exercising leadership in the international environmental arena, the United States may be able to sway or coerce other countries whose domestic mandate alone has not been sufficient to cause action. *See also* Shepard, *The Politics of Climate*, EPRI J., June 1988, at 15, quoting Rafe Pomerance. "The Montreal accords [on CFCs] would never have been reached without consistent American pressure on the world community over a 10-year period . . . . [W]e should show the same kind of foresight and perseverance in convincing the world to control greenhouse gas emissions." *Id.*

90. However, it is important not to lose sight of the fact that other countries will want the United States to participate in most agreements that are truly global in scope, since the United States is likely to be a significant part of the problem as well as the solution.

91. *See* H. SMITH, THE POWER GAME: HOW WASHINGTON WORKS (1988), on the potential and limitations of using the office of the Presidency as a bully pulpit.

92. This statement is true in both the domestic and international arena. Indeed, we would argue that the President stands to lose credibility if he does not articulate such priorities, at least implicitly. This articulation does not require stating that specific problems are unimportant, but rather that a small number of problems will receive immediate attention.

C. The General Theory Applied: Global Climate Change

Finally, we examine the implications of the general theory for a topical environmental issue. The prospect of global warming resulting from the greenhouse effect will remain an important issue for the next few years.[93] What does the preceding analysis suggest about the likely response to global climate change? Based on current scientific understanding, which is admittedly incomplete, serious efforts at slowing the release of greenhouse gases would require major changes in lifestyle and exorbitant expenditures.

In addition, pollution control activities spread their benefits unevenly. Reducing global warming would benefit some countries much more than others.[94] For example, while the rise in ocean levels that might follow global warming would seriously damage Bangladesh and New Zealand, land-locked Bolivia and Switzerland would probably suffer little harm. These difficulties will not block change forever, but we doubt that any major policy shifts will occur in the near future.[95] A coordinated strategy aimed at prevention would require both a much greater consensus on the scientific aspects of the problem and a much greater level of public concern than currently exist.[96]

Nations will, however, feel continuing pressure to appear active in addressing this issue. They will probably respond with a series of

93. *See* McDonald, *Scientific Basis for the Greenhouse Effect*, 7 J. POL'Y ANALYSIS & MGMT. 425 (1988), "Carbon dioxide and a wide variety of other gases, including methane, ozone, and freon, trap a portion of the earth's thermal radiation that would otherwise escape into space. This radiative trapping of energy produces the heating of the atmosphere popularly labeled the greenhouse effect." *Id. See also* WORLD METEOROLOGICAL ORGANIZATION, WMO/TD-NO. 225, DEVELOPING POLICIES FOR RESPONDING TO CLIMATIC CHANGE (April 1988); Mintzer, *Living in a Warmer World: Challenges for Policy Analysis and Management*, 7 J. POL'Y ANALYSIS & MGMT. 445 (1988); and U.S. ENVIRONMENTAL PROTECTION AGENCY, THE POTENTIAL EFFECTS OF GLOBAL CLIMATE CHANGE ON THE UNITED STATES (1988).

94. *See* Waterstone, *The Equity Aspects of Carbon Dioxide-Induced Climate Change*, 16 GEOFORUM 301, 302 (1985). The Soviet Union might actually enjoy a longer growing season if global temperatures continue to rise.

95. *See* Lave, *The Greenhouse Effect: What Government Actions Are Needed?*, 7 J. POL'Y ANALYSIS & MGMT. 460 (1988). We are not alone in these conclusions. Lave notes that because policy must be developed in the face of great uncertainty, programs should be sought that "are unlikely to be harmful or costly if the greenhouse consequences are more benign than predicted and likely to help if the worst happens." *Id. See* Schelling, *Anticipating Climate Change: Implications for Welfare and Policy*, ENVIRONMENT, Oct. 1984, at 34. The author suggests that it is unlikely that there will be substantial reductions in greenhouse gas-generating fossil fuels in the near term, since governments have already failed to reduce consumption of these fuels in the face of ample reasons to reduce energy dependency. *Id.*

96. There are two general categories of policy responses to the climate change problem. Preventive measures are aimed at minimizing the actual changes in climate, and require a thorough understanding of the physico-chemical processes. These actions by necessity must be taken with a global perspective in mind. Adaptation simply refers to how human settlements respond to incremental changes in local climate.

We think it likely that some countries will take unilateral preventive action. Such action could have a small impact on the problem, but is likely to have more symbolic than real value.

formal and informal meetings aimed at shaping and disseminating research findings, and giving the appearance of making progress. However, only when a much higher level of scientific consensus emerges will nations seriously consider making difficult economic sacrifices.

VI. CONCLUSIONS

International environmental agreements will probably become a more popular vehicle for addressing global environmental concerns. This Article has provided a framework for understanding the emergence of such agreements. The analysis suggests that domestic politics is a key factor in shaping these agreements, but that several other factors, such as the distribution of economic costs and benefits, public perceptions, and scientific consensus also play an important role. The various pressures to sign international environmental agreements will continue and the political benefits of concluding such agreements, at least for the foreseeable future, will remain important. However, many of the agreements will not have a dramatic effect on individual behavior. Those that do will acquire their authority from a large degree of scientific consensus, as well as a public perception of the great importance of the problem.

We also offer a somewhat different perspective on the appropriate role for the United States in shaping environmental agreements. The kernel of our argument is that more agreements are not necessarily good for the President or the public.[97] In short, environmental priorities need to be set if we are to develop policies that foster economic growth while enhancing environmental quality.

APPENDIX

Mulitilateral Treaties Signed by the United States

Treaty description	Signed	In Force	(for U.S.)
Regulation of whaling	1931	1935	
Nature/wildlife conservation for the Western Hemisphere	1940	1942	
Regulation of whaling (with schedule of regulations)	1946	1948	
Prevention of marine pollution by oil (superceded by 1978 protocol)	1954	1958	(1961)
Protocol to whaling regulations	1956	1959	

97. Selected departments and agencies of the bureaucracy, such as the State Department or the Environmental Protection Agency, may benefit from the proliferation of agreements.

APPENDIX

Mulitilateral Treaties Signed by the United States

Treaty description	Signed	In Force	(for U.S.)
Fishing and conservation of living resources of high seas	1958	1966	
Antarctica treaty	1959	1961	
Conservation of Atlantic tunas	1966	1969	
Exploration and use of space	1967	1967	
Intervention on high seas in case of oil pollution casualties	1969	1975	
Wetlands/waterfowl protection	1971	1975	(1986)
Prevention of marine pollution from dumping wastes and other matter	1972	1975	
Conservation of Antarctic seals	1972	1978	
Trade in endangered species	1973	1976	(6 mos. later)
Intervention on high seas for pollution sources other than oil	1973	1983	
Military use of environmental modification	1977	1978	(1980)
Pollution from ships	1978	1983	(supercedes 1954 protocol)
Long-range transboundary air pollution (LRTAP)	1979	1983	
Antarctic marine life	1980	1982	
Conservation of North Atlantic salmon	1982	1983	
Oil pollution in the Caribbean	1983	1986	
Protocol to LRTAP for financing of the monitoring/evaluation of air pollutants in Europe	1984	1988	
Vienna convention for protection of the ozone layer	1985	1988	
Montreal protocol on substances that deplete the ozone layer	1987	1989	
NO_x protocol to convention on LRTAP	1988	Not decided	

[13]

The Future of Environmental Law

William K. Reilly†

The world that I found when I left Yale College has changed a great deal, and it is still changing. Protection of the environment is still a tremendously important societal goal, but the problems that confront us and the kinds of solutions that we will have to craft to address them are very different. I would like to mention a number of major changes that I think have occurred —are occurring—which are going to affect the practice of environmental law for years to come.

First, the scale of environmental problems has changed enormously. In the late 1960s, lawyers like myself believed that environmental laws and regulations had to be strengthened and broadened. State and local laws often were inconsistent if they existed at all, pollution havens were notorious, and states were tempted to compete for new industry by avoiding enactment of environmental laws. Interstate transportation of pollution also posed equity problems. States with few environmental regulations could send their pollutants through the air or in the water to states that had stronger restrictions. To make matters worse, the technical understanding needed to sort through those problems was often unavailable at the state level.

Faced with this situation, the country did something that was unprecedented at the time. During the 1970s, we passed close to a dozen major environmental laws meant to protect us in a relatively comprehensive way. For the first time in history, an industrialized, technologically advanced nation enacted sweeping federal legislation to protect human health, natural systems, and the environment nationwide.

Nevertheless, those efforts were only a faint foreshadowing of the work that we have to do in the 1990s and beyond as we try to solve environmental problems on a global scale. As we face global warming trends, destruction of stratospheric ozone, and depletion of tropical rain forests, the political hurdles are daunting. If we thought it was difficult to convince Democrats and Republicans, large and small states, and high and low sulfur coal areas of the need to agree on a Clean Air Act in 1970, wait until we try to convince all of the nations of the world that they

† Administrator, United States Environmental Protection Agency.

should cut down on fossil fuel use to stop global warming. Yet that is exactly what we have to do if we are to manage the global environment in the years ahead. And there is no precedent for this multinational cooperation. We face a huge job in trying to overcome the political, economic, religious, and cultural differences that have separated nations for hundreds of years. Given these problems, we absolutely cannot act unilaterally. We must bring the rest of the world along. To do that, I think we must demonstrate by the effectiveness of our environmental actions here at home that we deserve a leading role in global environmental protection.

The second point I want to make is that the kinds and numbers of sources that contribute to so many serious environmental problems have proliferated enormously. Back in the 1960s, our task seemed relatively straightforward. We identified some of the major contributors to pollution. The pall of smog that hung over Pittsburgh or the fire that burned on the Cuyahoga River are obvious examples. What we had to do at that time was to convince the public that the pollution problems were intolerable and yet solvable, that the economic cost of addressing them was affordable and worth paying.

In large part, the environmental improvements that resulted from our actions are undeniable. When talking about the environmental problems that we face as a society today, we should acknowledge to the country that we have come a long way, and we should be proud of that fact. We made huge investments, and we got a lot for them. I personally think that the experience of environmental improvement in the 1970s is one of the great success stories of American life and history. We ought not to let the public forget that because they are going to be asked to make more sacrifices in the years ahead. They need to understand that these investments have, in fact, paid off before and will pay off again.

Reducing the pollution from so many large utility and industrial facilities in the past was one thing. We now have to face very serious environmental threats from millions of small, highly decentralized, and diversified sources. Reducing these threats is going to be a much more difficult job because the sources of many of our worst pollution problems today can be found in our homes, neighborhoods, and small businesses. For example, ground-level ozone pollution—smog—is caused by millions of automobiles, paint shops, bakeries, and print shops. I had a visit earlier this week from the Chemical Manufacturers' Association, which has done a very good job of reporting the toxic air, water, and land emissions associated with that industry. They told me, "We notice compliance by other industries is much less than that of the chemical industry, and the data that you have suggests that those industries cause a disproportionately large part of the problem." Well, they are absolutely right. The reality is that many other companies—print shops, large bakeries, dry cleaners—do not believe that they are contributing seriously to the pollution problems of our major cities, and yet they are. To control this pollution is going to require lifestyle-altering actions at the local level, actions that the federal government would have a very difficult time defining or implementing.

The South Coast Air Quality Basin is proposing to do away with drive-in restaurants and banks as part of its ozone control plan. Can you imagine the federal government, a Republican Administration's Environmental Protection Agency, even one run by a crazed tree-hugger, trying to get away with any such thing? Yet, that is what they are proposing in Los Angeles. Another good example is pollution of estuaries. I spent much of today learning about the problems of Long Island Sound. There are literally millions of small, decentralized sources of pollution along the coast itself and millions more located well inland. Lawn fertilizers and backyard garden insecticides used in Brattleboro, Vermont end up contributing pollution to Long Island Sound. Farm and ranch fertilizers, pesticides, and herbicides, used outside Bismarck, North Dakota end up as part of our problem in the Gulf of Mexico. Oil and gas residues washed off the streets of Twin Falls, Idaho end up in the Pacific Ocean. And there are many more examples like these.

In all of these cases, I think our national response is going to require the coordinated efforts of federal, state, and local governments, of businesses, and of individual families. There remains a major task of environmental education, of building the environmental ethic, and of changing personal behavior in fundamental ways. But our educational efforts are going to have to be increasingly sophisticated. The kinds of techniques that were effective for us in the 1970s are likely to be less relevant and perhaps less useful. I hope that in the future we are more successful in educating the public about risk so that they are less susceptible to fear and more capable of making the kinds of decisions that we expect informed citizens to make.

EPA has to base its decisions on data that are often incomplete, contradictory, or ambiguous. Moreover, if we can keep regulatory disagreements on a more scientific plane, the public will be much more willing to learn from the issues and then make up their own minds. None of us wants to read about the arcane details of risk assessment. What we all want is to be reassured that the people making the decisions have our own interests and values at heart and can be trusted. And that said, the fine print does not matter. I take as one of my principal responsibilities, and one of the things that I really hope to accomplish, is the creation of that kind of public trust in our regulatory programs.

But what does all this mean for young lawyers? First, I would say that you should pay much more attention to international law, diplomacy, and foreign languages than lawyers did twenty years ago. Second, I think you ought to pay more attention to local zoning laws, city codes, and state laws than lawyers did twenty years ago. One of the defects, one of the failings of the environmental movement in this country, has been an inability to organize in the state capitals to the same degree that the movement has organized in Washington. The really innovative ideas, the creative programs over the past eight to ten years, have come from the state level. For a variety of reasons, many new ideas will continue to come from there, and one of EPA's major tasks will be to encourage and cooperate with the local efforts.

The third point I want to make is that the enforcement of environmental laws is absolutely essential. I intend to give enforcement a very high priority. I think it is at the very heart of the integrity and the commitment of our regulatory programs. But in the environmental protection business of the future, proper incentives are going to become increasingly important. One in three of our municipal sanitary landfills will become obsolete in the next five years. That is going to pose a crisis of extraordinary impact in this society. We must encourage businesses to redesign manufacturing processes and to use less toxic materials. We generate far more hazardous and solid waste per capita than most other industrialized countries. That is a cause for discouragement to some; to me, it is a suggestion that we can do better. For example, in the early 1970s we reduced energy use per unit of GNP by forty percent, yet the economy continued to grow. Now the same kind of performance is required with respect to waste.

Fourth, I would like to suggest that we think about environmental law in a somewhat different way than we did in the 1960s.

As I look back on my own experience, I was trained to understand systems so as to perceive their vulnerabilities, the places at which they were susceptible to manipulation, and then to try to intervene in those systems and alter them to serve a specific interest. Environmental lawyers in the 1970s wrote a long list of laws to protect the environment, pollutant by pollutant, facility by facility, medium by medium. Taken together, those laws are now somewhat inconsistent or even conflicting—they give us little idea of the relative seriousness of the different environmental problems they were meant to solve. So I would hope to take a fresh look at environmental law, thinking in terms of systems, incentives, and multimedia approaches. We should not ask the question: How do I get that pollutant out of the air? But, where is the most efficient place to intervene in the system, across the spectrum of air, water, and land, to remove this threat to human health?

In a very real sense, we approach the decade of decision on the environment. We must first set an example here in the United States. We cannot lead if we are not out front at home. We intend and hope to do both. We are very determined to make a difference, to make our moment count, and to prepare the country for the next century. We need to move the environment from the margins of public policy where it has always been, and in my experience where it is in every other country of the world, and move it into the mainstream, both as a matter of domestic policy and foreign affairs.

Name Index

www.ingramcontent.com/pod-product-compliance
Lightning Source LLC
LaVergne TN
LVHW102106300926
849161LV00014B/3058
* 9 7 8 0 8 1 4 7 1 1 8 2 8 *